Quantitative Finance

Quantitative Finance

An Introduction to Investments, Asset Pricing, and Derivatives

Johan Walden

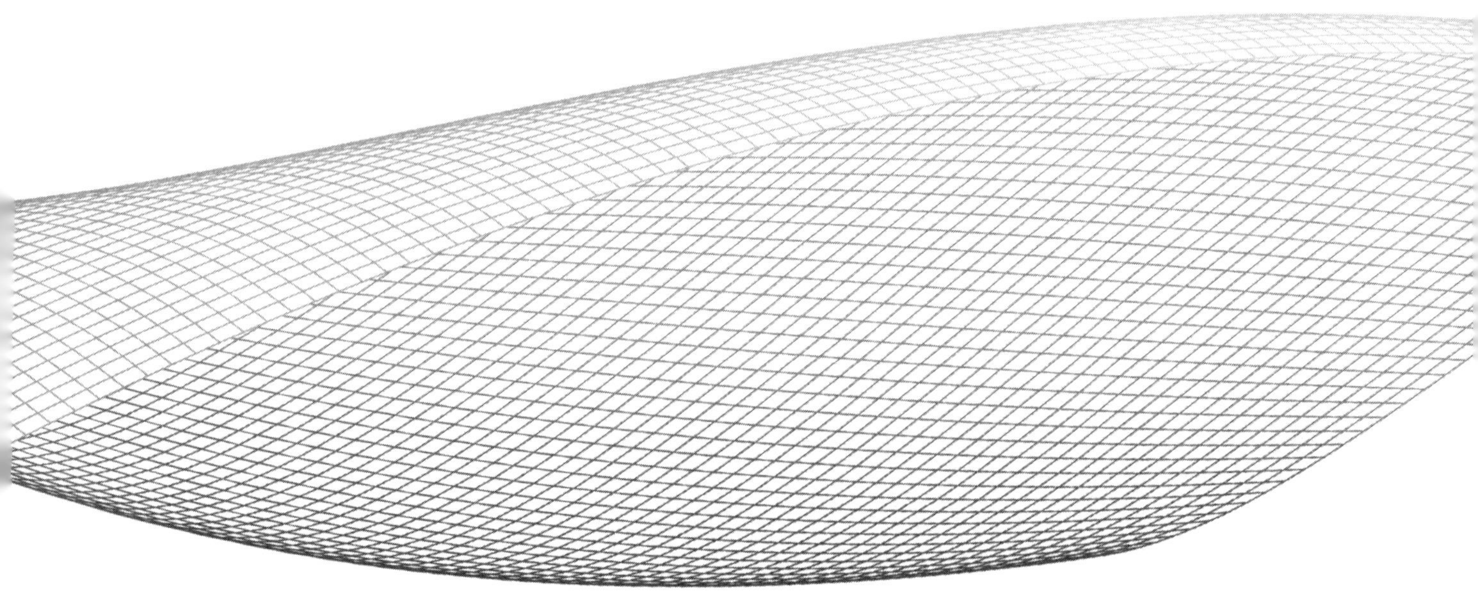

Princeton University Press
Princeton and Oxford

Published by Princeton University Press
41 William Street, Princeton, New Jersey 08540
99 Banbury Road, Oxford OX2 6JX

press.princeton.edu

GPSR Authorized Representative: Easy Access System Europe - Mustamäe tee 50, 10621 Tallinn, Estonia, gpsr.requests@easproject.com

ISBN 9780691270685
ISBN (e-book) 9780691285894
ISBN (web PDF) 9780691270715

Library of Congress Control Number: 2025934808

British Library Cataloging-in-Publication Data is available

Editorial: Hannah Paul and Josh Drake
Production Editorial: Theresa Liu
Text and Jacket/Cover Design: Wanda España
Production: Erin Suydam
Publicity: William Pagdatoon
Copyeditor: Alison Durham

Cover image by Johan Walden

This book has been composed in Minion Pro and Baskerville Display PT

Printed in the United States of America

10 9 8 7 6 5 4 3 2 1

MIX
Paper | Supporting responsible forestry
FSC® C008955
www.fsc.org

Contents

Quantitative Finance

CHAPTER 1 Introduction

This book provides an intermediate introduction to investments, asset pricing, and derivatives. The difficulty level is aimed to be in the sweet spot for a quantitative master's program in finance, somewhere between the MBA and PhD levels. It has been used in, and grew out of, multiple courses in UC Berkeley's Master of Financial Engineering program, in the University of Lausanne's Master of Science in Finance program, and in PhD-level asset pricing theory courses at UC Berkeley and the Stockholm School of Economics. The book may also be useful for some advanced undergraduate courses.

The book mainly focuses on theories and models for how investors and financial markets behave that were introduced in the second half of the 20th century. It studies how to think about making decisions under uncertainty and over time, how to pick an investment portfolio in the financial market, and—most extensively—how to characterize the prices and returns of financial assets in equity (stock) markets, bond markets, and derivative markets.

A wide range of topics are covered, and as we move through the material, it may from time to time be challenging to see how the different pieces fit together. The so-called asset pricing pyramid, shown in figure 1.1, provides an overarching conceptual framework to help navigate the material in such situations. The vertical dimension in this pyramid describes how specific the assumptions made in a particular theory or model are. Concepts at the base of the pyramid are general/generic, and we expect them to hold widely in financial markets. For example, payoff linearity of financial assets, the principle that the dividends paid by two units of an asset are twice those of the dividends paid by one unit, is something we expect to hold in general. Implications for asset prices that we can derive solely based on such general assumptions will consequently hold in general. A key such result is the existence of a so-called stochastic discount factor, which can be used to determine prices of financial assets.

Concepts high up in the pyramid depend on more specific assumptions. For example, the so-called capital asset pricing model, the CAPM, makes strong assumptions about how agents (a synonym of investors in this context) behave in the market. It is a so-called equilibrium model, in which asset prices need to be such that agents' aggregate demands equal the assets' aggregate supply, so that markets clear. These assumptions have strong implications for how the returns of financial assets behave—much stronger than implied by the existence of a stochastic discount

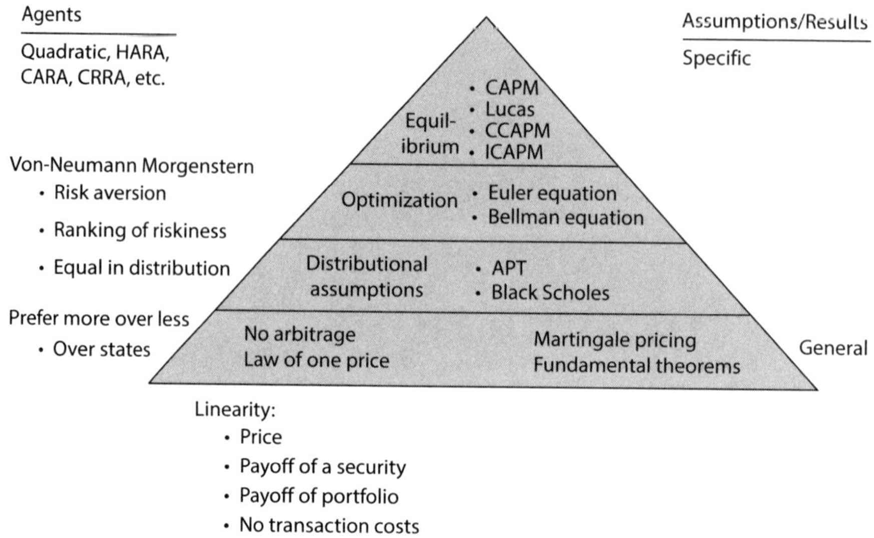

Figure 1.1: The asset pricing pyramid.

factor. It is great to have such strong results. Of course, the downside with being far up in the pyramid is that one can only trust that these results hold in environments where it is known that the specific underlying assumptions hold.

On the left-hand side of the asset pricing pyramid, we have listed assumptions made about the behavior of agents in financial markets. Again, at the bottom the assumptions are general, for example, that agents prefer more money over less. The assumptions at the top of the pyramid are much more specific, for example, with respect to their attitudes toward risk. We will frequently refer back to the asset pricing pyramid throughout the text.

This book is divided into three parts. Part I begins with an introduction to financial markets, leading to questions around how to make decisions under uncertainty, how to choose an investment portfolio, and how to determine what are appropriate prices and returns in financial markets. These questions are then the focus throughout the rest of part I. We first analyze investor preferences and decision-making under risk, cover fundamental concepts of expected utility theory, mean–variance utility, and other preference specifications, and introduce the concepts of risk aversion and risk rankings. In other words, we study the left-hand part in figure 1.1.

Building on the preference results, we then analyze the general portfolio choice problem in the mean–variance setting and in more general settings, leading to some workhorse equilibrium asset pricing models: the capital asset pricing model (CAPM), the Arrow–Debreu economy, the Lucas economy, the consumption CAPM, and arbitrage pricing theory (APT).

We relate these models to asset pricing puzzles and anomalies, and to factor models. Our main focus is on equity markets and to some extent bond markets, but we also mention other asset classes. Moreover, we touch upon the implications of the theory for real investments within publicly and privately held companies, providing a link to the corporate finance field. We use mathematical results from optimization theory, and so-called fixed-point theorems, to prove the existence of, and characterize, equilibrium. This part of the material lies in the upper part of the asset pricing pyramid.

Part II analyzes no-arbitrage asset pricing, with application to derivatives and bond markets. This theory lies at the very base of the asset pricing pyramid, and the results are therefore very general. We begin in a static discrete setting, and then gradually move to continuous-time models with diffusion processes. We cover forward contracts, futures, swaps, and options. Many of these financial instruments have been around for a long time, but have become increasingly popular over the past 50 years. They allow individuals and firms to manage their amount and kind of risk exposure, be it associated with changes in interest rates, exchange rates, stock prices, commodity prices, or default probabilities. We discuss how derivatives can be used to achieve various hedging and speculative objectives, introduce a general framework for derivatives pricing, and study several applications.

We cover the fundamental mathematical tools needed for the continuous-time theory: Itô processes, Itô's lemma, the martingale representation theorem, ordinary differential equations, stochastic differential equations, partial differential equations, Feynman–Kac's theorem, the Kolmogorov equations, the Black–Scholes PDE, and Girsanov's theorem. Finally, we discuss numerical methods. We cover three main classes of such numerical methods: binomial tree methods, finite difference methods, and Monte Carlo methods. We provide MATLAB code for some standard option problems, to understand the performance and general features of these methods. The mathematical level of chapters 6–8 is similar to part I (advanced undergraduate), whereas chapters 9–11 are more challenging. Consequently, a significant part of these later chapters is spent on understanding and developing the mathematical tools needed.

Part III covers a selection of more advanced topics. We discuss portfolio choice and equilibrium models in continuous time, with a focus on the Lucas one-tree exchange economy and the Cox–Ingersoll–Ross production economy. We introduce extensions of derivative pricing models: the constant elasticity of variance model, Merton's jump diffusion model, Heston's stochastic volatility model, and the variance gamma model. We also discuss the volatility index, VIX. Next, we introduce the Ross (2015) recovery theorem, in both the discrete- and continuous-time settings. We then discuss models with heterogeneous information and beliefs, with a focus on Hellwig's (1980) noisy rational expectations equilibrium model and Kyle's (1985) insider-trading model.

Finally, in the appendix, various mathematical concepts and results from set theory, topology, linear algebra, and calculus are stated.

1.1 Teaching Using This Book

The target audience for the material in this book is students in advanced quantitative master's programs in finance. The material may also be useful for advanced undergraduate courses and PhD courses.

The first main application of the book for teaching is for a three-unit (45 hours) asset pricing (or asset pricing theory) course. Part I of the book (chapters 2–5) together with chapters 6–7 in part II can be conveniently used for such a course, starting with a brief introduction to financial markets (chapter 2), followed by a treatment of different models for how agents make decisions under uncertainty and over time (chapter 3), which naturally leads to an analysis of the portfolio choice problem (chapter 4). These preliminaries are then used to introduce the main "classical," workhorse, equilibrium asset pricing models, the CAPM, and consumption-based models (static Arrow–Debreu model, Lucas model, consumption CAPM). In addition, the arbitrage pricing theory is introduced, showing how portfolio choice naturally leads to a factor asset pricing structure, even in the absence of equilibrium assumptions. Finally, chapters 6–7, cover the static no-arbitrage model, and especially the first and second fundamental theorems of asset pricing, portfolio replication, and risk-neutral pricing.

Variations of this course curriculum are possible. Sections 4.6 (challenges of empirically estimating expected returns), 4.7 (dynamic portfolio choice), and 5.3 (Black–Litterman model) are somewhat specific, and may be excluded. For students with knowledge of continuous-time finance, some pricing models from part II may also be covered, for example, section 10.3 on one-factor bond pricing models, and sections 12.1–12.3 on portfolio choice and equilibrium models in continuous time. Section 14.1, on recovery, does not require knowledge of continuous-time finance, and may easily be added for students interested in more recent developments, as may chapter 15 on information and disagreement in financial markets.

A note: In writing this part of the book, I have chosen a "classical" approach, where the initial focus is on individual decision-making and attitudes toward risk, followed by portfolio choice and equilibrium arguments, which eventually leads to asset pricing models and results. I am a very fond of this approach, rather than an alternative that pushes the analysis as far as possible under minimal assumptions, starting with absence of arbitrage, before making additional assumptions about agent behavior. It is also possible to take such an alternative approach, by first covering chapters 6–7, before moving on to part I.

The second main application of the book for teaching is for a two- or three-unit derivatives course (30–45 hours). Part II of the book (chapters 6–11) is designed for such a course. Chapter 7 begins with the static no-arbitrage model, and introduces as many of the fundamental concepts (absence of arbitrage, state prices, risk-neutral probabilities, replicating portfolios, etc.) in a simple setting. Chapter 8 introduces the multiperiod no-arbitrage model, providing a link between the discrete- and continuous-time models. Significant space is spent on the fundamental concepts of dynamic portfolio replication and filtrations as a way of representing information diffusion. These concepts are easier understood in a discrete model than in continuous time. Chapter 9 gradually introduces theory on differential equations and stochastic calculus, covering workhorse results that allow the derivation of the continuous-time model. Chapter 10 applies and extends the continuous-time methodology to analyze various additional assets, like bonds, and basket options. Finally, chapter 11 provides an introduction to numerical methods within continuous-time finance.

Variations are certainly also possible when designing the curriculum for such a derivatives course. The sections in chapter 10 are basically self-contained and independent, and may therefore be excluded at will. Chapter 11, on numerical methods, is also self-contained. More advanced material from chapters 12–14 may be included.

A note: Part II includes a lot of material focusing on understanding the theory and intuition that lead to derivative pricing formulas. In my experience, this is the right approach for a derivatives pricing course at the master's of finance level and above. Once the theory and intuition are understood, it is straightforward to look up and use specific derivative pricing formulas. But the specific formulas themselves do little to facilitate the understanding of the theory and underlying intuition.

The material in this book may also be used in several other courses. Chapters 3–4, and sections 5.1–5.3 may be used as the theoretical core in courses on investments, asset management, and portfolio management. Material in part I may be used for advanced readings in several core courses at the undergraduate and master's levels, including introduction to finance, financial markets, capital markets, and economic foundations of finance (chapters 2–5). The material may also be useful in several advanced undergraduate electives, for example, on asset pricing (chapters 2–5), derivatives (chapters 6–8), investments (chapters 3–5), and introduction to financial engineering (chapters 6–10).

1.2 On the Book's Origins and Approach

This book covers material I have taught over the years at UC Berkeley and elsewhere. The investments and asset pricing material in part I grew from the MFE Investments and Derivatives course in UC Berkeley's Master of Financial Engineering (MFE) program, MFE230A; the Asset Pricing and Long-Term Portfolio Management course, AP/LTPM, at University of Lausanne (UNIL), Switzerland; and Berkeley's PhD course in Asset Pricing Theory, PHD239A. I have also covered material from part I in the Theoretical Asset Pricing course, PhD404, at the Stockholm School of Economics, Sweden. Some of the discussions, on company valuation and real investments, relate to the core MBA Introduction to Finance course, MBA203, I taught at Berkeley, and also to the UNIL Valuation course.

The continuous-time material, part II, is most closely related to the Stochastic Calculus with Asset Pricing Applications course, MFE230Q, I taught at Berkeley, and to the Continuous Time Finance PhD course, PhD401, I taught at the Stockholm School of Economics, Sweden.

The material in part III has mainly been covered in PHD239A. Some of the mathematical preliminaries are covered in the Mathematical Foundations for Financial Engineers pre-program course for incoming Berkeley MFE students and, finally, some of the material in chapter 11, on numerical methods, has been covered in the pre-program computer programming course for incoming MFE students.

My goal has been to provide a theoretically rigorous treatment of the topics that are covered, combined with a lot of intuition. In Berkeley's MFE program, we are very proud of our students, who are quantitatively highly skilled, but also understand the underlying financial and economic intuition behind models in quantitative finance. Indeed, finding the right balance here is a key success factor for an MFE program. This has been my guiding principle when developing courses as well as for this text, and it has had multiple consequences.

In the trade-off between breadth and depth, I have often decided to cover fewer topics in more depth. Indeed, many of the theoretical results are proved in the main text. In my view, understanding how results come about—at a fairly detailed technical level—is key to *really* understanding a model also at the intuitive level. So I include proofs, not only for academic rigor but also to facilitate the learning process. In this spirit, I have tried to write proofs in a way that provides as much intuition as possible. A similar trade-off exists between going for the most general version of results versus making the mechanism behind them more transparent. Again, this is a question of finding the right balance. Here, I have often opted for less general results that are easier to grasp.

It will quickly become clear for anyone who reads this text that I *love* models. Models are invaluable in explaining the world around us, in structuring one's thinking, and in understanding causality—how one thing leads to another. Models are also excellent as pedagogical tools. A simple model is often worth a thousand pictures. Finally, models are fun! In the book, we dig into some workhorse models in quantitative finance and sort out how they work. I am personally not completely optimistic about the prospects of ever being able to "prove" which of many competing models is the "right one" for explaining the real world in practice. I leave it to others to make such value judgments, which are consequently largely absent from this text.

When writing the book, I have been guided by what works in the classroom. In my experience, the most efficient way of learning quantitative finance includes a lot of problem solving—going through examples and doing exercises. Consequently, this is how I have written the text, which has plenty of such examples and exercises. I often approach a topic by first discussing what we would like to achieve, and what the associated challenges are, rather than stating results up-front. For the learning process, this approach is highly efficient. Indeed, one of the core lessons I have learned, as a teacher, writer of academic papers, and management consultant, is how important it is to *always* know *why* I am working on something. My aim when writing this text has been that the reader at any point should be able to do a mini "elevator test," stepping back and explaining for themselves *what* we are doing and *why* we are doing it, in less than 30 seconds.

PART I

Investments and Asset Pricing

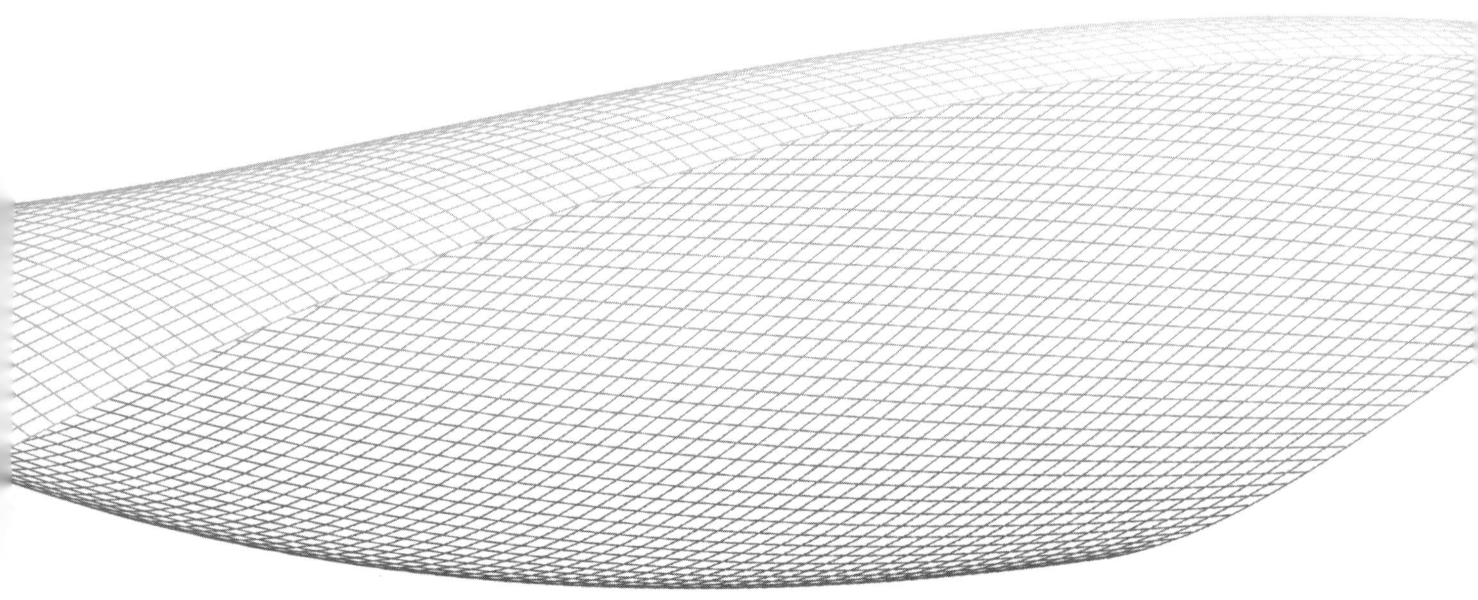

CHAPTER 2 Financial Markets

Financial markets are those markets in which *financial assets* are traded. In finance, we usually use the term *assets* rather than goods. An asset is anything that has economic value—i.e., it provides benefits that can be measured in dollars—and someone is willing to pay for it.

Recall that markets in general let individuals and other entities (firms, for example) meet and exchange goods in a manner that makes everyone better off. We will sometimes use the term *agent* instead of individual, in line with much of the theoretical literature. An agent is, roughly speaking, an individual who acts independently and makes his or her own decisions. Most often in our context, the agent is making investment decisions, in which case we will use the term *investor*.

Sometimes, the investment decision alone does not cover the complete decision environment an agent is facing. When we discuss equilibrium models, for example, an agent's decisions are also affected by other dimensions: human capital risk (employment, education, salary level, etc.), real estate (whether the agent owns a house, for example), and other factors. The term agent is therefore broader than the term investor.

Another complication arises under delegated management, that is, when an agent makes investment decisions on behalf of other agents. A mutual fund manager, for example, invests in assets on behalf of the mutual fundholders. Who is the investor in this case? The mutual fund manager, who is the agent that actually makes the decisions? The fundholder, whose capital is invested? Will they have the same objectives? If not, this leads to so-called agency problems. We will occasionally touch upon such agency problems, but mostly we will disregard them. So, most of the time, we will think of the investor as someone who both owns the capital and makes the investment decisions.

Consider a market for the exchange of goods, in which Ann, who owns potatoes but no rice, meets Bob, who owns rice but no potatoes. They agree to exchange potatoes for rice so that 2 pounds of rice is equivalent to 3 pounds of potatoes. In other words, the "exchange rate" they agree upon is 3 pounds of potatoes per 2 pounds of rice. Both Ann and Bob voluntarily participate in this market, because they are both "better off" after the exchange.

Next, consider a many-good market, in which lots of individuals participate. One way to organize this market would be for these individuals to enter into a large number of bilateral (two-agent) agreements where they exchange two or more goods with each other. The pairwise "exchange rates" may in this case vary across agent agreements, even for exchanges of identical goods. This setup roughly corresponds to an *over-the-counter* (OTC) market.

Another implementation of the market is through a *centralized exchange*. To avoid too many different exchange rates, a *numeraire* (currency), for example dollars (USD, \$) is introduced, and all goods are quoted in terms of this numeraire. So, instead of 3 pounds of potatoes per 2 pounds of rice, the price for potatoes may be quoted as \$4 per pound, and the price for rice as \$6 per pound. This allows the whole market to be expressed by N prices, where N is the number of goods, rather than in total $\frac{N(N-1)}{2}$ exchange rates needed between pairs of goods.

The agents can now decide how much to sell or buy of each good, once they know the prices. The prices are in turn set so that all markets clear, i.e., so that the total demand for each good equals total supply, in each market. This argument may seem somewhat circular (agents base their demand and supply on prices, and prices are set so that markets clear when based on all agents' demands), but it is possible to address this concern with the appropriate implementation of a market mechanism. Implementation may be a topic for an applied microeconomics course. For us, this classical concept of a market is just a starting point for our main objective: to understand investments and prices in financial markets!

2.1 Assets and Returns

Recall that an asset is anything that has economic value—i.e., it provides benefits that can be measured in dollars—and someone is willing to pay for it. Assets can be *real*, corresponding to the goods we just discussed. We are mainly interested in *financial assets*, which are also called *securities*. These are contractual claims to some of the benefits of ownerships of real assets. Examples of financial assets include common stock in a publicly traded company, corporate and treasury bonds, financial derivatives, certain types of real estate contracts—mortgages, collateralized mortgage obligations (CMOs), real estate investment trusts (REITs), etc.—and currencies.

What is special, and potentially confusing, about financial assets is that they often seem to represent a trade of "dollars for dollars." A buyer of a treasury bond, for example, pays a price, in dollars, to receive coupons and principal payments, in dollars. The time dimension is crucial here. A dollar today is not the same as a dollar tomorrow, so this contract represents an exchange of two different financial "goods."

For other assets, the actual future payment is unknown, with respect to size and potentially also to timing. The buyer of stocks in a publicly traded company faces uncertainty about the size and timing of future dividend payments. Of course, the stock can also be sold in the market, but its trading price there is not known in advance. *Financial economics* is the branch of economics that studies decisions, resource allocations, and markets, under uncertainty and over time. The focus on uncertainty and time is what is special about the markets we will study.

A conceptual way of defining a financial asset is through the cash flows its ownership generates in different *states* of the world over time, representing the two dimensions in figure 2.1. Note the initial cash flows of -3 in all states of the world, representing the negative cash flow associated with buying the asset at a known price.

Consider a risky investment in a publicly traded company. The history of such a company is often that it started as a privately held entity, usually financed with external capital through private investments or by bank debt. As the company grew, its capital needs increased and at some point it reached a scale at which solely relying on private funding was no longer feasible, or at least not efficient. At that point, it went through an initial public offering, in which ownership shares were sold to a broader investor base, shares which were from then on traded on an exchange, for example, on the New York Stock Exchange (NYSE) or the National Association of Securities Dealers Automated Quotations (NASDAQ). The details of how these exchanges operate vary somewhat, but they are both examples of centralized exchanges.

Bonds on the other hand are mainly traded in OTC markets, over the phone or through electronic communication networks (ECNs). Treasury securities, which are grouped into Treasury bills (with maturity less than a year), Treasury notes (with maturity between 1 and 10 years), and Treasury bonds (with maturity longer than 10 years), are usually considered risk-free. In contrast, corporate and municipal bonds are risky, although their riskiness is usually lower than the risk associated with stock ownership. Their risk and return distributions are also different. If held to maturity, a corporate bond's payout is fixed, as long as the issuer is not in distress.

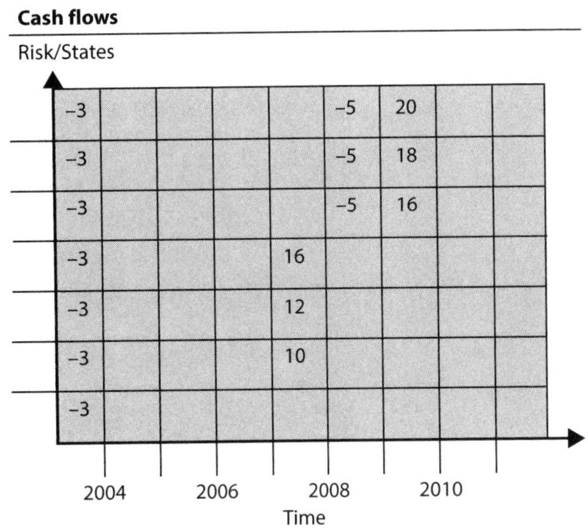

Figure 2.1: A financial asset, defined through the cash flows it generates in different states of the world over time.

Both treasury bonds and stocks of large companies traded on NYSE and NASDAQ are very *liquid* assets. Liquidity refers to the ease with which an asset can be purchased or sold. One way of defining such ease is through the difference between the prices a buyer and a seller can trade the asset at. Specifically, in a limit order market, there is a quoted bid price, at which a trader is willing to immediately buy the asset. Similarly, there is a quoted ask price at which a trader is willing to immediately sell the asset. The difference between the bid and the ask prices is called the *bid-ask spread*. The actual value of the asset lies somewhere between the bid and the ask, and half the spread represents the average cost for the buyer and seller of being able to trade immediately. How the price is affected by the number of shares being traded is also an important dimension of liquidity.

A useful assumption is that of a *perfect market*. In a perfect market, the bid and ask prices are the same, regardless of how many shares are traded. Moreover, the asset can be traded instantaneously and there are no commissions or other fees. In practice, perfect markets do not exist, but many markets may be close enough for the perfect market approximation to be reasonable. Whether a market is considered close to being perfect will also depend on the context. For a high-frequency trader, the bar would typically be much higher than for the retail trader who occasionally puts in an order.

2.2 Measuring Returns

A main focus for us will be on understanding returns on assets. In part I we work with discrete returns, which we now define. We consider an asset with price P_t at time t, which pays a stream of cash flows, $\{D_s\}_{s\geq t}$, over time. These cash flows may most easily be thought of as periodic dividend payments to the shareholders of a firm. They could also represent coupon payments from a bond, mortgage payments to a mortgage holder, etc. For an asset that does not make such payments, $D_s \equiv 0$.

What does time, t, measure? The appropriate length of a time period depends on the context. A passive investor with a long investment horizon may measure t in months or even years. An investor with an investment strategy based on news about firm fundamentals may have a daily, or even hourly, horizon. For example, traders who use news about a company's monthly sales figures, its customer base and suppliers, its product launches, etc., may focus on return measures at these horizons.[1] For high-frequency traders, whose profitability may depend on their ability to trade within milliseconds, microseconds, or even nanoseconds, such short time periods may be the appropriate horizon.

The price P_t is defined *ex dividend*, i.e., right after any dividend payment at t is made. A buyer of the asset at time t is thus assumed not to get the right to the D_t payment, but to all subsequent payments, as long as (s)he still owns the asset, including the D_T payment if the asset is sold at time T.

The one-period gross and net returns are defined by

$$\widetilde{R}_t = \widetilde{R}_{t,t+1} = \frac{P_{t+1} + D_{t+1}}{P_t}, \qquad \tilde{\mu}_t = \frac{P_{t+1} - P_t + D_{t+1}}{P_t} = \widetilde{R}_t - 1,$$

respectively. Note the tilde symbols above these terms, representing that the returns (usually) are random, i.e., they are not known in advance. For $\widetilde{R}_t$ and $\tilde{\mu}_t$, this means that their values will not be known until $t+1$.

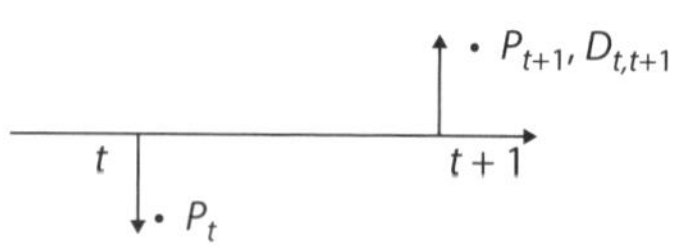

Figure 2.2: Measuring one-period returns.

The one-period return measures what will be earned by an investor who buys the asset at t, holds it for one period, and then sells it at $t+1$. As an example, consider a stock with price $P_t = 100$. An investor who purchases a share will realize a negative cash flow at t of -100, as shown in figure 2.2. At $t = 1$, the stock price has increased to $P_{t+1} = 105$. In addition, the stock pays a dividend at $t+1$ of $D_{t+1} = 3$. If the investor sells the asset at $t+1$, (s)he will collect total cash flows of $105 + 3 = 108$, earning a net return of $\tilde{\mu}_t = 8\%$, and a gross return of $\widetilde{R}_t = 1 + \tilde{\mu} = 1.08$. In other words, the total value of the position at $t+1$ is $V_{t+1} = P_{t+1} + D_{t+1} = 105 + 3 = 108$ (remember that the seller collects the dividend on the date of sale).

Assume now that the investor instead decides to hold onto the asset at $t = 1$, and instead sell at $t+2$. We are interested in the two-period return, $\widetilde{R}_{t,t+2}$, and we need to decide how to think about the dividend payment at $t+1$. In defining *total returns*, we assume that these are reinvested in the same asset. The investor thus uses the extra \$3 to buy $\frac{3}{105}$ additional shares of the stock. The value of the position at $t+2$ is then

$$\begin{aligned}
V_{t+2} &= \left(1 + \frac{D_{t+1}}{P_{t+1}}\right)(P_{t+2} + D_{t+2}) \\
&= \left(\frac{P_{t+1} + D_{t+1}}{P_{t+1}}\right)(P_{t+2} + D_{t+2}) \\
&= P_t\left(\frac{P_{t+1} + D_{t+1}}{P_t}\right)\left(\frac{P_{t+2} + D_{t+2}}{P_{t+1}}\right) \\
&= P_t\widetilde{R}_t\widetilde{R}_{t+1} \\
&\stackrel{\text{def}}{=} P_t\widetilde{R}_{t,t+2}.
\end{aligned}$$

[1] Such information is well known to affect stock prices. The share price of Apple, Inc., for example dropped by about 5% within 24 hours after its launch of the iPhone 5c in September 2013. This was widely explained by market concerns that the phone's sales price would be too high for it to compete with cheaper Android phones.

So, if the price of the asset increases to 115 at $t+2$ and it makes an additional dividend payment of $D_{t+2}=1$ at that point, $\widetilde{R}_{t+1}=\frac{115+1}{105}=1.0741$, so total returns between t and $t+2$ are

$$\widetilde{R}_{t,t+2}=1.08\times 1.0741=1.16,$$

corresponding to net returns of 16%.

We use this intuition to define the general k-period (compound total) returns,

$$\widetilde{R}_{t,t+k}=\prod_{\ell=1}^{k}\widetilde{R}_{t+\ell-1}.$$

It will also be convenient to define log-returns:

$$\tilde{\xi}_t=\ln(\widetilde{R}_t),\qquad \tilde{\xi}_{t,t+k}=\sum_{\ell=1}^{k}\tilde{\xi}_{t+\ell-1}.$$

Note that $\widetilde{R}_{t,t+k}$ denotes total returns over the k periods, *not* per-period/average returns. Average returns over k periods, from t to $t+k$, can be defined using arithmetic averages:

$$\bar{R}=\bar{R}^a=\frac{1}{k}\sum_{\ell=1}^{k}\widetilde{R}_{t+\ell-1},\qquad \bar{\mu}=\bar{\mu}^a=\bar{R}^a-1,$$

$$\bar{\xi}=\frac{1}{k}\sum_{\ell=1}^{k}\tilde{\xi}_{t+\ell-1}.$$

They may also be defined using geometric averages:

$$\bar{R}^g=\left(\prod_{\ell=1}^{k}\widetilde{R}_{t+\ell-1}\right)^{\frac{1}{k}}=e^{\bar{\xi}},\qquad \bar{\mu}^g=\bar{R}^g-1.$$

Whether it is most appropriate to use arithmetic or geometric averages depends on the context. In some cases there is no consensus in the field about which average is best to use. The two measures only yield the same result when returns are the same in each period, so it is important to know which measure is being used. As we will see, it follows from the famous *Jensen inequality* that the geometric average is always strictly lower than the arithmetic average when returns are not constant over time, $\bar{R}^g<\bar{R}^a$.

At t, the investor does not know future returns, but (s)he may know—or at least have beliefs about—the return distribution, the *cumulative distribution function* (c.d.f.) of returns,

$$\Phi(x)=\mathbb{P}(\widetilde{R}_t\leq x),$$

with associated probability density function (p.d.f.) $\phi(x)$. We define the expected return:

$$R_t=E[\widetilde{R}_t]=\int\widetilde{R}_t\,d\Phi=\int x\phi(x)\,dx,\qquad \mu_t=E[\tilde{\mu}_t]=R_t-1,$$

$$\xi_t=E[\tilde{\xi}_t]=\int\log(x)\phi(x)\,dx.$$

The return variance is

$$\sigma_t^2=\mathrm{Var}(\widetilde{R}_t)=\mathrm{Var}(\tilde{\mu}_t)=E[(\widetilde{R}_t-R_t)^2],$$

and the *return volatility* is $\sigma_t=\sqrt{\sigma_t^2}$.

The formulas above define population statistics. The corresponding sample statistics, based on historical observations, use the arithmetic average return, $\bar{\mu}^a$, to estimate one-period expected return, and the sample variance estimator (known at time $t+k$), to estimate variance,

$$\bar{\sigma}^2 = \frac{1}{k-1}\sum_{\ell=1}^{k}(\widetilde{R}_{t+\ell-1} - \bar{R}^a)^2.$$

Some other important statistics are

- population covariance of returns between assets i and j:

$$\sigma_{ij,t} = \mathrm{Cov}(\widetilde{R}_{i,t}, \widetilde{R}_{j,t}) = E[(\widetilde{R}_{i,t} - R_{i,t})(\widetilde{R}_{j,t} - R_{j,t})],$$

- population correlation of returns:

$$\rho_{ij,t} = \mathrm{Corr}(\widetilde{R}_{i,t}, \widetilde{R}_{j,t}) = \frac{\sigma_{ij,t}}{\sigma_{i,t} \times \sigma_{j,t}},$$

- sample covariance of returns:

$$\bar{\sigma}_{ij} = \frac{1}{k-1}\sum_{\ell=1}^{k}(\widetilde{R}_{i,t+\ell-1} - \bar{R}_i)(\widetilde{R}_{j,t+\ell-1} - \bar{R}_j),$$

- sample correlation of returns: $\bar{\rho}_{ij} = \frac{\bar{\sigma}_{ij}}{\bar{\sigma}_i \bar{\sigma}_j}$,
- *Sharpe ratio*: $S = \frac{R_t - R_t^f}{\sigma_t}$. Here, R_t^f is the one-period risk-free rate at t; see below. We will discuss the Sharpe ratio later on. It provides an important measure of the performance of an investment portfolio.

2.3 Bonds and Yields

A *bond* pays a *principal*, F, at its *maturity date*, T. It may also make periodic *coupon payments*, C, e.g., every year (annual payments) or every six months (semiannual payments). The *coupon rate*, c, expresses the fraction of the principal that is being paid in coupons per year.

Example 2.1. A 4% coupon bond making *annual* payments, with a principal of \$100 and a maturity date 5 years into the future is issued at $t=0$. It will make coupon payments of \$4 at $t=1, 2, 3, 4$, and 5. It will also make a (terminal) principal payment of \$100 at $t=5$.

Example 2.2. A 4% coupon bond making *semiannual* payments, with a principal of \$100 and a maturity date 5 years into the future is issued at $t=0$. It will make coupon payments of \$2 at $t=0.5, 1, 1.5, 2, 2.5, 3, 3.5, 4, 4.5$, and 5. It will also make a (terminal) principal payment of \$100 at $t=5$.

A coupon bond can be viewed as a portfolio of zero coupon bonds, so we focus on the pricing of zero coupon bonds. A T-bond is a risk-free bond that guarantees the holder \$1 at time T, and makes no other payments.[2] We denote the price of such a bond at time $t \leq T$ by $p(t, T)$.

[2] We focus exclusively on risk-free bonds, i.e., those issued by the Treasury, which are normally considered risk-free in nominal terms (as opposed to in real terms, which would account for inflation). In contrast, bonds may also be issued by companies, so-called corporate bonds, in which case they are typically not risk-free. In part I, we consider bond pricing under discrete compounding. In part II, we discuss models with continuous compounding.

The (zero coupon) *yield*, $y_{t,T}$, of a T-bond at time t is defined so that

$$p(t,T)=\frac{1}{(1+y_{t,T})^{T-t}},$$

i.e., so that the bond price is calculated by discounting the time-T payment over $T-t$ periods. If the per-period discount rate is constant, then $y_{t,T}=r$, for all t and T. The *forward rate*, $F_{t,s,T}$, is the per-period borrowing and lending rate (which are assumed to be the same) between s and T, that can be locked in at t, where $t<s<T$. It can be defined by the formula

$$1+F_{t,s,T}=\frac{(1+y_{t,T})^{(T-t)/(T-s)}}{(1+y_{t,s})^{(s-t)/(T-s)}}.$$

Example 2.3. Consider a borrower, who at time $t=2$ wants to ensure that (s)he gets to borrow \$100 at $s=3$, which will be paid back with interest at time $T=6$ (with no intermediate interest payments). The forward rate is $F_{2,3,6}=5\%$. This means that the borrower will need to pay back $\$100\times(1+5\%)^3\approx 115.76$ at $T=6$.

It is easy to show that the following formula holds:

$$(1+y_{t,T})^{T-t}=(1+F_{t,t,t+1})\times(1+F_{t,t+1,t+2})\times\cdots\times(1+F_{t,T-1,T}).$$

So the yield $y_{t,T}$ is roughly a geometric average of one-period forward rates between t and T. Technically, $1+y_{t,T}$ is a geometric average of $1+F_{t,t,t+1},\ldots,1+F_{t,T-1,T}$.

The one-period *spot rate* at time t is r_t, meaning that an investment of B at t grows to $B(1+r_t)$ at $t+1$. In other words, $r_t=y_{t,t+1}$. Since interest rates vary randomly in general, only r_t is known at t, whereas r_{t+k}, $k>0$, is not known until $t+k$. This randomness is different from the yield $y_{t+k}=y_{t,t+k}$, which is known at t for all $k>0$.

Consider the strategy of buying a one-period bond, and then reinvesting the total value after each period in a new one-period bond. So the investor

- deposits B at t, and gets $(1+r_t)B$ at $t+1$,
- deposits $B(1+r_t)$ at $t+1$, and gets $B(1+r_t)(1+r_{t+1})$ at $t+2$,
- deposits $B(1+r_t)(1+r_{t+1})$ at $t+2$, and gets $B(1+r_t)(1+r_{t+1})(1+r_{t+2})$ at $t+3$,
- ....

The gross return between t and $t+k$ is then

$$\widetilde{R}_{t,t+k}=(1+r_t)(1+r_{t+1})\cdots(1+r_{t+k-1}).$$

Since only r_t is known at t, this return is random when $k>1$. The geometric average returns are then $\bar{R}^g=\widetilde{R}_{t,t+k}^{1/k}$ and the arithmetic average returns are $\bar{R}^a=\frac{1}{k}\sum_{s=0}^{k-1}r_{t+s}$. We will use the notation $r_t^f=r_t$ and $R_t^f=1+r_t^f$ for the net and gross risk-free spot rates over one period. We often think of this as an annual spot rate, so that a period here represents a year.

2.4 Historical Returns and Important Questions

If we look at historical returns between 1928 and 2019,[3] measured by arithmetic averages, we find that the average annual stock market return ($\bar{\mu}^a$) was about 11.6% in nominal terms (corresponding to about 8.2% in real terms). Nominal geometric average returns ($\bar{\mu}^g$) were 9.7%.

[3]Data obtained from Aswath Damodaran's web page at NYU, Stern.

The nominal average return on short-term risk-free investments, so-called Treasury bills, was 3.4% during the same period. Thus, the return on the stock market in an average year was about 8% higher than the return from investing in short-term risk-free bonds. This difference, $\bar{R}^m - \bar{R}^f$, is the stock market's *risk premium*, also called the *equity premium*. The stock market's return volatility was about 20%. The return on long-term (Baa-rated) corporate bonds was significantly higher than the return on Treasury bills, with about 7.22% average returns (arithmetic, in nominal terms) over the period, and with a return volatility of about 7.2%.

This leads us to several important questions that we will focus on in part I:

1. **How to make decisions under uncertainty**. How can an investor evaluate an investment opportunity, or choose between several different such opportunities? Here, it is useful to distinguish between descriptive approaches, which aim at explaining and predicting how investors *do* behave, from normative approaches, which describe how investors *should* behave. Our focus is mainly on introducing a descriptive theory, although the two approaches overlap.[4]
2. **How to choose an appropriate investment portfolio**. Once we have a model for investor preferences under uncertainty, we can use it to analyze how investors choose their investment portfolios among a whole set of possible investment opportunities. We may distinguish between three different types of portfolio choices: asset allocation, asset selection, and consumption-savings allocation.
   - **Asset allocation**: How much capital to allocate to different asset classes (stocks, treasury bonds, corporate bonds, derivatives, real estate, private equity, etc.).
   - **Asset selection**: Which assets to invest in within a specific asset class.
   - **Consumption-savings allocation**: How much to consume versus how much to save for the future, e.g., for retirement.
3. **How to determine asset prices and returns**. What is the appropriate price/value of an asset in the market, and what are "reasonable" returns of an asset in the market? Here we may think about realized historical returns as well as expected future returns.

In addition, we will consider the following related questions:

4. **Horizon effects**. Just as time, t, can be measured in seconds or years, an investor's horizon may vary substantially, from a few weeks or shorter, up to many years or decades. How is the investment portfolio decision affected by the investment horizon?
5. **Performance metrics**. What are reasonable metrics for measuring the performance of an asset or portfolio? For example, the Sharpe ratio we mentioned before is a popular metric for measuring the performance of hedge funds. Why is the Sharpe ratio reasonable? Are there other, better, measures?

Finally, although our main focus is on understanding investment choices and returns in markets for publicly traded assets, our theory also has implications for other questions within corporate finance, for real investments (e.g., whether a company should invest in developing a new product) and for privately held (nontraded) assets, which we will touch upon.

We take a structured approach toward these questions. We begin by developing a general framework for how to approach investment decisions and asset pricing, making reasonable

[4]For example, a descriptive theory that predicts that investors who deviate from the theory will very quickly lose all their money clearly also has normative implications.

assumptions about what investors care about, i.e., what they value, when they invest, and how to model their investment choices. We then use the framework to develop powerful asset pricing formulas and models, which all have their advantages and disadvantages. We will discuss the general qualitative implications of these models, as well as their quantitative implications and how well they work in real markets.

We will derive some very nice and general results and, maybe even more importantly, we will also understand the limitations of our models. One key insight, we will see, is that there are many very important questions for which the best answer is "it depends." Knowing why it depends, and especially what it depends *on* is of great value in itself!

CHAPTER 3 Making Decisions under Uncertainty

To understand how to invest, we need to understand how agents make decisions in situations that involve uncertainty. There may also be a time dimension. For example, an investment opportunity may require an immediate investment of \$1000, and then pay back \$10,000 in five years, if things turn out well. The field of financial economics addresses economic environments that include uncertainty and/or a time dimension.

Probability theory offers an invaluable tool for modeling decisions under uncertainty. Consider, for example, a situation where an investor faces a risky investment opportunity, as follows: The investor may buy an instant lottery ticket for a price of $C = \$15$, drawn from a bowl. There are 100 tickets in the bowl, of which one is the winning ticket that instantaneously pays \$1000. The other tickets are worthless. How should the investor decide whether to buy the ticket or not?

One approach would be for the investor to compare the cost of buying the ticket with its *expected payoff*. Specifically, assuming that the bowl has been well shuffled, the investor may deduce that the chance of picking the winning ticket is $p = \mathbb{P}(\text{winning ticket}) = \frac{1}{100} = 1\%$, and the chance of picking a blank (one of the nonwinning tickets) is therefore $\mathbb{P}(\text{blank}) = 1 - p = 99\%$.

We can represent this payoff profile by a random variable, Π. Specifically, a *simple lottery*, $L = (a, b, p)$, is defined as a lottery that pays a with probability p, and b with probability $(1 - p)$. The lottery faced by the investor would then be represented by

$$L = \left(1000, 0, \frac{1}{100}\right).$$

We note that simple lotteries are closely related to Bernoulli distributed random variables. Recall that a random variable, ξ, has a *Bernoulli distribution*, $\xi \sim \text{Ber}(p)$, if $\mathbb{P}(\xi = 1) = p$, and $\mathbb{P}(\xi = 0) = 1 - p$. The payoff associated with the lottery $L = (a, b, p)$ is then $\Pi = b + (a - b)\xi$, where $\xi \sim \text{Ber}(p)$.

Going back to our investor, one way to decide whether buying the lottery ticket is worthwhile would be to compare the expected payoff from winning with the cost of buying the ticket, i.e., to calculate the net expected profit. The expected payoff is

$$E[\Pi] = p \times \$1000 + (1 - p) \times \$0 = \$10,$$

and the net expected profit is therefore

$$E[\Pi] - C = \$10 - \$15 = -\$5.$$

If the investor's rule is to invest if and only if expected net profits are strictly positive, then (s)he would therefore turn down the opportunity to invest in the lottery ticket. We summarize this expected-net-profit decision policy as follows:

Rule 1. Invest in a lottery with instantaneous payoffs Π if and only if the expected net profit is positive:

$$E[\Pi] - C > 0.$$

As a side note, we point out that the lottery ticket's cost can be "baked into" the lottery itself, by defining the lottery in terms of net payoffs. In the previous case, the net lottery would be defined as $L = (1000 - 15, 0 - 15, \frac{1}{100}) = (985, -15, \frac{1}{100})$. This is possible, since the payoffs are instantaneous. If the payoff would occur at a later date, netting would not capture the time dimension of the decision problem.

Is this a reasonable rule? If so, is it the only reasonable one? We do not want to impose strong restrictions on the tastes and preferences of investors, but our theory should rule out decision rules that are obviously damaging for an investor's wealth. Consider, for example, the lottery $L = (-100, -200, 0.5)$, which can be purchased at a price of \$15. This investment opportunity offers only downside: it leads to a net loss of either \$115 or \$215. So unless the investor gets other benefits from investing than the monetary payoff, we can conclude that the lottery should be avoided. Such nonmonetary benefits could include getting the opportunity to interact with the seller of the ticket, or knowing that the revenues from lottery sales go to a charitable cause. We will in general not take such nonmonetary benefits into account.

We assume that investors adhere to the following rule:

Rule 2. Invest in a project with instantaneous payoffs Π if the net profits are always positive:

$$\Pi - C > 0.$$

Rule 2 applies to investments for which the payoff is nonrandom, but also projects with random payoffs, as long as net profits are *always* positive. For example, the lottery $L = (85, 185, 0.5)$, defined over net payoffs, offers random profits of either \$85 or \$185, and we expect any investor to go ahead and invest even though the payoff is not known for sure. We note that rule 2 gives sufficient conditions for an investment to be preferable, by imposing much stronger conditions than rule 1. Indeed, for our lottery $L = (100, 0, \frac{1}{100})$, offered at the cost $C = 15$, rule 2 does not apply. The only thing we can deduce from rule 2 for that lottery is that it is not clear whether the lottery should be invested in. Does this mean that rule 1 is better than rule 2, since it provides explicit advice for lotteries that rule 2 is silent about? Not necessarily. Maybe rule 1 is "too confident" in its advice. Maybe some investors care about other properties of the lottery than expected payoffs. Rule 2 seems easier to justify. It should be valid for any investor who prefers more money over less. In the context of the asset pricing pyramid discussed in the introduction, rule 2 would be closer to the base than rule 1; see figure 1.1. We will further explore the topic later on in this chapter.

So far, we have studied situations where the investor either chooses to do nothing or buys the lottery ticket. What about a situation where the investor has to choose between the two mutually exclusive lotteries L^1 and L^2, with net payoffs Π^1 and Π^2, respectively? Since doing nothing is equivalent to accepting the lottery $(0, 1, 1)$, this situation actually provides an extension of our previous situation with only one lottery. The following decision rules provide extensions of the previous rules, when applied to lotteries defined over net payoffs:

Rule 3. Invest in the lottery with instantaneous payoffs Π^1 over the lottery with payoffs Π^2 if

$$E[\Pi^1] > E[\Pi^2].$$

Note that the rule does not take a stand on what to do if the expected payoffs are the same for the two lotteries.

Rule 4. Invest in a lottery with instantaneous payoffs Π^1 over one with payoffs Π^2 if it is always the case that

$$\Pi^1 - \Pi^2 > 0.$$

Again, rule 4 is based on stronger assumptions than rule 3 and seems very easy to justify, but does not always unambiguously determine what to do.

Should we expect reasonable investors to always adhere to rule 3? Consider the two lotteries $L^1 = (\$10\text{ million}, \$10\text{ million}, 50\%)$ and $L^2 = (\$30\text{ million}, \$0, 50\%)$. The first "lottery" thus offers a sure payment of \$10 million whereas for the second lottery, a toss of a fair coin determines whether the investor receives \$30 million or nothing. Note that rule 4 is silent about which of these two lotteries to choose, since the payoff can be higher for either of the lotteries. rule 3, however, unambiguously views lottery L^2 as preferable, since its expected payoffs are $E[\Pi^2] = \$15\text{ million} > E[\Pi^1] = \$10\text{ million}$.

When surveyed, many people actually rank lottery L^1 higher than L^2, usually arguing along the following lines:

> With \$10 million, I can do a lot of things (go to fancy restaurants, go on nice vacations, quit my job, etc.). It is true that I can do even more with \$30 million, but it is the initial \$10 million that makes the big difference.

In other words, the marginal cost of risking not getting the \$10 million by choosing L^2 over L^1 outweighs the marginal benefits of potentially getting the additional \$20 million. This argument captures the concept of *risk aversion*, which is consistent with rules 2 and 4, but *not* necessarily with rules 1 and 3.

3.1 Lotteries

We extend the concept of lotteries and associated decisions. We consider a class of lotteries, $\mathcal{L}$. The simple lotteries $L = (a, b, p)$, representing payoff a with probability $p \in [0, 1]$ (we also use the term payout), and b with probability $1 - p$, belong to $\mathcal{L}$. The associated random variable Π, or Π_L if we want to be specific, represents the payoff of such a lottery. The expected payoff of a simple lottery is $E[\Pi] = ap + b(1 - p)$. A special case is the scalar (real number) a, which represents the scalar lottery $(a, 0, 1)$, with the certain payoff a.

We introduce the operations of

- scaling: $L = (a, b, p) \;\Rightarrow\; kL = (ka, kb, p)$, and
- addition: $L = (a, b, p) \;\Rightarrow\; k + L = (k + a, k + b, p)$.

These operations keep us within the class of simple lotteries. We also introduce the concept of a *compound lottery*, $L = (L^1, L^2, p)$, where L^1 and L^2 are in turn lotteries. The compound lottery (L^1, L^2, p) represents a lottery that with probability p yields lottery L^1, and with probability $(1 - p)$, lottery L^2. In general, L^1 and L^2 can in turn be compound lotteries, allowing for a recursive definition of very complex lotteries. When $L^1=(a^1,b^1,p^1)$ and $L^2=(a^2,b^2,p^2)$ are simple lotteries, the resulting compound lottery is shown in figure 3.1.

We can also generalize the simple lottery concept to multievent simple lotteries

$$L=(a_1,a_2,\ldots,a_k;p_1,p_2,\ldots,p_{k-1}),\quad k>2.$$

Here, again letting the random variable Π represent the payoff of the general lottery, we have $\mathbb{P}(\Pi=a_n)=p_n$, $n=1,\ldots,k-1$, and $\mathbb{P}(\Pi=a_k)=1-p_1-\cdots-p_{k-1}$. It is clear that the mechanism to create complex compound lotteries from simple lotteries described above is sufficient to generate any general multievent lottery, at least in the eyes of investors who only care about the probabilities for different payoffs. For example, the compound lottery $((a^1,b^1,p^1),(a^2,b^2,p^2),p)$ is equivalent to the lottery $(a^1,b^1,a^2,b^2;p\times p^1,p\times(1-p^1),(1-p)\times p^2)$.

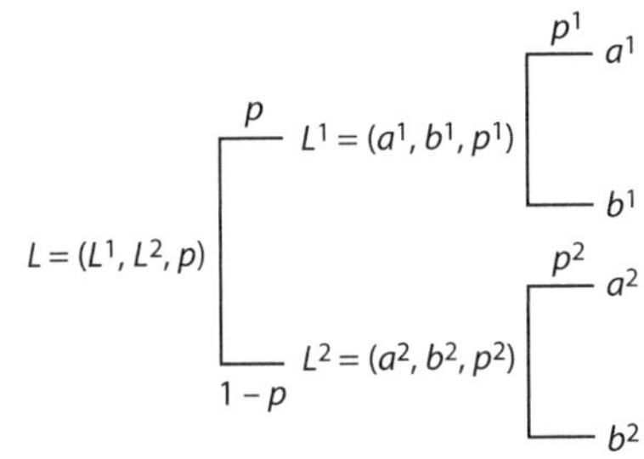

Figure 3.1: A compound lottery.

It will be convenient to write compound lotteries in their equivalent simple multievent form, in increasing order of payoffs: $L=(\Pi_1^L,\Pi_2^L,\ldots,\Pi_K^L;p_1,\ldots,p_{K-1})$, where $\Pi_1^L<\Pi_2^L<\cdots<\Pi_K^L$, $p_k>0$ for all k, and $\sum_{k=1}^{K-1}p_k<1$. We call this the *simple form*.

How should an investor rank lotteries in general? What are the conditions that make lottery L^1 "better than" lottery L^2 for a specific investor? Let us first study a specific lottery with a long history, which leads to the so-called *Saint Petersburg paradox*. We have considered compound lotteries that are generated from simple lotteries through a finite number of steps. But there is in theory nothing that prohibits us from defining lotteries using an infinite number of compounding steps. The Saint Petersburg paradox, which dates back to the early 18th century, is based on such a lottery. Specifically, Nicolas Bernoulli is known to have formulated the paradox in a letter in 1713. It was later given its name and analyzed by his cousin Daniel Bernoulli.[1]

The lottery is related to payoff of so-called doubling strategies within gambling, but with a better payoff than can be generated by such strategies. Specifically, consider the simple lottery $L^2=2=(2,0,1)$, which is used to construct the compound lottery $L^3=(2L^2,2,\frac{1}{2})\sim(4,2,\frac{1}{2})$. Lottery L^3 is in turn used to construct the lottery $L^4=(2L^3,2,\frac{1}{2})=(8,4,2;\frac{1}{4},\frac{1}{4})$. Recursively, we define

$$L^{k+1}=\left(2L^k,2,\frac{1}{2}\right),$$

and the infinite lottery

$$L^\infty=\lim_{k\to\infty}L^k.$$

The random payoffs Π^k are associated with the lottery L^k. It is easy to verify that $E[\Pi^k]=k$, so the expected payoff of Π^∞ is infinite.

Now, what should an investor/gambler be willing to pay for earning the right to the payoffs Π^∞ of the lottery L^∞? Equivalently, at what cost C would the investor be willing to take on the gamble with net payoffs $\Pi^\infty-C$? Clearly, under decision rule 3, the investor would be willing to pay an arbitrarily high amount. This is what Nicolas Bernoulli viewed as a paradox, since this seemed quite ridiculous, especially since the chance of winning a large amount is very small. Indeed, one verifies that $\mathbb{P}(\Pi^\infty>2^k)=2^{-k}$, $k\in\mathbb{N}$, so at a cost of $C=2^{14}=16{,}384$, the probability of a positive net payoff would be far lower than one in a thousand. For many risk-averse investors, the argument

[1] From the Swiss town of Basel, many members of the Bernoulli family provided tremendous contributions within mathematics, physics, probability theory, and insurance, from the 17th century onward. In addition to Daniel and Nicolas, other notable members include Jacob I and II, and Johann I, II, and III (the aforementioned Bernoulli distribution being named after Johann I).

of infinite expected net payoffs would actually not be persuasive; they would only be willing to pay a fairly modest amount for the lottery. Note also that rule 4 is not very helpful in this case, since it will not be able to provide any recommendation when the cost of the lottery is higher than 2, in which case there are some outcomes with net negative payoffs and others with net positive payoffs.

Daniel Bernoulli proposed a resolution to the paradox, by suggesting that gamblers, instead of the actual payoff, should associate something he called *moral utility* with the payoff, and that it would be the expected value of this moral utility that would govern how much they would be willing to pay. Specifically, the moral utility amount $u(\Pi) = \log_2(\Pi)$ would be associated with the payoff Π. Under this assumption, the moral utility associated with the lottery L^∞ would be

$$\begin{aligned} U(\Pi^\infty) &= \sum_k p_k \log_2(\Pi_k) \\ &= \frac{1}{2}\log_2(2) + \frac{1}{2^2}\log_2(4) + \frac{1}{2^3}\log_2(8) + \cdots \\ &= \sum_{k=1}^{\infty} \frac{k}{2^k} \\ &= 2, \end{aligned}$$

which can be derived using power series arguments.[2] Note that this moral utility is not measured in dollar terms, so it is a bit unclear what it represents. The idea here is that the moral utility associated with two lotteries can be used to compare and thereby rank them, leading to the following decision rule:

Rule 5. Invest in the lottery with instantaneous payoffs Π^2 over the lottery with payoffs Π^1 if

$$U(\Pi^2) > U(\Pi^1).$$

Now consider the scalar lottery $(4, 0, 1)$, with payoffs $\Pi \equiv 4$. The moral utility associated with this lottery is $U(\Pi) = 1 \times \log_2(4) = 2 = U(\Pi^\infty)$. The certain payoff of 4 would therefore provide the same moral utility to the investor as the lottery L^∞. A higher certain payoff would be preferred by the investor over the lottery, and for a lower certain payoff the investor would prefer the lottery. The terminology we use for this threshold payment is that the *certainty equivalent* of L^∞ is $1 \times \log_2(4) = 2$.

Definition 3.1. The *certainty equivalent* of a lottery is the certain payment CE that makes the investor indifferent between the lottery and the certain payment, $U(\Pi) = U(\text{CE})$.

Note that this is not quite the same as the investor being willing to pay 4 for the lottery. In fact, the moral utility associated with the net payment $L^\infty - 4$ is

$$\begin{aligned} U(\Pi^\infty - 4) &= \frac{1}{2}\log_2(2-4) + \frac{1}{2^2}\log_2(4-4) + \frac{1}{2^3}\log_2(8-4) + \cdots \\ &= -\infty, \end{aligned}$$

where we have defined the moral utility of nonpositive payoffs to be negative infinity.

[2] Specifically, for a real number x, such that $|x| < 1$, we have the geometric series formula $\sum_{k=0}^\infty x^k = \frac{1}{1-x} \overset{\text{def}}{=} G(x)$. Here, $G(x)$ is a real analytic function, which implies that its derivative can be calculated by termwise derivatives of the elements in its infinite power series $G'(x) = \sum_{k=1}^\infty kx^{k-1}$. But we also know that $G'(x) = \frac{1}{(1-x)^2}$, and thus $\sum_{k=1}^\infty kx^k = x\sum_{k=1}^\infty kx^{k-1} = xG'(x) = \frac{x}{(1-x)^2}$, which when $x = \frac{1}{2}$ gives us $\frac{(1/2)}{(1-1/2)^2} = 2$, in line with the formula.

So Bernoulli's decision rule based on moral utility is drastically different from the decision rule based on expected payoffs: under the former rule, the lottery L^{∞} has a certainty equivalent of 4. Under the latter, its certainty equivalent is infinite.

3.2 Expected Utility

The logarithmic moral utility function chosen by Bernoulli seems a bit arbitrary. More generally, an *expected utility* function, $u\colon \mathbb{R} \to \mathbb{R}$, can be used to extend rule 5, to evaluate different lotteries by comparing the associated expected utility,

$$U(\Pi) = E[u(\Pi)] = \sum_k u(\Pi_k)p_k,$$

of each lottery. We assume that the function u is strictly increasing and continuous. We will also often assume that

- u is strictly concave, and
- u is twice continuously differentiable.

An expected utility function that satisfies these additional conditions will then have $u' > 0$, and $u'' < 0$. We sometimes assume that the expected utility function is only defined on a subinterval of the real line, $U\colon K \to \mathbb{R}$, where K is an interval, which is closed, half-open, or open, and may be unbounded.

The reason we often assume that the expected utility function is strictly concave is because it captures the concept of risk aversion that we discussed earlier. Specifically, *Jensen's inequality* states the following:

Proposition 3.1 (Jensen's inequality). *For a strictly concave function, f, the following inequality is satisfied:*

$$u(E[\Pi]) > E[u(\Pi)],$$

for any nondegenerate random variable, Π.

Jensen's inequality in an expected utility setting thus says that an investor always prefers to receive the expected payoff of a risky lottery over the lottery itself. In other words, the certainty equivalent of a lottery is lower than its expected payoffs. We will soon introduce some utility functions that are commonly used.

We stress that the expected utility representation does not necessarily mean that the investor associates a numerical value (the expected utility) with a lottery. In fact, this is most likely *not* the case. It simply provides an intermediate step that allows the investor to rank lotteries, by using rule 5.

3.2.1 Axiomatic Derivation

The expected utility rule may still seem quite arbitrary, but it has an axiomatic foundation, which was originally introduced by von Neumann and Morgenstern; see von Neumann and Morgenstern (1944). To follow their approach, we introduce some new notation that captures an investor's ranking of different lotteries.

We write $L^1 \succeq L^2$ if an investor *weakly prefers* lottery L^1 over L^2, without making any assumption yet about how the investor makes that decision. We also write $L^1 \succ L^2$, denoting that the investor *strictly prefers* L^1 over L^2. This describes a situation when the investor weakly prefers L^1

over L^2, and does *not* weakly prefer L^2 over L^1, i.e., $\neg(L^2 \succeq L^1)$. If $L^2 \succeq L^1$ and $L^1 \succeq L^2$, we say that the agent is *indifferent* between the two lotteries, and write $L^1 \sim L^2$.

We call $\succeq$ the investor's *preference relation*, which describes the following decision rule:

Rule 6. Invest in lottery L^1 over lottery L^2 if

$$L^1 \succ L^2.$$

If the investor is indifferent between the two lotteries, $L^1 \sim L^2$, (s)he is equally happy with any of the two.

So far, rule 6 does not really tell us anything, since we make no assumptions about the preference relation. We therefore impose restrictions on these preferences. For technical reasons, we focus on a subset of the class of lotteries $\mathcal{L}^0_{[a,b]} \subset \mathcal{L}$, with a finite set of possible outcomes. For a lottery to belong to this class, $L \in \mathcal{L}^0_{[a,b]}$, the associated payoff, Π, must satisfy $-\infty < a \leq \Pi \leq b < \infty$, and $|\operatorname{range}(\Pi)| < \infty$. For future reference, we also define $\mathcal{L}^0 = \bigcup_{-\infty<a<b<\infty} \mathcal{L}^0_{[a,b]}$. Each lottery in $\mathcal{L}^0$ has a finite range, and any finite set of such lotteries jointly belongs to some $\mathcal{L}^0_{[a,b]}$. These are the lotteries that can be generated from simple lotteries, by taking a finite number of compounding steps.

We now make the following assumptions about the preference relation $\succeq$, defined over $\mathcal{L}^0_{[a,b]} \times \mathcal{L}^0_{[a,b]}$:

Assumption 3.1.

C1. Completeness: At least one of $L^1 \succeq L^2$ and $L^2 \succeq L^1$ always holds.
C2. Transitivity: If $L^1 \succeq L^2$ and $L^2 \succeq L^3$, then $L^1 \succeq L^3$.
C3. Continuity: If $L^n \to L$, $\hat{L}^n \to \hat{L}$, and $L^n \succeq \hat{L}^n$ for all n, then $L \succeq \hat{L}$.

We call these assumptions *axioms*. Axioms are assumptions based on "first principles." They are unprovable (that is why they need to be assumptions), but have the flavor of being self-evident, or at least widely accepted, or even just particularly useful as a starting point for a theory.

The initial two assumptions are very natural: the first simply means that the investor can compare any two lotteries in $\mathcal{L}^0_{[a,b]}$, and the second that if (s)he finds L^1 at least as good as L^2, and L^2 at least as good as L^3, then L^1 is viewed as at least as good as L^3. Together, they indicate that the preference relation is a so-called *weak order* (also called a total preorder), whereas the strict preference relation, $\succ$, is a *strict weak order*. Note that for a weak order, the strict preference $L^1 \succ L^2$ can be simplified to $\neg(L^2 \succeq L^1)$, since the preference relation is complete, so $\neg(L^2 \succeq L^1) \Rightarrow L^1 \succeq L^2$.

The third assumption is more technical. It specifies that if two sequences of lotteries converge to lotteries, and one sequence elementwise dominates the other, then its limit dominates the limit of the other. We actually need to formally define what it means for a sequence of lotteries to converge for this condition to even make sense. We do this by introducing a distance function—a metric—over lotteries (see appendix B.1). The metric we use measures the average distance between the cumulative distribution functions associated with the lotteries' payoffs, i.e., we define the distance function

$$d(L^1, L^2) = \frac{1}{b-a} \int_a^b |F_{\Pi^1}(x) - F_{\Pi^2}(x)|\, dx,$$

where F_{Π^1} and F_{Π^2} denote the cumulative distribution functions associated with the two lotteries. A consequence of the continuity assumption is that an investor is indifferent between any two lotteries that have the same associated cumulative distribution function or, equivalently, the same simple form. In other words, with this distance function we are implicitly imposing the so-called *reduction of compound lotteries* axiom, ROCL. Thus, if we (as is usual in mathematics) write $L^1 = L^2$ when $d(L^1, L^2) = 0$, it follows that $L^1 = L^2 \Rightarrow L^1 \sim L^2$. This can be seen as follows: Assume that L^1 and L^2 represent the same lottery, so that $d(L^1, L^2) = 0$. It then follows that the sequence $L^1, L^1, \dots, L^1, \dots$, converges to both L^1 and L^2, as does the sequence $L^2, L^2, \dots, L^2, \dots$. Now assume $L^1 \succ L^2$. Then from C3, since the first sequence converges to L^2 and the second to L^1, it follows that $L^2 \succeq L^1$, which leads to a contradiction. A similar contradiction arises if $L^2 \succ L^1$. It must therefore be that $L^1 \sim L^2$.

The above assumptions are similar to those made in the field of microeconomics about how agents rank bundles of consumption goods, as you may recognize. Assumption 3.1 does not really build upon the specific type of "goods" we are studying, namely lotteries. The following assumption on the other hand does:

Assumption 3.2.

C4. Independence axiom: $L^1 \succeq L^2$ if and only if $(L^1, L^*, p) \succeq (L^2, L^*, p)$ for all lotteries L^1, L^2, L^*, and $p \in [0, 1]$.

Assumption C4 seems quite natural. It states that if two compound lotteries are such that they lead to the same lottery, L^*, with the same probability, $1 - p$, then their ranking is determined by the ranking of their alternative outcomes (which occur with common probability p), treated as lotteries on their own. Note that as a special case of the independence axiom (obtained by choosing $L^* = L^2$), if $L^1 \succeq L^2$, then $(L^1, L^2, p) \succeq L^2$ for all p. This in turn implies that

$$L^1 \sim L^2 \;\Rightarrow\; (L^1, L^2, p) \sim L^2, \;\; \forall p. \tag{3.1}$$

Finally, we make the assumption of the existence of a maximum and a minimum lottery:

Assumption 3.3.

C5. Existence of extremes: There exists a lottery $\bar{L}$, such that $\bar{L} \succeq L$ for all $L \in \mathcal{L}^0_{[a,b]}$, and a lottery $\underline{L}$, such that $L \succeq \underline{L}$ for all $L \in \mathcal{L}^0_{[a,b]}$.

We would think that the lotteries $\bar{L} = b$ and $\underline{L} = a$, $b > a$, would be such extreme lotteries (as long as the investor prefers more over less), but this is strictly speaking not necessary for the result, just that such extreme lotteries exist.

One can show that for a preference relation that satisfies the above assumptions, the following result holds:

Corollary 3.1. *Under assumptions* C1–C5, *the following properties are satisfied:*

C6. *Continuity* (2)*: For lotteries L^1, L^2, L^3, such that $L^1 \succ L^2 \succ L^3$, there exists a p such that $(L^1, L^3, p) \sim L^2$.*

C7. *Dominance: If $L^1 \succ L^2$, then $(L^1, L^2, p_1) \succeq (L^1, L^2, p_2)$ if and only if $p_1 \geq p_2$.*

Note that C7 also holds with strict inequalities, i.e., $(L^1, L^2, p_1) \succ (L^1, L^2, p_2)$ if and only if $p_1 > p_2$.[3] It is valuable to get some further intuition for how these assumptions lead to C6 and C7, so let us show the results formally.

[3] This follows, because when it is not the case that $p_1 \geq p_2$—i.e., when $p_2 > p_1$—it is not the case that $(L^1, L^2, p_1) \succeq (L^1, L^2, p_2)$—i.e., $(L^1, L^2, p_2) \succ (L^1, L^2, p_1)$.

Proof of corollary 3.1. We first show C7. Assume $p_1 \geq p_2$, and note that

$$(L^1, L^2, p_1) = (L^1, L^3, p_1 - p_2),$$
$$(L^1, L^2, p_2) = (L^2, L^3, p_1 - p_2),$$

where $L^3 = (L^1, L^2, \frac{p_2}{1-p_1+p_2})$. So, by the independence axiom, $(L^1, L^2, p_1) \succeq (L^1, L^2, p_2)$ if and only if $L^1 \succeq L^2$ when $p_1 \geq p_2$, proving the sufficiency part. For $p_2 \geq p_1$, simply switching L^1 and L^2 in the argument shows that $(L^1, L^2, p_1) \succeq (L^1, L^2, p_2)$ if and only if $L^2 \succeq L^1$, proving necessity.

To show C6, define $A = \{p : (L^1, L^3, p) \succeq L^2\}$. It follows that $1 \in A$, since $(L^1, L^3, 1) = L^1 \succeq L^2$, and from C7 that if $p_2 \in A$, and $p_1 > p_2$, then $p_1 \in A$. Moreover, because of C3, A is a closed set. This can be seen by defining $p^* = \inf A < 1$, taking the sequence of lotteries $\hat{L}^n = (L^1, L^3, p^* + \frac{\epsilon}{n})$, which converges to $L = (L^1, L^3, p^*)$ and satisfies $\hat{L}^n \succeq L^2$ for all n, which via C3 then implies that $L = (L^1, L^3, p^*) \succeq L^2$, and thus $p^* \in A$, so indeed $A = [p^*, 1]$ for some $p^* < 1$. So, for all $(L^1, L^3, p^*) \succeq L^2$ and, moreover, for all $p < p^*$, $L^2 \succ (L^1, L^3, p)$ (since $p \notin A$). Another application of assumption C3 then implies that $L^2 \succeq (L^1, L^3, p^*)$, so both results together imply that $(L^1, L^3, p^*) \sim L^2$. In addition, it is clear that p^* is unique, from the strict inequality version of C7. □

We show that preferences that satisfy assumptions C1–C5 have an expected utility representation, as discussed in von Neumann and Morgenstern (1944):

Theorem 3.1 (Von Neumann–Morgenstern expected utility theorem). *Consider a preference relation that satisfies axioms C1–C5. Then there exists a utility function $u\colon [a, b] \to \mathbb{R}$, so that lotteries in $\mathcal{L}^0_{[a,b]}$ can be ranked by their associated expected utilities,*

$$U(L) = \sum_k u(\Pi_k) p_k,$$

i.e., $L_1 \succeq L_2$ if and only if $U(L_1) \geq U(L_2)$.

Proof. The result follows trivially when $\bar{L} \sim \underline{L}$, by defining $u(x) \equiv 1$. We therefore focus on the case when $\bar{L} \succ \underline{L}$. We define the function $U(L) = p$, where p is the probability that makes the investor indifferent between $(\bar{L}, \underline{L}, p)$ and L, i.e., p is chosen such that $(\bar{L}, \underline{L}, p) \sim L$. There exists such a probability by C6, and it is unique by C7 for any L such that $\bar{L} \succ L \succ \underline{L}$. For the case when $L \sim \bar{L}$, $\bar{L} = (\bar{L}, \underline{L}, 1) \sim L$, so $p = 1$ is a solution in this case, and since $L \sim \bar{L} \succ (\bar{L}, \underline{L}, p)$ for all $p < 1$ (via the strict inequality version of C7), this is the unique solution. Similarly, when $L \sim \underline{L}$, it follows that $p = 0$ is the unique solution.

By another application of C7 it follows that

$$U(L^1) > U(L^2) \quad \Leftrightarrow \quad L^1 \succ L^2,$$

and also that $U(L^1) \geq U(L^2)$ if and only if $L^1 \succeq L^2$, i.e., the higher the p associated with the equivalent lottery $(\bar{L}, \underline{L}, p)$, the "better" the lottery is.

It remains to be shown that $U(L)$ can be written as an expected utility, $U(L) = E[u(\Pi^L)]$, for some utility function u. Define $u(x) = U(x)$ for the degenerate lottery x with payout $\Pi \equiv x$, i.e., the lottery $(\Pi, 0, 1)$. Obviously, $u(x) = E[u(\Pi)]$, so for such degenerate lotteries, the U function represents expected utility.

Now consider the compound lottery $L^* = (L^1, L^2, p^*)$, with payout Π^*, and assume that $U(L^1) = E[u(\Pi^1)] = p_1$, and $U(L^2) = E[u(\Pi^2)] = p_2$. We then have

$$\begin{aligned}(L^1, L^2, p^*) &\sim ((\bar{L}, \underline{L}, p_1), L^2, p^*) \\ &\sim ((\bar{L}, \underline{L}, p_1), (\bar{L}, \underline{L}, p_2), p^*) \\ &\sim (\bar{L}, \underline{L}, p^* p_1 + (1 - p^*) p_2).\end{aligned}$$

The first two relations follow from C4, and the third from C3. Therefore,

$$U(L^*) = U((L^1, L^2, p^*)) = p^* p_1 + (1 - p^*) p_2 = p^* E[u(\Pi^1)] + (1 - p^*) E[u(\Pi^2)] = E[u(\Pi^*)].$$

The rightmost equality in the above expression follows from the law of iterated expectations, which in this context states that $E[u(\Pi^*)] = E[E[u(\Pi^*)|q]]$, where $q = 1$ if the p^* lottery leads to lottery $(\bar{L}, \underline{L}, p_1)$, and $q = 2$ if it leads to lottery $(\bar{L}, \underline{L}, p_2)$; see figure 3.2.

Because any lottery $L \in \mathcal{L}^0_{[a,b]}$ can be recursively constructed from scalar lotteries $(L^x = x)$ via a finite sequence of binary compounding steps, an induction argument implies that any such lottery has the expected utility specification $U(L) = E[u(\Pi^L)]$. We are done! □

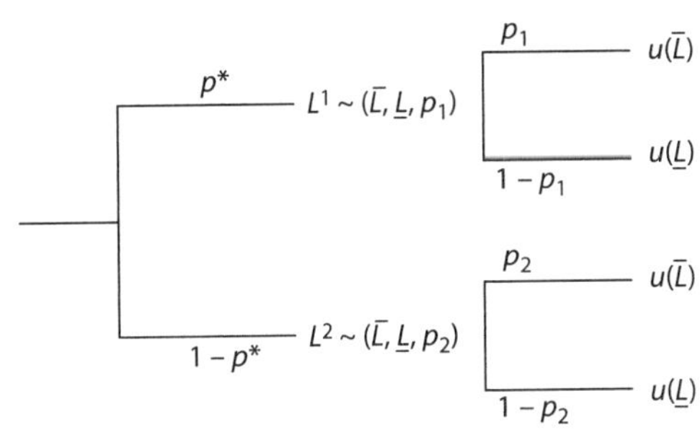

Figure 3.2: Law of iterated expectations (LIE) for a compound lottery.

It is easy to show that C3 implies that the expected utility function is continuous, and therefore also that the range of u is the whole of the interval $[0, 1]$. Although it does not follow from the expected utility theorem directly, we will always assume that u is strictly increasing, to capture our assumption that investors prefer more money over less. We also usually assume that the utility function u is strictly concave, to capture risk aversion, and, for technical reasons, that it is twice continuously differentiable, $u \in C^2$, which then makes strict concavity equivalent to the condition $u'' < 0$. Finally, we will often extend the interpretation of the expected utility to cover all lotteries in $\mathcal{L}$—with potentially an infinite number of outcomes that may be unbounded—as long as $E[u(\Pi^L)]$ is finite.

In light of the expected utility theorem, it is clear that for preferences satisfying assumptions C1–C5, rule 6 is equivalent to the following one:

Rule 7. Invest in lottery L^1 with payoffs Π^1 over lottery L^2 with payoffs Π^2, if

$$E[u(\Pi^1)] > E[u(\Pi^2)].$$

One also verifies immediately (do this as an exercise) that the expected utility function $v(x) \stackrel{\text{def}}{=} a \times u(x) + b$, for constants $a \in \mathbb{R}_{++}$, and $b \in \mathbb{R}$, represents identical preferences to the utility function u, and thus leads to identical decisions under rule 7. Also note that the risk-neutral case, in which only expected payoffs matter, in line with decision rule 1, is a special case of rule 7 for which $u(x) \equiv x$. Since this function is not strictly concave, this expected utility function does not represent that of a risk-averse investor. An investor with expected utility function $u(x) \equiv x$ is called *risk neutral*. An investor with a strictly convex expected utility function (i.e., $u'' > 0$, if $u \in C^2$) is called *risk loving*.

Example 3.1 (The Allais paradox). Consider the lotteries

- $L^1 = (10000, 0, 0.1)$,
- $L^2 = (15000, 0, 0.09)$,

- $L^3 = 10000$,
- $L^4 = (15000, 0, 0.9)$.

(a) Rank L^1 versus L^2, using your personal preferences.
(b) Rank L^3 versus L^4, using your personal preferences.
(c) Is your joint ranking of the two pairs of lotteries above consistent with expected utility preferences?

When surveyed, many people reveal rankings that violate the independence axiom for these lotteries. Specifically, they strictly prefer L^2 over L^1, since that lottery pays much more in the good state, which occurs with only a slightly lower probability than for L^1. They also prefer L^3 over L^4, since they like being sure of getting the payout guaranteed by L^3, even though it is somewhat lower than what L^4 may pay. Now, since L^1 may be viewed as a compound lottery $L^1 = (L^3, 0, 0.1)$, as may $L_2 = (L^4, 0, 0.1)$, the independence axiom implies that $L^1 \succ L^2 \Leftrightarrow L^3 \succ L^4$, so these preferences are jointly inconsistent with expected utility preferences.

3.3 State Spaces

In probability theory and statistics, we often work with different "states of the world." Two such different states could, for example, represent whether there is a recession in the economy or not. Or a state—one among many—may be defined by the joint outcome of all stock prices in the market on a given date. State spaces provide a helpful representation here, beyond the axiomatic theory we introduced for lotteries, allowing us to put some more structure on the randomness.

We define a *probability space* as a triplet $(\Omega, \mathbb{P}, \mathcal{F})$, where the *state space* $\Omega = \{\omega_1, \ldots, \omega_M\}$ represents the possible states that may occur, $\mathbb{P}$ defines probabilities, and $\mathcal{F}$ is a set of events. An *event* is defined as a set of states, so $\mathcal{F}$ is therefore a set of subsets of Ω. The probability measure $\mathbb{P}$ is defined over these events, $\mathbb{P}\colon \mathcal{F} \to [0, 1]$. We will discuss the properties of $\mathcal{F}$ later, but for now we simply assume that it contains all the possible subsets of Ω: $\mathcal{F} = 2^{\Omega}$. The probability measure can then be defined by the probability it assigns to the singleton events: $p_i = \mathbb{P}(\{\omega_i\})$, $i = 1, 2, \ldots, M$.

The lottery, $L = (\Pi_1, \Pi_2, p)$, for example, can be represented by the state space $\Omega = \{\omega_1, \omega_2\}$, where the lottery pays off Π_1 in state ω_1 which occurs with probability p, and Π_2 in state ω_2 which occurs with probability $1 - p$. We will use such a state space representation of a lottery when we wish to put more structure on the environment.

An immediate advantage of this approach is that it allows us to model random outcomes across lotteries and assets that are dependent. For example, imagine the lotteries $L^1 = (2, 0, \frac{1}{4})$ with associated payoffs Π^1, and $L^2 = (1, 0, \frac{1}{2})$ with associated payoffs Π^2, where lottery L^2 always pays 1 if lottery L^1 pays 2. There is no immediate way of modeling this relation without putting more structure on how events are related, but it is easy if we use a state space.[4] We define $\Omega = \{\omega_1, \omega_2, \omega_3\}$, where ω_1 represents the event $(\Pi^1, \Pi^2) = (2, 1)$, ω_2 the event $(\Pi^1, \Pi^2) = (0, 1)$, and ω_3 the event $(\Pi^1, \Pi^2) = (0, 0)$. The probabilities for these events are then $p_1 = \mathbb{P}(\{\omega_1\}) = 0.25$, $p_2 = \mathbb{P}(\{\omega_2\}) = 0.25$, and $p_3 = \mathbb{P}(\{\omega_3\}) = 0.5$. So these two dependent lotteries could easily be handled within the framework of a probability space.

[4]This is not a flaw of the lottery framework in any way. That framework was designed to specifically handle agent attitudes to risk, whereas a richer framework is useful if we want to model the stock market, for example.

We will often work with continuous state spaces. Specifically, we use the following setting:

- A random variable, $\widetilde{X}$, with probability density function (p.d.f.) f and cumulative distribution function (c.d.f.) F:
  - $F(x) = \mathbb{P}(\widetilde{X} \leq x) = \int_{-\infty}^{x} f(x)\, dx$.
  - We have $F(\infty) = 1$ and $F(-\infty) = 0$.
  - The cumulative distribution function $F(x) = \mathbb{P}(\widetilde{X} \leq x)$ is defined even if $\widetilde{X}$ does not have a p.d.f., because there are discrete outcomes that occur with strictly positive probability. In this case, F is right continuous for all x, $F(x) = \lim_{h \searrow 0} F(x+h)$, but may have discontinuities when approached from the left, so it may be the case that $F(x) \neq \lim_{h \nearrow 0} F(x+h)$.
- A utility function, u, defined on $\mathbb{R}$, $\mathbb{R}_+$, or $\mathbb{R}_{++}$, such that
  - u is twice continuously differentiable, strictly increasing, and strictly concave, so that $u' > 0$ and $u'' < 0$.

Expected utility is then

$$U = E[u(x)] = \int u(x)\, dF(x) = \int u(x) f(x)\, dx.$$

3.4 Quantifying Risk Aversion

The concavity of the utility function makes the investor risk averse. We would like to have a quantitative measure of "how risk averse" an expected utility function is at a specific wealth level. Pratt (1964) addresses this question by looking at how an investor trades off higher expectations against higher volatility for very "small" lotteries. Specifically, consider an expected-utility-maximizing agent with current wealth W, who faces a "small" lottery: $L = (\sigma, -\sigma, \frac{1}{2})$, where $0 < \sigma \ll 1$, with associated payoff Π. It follows that

- $E[\Pi] = 0$, and
- $\mathrm{Var}[\Pi] = \sigma^2$.

If the investor is risk averse, (s)he will not want to take on this lottery, since it adds risk with zero expected payoffs, i.e., $E[u(W + \Pi)] < E[u(W)] = u(W)$. Another way to make the investor unhappier is simply to charge a risk-free fee C, leading to utility $u(W - C)$. Indeed, we can choose C to make the investor indifferent between being charged the fee and taking on the lottery, i.e., such that

$$u(W - C) = E[u(W + \Pi)]. \tag{3.2}$$

In other words, $-C$ is the agent's certainty equivalent associated with the lottery. Intuitively, the higher the fee the agent is willing to pay to avoid the lottery, the more risk averse (s)he is. Since the lottery is small, we can do a Taylor expansion[5] on both sides of (3.2), to get

$$u(W) - Cu'(W) = u(W) + \frac{1}{2}(u'(W)(\sigma) + u'(W)(-\sigma))$$
$$+ \frac{1}{2}u''(W)\frac{1}{2}(\sigma^2 + \sigma^2) + O(|\sigma|^3 + |C|^2),$$

[5] See Taylor's theorem in appendix C. The term $O(x)$ here represents the "big O" order function.

leading to

$$C = -\frac{1}{2}\frac{u''(W)}{u'(W)}\sigma^2 + O(|\sigma|^3).$$

This motivates the definition of the *absolute risk aversion* (ARA) coefficient,

$$\text{ARA} = -\frac{u''(W)}{u'(W)},$$

which is such that

$$C = \frac{\sigma^2}{2}\,\text{ARA} + O(|\sigma|^3).$$

The absolute risk-aversion coefficient thus determines how costly an agent thinks it is to be forced to take on a small lottery, per unit of variance. Sometimes it is useful to use the reciprocal of absolute risk aversion, which is called *risk tolerance*:

$$T(W) = \frac{1}{\text{ARA}(W)} = -\frac{u'(W)}{u''(W)}.$$

The ARA typically depends on the agent's wealth level, i.e., it is in general a function of W. For CARA utility, however, one verifies that it is independent of wealth, $\text{ARA} = \gamma$ for all wealth levels, W.

Example 3.2 (CARA preferences). The CARA utility functions are specified as

$$u(x) = -e^{-\gamma x}, \quad \gamma > 0.$$

One verifies that agents with these preferences have constant absolute risk aversion, thereby the name of the utility function, $\text{ARA} = \gamma$, regardless of W. They also have constant risk tolerance, $T(W) = \frac{1}{\gamma}$.

We also introduce the concept of relative risk aversion. Consider an agent with wealth W, who faces a lottery $L = (\sigma W, -\sigma W, \frac{1}{2})$, with

- $E[\Pi] = 0$,
- $\text{Var}[\Pi] = \sigma^2 W^2$.

Compared with the previous situation, the risk (standard deviation) of the lottery is expressed in units of the agent's wealth. For a very wealthy agent (with high W), the same σ therefore represents a much riskier lottery in dollar terms than for a poor agent (with low W). A Taylor expansion for small σ gives us

$$\begin{aligned} u(W) - cWu'(W) = u(W) &+ \frac{1}{2}u'(W)((\sigma W) + (-\sigma W)) \\ &+ \frac{1}{2}u''(W)\frac{1}{2}(\sigma^2 W^2 + \sigma^2 W^2) + O(|\sigma|^3 + |c|^2), \end{aligned}$$

implying that the certainty equivalent, CE, in terms of the fraction of wealth the agent would be willing to give up to avoid the lottery, is

$$\text{CE} \approx \frac{\sigma^2}{2} W \frac{u''(W)}{u'(W)} \stackrel{\text{def}}{=} -\frac{\sigma^2}{2}\,\text{RRA}(W).$$

We therefore define the *relative risk aversion* (RRA) coefficient at wealth W:

$$\text{RRA}(W) = -W\frac{u''(W)}{u'(W)} = W \times \text{ARA}(W).$$

As for constant absolute risk aversion, we may consider preferences with constant relative risk aversion (CRRA), i.e., such that $\mathrm{RRA}(W) = \gamma$ regardless of $W > 0$.

Example 3.3 (CRRA preferences). The constant relative risk-aversion preferences have $\mathrm{RRA} = \gamma$ regardless of wealth, where $\gamma > 0$.

- Their specification is

$$u(x) = \begin{cases} \frac{x^{1-\gamma}}{1-\gamma}, & \gamma \neq 1, \\ \ln(x), & \gamma = 1. \end{cases}$$

- When $\gamma \neq 1$, this is *power utility*.
- When $\gamma = 1$, this is *logarithmic utility*.

We show a few examples of utility functions associated with CRRA preferences in figure 3.3.

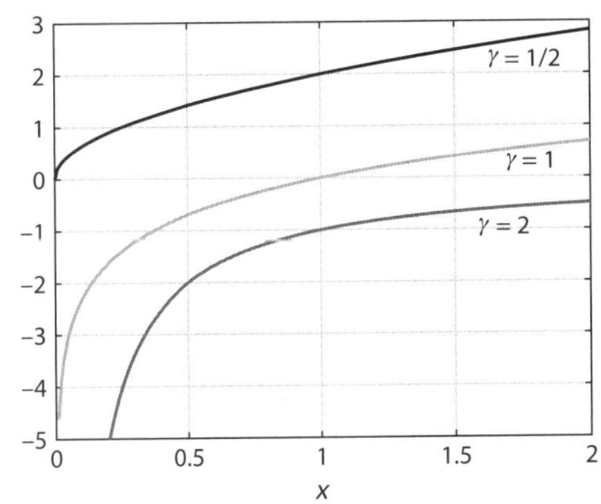

Figure 3.3: CRRA utility functions.

It may be argued that CRRA preferences should be better at describing investors' behavior in practice than CARA preferences. Specifically, it seems like a stretch to assume that someone should be willing to pay the same amount for the lottery $L(10000, 0, \frac{1}{2})$, regardless of whether their wealth is a few dollars or in the billions. CARA preferences are still used a lot in the literature, often because they make the analysis very tractable. This is usually fine, but one should be aware that when calibrating a model with CARA preferences, one needs to think carefully about the appropriate choice of γ. Of course, both CARA and CRRA preferences provide tight specifications of agent preferences and therefore belong high up in the asset pricing pyramid; see figure 1.1.

Note that CRRA utilities are only defined for positive values. When the wealth approaches zero, an investor with these preferences becomes infinitely risk averse. So an investor with CRRA preferences would never accept a lottery that has any chance, regardless of how small, of leading to negative wealth. A less dramatic utility specification for negative wealth is one for which $\mathrm{ARA}(W) \sim |W|^n$ for $W \leq -c$, for some constant $c > 0$. For example, an expected utility function that satisfies

$$u(x) = -e^{|x|^n}, \quad n \geq 2, \; x \leq -1,$$

will have

$$\mathrm{ARA}(W) = n|W|^{n-1} + (n-1)\frac{1}{|W|}, \quad W \leq -1.$$

For $x > 0$, the risk-averse expected utility function may obviously not behave like $-e^{x^n}$, which would be decreasing in wealth. We therefore use another specification for $x > -1$. In the case above, we can for example use the following extension, defined on the whole of the real line, $\mathbb{R}$:

$$u_H(x; n) = \begin{cases} -e^{|x|^n}, & x \leq -1, \\ -\frac{n}{2n-1} e^{-(2n-1)(x+1)+1} - \frac{n-1}{2n-1} e, & x > -1. \end{cases} \tag{3.3}$$

This extension, where "H" stands for "high" (risk aversion), makes u twice continuously differentiable on the whole of $\mathbb{R}$, with $\mathrm{ARA} = 2n - 1$ when $x \geq -1$. Similarly, we introduce utility functions that have very low risk aversion, representing utilities that are close to risk neutral. One such utility specification is

$$u_L(x;\epsilon) = x - \epsilon\left(x\tan^{-1}(x) - \frac{1}{2}\log(1+x^2)\right), \quad 0 < \epsilon < \frac{2}{\Pi} \tag{3.4}$$

(where "L" stands for "low" risk aversion). This function has $u_L' = 1 - \epsilon\tan^{-1}(x)$, $u_L'' = -\frac{\epsilon}{1+x^2}$, and thus

$$\text{ARA} = \frac{\epsilon}{(1+x^2)(1-\epsilon\tan^{-1}(x))},$$

which tends toward zero when x tends to $\pm\infty$.

A risk-averse expected utility function implies a preference for *consumption smoothing*. As before, consider a risk-averse investor with wealth W, who faces the lottery $L(\sigma, -\sigma, \frac{1}{2})$. So far, we have not discussed what the agent will actually *do* with the wealth, but money itself cannot be "eaten." Rather, the utility associated with wealth represents the utility that can be created by buying and consuming goods (food, cars, vacations, etc.). With such a consumption-based interpretation, an agent's utility is really over consumption, $u(c)$. Here we may think of a very simple environment in which there is only one consumption good, or, equivalently, in which we measure an agent's total consumption in units of a *representative good*.

Now consider a risk-averse agent who will receive a random endowment of the consumption good, $\tilde{c}$, which is then consumed. The expected utility associated with this endowment is then

$$U = E[u(\tilde{c})].$$

The reason we have been able to use the specification over wealth is because money can be used to buy consumption goods. In particular, if the price of one unit of the good is a dollar, and the investor has no motive to save any of the random wealth $\widetilde{W}$, we immediately get $\tilde{c} = \widetilde{W}$, so our previous specification over wealth is justified:

$$U = E[u(\widetilde{W})].$$

Keeping in mind that there is an underlying consumption good specification is often useful, especially if we wish to understand how the real economy is related to financial markets. We will discuss this further in the asset pricing part of the text. At this point, we just mention the implication for consumption smoothing. Specifically, Jensen's inequality implies that the agent ex ante prefers consuming the amount c for sure, rather than $c+\sigma$ with a 50% chance and $c-\sigma$ with a 50% chance. This is the "real consumption version" of risk-averse preferences.

More generally, a risk-averse agent always ex ante prefers consuming $E[\tilde{c}]$ for sure rather than the random amount $\tilde{c}$. An interpretation is that the agent would like to smooth consumption across states, by moving consumption from the high-consumption states to the low-consumption states. In the example above, the agent would like to move the consumption σ from the $c+\sigma$ state to the $c-\sigma$ state, leading to consumption c in both states. Such a consumption smoothing motive may help explain why expected returns of assets vary over the business cycle, for instance.

Finally, we provide another characterization of increased risk aversion that relies directly on the utility functions:

Proposition 3.2. *Consider two expected utility functions, u_1 and u_2, such that for some x, $u_1'(x) = u_2'(x)$. Assume that the ARA associated with u_1 is higher than the ARA associated with u_2 at every wealth level:*

$$\text{ARA}_1(y) > \text{ARA}_2(y), \quad \forall y.$$

Then $u_1'(y) > u_2'(y)$ for all $y < x$, and $u_1'(y) < u_2'(y)$ for all $y > x$. If, in addition, $u_1(x) = u_2(x)$, then $u_1(y) < u_2(y)$ for all $y \neq x$.

Proof. Define $z_n(x) = \ln(u_n'(x))$, $n \in \{1, 2\}$. It follows that $z_n' = -\text{ARA}_n(x)$. From the fundamental theorem of calculus, $z_n(y) = z_n(x) - \int_x^y \text{ARA}_n(s)\, ds$, for $y > x$. If $\text{ARA}_1(y) > \text{ARA}_2(y)$, it then follows that $z_1(y) < z_2(y)$, and since the logarithm is monotonically increasing, that $u_1'(y) < u_2'(y)$. Another application of the fundamental theorem of calculus to $u_n'(x)$ implies the second result, $u_1(y) < u_2(y)$, and an identical argument can be made for $y < x$. □

Proposition 3.2 captures the idea that utility functions have "higher curvature," the higher the risk aversion they are associated with. Note that since expected utility functions are invariant to affine transformations, $u \mapsto au + b$, where $a > 0$, one can always rescale so that the conditions $u_1(x) = u_2(x)$, $u_1'(x) = u_2'(x)$ are satisfied.

3.5 Subjective Expected Utility Theory

In the expected utility theory we developed, we assumed that the probabilities for the different outcomes were objectively known. In practice, many decision problems that include risk are such that investors do not objectively know probabilities for different outcomes. Savage (1954) developed an axiomatic theory, *subjective expected utility* (SEU) theory, under which investors behave as if they are expected utility maximizers even if probabilities are not known, with their own subjective beliefs about these probabilities.

In Savage's model, agents may take "acts," which are actions that we here represent by the calligraphic symbol $\mathcal{A}$. These acts determine the payoffs they receive in different states of the world. The setting corresponds to one with lotteries, but with unknown probabilities, e.g., $L = (0, 1, p)$, where no information is given about p. Similar axioms to expected utility theory ensure that an agent in the model behaves (i.e., ranks consequences of acts) as if (s)he is an expected utility maximizer with some personal, subjective, probability estimate, $0 \leq p \leq 1$.

A key axiom in the theory is the so-called *sure thing principle*, which in Savage's theory replaces the independence axiom, and which states that

$$\text{if both } \mathcal{A}|E \text{ and } \mathcal{A}|\neg E, \text{ then } \mathcal{A}.$$

This principle states that if the agent views it as optimal to take act/action $\mathcal{A}$ if the event E occurs, and also if it does not occur (i.e., if $\neg E$ occurs), then the agent should take the action $\mathcal{A}$, even without knowledge about whether E occurs or not. This seems to make a lot of sense at first sight, but it is relatively straightforward to come up with counterexamples when the sure-thing principle is violated, if one allows the act $\mathcal{A}$ to affect the (subjective) likelihood for the event E to occur.

Savage's theorem now states that an agent whose acts satisfy the axioms behaves as if maximizing expected utility, using a subjective probability distribution over states.

3.6 Ambiguity Aversion

In experiments, Ellsberg (1961) showed that people deviate from Savage's predictions in situations where probabilities are not known. One such experiment is as follows: Consider an urn that contains 90 balls, each of which is either red, blue, or yellow. You know that there are 30 red balls, but not the number of blue or yellow balls, just that there are in total 60 balls that are either blue or yellow. You get to play a lottery-like game where you pick a ball from the urn with a blindfold on (so you do not see the color of the ball you pick). Your reward depends on which of the following four lotteries you have selected before picking the ball:

- L^{R}: Earn \$100 if the ball you picked is red.
- L^{B}: Earn \$100 if the ball you picked is blue.
- L^{NR}: Earn \$100 if the ball you picked is not red.
- L^{NB}: Earn \$100 if the ball is you picked is not blue.

How would you rank these four "lotteries"? Many people have the following ranking:

$$L^{\mathrm{NR}} \succ L^{\mathrm{NB}} \succ L^{\mathrm{R}} \succ L^{\mathrm{B}}. \tag{3.5}$$

An argument for why L^{R} is preferred to L^{B} goes something along the lines "I know that I have a $\frac{1}{3}$ chance of earning the reward if I choose L^{R}, whereas the chance can be anywhere between 0 and $\frac{2}{3}$ if I pick L^{B}. So L^{B} seems riskier than L^{R} and I therefore prefer L^{R}. A similar argument leads to L^{NR} dominating L^{NB}.

These two rankings together are inconsistent with subjective expected utility theory, however. Under Savage's axioms, an agent will have a subjective probability estimate of the probability for a randomly chosen ball to be blue, p. If $p < \frac{1}{3}$, then $L^{\mathrm{R}} \succ L^{\mathrm{B}}$. But in that case $L^{\mathrm{NB}} \succ L^{\mathrm{NR}}$. Similarly, if the subjective probability $p > \frac{1}{3}$, $L^{\mathrm{B}} \succ L^{\mathrm{R}}$ and $L^{\mathrm{NR}} \succ L^{\mathrm{NB}}$. Finally, if $p = \frac{1}{3}$, $L^{\mathrm{R}} \sim L^{\mathrm{B}}$ and $L^{\mathrm{NB}} \sim L^{\mathrm{NR}}$. So no p leads to the ranking (3.5), and thus subjective expected utility does not explain this ranking.

This preference in favor of situations where risks (probabilities) are known that many people reveal, like the L^{R} lottery, over those where they are unknown, like the L^{B} lottery, is called *ambiguity aversion*. It has been suggested to help explain several situations where people behave in a manner that seems to be "more risk averse" than can be explained by standard expected utility theory with "reasonable risk aversion." Gilboa and Schmeidler (1989) introduced an axiomatic theory of ambiguity aversion, and an extensive literature has since developed.

3.7 Behavioral Economics and Decision-Making

The field of behavioral economics studies the behavior of people in practice, and how it deviates from rational decision-making, including deviations from expected utility theory. Kahneman and Tversky (1979) initiated this field.[6] In a careful experimental study, they provided evidence that people deviate from the predictions of expected utility theory. They proposed *prospect theory* as an alternative framework that is more in line with the actual behavior they found in their experiments.

In the paper, subjects revealed the following (joint) preferences:

1. $(0, 0, 1) \succ (\$110, -\$100, 0.5)$,
2. $(\$500, 0, 1) \succ (\$1000, 0, 0.5)$,
3. $(-\$1000, 0, 0.5) \succ (-\$500, 0, 1)$,
4. $(\$5000, 0, 0.001) \succ (\$5, 0, 1)$,
5. $(-\$5, 0, 1) \succ (-\$5000, 0, 0.001)$.

[6] Daniel Kahneman and Amos Tversky are, together with Richard Thaler, viewed as the founding fathers of behavioral economics.

These rankings are in several ways inconsistent with risk-averse expected-utility-maximizing behavior. As an exercise, see if you can find three violations of a hypothesized ranking based on the expected utility $U = E[u(\Pi)]$, where u is a twice continuously differentiable, strictly increasing, and strictly concave utility function.

Kahneman and Tversky suggested a ranking based on $\widehat{U} = \mathcal{F}[\hat{u}, \Pi]$, where the continuous function $\hat{u}$ is concave over gains, but convex over losses, and has a "kink," i.e., a discontinuity in its slope, at the so-called reference point where $\Pi = 0$.

The function $\mathcal{F}$ has a similar role to taking an expectation of $\hat{u}$, but it weighs probabilities nonlinearly. Specifically,

$$\widehat{U} = \sum_k \hat{u}(\Pi_k)F(p_k),$$

where low probabilities are overweighted by the nonlinear increasing function, F, and high probabilities are underweighted. This is in contrast to the standard expected utility specification:

$$U = \sum_k u(\Pi_k)p_k.$$

Examples of what the functions $\hat{u}$ and F may look like are provided in figure 3.4.

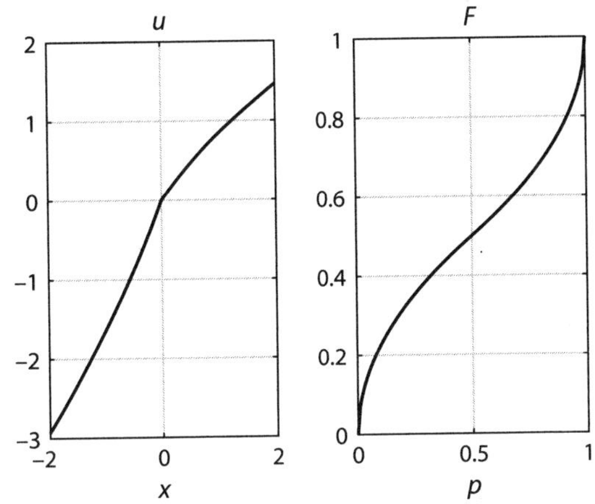

Figure 3.4: Prospect theory: Kinked utility function and nonlinear probability weightings.

3.8 Introducing a Time Dimension

A lottery that pays off today is not the same as one that pays off several years into the future. So far we have ignored this time dimension. A standard way of taking time into account within the expected utility framework is to specify a dynamic *time-separable* expected utility function. Consider the two-date utility

$$U_0 = u(c_0) + \delta E[u(c_1)].$$

Here, c_0 denotes how much the agent consumes at $t = 0$, which is known (nonrisky), and c_1 is consumption at $t = 1$, which typically is risky. The parameter $0 < \delta \leq 1$ is a *personal discount factor*, representing that the agent is impatient (when $\delta < 1$) and prefers to consume earlier rather than later.

Here, the argument in the utility function is consumption (not wealth). Later on, we will let the agent decide how to split his or her wealth into consumption in different time periods. The split will affect the agent's expected utility. Since u is concave, it will typically not be optimal for the agent to use all wealth for consumption in either time period. Instead, a balanced approach will lead to higher expected utility—another form of consumption smoothing that we will return to later on.

The extension to more than two time periods is straightforward, leading to

$$U_0 = \sum_{t=0}^{T} \delta^t E[u(c_t)]. \tag{3.6}$$

In general, it is possible to make the utility function time dependent, $u_t(\cdot)$. However, it is more common to assume the same utility function in each time period. We can also rewrite (3.6) in recursive two-date form. We define $U_T = u(c_T)$, and for $t = T-1, T-2, \ldots, 0$,

$$U_t = u(c_t) + \delta E_t[U_{t+1}].$$

In words, the expected utility at t is the sum of the contribution to utility at t and the discounted expected utility at $t+1$ of all future periods, as summarized by U_{t+1}. This formulation will be very helpful in future chapters, allowing us to use *dynamic programming* to solve multiperiod problems. We can rewrite it this way because of the *law of iterated expectations* (LIE), which states that $E_t[E_s[\widetilde{X}]] = E_t[\widetilde{X}]$, $s \geq t$. So, for example, with three periods,

$$U_0 = u(c_0) + \delta E_0[u(c_1) + \delta u(c_2)] = u(c_0) + \delta E_0[u(c_1) + \delta E_1[u(c_2)]] = u(c_0) + \delta E_0[U_1].$$

Example 3.4. Consider an infinitely lived investor with logarithmic preferences,

$$U_0 = E_0\left[\sum_{t=0}^{\infty} \delta^t \ln(\tilde{c}_t)\right],$$

where the consumption dynamics are $\tilde{c}_{t+1} = \tilde{c}_t \times e^{\tilde{x}_t}$, and where $\tilde{x}_t \sim N(\mu, \sigma^2)$, $t = 1, 2, \ldots$, are independent and identically distributed (i.i.d.) random variables with normal distributions, and c_0 is known. To calculate expected utility, we note that

$$\tilde{c}_t = c_0 e^{\sum_{k=1}^{t} \tilde{x}_t},$$

and therefore

$$E_0[\ln(\tilde{c}_t)] = \ln(c_0) + E_0\left[\sum_{k=1}^{t} \tilde{x}_t\right] = \ln(c_0) + t\mu.$$

It follows that

$$\begin{aligned} U_0 &= \sum_{t=0}^{\infty} \delta^t (\ln(c_0) + t\mu) \\ &= \frac{1}{1-\delta} \ln(c_0) + \mu \sum_{t=1}^{\infty} t\delta^t \\ &= \frac{1}{1-\delta} \ln(c_0) + \mu \frac{\delta}{(1-\delta)^2} \\ &= \frac{1}{1-\delta}\left(\ln(c_0) + \mu \frac{\delta}{1-\delta}\right). \end{aligned}$$

Here we used the geometric summation formula introduced earlier in this chapter when discussing moral utility (see footnote 2 on page 22). As we will see, the case with logarithmic utility is often very tractable in dynamic problems. One reason, as seen here, is that it turns products into sums, by the law of logarithms. Total returns are geometric because of compounding, so their logarithms become sums. Sums of random variables are in turn conveniently handled in probability theory, for example by applying the central limit theorem for i.i.d. random variables.

3.9 Epstein–Zin Preferences

An investor with time-separable expected utility preferences does not care about the timing of uncertainty resolution. This is a consequence of the law of iterated expectations.

Consider, for example, the two alternatives in figure 3.5. The investor has square-root utility and a personal discount factor $\delta = 1$,

$$U_0 = \sqrt{c_0} + E_0[\sqrt{c_1} + \sqrt{c_2}],$$

and is comparing the two different alternatives V1 (version 1) and V2 (version 2). In both cases, consumption at $t = 0$ and $t = 1$ is 1, whereas consumption is 1 or 2 at $t = 2$, with 50% probability each. The only difference is that in V1 the investor finds out at $t = 1$ about time 2 consumption (early uncertainty resolution), whereas in V2 the information is only revealed at $t = 2$ (late uncertainty resolution).

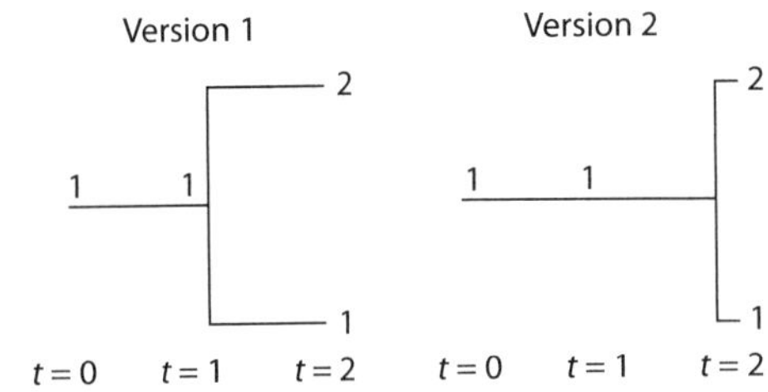

Figure 3.5: Different timing of uncertainty resolution, with three dates.

Under V1, at $t = 1$, the investor's expected utility can then either be $U_1 = \sqrt{1} + \sqrt{2}$, or $U_1 = \sqrt{1} + \sqrt{1}$. The expected utility at $t = 0$ is then

$$U_0 = \sqrt{c_0} + E_0[U_1] = 1 + \frac{1}{2} \times (1 + \sqrt{2}) + \frac{1}{2}(1 + 1) = 2\frac{1}{2} + \frac{\sqrt{2}}{2}.$$

Under V2, at $t = 1$, the investor's expected utility is, for sure,

$$U_1 = \sqrt{c_1} + E[\sqrt{c_2}] = \sqrt{1} + \frac{1}{2} \times \sqrt{2} + \frac{1}{2} \times 1 = 1\frac{1}{2} + \frac{\sqrt{2}}{2},$$

since no information about the outcome of the lottery has arrived yet. At $t = 0$, the utility is then

$$U_0 = \sqrt{1} + E_0\left[1\frac{1}{2} + \frac{\sqrt{2}}{2}\right] = 2\frac{1}{2} + \frac{\sqrt{2}}{2}.$$

So the expected utility is the same regardless of whether there is early or late uncertainty resolution in this case, under the expected utility specification.

Now, there are many situations where many people *do* seem to care about the timing of uncertainty resolution. For example, parents might withhold the information that the family pet was hit by a car from their children, to allow them to enjoy their spring break vacation trip. Also, someone might decide not to take a diagnostic test that will reveal whether they have a rare disease that will develop later in life, for which there is no cure. In both cases, late uncertainty resolution is preferred. On the other hand, some people may think surprise parties "waste" the happiness associated with anticipating the event. They would rather have been told in advance, thus preferring early uncertainty resolution, so that they could have been happy thinking about the upcoming event.

Note that it is important in these examples that the revelation of information does not allow the agent to take action, conditioned on the revealed information. The timing of revelation just determines when they find out what will happen. If there is an efficient cure for the disease available in the example above, that needs to be taken immediately to be effective, this introduces a rationale for preferring early uncertainty resolution also in the expected utility setting.

Epstein–Zin (EZ) preferences allow agents to care about the timing of uncertainty resolution. The specification is defined recursively (just like expected utility, EU, preferences can also be defined recursively, using the law of iterated expectations). In the two-date economy, the utility specification is

$$U = \left(c_0^{1-\rho} + \delta E[\tilde{c}_1^{1-\gamma}]^{\frac{1-\rho}{1-\gamma}}\right)^{\frac{1}{1-\rho}}. \tag{3.7}$$

Here, $\psi = \frac{1}{\rho}$ is the *coefficient of intertemporal substitution*, and γ is as usual the risk-aversion coefficient. With this specification, γ governs consumption smoothing over states and ψ consumption smoothing over time, a point we will discuss later.

One sees that when $\gamma = \frac{1}{\psi}$, the EZ preferences reduce to CRRA preferences with risk-aversion coefficient γ, because

$$U = (c_0^{1-\gamma} + \delta E[\tilde{c}_1^{1-\gamma}])^{\frac{1}{1-\gamma}} = ((1-\gamma)U^{\text{EU}})^{\frac{1}{1-\gamma}}.$$

Specifically, focusing on $\gamma \neq 1$ (the logarithmic case needs to be handled separately but leads to the same conclusion), $U^{\text{EU}} = \frac{U^{1-\gamma}}{1-\gamma}$, for arbitrary positive values of U_a and U_b,

$$U_a > U_b \;\Leftrightarrow\; \frac{U_a^{1-\gamma}}{1-\gamma} > \frac{U_b^{1-\gamma}}{1-\gamma},$$

where the right-hand side represents CRRA expected utility, so the rankings of lotteries are the same. EZ preferences are therefore indeed the same as CRRA preferences in this case, i.e., CRRA preferences are a special case of EZ preferences. In contrast to the EU setting, EZ preferences are in general *not* time separable.

With more than two periods, EZ preferences are defined recursively:

$$U_t = \left(c_t^{1-\rho} + \delta E[U_{t+1}^{1-\gamma}]^{\frac{1-\rho}{1-\gamma}}\right)^{\frac{1}{1-\rho}},$$

with the terminal period utility

$$U_T = c_T.$$

Let us revisit the two examples, V1 and V2, with EZ preferences. Specifically, assume the preferences

$$U_0 = (\sqrt{c_0} + E_0[U_1^{-1}]^{-\frac{1}{2}})^2, \quad U_1 = (\sqrt{c_1} + E_1[U_2^{-1}]^{-\frac{1}{2}})^2, \quad U_2 = c_2.$$

This corresponds to the parameters $\rho = \frac{1}{2}$, $\gamma = 2$, and $\delta = 1$. It follows that

$$1-\gamma = -1, \quad \frac{1-\rho}{1-\gamma} = -\frac{1}{2}, \quad \frac{1}{1-\rho} = 2.$$

Note also that $\rho \neq \gamma$, so this is not a case that reduces to CRRA utility.

We begin with the case of early uncertainty resolution: We have, at $t = 2$, two possible utilities:

$$U_{21} = 1, \tag{3.8}$$

$$U_{22} = 2. \tag{3.9}$$

At $t = 1$, it is already known which of these outcomes will materialize, so there are two possible values of U_1:

$$U_{11} = \left(1^{\frac{1}{2}} + \left(\frac{1}{U_{21}}\right)^{-\frac{1}{2}}\right)^2 = 4$$

and

$$U_{12} = \left(1^{\frac{1}{2}} + \left(\frac{1}{U_{22}}\right)^{-\frac{1}{2}}\right)^2 \approx 5.828.$$

At $t = 0$, this then leads to the utility

$$U_0^{\text{V1}} = \left(1^{\frac{1}{2}} + \left(\frac{1}{2}\frac{1}{U_{11}} + \frac{1}{2}\frac{1}{U_{12}}\right)^{-\frac{1}{2}}\right)^2 \approx 10.10.$$

Let us now compare this with the case of late uncertainty resolution. At $t = 2$, we have the same two possible utilities (3.8, 3.9) as in the previous case. At $t = 1$, it is not known which of these two outcomes will materialize, so there is only one utility:

$$U_1 = \left(1^{\frac{1}{2}} + \left(\frac{1}{2}\frac{1}{U_{21}} + \frac{1}{2}\frac{1}{U_{22}}\right)^{-\frac{1}{2}}\right)^2 \approx 4.643,$$

and at $t=0$ we then get

$$U_0^{V2}=\left(1^{\frac{1}{2}}+\left(\frac{1}{U_1}\right)^{-\frac{1}{2}}\right)^2\approx 9.952.$$

So, since $U_0^{V2}<U_0^{V1}$, this EZ agent prefers early uncertainty resolution. One can show that when $\frac{1}{\psi}<\gamma$, early uncertainty resolution is preferred, whereas when $\frac{1}{\psi}>\gamma$, late uncertainty resolution is preferred. Indeed, expanding the time-0 utility under the two different cases, $\{E,L\}$, representing early and late uncertainty resolution, we get

$$U_{L,0}^{1-\rho}=c_0^{1-\rho}+\delta E_0\big[\big(c_1^{1-\rho}+\delta E_1[c_2^{1-\gamma}]^{\frac{1-\rho}{1-\gamma}}\big)^{\frac{1-\gamma}{1-\rho}}\big],$$
$$U_{E,0}^{1-\rho}=c_0^{1-\rho}+\delta E_0\big[\big(c_1^{1-\rho}+\delta (c_2^{1-\gamma})^{\frac{1-\rho}{1-\gamma}}\big)^{\frac{1-\gamma}{1-\rho}}\big].$$

We focus on the case $0<\rho<\gamma<1$, and define $\theta=\frac{1-\rho}{1-\gamma}>1$.

Clearly, early uncertainty resolution being preferred, $U_{L,0}\le U_{E,0}$, is equivalent to

$$E_0\big[(c_1^{1-\rho}+\delta E_1[c_2^{1-\gamma}]^{\theta})^{\frac{1}{\theta}}\big]\le E_0\big[(c_1^{1-\rho}+\delta (c_2^{1-\gamma})^{\theta})^{\frac{1}{\theta}}\big]. \tag{3.10}$$

Define the function $F_\theta(x)=(c_1^{1-\rho}+\delta x^{\theta})^{\frac{1}{\theta}}$, and verify that F is strictly convex when $\theta>1$ ($F_\theta''>0$), and also that F_θ is strictly concave when $\theta<1$. Then (3.10) can be written

$$E_0[F_\theta(E_1[c_2^{1-\gamma}])]\le E_0[F_\theta(c_2^{1-\gamma})].$$

The result now follows from Jensen's inequality ($F(E[x])\le E[F(x)]$ when F is convex) and the law of iterated expectations, since

$$E_0[F_\theta(E_1[c_2^{1-\gamma}])]\le E_0[E_1[F_\theta(c_2^{1-\gamma})]]=E_0[F_\theta(c_2^{1-\gamma})].$$

Altogether, the result then follows: $U_{L,0}\le U_{E,0}$, where the inequality is strict except in the deterministic case, when there is no uncertainty. The agent therefore prefers *early* uncertainty resolution in general. Equivalent arguments lead to the result for other parameter regions of ρ and γ, taking into account that $U^{1-\rho}$ is decreasing in U when $\rho>1$.

In the example above, $\frac{1}{\psi}=\rho=\frac{1}{2}<2=\gamma$, so we are indeed in the region of preference for early uncertainty resolution, just like we saw in the numerical example.

3.10 Defining Increased Riskiness

So far we have focused on what makes an investor prefer one lottery over another based on preferences, with the understanding that the rankings we derived would be investor specific, so that one investor may prefer lottery L^1 over L^2, whereas another may prefer L^2 over L^1. When thinking about several investors at the same time, say all the investors, $i\in\mathcal{I}$, in some set, $\mathcal{I}$, it is therefore more informative to write $L^1\succeq_i L^2$, to clarify that the ranking is with respect to the preferences of investor *i*. We may also represent the agents by their actual utility functions, $u\in\mathcal{U}$, and write $L^1\succeq_u L^2$ to denote that the ranking holds with respect to the agent with expected utility function u.

How can we determine whether lottery L^1 is "objectively better" than L^2? How can we determine whether it is "objectively riskier"? These question were asked by Rothschild and Stiglitz (1970, 1971). Their idea was to look at a large set of expected utility functions, representing agent behavior that could be considered reasonable, and view L^1 as better/less risky than L^2 if all agents in the set agree on this ranking. Note that, with this approach, we expect to get a much weaker ranking than when we focus on an individual agent's ranking over lotteries. An individual agent will always be able to compare two lotteries and conclude that one is weakly better than the other, since individual preference relations are complete.

In contrast, when we require multiple agents to agree, we would expect there to be many situations where one agent strictly prefers L^1 to L^2, whereas another agent strictly prefers L^2 to L^1. One may think of introducing some type of "majority rule" in this case, but since we are not making any specific assumptions about the agents' actual preferences, just that they belong to $\mathcal{U}$, a huge set, this would be challenging. Rather, we view this as a situation where the lotteries cannot be ranked, with the understanding that there will be many such situations of lotteries that cannot be ranked.

Two reasonable sets of preferences are

$$\mathcal{U}^1 = \{u : u \in C^1, u \text{ is strictly increasing}\},$$

$$\mathcal{U}^2 = \{u : u \in C^2, u \text{ is strictly increasing and strictly concave}\}.$$

It follows that $\mathcal{U}^2$ is a strict subset of $\mathcal{U}^1$. Therefore, if all agents in $\mathcal{U}^1$ prefer L^1 over L^2, all agents in the smaller set $\mathcal{U}^2$ also prefer L^1 over L^2. In general, the larger we make the set $\mathcal{U}$, the more agents need to agree for a lottery to be objectively preferred over another, and the weaker the ranking we therefore expect to get.

Let us consider two lotteries, L^1 and L^2, defined over the probability space $(\Omega, \mathcal{F}, \mathbb{P})$. As we discussed before, these lotteries can simply be viewed as random variables on $\Omega = \{\omega_1, \ldots, \omega_N\}$. Assume that L^1 *statewise dominates* L^2, in that $L^1(\omega_n) \geq L^2(\omega_n)$ for all states, $\omega_n \in \Omega$. It follows immediately that any agent with expected utility $u \in \mathcal{U}^1$ prefers L^1 over L^2, since

$$E[u(L^1)] = \sum_n u(L^1(\omega_n))\mathbb{P}(\omega_n) \geq \sum_n u(L^2(\omega_n))\mathbb{P}(\omega_n) = E[u(L^2)].$$

The ranking will be strict if $L^1(\omega_n) > L^2(\omega_n)$ in at least one state that occurs with strictly positive probability. We have thus shown the following result:

State	p	Payout L1	Payout L2
• 1	0.1	2	3
• 2	0.3	4	5
• 3	0.3	6	7
• 4	0.3	1	3

Figure 3.6: Lotteries with statewise dominance.

Proposition 3.3. *If lottery L^1 dominates L^2 statewise, then all investors with utility functions in $\mathcal{U}^1$ prefer L^1 over L^2.*

Example 3.5. Consider the two lotteries L^1 and L^2 defined over the state space $\Omega = \{1, 2, 3, 4\}$, with associated probabilities $p_i = \mathbb{P}(i)$, and payouts described in figure 3.6. It follows that L^2 dominates L^1 statewise.

This result is very intuitive, but unfortunately it imposes a lot of restrictions on the lotteries L^1 and L^2. If L^1 and L^2 are independent random variables, for example, it can only be applied if $\min L^1 \geq \max L^2$. A related concept to statewise dominance arises in no-arbitrage asset pricing theory, which we will cover later in this text. An arbitrage opportunity is basically an investment that strictly dominates the trivial lottery statewise.

We can build upon the idea behind this result, and expand it, by noting that expected utility maximizers do not care about the actual states they receive payouts in, just about the probabilities for those states. For example, in figure 3.6, consider a modified version $\hat{L}^2$ of the lottery L^2, for which the payouts in states 2 and 3 are switched, i.e., $\hat{L}^2(2) = 7$ and $\hat{L}^2(3) = 5$. In states 1 and 4, the lottery pays the same as before, $\hat{L}^2(1) = 3$ and $\hat{L}^2(4) = 3$. Since the probabilities for states 2 and 3 are the same, the expected utility associated with $\hat{L}^2$ is the same as with L^2, and it must therefore be that $\hat{L}^2$ is also preferred over L^1 by all agents in $\mathcal{U}^1$. However, L^2 does not dominate L^1 statewise, since $\hat{L}^2(3) = 5 < 6 = L^1(3)$.

The concept of first-order stochastic dominance (FSD) "anonymizes" states by focusing on the distributions of payouts rather than on the actual states in which they occur. For the lottery L, with the associated payout Π_L, define cumulative distribution function $F_L(x) = \mathbb{P}(\Pi_L \le x)$.

Definition 3.2. Lottery L^1 is said to weakly *first-order stochastically dominate* lottery L^2, $L^1 \succeq_{\text{FSD}} L^2$, if

$$F_{L^1}(x) \le F_{L^2}(x), \quad \forall x.$$

If the inequality is also strict for some x, then the lottery L^1 is said to strictly FSD L^2, $L^1 \succ_{\text{FSD}} L^2$.

We also write $F_{L^1} \succeq_{\text{FSD}} F_{L^2}$, focusing directly on the lotteries' cumulative distribution functions rather than on the lotteries themselves.

Theorem 3.2. *If $F_{L^1} \succeq_{FSD} F_{L^2}$, then any investor with utility function in $\mathcal{U}^1$ weakly prefers L^1 over L^2, $E[u(\Pi_{L^1})] \ge E[u(\Pi_{L^2})]$. If $F_{L^1} \succ_{FSD} F_{L^2}$, then any investor with utility function in $\mathcal{U}^1$ strictly prefers L^1 over L^2, $E[u(\Pi_{L^1})] > E[u(\Pi_{L^2})]$.*

Proof. For simplicity, we focus on lotteries in $\mathcal{L}^0$, $L^1, L^2 \in \mathcal{L}^0_{[a,b]}$, for some finite interval $[a, b]$. Obviously, $F_{L^1}(b) = F_{L^2}(b) = 1$, since F_{L^n} is a c.d.f. of a random variable with support in $[a, b]$. We also choose a to be lower than the minimum payout, $a < \min\{\min L^1, \min L^2\}$, so that $F_{L^1}(a) = F_{L^2}(a) = 0$.

Assume that $F_{L^1} \succeq_{\text{FSD}} F_{L^2}$. For an expected utility function $u \in \mathcal{U}^1$ we have

$$U(L^1) = \int_a^b u(x)\, dF_{L^1}(x),$$

$$U(L^2) = \int_a^b u(x)\, dF_{L^2}(x).$$

We recall the integration by parts rule:

$$\int_a^b g\, dH = [gH]_a^b - \int_a^b g(x)H(x)\, dx,$$

so

$$\int_a^b u(x)\, dF_{L^n} = [uF_{L^n}]_a^b - \int_a^b u'(x)F_{L^n}(x)\, dx$$

$$= u(b) \times 1 - u(a) \times 0 - \int_a^b u'(x)F_{L^n}(x)\, dx,$$

and therefore

$$U(L^1) - U(L^2) = \int_a^b u'(x)(F_{L^2}(x) - F_{L^1}(x))\, dx.$$

Since $u'(x) > 0$, and $F_{L^1}(x) \le F_{L^2}(x)$ (because $L^1 \succeq_{\text{FSD}} L^2$), it follows that

$$U[L^1] - U[L^2] \ge 0,$$

and therefore that the investor prefers L^1 over L^2. Since the utility function u was an arbitrary function in $\mathcal{U}^1$, this proves the result. An identical argument shows the strict preference when $F_{L^1} \succ_{\text{FSD}} F_{L^2}$.

Although not part of the formulation of the proposition, the result is really an if-and-only-if result in the sense that if it is *not* the case that $L^1 \succeq_{\text{FSD}} L^2$ (which, since FSD provides a weak ranking, does *not* imply that $L^2 \succeq_{\text{FSD}} L^1$), then there exists a utility function, $u \in \mathcal{U}^1$, such that

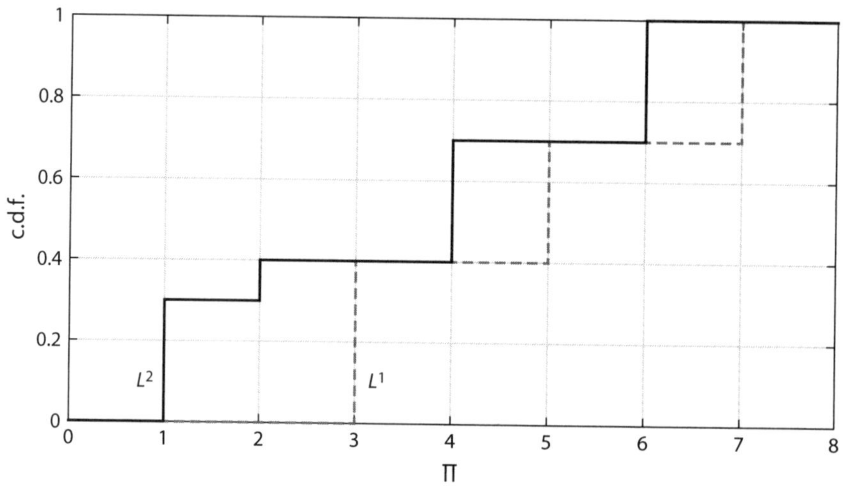

Figure 3.7: First-order stochastic dominance.

$U(L^1) < U(L^2)$. To show this, choose an interval $R = [x, x+\epsilon] \subset [a, b]$, such that $F_{L^1}(y) - F_{L^2}(y) \geq \epsilon$ for all $y \in [x, x+\epsilon]$. Here, $x \in [a, b)$, and $\epsilon > 0$ can be arbitrarily close to zero as long as it is strictly positive. Such an interval, R, must necessarily exist, since $F_{L^1}(x) > F_{L^2}(x)$ for some x, and both functions are right continuous. Now choose a utility function $u \in \mathcal{U}^1$, such that $u'(y) = 1$ for $y \in [x + \frac{\epsilon}{4}, x + \frac{3\epsilon}{4}]$, and $u'(y) = \frac{\epsilon}{4(b-a)}$ for $y \in [a, b] \backslash R$. We then have

$$\begin{aligned}
U(L^1) - U(L^2) &= \int_a^b u'(x)(F_{L^2}(x) - F_{L^1}(x))\, dx \\
&= \int_{x \in [a,b] \backslash R} u'(x)(F_{L^2}(x) - F_{L^1}(x))\, dx + \int_{x \in R} u'(x)(F_{L^2}(x) - F_{L^1}(x))\, dx \\
&\leq \frac{\epsilon}{4(b-a)} \times (b - a - \epsilon) - \frac{\epsilon}{2} \times 1 \\
&\leq -\frac{\epsilon}{4}.
\end{aligned}$$

Thus, $U(L^1) < U(L^2)$ for the agent with utility function u or, equivalently, $L^2 \succ_u L^1$. □

We see that first-order stochastic dominance can be determined by comparing the c.d.f.s of two lotteries. An example is given in figure 3.7, in which the dash-dotted line represents the c.d.f. of lottery L^1, which first-order stochastically dominates lottery L^2, whose c.d.f. is represented by the solid line.

First-order stochastic dominance captures better-than rankings for a very large set of investors—those with increasing expected utility functions. Even risk-loving investors will agree that they prefer one lottery over another if it first-order stochastically dominates that lottery. So the concept has little to do with risk aversion. To develop a measure that is focused on risk aversion, we look at the class $\mathcal{U}^2$ of utility functions, which only include risk-averse investors, i.e., those with strictly concave utility functions. Consider the lotteries L^1 and L^2 with associated cumulative distribution functions F_{L^1} and F_{L^2}, and assume that $\int_{-\infty}^{0} F_{L^1}(x)\, dx < \infty$ and $\int_{-\infty}^{0} F_{L^2}(x)\, dx < \infty$, which will be the case as long as neither lottery has a very heavy-tailed distribution. For lotteries in

$\mathcal{L}^0$, the condition will automatically be satisfied. It will be easiest to focus on such lotteries, since it avoids some technical issues, e.g., ensuring that expected utility is finite.[7]

Definition 3.3. Lottery L^1 is said to weakly *second-order stochastically dominate* lottery L^2, $L^1 \succeq_{SSD} L^2$, if

$$\int_{-\infty}^{x} F_{L^1}(s)\, ds \leq \int_{-\infty}^{x} F_{L^2}(s)\, ds, \quad \forall x.$$

If the inequality is also strict for some x, then the lottery L^1 is said to strictly SSD L^2, $L^1 \succ_{SSD} L^2$.

We now have the following result:

Theorem 3.3. *If $L^1 \succeq_{SSD} L^2$, then any investor with utility function in $\mathcal{U}^2$ weakly prefers L^1 over L^2, $E[u(\Pi_{L^1})] \geq E[u(\Pi_{L^2})]$. If $F_{L^1} \succ_{SSD} F_{L^2}$, then any investor with utility function in $\mathcal{U}^2$ strictly prefers L^1 over L^2, $E[u(\Pi_{L^1})] > E[u(\Pi_{L^2})]$.*

Proof. Just like for FSD, we focus on lotteries in $\mathcal{L}^0$, $L^1, L^2 \in \mathcal{L}^0_{[a,b]}$ for some finite interval $[a, b]$, such that a is below the minimum payout. We define

$$G_{L^n}(x) = \int_a^x F_{L^n}(s)\, ds, \quad n \in \{1, 2\},$$

and note that $G_{L^n}(a) = 0$. Again, we use the integration by parts rule to arrive at

$$\begin{aligned}\int_a^b u(x)\, dF_{L^n} &= [uF_{L^n}]_a^b - \int_a^b u'(x) F_{L^n}(x)\, dx \\ &= u(b) \times 1 - u(a) \times 0 - \int_a^b u'(x) F_{L^n}(x)\, dx.\end{aligned}$$

However, instead of stopping here as we did in the proof for FSD, we apply the rule again to get

$$\begin{aligned}\int_a^b u(x)\, dF_{L^n} &= u(b) - \int_a^b u'(x) F_{L^n}(x)\, dx \\ &= u(b) - [u' G_{L^n}]_a^b + \int_a^b u''(x) G_{L^n}(x)\, dx \\ &= u(b) - u'(b) G_{L^n}(b) + \int_a^b u''(x) G_{L^n}(x)\, dx.\end{aligned}$$

We therefore get

$$U(L^1) - U(L^2) = -u'(b)(G_{L^1}(b) - G_{L^2}(b)) + \int_a^b u''(x)(G_{L^1}(x) - G_{L^2}(x))\, dx.$$

Since $u' > 0$ and $u'' < 0$ for all $u \in \mathcal{U}^2$, it follows that $U(L^1) - U(L^2) \geq 0$. As is the case for FSD, the argument also goes through with strict inequalities, and one can show that the reverse "only-if" result holds, namely that if L^1 does *not* SSD L^2, then there exists a utility function, $u \in \mathcal{U}^2$, such that $L^2 \succ_u L^1$. □

[7] For a very risk-averse investor, expected utility may be negatively infinite even if the lottery is thin tailed. For example, a risk-averse investor with utility function $u(x) \sim -e^{x^2}$ when $x < -1$ would have negatively infinite expected utility even for a standard normally distributed lottery with payoff $\Pi \sim N(0, 1)$.

Note that if $L^1 \succeq_{SSD} L^2$, then it must be the case that $E[\Pi^1] \geq E[\Pi^2]$, since

$$E[\Pi^n] = \int_a^b x\, dF_{L^n} = b - \int_a^b F_{L^n}(x)\, dx$$
$$= b - [G_{L^n}]_a^b = b - G_{L^n}(b),$$

so $E[\Pi^1] - E[\Pi^2] = G_{L^2}(b) - G_{L^1}(b)$, which is nonnegative when $L^1 \succeq L^2$. This should come as no surprise, since there are utility functions in $\mathcal{U}^2$ that are arbitrarily close to risk neutral, and a risk-neutral investor only cares about expectations. If $E[\Pi^1] < E[\Pi^2]$, there would therefore be such an almost-risk-neutral investor who would prefer L^2 over L^1. That the expected payout of L^1 is at least as high as the expected payout of L^2 ($E[\Pi^1] \geq E[\Pi^2]$) is thus a necessary condition for L^1 to second-order stochastically dominate L^1. However, it is not sufficient. The dominating lottery also needs to be weakly less risky than the dominated lottery in a sense we yet need to define. Before we do this, however, we state a property of SSD that is very intuitive, and also easy to show:

Proposition 3.4. *If $L^1 \succeq_{SSD} L^2$, then $L^1 + q_1 \succeq_{SSD} L^2 + q_2$ for constants $q_1 \geq q_2$.*

Intuitively, adding risk-free positive payoffs to a lottery always makes it more attractive.

Definition 3.4. The lottery L^1 is (weakly) *less risky* than L^2 if

$$L^1 - E[\Pi^1] \succeq_{SSD} L^2 - E[\Pi^2].$$

There are many different definitions of risk within finance. To be completely unambiguous here, one may state that *lottery L^1 is weakly less risky than L^2 based on second-order stochastic dominance.* This is the most general measure of risk we will use in this text. We immediately get the following result:

Proposition 3.5. *For two lotteries with the same expected payouts, L^1 and L^2, all agents in $\mathcal{U}^2$ prefer L^1 over L^2 if and only if L^1 is less risky than L^2.*

When discussing portfolio choice and the capital asset pricing model, in the next chapters, we will often work with variance (or, equivalently, standard deviation) as a measure of the riskiness of a portfolio of assets. As we will see, that measure works very well for some specific choices of utility functions that belong to a very small subset of $\mathcal{U}^2$. It therefore provides a strong ranking of riskiness. Specifically, an investor with an expected utility function $u(x) = x - ax^2$, where $a > 0$ is chosen appropriately small, so that the utility function is increasing on the range of possible payouts, will only care about the mean and variance of a lottery. Our definition above, which is based on SSD, is weaker than a definition that ranks risks based on variance, since investors with utility functions in $\mathcal{U}^2$ who take into account properties of lotteries other than expected payouts and variance (for instance skewness and kurtosis) must also agree on SSD rankings. The next result thus follows:

Proposition 3.6. *A necessary condition for the lottery L^1 to be less risky than L^2 is that* $\text{Var}(\Pi^1) \leq \text{Var}(\Pi^2)$.

In the context of the asset pricing pyramid, see figure 1.1, a risk ranking based on variance belongs at the top of the pyramid, whereas a ranking based on $\mathcal{U}^1$ or $\mathcal{U}^2$ belongs somewhere in the middle—being based on expected utility preferences, but not taking a stance on the actual utility function.

Definitions 3.3 and 3.4, together with theorem 3.3, provide a strong characterization of what it means for a lottery to be more risky than another, in terms of the function $G(x) = \int_{-\infty}^{x} F(x)\, dx$:

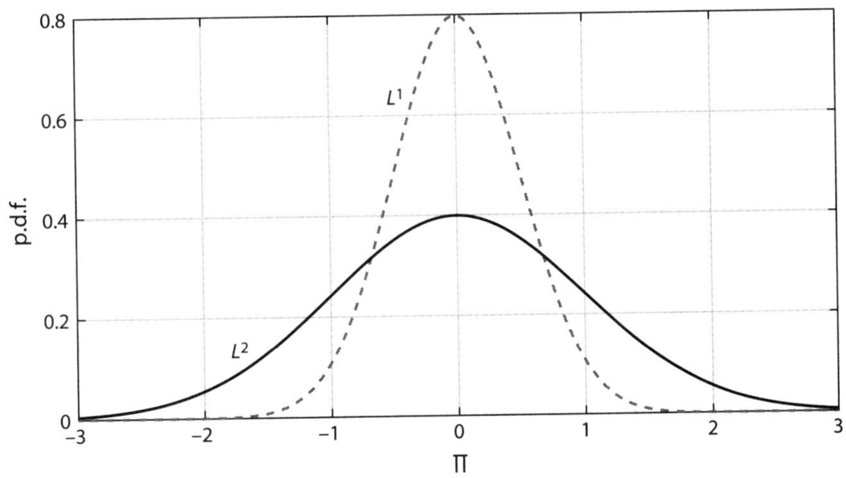

Figure 3.8: Second-order stochastic dominance.

the larger the value of this function, the riskier the lottery. An example of two lotteries is given in figure 3.8. The lottery with the solid line p.d.f., L_2, is riskier than the lottery with the dash-dotted line p.d.f., L_1. For instance, it has a higher standard deviation. The intuition for what it means for G_{L^2} be larger than G_{L^1} is not immediately clear though, at least not as clear as the interpretation of higher variance, which means that the "spread" of the payoff is higher.

A useful concept for understanding increased riskiness when using second-order stochastic dominance is in terms of a mean-preserving spread.

Definition 3.5. Consider two random variables, Π_{L^1} and Π_{L^2}, with the same mean, $E[\Pi_{L^1}] = E[\Pi_{L^2}]$. The random variable Π_{L^2} is said to be a *mean-preserving spread* of Π_{L^1} if

$$\Pi_{L^2} =^d \Pi_{L^1} + z,$$

where $E[z|\Pi_{L^1}] = 0$, for all realizations of Π_{L^1}.

Here, the symbol $=^d$ means that the random variables are equal in distribution, i.e., that their c.d.f.s are identical: $F_{L^1}(x) = F_{L^2}(x)$ for all x. The condition that $E[z|\Pi_{L^1}] = 0$ means that z is *conditionally independent* of Π_{L^1}. A special case for which z is conditionally independent of Π_{L^1} is when z and Π_{L^1} are independent.

Theorem 3.4. *The following three statements are equivalent for two lotteries, L^1 and L^2, with the same expectation, $E[\Pi_{L^1}] = E[\Pi_{L^2}]$:*

(a) *All agents in $\mathcal{U}_2$ prefer L^1 to L^2.*
(b) $F_{L^1} \succeq_{SSD} F_{L^2}$.
(c) *F_{L^2} is a mean-preserving spread of F_{L^1}.*

Proof. Note that (a) and (b) are equivalent per theorem 3.3. We use the law of iterated expectations to show that (c) implies (a). We have

$$\begin{aligned} E[u(\Pi_{L^2})] &= E[E[u(\Pi_{L^1} + z|\Pi_{L^1})]] \\ &\le E[u(\Pi_{L^1})]. \end{aligned}$$

Here we use Jensen's inequality and the fact that $E[\Pi_{L^1} + z|\Pi_{L^1}] = \Pi_{L^1}$. The reverse implication is proved in Rothschild and Stiglitz (1970), and goes a bit outside the scope of this text, so we omit it; see also Ingersoll (1987). □

3.11 Exercises

1. Consider the following utility functions:

   - $u(x) = \ln(x)$,
   - $u(x) = -e^{-\gamma x}$,
   - $u(x) = \frac{x^{1-\gamma}}{1-\gamma}$.

   Check that they are well behaved ($u' > 0$, $u'' < 0$), or state any parameter restrictions that are needed to ensure that they are. Compute the absolute and relative risk-aversion coefficients. How does risk aversion change with x?

2. Consider an investor with constant absolute risk-aversion (CARA) expected utility, $u(W) = -e^{-\gamma W}$, where γ denotes the coefficient of absolute risk aversion. Assume that the investor's current wealth is $W = 0$, and consider the following three lotteries:

   - $L^1 = (5, 0, 0.9)$,
   - $L^2 = (10, 0, 0.9)$,
   - $L^3 = (4, 0.1, 0.9)$.

   (a) Rank the three lotteries for an investor with $\gamma = 1$, and calculate the certainty equivalent for the three lotteries.
   (b) Do the same calculations as in (a) for an investor with $\gamma = 4$.

3. Would an investor with CARA expected utility $u(x) = -e^{-\gamma x}$, $\gamma = 1$, and wealth $W = 3$ accept the lottery $L = (1, -1, 0.9)$?

4. What risk-aversion coefficient, $\gamma > 0$, would make a CARA investor facing the lottery in question 3 above indifferent between accepting the lottery or not.

5. Show that the constant absolute risk-aversion coefficient, ARA, is invariant to linear transformations of the underlying utility function, $u(x) \mapsto au(x) + b$, $a > 0$, $b \in \mathbb{R}$.

6. You are exposed to the lottery $(1000, -1000, 0.5)$. Someone offers to take on the lottery, if you pay them 500. Your utility function is logarithmic. At what wealth levels are you willing to pay 500 to avoid the lottery?

7. Consider an investor with CARA utility, wealth $W = 10$, and risk aversion $\gamma = 0.1$, who is given the opportunity to buy a lottery ticket $L = (100, 0, 0.01)$.

   (a) How much would the investor be willing to pay for the ticket?
   (b) If the investor instead had wealth $W = 100$, what would he/she be willing to pay for the ticket?
   (c) Do the same calculations as in (a) and (b) for an investor with log-utility, $u(x) = \ln(x)$. You will need to find the solution numerically.

8. Consider three CARA investors, $i \in \{1, 2, 3\}$, with risk-aversion coefficients, $\gamma_1 = 0.5$, $\gamma_2 = 1$, $\gamma_3 = 2$, and wealths $W^1 = 10$, $W^2 = 100$, $W^3 = 1000$, respectively. They are bidding against

each other in an auction to buy the lottery $L = (0, 5, 10; 0.8, 0.1)$, written in simple form (see page 21). The lottery thus has two winning prize levels (a 10% chance of winning 5, and a 10% chance of winning 10). Who will buy the lottery and at what price, P?

9. Consider an investor with log-utility and wealth $W = 2$, and a lottery $L = (3, 0, 0.5)$.

   (a) If the investor already owns the lottery, what is the minimum price at which (s)he will be ready to sell it?
   (b) If the investor does not own the lottery yet, what is the maximum price at which (s)he will be ready to buy it?
   (c) If the economy consists only of the two investors described above, one who owns the lottery (which is indivisible) and one who may potentially buy it, will they trade the lottery with each other? Explain!

10. The only investment opportunity available in a market, asset A, costs \$1000 and offers (immediate) net returns of -5% with 10% probability, and +30% with 90% probability. So the net payoff of asset A when interpreted as a lottery is $(-1000 + 950, -1000 + 1300, 0.1)$. A competitor is planning to introduce another asset, B, that also costs \$1000, which will offer net returns of -10% with 1% probability, and +40% with 99% probability, corresponding to the lottery $(-1000 + 900, -1000 + 1400, 0.01)$.

    (a) Consider a CRRA investor with risk-aversion coefficient $\gamma = 2$ and wealth $W = \$1000$. How would this investor rank the three alternatives: (i) invest in A, (ii) invest in B, and (iii) invest in neither?
    (b) The competitor wants *every* investor to prefer asset B over asset A, and therefore considers selling it for a lower price than \$1000. At what price, P_1, would every investor with an *increasing* expected utility function prefer asset B over asset A? At what price, P_2, would every investor with a *risk-averse* expected utility function prefer asset B over asset A?

11. Consider two uniformly distributed random variables, $\widetilde{X}_1$ and $\widetilde{X}_2$, with support on $[-1, 1]$ and $[-2, 2]$, respectively. Their respective probability density functions are then $f_1 = \frac{1}{2}\chi_{[-1,1]}$, and $f_2 = \frac{1}{4}\chi_{[-2,2]}$, where the indicator function χ_A on the set A is defined such that

$$\chi_A(x) = \begin{cases} 1, & x \in A, \\ 0, & x \notin A. \end{cases} \tag{3.11}$$

    Their c.d.f.s are F_1 and F_2.

    (a) Does F_1 first-order stochastically dominate F_2?
    (b) Does F_1 second-order stochastically dominate F_2?

12. Ann, Bob, and Charles are choosing between three different lotteries,

$$L^1 = (0, 5, 10; 0.25, 0.5),$$

$$L^2 = (0, 5, 10; 0.5, 0),$$

$$L^3 = (0, 5, 10; 0, 0.5),$$

    written in simple form (see page 21).

Ann, Bob, and Charles are all expected utility maximizers. Ann has a logarithmic utility function $u^A(x) = \ln(\beta + x)$, $\beta > 0$, whereas Bob has CARA utility $u^B(x) = -e^{-\gamma x}$, $\gamma > 0$. Finally, Charles—who goes by the nickname "Daredevil Charlie"—has the utility function $u^C(x) = e^{\alpha x}$ for some $\alpha > 0$.

What can we say about how Ann, Bob, and Charles rank these three lotteries, without further knowledge about the parameters, α, β, and γ? Is there a lottery that all three of them rank the highest? If so, what about the other two lotteries?

13. Consider the following class of lotteries $\{L^\alpha\}_{0<\alpha<\infty}$, defined by

$$L^\alpha = \left(1 - \alpha, 1 + \frac{1}{\alpha}, \frac{1}{1+\alpha^2}\right).$$

Recall that the lottery $L = (u, v, p)$ pays u with probability p and v with probability $1 - p$.

(a) Calculate the expected value and variance of the random payoff $\tilde{x}^\alpha$ associated with the lottery L^α.

(b) Consider an agent with CARA expected utility preferences, $U = E[-e^{-\tilde{x}}]$, over lotteries with payoffs $\tilde{x}$. Calculate the expected utility U^α the agent associates with the lottery L^α.

(c) Calculate $\lim_{\alpha\to 0} U^\alpha$ and $\lim_{\alpha\to\infty} U^\alpha$.

(d) One can show that $\frac{dU^\alpha}{d\alpha} < 0$. What are the implications with respect to which lotteries the agent would be willing to accept?

(e) Does the agent behave like a mean variancc optimizer? Explain!

CHAPTER 4

Choosing an Investment Portfolio

4.1 Introduction

We use our results from the previous chapter to analyze how to choose an investment portfolio. We consider an investor with expected utility preferences and utility function u, which is smooth (three times continuously differentiable) and concave. The investor's initial wealth is $W_0 > 0$. There is a bank account available that offers the interest rate r^f and, as before, we also define $R^f = 1 + r^f$. Equivalently, the current price of a zero coupon bond that pays F in the next period is $\frac{F}{1+r^f}$.

In most parts of this chapter, we assume that there is only one period. So investments occur at $t = 0$, and returns are realized at $t = 1$. We may think of the time period as a year. We initially disregard any consumption motives the investor may have at $t = 0$, so all wealth is invested. To avoid any motives to "stuff money in the mattress," we assume that $r^f > 0$. An investment in risk-free bonds of V dollars at time 0 will then grow to

$$V \times (1 + r^f) = VR^f$$

dollars at $t = 1$.

We make the following assumptions of a *perfect market*:

- Fractional holdings are possible, as is short-selling. So, for example, an investor can buy 1.532 shares, or −63.5 shares of a stock.
- There is no bound on how many units of an asset (e.g., stock shares) can be purchased or sold.
- There are no transaction costs or bid-ask spreads.
- Price linearity: the cost of c units of an asset is c times the cost of one unit.
- Payoff linearity: the payoff of c units of an assets is c times the payoff of one unit.
- Linearity across assets: the price and payoff of a portfolio of different assets are the sums of the prices and payoffs of the individual assets.

For the time being, we assume that there is only one risky asset, a "stock," which is available at the time-0 price, P_0, per share. Its value is $\widetilde{P}_1$ per share at time 1. For simplicity, we assume that the stock does not pay dividends, so its total return is then

$$\tilde{\mu} = \frac{\widetilde{P}_1 - P_0}{P_0}.$$

We also assume that the return distribution is associated with a continuous probability density function. We have

(i) the expected return of $\tilde{\mu}$ is $\mu = E[\tilde{\mu}]$,
(ii) the variance of $\tilde{\mu}$ is $\sigma^2 = \text{Var}(\tilde{\mu}) > 0$,
(iii) the probability density function of $\tilde{\mu}$ is $\phi(x)$, and
(iv) V dollars invested in the stock at $t = 0$ grow to $V(1 + \tilde{\mu})$ dollars at $t = 1$.

Although we use the term "stock" for the risky asset, it may be more intuitive to think of it as an investment in a broad market portfolio of stocks, for example, in an index fund.

We next write down the investor's *budget constraint*. As mentioned, we initially do not consider investor consumption at time 0. For later use, we still include a term for consumption at time 0, C_0, which we for the time being set to zero. Since the bank's interest rate is positive, an investor who invests V in stock and consumes C_0 always deposits the remaining $W_0 - V - C_0$ in the bank and earns interest. The investor's budget constraint is therefore

$$\begin{aligned} W_1 &= (W_0 - V - C_0)(1 + r^f) + V(1 + \tilde{\mu}) \\ &= (W_0 - C_0)(1 + r^f) + V(\tilde{\mu} - r^f). \end{aligned}$$

When $C_0 = 0$, this reduces to

$$\begin{aligned} W_1 &= W_0(1 + r^f) + V(\tilde{\mu} - r^f) \\ &= W_0(1 + r^f + \alpha(\tilde{\mu} - r^f)) \\ &= W_0(R^f + \alpha(\tilde{\mu} - r^f)). \end{aligned}$$

Here, $\alpha = \frac{V}{W_0}$ is the fraction of wealth the investor allocates to the risky asset.

We explore the return distribution on the investor's portfolio, as a function of the fraction of wealth invested in the risky asset, α. We mention some special cases:

- When $\alpha = 0$, the investor deposits all the wealth in the bank account and stays away from the stock.
- When $\alpha = 1$, the investor puts all the wealth in the stock.
- When $\alpha > 1$, the investor borrows from the bank to invest in the stock (leveraged position).
- When $\alpha < 0$, the investor short-sells the stock.
- When $0 < \alpha < 1$, the investor buys both the bond and the stock.

In figure 4.1, we show the return distributions of wealth for a specific case, with normally distributed stock returns: $\tilde{\mu} \sim N(\mu, \sigma^2)$, $\mu = 12\%$, $\sigma = 15\%$, $r^f = 5\%$, leading to the return distribution

$$\frac{W_1}{W_0} = 1 + r^f + \alpha(\tilde{\mu} - r^f) \sim N(1 + r^f + \alpha(\mu - r^f), \alpha^2\sigma^2).$$

In the leftmost panel, the investor puts most wealth in the bond, leading to quite low expected returns and very little risk. In the middle panel, the investor puts all money in the stock, increasing expected returns but also risk (the spread of the potential returns is higher). In the rightmost panel, the investor borrows money from the bank to invest in the stock ($\alpha = 2$), further increasing expected returns and also risk.

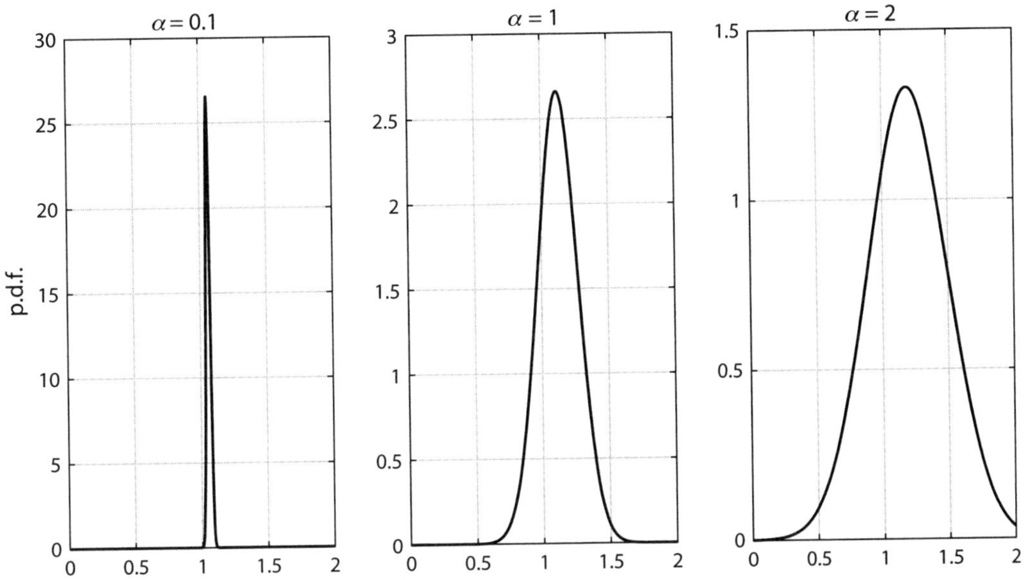

Figure 4.1: Portfolio return distribution (p.d.f.) for different investment levels, $\alpha = 0.1$, $\alpha = 1$, and $\alpha = 2$.

So what level of investments in the risky asset, α^*, should the investor choose? The level that maximizes expected utility of wealth at $t = 1$, $E[u(W_1)]$, of course! This leads to the following maximization problem:

$$\begin{aligned}\alpha^* &= \arg\max_\alpha E[u(W_1)]\\ &= \arg\max_\alpha E\big[u\big(W_0(1 + r^f + \alpha(\tilde{\mu} - r^f))\big)\big]\\ &= \arg\max_\alpha \int u\big(W_0(1 + r^f + \alpha(\tilde{\mu} - r^f))\big)\phi(x)\, dx.\end{aligned}$$

The number of dollars invested in the stock is then $V^* = W_0\alpha^*$. We sometimes write $\alpha^*(W_0)$ and $V^*(W_0)$ when we want to stress the potential dependence of these variables on investor wealth.

We return to the questions we asked earlier, of how much should be invested in stocks, and specifically ask ourselves the following questions:

- When will the investor stay away from the stock, i.e., choose $\alpha^* = 0$?
- Will the investor ever short-sell the stock?
- Will the investor increase the amount invested in stocks when wealth increases?
  - Is $V^*(W_0)$ increasing in wealth, W_0?
  - Is $\alpha^*(W_0)$ increasing in wealth, W_0?

The properties of the expected utility function allow us to immediately answer the first two questions:

Theorem 4.1. *As long as the expected return on the stock is higher than the risk-free rate, the investor invests a positive amount in the stock, regardless of its riskiness. Specifically,*

- $\alpha^* > 0$ *when* $\mu > r^f$,
- $\alpha^* < 0$ *when* $\mu < r^f$,
- $\alpha^* = 0$ *when* $\mu = r^f$.

Proof. The investor solves

$$\max_{\alpha} U = \max_{\alpha} \int_{-\infty}^{\infty} u\big(W_0(1+r^f+\alpha(x-r^f))\big)\phi(x)\,dx.$$

We can write $U = U(\alpha)$, and the *first-order condition* (FOC) is then $\frac{dU}{d\alpha}(\alpha^*) = 0$, implying

$$0 = \int_{-\infty}^{\infty} u'\big(W_0(1+r^f+\alpha^*(x-r^f))\big)(x-r^f)\phi(x)\,dx. \tag{4.1}$$

Here we are technically using the fact that we can switch the order of differentiation and integration, $\frac{d}{d\alpha}[\int_{-\infty}^{\infty} f(x,\alpha)\,dx] = \int_{-\infty}^{\infty} \frac{d}{d\alpha}[f(x,\alpha)]\,dx$. There are a large number of such "switches of order are OK for linear operators" results in mathematics (both differentiation and integration are linear operations, with the linearity concept appropriately defined). Examples include the commutativity of multiplication—$a(bx) = b(ax)$—which can be viewed as switching the orders of the linear operators $x \mapsto ax$ and $x \mapsto bx$, and Fubini's theorem in measure theory, which allows one to switch the order of integration for integrals over multiple variables.

To show that it is OK to switch the order of differentiation and integration, one usually relies on Lebesgue's dominated convergence theorem, in combination with some additional assumptions about the function—for example, that its absolute derivative ($|x \times u' \times \phi(x)|$ in this case) is not "too large." Specifically, if $\tilde{\mu}$ has compact support, i.e., if $\phi(x) = 0$ when $x \notin [a, b]$ for some finite interval $[a, b]$, then switching the order is OK. More generally, as long as

$$\sup_x |x| \times u'\big(W_0(R^f+\alpha(x-r^f))\big) \times \phi(x) \le M < \infty$$

for all α in some neighborhood around 0, $\alpha \in (\underline{\alpha}, \bar{\alpha})$, $\underline{\alpha} < 0 < \bar{\alpha}$, then it is OK to switch the order for such α. Intuitively, the general condition means that the distribution of ϕ decreases fast enough in the tails, so that there will not be arbitrarily high contributions to expected utility from far out in these tails (in the left tail of x if $\alpha > 0$ and in the right tail if $\alpha < 0$). For standard choices of utility functions and risk distributions, this switching condition is satisfied.

Now, if the agent chooses $\alpha = 0$,

$$\begin{aligned}
\left.\frac{dU}{d\alpha}\right|_{\alpha=0} &= \int_{-\infty}^{\infty} W_0 u'\big(W_0(1+r^f+\alpha(\tilde{\mu}-r^f))\big)(x-r^f)\phi(x)\,dx \\
&= W_0 u'(W_0(1+r^f)) \int_{-\infty}^{\infty} (x-r^f)\phi(x)\,dx \\
&= W_0 u'(W_0(1+r^f))(\mu - r^f).
\end{aligned}$$

So $U'(0) > 0$ if $\mu > r^f$, $U'(0) < 0$ if $\mu < r^f$, and $U'(0) = 0$ if $\mu = r^f$.

The concavity of u then implies the result. For simplicity, we assume that it is also OK to switch the order of differentiation and integration when differentiating a second time. Specifically,

$$\sup_x \big|x^2 u''\big(W_0(R^f+\alpha(x-r^f))\big)\big|\phi(x) \le M' < \infty$$

for all $\alpha \in (\underline{\alpha}, \bar{\alpha})$, $\underline{\alpha} < 0 < \bar{\alpha}$. This gives us

$$\frac{d^2U}{d\alpha^2} = \int_{-\infty}^{\infty} W_0^2 u''\big(W_0(1+r^f+\alpha(\tilde{\mu}-r^f))\big)(x-r^f)^2\phi(x)\,dx < 0.$$

So $U(\alpha)$ is strictly concave, i.e., $U'(\alpha)$ is strictly decreasing in α. When $\mu = r^f$, this immediately implies that $\alpha^* = 0$, since the first-order condition being satisfied for a strictly concave function is sufficient for a global maximum. For $\mu > r^f$, $U'(0) > 0$, and α^* must therefore be strictly positive. Note that we may technically have $\alpha^* = +\infty$ if the agent is sufficiently close to risk neutral. For example, with the low-risk aversion $u(x) = u_L(x;\epsilon)$ that we described earlier, with initial wealth $W_0 = 0$, the risk $\tilde{\mu} \sim N(1,1)$, and $r^f = 0$, we get

$$\begin{aligned}\frac{dU_L}{dV} &= \int_0^\infty u'(W_0 + V(x - r^f))(x - r^f)\phi(x)\,dx\\&= \frac{1}{\sqrt{2\pi}}\int_{-\infty}^{\infty}(1 - \epsilon\tan^{-1}(Vx))e^{-(x-1)^2/2}\,dx\\&= 1 - \epsilon\frac{1}{\sqrt{2\pi}}\int_{-\infty}^{\infty}\tan^{-1}(Vx)xe^{-(x-1)^2/2}\,dx.\end{aligned}$$

Now, $|\tan^{-1}(Vx)| \leq \frac{\pi}{2}$ regardless of V and x, and for large $V \gg 0$, $\tan^{-1}(Vx) \to \frac{\pi}{2}\,\mathrm{sign}(x)$, for all $x \neq 0$, so by dominated convergence,

$$\lim_{V\to\infty}\frac{1}{\sqrt{2\pi}}\int_{-\infty}^{\infty}\tan^{-1}(Vx)xe^{-(x-1)^2/2}\,dx = \frac{\sqrt{\pi}}{2\sqrt{2}}\int_{-\infty}^{\infty}|x|e^{-(x-1)^2/2}\,dx \approx 1.83254,$$

and thus $\frac{dU_L}{dV} \geq 1 - 1.183254\epsilon > 0$ for all α, when $\epsilon < \frac{1}{1.183254}$. So the marginal utility of increasing risky investments for such a close-to-risk-neutral investor is always positive in this case, and formally $\alpha^* = +\infty$.

The example of an investor with utility function u_L falls within the scope of our proof. Indeed, $U_L'(0) > 0$ and $U_L''(0) < 0$. It is simply that we never verify that there is an α^* for which $U'(\alpha^*) = 0$ in the proof.

Another example, which falls outside the proof, is when the expected utility function is one of high risk aversion. Specifically, consider the utility function $u_H(x;n)$ discussed before, with $n > 2$. It is easy to verify that

$$\int_{-\infty}^{\infty} u_H\big(W_0(R^f + \alpha(x - r^f)); n\big)\phi(x)\,dx = -\infty$$

whenever $\alpha \neq 0$ and $\tilde{\mu} \sim N(\mu, \sigma^2)$, $\sigma > 0$. Indeed, the investor is so risk averse that regardless of how small α is (positive or negative), the contribution to expected utility blows up as x becomes more and more negative. This investor will therefore always choose $\alpha = 0$, regardless of μ and σ^2. The reason that this example falls outside our proof is that the boundedness requirements do not hold. Indeed,

$$\lim_{x\to-\infty}|x|u_H'\big(W_0(R^f + \alpha(x - r^f)); n\big)\phi(x) = \infty,$$

for all $\alpha > 0$ in this case. We have shown the result. □

Theorem 4.1 provides a very general result, modulo some technical constraints related to finite expected utility, as discussed in the proof of the theorem. Henceforth, we assume that such technical constraints are satisfied, and that there is a finite optimal investment level, $-\infty < \alpha^* < \infty$. The result holds regardless of the distribution of stock returns and expected utility function, beyond the constraint that the investor is risk averse. Note that the result could have equivalently been formulated in terms of $V^* = \alpha^* W_0$.

Example 4.1. Consider an investor with CARA utility, $u(x) = -e^{-\gamma x}$. The stock's returns are normally distributed, $\tilde{\mu} \sim N(\mu, \sigma^2)$. Its probability density function is therefore $\phi(x) = \frac{1}{\sqrt{2\pi\sigma^2}}e^{-(x-\mu)^2/2\sigma^2}$. The risk-free rate is $r^f > 0$, and $R^f = 1 + r^f$. We use the following formula for the expectation of the exponential of a normally distributed random variable, $\widetilde{X} \sim N(a, b^2)$:

$$E[e^{-c\widetilde{X}}] = \frac{1}{\sqrt{2\pi b^2}} \int e^{-cx-(x-a)^2/2b^2}\, dx = e^{-c(a-cb^2/2)}, \tag{4.2}$$

and the dollar-value form of the investor's budget constraint:

$$W_1 = W_0 R^f + V(\tilde{\mu} - r^f).$$

The investor's maximization problem is max $E[u(W_1)]$, leading to

$$\begin{aligned} V^* &= \arg\max_V -E[e^{-\gamma(W_0R^f + V(\tilde{\mu}-r^f))}] \\ &= \arg\min_V E[e^{-\gamma V(\tilde{\mu}-r^f)}] \\ &= \arg\min_V e^{-\gamma(V(\tilde{\mu}-r^f) - V^2\gamma\sigma^2/2)} \\ &= \arg\max_V e^{V(\mu-r^f) - V^2\gamma\sigma^2/2}. \end{aligned}$$

The first-order condition is then

$$\mu - R^f = V^*\gamma\sigma^2,$$

so

$$V^* = \frac{\mu - R^f}{\gamma\sigma^2}. \tag{4.3}$$

The dollar amount invested in the stock in this case does not depend on the investor's wealth level, W_0. This is related to the fact that absolute risk aversion is constant under the CARA expected utility specification.

We note that $E[W_1] = W_0R^f + V(\mu - R^f)$, and $\text{Var}(W_1) = V^2\sigma^2$. So a *mean-variance* optimizing investor arrives at the same portfolio by solving

$$\begin{aligned} V^* &= \arg\max_V E[W_1] - \frac{\gamma}{2}\text{Var}[W_1] \\ &= \arg\max_V V(\mu - R^f) - \frac{\gamma}{2}V^2\sigma^2. \end{aligned}$$

For the specific combination of CARA investors and normally distributed risks, the problem therefore simplifies to that of an investor with the utility specification $U(\tilde{x}) = E[\tilde{x}] - \frac{\gamma}{2}\text{Var}[\tilde{x}]$, a convenient property that has been used in many models in the finance literature.

We next analyze how the amount invested in the stock—either defined in dollar terms, V^*, or in terms of fraction of wealth, α^*—depends on investor risk aversion and wealth. We first compare two agents with different degrees of risk aversion.

Theorem 4.2. *Consider two investors, with absolute risk aversion* $\text{ARA}_1(W)$ *and* $\text{ARA}_2(W)$*, respectively. If* $\text{ARA}_1(W) > \text{ARA}_2(W)$ *for all* W*, then*

- $V_1^*(W) < V_2^*(W)$ *for all* W*, and*
- $\alpha_1^*(W) < \alpha_2^*(W)$ *for all* W*.*

Proof. Rescale the utility functions so that $u_1'(WR^f) = u_2'(WR^f)$. From proposition 3.2 it follows that $u_1'(x) < u_2'(x)$ when $x > WR^f$, and $u_1'(x) > u_2'(x)$ when $x < WR^f$. Now,

$$\left.\frac{dU_1}{dV}\right|_{V_1^*} = \int_{-\infty}^{\infty} u_1'(WR^f + V_1^*(x - r^f))(x - r^f)\phi(x)\, dx = 0$$

for investor 1's optimal fraction of investments, α_1^*. At this fraction, for agent 2,

$$
\begin{aligned}
\left.\frac{dU_2}{dV}\right|_{V_1^*} &= \int_{-\infty}^{\infty} u_2'(WR^f + V_1^*(x-r^f))(x-r^f)\phi(x)\,dx \\
&= -\int_{-\infty}^{r^f} u_2'(WR^f + V_1^*(x-r^f))(r^f-x)\phi(x)\,dx \\
&\quad + \int_{r^f}^{\infty} u_2'(WR^f + V_1^*(x-r^f))(x-r^f)\phi(x)\,dx \\
&> -\int_{-\infty}^{r^f} u_1'(WR^f + V_1^*(x-r^f))(r^f-x)\phi(x)\,dx \\
&\quad + \int_{r^f}^{\infty} u_1'(WR^f + V_1^*(x-r^f))(x-r^f)\phi(x)\,dx \\
&= 0.
\end{aligned}
$$

The expected utility for investor 2 is therefore increasing in V at V_1^*, and since U_2 is concave, see the proof of Theorem 4.1, the optimal investment level for investor 2 is higher, $V_2^* > V_1^*$, showing the first part of the proof.

The second part of the proof, the results for α^*, then also follows immediately since $\alpha^* = \frac{V^*}{W}$. □

The following result compares the demand for the risky asset by an investor, across different wealth levels (see Arrow 1971):

Theorem 4.3. *Consider an investor with absolute risk-aversion function* ARA(W), *and relative risk-aversion function* RRA(W), *respectively.*

- *Absolute risk aversion:*
  - *If* $\text{ARA}'(W) < 0$, *then* $V^*(W)$ *is increasing in* W.
  - *If* $\text{ARA}'(W) > 0$, *then* $V^*(W)$ *is decreasing in* W.
  - *If* $\text{ARA}'(W) = 0$, *then* $V^*(W)$ *does not depend on* W.
- *Relative risk aversion:*
  - *If* $\text{RRA}'(W) < 0$, *then* $\alpha^*(W)$ *is increasing in* W.
  - *If* $\text{RRA}'(W) > 0$, *then* $\alpha^*(W)$ *is decreasing in* W.
  - *If* $\text{RRA}'(W) = 0$, *then* $\alpha^*(W)$ *does not depend on* W.

Proof. We first show the ARA results. Consider the investor's portfolio choice problem with wealth W and utility u_1:

$$\max_V U_1 = \max_V \int_{-\infty}^{\infty} u_1(WR^f + V(x-r^f))\phi(x)\,dx,$$

leading to optimal investments, V^*. Now consider a richer investor with the same utility function, but with wealth $\widehat{W} = W + A$, $A > 0$, solving

$$
\begin{aligned}
\max_V U_2 &= \max_V \int_{-\infty}^{\infty} u_1(\widehat{W}R^f + V(x-r^f))\phi(x)\,dx, \\
&= \max_V \int_{-\infty}^{\infty} u_1(AR^f + WR^f + V(x-r^f))\phi(x)\,dx.
\end{aligned}
$$

We define the new utility function $u_2(x) \stackrel{\text{def}}{=} u_1(AR^f + x)$, and note that if ARA is decreasing in wealth, then $\text{ARA}_2 < \text{ARA}_1$. We can then write the maximization problem for the second investor as

$$\max_V U_2 = \max_V \int_{-\infty}^{\infty} u_2(WR^f + V(x - r^f))\phi(x)\,dx.$$

It follows from theorem 4.2 that $V_2^* > V_1^*$.

An identical argument shows the results for increasing absolute risk aversion. Finally, we know from before that investments are independent of wealth for CARA utility, which is the utility function for which ARA is independent of wealth. We have therefore shown all the ARA results.

To show RRA results, we have to work a little bit harder. Specifically, consider two investors with the same utility functions with decreasing relative risk aversion in wealth ($\text{RRA}'(W) < 0$), and wealths W^1 and W^2, respectively, with $W^2 > W^1$. The first investor solves

$$\max_\alpha U_1 = \max_\alpha \int_{-\infty}^{\infty} u_1\big(W^1(R^f + \alpha(x - r^f))\big)\phi(x)\,dx,$$

leading to optimal fraction of investments, α^*. Now consider the second investor, who maximizes

$$\max_\alpha U_2 = \max_\alpha \int_{-\infty}^{\infty} u_1\big(W^2(R^f + \alpha(x - r^f))\big)\phi(x)\,dx.$$

Define $u_2(x) = u_1\big(\frac{W^2}{W^1}x\big)$, and verify that $\text{ARA}_2(W^1) = \frac{W^2}{W^1}\text{ARA}_1(W^2)$. Now, since $\text{RRA}(W) = W \times \text{ARA}(W)$,

$$\begin{aligned}\text{RRA}_1(W^2) < \text{RRA}_1(W^1) \;&\Leftrightarrow\; \frac{W^2}{W^1}\text{ARA}_1(W^2) < \text{ARA}_1(W^1)\\ &\Leftrightarrow\; \text{ARA}_2(W^1) < \text{ARA}_1(W^1).\end{aligned}$$

We rewrite the second investor's problem as

$$\max_\alpha U_2 = \max_\alpha \int_{-\infty}^{\infty} u_2\big(W^1(R^f + \alpha(x - r^f))\big)\phi(x)\,dx.$$

Since $\text{ARA}_2(W^1) < \text{ARA}_1(W^1)$, it follows from theorem 4.2 that $\alpha_2^* < \alpha_1^*$. An identical argument for increasing RRA ($\text{RRA}'(W) > 0$) can be made, and we know from before that when RRA is constant, α does not depend on wealth. We are done. □

So whether increased wealth makes the investor increase the *dollar amount* invested in the risky asset depends on how the absolute risk-aversion coefficient changes with wealth, and whether (s)he increases the *fraction of wealth* invested depends on how the relative risk-aversion coefficient changes. Thus, already in this very stylized setting with one risky asset, we see that further assumptions about investor preferences are needed (in this case, the behavior of the risk-aversion coefficients when wealth changes) to answer fundamentally important questions.

It may seem counterintuitive that an investor would decrease the dollar amount invested in the stock—which has higher expected returns than the bond—when becoming wealthier, and one may therefore wish to rule out expected utility specifications with increasing absolute risk aversion (so-called IARA preferences).

4.2 Multiple Risky Assets

We next study the setting with multiple risky assets. This allows us to address the asset selection question we discussed earlier. Specifically, we can view the bond versus stock decision as an asset allocation choice, leading to the decomposition of the total wealth portfolio into a bond portfolio, in which the fraction $1-\alpha_0$ of wealth is invested, and a stock portfolio in which the remaining fraction α_0 is selected. But, with thousands of stocks available, how should the stock portion of the portfolio be allocated between these stocks? This is the asset selection problem.

In general, we expect the answer to the asset selection problem to depend on the investor's preferences and wealth. Indeed, we may conjecture that because of the large class of possible utility functions (for instance, the set $\mathcal{U}^2$), it will be very difficult for an investment adviser to help solve the asset selection problem—which is very high-dimensional when there are many assets to choose between—without very detailed knowledge about the investor's preferences. This turns out to be the case in general, but for some important special cases there are really powerful results showing that the optimal investment will be very similar across investors. In some very specific cases, the investment problem even "collapses" so that all investors basically choose the same portfolio of risky assets, making life easy for the investment adviser!

We first provide an example with three assets, in which no such collapse occurs: Consider an investor with utility function

$$u(x)=\begin{cases} x-\frac{1}{8}x^2, & x\le 4-\epsilon,\\ -\frac{\epsilon^2}{4}e^{-(x-4)/\epsilon-1}+2+\frac{\epsilon^2}{8}, & x>4-\epsilon, \end{cases}$$

where $0<\epsilon\ll 1$. This utility function may seem a bit cumbersome, but it is really its quadratic behavior when $x\le 4-\epsilon$ that is important for us. When $\epsilon\to 0$, it converges to the function

$$\hat{u}(x)=\begin{cases} x-\frac{1}{8}x^2, & x\le 4,\\ 2, & x>4. \end{cases}$$

However, $\hat{u}$ does not belong to $\mathcal{U}^2$, since it is not increasing, nor strictly concave when $x>4$, whereas its approximation when $\epsilon>0$ does belong to $\mathcal{U}^2$. That is why we choose the more cumbersome utility function, u. The utility function is shown as the solid line in figure 4.2, where $\epsilon=0.001$ has been chosen.

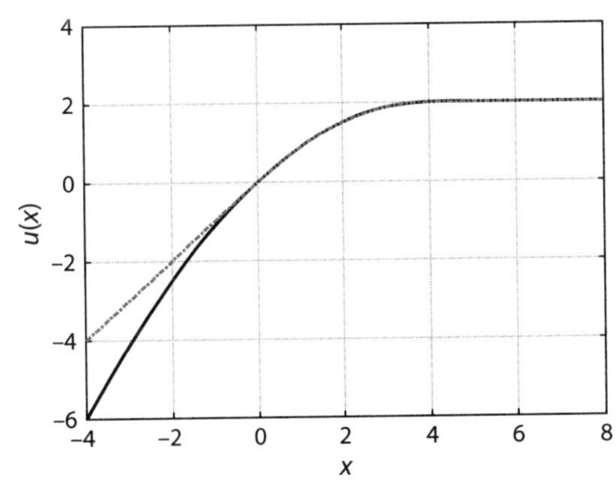

Figure 4.2: Different utility functions.

We will make heavy use of vectors and matrices when analyzing multi-asset models. The transpose of the row vector (a,b,c), which has three elements, is the column vector $(a,b,c)'\in\mathbb{R}^3$. We also use the notation $(a,b,c)^T$ for the transpose. Further notation is provided in appendix B.

There are three assets, 0, 1, and 2, all with price 1 at time 0. Asset 0 is risk-free (a bond). We use a state space formulation of their payoffs. Specifically, there are three states, $\Omega=\{\omega_1,\omega_2,\omega_3\}$, with associated probabilities $p_i=\mathbb{P}(\omega_i), p_1=p_2=p_3=\frac{1}{3}$. The total returns of these assets (which are the same as their dollar payments since they each cost one dollar) are represented by the vectors

$$\pi^i=(\widetilde{R}_i(\omega_1),\widetilde{R}_i(\omega_2),\widetilde{R}_i(\omega_3))',\quad i=0,1,2.$$

The payoffs of the assets are

- risk-free asset: payoff 1 in all states, $\pi^0 = (1, 1, 1)'$, so $r^f = 0$;
- risky asset 1: payoff $\pi^1 = (0, 4, 0)'$;
- risky asset 2: payoff $\pi^2 = (0, 0, 5)'$.

The investor's wealth is W, where $0 \leq W < 4 - \frac{81}{40}\epsilon$.

The investor chooses the number of dollars to invest in risky assets 1 and 2, V_1 and V_2, respectively, and invests the remaining wealth $W - V_1 - V_2$ in the risk-free asset. The maximization problem is then

$$\begin{aligned}\arg\max_{V_1,V_2} E[u(W_1)] &= \arg\max_{V_1,V_2} E[u(W - V_1 - V_2 + V_1\pi_1 + V_2\pi_2)] \\ &= \arg\max_{V_1,V_2} \frac{1}{3}\big(u(W - V_1 - V_2) + u(W + 3V_1 - V_2) \\ &\qquad + u(W - V_1 + 4V_2)\big).\end{aligned}$$

This is a standard concave optimization problem in two variables.

Recall the following result on multivariate (unconstrained) concave optimization:

Theorem 4.4. *Consider the twice continuously differentiable multivariate $F\colon \mathbb{R}^N \to \mathbb{R}$, which is* strictly concave *in that*

$$F(\lambda\mathbf{x} + (1-\lambda)\mathbf{y}) > \lambda F(\mathbf{x}) + (1-\lambda)F(\mathbf{y}),$$

for all $\mathbf{x} \neq \mathbf{y}$ and $\lambda \in (0,1)$. Define the gradient operator, $(\nabla F) = \left(\frac{\partial F}{\partial x_1}, \frac{\partial F}{\partial x_2}, \ldots, \frac{\partial F}{\partial x_N}\right)' \in \mathbb{R}^N$. *A necessary and sufficient condition for $\mathbf{x}$ to define a unique global maximum of F is that the* first-order condition *(FOC)*

$$(\nabla F)(\mathbf{x}) = \mathbf{0} \tag{4.4}$$

is satisfied.

For a smooth function, F, concavity is determined by the properties of the function's *Hessian*, as shown by the following result:

Proposition 4.1. *Define the Hessian, $\mathbf{H}\colon \mathbb{R}^N \to \mathbb{R}^{N\times N}$, of a twice continuously differentiable function $F\colon \mathbb{R}^N \to \mathbb{R}$ by $\mathbf{H}_{ij} = \frac{\partial^2 F}{\partial x_i \partial x_j}$, i.e.,*

$$\mathbf{H} = \begin{bmatrix} \frac{\partial^2 F}{\partial x_1^2} & \frac{\partial^2 F}{\partial x_1 \partial x_2} & \cdots & \frac{\partial^2 F}{\partial x_1 \partial x_N} \\ \frac{\partial^2 F}{\partial x_2 \partial x_1} & \frac{\partial^2 F}{\partial x_2^2} & \cdots & \frac{\partial^2 F}{\partial x_2 \partial x_N} \\ \vdots & \vdots & \cdots & \vdots \\ \frac{\partial^2 F}{\partial x_N \partial x_1} & \frac{\partial^2 F}{\partial x_N \partial x_2} & \cdots & \frac{\partial^2 F}{\partial x_N^2} \end{bmatrix}.$$

A necessary and sufficient condition for F to be strictly concave is that $\mathbf{H}(\mathbf{x})$ is negative definite for each $\mathbf{x} \in \mathbb{R}$.

Further material on vectors and matrices can be found in appendix B, and on multivariate optimization in appendix C.

Many of the optimization problems in quantitative finance, including the one we are currently studying, are smooth and strictly concave, in which case the problem is solved by finding a solution to the first-order conditions (4.4).

The first-order conditions in our example are

$$0=\frac{1}{3}\Big(1+\frac{1}{4}(W-V_1-V_2)-\frac{3}{4}(W+3V_1-V_2)+\frac{1}{4}(W-V_1+4V_2)\Big),$$
$$0=\frac{1}{3}\Big(2+\frac{1}{4}(W-V_1-V_2)+\frac{1}{4}(W+3V_1-V_2)-\frac{4}{4}(W-V_1+4V_2)\Big).$$

Technically, these first-order conditions are correct only if the solution lies in the region such that $u(W_1)<4-\epsilon$, for all realizations, $\omega\in\Omega$. One can verify that this will indeed be the case here.

It follows that the solution is

$$V_1^*=\frac{15}{81}(4-W),\quad V_2^*=\frac{14}{81}(4-W).$$

So the *amount* invested in the risky assets varies with W, and thus the solution to the sector allocation problem depends on the investor's wealth,

$$\alpha_0^*=\frac{V_1^*+V_2^*}{W}=\frac{29}{81}\times\frac{4-W}{W},$$

and

$$V_0^*=V_1^*+V_2^*=\alpha_0 W=\frac{29}{81}(4-W).$$

But the solution to the asset selection problem does *not* depend on wealth, since the investment in stock 1 as a fraction of the total risky investment is

$$\frac{V_1^*}{V_1^*+V_2^*}=\frac{15}{29},$$

which is independent of W! So the investment adviser would not need to know the investor's wealth to find the optimal investment mix among risky assets. Regardless of wealth, the investor should choose a portfolio with the fraction $\frac{15}{29}$ in stock 1, and the remaining $\frac{14}{29}$ in stock 2. Equivalently, the investor could invest in a mutual fund which has invested in this asset mix. This is very nice invariance result!

How general is this result? Unfortunately, it is not general at all. For example, we can adjust the utility function, so that $u(x)=x$ for $x<0$, in line with the dash-dotted line in figure 4.2, i.e.,

$$u(x)=\begin{cases} x, & x<0,\\ x-\frac{1}{8}x^2, & 0\le x\le 4-\epsilon,\\ -\frac{\epsilon^2}{4}e^{-(x-4)/\epsilon-1}+2+\frac{\epsilon^2}{8}, & x>4-\epsilon,\end{cases}$$

and further assume that $0\le W\le 1$. One verifies that the investor's optimal portfolio in this case becomes

$$V_1^*=\frac{124-55W}{121},\quad V_2^*=\frac{108-44W}{121}(4-W),$$

and thus

$$\frac{V_1^*}{V_1^*+V_2^*}=\frac{124-55W}{232-99W},$$

which *does* depend on wealth. In this situation, the investment adviser would therefore need to know the investor's wealth to be able to provide sound advice about which mutual fund to invest in. Now, asking about investor wealth and then giving advice may seem quite straightforward. But this was of course just for our mini-example, with two risky assets. When there are a large number of risky assets and a large class of possible utility functions, the whole of $\mathcal{U}^2$, for instance, one can

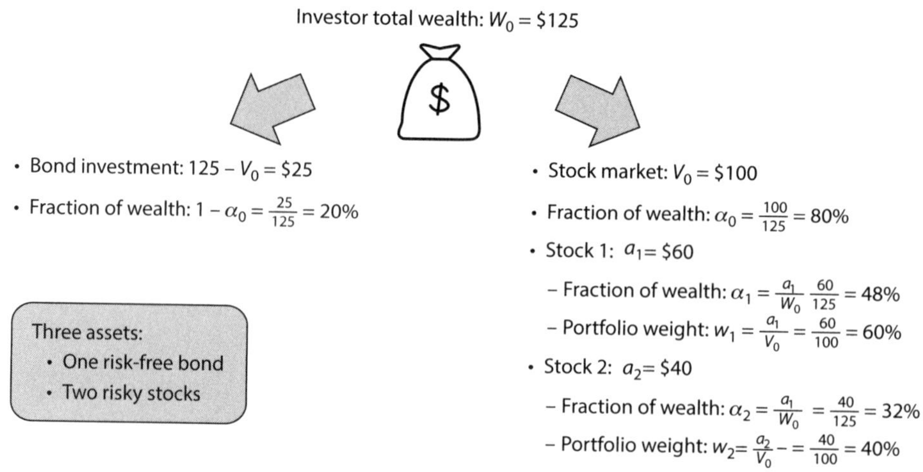

Figure 4.3: Notation used in the portfolio choice problem.

imagine the advisor having to ask thousands of questions before being able to give sound advice. We need a systematic approach to find out when the situation may be simplified so that we get the type of invariance result above.

4.3 General Problem

We analyze the general problem, with N risky assets, a risk-free bond, and an investor with wealth W_0 and expected utility function u. We use the following notation:

- the bond's return is $R^f = 1 + r^f$;
- the assets' returns are $\widetilde{R}_1, \ldots, \widetilde{R}_N$; also, $\tilde{\mu}_n = \widetilde{R}_n - 1$;
- the assets' expected returns are $R_n = E[\widetilde{R}_n] = 1 + \mu_n$.

Note that here the subscript n represents which asset we are referring to. In the introduction, the subscript t represented time.

We want the flexibility to analyze several variations of the setup, just like we switched between the fraction α and dollar amount V in the one-stock problem, so we introduce some additional notation. The agent invests the fraction $1 - \alpha_0$ of wealth in the risk-free asset and the total fraction α_0 in risky assets. The fraction of wealth invested in risky asset n is α_n, which we also represent by the vector $\alpha = (\alpha_1, \ldots, \alpha_N)'$. Of the total investment in risky assets, which is $V_0 = \alpha_0 W_0$, the fraction w_n is invested in asset n. This implies that

$$\alpha_n = w_n \alpha_0.$$

The difference between the left- and right-hand sides of this expression is thus that the left-hand side is the fraction of total wealth (W_0), whereas w_n is the fraction of risky investments (V). It follows that $\sum_n w_n = 1$. The dollar amount invested in risky asset n is a_n, which then implies that $a_n = \alpha_n W_0 = w_n V_0$. An example with two risky assets is given in figure 4.3, which clarifies the relation between the different terms.

We can write the return of a risky portfolio as

$$\widetilde{R}^p = \sum_n w_n \widetilde{R}_n = \mathbf{w}'\widetilde{\mathbf{R}},$$

where the vectors are $\mathbf{w}=(w_1,\ldots,w_N)'$ and $\widetilde{\mathbf{R}}=(\widetilde{R}_1,\ldots,\widetilde{R}_N)'$. We also define $\tilde{\mu}=(\tilde{\mu}_1,\ldots\tilde{\mu}_N)'$,

$$\tilde{\mu}^p=\mathbf{w}'\tilde{\mu},$$

and

$$\mu^p=E[\tilde{\mu}^p]=\mathbf{w}'\mu.$$

The investor's budget constraint is

$$\begin{aligned} W_1&=W_0(1-\alpha_0)R^f+\alpha_0 W_0\mathbf{w}'\widetilde{\mathbf{R}}\\ &=W_0(R^f+\alpha_0\mathbf{w}'\tilde{\mu}^e), \end{aligned}$$

where $\tilde{\mu}^e=\tilde{\mu}-r^f\mathbf{1}$ is the vector of *excess returns* of the risky assets over the risk-free asset, with associated expected value $\mu^e=E[\tilde{\mu}^e]$, and where $\mathbf{1}=(1,1,\ldots,1)'$ is an N-vector of ones.

The investor's optimization problem is

$$\max_{\mathbf{w},\alpha_0} E[u(W_0(R^f+\alpha_0\mathbf{w}'\tilde{\mu}^e))],$$

such that

$$\mathbf{w}'\mathbf{1}=1.$$

Our first concern is with the asset selection problem, and specifically what can be said in general about the portfolio, $\mathbf{w}$, an investor will/should choose. Ideally, we would like a result along the lines of "all investors with expected utility functions in $\mathcal{U}^2$ (where we defined the class of utility functions $\mathcal{U}^2$ on page 40) should choose the same portfolio, $\mathbf{w}^*$, regardless of wealth, W_0," without any further restrictions on risk distributions. This would make life simple for our investment adviser.

Unfortunately, such results are only valid under very specific assumptions about return distributions and/or utility functions (much smaller classes than $\mathcal{U}^2$). The following theorem by Cass and Stiglitz (1970) is the most general that holds without further constraints on return distributions:

Theorem 4.5 (Cass and Stiglitz 1970). *The optimal risky portfolio, $\mathbf{w}^*$, is independent of wealth for all risk distributions if and only if agents have so-called hyperbolic absolute risk aversion (HARA) utility, i.e., if their utility functions are such that*

- $u'(x)=(ax+b)^{-\gamma}$, *or*
- $u'(x)=ce^{-\gamma x}$,

where a, b, c, and γ are constants.

The class of HARA utility functions includes CARA utility and CRRA utility, as well as some other functions (when $b\neq 0$), but is of course much smaller than $\mathcal{U}^2$.

Example 4.2 (Multivariate returns and mean–variance preferences). Consider a market in which returns are multivariate normally distributed,

$$\tilde{\mu}\sim N(\mu,\Sigma),$$

with expected return vector $\mu\in\mathbb{R}^N$, covariance matrix $\Sigma\in\mathbb{R}^{N\times N}$, and we assume that Σ is invertible. We use the following algebraic property of multivariate normal distributions:

$$\widetilde{X}\sim N(\mu,\Sigma)\ \Rightarrow\ \mathbf{a}'\widetilde{X}\sim N(\mathbf{a}'\mu,\mathbf{a}'\Sigma\mathbf{a}),\quad \mathbf{a}\in\mathbb{R}^N.$$

The budget constraint is

$$W_1 = W_0(R^f + \alpha'(\widetilde{\mathbf{R}} - R^f \mathbf{1})) = W_0 R^f + \mathbf{a}'(\tilde{\mu} - r^f \mathbf{1}),$$

implying

$$W_1 \sim N(W_0 R^f + \mathbf{a}'(\mu - r^f \mathbf{1}), \mathbf{a}'\Sigma\mathbf{a}).$$

The investor solves

$$\max_{\mathbf{a}\in\mathbb{R}^N} E[u(W_1)].$$

Since returns are normally distributed for each portfolio choice $\mathbf{a}$, expected utility as a function of $\mathbf{a}$ is

$$E[u(W_1)|\mathbf{a}] = -e^{-\gamma(W_0 R^f + \mathbf{a}'(\mu - r^f \mathbf{1}) - \gamma \mathbf{a}'\Sigma\mathbf{a}/2)}.$$

Thus, the investor will behave as a mean–variance investor in this multi-asset setting too.

The investor with mean–variance preferences $U(\tilde{x}) = E[\tilde{x}] - \frac{\gamma}{2}\,\mathrm{Var}(\tilde{x})$ chooses the portfolio

$$\mathbf{a}^* = \arg\max_{\mathbf{a}} \mathbf{a}'(\mu - r^f \mathbf{1}) - \frac{\gamma}{2}\mathbf{a}'\Sigma\mathbf{a},$$

leading to

$$\mathbf{a}^* = \frac{1}{\gamma}\Sigma^{-1}(\mu - r^f \mathbf{1}) = \frac{1}{\gamma}\Sigma^{-1}\mu^e,$$

which is then also the portfolio the CARA investor chooses. The expected utility from choosing this portfolio is

$$U = -e^{-\gamma(W_0 R^f + \frac{1}{2\gamma}(\mu_e'\Sigma^{-1}\mu_e))},$$

so the certainty equivalent for the investor, associated with being able to invest in the risky assets, is

$$\mathrm{CE} = \frac{1}{2\gamma}\mu_e'\Sigma^{-1}\mu_e.$$

We see that the certainty equivalent is lower, the higher the risk aversion. This is natural, since a very risk-averse investor will not see much benefit in investing in risky assets even if these have high expected returns, and therefore only invest modestly in such assets. An investor with low risk aversion, however, will appreciate the higher expected returns offered by these assets, and invest a significant amount in them.

4.4 Modern Portfolio Theory

We now look further into the portfolio choice problem in a mean–variance setting, initially focusing on the case with no risk-free asset. This follows the original approach to portfolio choice under risk aversion; see Roy (1952) and especially the so-called *modern portfolio theory* introduced in Markowitz (1952). The approach makes strong assumptions about investor preferences, and as a consequence it is possible to derive very strong results. Even if these assumptions may be viewed as too strong, our approach provides a great benchmark model against which more advanced models can be compared. In the context of the asset pricing pyramid (see figure 1.1), modern portfolio theory belongs at the top of the pyramid.

The key assumption we make is that the investor only cares about the first two moments of portfolio returns: $U = U(\mu_p, \sigma_p^2)$, and that (s)he

- likes higher expected returns, $u_1' > 0$,
- dislikes higher variance, $u_2' < 0$, and
- only cares about portfolio returns.

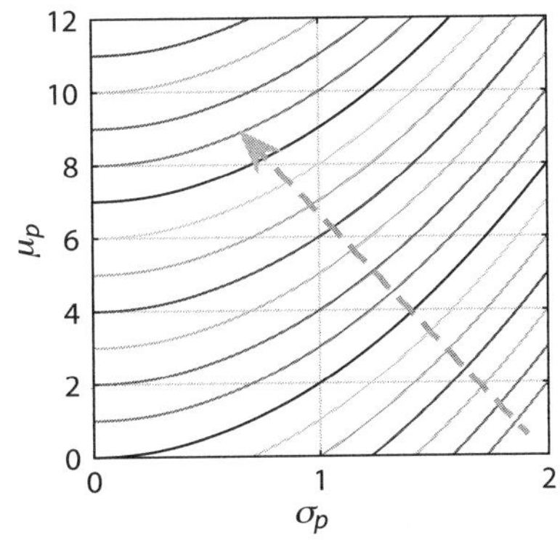

Figure 4.4: Indifference curves under the CARA-normal setting.

The third point above deserves to be emphasized. The assumption is very natural, given the expected utility approach we have taken, which focuses exclusively on the distribution of outcomes. Upon further thought, however, one may envision other motives than portfolio returns that could affect an investor's portfolio choice. For example, the investor may live close to a company's headquarters and therefore think it is fun to buy the company's stock and support the local community. Or the investor may like the products a company produces and sells, and purchase stocks as a signal of approval.[1] All such motives are ruled out here—strong results require strong assumptions.

The CARA-normal setting falls within this setting, with $u(\mu_p, \sigma_p^2) = \mu_p - \frac{\gamma}{2}\sigma_p^2$, but other functional forms of $u(\mu_p, \sigma_p^2)$ are also possible, e.g., $u(\mu_p, \sigma_p^2) = \frac{e^{\mu_p}}{1+\sigma_p^4}$. One way of visualizing the investor's trade-off between mean and variance is to show their so-called *indifference curves*, which are defined as the level sets $\{(\sigma_p, \mu_p) : u(\mu_p, \sigma_p^2) = c\}$, for some constant, c (one usually plots these graphs with σ_p on the x-axis, for historical reasons). In figure 4.4, the indifference curves under the CARA-normal setting are shown.

Another set of utility functions that leads to mean–variance preferences (under the expected utility framework) are the quadratic ones,

$$u(x) = x - ax^2, \quad a > 0.$$

Here we must ensure that $x < \frac{1}{2a}$ for the utility specification to make sense, since for higher x, the utility is decreasing in x. When calculating $E[u(\tilde{\mu})]$, this then implies that $\mu = E[\tilde{\mu}] < \frac{1}{2a}$. Figure 4.5 shows quadratic utility functions for a few values of a.

The level sets are of the form $C = E[u(x)] = \mu - aE[x^2] = \mu - a(\sigma^2 + \mu^2)$. Equivalently, we can define $r^2 = \frac{1}{4a^2} - \frac{C}{a}$, and write the level sets as

$$r^2 = \sigma^2 + \left(\mu - \frac{1}{2a}\right)^2, \quad r > 0.$$

These level sets are then circles centered at $(\sigma, \mu) = (0, \frac{1}{2a})$, with radius r, as shown in figure 4.6. Only the lower halves of these level sets, for which $\mu < \frac{1}{2a}$, correspond to the economically meaningful indifference curves, since when $\mu > \frac{1}{2a}$, the level sets are such that they suggest lower utility for higher μ, all else equal.

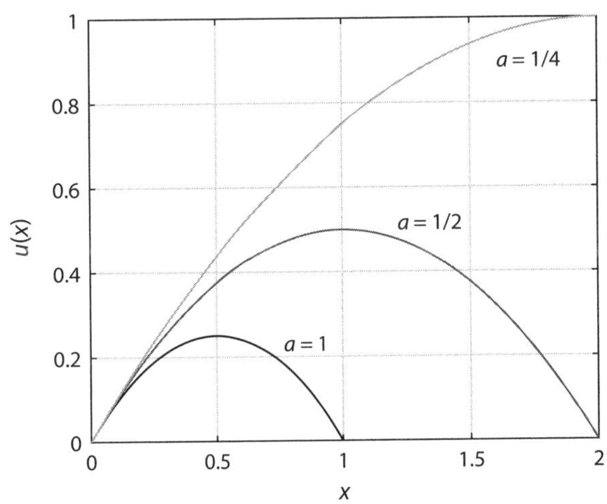

Figure 4.5: Quadratic utility functions.

From our earlier notation, we have the return vector $\tilde{\mu} = (\tilde{\mu}_1, \ldots, \tilde{\mu}_N)'$, with expected returns $\mu = E(\tilde{\mu}) \in \mathbb{R}^N$. We also define $\sigma_{ij} = \mathrm{Cov}(\tilde{\mu}_i, \tilde{\mu}_j)$, the standard deviations $\sigma_i = \sqrt{\sigma_{ii}}$, the pairwise correlations $\rho_{ij} = \frac{\sigma_{ij}}{\sigma_i\sigma_j}$, and the covariance matrix $\Sigma = [\sigma_{ij}]_{ij} \in \mathbb{R}^{N\times N}$.

[1] My son—who loves computer games—chose to buy two shares of Nintendo stock as his first investment, even though he was not bullish about the company's future prospects, given the strong competition in the game-consoles market.

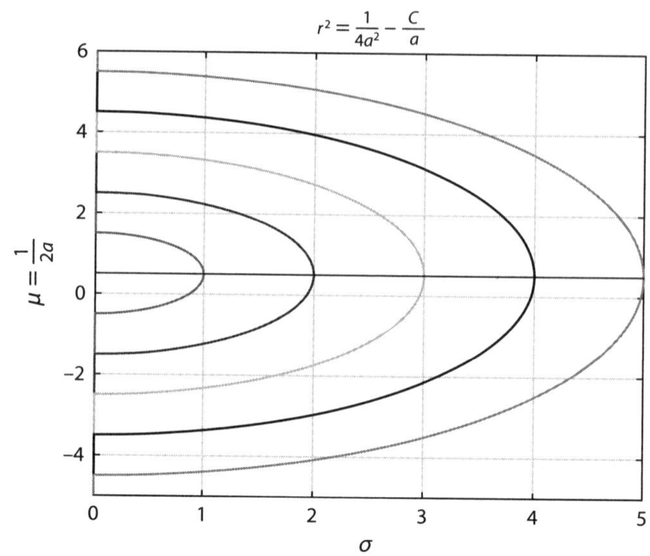

Figure 4.6: Indifference curves with quadratic utility functions.

We make the following assumptions:

- Σ is invertible, and
- $\mu_i \neq \mu_j$ for some i, j.

Again, note that there is no risk-free asset. Also recall that the portfolio return, given that $\mathbf{w}'\mathbf{1} = 1$, is $\tilde{\mu}_p = \mathbf{w}'\tilde{\mu}$, with expected value $\mu_p = \mathbf{w}'\mu$ and standard deviation $\sigma_p^2 = \mathbf{w}'\Sigma\mathbf{w}$. Finally, note that a covariance matrix is always symmetric and positive semidefinite and, moreover, that since Σ is invertible, it follows that it is *symmetric positive definite* (SPD).

Now consider a mean–variance optimizing investor who has decided to choose a portfolio with expected return μ_0, i.e., to pick a $\mathbf{w}$ such that $\mathbf{w}'\mu = \mu_0$. Of course, the portfolio must also satisfy $\mathbf{w}'\mathbf{1} = 1$, but we make no further restrictions, and, for example, allow for possible short-selling of stocks. Which portfolio should the investor choose? Since variance is disliked, (s)he will solve

$$\begin{aligned} &\min_{\mathbf{w}} \frac{1}{2}\mathbf{w}'\Sigma\mathbf{w}, \\ &\text{s.t. } \mathbf{w}'\mathbf{1} = 1, \\ &\qquad \mathbf{w}'\mu = \mu_0. \end{aligned}$$

This constrained optimization problem can be solved using standard Lagrangian optimization techniques; see appendix C. Specifically, define the scalars

$$\begin{aligned} A &= \mathbf{1}'\Sigma^{-1}\mathbf{1}, \\ B &= \mathbf{1}'\Sigma^{-1}\mu, \\ C &= \mu'\Sigma^{-1}\mu, \\ \Delta &= AC - B^2. \end{aligned}$$

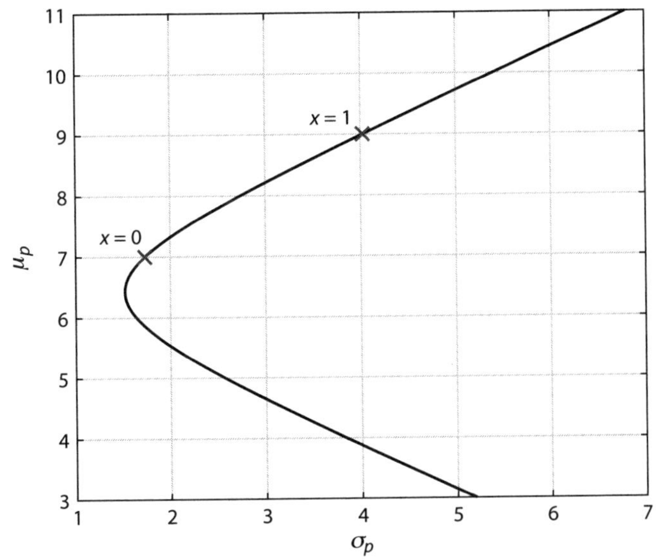

Figure 4.7: Feasible standard deviation/expected returns combinations, two risky assets.

One can show that $\Delta > 0$.[2]

Example 4.3. It is useful to gain intuition in a mini-example, with only two risky assets. Consider the expected return vector and covariance matrix

$$\mu = \begin{bmatrix} 9 \\ 7 \end{bmatrix}, \quad \Sigma = \begin{bmatrix} 16.2 & 5.4 \\ 5.4 & 3 \end{bmatrix}.$$

The portfolio is $\mathbf{w} = (x, 1-x)'$, implying

$$\mu_p = 9x + 7(1-x),$$
$$\sigma_p^2 = 16.2x^2 + 2 \times 5.4x(1-x) + 3(1-x)^2.$$

We show the possible standard-deviation–expected-return combinations, (σ_p, μ_p), in figure 4.7. The two crosses correspond to investing everything in assets 1 and 2, respectively. Points on the curve outside the region between the crosses correspond to short-selling one of the assets (asset 2 for the points above the $x = 1$ cross, and asset 1 for the points below the $x = 0$ cross). Of course, since there is only one point on the curve for each value of μ_0 in this mini-example, there is nothing for the investor to optimize—each μ_0 is associated with a unique portfolio.

The minimization problem when there are more than two assets can be visualized as in figure 4.8. The objective is to find a point on the so-called *minimum variance frontier* that minimizes σ_p given $\mu_p = \mu_0$. In the figure, the feasible (σ_p, μ_p) combinations given portfolios of the

[2]Specifically, since Σ is SPD, so is Σ^{-1}, so Σ^{-1} can be used to define an inner product: $\langle \mathbf{x}, \mathbf{y} \rangle \stackrel{\text{def}}{=} \mathbf{x}'\Sigma^{-1}\mathbf{y}$. The Cauchy–Schwarz inequality then implies that $(\langle \mu, \mathbf{1} \rangle)^2 < \langle \mu, \mu \rangle \times \langle \mathbf{1}, \mathbf{1} \rangle$ when $\mu \nparallel \mathbf{1}$, i.e., $B^2 < AC$. Of course, $\mu \nparallel \mathbf{1}$, since μ contains at least two elements with different values, per assumption.

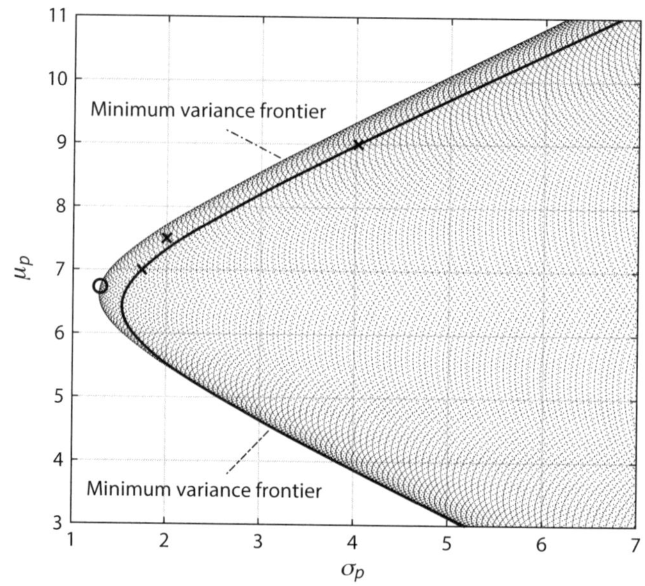

Figure 4.8: Minimum variance frontier with three risky assets.

form $\mathbf{w} = (x, y, 1 - x - y)'$ are shown, for an extension of the example we just studied, with three assets and

$$\mu = \begin{bmatrix} 9 \\ 7 \\ 7.5 \end{bmatrix}, \quad \Sigma = \begin{bmatrix} 16.2 & 5.4 & 4.03 \\ 5.4 & 3 & 1.38 \\ 4.03 & 1.38 & 4 \end{bmatrix}.$$

The line from the previous figure is included, but we see that it is possible to move even higher up to the left in the figure—in the direction that mean–variance optimizing investors like, by including the third asset. The boundary of the region with feasible risk-return profiles is given by the solutions to the problem $\min \sigma_p | \mu_p$. We call this boundary the *minimum variance frontier.* Note that neither of the risk-return profiles offered by individual stocks, represented by the crosses, lies on the minimum variance frontier. In general, the minimum variance frontier contains nondegenerate portfolios of assets. The qualitative behavior of the problem thus changed a lot when we went from two to three stocks. However, the qualitative behavior remains similar when we move from three to $N > 3$ stocks. The feasible region has the same parabolic shape as in figure 4.8 when we add more stocks, although the region increases in size, moving the minimum variance frontier to the left.

Note that there is a *global minimum variance portfolio*—the leftmost point in the region of feasible (σ_p, μ_p) combinations. We would expect a very risk-averse investor to choose a portfolio somewhere near this point. One can show that the global minimum variance portfolio is $\frac{1}{\mathbf{1}'\Sigma^{-1}\mathbf{1}}\Sigma^{-1}\mathbf{1}$.

The Lagrangian optimization problem takes the form

$$\min_{\mathbf{w}} \mathcal{L}, \quad \text{where } \mathcal{L} \stackrel{\text{def}}{=} \frac{1}{2}\mathbf{w}'\Sigma\mathbf{w} - \lambda_1(\mathbf{w}'\mathbf{1} - 1) - \lambda_2(\mathbf{w}'\mu - \mu_0)$$

(see appendix C.5) leading to the first-order conditions

$$\Sigma\mathbf{w} = \lambda_1 \mathbf{1} + \lambda_2 \mu,$$

$$\mathbf{w}'\mathbf{1} = 1,$$

$$\mathbf{w}'\mu = \mu_0.$$

The first equation implies that

$$\mathbf{w} = \lambda_1 \Sigma^{-1}\mathbf{1} + \lambda_2 \Sigma^{-1}\mu,$$

and premultiplying this equation with $\mathbf{1}'$ and μ', respectively, leads to the system of two equations with two unknowns,

$$1 = \lambda_1 A + \lambda_2 B,$$

$$\mu_0 = \lambda_1 B + \lambda_2 C,$$

with solution

$$\lambda_1 = \frac{C - B\mu_0}{AC - B^2},$$

$$\lambda_2 = \frac{A\mu_0 - B}{AC - B^2}.$$

Defining the normalized portfolios

$$\mathbf{w}_A = \frac{1}{A}\Sigma^{-1}\mathbf{1},$$

$$\mathbf{w}_B = \frac{1}{B}\Sigma^{-1}\mu,$$

which each have weights that sum to 1, we can write this as

$$\mathbf{w} = a\mathbf{w}_A + b\mathbf{w}_b,$$

where

$$\mathbf{w}_A = \frac{1}{A}\Sigma^{-1}\mathbf{1},$$

$$\mathbf{w}_B = \frac{1}{B}\Sigma^{-1}\mu,$$

$$a = \frac{AC - AB\mu_0}{AC - B^2},$$

$$b = \frac{AB\mu_0 - B^2}{AC - B^2}.$$

Note that $b = 1 - a$, and that $\mathbf{w}_A$ is the global minimum variance portfolio.

Thus, even if there are thousands of stocks available, all investors will choose to invest in some combination of the two portfolios $\mathbf{w}_A$ and $\mathbf{w}_B$! An interpretation is that it would be sufficient to have two mutual funds to satisfy the needs of all investors in the market, who would then not need to invest directly in stocks. We summarize this in the following theorem:

Theorem 4.6 (Two-fund separation theorem). *In the absence of a risk-free asset, all mean–variance optimizing investors choose a linear combination of two investment portfolios,*

$$\mathbf{w} = \zeta\mathbf{w}_A + (1 - \zeta)\mathbf{w}_B,$$

where

- $\mathbf{w}_A = \frac{1}{A}\Sigma^{-1}\mathbf{1}$, $A = \mathbf{1}'\Sigma^{-1}\mathbf{1}$,
- $\mathbf{w}_B = \frac{1}{B}\Sigma^{-1}\mu$, $B = \mathbf{1}'\Sigma^{-1}\mu$.

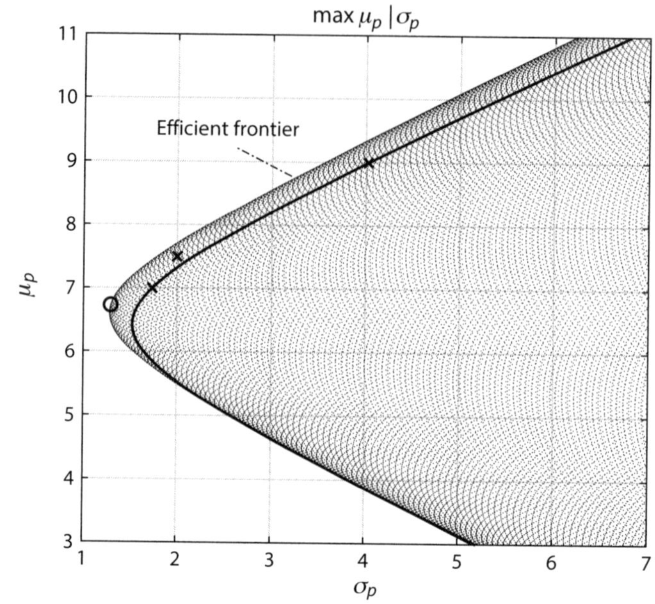

Figure 4.9: Efficient frontier with three assets.

Note that there are points on the minimum variance frontier that a mean–variance investor would never choose. Specifically, the points on the frontier with expected returns below that of the global minimum variance portfolio can always be improved upon by choosing a portfolio with higher expected returns and the same volatility, moving vertically up to a higher point on the frontier. Such points are not efficient. The *efficient frontier* contains the subset of points on the minimum variance frontier for which no points with higher expected returns and the same volatility exist, as shown in figure 4.9. This corresponds to the points that maximize μ_p, given σ_p.

This analysis so far has been for the case when there is no risk-free asset available. We have already looked at the case with a risk-free asset with returns r^f, within the CARA-normal framework. In that case, the preferences were of the linear form $U = \mu_p - \frac{\gamma}{2}\sigma_p^2$. Under general mean–variance preferences, the optimization problem for the investor who wishes to ensure the expected returns μ_0 becomes

$$\min_{\alpha} \frac{1}{2}\alpha'\Sigma\alpha,$$
$$\text{s.t. } \mu_0 = r^f + \alpha'(\mu - r^f\mathbf{1}).$$

Here, $\alpha \in \mathbb{R}^N$ is the part of the portfolio that is invested in risky assets, as discussed before (recall the difference between $\mathbf{w}$ and α). So the weights do not have to sum to 1, since it is possible to lend to or borrow from the bank (or, equivalently, buy or sell the risk-free bond). Using the Lagrangian, one verifies that the solution is

$$\alpha = \frac{\mu_0 - r^f}{A(r^f)^2 - 2r^f B + C}\Sigma^{-1}(\mu - r^f\mathbf{1}).$$

Note that since Σ^{-1} is SPD, $0 < (\mu - r^f\mathbf{1})'\Sigma^{-1}(\mu - r^f\mathbf{1}) = A(r^f)^2 - 2r^f B + C$, so the denominator in this expression is strictly positive. The normalized stock portfolio is then

$$\mathbf{w} = \frac{\alpha}{\mathbf{1}'\alpha} = \frac{1}{B - Ar^f}\Sigma^{-1}(\mu - r^f\mathbf{1}).$$

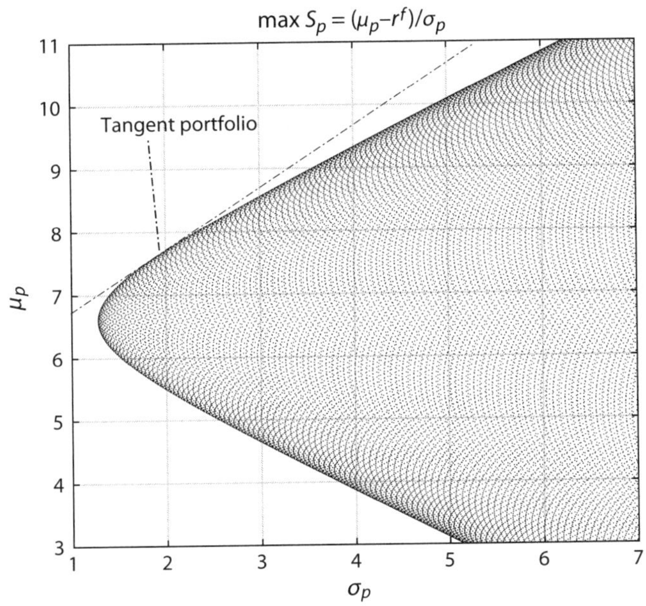

Figure 4.10: Maximizing the Sharpe ratio.

Thus, in the case with a risk-free asset, all investors invest in the *same* portfolio $\mathbf{w}$, and one mutual fund would be sufficient to serve the whole market of investors! We have shown the following result:

Theorem 4.7 (One-fund separation theorem). *When a risk-free asset is available, all mean–variance-optimizing investors choose the same portfolio of risky assets,*

$$\mathbf{w} = \frac{1}{B - Ar^f} \Sigma^{-1}(\mu - r^f \mathbf{1}).$$

Note that the one-fund separation theorem does not mean that all investors choose identical total portfolios. They will differ in how much of their wealth they invest in the market, α_0, depending on their risk aversion. But given α_0, they all invest in the same *risky* portfolio, $\mathbf{w}$ (recall that $\alpha = \alpha_0 \mathbf{w}$).

It is possible to show that the portfolio $\mathbf{w}$ in the one-fund separation theorem is the portfolio with the highest Sharpe ratio of all possible portfolios, S_p^*; see figure 4.10. The portfolio is called the *tangent portfolio* (or tangency portfolio), since it lies on the line $r^f + \alpha_0 S_p^*$ (as a function of α_0) that forms a tangent to the efficient frontier. An alternative way of solving the investor's problem is therefore to focus on the Sharpe ratio maximization problem.

Proposition 4.2. *The portfolio chosen by the mean–variance investor is the tangent portfolio, which maximizes portfolio Sharpe ratio, S_p.*

Proof. Consider the maximization problem

$$\max_{\mathbf{w}} S(\mathbf{w}) = \frac{\mu_p - r^f}{\sigma_p} = \frac{\mathbf{w}'(\mu - r^f \mathbf{1})}{\sqrt{\mathbf{w}'\Sigma\mathbf{w}}}.$$

The first-order condition is $\nabla_{\mathbf{w}} S = \mathbf{0}$. To calculate this, we use the formula $\nabla_{\mathbf{w}}(\mathbf{w}'\Sigma\mathbf{w})^{1/2} = \frac{1}{2}\frac{2\Sigma\mathbf{w}}{(\mathbf{w}'\Sigma\mathbf{w})^{1/2}}$, which follows from a multivariate version of the chain rule. We also have the rule from calculus, $(\frac{f}{g})' = \frac{f'}{g} - \frac{fg'}{g^2}$. Altogether we get

$$\nabla_{\mathbf{w}} S = \mathbf{0} = \frac{\mu - r^f \mathbf{1}}{\sqrt{\mathbf{w}'\Sigma\mathbf{w}}} - \frac{\Sigma\mathbf{w}}{(\mathbf{w}'\Sigma\mathbf{w})^{3/2}} \mathbf{w}'(\mu - r^f \mathbf{1}),$$

and thus

$$\mu - r^f \mathbf{1} = \frac{\Sigma\mathbf{w}}{(\mathbf{w}'\Sigma\mathbf{w})} \mathbf{w}'(\mu - r^f \mathbf{1}).$$

This still looks quite nasty as an equation for $\mathbf{w}$, but the key here is that $\frac{1}{(\mathbf{w}'\Sigma\mathbf{w})}\mathbf{w}'(\mu - r^f\mathbf{1})$ is just a constant, let us call it C, which then gives us

$$\mu - r^f \mathbf{1} = C\Sigma\mathbf{w}.$$

So

$$\mathbf{w}^* = \frac{1}{C}\Sigma^{-1}(\mu - r^f \mathbf{1}),$$

and $\frac{1}{C}$ is then just the same normalization constant that we had before to ensure $\mathbf{1}'\mathbf{w} = 1$. We arrive at

$$\mathbf{w}^* = \frac{1}{\mathbf{1}'\Sigma^{-1}(\mu - r^f \mathbf{1})} \Sigma^{-1}(\mu - r^f \mathbf{1}),$$

which is the same portfolio that we derived before, with associated Sharpe ratio, S_p^*. □

Once S_p^* and the associated portfolio $\mathbf{w}$ are known, the investor's final optimization problem is to choose the fraction of wealth, α_0, to allocate to the risky portfolio, corresponding to picking a point on the dotted line in figure 4.10, and to invest the remaining fraction $1 - \alpha_0$ in the risk-free asset.

Example 4.4. Consider the multivariate CARA-normal framework. Returns are

$$\tilde{\mu} \sim N(\mu, \Sigma), \quad \mu \in \mathbb{R}^N, \ \Sigma \in \mathbb{R}^{N \times N},$$

and we assume that Σ is invertible. We use the algebraic property of multivariate normal distributions, that $\widetilde{X} \sim N(\mu, \Sigma) \Rightarrow \mathbf{a}'\widetilde{X} \sim N(\mathbf{a}'\mu, \mathbf{a}'\Sigma\mathbf{a})$. The investor's budget constraint is $W_1 = W_0(R^f + \alpha'(\tilde{\mu} - r^f \mathbf{1})) = W_0 R^f + \mathbf{a}'(\tilde{\mu} - r^f \mathbf{1})$, where because of the algebraic property, $W_1 \sim N(W_0 R^f + \mathbf{a}'(\tilde{\mu} - r^f \mathbf{1}), \mathbf{a}'\Sigma\mathbf{a})$, and the investor's optimization problem is

$$\max_{\mathbf{a} \in \mathbb{R}^N} E[u(W_1)].$$

So, given the vector $\mathbf{a}$, $\widetilde{W}_1$ is univariate normally distributed. We know from before that the optimization problem has a mean–variance formulation. We can find the solution in the multivariate case by solving the following mean–variance optimization problem:

$$\mathbf{a}^* = \arg\max_{\mathbf{a}} F(\mathbf{a}) \stackrel{\text{def}}{=} \mathbf{a}'(\mu - r^f \mathbf{1}) - \frac{\gamma}{2}\mathbf{a}'\Sigma\mathbf{a},$$

leading to the optimal portfolio

$$\mathbf{a}^* = \frac{1}{\gamma}\Sigma^{-1}(\mu - r^f \mathbf{1}).$$

This follows from the FOC, $\nabla F = (\mu - r^f \mathbf{1}) - \gamma\Sigma\mathbf{a} = \mathbf{0}$. So the portfolio chosen by the CARA investor is the same as that chosen by a mean–variance investor.

4.4.1 Restrictions on Risk Distributions

The previous approach makes very strong assumptions about utility functions, but allows for almost arbitrary risk distributions as long as these are not too heavy tailed, so that portfolio variances are well defined and finite. An alternative approach is to restrict the class of risk distributions, so that results for a larger class of utility functions hold. We can think of the joint problem of choosing the class of risk distributions $\mathcal{R}$ and utility functions $\mathcal{U}$, within which strong portfolio implications can be derived. The larger is $\mathcal{R}$, the smaller $\mathcal{U}$ needs to be and vice versa.

The following result shows that if we restrict ourselves to the class of multivariate normal risk distributions, then the whole class $\mathcal{U}^2$ of utility functions is covered by the mean–variance efficiency analysis (as long as risk aversion is such that expected utility is finite for any $\tilde{\mu} \sim N(\mu, \sigma^2)$, $E[u(\tilde{\mu})] > -\infty$).

Theorem 4.8. *If risks are multivariate normally distributed, i.e., $\tilde{\mu} \sim N(\mu, \Sigma)$, then any risk-averse expected-utility-maximizing investor will choose a mean–variance-efficient portfolio.*

Proof. As we noted before, if $\tilde{\mu} \sim N(\mu, \Sigma)$, it follows that $\mathbf{w}'\tilde{\mu} \sim N(\mu_p, \sigma_p^2)$, where $\mu_p = \mathbf{w}'\mu$, and $\sigma_p^2 = \mathbf{w}'\Sigma\mathbf{w}$. The investor, with wealth $W_0 > 0$, then has expected utility

$$\begin{aligned} U &= E[u(W_0\mathbf{w}'\tilde{\mu})] \\ &= \int u(W_0(\mu_p + \sigma_p x))\phi(x)\,dx, \end{aligned}$$

where $\phi(x) = \frac{1}{\sqrt{2\pi}}e^{-\frac{x^2}{2}}$ is the p.d.f. of the standard normal distribution. So only the first two moments of the portfolio risk distribution actually matter for the investor's expected utility: $U = U(\mu_p, \sigma_p^2)$. It also follows that

$$\begin{aligned} \frac{\partial U}{\partial \mu_p} &= \int W_0 u'(\cdot)\phi(x)\,dx > 0, \\ \frac{\partial U}{\partial \sigma_p} &= \int W_0 x u'(\cdot)\phi(x)\,dx < 0 \end{aligned}$$

(since u' is decreasing), so within this class of risk distributions, the expected-utility-maximizing agent can be treated like an agent with mean–variance preferences, as analyzed before. Thus, the investor will choose a mean–variance-efficient portfolio. □

From what we know about the equivalence of the second-order stochastic domain of risks and the ranking by agents in $\mathcal{U}^2$, this immediately implies the following result:

Theorem 4.9. *If risks are multivariate normally distributed, two portfolios with the same expected returns are SSD ranked by their variances.*

These results are thus very general with respect to utility functions but, unfortunately, the assumption of normally distributed risks is unreasonable in many situations. In particular, the assumption allows neither limited liability, since normally distributed risks are unbounded from below, nor risks with heavier tails than normal distributions, as many financial risks are known to be.

By inspecting the proof of theorem 4.8, it quickly becomes clear that the result can be generalized. Specifically, it is not the actual normal p.d.f., ϕ, that does the trick in the proof. Rather, it is that the portfolios have the same type of risk distribution as the original risks, scaled by σ_p and translated by μ_p. We take this as a starting point to introduce a more general class of risks than the multivariate normally distributed class.

Definition 4.1. A multivariate random variable $\tilde{\mathbf{x}} = (\tilde{x}_1, \ldots, \tilde{x}_N)$ is said to belong to the class of *elliptical distributions* if its (multivariate) probability density function is of the form $\phi(\mathbf{x}) = kf((\mathbf{x}-\mu)'\Sigma^{-1}(\mathbf{x}-\mu)')$ for a nonnegative function $f: \mathbb{R}_+ \to \mathbb{R}_+$, and with scaling coefficient $k > 0$, vector of expected returns μ, and SPD covariance matrix proportional to Σ.

This definition hardwires the well-known properties of the joint distribution function of multivariate normal distributions, specifically, that the level sets of such multivariate distributions are of the form $(\mathbf{x}-\mu)'\Sigma^{-1}(\mathbf{x}-\mu) = c^2$, which in turn implies that the portfolio return $\tilde{x}_p = \mathbf{w}'\tilde{\mathbf{x}}$ can be written as $\tilde{x}_p = \mu_p + \sigma_p \tilde{x}$, where $\tilde{x}$ has the p.d.f. $f(x^2)$, $\mu_p = \mathbf{w}'\mu$, and $\sigma_p^2 = \mathbf{w}'\Sigma\mathbf{w}$. An identical argument to the one leading to theorem 4.8 therefore gives us the following result:

Theorem 4.10. *If risks are multivariate elliptical distributed, then any expected-utility-maximizing investor will choose a mean–variance-efficient portfolio.*

Also, the next result follows immediately:

Theorem 4.11. *If risks are multivariate elliptical distributed, two portfolios with the same expected returns are SSD ranked by their variances*

General elliptical distributions may be bounded, or have heavier tails than normal distributions. So mean–variance portfolio optimization can be modeled in such environments, for example, with firms that have limited liability, and which can therefore not have unboundedly negative returns. However, the restriction imposed on the joint behavior of assets by the elliptical level set property of the p.d.f. is quite specific.

4.4.2 Hedging Portfolio

In practice, an agent may be exposed to wealth risk that is unrelated to investments. For example, a personal unemployment shock will likely affect the agent's wealth negatively. Consider an agent with mean–variance preferences over total wealth, $\widetilde{W}$, $U(\widetilde{W}) = E[\widetilde{W}] - \frac{\gamma}{2}\operatorname{Var}(\widetilde{W})$. As before, there are N risky assets, and for simplicity we assume that the risk-free rate is zero, $r^f = 0$. The returns on the risky assets are multivariate normally distributed, $\tilde{\mu} \sim N(\mu, \Sigma)$, and the agent's initial wealth is W_0. (S)he is also exposed to a personal shock $\tilde{x}$, where $\tilde{x} \sim N(x, \sigma_x^2)$. The budget constraint is therefore

$$\widetilde{W} = W_0 + \mathbf{a}'\tilde{\mu} + \tilde{x}.$$

Now recall the standard formula from probability theory,

$$\operatorname{Var}(\tilde{y} + \tilde{z}) = \operatorname{Var}(\tilde{y}) + \operatorname{Var}(\tilde{z}) + 2\operatorname{Cov}(\tilde{y}, \tilde{z}),$$

and define the vector η, with elements $\eta_i = \operatorname{Cov}(\tilde{\mu}_i, \tilde{x})$. It then follows that

$$E[\widetilde{W}] = W_0 + \mathbf{a}'\mu + x, \quad \operatorname{Var}(\widetilde{W}) = (\mathbf{a}'\Sigma\mathbf{a} + \sigma_x^2 + 2\mathbf{a}'\eta),$$

leading to the investor's optimization

$$\max_{\mathbf{a}} W_0 + \mathbf{a}'\mu + x - \frac{\gamma}{2}(\mathbf{a}'\Sigma\mathbf{a} + \sigma_x^2 + 2\mathbf{a}'\eta),$$

with FOC

$$\mu - \gamma(\Sigma\mathbf{a} + \eta) = 0,$$

and solution

$$\mathbf{a} = \Sigma^{-1}\Big(\frac{1}{\gamma}\mu - \eta\Big).$$

When $\eta = \mathbf{0}$, which occurs when there is no $\tilde{x}$ risk or more generally when $\tilde{x}$ risk is uncorrelated with asset returns, this reduces to the previous formula,

$$\mathbf{a} = \frac{1}{\gamma}\Sigma^{-1}\mu.$$

The difference between these two portfolios, $\Sigma^{-1}\eta$, denotes the agent's *hedging portfolio*. It is straightforward to gain an intuition about this portfolio when Σ is a diagonal matrix, i.e., when asset returns are uncorrelated. In this case, Σ^{-1} is also diagonal, so in assets with positive η_i, i.e., assets with positive correlation between the personal shock and the asset's returns, the agent decreases investments. This is intuitive: since the agent is already exposed to risk associated with the ith asset, through the personal shock, (s)he decreases exposure in the investment portfolio. When $\eta_i < 0$, i.e., when there is negative correlation between the personal shock and the asset's returns, the agent increases investments in the asset. This is also intuitive: since the personal shock offers a hedge (insurance) against the ith asset's risk, (s)he is willing to invest more in that asset. Low returns in the asset tend to be offset by high realizations of the personal shock, which decreases total risk.

4.4.3 The Power of Diversification

One thing that makes the mean–variance-efficient portfolios $\mathbf{w} = \zeta\mathbf{w}_A + (1-\zeta)\mathbf{w}_B$ "good" is that they do not expose the investor to more risk (i.e., variance) than needed. One force at play here is that of *diversification*, which is a very old and powerful idea for how total risk can be spread when multiple risk sources are available. Indeed, this idea has been around much longer than modern portfolio theory. The idiom "Don't put all your eggs in one basket," dates back at least to the early 17th century.[3]

The presence of a diversification effect is not completely transparent from inspection of the portfolios

- $\mathbf{w}_A = \frac{1}{A}\Sigma^{-1}\mathbf{1}$, $A = \mathbf{1}'\Sigma^{-1}\mathbf{1}$ and
- $\mathbf{w}_B = \frac{1}{B}\Sigma^{-1}\mu$, $B = \mathbf{1}'\Sigma^{-1}\mu$.

Indeed, other forces are also at play when selecting $\mathbf{w}$. The potential of using the whole correlation structure between assets, including possibly negative correlation, to minimize portfolio variance, shows up in the Σ^{-1} parts of the portfolio terms. The importance of individual assets' expected returns shows up in the μ parts. That diversification is also an important part of the formula is easiest to see in the special case when the asset returns are i.i.d. (so $\mu \propto \mathbf{1}$ and $\Sigma \propto \mathbf{I}$). In this case, we have the following general result:

Theorem 4.12 (Samuelson 1967). *If the returns of the N assets are i.i.d., a risk-averse investor invests in the "$\frac{1}{N}$ portfolio" (pronounced "one over N portfolio"),*

$$\mathbf{w} = \frac{1}{N}\mathbf{1},$$

i.e., the investor maximally diversifies investments.

[3] In *Don Quixote* (from 1605), Miguel de Cervantes wrote, "It is the part of a wise man to keep himself today for tomorrow, and not venture all his eggs in one basket," but the saying had likely been around earlier than that.

Samuelson (1967) proves the result using the N-dimensional symmetry of the agent's maximization problem in the i.i.d. case, together with the concavity of the optimization problem. By simply plugging in the $\frac{1}{N}$ portfolio as a candidate solution, he shows that it satisfies the first- and second-order conditions necessary and sufficient for a global maximum.[4]

4.5 Including Consumption at $t=0$

So far, we have focused on the static setting for our analysis of investments under risk. We extend the setting to two dates, to see how risk aversion affects incentives to save. Consider an investor who consumes at time 0, invests what is not to consumed in a risky asset, and consumes the resulting wealth at time 1. The portfolio choice problem is thus trivial. There is only one asset, with risky returns $\widetilde{R}$. The investor's decision is how much to invest in that asset and how much to consume immediately.

We need to specify the investor's utility as a function of consumption at both points in time. We use the two-period expected utility specification from chapter 3. Specifically, assume that $u \in \mathcal{U}^2$ is an expected utility function, and define the total expected utility of consuming c_0 at time 0 and c_1 at time 1 as

$$U = u(c_0) + \delta E[u(c_1)].$$

Here, $0 < \delta < 1$ is the investor's *personal discount factor*, representing that (s)he is impatient, preferring to consume earlier rather than later. The budget constraint is $c_1 = W_1 = (W_0 - c_0)\widetilde{R} = S\widetilde{R} = sW_0\widetilde{R}$. Here, S represents the nominal savings and $s = \frac{W_0 - c_0}{W_0}$ is the investor's savings rate, i.e., savings as a fraction of total wealth. We are interested in how the investor's savings, or equivalently, her/his savings rate s, depends on the risk characteristics of the investment, $\widetilde{R}$.

The investor's maximization problem is

$$\max_{c_0} u(c_0) + \delta E[u((W - c_0)\widetilde{R})],$$

leading to the first-order condition

$$u'(c_0) = \delta E[u'((W - c_0)\widetilde{R})\widetilde{R}].$$

Let us focus on the CRRA utility case, with $u'(x) = x^{-\gamma}$. With this utility function, the first-order condition can be written

$$c_0^{-\gamma} = \delta E[(W_0 - c_0)^{-\gamma}\widetilde{R}^{1-\gamma}] = \delta (W_0 - c_0)^{-\gamma} E[\widetilde{R}^{1-\gamma}],$$

which in turn leads to

$$\left(\frac{W_0 - c_0}{c_0}\right)^{\gamma} = \delta E[\widetilde{R}^{1-\gamma}].$$

Note that

$$\frac{W_0 - c_0}{c_0} = \frac{s}{1-s} = \frac{1}{\frac{1}{s} - 1},$$

so the left-hand side of the equation above is increasing in s, regardless of $\gamma > 0$.

[4] A note: The argument is based on the variance being finite. For very heavy-tailed risk distributions, diversification is actually known to increase riskiness, as observed by Mandelbrot and Fama in the 1960s. For such heavy-tailed risks, an investor would choose minimal diversification, by holding only one asset.

Now let us consider the behavior of the right-hand side,

$$\delta E[\widetilde{R}^{1-\gamma}],$$

for two different assets, $\widetilde{R}_1$ and $\widetilde{R}_2$, with the same mean, but where the first asset second-order stochastically dominates the first, $\widetilde{R}_1 \succ_{\text{SSD}} \widetilde{R}_2$. In other words, the second asset is riskier than the first. We initially consider the case when $\gamma < 1$, so that the mapping $x \mapsto x^{1-\gamma}$ is strictly concave. The expectation can therefore be viewed as an "expected utility" with the "utility function" $u(x) = x^{1-\gamma}$, and it follows from our earlier results on second-order stochastic dominance that

$$\delta E[\widetilde{R}_1^{1-\gamma}] > \delta E[\widetilde{R}_2^{1-\gamma}].$$

Since the left-hand side is increasing in s, it must be that the investor's chosen savings rate when exposed to the first risk is *higher* than when exposed to the second, $s_1 > s_2$. The reverse result holds when $\gamma > 1$, which can be seen by noting that the "utility function" $u(x) = -x^{\gamma-1}$ is strictly concave in this case, so $s_2 < s_1$ when $\gamma < 1$. For the knife-edge, $\gamma = 1$, the savings rate is the same for both assets, $s_1 = s_2$.

So an investment adviser who is asked what the appropriate savings rate is under different environments—high-risk versus low-risk periods, for instance—would need to know how risk averse the investor is to be able to provide advice. The risk-aversion coefficient thus influences the intertemporal decision. We should not be surprised about such dependence, although we would not have been able to predict the direction of the effect without the above analysis, since we saw such an effect before when discussing consumption smoothing across states. Indeed, the savings result is closely related to consumption smoothing incentives, but over time rather than across states.

The following theorem generalizes our result to a larger class of utility functions, although still a small subset of $\mathcal{U}^2$:

Theorem 4.13 (Rothschild and Stiglitz 1971). *If two risks, $\widetilde{R}_1$ and $\widetilde{R}_2$, are such that $E[\widetilde{R}_1] = E[\widetilde{R}_2]$, and $\widetilde{R}_1$ strictly second-order stochastically dominates $\widetilde{R}_2$, then*

- *if* $\text{RRA}' \leq 0$ *and* $\text{RRA} > 1$, *then the investor saves more under risk* 2, $s_2 > s_1$;
- *if* $\text{RRA}' \geq 0$ *and* $\text{RRA} < 1$, *then the investor saves more under risk* 1, $s_1 > s_2$.

The fact that the risk-aversion coefficient influences both attitudes toward risk and intertemporal decisions, e.g., savings, has been viewed as a weakness of the expected utility framework, making it inconsistent with several empirical facts. The following example shows how risk aversion completely determines savings in extreme cases:

Example 4.5. Consider the two-date model with risk-free investment, so that $\widetilde{R} \equiv 1$, and time-separable CRRA utility,

$$U = \frac{c_0^{1-\gamma}}{1-\gamma} + \delta E\left[\frac{c_0^{1-\gamma}}{1-\gamma}\right].$$

A similar argument to before leads to the solution

$$\left(\frac{1}{\delta}\right)^{\frac{1}{\gamma}} = \frac{1}{s} - 1.$$

Note that $s = \frac{1}{2}$ corresponds to complete consumption smoothing, $c_0 = c_1$. The investor's savings rate will move closer to $s = \frac{1}{2}$ when γ increases, and converge to $s = \frac{1}{2}$ when γ tends to infinity, regardless of the personal discount rate, δ. Intuitively, the consumption smoothing incentives become completely dominating when the investor's risk aversion grows without bounds. This forced link between γ and s does not seem to capture the real-world behavior of investors very well.

To break this link, Epstein–Zin (EZ) preferences, which we studied in chapter 3, may be used. Recall that these can be written as (in the special case with two dates)

$$U=\left((1-\delta)c_0^{1-\rho}+\delta E[\tilde{c}_1^{1-\gamma}]^{\frac{1-\rho}{1-\gamma}}\right)^{\frac{1}{1-\rho}}.$$

Here,

$$\psi=\frac{1}{\rho}$$

is the coefficient of *elasticity of intertemporal substitution* (EIS), and γ is the risk-aversion coefficient, as usual.[5]

One can show that with the EZ specification, γ governs consumption smoothing incentives across states and ψ consumption smoothing incentives over time. Also, recall that when $\gamma=\frac{1}{\psi}$, EZ preferences reduce to CRRA preference, i.e., in that case,

$$U\propto\left(c_0^{1-\gamma}+\delta E[\tilde{c}_1^{1-\gamma}]\right)^{\frac{1}{1-\gamma}}.$$

We see the effect in our example with no risk ($\widetilde{R}\equiv 1$) and Epstein–Zin preferences. In this case, utility reduces to

$$\begin{aligned}U&=\left((1-\delta)c_0^{1-\rho}+\delta((W_0-c_0)^{1-\gamma})^{\frac{1-\rho}{1-\gamma}}\right)^{\frac{1}{1-\rho}}\\&=((1-\delta)c_0^{1-\rho}+\delta(W_0-c_0)^{1-\rho})^{\frac{1}{1-\rho}}\\&=W_0((1-\delta)s^{1-\rho}+\delta(1-s)^{1-\rho})^{\frac{1}{1-\rho}},\end{aligned}$$

leading to first-order conditions for savings,

$$(1-\delta)s^{-\rho}=\delta(1-s)^{-\rho},$$

and the optimal savings rate

$$s^*=\frac{1}{1+(\frac{\delta}{1-\delta})^{\frac{1}{\rho}}}.$$

These EZ preferences therefore achieve the goal of separating attitudes toward risk (which are governed by γ) from attitudes toward consumption smoothing over time (which are governed by ρ).

4.6 The Challenge of Estimating Expected Returns

We have assumed that the investor knows the expected return vector, μ, and covariance matrix, Σ. Where does this information come from in practice? If the investor has observed historical returns for some time, (s)he can use standard statistical estimation methods, under the (not completely

[5]Here we use a slightly different parametrization from before, with $(1-\delta)$ in front of the c_0 consumption term. This can be transformed into our previous specification by multiplying by the constant $(\frac{1}{1-\delta})^{\frac{1}{1-\rho}}$, and defining $\hat{\delta}=\frac{\delta}{1-\delta}$. Of course, the preferences are invariant to multiplication by a positive constant.

innocent) assumption that the past reflects the future, e.g., because returns are i.i.d. over time. Let us see in an example how well this works in practice.

Consider a so-called one-factor market model with N stocks, where there are two sources of risks for individual stock returns: a common shock, ξ_0, and a firm-specific shock, ξ_n, $n=1,\dots,N$. All these shocks are independent and normally distributed. The time-t return of stock n can be written

$$\tilde{\mu}_{n,t} = r^f + r^e + \sigma_S \xi_{0,t} + \sigma_I \xi_{n,t}, \quad \xi_{m,t} \sim N(0,1),\ t=1,2,\dots,T,\ m=0,1,\dots,N.$$

Here, σ_I, and σ_S are common constants for all stocks. The expected return vector is of the form $\mu = r^m \mathbf{1}$ in each time period, $r^m = r^f + r^e$.

It follows that the covariance matrix is of the form

$$\Sigma = \sigma_I^2 \mathbf{I} + \sigma_S^2 \mathbf{1}\mathbf{1}'.$$

This so-called *market model* is very simple, while still capturing a lot of the real market: diversification of idiosyncratic (firm-specific) risk, a market return factor (which we will see is a natural outcome from the equilibrium analysis in the next chapter), and it is simple to calibrate to aggregate market behavior. Most importantly, if estimating the parameters needed to solve the portfolio choice problem is challenging in this simple environment, it will likely be even harder in practice.

We use the following parameters, which roughly fit the US stock market in the 20th century:

- $r^f = 5\%$ per year,
- $r^m = 11\%$ per year,
- $r^e = r^m - r^f = 6\%$ per year,
- $\sigma_S = 15\%$ per year,
- $\sigma_I = 30\%$ per year.

As a benchmark, let us study an investor who knows μ and Σ, and who solves the portfolio choice problem to get

$$\mathbf{w} = \frac{1}{\mathbf{1}'\Sigma^{-1}(\mu - r^f\mathbf{1})}\Sigma^{-1}(\mu - r^f\mathbf{1}) = \frac{1}{N}\mathbf{1},$$

and who would therefore invest the same fraction of wealth in each of the N stocks. This is unsurprising, since the problem is symmetric (see section 4.4.3). The resulting portfolio is maximally diversified and achieves the highest Sharpe ratio. Let us focus on the case with $N=100$ stocks. The Sharpe ratio of the optimal portfolio in this case is $S_p = 0.3922$. When $N \to \infty$, the Sharpe ratio converges to 0.4, the intuition being that all firm-specific risk is diversified away and the Sharpe ratio of the remaining common risk is $\frac{r^m - r^f}{\sigma_S} = \frac{6\%}{15\%} = 0.4$.

Now consider an investor who does not know the expected returns of the different stocks, but has to estimate them from the data. For simplicity, we assume that the covariance matrix Σ is known, which makes life a bit simpler for the investor.[6] We assume annual observations for T years of the 100 stocks. The investor knows that the joint return distribution is identical in each period, and uses standard maximum likelihood estimation to get the estimated expected

[6]This is not unreasonable. As we will discuss in the second part of the book, it is much easier to draw inferences about second moments than about first moments in these models.

return vector

$$\bar{\mu} = \frac{1}{T}\sum_{t=1}^{T}\tilde{\mu}_t,$$

leading to the portfolio

$$\bar{\mathbf{w}} = \frac{1}{\mathbf{1}'\Sigma^{-1}(\bar{\mu} - r^f\mathbf{1})}\Sigma^{-1}(\bar{\mu} - r^f\mathbf{1}).$$

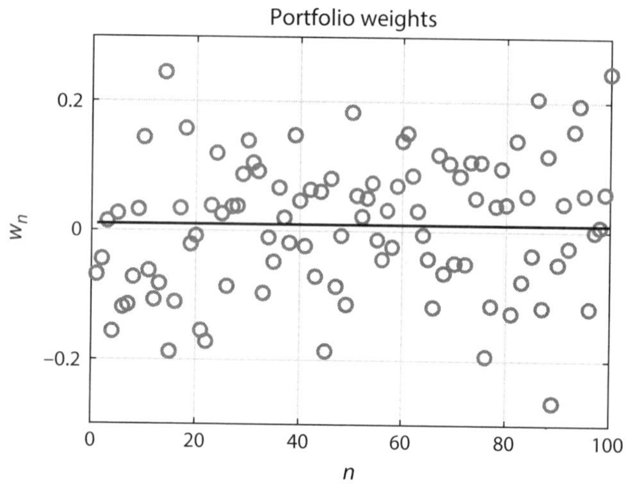

Figure 4.11: Portfolio weights, $\bar{\mathbf{w}}$, obtained when solving the portfolio problem with estimated expected returns, $\bar{\mu}$.

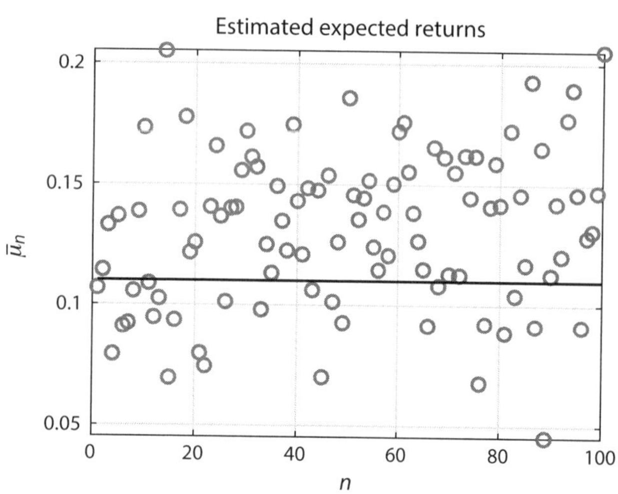

Figure 4.12: Estimated expected returns, $\bar{\mu}$.

In figure 4.11, we simulate returns, with $T = 10$, $N = 100$, and see which portfolio the investor chooses. On the x-axis we have enumerated the stocks, and on the y-axis the portfolio weights are shown, which of course sum to 1. We see that the portfolio is *very* far away from the optimal portfolio, which has $w_n = \frac{1}{100}$ for all N. How good is the estimated portfolio? The Sharpe ratio of this portfolio (based on the actual expected return vector, μ), is $\bar{S}_p = 0.0443$, which is barely higher than 0, and far below the maximum Sharpe ratio of $S_p = 0.3922$.

What is going on? We see that the investor's portfolio based on $\bar{\mu}$ is highly leveraged. Indeed, the investor puts much more than 1% in many of the stocks, financed by borrowing (short-selling) in the other stocks. A measure of how highly leveraged a portfolio is, is the sum of absolute portfolio weights: $\sum_n |w_n| = 13.25$, i.e., it is leveraged over 12 times. This is not a well-diversified portfolio. Rather, it is highly speculative. Figure 4.12 shows the estimated expected returns that the portfolio is based on. We see that the estimates are highly inaccurate: estimated expected returns vary between about −10% and +40%. If these were the actual expected returns, a highly leveraged portfolio would be justified, to take advantage of the return discrepancies. But the actual expected returns are $\mu_n = 11\%$ for all stocks, so there is no discrepancy in reality.

Now, one may argue that it is unsurprising that the estimates are so lousy since we only have 10 observations. What if we had daily return observations for the 10 years instead, say 250 trading-day observations per year, so instead of 10 observations, there would be 2500 over the 10-year period? Unfortunately, that would not help at all. One can show that only the total return between 0 and T matters for the estimate; the frequency of observations is irrelevant in this example. Increasing the length of the total sample period, T, helps though. How large would T have to be to get sufficiently good estimates to avoid spurious speculation in the chosen portfolio?

We get an idea from the standard error estimate. Recall that for an i.i.d. sequence of random variables $\tilde{\mu} \sim N(\mu, \sigma^2)$, if μ is estimated by its sample mean from T observations and σ is known, the standard error is

$$s \stackrel{\text{def}}{=} \frac{\sigma}{\sqrt{T}},$$

and we know that with a 95% likelihood,

$$|\bar{\mu} - \mu| < 1.96s.$$

As an example, if we plug in the parameters

- $\mu = 11\%$ per year,
- $\sigma = 33\%$ per year,
- $T = 100$ years,

the confidence interval is then about 6.5%, i.e., there is a 5% chance that $|\bar{\mu} - \mu| > 6.5\%$, even with 100 years of observations.

In words, even with a hundred years of observations (no matter how frequent), there is a reasonable chance that the estimated value of μ is as low as 4.5% or as high as 17.5%. With a hundred stocks, there will therefore very likely be huge variations in estimated expected returns among them purely because of noise, even with *a hundred years of observations*, and even if *the expected return on each stock is the same during the whole period*, conditions that are not satisfied in practice. This challenge is not unique for maximum likelihood estimation. It is a genuine property of the estimation problem, due to the high noise-to-signal ratio of stocks in the market. It will, for example, still be present if we switch to Bayesian estimation.

The challenge poses a major hurdle to the practical application of portfolio choice. Potential ways of addressing it include the following:

- Use additional information—about the individual firm, its sector, industry, etc.—to draw inferences about its prospects. This may require actual knowledge about the firm's business and operations; see, for example, Copeland, Koller, and Murrin (1994).
- Use robust estimators, e.g., which do not allow for negative portfolio weights, or shrinkage estimators; see, for example, Fabozzi, Focardi, and Kolm (2006).
- Use simple investing rules that are not based on estimation (e.g., simply choose $w_n = \frac{1}{N}$); see, for example DeMiguel, Garlappi, and Uppal (2009).
- Use equilibrium analysis to include additional information in the portfolio choice problem; see, for example, Black and Litterman (1991). We will discuss this approach further in the next chapter.

4.7 Dynamic Portfolio Choice

Consider a CARA investor who in a two-period economy, $t = 0, 1, 2$, maximizes expected utility of terminal wealth, W_2. The returns of the N stocks are multivariate normally distributed, with the same covariance matrix in both periods, but the expected returns may differ: $\tilde{\mu}_0 \sim N(\mu_0, \Sigma)$, $\tilde{\mu}_1 \sim N(\mu_1, \Sigma)$. At $t = 0$, the distribution of $\tilde{\mu}_0$ is known. However, the distribution of $\tilde{\mu}_1$ may not be known until $t = 1$. For example, it may depend on the realization of $\tilde{\mu}_0$.[7] We may assume that

[7] In this case, the investor may have more precise information about the distribution of $\tilde{\mu}_1$ at $t = 1$ than at $t = 0$, and be able to use that information when choosing the $t = 1$ portfolio. The variance matrix at $t = 1$, Σ, reflects the information available at $t = 1$ in this case.

$$\tilde{\mu}_0 = \mu_0 + \mathbf{Z}\tilde{\xi}_0,$$

$$\tilde{\mu}_1 = \mu_1 + \mathbf{Z}\tilde{\xi}_1,$$

where, $\mathbf{Z} \in \mathbb{R}^{N\times N}$, $\Sigma = \mathbf{ZZ}' \in \mathbb{R}^{N\times N}$ is symmetric positive definite, $\tilde{\xi}_0 \sim N(\mathbf{0}, \mathbf{I})$, $\tilde{\xi}_1 \sim N(\mathbf{0}, \mathbf{I})$, and $\tilde{\xi}_0 \in \mathbb{R}^N$ and $\tilde{\xi}_1 \in \mathbb{R}^N$ are independent.

The risk-free rate is $r^f = 0$ in both periods, leading to the following budget constraints when the investor invests $\mathbf{a}_0 \in \mathbb{R}^N$ in period 0 and $\mathbf{a}_1 \in \mathbb{R}^N$ in period 1:

$$W_1 = W_0 + \mathbf{a}_0'\tilde{\mu}_0,$$

$$W_2 = W_1 + \mathbf{a}_1'\tilde{\mu}_1.$$

How will the investor behave at $t = 0$ and $t = 1$? We solve the problem by *backward induction.* Specifically, we start with the $t = 1$ problem. At $t = 1$, the investor solves the one-period problem, which we covered in Example 4.2, leading to investment portfolio

$$\mathbf{a}_1 = \frac{1}{\gamma}\Sigma^{-1}\mu_1,$$

and expected utility

$$J_1 = \max_{\mathbf{a}_1} E_1[u(W_2)] = -e^{-\gamma(W_1 + \frac{1}{2\gamma}\mu_1'\Sigma^{-1}\mu_1)}.$$

Here, $J_1(W_1)$ is the *indirect utility function,* also called the *derived utility function,* that takes into account that the investor chooses the optimal portfolio at $t = 1$.

Next consider the investor's problem at $t = 0$, $U_0 = \max E_0[U(W_2)]$. The law of iterated expectations implies that

$$J_0 = \max_{\mathbf{a}_0, \mathbf{a}_1} E_0[E_1[u(W_2)]] = \max_{\mathbf{a}_0} E_0[J_1]$$

$$= \max_{\mathbf{a}_0} -E_0\left[e^{-\gamma(W_0 + \mathbf{a}_0'\tilde{\mu}_0 + \frac{1}{2\gamma}\mu_1'\Sigma^{-1}\mu_1)}\right].$$

Now, if μ_1 does not depend on what happened before $t = 1$, the $t = 0$ investment is the solution to another one-period problem, yielding the portfolio

$$\mathbf{a}_0 = \frac{1}{\gamma}\Sigma^{-1}\mu_0, \tag{4.5}$$

and utility

$$J_0 = -e^{-\gamma(W_0 + \frac{1}{2\gamma}\mu_0'\Sigma^{-1}\mu_0 + \frac{1}{2\gamma}\mu_1'\Sigma^{-1}\mu_1)}.$$

The extra term, $\frac{1}{2\gamma}\mu_1'\Sigma^{-1}\mu_1$, is just a constant in this case, and therefore does not impact the investor at $t = 0$.[8] So the investor effectively behaves the same way in each of the periods as in the static problem.

Consider now the situation when the distribution of $\tilde{\mu}_1$ depends on $\tilde{\mu}_0$. Specifically, let us assume that $\mu_1 = \mu_0 - \mathbf{A}\tilde{\xi}_0$, i.e.,

$$\tilde{\mu}_1 \sim N(\mu_0 - \mathbf{A}\tilde{\xi}_0, \Sigma).$$

Since $\tilde{\mu}_0$ is known at $t = 1$, when the investor chooses the investment portfolio for the second period, that information can be used when investing at $t = 1$. The investor will then choose the

[8] This result is not true in general, but depends on the CARA utility function. It also holds for CRRA utility in this case.

portfolio

$$\mathbf{a}_1 = \frac{1}{\gamma}\Sigma^{-1}(\mu_0 - \mathbf{A}\tilde{\xi}_0),$$

and his/her expected utility is

$$J_1 = \max_{\mathbf{a}_1} E_1[u(W_2)] = -E\left[e^{-\gamma(W_1 + \frac{1}{2\gamma}(\mu_0 - \mathbf{A}\tilde{\xi}_0)'\Sigma^{-1}(\mu_0 - \mathbf{A}\tilde{\xi}_0))}\right].$$

How will the investor behave at $t=0$? One may conjecture that since the return distribution in the first period is the same, $\tilde{\mu}_0 \sim N(\mu_0, \Sigma)$, as when $\tilde{\mu}_1$ did not depend on what happened between $t=0$ and $t=1$, the investor should choose the same portfolio at $t=0$ as before. This intuition is—except in very special cases—incorrect! Instead, as we will see, the investor will take into account that the returns in the first period are related to the returns in the second, and adjust the initial portfolio, $\mathbf{a}_0$, to take advantage of this relation. Let us first work out the algebra and then discuss the intuition behind the results.

It is easy to see that the law of iterated expectations implies that the investor's problem at $t=0$ is

$$\begin{aligned}
J_0 &= \max_{\mathbf{a}_0,\mathbf{a}_1} E_0[E_1[u(W_2)]] = \max_{\mathbf{a}_0} E_0[J_1] \\
&= \max_{\mathbf{a}_0} -E_0\left[e^{-\gamma(W_0 + \mathbf{a}_0'(\mu_0 + \mathbf{Z}\tilde{\xi}_0) + \frac{1}{2\gamma}(\mu_0 - \mathbf{A}\tilde{\xi}_0)'\Sigma^{-1}(\mu_0 - \mathbf{A}\tilde{\xi}_0))}\right] \\
&= \max_{\mathbf{a}_0} -\underbrace{e^{-\gamma(W_0 + \mathbf{a}_0'\mu_0)}}_{K} E_0\left[e^{-\gamma((\mathbf{Z}'\mathbf{a}_0)'\tilde{\xi}_0 + \frac{1}{2\gamma}(\mu_0 - \mathbf{A}\tilde{\xi}_0)'\Sigma^{-1}(\mu_0 - \mathbf{A}\tilde{\xi}_0))}\right] \\
&= \max_{\mathbf{a}_0} -KE_0\left[e^{-\gamma((\mathbf{Z}'\mathbf{a}_0)'\tilde{\xi}_0 + \frac{1}{2\gamma}(\mu_0'\Sigma^{-1}\mu_0 - 2(\mathbf{A}'\Sigma^{-1}\mu_0)'\tilde{\xi}_0 + \tilde{\xi}_0'(\mathbf{A}'\Sigma^{-1}\mathbf{A})\tilde{\xi}_0))}\right] \\
&= \max_{\mathbf{a}_0} -Ke^{-\frac{1}{2}\mu_0'\Sigma^{-1}\mu_0} E_0\left[e^{(\underbrace{\mathbf{A}'\Sigma^{-1}\mu_0 - \gamma\mathbf{Z}'\mathbf{a}_0}_{\mathbf{b}})'\tilde{\xi}_0 - \frac{1}{2}\tilde{\xi}_0'(\underbrace{\mathbf{A}'\Sigma^{-1}\mathbf{A}}_{\mathbf{B}})\tilde{\xi}_0}\right] \\
&= \max_{\mathbf{a}_0} -Ke^{-\frac{1}{2}\mu_0'\Sigma^{-1}\mu_0} \det(\mathbf{I} + \mathbf{B})^{-1/2} e^{\frac{1}{2}\mathbf{b}'(\mathbf{I}+\mathbf{B})^{-1}\mathbf{b}}.
\end{aligned} \tag{4.6}$$

Here we used the lemma below in the last step, together with the fact that $\tilde{\xi}_0 \sim N(\mathbf{0}, \mathbf{I})$, and that $\mathbf{A}'\Sigma^{-1}\mathbf{A}$ is symmetric and positive semidefinite.

Lemma 4.1. *Consider a random variable,* $\tilde{\mathbf{x}} \sim N(\mu, \Sigma) \in \mathbb{R}^N$*, a symmetric positive semidefinite matrix,* $\mathbf{B} \in \mathbb{R}^{N\times N}$*, and a vector,* $\mathbf{b} \in \mathbb{R}^N$*. Then*

$$E\left[e^{\mathbf{b}'\tilde{\mathbf{x}} - \frac{\tilde{\mathbf{x}}'\mathbf{B}\tilde{\mathbf{x}}}{2}}\right] = \det(\mathbf{I} + \Sigma\mathbf{B})^{-1/2} e^{\frac{1}{2}\mathbf{q}'(\Sigma^{-1}+\mathbf{B})^{-1}\mathbf{q} - \frac{1}{2}\mu'\Sigma^{-1}\mu},$$

where $\mathbf{q} = \Sigma^{-1}\mu + \mathbf{b}$.

Proof. From the formula for the probability density function of the multivariate distribution, we know that for $\tilde{\mathbf{x}} \sim N(\mu, \Sigma)$, the p.d.f. is

$$f(\mathbf{y}) = \frac{1}{(2\pi \det(\Sigma))^{1/2}} e^{-\frac{(\mathbf{y}-\eta)'\Sigma^{-1}(\mathbf{y}-\eta)}{2}},$$

and thus

$$\frac{1}{(2\pi \det(\Sigma))^{1/2}} \int_{\mathbf{y}\in\mathbb{R}^N} e^{-\frac{(\mathbf{y}-\mu)'\Sigma^{-1}(\mathbf{y}-\mu)}{2}}\, dV(\mathbf{y}) = 1.$$

Here the integral $\int f(\mathbf{y})\, dV(\mathbf{y})$ denotes the volume integral $\int\int \cdots \int f(\mathbf{y})\, d\mathbf{y}_1\, d\mathbf{y}_2 \cdots d\mathbf{y}_N$.

We have

$$
\begin{aligned}
&E[e^{\mathbf{b}'\tilde{\mathbf{x}}-\frac{\tilde{\mathbf{x}}'\mathbf{B}\tilde{\mathbf{x}}}{2}}]\\
&=\frac{1}{(2\pi\,\det(\Sigma))^{1/2}}\int_{\mathbf{y}\in\mathbb{R}^N} e^{-\frac{(\mathbf{y}-\mu)'\Sigma^{-1}(\mathbf{y}-\mu)}{2}+\mathbf{b}'\mathbf{y}-\frac{\mathbf{y}'\mathbf{B}\mathbf{y}}{2}}\,dV(\mathbf{y})\\
&=\frac{1}{(2\pi\,\det(\Sigma))^{1/2}}\int_{\mathbf{y}\in\mathbb{R}^N} e^{-(\frac{\mathbf{y}'\Sigma^{-1}\mathbf{y}}{2}+\frac{\mu'\Sigma^{-1}\mu}{2}-2\frac{\mu'\Sigma^{-1}\mathbf{y}}{2})+\mathbf{b}'\mathbf{y}-\frac{\mathbf{y}'\mathbf{B}\mathbf{y}}{2}}\,dV(\mathbf{y})\\
&=\frac{1}{(2\pi\,\det(\Sigma))^{1/2}}\int_{\mathbf{y}\in\mathbb{R}^N} e^{-(\frac{\mathbf{y}'(\Sigma^{-1}+\mathbf{B})\mathbf{y}}{2}+\frac{\mu'\Sigma^{-1}\mu}{2}-2\frac{(\Sigma^{-1}\mu+\mathbf{b})'\mathbf{y}}{2})}\,dV(\mathbf{y})\\
&=\frac{1}{(2\pi\,\det(\Sigma))^{1/2}}\int_{\mathbf{y}\in\mathbb{R}^N} e^{-(\frac{(\mathbf{y}-(\Sigma^{-1}+\mathbf{B})^{-1}\mathbf{q})'(\Sigma^{-1}+\mathbf{B})(\mathbf{y}-(\Sigma^{-1}+\mathbf{B})^{-1}\mathbf{q})}{2}+\frac{\mu'\Sigma^{-1}\mu}{2}-\frac{\mathbf{q}'(\Sigma^{-1}+\mathbf{B})^{-1}\mathbf{q}}{2})}\,dV(\mathbf{y})\\
&=\frac{\det((\Sigma^{-1}+\mathbf{B})^{-1})^{1/2}}{\det(\Sigma)^{1/2}}e^{\frac{\mu'\Sigma^{-1}\mu}{2}-\frac{\mathbf{q}'(\Sigma^{-1}+\mathbf{B})^{-1}\mathbf{q}}{2}}\\
&=\frac{1}{\det(\Sigma(\Sigma^{-1}+\mathbf{B}))^{1/2}}e^{\frac{1}{2}\mathbf{q}'(\Sigma^{-1}+\mathbf{B})^{-1}\mathbf{q}-\frac{1}{2}\mu'\Sigma^{-1}\mu}\\
&=\det(\mathbf{I}+\Sigma\mathbf{B})^{-\frac{1}{2}}e^{\frac{1}{2}\mathbf{q}'(\Sigma^{-1}+\mathbf{B})^{-1}\mathbf{q}-\frac{1}{2}\mu'\Sigma^{-1}\mu}.
\end{aligned}
$$

□

Now,

$$
\begin{aligned}
\mathbf{b}'(\mathbf{I}+\mathbf{B})^{-1}\mathbf{b}&=(\mathbf{A}'\Sigma^{-1}\mu_0-\gamma\mathbf{Z}'\mathbf{a}_0)'(\mathbf{I}+\mathbf{A}'\Sigma^{-1}\mathbf{A})^{-1}(\mathbf{A}'\Sigma^{-1}\mu_0-\gamma\mathbf{Z}'\mathbf{a}_0)\\
&=\mu_0'\Sigma^{-1}\mathbf{A}(\mathbf{I}+\mathbf{A}'\Sigma^{-1}\mathbf{A})^{-1}\mathbf{A}'\Sigma^{-1}\mu_0+\gamma^2\mathbf{a}_0'\mathbf{Z}(\mathbf{I}+\mathbf{A}'\Sigma^{-1}\mathbf{A})^{-1}\mathbf{Z}'\mathbf{a}_0\\
&\quad-2\gamma\mathbf{a}_0'\mathbf{Z}(\mathbf{I}+\mathbf{A}'\Sigma^{-1}\mathbf{A})^{-1}\mathbf{A}'\Sigma^{-1}\mu_0,
\end{aligned}
$$

and this allows us to write

$$
J_0=\max_{\mathbf{a}_0}K'e^{-\gamma(\mathbf{a}_0'(\mathbf{I}+\mathbf{Z}(\mathbf{I}+\mathbf{A}'\Sigma^{-1}\mathbf{A})^{-1}\mathbf{A}'\Sigma^{-1})\mu_0-\frac{\gamma}{2}\mathbf{a}_0'\mathbf{Z}(\mathbf{I}+\mathbf{A}'\Sigma^{-1}\mathbf{A})^{-1}\mathbf{Z}'\mathbf{a}_0)}. \tag{4.7}
$$

Here, the extra identity matrix, **I**, in the leftmost term in the exponent comes from the previously defined term K, and the term K' does not depend on $\mathbf{a}_0$. The first-order condition for an optimum in $\mathbf{a}_0$ is then

$$
\gamma\mathbf{Z}(\mathbf{I}+\mathbf{A}'\Sigma^{-1}\mathbf{A})^{-1}\mathbf{Z}'\mathbf{a}_0=(\mathbf{I}+\mathbf{Z}(I+\mathbf{A}'\Sigma^{-1}\mathbf{A})^{-1}\mathbf{A}'\Sigma^{-1})\mu_0,
$$

which is equivalent to

$$
\gamma\mathbf{a}_0=(\mathbf{Z}^{-1})'(\mathbf{I}+\mathbf{A}'\Sigma^{-1}\mathbf{A})\mathbf{Z}^{-1}(\mathbf{I}+\mathbf{Z}(\mathbf{I}+\mathbf{A}'\Sigma^{-1}\mathbf{A})^{-1}\mathbf{A}'\Sigma^{-1})\mu_0.
$$

After some further algebra, we arrive at

$$
\mathbf{a}_0=\frac{1}{\gamma}(\Sigma^{-1}+(\mathbf{A}\mathbf{Z}^{-1})'\Sigma^{-1}(\mathbf{A}\mathbf{Z}^{-1}+\mathbf{I}))\mu_0.
$$

When $\mathbf{A}=\mathbf{0}$, this collapses to the previous solution (4.5), but when $\mathbf{A}\neq\mathbf{0}$, the investor will in general adjust the portfolio to take into account the varying *investment opportunity set*. The term

$$
\mathbf{H}=(\mathbf{A}\mathbf{Z}^{-1})'\Sigma^{-1}(\mathbf{A}\mathbf{Z}^{-1}+\mathbf{I})\mu_0
$$

captures the *hedging portfolio* component of the investment, i.e., the adjustment the investor makes to take into account that the next period's returns also affect the returns in future periods. This contrasts with the behavior of a *myopic* investor, who would only consider the distribution of $\tilde{\mu}_0$ when choosing the portfolio at time 0. Note that since $\tilde{\mu}_0 - \mu_0 = \mathbf{Z}\tilde{\xi}_0$, we can alternatively write

$$\tilde{\mu}_1 \sim N(\mu_0 - \mathbf{C}(\tilde{\mu}_0 - \mu_0), \Sigma),$$

where $\mathbf{C} = \mathbf{A}\mathbf{Z}^{-1}$. Under this representation, the hedging portfolio component can then be written as

$$\mathbf{H} = \mathbf{C}'\Sigma^{-1}(\mathbf{C} + \mathbf{I})\mu_0.$$

Which type of investor will behave myopically? The only investor that behaves myopically regardless of the return distributions in the two periods (and regardless of how they are related) is the investor with logarithmic utility (i.e., CRRA with $\gamma = 1$), which is due to the fact that the effects of individual returns in different periods are separated for the investor with logarithmic utility. Specifically, consider the investor who invests in the portfolio w_0 at time 0 and w_1 at time 1. Here, $(\mathbf{w}_t)_i$ represents the fraction of time-t wealth invested in risky asset i, and since lending or borrowing is possible, there are no constraints, $\mathbf{w}_t \in \mathbb{R}^N$. The returns are $\tilde{\mu}_0$ and $\tilde{\mu}_1$ in the two periods. In contrast to the case with CARA utility, we need to assume a lower bound for the return of each asset, since the investor with logarithmic utility would never invest in an asset with no such lower bound.[9]

As before, the risk-free rate is $r^f = 0$ in both periods. The budget constraint then becomes

$$W_1 = W_0(1 + \mathbf{w}_0'\tilde{\mu}_0),$$
$$W_2 = W_1(1 + \mathbf{w}_1'\tilde{\mu}_1) = W_0(1 + \mathbf{w}_0'\tilde{\mu}_0)(1 + \mathbf{w}_1'\tilde{\mu}_1).$$

The log-investor's expected utility is then

$$U_0 = E_0[\ln(W_0(1 + \mathbf{w}_0'\tilde{\mu}_0)(1 + \mathbf{w}_1'\tilde{\mu}_1))] = \ln(W_0) + E_0[\ln(1 + \mathbf{w}_0'\tilde{\mu}_0)] + E_0[\ln(1 + \mathbf{w}_1'\tilde{\mu}_1)].$$

It is clear that the logarithmic utility specification does something very special here. Due to the multiplicative feature of compound returns, when we take the logarithm, the contributions to expected utility in the two periods are completely separated. As a consequence, it is irrelevant how the distribution of $\tilde{\mu}_1$ is related to the realization of $\tilde{\mu}_2$ in the choice of optimal time-0 portfolio, $\mathbf{w}_0$. The contribution to U_0 from time-2 investments, $E_0[\ln(\mathbf{w}_1'\tilde{\mu}_1)]$, will obviously depend on the distributional properties of $\tilde{\mu}_0$, which may depend on what happened between times 0 and 1, and specifically on $\tilde{\mu}_1$. However, the choice at time 0, of $\mathbf{w}_0$, is uncoupled from that term.

Another way of viewing this is to define $F_1(\tilde{\mu}_0) = \max_{\mathbf{w}_1} E_1[\ln(1 + \mathbf{w}_1'\tilde{\mu}_1|\tilde{\mu}_0)]$. Note that F_1 does not depend on $\mathbf{w}_0$. The time-0 maximization problem of $\mathbf{w}_0$ then becomes

$$U_0 = \max_{\mathbf{w}_0} \ln(W_0) + E_0[\ln(1 + \mathbf{w}_0'\tilde{\mu}_0)] + E_0[F_1(\tilde{\mu}_0)].$$

Because of the independence of the first and third terms of $\mathbf{w}_0$, this can be solved by maximizing

$$\max_{\mathbf{w}_0} E_0[\ln(1 + \mathbf{w}_0'\tilde{\mu}_0)],$$

i.e., the investor is myopic when choosing portfolio $\mathbf{w}_0$ at $t = 0$! Compare this with the optimization for the CARA investor (4.6) which is of the form

$$U_0 = -E_0\left[e^{-\gamma \mathbf{a}_0'\tilde{\mu}_0} F_2(\tilde{\mu}_0)\right],$$

[9] Strictly speaking, this is only the case in discrete-time models.

where the function F_2 represents the contribution to expected utility under the optimal investment at time 1. With CARA utility, $\mathbf{a}_0$ is therefore coupled with the function $F_2(\tilde{\mu}_0)$, which will impact the investor's choice of $\mathbf{a}_0$, and lead to deviations from the myopic behavior.

4.7.1 Growth Optimal Portfolios

Consider an investor with a very long horizon, caring about W_T for a very large T. So the investor maximizes $E[u(W_T)]$, i.e., there is no intermediate consumption.

As before, the investor's current wealth is W_0. Consider the CRRA utility case:

$$u(x) = \frac{x^{1-\gamma}}{1-\gamma}.$$

For simplicity, we focus on the situation when there are only two assets: one risk-free asset, with return $R_t^f \equiv 1$ in each period, and one risky asset, with i.i.d. returns $\tilde{\mu}_t$. Moreover, we assume that the investor is restricted to choosing the same fraction, α, of wealth invested in the risky asset in each period. This myopic behavior can actually be shown to be optimal for general CRRA utility functions when returns are i.i.d., just like we showed myopic behavior in general (not necessarily with i.i.d. returns) for logarithmic utility (i.e., CRRA with $\gamma = 1$).

The wealth after T periods in this case is

$$W_T = W_0(1+\alpha(\tilde{\mu}_1 - 1))(1+\alpha(\tilde{\mu}_2 - 1)) \cdots (1+\alpha(\tilde{\mu}_T - 1)).$$

Now we use the following property for independent random variables, $\widetilde{X}$ and $\widetilde{Y}$:

$$E[F(\widetilde{X})G(\widetilde{Y})] = E[F(\widetilde{X})]E[G(\widetilde{Y})],$$

for general functions F and G, which in our context implies

$$\begin{aligned} E[((1+\alpha(\tilde{\mu}_1 - 1))(1+\alpha(\tilde{\mu}_2 - 1)))^{1-\gamma}] &= E[(1+\alpha(\tilde{\mu}_1 - 1))^{1-\gamma}(1+\alpha(\tilde{\mu}_2 - 1))^{1-\gamma}] \\ &= E[(1+\alpha(\tilde{\mu}_1 - 1))^{1-\gamma}]E[(1+\alpha(\tilde{\mu}_2 - 1))^{1-\gamma}] \\ &= \left(E[(1+\alpha(\tilde{\mu}_1 - 1))^{1-\gamma}]\right)^2. \end{aligned}$$

When applied T times, this leads to the investor's expected utility,

$$E[u(W_T)] = \frac{W_0^{1-\gamma}}{1-\gamma} E[(1+\alpha(\tilde{\mu}_1 - 1))^{1-\gamma}]^T.$$

The FOC with respect to α is then

$$E[(\tilde{\mu}_1 - 1)(1+\alpha(\tilde{\mu}_1 - 1))^{-\gamma}] = 0. \tag{4.8}$$

We can relate this FOC to the problem of finding a so-called *growth (rate) optimal portfolio*. Specifically, define $\tilde{y}_t = \log(1+\alpha(\tilde{\mu}_t - 1))$, with associated expected value $E[\tilde{y}_t] = \mu_y$. Clearly,

$$\frac{1}{T}\log\left(\frac{W_T}{W_0}\right) \stackrel{\text{def}}{=} \widetilde{Y}_T = \frac{1}{T}\sum_{t=1}^{T} \tilde{y}_t.$$

Equivalently, we have $W_T = W_0 e^{\widetilde{Y}_T T}$.

Now, since the variables $\tilde{y}_t$ are i.i.d., the strong law of large numbers implies that

$$\widetilde{Y}_T \to_{\text{a.s.}} \mu_y,$$

so the investor with the highest μ_y will (almost surely, see section 8.3) outperform—and become wealthier than—all other investors in the long run! This is the famous Kelly (1956) criterion for a growth optimal portfolio, which sounds very reasonable, although it was not derived from an expected utility formulation. However, since the maximization problem for the growth optimal portfolio,

$$\max_{\alpha} \mu_y = \max_{\alpha} E[\ln(1+\alpha(\tilde{\mu}_1 - 1))],$$

is the same as for the CRRA investor with logarithmic utility, $\gamma = 1$ (one shows easily that the logarithmic utility leads to the same FOC as in (4.8), when $\gamma = 1$), the log-utility investor actually chooses the growth optimal portfolio!

The log-utility investor thus outperforms all other investors in the long run. Indeed, it follows that $E[W_T^{\gamma}]/E[W_T^{1}] \to 0$ as $T \to \infty$, for $\gamma \neq 1$, where W_T^{γ} is the wealth of the investor with risk-aversion coefficient γ at T. This opens up the question of whether we can rationalize *any* other utility function than log-utility in the longer horizon. Indeed, why would an investor voluntarily choose to almost surely be dominated by another investor (one can show almost sure dominance of any CRRA investor with $\gamma \neq 1$)?

The key to the answer is that expected utility maximization is not the same as maximization of long-term growth rate. Indeed, consider the example where a risk-neutral and a risk-averse investor get to enter into a favorable coin-toss gamble many times in a row. As before, we assume $R^f = 1$. The fair coin has $p = \frac{1}{2}$ for heads (and $p = \frac{1}{2}$ for tails). The investor may bet anything from 0 up to his/her total wealth W_t, at time t. The payoff for a dollar betted is 3 if the outcome is heads and 0 if it is tails. So the expected payoff is $\frac{3+0}{2} = 1.5$ and the expected return is also $R = 1.5$.

The risk-neutral investor views this as a great bet and goes all in every time, betting the whole of W_t at time t. At time T, his/her wealth is therefore $3^T W_0$ with probability 2^{-T}, and 0 with probability $1 - 2^{-T}$. The log-utility investor on the other hand solves

$$\max_{\alpha} \ln(1+\alpha(3-1))\frac{1}{2} + \ln(1+\alpha(0-1))\frac{1}{2},$$

leading to the investment $\alpha = \frac{1}{4}$. Thus, the log-investor bets $\frac{1}{4}$ of total wealth in each period. The expected growth rate is then

$$\mu_y = \ln\left(1+\frac{1}{4}(3-1)\right)\frac{1}{2} + \ln\left(1+\frac{1}{4}(0-1)\right)\frac{1}{2} \approx 0.05889,$$

and in the long run the log-utility investor's wealth will therefore with high likelihood be fairly close to $W_0 e^{\mu_y T}$. Thus, the log-utility investor will very likely be wealthier than the risk-neutral investor. But note that the *expected* wealth of the risk-neutral investor after T periods is

$$E[W_T] = \left(\frac{3}{2}\right)^T W_0,$$

whereas the expected return for the log-utility investor over a period is

$$\left(1+\frac{1}{4}(3-1)\right)\frac{1}{2} + \left(1+\frac{1}{4}(0-1)\right)\frac{1}{2} = \frac{9}{8},$$

and therefore after T periods,

$$E[W_T] = \left(\frac{9}{8}\right)^T W_0.$$

This is lower than the expected wealth of the risk-neutral investor. From this perspective, it is not clear at all that log-utility preferences should have precedence over other utility functions.

A EUROPEAN ROULETTE EXAMPLE Consider a generalized version of the example we studied at the beginning of section 4.2. This was a complete market example (see section 5.4.2), in which there were as many assets with linearly independent payoffs as there were states. Similarly, here we assume that there are N states and equally many assets, each of which has the time-0 price 1 and pays θ^n if state n occurs, and 0 otherwise, i.e., their payoffs are given by $\theta^n\delta_n$, where $\delta_n \in \mathbb{R}^N$ is the vector of returns of asset n in the N different states (see also the definition in appendix B, page 436),

$$(\delta_n)_{n'} = 1 \text{ if } n = n', \quad (\delta_n)_{n'} = 0 \text{ if } n \neq n'.$$

The assets δ_n are so-called Arrow–Debreu securities, which we will discuss later. The probability for state n to occur is p_n.

The log-utility investor's maximization problem is now

$$\max_{w_1,\ldots,w_N} \sum_{n=1}^{N} \ln(w_n\theta^n)p_n, \quad \text{s.t.} \sum_n w_n = 1.$$

Because of the law of logarithms, $\ln(AB) = \ln(A) + \ln(B)$, this is equivalent to the problem

$$\max_{w_1,\ldots,w_N} \sum_{n=1}^{N} \ln(w_n)p_n, \quad \text{s.t.} \sum_n w_n = 1,$$

i.e., the investor will only care about probabilities in the optimization, not actual returns (the returns will matter for the expected utility, but not in the choice of portfolio weights). One verifies that the solution to this problem is

$$w_n = p_n, \quad n = 1, \ldots, N,$$

leading to the utility

$$U = \sum_n \ln(p_n)p_n + \sum_n \ln(\theta^n)p_n + \ln(W).$$

This problem is closely related to the entropy concept in information theory. The *entropy* of a probability distribution is defined as

$$H(\{p_n\}_n) \stackrel{\text{def}}{=} -\sum_n \ln(p_n)p_n.$$

The utility may therefore be expressed as

$$U = -H + \sum_n \ln(\theta^n)p_n + \ln(W),$$

where only H is determined by the portfolio choice of the investor.

For example, consider the game of European roulette. There are 37 numbers on the roulette wheel between 0 and 36, of which 18 are red, 18 are black, and 1 (the number 0) is green. The wheel is spun, and a ball lands in the pocket associated with each of these numbers with equal probability, $\frac{1}{37}$. The probabilities of landing on a red number and landing on a black number are then equal, $p^r = p^b = \frac{18}{37}$, and the probability of landing on the green number is $p^g = \frac{1}{37}$. The payoffs of betting on the colors red or black are equal, $\theta^r = \theta^b = 2 = \frac{36}{18}$, and the payoff of betting on green (i.e., on the number 0) is $\theta^g = 36$.

The log-utility investor will in this case bet $w_r = w_b = \frac{18}{37}$ of his/her wealth on each red and black, and $w_g = \frac{1}{37}$ on green. The expected utility will then be

$$U = \ln\left(\frac{18}{37} \times \frac{36}{18}\right)\frac{18}{37} + \ln\left(\frac{18}{37} \times \frac{36}{18}\right)\frac{18}{37} + \ln\left(\frac{1}{37} \times 36\right)\frac{1}{37} + \ln(W)$$
$$= \ln\left(\frac{36}{37}\right) + \ln(W).$$

Note that this assumes that there are no other investment alternatives. The expected net return on this investment is negative, and the expected utility is therefore less than is achieved by simply staying away from the roulette table, $U = \ln(W)$, since $\ln(\frac{36}{37}) < 0$. So *not* playing roulette first-order stochastically dominates playing. This example should therefore, by no means, be interpreted as supportive of "investing" in the roulette table!

4.7.2 Universal Portfolios

The analysis in the previous section was based on the assumption that the probabilities for different outcomes were known. What if they are unknown? They could even change period by period. Achieving the growth optimal rate would seem out of reach in this case. Surprisingly, however, it is possible to asymptotically reach the same growth rate without *any* information about returns. This follows from the theory of *universal portfolios* (see Cover 1991).

To capture the idea, let us begin with a simplified situation with three stocks, where the investor allocates his/her portfolio of, say $W = \$100$, once and for all, at $t = 0$, and then does not get to rebalance again before T. The three stocks' returns, $\tilde{\mu}^n$, $n = 1, 2, 3$, are i.i.d. over time, with associated expected log-returns μ_y^n. Assume that the investor has no idea about which stock has the highest μ_y^n, and wants to avoid the risk of missing out on the winner. What should (s)he do? A natural approach is to put $\frac{1}{3}$ in each of the stocks. This strategy ensures a terminal wealth of at least $\frac{1}{3}$ of what would be obtained by investing only in the stock with the highest growth rate. So, in the long run,

$$\frac{W_T}{W_0} \geq \frac{1}{3}\frac{W_T^{\max}}{W_0}, \text{ a.s.}$$

We emphasize again that we allow *no* rebalancing of investments over time. It follows that

$$\frac{1}{T}\ln\left(\frac{W_T}{W_0}\right) \geq \frac{1}{T}\ln\left(\frac{W_T^{\max}}{W_0}\right) - \frac{1}{T}\ln(3), \text{ a.s.,}$$

and thus that for large T, the asymptotic growth rates of these two strategies are the same! Thus, even without knowledge about the return distributions, a diversification strategy can achieve close to maximal growth in the long run.

We now extend this argument to the case where the investor is allowed to rebalance in each period. Specifically, we allow the investor to choose portfolio weights, $\mathbf{w} = (w_1, w_2, \ldots, w_N)' \in \bar{S}^N$. Here, $\bar{S}^N$ is the (closed) N-dimensional unit simplex,

$$\bar{S}^N = \left\{\mathbf{x} \in \mathbb{R}_+^N : \sum_{n=1}^N \mathbf{x}_n = 1\right\}.$$

Specifically, consider our previous example, with N assets—Arrow–Debreu securities—each of which offers a conditional return of θ^n in each period, if state n occurs, and pays zero otherwise. As derived before, the investor will choose the portfolio with $w_n = \mathbf{p}_n$ in this case, where $\mathbf{p}_n$ is the probability for state n to occur. When the investor does not know the probabilities, a similar argument to before suggests that (s)he should split the wealth evenly between *all* possible investment strategies, i.e., put an equal amount in each $\mathbf{w} \in \bar{S}^N$, where $\bar{S}^N$, as before, is the N-dimensional unit simplex. Assume that the investor has one dollar to spread among these stocks, i.e., $W_0 = 1$.

Since there are an infinite number of such portfolios, this means that nothing is invested in each portfolio, but we can take an infinitesimal interpretation. Indeed, we can view the investment as forming a portfolio of an infinite number of constituent portfolios, for different probability vectors, $\mathbf{p} = (\mathbf{p}_1, \ldots, \mathbf{p}_N)' \in \bar{S}^N$, each with optimal investment $\mathbf{a}(\mathbf{p}) = \mathbf{w}(\mathbf{p}) = \mathbf{p}$. The total investment will then be the sum (or integral of all investments), i.e.,

$$\mathbf{w}^0 = \int_{\mathbf{p}\in\bar{S}^N} \mathbf{w}(\mathbf{p})\, d\lambda(\mathbf{p}) = \int_{\mathbf{p}\in\bar{S}^N} \mathbf{p}\, d\lambda(\mathbf{p}) = \frac{1}{N}\mathbf{1}_N. \tag{4.9}$$

Here the integral $\int_{\mathbf{p}\in\bar{S}^N} d\lambda(\mathbf{p})$ denotes the surface integral on the unit simplex.

So the investor invests an equal amount in each stock. Also, at the constituent portfolio level, $\mathbf{w}^0(\mathbf{p}) = \mathbf{p}$.

Now assume that state n occurs in the first period. The total value of the portfolio is then

$$W_1 = \mathbf{w}_n^0 \theta^n = \frac{\theta^n}{N}.$$

We can also interpret this in terms of all the constituent portfolios, specifically, the investment in portfolio $\mathbf{p}$ will have grown to

$$\mathbf{a}^0(\mathbf{p})_n \theta^n.$$

With this interpretation, we can write the total wealth at time 1 as

$$W_1 = \int_{\mathbf{p}\in\bar{S}^N} \mathbf{a}^0(\mathbf{p})_n \theta^n\, d\lambda(\mathbf{p}) = \theta^n \int_{\mathbf{p}\in\bar{S}^N} (\mathbf{p})_n\, d\lambda(\mathbf{p}).$$

Now the investor should rebalance each of the constituent portfolios according to the $\mathbf{w} = \mathbf{p}$ rule in each period. So the rebalanced $\mathbf{p}$-portfolio will be (in dollar terms)

$$\mathbf{a}^1(\mathbf{p}) = \mathbf{a}^0(\mathbf{p})_n \theta^n \mathbf{p}.$$

Integrating up the new total portfolio, we get

$$\mathbf{a}^1 = \int_{\mathbf{p}\in\bar{S}^N} \mathbf{a}^0(\mathbf{p})_n \theta^n \mathbf{p}\, d\lambda(\mathbf{p}) = \theta^n \int_{\mathbf{p}\in\bar{S}^N} (\mathbf{p})_n \mathbf{p}\, d\lambda(\mathbf{p}), \tag{4.10}$$

and the new total portfolio is then

$$\mathbf{w}^1 = \frac{1}{W_1}\theta^n \int_{\mathbf{p}\in\bar{S}^N} \mathbf{a}^1(\mathbf{p})_n \mathbf{p}\, d\lambda(\mathbf{p}) = \frac{\int_{\mathbf{p}\in\bar{S}^N} \mathbf{a}^1(\mathbf{p})_n \mathbf{p}\, d\lambda(\mathbf{p})}{\int_{\mathbf{p}\in\bar{S}^N} \mathbf{a}^0(\mathbf{p})_n\, d\lambda(\mathbf{p})}. \tag{4.11}$$

The same updating rule will then be carried out at $t = 2, 3, \ldots$, leading to

$$\mathbf{a}^{t+1}(\mathbf{p}) = \mathbf{a}^t(\mathbf{p})_{n_t} \theta^{n_t} \mathbf{p}, \tag{4.12}$$

$$\mathbf{a}^{t+1} = \theta^{n_t} \int_{\mathbf{p}\in\bar{S}^N} \mathbf{a}^t(\mathbf{p})_{n_t} \mathbf{p}\, d\lambda(\mathbf{p}), \tag{4.13}$$

where state n_t was realized at time t. This leads to wealth

$$W_{t+1} = \mathbf{1}'\mathbf{a}^t = \theta^n \int_{\mathbf{p}\in\bar{S}^N} \mathbf{a}^t(\mathbf{p})_{n_t}\, d\lambda(\mathbf{p}), \tag{4.14}$$

and the total portfolio

$$\mathbf{w}^{t+1} = \frac{1}{W_{t+1}} \theta^{n_t} \int_{\mathbf{p}\in\bar{S}^N} \mathbf{a}^{t+1}(\mathbf{p})_{n_t} \mathbf{p}\, d\lambda(\mathbf{p}) = \frac{\int_{\mathbf{p}\in\bar{S}^N} \mathbf{a}^t(\mathbf{p})_{n_t} \mathbf{p}\, d\lambda(\mathbf{p})}{\int_{\mathbf{p}\in\bar{S}^N} \mathbf{a}^t(\mathbf{p})_{n_t}\, d\lambda(\mathbf{p})}. \tag{4.15}$$

We call the strategy implemented by (4.9, 4.13–4.15) the *universal portfolio strategy* (UPS), and the realized wealth of this strategy at time T is W_T^{UPS}. Now consider a strategy that chooses the same portfolio, $\mathbf{w}$, in each period. We call such a strategy a *constant rebalanced portfolio*. The following result can be shown:

Theorem 4.14 (Asymptotic optimality of the universal portfolio strategy). *Consider the optimal constant rebalanced portfolio strategy* $\mathbf{w}$ *that maximizes the wealth at* T*:*

$$W_T^* = \max_{\mathbf{w}\in\bar{S}^N} W_T = \max_{\mathbf{w}\in\bar{S}^N} W_0 \prod_{t=0}^{T-1} \theta^{n_t}(\mathbf{w})_{n_t}.$$

Asymptotically, the universal portfolio strategy achieves the same growth rate as the optimal constant rebalanced portfolio strategy:

$$\lim_{T\to\infty} \left(\frac{1}{T} \ln\left(\frac{W_T^{UPS}}{W_0}\right) - \frac{1}{T} \ln\left(\frac{W_T^*}{W_0}\right)\right) = 0.$$

Note that the return terms θ^{n_t} actually cancel out in the definition of $\mathbf{w}^{t+1}$, and therefore do not impact the portfolio (although they do impact the actual wealth). The following iteration therefore also implements the UPS:

$$\hat{\mathbf{a}}^0(\mathbf{p}) = \mathbf{p},$$

$$\hat{\mathbf{a}}^{t+1}(\mathbf{p}) = \hat{\mathbf{a}}^t(\mathbf{p})_{n^t} \mathbf{p},$$

$$\mathbf{w}^{t+1} = \frac{\int_{\mathbf{p}\in\bar{S}^N} \hat{\mathbf{a}}^{t+1}(\mathbf{p})\, d\lambda(\mathbf{p})}{\int_{\mathbf{p}\in\bar{S}^N} \hat{\mathbf{a}}^t(\mathbf{p})_{n^t}\, d\lambda(\mathbf{p})}.$$

This iteration shows that only the realization $\{n_t\}_t$ matters for the chosen weights, and not the returns, $\{\theta^n\}_n$, nor the true probabilities, $\mathbf{p}$.

Note the generality of this theorem in that it is not based on any statistical assumptions about probabilities—indeed, they may change over time in an arbitrary fashion and the result still holds. The result holds for *arbitrary* realizations. Finally, the time-T portfolio maximization when choosing the optimal constant rebalanced portfolio strategy is done ex post, after the returns have been realized. It is quite remarkable that the UPS manages to receive the same asymptotic growth rate without any knowledge of risk distributions. The intuition for why it performs so well lies in how it chooses *all* possible constant rebalanced portfolios, and thereby also the one that will realize the optimal outcome.

Note that the one thing the optimal constant rebalanced portfolio does not do is change the portfolio weights over time. Someone with perfect foresight about the realization would choose the time-varying portfolios $\mathbf{w}^t = \delta_{n_t}$ (assuming short-selling was not allowed), and thereby achieve the growth $W_T = W_0 \prod_{t=0}^{T-1} \theta^{n_t}$, which would (typically) be much higher than that of the optimal constant rebalanced portfolio.

AN EXAMPLE WITH THREE STATES Consider the case with three states and three assets, $N = 3$, with conditional returns θ^1, θ^2, and θ^3 in the different states. The UPS investor chooses the initial portfolio $\mathbf{w}^0 = (\frac{1}{3}, \frac{1}{3}, \frac{1}{3})'$, i.e., invests an equal fraction in each asset. Now assume that the first state is realized in the first period, $n^1 = 1$. This leads us to

$$\begin{aligned}
\hat{\mathbf{a}}^0(\mathbf{p}) &= \mathbf{p}, \\
\hat{\mathbf{a}}^1(\mathbf{p}) &= (\mathbf{p})_1\mathbf{p}, \\
\mathbf{w}^1 &= \frac{\int_{\mathbf{p}\in\bar{S}^N} (\mathbf{p})_1\mathbf{p}\, d\lambda(\mathbf{p})}{\int_{\mathbf{p}\in\bar{S}^N} (\mathbf{p})_1\, d\lambda(\mathbf{p})} \\
&= \left(\frac{q_1}{q}, \frac{q_2}{q}, \frac{q_3}{q}\right)',
\end{aligned}$$

where

$$\begin{aligned}
q_1 &= \int_0^1 \int_0^{1-\mathbf{p}_1} \mathbf{p}_1^2\, d\mathbf{p}_2\, d\mathbf{p}_1 = \frac{1}{12}, \\
q_2 &= \int_0^1 \int_0^{1-\mathbf{p}_1} \mathbf{p}_1\mathbf{p}_2\, d\mathbf{p}_2\, d\mathbf{p}_1 = \frac{1}{24}, \\
q_3 &= \int_0^1 \int_0^{1-\mathbf{p}_1} \mathbf{p}_1\mathbf{p}_3\, d\mathbf{p}_2\, d\mathbf{p}_1 = \frac{1}{24}, \\
q &= \int_0^1 \int_0^{1-\mathbf{p}_1} \mathbf{p}_1\, d\mathbf{p}_2\, d\mathbf{p}_1 = \frac{1}{6}.
\end{aligned}$$

Altogether, we then have

$$\mathbf{w}^1 = \begin{bmatrix} \frac{2}{4} \\ \frac{1}{4} \\ \frac{1}{4} \end{bmatrix}.$$

Next assume that state 1 is realized in the second period. A similar argument leads us to $\mathbf{w}^2 = (\frac{q_1}{q}, \frac{q_2}{q}, \frac{q_3}{q})'$, where

$$\begin{aligned}
q_1 &= \int_0^1 \int_0^{1-\mathbf{p}_1} \mathbf{p}_1^3\, d\mathbf{p}_2\, d\mathbf{p}_1 = \frac{1}{20}, \\
q_2 &= \int_0^1 \int_0^{1-\mathbf{p}_1} \mathbf{p}_1^2\mathbf{p}_2\, d\mathbf{p}_2\, d\mathbf{p}_1 = \frac{1}{60}, \\
q_3 &= \int_0^1 \int_0^{1-\mathbf{p}_1} \mathbf{p}_1^2\mathbf{p}_3\, d\mathbf{p}_2\, d\mathbf{p}_1 = \frac{1}{60}, \\
q &= \int_0^1 \int_0^{1-\mathbf{p}_1} \mathbf{p}_1^2\, d\mathbf{p}_2\, d\mathbf{p}_1 = \frac{1}{12},
\end{aligned}$$

so

$$\mathbf{w}^2 = \begin{bmatrix} \frac{3}{5} \\ \frac{1}{5} \\ \frac{1}{5} \end{bmatrix}.$$

If, on the other hand, the second state was realized in the second period, the calculation leads to

$$\mathbf{w}^2 = \begin{bmatrix} \frac{2}{5} \\ \frac{2}{5} \\ \frac{1}{5} \end{bmatrix}.$$

We are beginning to see a structure here. Indeed, by noting that the integrals used to calculate the portfolio weights are equivalent to integrals over statistical *Dirichlet distributions*, which are multivariate versions of the more standard *beta distributions*, one can derive the following portfolio weight formula for the holding at time t in the general case with N possible outcomes, and where the number of realizations of the different states is $m_1, m_2, \ldots, m_N$ (where $m_k \geq 0$ for all k, and $\sum_k m_k = t$):

$$\mathbf{w}^t = \left(\frac{m_1+1}{t+N}, \frac{m_2+1}{t+N}, \ldots, \frac{m_N+1}{t+N}\right)'. \tag{4.16}$$

Interestingly, the portfolio in (4.16) is the same as that which a Bayesian investor with logarithmic utility and Dirichlet $B(\mathbf{1})$ distributed prior would invest in. We state this in the following corollary:

Corollary 4.1. *A Bayesian log-utility investor with* $B(\mathbf{1})$ *distributed prior about* $\mathbf{p} \in S^M$ *invests in the UPS portfolio* (4.16) *in each time period.*

Finally, the time-t wealth of the investor is

$$W_t = \left(\prod_{k=1}^{N} (\theta^k)^{m_k}\right) \frac{\prod_{k=1}^{N} \left(\prod_{s=0}^{m_k-1} (1+s)\right)}{\prod_{s=0}^{t-1} (N+s)}.$$

This expression looks quite involved, but it is actually straightforward. The leftmost term represents the actual realized returns, whereas the ratio to the right in the expression represents the cumulative product of portfolio weights, taking into account that the order in which realizations occur is irrelevant.

4.8 Exercises

1. A CARA expected utility investor with risk-aversion coefficient $\gamma > 0$ considers investing in a market with three risky assets with multivariate normal returns, $\tilde{\mu} \sim N(\mu, \Sigma)$, where

$$\mu = \begin{bmatrix} 1 \\ 2 \\ 3 \end{bmatrix}, \quad \Sigma = \begin{bmatrix} 3 & 0 & 0 \\ 0 & 2 & 0 \\ 0 & 0 & 1 \end{bmatrix}. \tag{4.17}$$

   There is no risk-free asset in the market.

   (a) What portfolio, $\mathbf{w} = (w_1, w_2, w_3)'$, will the investor choose?
   (b) What is the limit portfolio that an investor with $\gamma \to \infty$ will choose? Explain intuitively, in one sentence, why this portfolio is chosen in the limit.

2. Consider an investor who minimizes the variance of his/her portfolio of two assets with means $\mu_1 < \mu_2$ and variances $\sigma_1^2 < \sigma_2^2$ correspondingly, and the correlation of returns is ρ.

   (a) Derive the weights of two assets in the investor's optimal portfolio (global minimum variance portfolio).

(b) Assume that the investor's portfolio is long-only, i.e., that short-selling is not allowed. Compare formally μ_1, μ_2, and the expected return of the portfolio when $\rho \in \{-1, 0, 1\}$.

(c) Assume again that $\rho = 1$, but relax the assumption that the portfolio is long-only. Compute the expected return and variance of the optimal portfolio in this case. How do they compare to the expected return and variance of the long-only portfolio with the same correlation between asset returns?

3. Consider a CARA investor with an absolute risk aversion of 1 who solves a one-period optimal portfolio problem.

   (a) Assume there are only two assets available. They both have an expected return of $\frac{1}{6}$ and a variance of 1; return covariance is $\frac{1}{2}$. Compute the optimal portfolio, its expected return, and variance. How does it compare with the case when only one such asset is available?

   (b) Assume a third asset becomes available. It has the same expected return and variance as the other two assets. Its covariances with the two existing assets are both $\frac{1}{2}$. Compute the optimal portfolio of three assets, its expected return, and its variance. How does it compare with the case when only two assets are available?

   (c) Assume instead that the third asset has covariances of $\frac{1}{2}$ and 0 with the existing assets. How does your answer to the previous question change?

4. Consider a market with three risky assets (stocks), with expected returns $\mu_1 = 11\%$, $\mu_2 = 6\%$, and $\mu_3 = 9\%$, and standard deviations $\sigma_1 = 0.5$, $\sigma_2 = 0.6$, and $\sigma_3 = 0.4$. The assets' returns are independent. There is also a risk-free asset offering returns $r^f = 1\%$.

   (a) Calculate the stock portfolio, $\mathbf{w}$ (in terms of fraction of risky investments, i.e., such that $\sum_i w_i = 1$), that a mean–variance investor would choose in this market.

   (b) Stock 2 has lower expected return and higher standard deviation than the other two stocks, and therefore seems to be dominated by them. Would a mean–variance investor still choose to invest a positive amount in that stock? If so, why?

   (c) Assume the stock returns are multivariate normally distributed, $\tilde{\mu} \sim N(\mu, \Sigma)$, with the above-defined moments. Calculate the stock portfolio $\mathbf{a} = (a_1, a_2, a_3)'$ (measured in dollars, so that a_i is the number of dollars invested in stock i) that a CARA investor with risk-aversion coefficient $\gamma = \frac{1}{10{,}000}$ would choose.

   (d) Assume that the stock returns are multivariate normally distributed, $\tilde{\mu} \sim N(\mu, \Sigma)$, with the above-defined moments. Calculate the stock portfolio $\mathbf{w}$ that a CRRA investor with risk-aversion coefficient 1 (i.e., with log-utility) would choose.

5. Consider an investor who maximizes the utility $E(R_p) - \frac{\lambda}{2} V(R_p)$, where R_p is the return of the portfolio of N assets with mean μ (column vector of size $N \times 1$) and variance–covariance matrix Σ ($N \times N$ matrix), by choosing a vector of portfolio weights $\mathbf{w}$ ($N \times 1$ column vector) under the constraint that the sum of portfolio weights must be equal to 1.

   (a) Write down a Lagrangian for this constrained optimization problem.

   (b) Solve it for the optimal portfolio weights $\mathbf{w}^*$.

   (c) Recognize an expression for asset weights in the global minimum variance portfolio (GMVP) $\mathbf{w}^*_{\text{GMVP}}$ to rewrite the optimal solution as

$$\mathbf{w}^* = \mathbf{w}^*_{\text{GMVP}} + \frac{1}{\lambda}\Sigma^{-1}(\mu - (\mu'\mathbf{w}^*_{\text{GMVP}})\mathbf{1}).$$

Assume that $\mu = m \times \mathbf{1}$, where m is scalar. What is the optimal portfolio in this case?

6. Consider an expected-utility-maximizing investor with utility function

$$u_L(x;\epsilon) = x - \frac{1}{10}\left(x\tan^{-1}(x) - \frac{1}{2}\log(1+x^2)\right).$$

As discussed in the main text, this utility function is increasing and close to linear, but still "mildly" risk averse (concave). Consider a one-period market with a risk-free asset with net returns $r^f = 0$, and a risky asset with net returns $\tilde{\mu}$, where the p.d.f. for $\tilde{\mu}$ is

$$\phi(x) = \frac{2}{\pi}\frac{|x|}{1+x^4}.$$

The investor's wealth is $W = 10$. What fraction, α, will (s)he invest in the risky asset?

7. Consider an intertemporal saving problem

$$\max_S E[u(W_0 - S) + \delta u(S\widetilde{R})],$$

where W_0 is the initial wealth, S is a chosen saving amount, and $\widetilde{R}$ is a gross return on a risky asset with mean μ and variance σ^2. Assume that the agent has mean–variance preferences, i.e.,

$$u(\tilde{x}) = E(x) - \frac{\gamma}{2}V(x).$$

   (a) Compute the optimal saving S^*.
   (b) Assume that the risky asset's payoff distribution has changed such that the new payoff second-order stochastically dominates the old payoff, but the expected return remains the same. Does the optimal savings level increase or decrease?

8. Consider a mean–variance investor in a market with two risky stocks with (multivariate) normally distributed returns $\tilde{\mu}_i \sim N(\mu_i, \sigma_i^2)$, $i \in \{1,2\}$, $\mu_1 = 0.15$, $\mu_2 = 0.16$, $\sigma_1 = \sigma_2 = 0.4$. The correlation between the two stocks' returns is $\text{Corr}(\tilde{\mu}_1, \tilde{\mu}_2) = 0.5$. There is also a risk-free asset with return $r^f = 0.02$.

   The investor's target return on her/his portfolio is 10%. Which portfolio $(\alpha_0, \alpha_1, \alpha_2)'$ should (s)he choose? Here, $\alpha_0, \alpha_1, \alpha_2$ represents her/his investment (in terms of fraction of wealth) in the risk-free asset, stock 1, and stock 2, respectively

9. *Dynamic portfolio choice*: Consider a CARA investor with expected utility function $u(x) = -e^{-\gamma x}$, who in a two-period economy, $t = 0, 1, 2$, maximizes expected utility of terminal wealth, $E[u(W_2)]$. There are two stocks in the economy, and a bond with risk-free returns $r^f = 0$. The returns on the two stocks in each period are

$$\tilde{\mu}_{t,i} = \mu_{t,i} + \sigma_i \tilde{\xi}_{t,i}, \quad i \in \{1,2\},\ t \in \{0,1\},$$

where $\tilde{\xi}_{t,i} \sim N(0,1)$ are independent across stocks (i) and time (t). Note that the volatility terms, σ_i, do not depend on time.

   Assume that $\mu_{0,2} = \mu_{1,2} = 0$, $\mu_{0,1} = q > 0$, and

$$\mu_{1,1} = q - k\tilde{\mu}_{0,2}, \quad k \in \mathbb{R}.$$

Thus, $\mu_{1,1}$, and thereby also the distribution of $\tilde{\mu}_{1,1}$, depends on the return on stock 2 in the previous period (when $k \neq 0$).

(a) Derive a formula for the investor's (dollar) investments in the two stocks at time 0, $\mathbf{a}_0 = (a_{0,1}, a_{0,2})'$, as a function of γ, q, k, σ_1, and σ_2.

(b) Compare qualitatively the investor's time-0 investment in asset 2, $a_{0,2}$, when $k = 0$ and when $k > 0$, respectively. Explain these investment behaviors and why they differ.

CHAPTER 5 Determining the Prices of Assets

5.1 Equilibrium Pricing

When we studied the portfolio choice problem, we took the return distributions as given. In reality, these distributions will be determined by market clearance. Specifically, prices are set such that agents' total demand for assets, determined by the assets' return distributions, equals supply. But return distributions are influenced by prices. In equilibrium prices should be consistent with both market clearance and the return distributions they imply.

Let us consider an example. Assume that there are M CARA investors, each with risk-aversion coefficient γ. Here, M is a large number so each agent is "small," in having very limited impact on market-clearing prices. Specifically, in line with our perfect market assumptions, we assume that each agent acts as a *price taker*, taking prices as fixed regardless of their own demand.

The risk-free rate is also fixed, R^f. In other words, the risk-free bond is in perfectly elastic supply. There is one publicly traded firm, with S shares traded in the market. This is a one-period model, so the stock is traded at time 0, then the firm produces and sells its product, and at $t=1$ it pays the net profits as a dividend to its shareholders and then liquidates. Specifically, we assume that the dividend per share at that point is $\widetilde{D}\sim N(a,b^2)$. In this stylized setting, dividends may thus be negative.

Now, given the time-0 price of P_0, the (total) return on investing in the stock is

$$\widetilde{R}=\frac{\widetilde{D}}{P_0}\sim N\left(\frac{a}{P_0},\frac{b^2}{P_0^2}\right). \tag{5.1}$$

This, in turn, leads to an individual agent's (dollar) demand,

$$d=\frac{\frac{a}{P_0}-R^f}{\gamma\frac{b^2}{P_0^2}};$$

see (4.3). Since there are S shares in total, the total dollar supply is SP_0, and the total dollar demand is Md. The market-clearing condition, $SP_0=Md$, is then

$$M\frac{\frac{a}{P_0}-R^f}{\gamma\frac{b^2}{P_0^2}}=SP_0,$$

and by reordering terms we get

$$P_0 = \frac{1}{R^f}\left(a - \frac{S}{M}\gamma b^2\right). \tag{5.2}$$

The price then determines the return distribution, as characterized by $\mu = E[\widetilde{R}] - 1$, and $\sigma^2 = \mathrm{Var}(\widetilde{R})$, through (5.1).

In contrast to the problems we have studied so far, μ and σ are not arbitrary in this example. Their values are determined by the primitives in the economy, in terms of total supply and demand (governed by S and M), production technology (a and b), and preferences of market participants (γ). The equilibrium price (5.2) is very intuitive. First, the price decreases if the risk-free rate increases. Naturally, demand for the stock decreases, all else equal, if the bond offers higher returns.

But in equilibrium, all else is *not* equal. For the stock market to clear, the stock needs to become more competitive, which it does by offering higher expected returns, via a lower time-0 price ($\widetilde{D}$ is exogenously fixed). Note that the risk premium is zero when $P_0 = \frac{a}{R^f}$, since in this case $\mu = \frac{a}{a/R^f} - 1 = R^f - 1$.

The price is increasing in a, which is unsurprising since higher expected dividend payoffs, all else equal, make the stock a more favorable investment. Since the market needs to clear, the price needs to increase if a increases. A similar argument for risk implies that the price is decreasing in b^2, since agents are risk averse.

Finally, the ratio between the number of company shares and the number of investors in the market, $\frac{S}{M}$, determines the price. When $\frac{S}{M}$ is close to zero, each agent bears little risk in equilibrium, and therefore requires only a small risk premium for taking on the risk. So P_0 is close to $\frac{a}{R^f}$. When $\frac{S}{M}$ is large, each agent bears a lot of risk and needs to be compensated with a high risk premium. So P_0 is a lot lower than $\frac{a}{R^f}$ in this case.

AN EXAMPLE WITH HETEROGENEOUS INFORMATION Consider an economy with in total M CARA investors, M_1 of which have risk-aversion coefficients γ_1, and the remaining $M_2 = M - M_1$ have risk-aversion coefficients γ_2. There is one firm in the economy, which at time 1 pays a liquidating dividend of $\widetilde{D}$ dollars to its shareholders. The number of outstanding shares of the firm is S. We define the harmonic weighted-average risk-aversion coefficient, $\bar{\gamma}$, according to the formula

$$\frac{1}{\bar{\gamma}} = \frac{1}{M}\left(\frac{M_1}{\gamma_1} + \frac{M_2}{\gamma_2}\right).$$

The risk-free rate is R^f.

The liquidating dividend is random, and depends on the realization of two shocks: customer demand for the company's product and the future oil price,

$$\widetilde{D} = \tilde{\xi}_1 + \tilde{\xi}_2,$$

where $\tilde{\xi}_1 \sim N(a_1, b_1^2)$ and $\tilde{\xi}_2 \sim N(a_2, b_2^2)$ are independent.

(a) Consider first the situation in which the realizations of $\tilde{\xi}_1$ and $\tilde{\xi}_2$ are unknown to all investors. We derive an expression for the market-clearing stock price as a function of $\bar{\gamma}, a_1, a_2, b_1, b_2, S, M$, and R^f.

For the investors with risk-aversion parameter γ_1, their maximization problem is

$$\max_{A_1} E[-e^{-\gamma_1 \widetilde{W}_1^1}],$$

where

$$\widetilde{W}_1^1 \sim N\Big(W_0^1 R^f + A_1\Big(\frac{a}{P_0} - R^f\Big), \Big(\frac{A_1}{P_0}\Big)^2 b^2\Big),$$

$a \stackrel{\text{def}}{=} a_1 + a_2$, and $b^2 \stackrel{\text{def}}{=} b_1^2 + b_2^2$. Solving this yields

$$A_1 = \frac{\frac{a}{P_0} - R^f}{\frac{\gamma_1 b^2}{P_0^2}},$$

and by symmetry,

$$A_2 = \frac{\frac{a}{P_0} - R^f}{\frac{\gamma_2 b^2}{P_0^2}}.$$

By market clearing,

$$M_1 A_1 + M_2 A_2 = S P_0.$$

Substituting in,

$$M_1\left[\frac{\frac{a}{P_0} - R^f}{\frac{\gamma_1 b^2}{P_0^2}}\right] + M_2\left[\frac{\frac{a}{P_0} - R^f}{\frac{\gamma_2 b^2}{P_0^2}}\right] = SP_0 \;\Rightarrow\; \Big(\frac{M_1}{\gamma_1} + \frac{M_2}{\gamma_2}\Big)\left(\frac{\frac{a}{P_0^2} - R^f}{\frac{b^2}{P_0^2}}\right) = SP_0.$$

Solving for the price P_0 yields

$$P_0 = \frac{1}{R^f}\Big(a_1 + a_2 - \frac{\gamma S}{M}(b_1^2 + b_2^2)\Big).$$

(b) Now consider the situation where the M_1 investors with risk aversion γ_1 actually *know* what customer demand is, i.e., they know the realization $\tilde{\xi}_1 = x$ already at time 0. We may think of this as these investors having surveyed potential customers so that they know what the product demand will be—information that the M_2 investors do not have. For simplicity, we assume that $\gamma_1 = \gamma_2 = \bar{\gamma}$, i.e., that the two groups have the same risk-aversion coefficients.

Let us derive an expression for the market-clearing stock price as a function of γ, a_1, a_2, b_1, b_2, S, M_1, M_2, and R^f.

The difference here, compared with (a), is that for the M_1 investors who know the realization of the first risk, the dividend distribution is $\widetilde{D} \sim N(x + a_2, b_2^2)$, while for the M_2 investors $\widetilde{D} \sim N(a, b^2)$. Solving the same type of maximization problem yields the following market-clearing condition:

$$M_1 \frac{x + a_2}{b_2^2} + M_2 \frac{a_1 + a_2}{b_1^2 + b_2^2} - R^f P_0\Big(\frac{M_1}{b_2^2} + \frac{M_2}{b_1^2 + b_2^2}\Big) = \bar{\gamma} S,$$

or, equivalently, defining

$$c = \frac{b_1^2 + b_2^2}{b_1^2 + 2b_2^2} \qquad \in (0, 1),$$

$$\widehat{M} = 2M_1 c + 2M_2(1 - c) \qquad \in 2(\min(M_1, M_2), \max(M_1, M_2)),$$

$$\bar{b}^2 = \frac{2}{\frac{1}{b_1^2 + b_2^2} + \frac{1}{b_2^2}} \qquad \in (b_2^2, b_1^2 + b_2^2),$$

we obtain

$$M_1c(x+a_2)+M_2(1-c)(a_1+a_2)-R^f P_0\frac{\widehat{M}}{2}=\bar{\gamma}S\frac{\bar{b}^2}{2},$$

so that

$$P_0=\frac{1}{R^f}\Big(\frac{2M_1c}{\widehat{M}}(x+a_2)+\frac{2M_2(1-c)}{\widehat{M}}(a_1+a_2)-\frac{\bar{\gamma}S}{\widehat{M}}\bar{b}^2\Big).$$

Note that this price is more informative than the price in (a), since the information about the first shock, $\tilde{\xi}_1=x$, is partly incorporated into the price in (b). In particular,

$$\frac{2M_1c}{\widehat{M}}(x+a_2)+\frac{2M_2(1-c)}{\widehat{M}}(a_1+a_2)$$

will be closer to $\tilde{x}_1+\tilde{x}_2$ than a_1+a_2. The larger the fraction of informed investors, $\frac{M_1}{M_1+M_2}$, the closer $2M_1c$ will be to $\widehat{M}$, and the more the price will reflect this information.

We may think of this example as a simple way of understanding how information is gradually incorporated into asset prices, as market participants find out new information about a firm over time, making prices more and more informative.

5.2 Capital Asset Pricing Model, CAPM

We can apply the previous arguments to a market with N risky assets, which will lead us to the celebrated *capital asset pricing model* (CAPM). We do this with mean–variance maximizing agents, but the CARA-normal framework with multivariate risks would yield the same result. Recall that the mean–variance investor who wishes to realize expected returns of μ_0 will choose the following investment:

$$\alpha=\frac{\mu_0-r^f}{A(r^f)^2-2r^fB+C}\Sigma^{-1}(\mu-r^f\mathbf{1}),$$

$$\mathbf{w}_m=\frac{\alpha}{\mathbf{1}'\alpha}=\frac{1}{B-Ar^f}\Sigma^{-1}(\mu-r^f\mathbf{1}),$$

so the risky portfolio is the same regardless of μ_0. We define the portfolio's return $\tilde{\mu}_m=\mathbf{w}_m'\tilde{\mu}$, with expected return $\mu_m=E[\tilde{\mu}_m]=\mathbf{w}_m'\mu$, and variance $\sigma_m^2=\mathrm{Var}(\tilde{\mu}_m)=\mathbf{w}_m'\Sigma\mathbf{w}_m$.

The next result will be key to the CAPM formula that expresses the expected return on an individual stock:

Theorem 5.1. *Define the vector $\beta=(\beta_1,\ldots,\beta_N)'$ with elements*

$$\beta_n=\frac{\mathrm{Cov}(\tilde{\mu}_n,\tilde{\mu}_m)}{\sigma_m^2}.$$

Then the following (vector) relationship holds between assets' expected returns and β's:

$$\mu-r^f\mathbf{1}=(\mu_m-r^f)\beta. \tag{5.3}$$

Proof. Recall that $\mu^e=\mu-r^f\mathbf{1}$, and $\mu_m^e=\mu_m-r^f=\mathbf{w}_m'\mu^e$. An equivalent formulation of (5.3) is therefore

$$\mu^e=\beta\mu_m^e.$$

Also, per definition, $\beta=\frac{1}{\mathbf{w}_m'\Sigma\mathbf{w}_m}\Sigma\mathbf{w}_m$. Moreover, we have $\mathbf{w}_m=(B-Ar^f)^{-1}\Sigma^{-1}\mu^e$, so $\Sigma\mathbf{w}_m=(B-Ar^f)^{-1}\mu^e$.

Now,

$$\begin{aligned}\beta\mu_m^e = \beta\mathbf{w}_m'\mu^e &= \frac{1}{\mathbf{w}_m'\Sigma\mathbf{w}_m}(\Sigma\mathbf{w}_m)(\mathbf{w}_m'\mu^e)\\ &= \frac{1}{(A-Br^f)^{-2}((\mu^e)'\Sigma^{-1}\mu^e)}(B-Ar^f)^{-2}\mu^e((\mu^e)'\Sigma^{-1}\mu^e)\\ &= \mu^e.\end{aligned}$$

□

Equation (5.3) states that the risk premium on asset i is a linear function of how much the asset's returns covary with the returns of the mean–variance-efficient portfolio, $\tilde{\mu}^e$. The coefficient $\beta_i = \frac{\text{Cov}(\tilde{\mu}_i,\tilde{\mu}_m)}{\text{Var}(\tilde{\mu}_m)}$ scales this covariance with the variance of this mean–variance-efficient portfolio. Note that this result does not depend on equilibrium arguments. It is a technical property of the mean–variance-efficient portfolio. Since the portfolio $\mathbf{w}_m$ depends on the risk premium vector μ^e, it should not come as a complete surprise that such a relationship may arise. Indeed, an asset that has a very high expected return should have a high associated portfolio weight, and thus have a higher covariance with $\tilde{\mu}^e = \mathbf{w}_m'\tilde{\mu}$, all else equal. Under the weak assumptions of modern portfolio theory, there will always exist a mean–variance-efficient portfolio with the property defined by (5.3)!

The general equilibrium argument made by Sharpe, Lintner, and Treynor is now based on the observation that if all investors in the market are mean–variance investors, they will all choose the same investment portfolio. That is, investor k's dollar demand for stock i is $d_{k,i} = c_k(\mathbf{w}_m)_i$, and the total demand for stock i of the K investors is then $\sum_{k=1}^K d_{k,i} = C(\mathbf{w}_m)_i$, where $C = \sum_{k=1}^K c_k$. The price of stock i is P_i and the supply is S_i, $i = 1, \ldots, N$. The market-clearing condition for stock i is then $S_iP_i = C(\mathbf{w}_m)_i$, leading to

$$(\mathbf{w}_m)_i = \frac{S_iP_i}{\sum_{i=1}^N S_iP_i}.$$

In equilibrium, the mean–variance-efficient portfolio must therefore be the *market portfolio*, i.e., each stock's portfolio weight is its market value as a share of the total stock market value. In other words, investors do not need to know Σ and μ^e to "find" the mean–variance-efficient portfolio. They can simply invest in a value-weighted market index fund!

Theorem 5.2 (Capital asset pricing model). *The expected return on any stock, μ_n, is*

$$\mu_n = r^f + \beta_n(r^m - r^f),$$

where r^m is the expected return on the market portfolio, r^f is the risk-free rate, and

$$\beta_n = \frac{\text{Cov}(\tilde{\mu}_n, \tilde{r}^m)}{\sigma_m^2}$$

is the covariance between the stock's return and the market's return, scaled by the variance of the market's return.

In other words, the market portfolio is mean–variance efficient. This is a wonderful result, providing a very strong characterization of asset returns. Of course, being based on mean–variance investors, the CAPM makes very strong assumptions, and therefore belongs high up in the asset pricing pyramid; see figure 1.1.

5.2.1 CARA-Normal CAPM Model

A useful equilibrium setting that leads to equilibrium in which CAPM holds is the CARA/normal framework with multiple stocks. Since investors are mean–variance optimizers in this setting, the CAPM will indeed hold. We can derive the equilibrium prices following a similar approach to section 5.1. Specifically, assume the vector $\mathbf{S}$ describes the number of shares available of the N stocks, and that the vector of terminal dividends per share has the distribution $\widetilde{\mathbf{D}} \sim N(\mathbf{a}, \Sigma)$. The vector of asset prices at $t=0$ is $\mathbf{P}_0$, and the vector of total returns is then

$$\widetilde{\mathbf{R}} = \Lambda_{\mathbf{P}_0}^{-1}\widetilde{\mathbf{D}} \sim N(\Lambda_{\mathbf{P}_0}^{-1}\mathbf{a}, \Lambda_{\mathbf{P}_0}^{-1}\Sigma\Lambda_{\mathbf{P}_0}^{-1}).$$

This, in turn, leads to an individual agent's (dollar) demand vector

$$\mathbf{d} = \frac{1}{\gamma}(\Lambda_{\mathbf{P}_0}^{-1}\Sigma\Lambda_{\mathbf{P}_0}^{-1})^{-1}(\Lambda_{\mathbf{P}_0}^{-1}\mathbf{a} - R^f\mathbf{1}).$$

As before, we assume M investors who all have the risk-aversion coefficient γ, so the market-clearing condition becomes $M\mathbf{d} = \Lambda_{\mathbf{P}_0}\mathbf{S}$, i.e.,

$$\frac{M}{\gamma}(\Lambda_{\mathbf{P}_0}^{-1}\Sigma\Lambda_{\mathbf{P}_0}^{-1})^{-1}(\Lambda_{\mathbf{P}_0}^{-1}\mathbf{a} - R^f\mathbf{1}) = \Lambda_{\mathbf{P}_0}\mathbf{S},$$

which after some algebra gives us

$$\mathbf{P}_0 = \frac{1}{R^f}\left(\mathbf{a} - \frac{\gamma}{M}\Sigma\mathbf{S}\right). \tag{5.4}$$

This is a useful formula to have when one is interested in actual sizes (in dollar terms), not only returns. It allows us to understand equilibrium in terms of demand and supply. The rightmost term in (5.4) shows how the covariances between dividend payments of different stocks affect their prices, compared with the expected payoff discounted at the risk-free rate.

EXAMPLE: SYMMETRIC ONE-FACTOR MARKET MODEL Consider the following model, where the dividend payouts are given by

$$\widetilde{D}_n = a + b\tilde{\xi}_0 + c\tilde{\xi}_n, \qquad n = 1, \ldots, N,$$

where $\tilde{\xi}_n \sim N(0, 1)$ are i.i.d. normally distributed, $n = 0, \ldots, N$. The factor $\tilde{\xi}_0$ is systematic and affects all the stocks, whereas the $\tilde{\xi}_n$ risks, $n = 1, \ldots, N$, represent idiosyncratic risks that only affect one stock. One calculates the covariance matrix $\Sigma = c^2\mathbf{I} + b^2\mathbf{1}\mathbf{1}'$, and the vector of expected payouts, $\mathbf{a} = a\mathbf{1}$. Assume that there are S shares available of each stock, $\mathbf{S} = S\mathbf{1}$, and that the risk-free rate is normalized to $R^f = 1$. The equilibrium price vector is then

$$\mathbf{P}_0 = \frac{1}{R^f}\left(\mathbf{a} - \frac{\gamma}{M}\Sigma\mathbf{S}\right) = a\mathbf{1} - \frac{\gamma S}{M}(c^2 + b^2N)\mathbf{1}.$$

So all the stock prices are the same,

$$P_n = a - \frac{\gamma S}{M}(c^2 + b^2N), \qquad n = 1, \ldots, N,$$

which is unsurprising since all the firms are identical (in distribution). The equilibrium price function is similar to the one-stock case (5.2), but with a major difference: the price discount attributed to the systematic factor is scaled by a factor N, the number of stocks. This risk is not diversified away in the market portfolio, and the investor's exposure to the systematic risk is therefore N

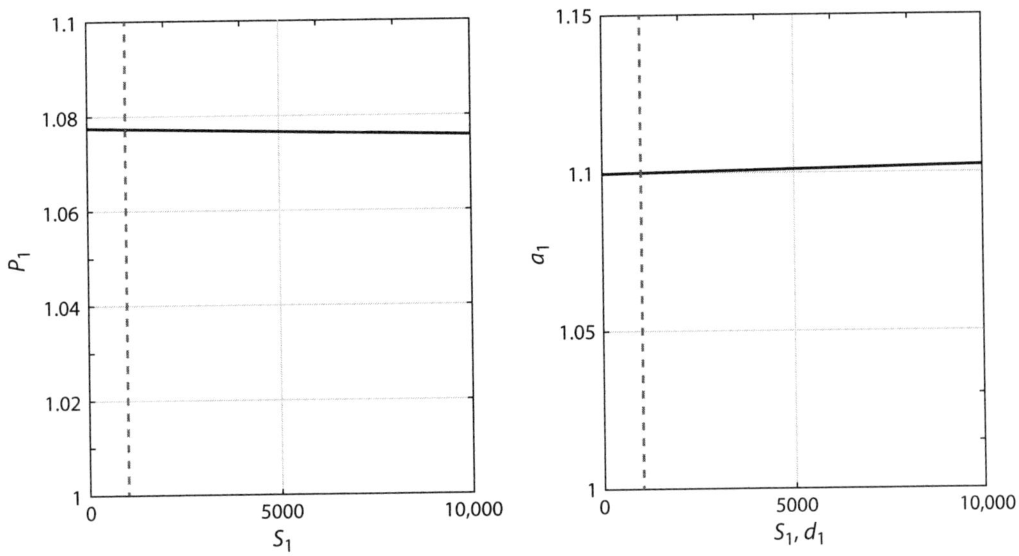

Figure 5.1: Equilibrium demand and supply in the CARA-normal CAPM model.

times the exposure in an individual stock. The idiosyncratic risks, $\tilde{\xi}_n$, on the other hand, are just present in one stock and therefore there is no scaling for these, i.e., c^2 is not multiplied by N in the price function. The distinction between the price discount associated with $\tilde{\xi}_0$ risk (high) and with $\tilde{\xi}_n$ risk (low) is one of the major implications of the CAPM, related to our earlier diversification discussion.

Another interpretation of this insight is through the lens of investor demand. Recall that demand for a good may be elastic (price sensitive) or inelastic (price insensitive). One reason for highly elastic demand is that there exist good substitutes: if the price increases consumers switch to substitutes, and if it decreases consumers switch from substitutes to the good. There is therefore not much room for prices to change for goods with elastic demand.

In our CAPM model, investors only care about portfolio return distributions. The idiosyncratic risk represents the firm-specific component of the stock investment, but since investors are almost risk neutral toward this risk, we expect demand functions to be highly elastic when N is large. We verify this intuition in an example. Consider the symmetric one-factor market model with parameters $N = 1000$, $M = 10^6$, $\gamma = 1$, $b = 0.15$, $c = 0.4$, $S = 1000$, $a = 1.1$. One verifies that the equilibrium price of each stock is $P_0 = 1.0774$, corresponding to a risk premium of about 2% $(\frac{1.1}{1.0773} - 1 \approx 0.021)$.

Holding the supply of stock 2 fixed at 1000, we study the equilibrium price of asset 1, as a function of its supply, S_1. Using (5.4), we verify that the price function is

$$P_1 = a - \frac{\gamma}{M}(b^2(N-1)S + (b^2 + c^2)S_1), \tag{5.5}$$

as shown by the solid line in the left-hand panel of figure 5.1. We see that the equilibrium price is almost flat in S_1. Indeed, it barely decreases when the stock supply increases from 0 to 10,000. This is because each of the other 999 stocks is an almost perfect substitute for stock 1.

In the right-hand panel of the figure, we show how investors' aggregate demand for stock 1, d_1, depends on the expected payoffs, a_1, keeping all other parameters fixed (with $S_1 = S = 1000$).

Here we calculate the market demand function in number of shares as

$$\mathbf{d}^S = \frac{M}{\gamma}\Sigma^{-1}(\mathbf{a} - P_0\mathbf{1}),$$

and using the property $\Sigma^{-1} = (c^2\mathbf{I} + b^2\mathbf{1}\mathbf{1}')^{-1} = \frac{1}{c^2}\mathbf{I} - \frac{b^2}{c^2(c^2+b^2N)}\mathbf{1}\mathbf{1}'$, we get

$$d_1^S = \frac{M}{\gamma}\left(\frac{1}{c^2}(a_1 - P_0) - \frac{b^2}{c^2(c^2+b^2N)}(a_1 + (N-1)a - NP_0)\right).$$

The line in the right-hand panel of the figure shows this demand function as a function of a_1. It is almost flat, so demand is almost perfectly elastic.

It has been suggested that, in practice, demand curves for stocks are quite far from perfectly elastic; see, e.g., Petajisto (2009). A possible way for sloping demand curves to arise is if there is some type of segmentation, such that investors only participate in a subset of markets. In such a situation, the diversification benefits in the market effectively go down. As an extreme example, assume that $M = N$, and the market is perfectly segmented, so that each investor only invests in one stock: the market-clearing price as a function of S_1 is then

$$P_1 = a - \gamma(b^2 + c^2)S_1,$$

which has an M times higher slope than the price function in the market without segmentation (5.5). Petajisto (2009) introduces a model in which individual investors only have direct access to investments in the market portfolio. Active money managers invest in individual stocks, on behalf of the individual investors. But these money managers are specialized and only invest in a small number of stocks. It is the money managers' demand functions that determine market clearing in markets for individual stocks. If the managers are risk averse, demand curves in individual stocks will be downward sloping, more so than when individual investors have direct access to these markets. This is an example of an economy with frictions, where agency problems arise when the money managers' objective functions deviate from those of their clients.

EXAMPLE: EQUILIBRIUM, IMPACT INVESTING, AND DIVESTING A potential application of the model is for understanding the equilibrium effects of impact investing. Impact investing aims at reducing social and environmental costs in society through investment choices. One tool through which this can be achieved is through divestment. The idea is that if investors avoid companies that impose environmental costs on society, then the cost of capital for these firms or, equivalently, their required (expected) returns in the market increase, which makes it more difficult for them fund their investments.

Recall that we showed the following equilibrium price for a representative firm:

$$P = \frac{1}{R^f}(a - qb^2), \quad q = \frac{\gamma S}{M},$$

where R^f is the risk-free rate, a is the expected payoff of the firm, b^2 is the variance of the payoff, and q depends on the risk aversion (γ), supply (S), and demand (M) in the market. The idea is that if fewer investors are willing to invest, so that M is lower, the price of the firm decreases—and, equivalently, its required expected returns increase. As a consequence, the firm will require higher expected returns for these types of investments, i.e., its cost of capital increases, causing fewer such investments to occur in the future.

How large will the divestment effect be in an equilibrium model with many stocks and CARA investors?[1] To this end, consider an economy with $2M$ price-taking CARA investors, each maximizing expected utility

$$U = E[-e^{-\gamma \widetilde{W}_1}]. \tag{5.6}$$

The gross risk-free rate in the economy is $R^f = 1$, and there are N publicly traded firms. The terminal dividend paid by firm n is

$$\widetilde{D}_n = 1 + b\xi_0 + a\xi_n, \quad n = 1, \ldots, N,$$

where ξ_n, $n = 0, \ldots, N$, are i.i.d. normally distributed random variables, $\xi_n \sim N(0,1)$, $a > 0$, and $b \geq 0$. There is one share available of each stock $S_n = S = 1$, $n = 1, 2, \ldots, N$, each paying the dividend $\widetilde{D}_n$. Note that $\mathrm{Var}(\widetilde{D}_n) = a^2 + b^2$, and $\mathrm{Cov}(\widetilde{D}_n, \widetilde{D}_m) = b^2$, when $n \neq m$. The covariance matrix of the vector $\widetilde{D} = (\widetilde{D}_1, \ldots, \widetilde{D}_N)'$ is then $\Sigma = a^2\mathbf{I} + b^2\mathbf{1}\mathbf{1}'$.

The firms' stock prices at time 0, P_n, are determined by market clearing, and $\mathbf{P} = (P_1, P_2, \ldots, P_N)'$. Following our earlier argument, the vector of stock returns has the following distribution:

$$\tilde{\mu} \sim N(\mu, \widehat{\Sigma}), \quad \mu = \Lambda_{\mathbf{P}}^{-1}\mathbf{1}, \ \widehat{\Sigma} = \Lambda_{\mathbf{P}}^{-1}\Sigma\Lambda_{\mathbf{P}}^{-1}, \ \Lambda_{\mathbf{P}} = \mathrm{diag}(\mathbf{P}).$$

Let us first assume that the investors do not distinguish between the different companies, i.e., they all treat each company the same, and only care how it contributes to the risk and return of their investment portfolio. This leads to the equilibrium market-clearing condition

$$S\mathbf{P} = \frac{2M}{\gamma}\widehat{\Sigma}^{-1}(\mu - R^f\mathbf{1}).$$

Moreover, let us assume that there are $N = 500$ stocks in the market.

To calibrate the model so that it fits the real market, we assume that the market's risk premium is $\mu^e = \frac{\mathbf{P}'\mu}{\mathbf{1}'\mathbf{P}} - R^f = 6\%$, the (forward) market volatility is $\sigma^m = \sigma(\frac{\mathbf{1}'\widetilde{D}}{N}) = 15\%$, and the (forward) volatility of each individual stock's return is $\sigma^i = \sigma(\widetilde{D}_n) = 45\%$.

Since the economy is symmetric, all stocks have the same equilibrium price, $\mathbf{P} = P\mathbf{1}$. We also have $\mathbf{P}'\mu = \mathbf{P}'\Lambda_{\mathbf{P}}^{-1}\mathbf{1} = N$, and since $\mu^e = \frac{1}{P} - R^f = 6\%$, we get

$$P = \frac{1}{1.06}.$$

To recover the values of a, b, and $q = \frac{\gamma S}{M}$, such that the postulated values of μ^m, σ^m, and σ^i are matched in equilibrium, we calculate

$$\mathrm{Var}\left(\frac{\mathbf{1}'\widetilde{D}}{N}\right) = \frac{1}{N^2}\left(\frac{a}{N} + b^2\right) = (15\%)^2$$

and

$$\mathrm{Var}(\widetilde{D}_n) = a^2 + b^2 = (45\%)^2.$$

Solving for a^2 and b^2 yields $a^2 \approx 0.18036$, and $b^2 \approx 0.02214$.

Finally, for the covariance matrix of returns, we have

$$\widehat{\Sigma} = \frac{1}{P^2}(a^2\mathbf{I} + b^2\mathbf{1}\mathbf{1}'),$$

[1] Berk and van Binsbergen (2025) study the equilibrium impact of divestments in a more advanced setting.

which leads to

$$\begin{aligned}\widehat{\Sigma}^{-1}(\mu - R^f\mathbf{1}) &= P^2\frac{1}{a^2}\Big(\mathbf{I} - \frac{b^2}{a^2+Nb^2}\mathbf{1}\mathbf{1}'\Big)\Big(\frac{1}{P}\mathbf{1} - R^f\mathbf{1}\Big)\\ &= P^2\frac{\mu^e}{a^2}\Big(\mathbf{I} - \frac{b^2}{a^2+Nb^2}\mathbf{1}\mathbf{1}'\Big)\mathbf{1}\\ &= P^2\frac{\mu^e}{a^2}\Big(1 - \frac{Nb^2}{a^2+Nb^2}\Big)\mathbf{1},\end{aligned}$$

and since $S\Lambda_{\mathbf{P}}\mathbf{1} = \frac{2M}{\gamma}\widehat{\Sigma}^{-1}(\mu - R^f\mathbf{1})$, to

$$q = 2P\frac{\mu^e}{a^2}\Big(1 - \frac{Nb^2}{a^2+Nb^2}\Big).$$

Plugging in the values of μ^e, a^2, b^2, and N, we arrive at

$$q \approx 0.0100626.$$

Next we study an alternative economy, where we assume that firms $n = 1, \ldots, \frac{N}{2}$ are "green"(i.e., environmentally friendly), whereas stocks $n = \frac{N}{2} + 1, \ldots, N$ are "brown" (not environmentally friendly). Moreover, we assume that investors $m = 1, \ldots, M$ decide to invest only in green stocks. They thus choose to maximize expected utility in (5.6), using investment portfolios that only contain stocks $n = 1, \ldots, \frac{N}{2}$. Indeed, for the green investors it is as if the brown stocks do not exist, i.e., as if there are only $\frac{N}{2}$ stocks in the market. The remaining investors, $m = M + 1, \ldots, 2M$ are ignorant about the distinction between green and brown stocks, and continue to maximize (5.6) using the whole universe of N stocks. We can think of the situation as equivalent to one where the green investors only have access to the green stocks, and therefore form their demand functions based on these. Since there are more investors willing to invest in green stocks, we expect the market price of these to be higher. But the size of the effect needs to be determined in equilibrium, by market clearing.

We wish to derive a formula for the equilibrium prices P^g and P^b of green and brown stocks in this alternative setting. We first calculate the demand of the green investors that only have access to the green stocks. To do this we use a smaller covariance matrix that only contains the variances and covariances of the green stocks, $\widehat{\Sigma}_g \in \mathbb{R}^{\frac{N}{2}\times\frac{N}{2}}$. Specifically, $\widehat{\Sigma}_g$ represents the upper-left $\frac{N}{2} \times \frac{N}{2}$ corner of $\widehat{\Sigma}$. The demand of the green investors for the green stocks is

$$\begin{aligned}\mathbf{D}_g &= \frac{M}{\gamma}\widehat{\Sigma}_g^{-1}(\mu_g - R^f\mathbf{1}_{\frac{N}{2}})\\ &= \frac{M}{\gamma}\Lambda_{\mathbf{P}_g}\Sigma_g^{-1}\Lambda_{\mathbf{P}_g}(\Lambda_{\mathbf{P}_g}^{-1}\mathbf{1}_{\frac{N}{2}} - R^f\mathbf{1}_{\frac{N}{2}})\\ &= \frac{M}{\gamma}\Lambda_{\mathbf{P}_g}\Sigma_g^{-1}(\mathbf{1}_{\frac{N}{2}} - R^f P_g\mathbf{1}_{\frac{N}{2}})\\ &= \frac{M}{\gamma}P_g I\Sigma_g^{-1}(\mathbf{1}_{\frac{N}{2}} - R^f P_g\mathbf{1}_{\frac{N}{2}})\\ &= \frac{M}{\gamma}P_g(1 - R^f P_g)\Sigma_g^{-1}\mathbf{1}_{\frac{N}{2}}\end{aligned}$$

$$
\begin{aligned}
&= \frac{M}{\gamma} P_g(1 - R^f P_g) \frac{1}{a^2}\Big(\mathbf{I} - \frac{b^2}{a^2 + b^2 \frac{N}{2}} \mathbf{1}_{\frac{N}{2}} \mathbf{1}'_{\frac{N}{2}}\Big) \mathbf{1}_{\frac{N}{2}} \\
&= \frac{M}{\gamma} P_g(1 - R^f P_g) \frac{1}{a^2}\Big(1 - \frac{b^2 \frac{N}{2}}{a^2 + b^2 \frac{N}{2}}\Big) \mathbf{1}_{\frac{N}{2}} \\
&= \frac{M}{\gamma} P_g(1 - R^f P_g) \frac{2}{2a^2 + b^2 N} \mathbf{1}_{\frac{N}{2}},
\end{aligned}
$$

where $\mathbf{1}_{\frac{N}{2}}$ is an $\frac{N}{2}$-dimensional vector of 1's, and $\mathbf{P}_g = P_g \mathbf{1}_{\frac{N}{2}}$ is an $\frac{N}{2}$-vector of prices of green stocks. Including the brown stocks, which the green investors do not demand, we get

$$
\mathbf{D}_g^{\text{TOT}} = \frac{M}{\gamma} P_g(1 - R^f P_g) \frac{2}{2a^2 + b^2 N} \begin{bmatrix} \mathbf{1}_{\frac{N}{2}} \\ \mathbf{0}_{\frac{N}{2}} \end{bmatrix}.
$$

We next calculate the demand of the brown investors, who select among the whole universe of N stocks:

$$
\begin{aligned}
\mathbf{D}_b &= \frac{M}{\gamma} \widehat{\Sigma}^{-1}(\mu - R^f \mathbf{1}) \\
&= \frac{M}{\gamma} \Lambda_{\mathbf{P}} \Sigma^{-1} \Lambda_{\mathbf{P}} (\Lambda_{\mathbf{P}}^{-1} \mathbf{1} - R^f \mathbf{1}) \\
&= \frac{M}{\gamma} \Lambda_{\mathbf{P}} \Sigma^{-1} (\mathbf{1} - R^f \mathbf{P}) \\
&= \frac{M}{\gamma} \Lambda_{\mathbf{P}} (\Sigma^{-1} \mathbf{1} - R^f \Sigma^{-1} \mathbf{P}).
\end{aligned}
$$

Because of symmetry, we know that $\mathbf{P} = (P_g \mathbf{1}'_{\frac{N}{2}}, P_b \mathbf{1}'_{\frac{N}{2}},)'$, which allows us to calculate $\Sigma^{-1}\mathbf{1}$ and $\Sigma^{-1}\mathbf{P}$ as

$$
\begin{aligned}
\Sigma^{-1}\mathbf{1} &= \frac{1}{a^2}\Big(\mathbf{I} - \frac{b^2}{a^2 + b^2 N} \mathbf{1}\mathbf{1}'\Big)\mathbf{1} \\
&= \frac{1}{a^2}\Big(1 - \frac{b^2 N}{a^2 + b^2 N}\Big)\mathbf{1} \\
&= \frac{1}{a^2 + b^2 N}\mathbf{1},
\end{aligned}
$$

$$
\begin{aligned}
\Sigma^{-1}\mathbf{P} &= \frac{1}{a^2}\Big(\mathbf{I} - \frac{b^2}{a^2 + b^2 N} \mathbf{1}\mathbf{1}'\Big)\mathbf{P} \\
&= \frac{1}{a^2}\Big(\mathbf{P} - \frac{b^2}{a^2 + b^2 N} \mathbf{1}\mathbf{1}'\mathbf{P}\Big) \\
&= \frac{1}{a^2}\Big(\mathbf{P} - \frac{b^2}{a^2 + b^2 N} \frac{N(P_g + P_b)}{2} \mathbf{1}\Big).
\end{aligned}
$$

So the demand by the brown investors is given by

$$
\begin{aligned}
\mathbf{D}_b &= \frac{M}{\gamma} \Lambda_{\mathbf{P}} (\Sigma^{-1} \mathbf{1} - R^f \Sigma^{-1} \mathbf{P}) \\
&= \frac{M}{\gamma} \Lambda_{\mathbf{P}} \Big(\frac{1}{a^2 + b^2 N}\mathbf{1} - \frac{R^f}{a^2}\Big(\mathbf{P} - \frac{b^2}{a^2 + b^2 N} \frac{N(P_g + P_b)}{2}\mathbf{1}\Big)\Big) \\
&= \frac{M}{\gamma} \Big(\frac{1}{a^2 + b^2 N}\Lambda_{\mathbf{P}}\mathbf{1} - \frac{R^f}{a^2}\Lambda_{\mathbf{P}}\Big(\mathbf{P} - \frac{b^2}{a^2 + b^2 N} \frac{N(P_g + P_b)}{2}\mathbf{1}\Big)\Big) \\
&= \frac{M}{\gamma} \Big(\frac{1}{a^2 + b^2 N}\mathbf{P} - \frac{R^f}{a^2}\Big(\Lambda_{\mathbf{P}}\mathbf{P} - \frac{b^2}{a^2 + b^2 N} \frac{N(P_g + P_b)}{2}\mathbf{P}\Big)\Big).
\end{aligned}
$$

Now, for the market-clearing condition, we know that the sum of the demands from the green and brown investors must be equal to the supply (which has not changed). So we have

$$
\begin{aligned}
S\Lambda_{\mathbf{P}}\mathbf{1} &= \mathbf{D}_b + \mathbf{D}_g^{\mathrm{TOT}} \\
&= \frac{M}{\gamma}\left(\frac{1}{a^2+b^2N}\mathbf{P} - \frac{R^f}{a^2}\left(\Lambda_{\mathbf{P}}\mathbf{P} - \frac{b^2}{a^2+b^2N}\frac{N(P_g+P_b)}{2}\mathbf{P}\right)\right) \\
&\quad + \frac{M}{\gamma}P_g(1-R^fP_g)\frac{2}{2a^2+b^2N}\begin{bmatrix}\mathbf{1}_{\frac{N}{2}}\\ \mathbf{0}_{\frac{N}{2}}\end{bmatrix} \\
\Rightarrow\ \mathbf{P} &= \frac{1}{q}\left(\frac{1}{a^2+b^2N}\mathbf{P} - \frac{R^f}{a^2}\left(\Lambda_{\mathbf{P}}\mathbf{P} - \frac{b^2}{a^2+b^2N}\frac{N(P_g+P_b)}{2}\mathbf{P}\right)\right) \\
&\quad + \frac{1}{q}P_g(1-R^fP_g)\frac{2}{2a^2+b^2N}\begin{bmatrix}\mathbf{1}_{\frac{N}{2}}\\ \mathbf{0}_{\frac{N}{2}}\end{bmatrix}.
\end{aligned}
$$

This vector equation defines a system of N equations for the prices of the green and brown stocks. However, there are effectively only two equations (since the equations are identical within the two $\frac{N}{2}$ "blocks"), one with P_g and one with P_b on the left-hand side, giving us

$$
\begin{cases}
P_g = \frac{1}{q}\left(\frac{1}{a^2+b^2N}P_g - \frac{R^f}{a^2}\left(P_g^2 - \frac{b^2}{a^2+b^2N}\frac{N(P_g+P_b)}{2}P_g\right)\right) \\
\qquad + \frac{1}{q}P_g(1-R^fP_g)\frac{2}{2a^2+b^2N}, \\
P_b = \frac{1}{q}\left(\frac{1}{a^2+b^2N}P_b - \frac{R^f}{a^2}\left(P_b^2 - \frac{b^2}{a^2+b^2N}\frac{N(P_g+P_b)}{2}P_b\right)\right).
\end{cases}
$$

Solving this system, we arrive at

$$
\begin{aligned}
P_g &= \frac{2-q(a^2-b^2N)}{2R^f}, \\
P_b &= \frac{2(2a^2+b^2N)-(a^2+b^2N)(4a^2+b^2N)q}{2(2a^2+b^2N)R^f}.
\end{aligned}
$$

Using the values of a, b, and q that we derived in the symmetric economy, the equilibrium prices are $P_g = 0.943396$ and $P_b = 0.94161$. We know that the expected returns are given by $\mu = \Lambda_{\mathbf{P}}^{-1}\mathbf{1}$, so $\mu_g = 1.06$ and $\mu_b = 1.06201$. Finally, the difference between the prices of the green and brown stocks in this case is $P_g - P_b = 0.00178625$.

Because the differences in prices and returns are very small—about 0.2% in expected returns between brown and green stocks, even though half of the investor population choose to divest—it is clear that within this framework we expect divesting to have only a marginal effect in reallocating capital from brown to green investments.

The result is natural, taking into account the flat demand curves we encountered in the previous example. Even a substantial shock will have limited impact on prices when the stocks are almost perfect substitutes. If the green and brown stocks were more "different," for example in that they were exposed to independent factor shocks, so that all green stocks were affected by one type of shock and all brown stocks by another, then the impact on cost of capital would be larger, because these shocks would then not be diversifiable. In other words, there needs to be enough heterogeneity between the firms to break the strong force toward highly elastic aggregate demand functions in these markets.

5.2.2 CAPM via a Regression

We can interpret CAPM through the lens of a regression or, equivalently, a projection operator. Recall that for an arbitrary vector, $\mathbf{x}$, the matrix $\mathbf{A} = \frac{1}{\mathbf{x}^T\mathbf{x}}\mathbf{x}\mathbf{x}^T$ is a projection operator that projects any vector onto the span of $\mathbf{x}$, i.e., such that $\mathbf{y} = \mathbf{A}\mathbf{y} + \epsilon$, where $\epsilon \perp \mathbf{x}$; see appendix B.4. In the context of the CAPM, we equivalently have

$$\tilde{\mu}_n^e = \frac{\langle \tilde{\mu}_n^e, \tilde{r}_e^m \rangle}{\langle \tilde{r}_e^m, \tilde{r}_e^m \rangle} \tilde{r}_e^m + \tilde{\epsilon}_n, \quad \text{where } \tilde{\epsilon}_n \perp \tilde{r}_e^m,$$

i.e., an asset's returns are decomposed into a market component—by projecting them onto market returns—and an idiosyncratic component that is orthogonal to the market.

An equivalent interpretation is via a regression. We have

$$\begin{aligned}\tilde{\mu}_n^e &= \frac{\mathrm{Cov}(\tilde{\mu}_n^e, \tilde{r}_e^m)}{\mathrm{Var}(\tilde{r}_e^m)} \tilde{r}_e^m + \tilde{\epsilon}_n \\ &= \beta_i \tilde{r}_e^m + \tilde{\epsilon}_n,\end{aligned}$$

where $\mathrm{Cov}(\tilde{r}_e^m, \tilde{\epsilon}_n) = 0$, $E[\tilde{\epsilon}_n] = 0$. The coefficient β_n is the regression coefficient of a univariate regression of firm returns on the market portfolio. Risk in the $\tilde{r}_e^m$-direction is priced, in that it comes with a risk premium over the risk-free rate. Risk orthogonal to $\tilde{r}_e^m$ is unpriced and has no risk premium over the risk-free rate, $E[\tilde{\epsilon}_n] = 0$.

5.2.3 CAPM with Unknown Market Portfolio

Assume that we do not know what the market portfolio is, but we believe that its returns lie in the span of $\tilde{r}^1$ and $\tilde{r}^2$, $\tilde{r}_e^m = q_1\tilde{r}^1 + q_2\tilde{r}^2$. Here, $\tilde{r}^1$ and $\tilde{r}^2$ could be returns on portfolios of traded assets, $\tilde{r}^i = w_i'\tilde{\mu}^e$, but could also represent untraded risks.

From the previous projection/regression interpretation of the CAPM, we know that

$$\tilde{\mu}_n^e = \beta_n(q_1\tilde{r}^1 + q_2\tilde{r}^2) + \tilde{\epsilon}_n, \quad \tilde{\epsilon}_n \perp (q_1\tilde{r}^1 + q_2\tilde{r}^2).$$

Now, if we project the firm's excess returns $\tilde{\mu}_n^e$ onto S, the span of $\{\tilde{r}^1, \tilde{r}^2\}$, so that

$$\tilde{\mu}_n^e = \gamma_1\tilde{r}^1 + \gamma_2\tilde{r}^2 + \tilde{\xi}_n, \quad \tilde{\xi}_n \perp S,$$

it follows, again from the property of projection operators, that $\tilde{\xi}_n \perp q_1\tilde{r}^1 + q_2\tilde{r}^2 = \tilde{r}_e^m$, and therefore, because the CAPM holds, that $E[\tilde{\xi}_n] = 0$.

Thus, the following two-factor relation holds:

$$E[\tilde{\mu}_n^e] = \gamma_1 E[\tilde{r}^1] + \gamma_2 E[\tilde{r}^1],$$

i.e., we have a two-factor representation of the cross section of expected returns.[2] This argument is straightforward to generalize to $Q > 2$ factors, leading to a *multifactor model*.

Empirically, multifactor models have been shown to explain the cross section of expected returns better than the CAPM. Fama and French (1993) introduce a three-factor model where a size factor (SMB) and a value factor (HML) are included, in addition to the market factor, so that

$$E[\tilde{\mu}_n^e] = \beta_m E[\tilde{r}_m^e] + \beta_{\mathrm{SMB}} E[\tilde{r}_{\mathrm{SMB}}^e] + \beta_{\mathrm{HML}} E[\tilde{r}_{\mathrm{HML}}^e].$$

[2]Note that in general $\gamma_1 \neq q_1$ and $\gamma_2 \neq q_2$.

The size factor is defined by a portfolio that is long (i.e., it buys) small firms, as measured by market capitalization, and short (i.e., it short-sells) large firms. The factor's origins can be traced to Banz (1981), who observed a size effect—that small firms tend to have higher realized returns than predicted by the CAPM, whereas large firms tend to have lower realized returns. The acronym SMB stands for small-minus-big.

The value factor is defined by a portfolio that is long so-called value firms and short so-called growth firms. There are several ways to define what is a value firm. The approach taken in Fama and French (1993) is to look at a firm's book-to-market ratio, i.e., the ratio of the firm's book value of equity to its market value of equity. Firms with high ratios are value firms, whereas firms with low ratios are growth firms (they have relatively high market values, suggesting that they are expected to grow rapidly in the future). The origins of this factor may be traced back to the value investment strategy developed by Graham and Dodd (1934). The acronym HML stands for high-minus-low.

Other factors that have been shown to empirically explain the cross section of expected returns include the momentum factor (Jegadeesh and Titman (1993) and Carhart (1997)), the investment factor, and the profitability factor, see Hou et al. (2015) and Fama and French (2015). The theoretical argument above provides one rationale for using multifactor models. We will return to multifactor models in section 5.5, and provide another rationale.

5.3 Black–Litterman Model

We have seen the challenges associated with portfolio choice that are related to the estimation of expected returns of all individual stocks in the market. The CAPM allows us to get around this challenge by piggybacking on the market itself. Specifically, since according to the CAPM the market chooses the mean–variance-efficient portfolio—or equivalently, the portfolio with the maximum Sharpe ratio—we can obtain the optimal portfolio by simply investing in the market. These two approaches, pick a portfolio based on estimating all expected returns, versus investing in the market portfolio, are at the opposite ends of the spectrum: either we rely completely on our own information about all the assets in the market, or we do not use any such information at all.

What if we have some private views of our own, for example, about the prospects of stocks in a specific sector, which we would like to incorporate into our portfolio decision, without having to take a stand on the returns of all stocks in the market?

Black and Litterman introduced a model that allows an investor to combine such private views with the piggybacking that the CAPM allows; see Black and Litterman (1991, 1992) and He and Litterman (2002). Their model is based on Bayesian inference. Recall Bayes' rule, which states that if A and B represent two events, such that $\mathbb{P}(A) > 0$, then

$$\mathbb{P}(B|A) = \frac{\mathbb{P}(A|B)\mathbb{P}(B)}{\mathbb{P}(A)},$$

or, equivalently,

$$\mathbb{P}(B|A) = \frac{\mathbb{P}(A \cap B)}{\mathbb{P}(A)}.$$

Here, $\mathbb{P}(B|A)$ is the conditional probability for event B occurring, given that event A (which has a strictly positive probability) occurs, and $\mathbb{P}(A \cap B)$ is the joint probability for A and B occurring.

The use of Bayes' rule for incorporating new information is often defined as a requirement for rational investor behavior, for example when combining expected utility preferences with gradual arrival of information. We will see examples of this later when discussing models with asymmetric information.

A standard application of Bayesian updating is given by the following example: Assume the random variable $\tilde{y}$ is normally distributed with variance ρ^2, conditional on knowing its expectation, μ:

$$\tilde{y} = \mu + \rho\xi_1, \quad \xi_1 \sim N(0,1).$$

The parameter μ is unknown, but it is known also to be normally distributed:

$$\mu = \theta + \sigma\xi_2, \quad \xi_2 \sim N(0,1),$$

where ξ_1 and ξ_2 are independent. The unconditional expected value of $\tilde{y}$ is then $E[\tilde{y}] = E[E[\tilde{y}|\mu]] = E[\mu] = \theta$, and its unconditional variance is $\mathrm{Var}(\tilde{y}) = \sigma^2 + \rho^2$. Note that the unconditional variance of $\tilde{y}$ is higher than the conditional variance, which is ρ^2. This is intuitive, since knowledge of μ allows one to form a more precise estimate of the expectation of $\tilde{y}$.

What if one does not know μ, but can draw some inferences based on noisy information? For example, maybe one knows the realization of a random variable $\tilde{z} = \mu + \tau\xi_3$, where $\xi_3 \sim N(0,1)$ is independent of ξ_2 and ξ_1. Indeed, $\tilde{z}$ will provide some information about μ, and thereby about $\tilde{y}$, since its realization will likely not be very far away from μ, at least if τ is small. By applying Bayes' rule, we make this argument precise. Specifically, given the observation $\tilde{z} = z$, we can calculate the *posterior* probability density function of μ:

$$\begin{aligned} p(\mu|z) &= \frac{p(z|\mu)p(\mu)}{p(z)} \\ &= \frac{\frac{1}{\sqrt{2\pi\tau^2}} e^{-(z-\mu)^2/(2\tau^2)} \frac{1}{\sqrt{2\pi\sigma^2}} e^{-(\mu-\theta)^2/(2\sigma^2)}}{\int \frac{1}{\sqrt{2\pi\tau^2}} e^{-(z-\mu)^2/(2\tau^2)}\, dz} \\ &= \frac{1}{\sqrt{2\pi q^2}} e^{-\frac{(\mu-v)^2}{2q^2}}, \end{aligned}$$

where

$$q^2 = \frac{1}{\frac{1}{\sigma^2} + \frac{1}{\tau^2}} \quad \text{and} \quad v = \frac{\tau^2}{\sigma^2+\tau^2}\theta + \frac{\sigma^2}{\sigma^2+\tau^2} z.$$

Thus, the posterior distribution of μ is

$$\mu | \tilde{z} = z \sim N(v, q^2).$$

The calculation is based on the standard integration formula for Gaussian kernels: $\frac{1}{\sqrt{2\pi}} \int e^{-x^2/2} dx = 1$. leading to a special case of the so-called projection theorem; see chapter 15.

Note that the expected value of μ, $E[\mu|\tilde{z} = z] = v$, is a weighted average of the unconditional expectation, θ, and the realization of $\tilde{z}$. If τ^2 is relatively high compared with σ^2, then the observation of $\tilde{z}$ does not provide much information (since it is so noisy), and the posterior expectation will be close to the prior, θ. When τ^2 is low compared with σ^2, on the other hand, $\tilde{z}$ contains a lot of information about μ, and much weight is therefore put on z. Note also that $q^2 < \min(\sigma^2, \tau^2)$, so the posterior variance of μ is lower than both the prior variance and the conditional variance of $\tilde{y}$ given μ. Finally, note that $E[\tilde{y}|\tilde{z}] = v$, and $\mathrm{Var}(\tilde{y}|\tilde{z} = z) = q^2 + \rho^2 < \sigma^2 + \rho^2$, so knowledge about $\tilde{z}$ is also helpful for predicting $\tilde{y}$.

In general, Bayesian updating can lead to complicated formulas. The neat closed-form expressions in the previous example are by no means guaranteed. The reason it worked out so nicely in this case is that the normal distribution assumed for μ, $p(\mu)$, is the *conjugate prior* of the normal posterior distribution $p(\mu|z)$. Thus, we stay within the class of normal distributions when updating. This is another great property of normal distributions. This also means that we can repeat the updating iteratively if additional i.i.d. observations are made, $\tilde{z}_1$, $\tilde{z}_2$, etc., staying within the class of normal distributions in each step.

A generalized version of the updating in the example, for multivariate normal distributions, is provided in the following standard result:

Proposition 5.1. *Consider the parameter vector $\mu \in \mathbb{R}^N$, with distribution*

$$\mu \sim N(\theta, \Sigma),$$

where θ is an N-vector, Σ is an $N \times N$ SPD matrix, and assume the K-vector $\mathbf{z}$ is defined as

$$\mathbf{z} = \mathbf{X}'\mu + \epsilon,$$

where $\mathbf{X}$ is an $N \times K$ matrix,

$$\epsilon \sim N(\mathbf{0}, \Omega)$$

is a K-random vector, Ω is a $K \times K$ SPD matrix, and ϵ is independent of μ.

Then the posterior distribution of μ, given $\mathbf{z}$, is

$$\mu|\mathbf{z} \sim N(\mathbf{v}, \mathbf{Q}),$$

where

$$\mathbf{Q} = (\Sigma^{-1} + \mathbf{X}\Omega^{-1}\mathbf{X}')^{-1}$$

and

$$\mathbf{v} = \mathbf{Q}(\Sigma^{-1}\theta + \mathbf{X}\Omega^{-1}\mathbf{z}).$$

In the one-dimensional case, $N = 1$, the proposition collapses to the example we just studied, where $\tilde{z} = \mu + \epsilon$, and $\epsilon \sim N(0, \tau^2)$. When $N > 1$, the proposition is based on observing linear combinations of the elements in the μ-vector with noise, and is therefore more complicated. Note also that if we have the multivariate random variable

$$\tilde{\mathbf{y}} \sim N(\mu, \mathbf{T}),$$

then the posterior distribution of $\tilde{y}$ is

$$\tilde{\mathbf{y}}|\mathbf{z} \sim N(\mathbf{v}, \mathbf{T} + \mathbf{Q}).$$

Proposition 5.1 can be used to understand the Black–Litterman model. We consider an investor who has some “views” about the returns of specific portfolios of assets. For example, a view may be that the average expected excess return on the five major stocks that dominate the telecommunications industry is 15% next year. Here, and in the rest of this section, we use the notation μ for the vector of excess returns rather than μ^e, to be consistent with the above notation. Such a view can then be thought of as corresponding to an element, z_k, in the $\mathbf{z}$-vector, $\mathbf{z} = (z_1, \ldots, z_K)'$. Specifically, defining the $\mathbf{x}^1$-vector that has elements $(\mathbf{x}^1)_n = \frac{1}{5}$ for the five dominant telecommunications stocks, and 0 for all the other assets in the market, $(\mathbf{x}^1)_n = 0$, $n = 6, \ldots, N$, this view would correspond to

$$z_1 = E[(\mathbf{x}^1)'\mu] = 15\%.$$

We have written this as an expectation to allow for prior uncertainty about the expected return vector, in line with the Bayesian updating example. Stacking together K such views in the $\mathbf{X}$-matrix, with expected values in the $\mathbf{z}$-vector, and also accounting for some perceived uncertainty by the investor about these views, as well as correlated errors, we summarize the views in the following equation:

$$\mathbf{X}'\mu \sim N(\mathbf{z}, \Omega).$$

Here, Ω is the $K \times K$ SPD covariance matrix, which represents how confident the investor is about these views and their covariances. In Black–Litterman's original paper, Ω is assumed to be diagonal, so that errors are uncorrelated across views.

Now, the number of views is typically much lower than the number of assets, $K \ll N$. Indeed, if $K = N$, and $\mathbf{X}$ were invertible, $E[\mu] = (\mathbf{X}^{-1})'\mathbf{z}$ could be calculated from the views. Additional information about $E[\mu]$ is gained from the CAPM. This is where the Black–Litterman model is based on an equilibrium argument, since the CAPM is an equilibrium model. From the one-fund separation theorem, we know that all investors (except the one we are focusing on, who is assumed to have negligible impact on the market) will hold the market portfolio, which is mean–variance efficient with respect to their information. So, if the return vector is

$$\tilde{\mu} \sim N(\mu, \Sigma),$$

then the market portfolio is $\mathbf{w} = \frac{1}{a}\Sigma^{-1}\mu$, where the constant a is related to the aggregate risk aversion in the economy.

In contrast to μ, the market's portfolio weights are observable, potentially with some noise. We can use this to draw inferences about μ, by rewriting

$$\mu = a\Sigma\mathbf{w} + \epsilon.$$

Here, the noise term $\epsilon \sim N(0, b\Sigma)$ accounts for uncertainty in this observation, for which the specific covariance matrix $b\Sigma$ is assumed to be essentially the same as the covariance matrix between asset returns (except for the scaling factor, b). This is in line with the original setup in Black and Litterman's model. The investor uses the information about the market portfolio to form a prior belief about the distribution of μ:

$$\mu \sim N(a\Sigma\mathbf{w}, b\Sigma).$$

The setup is now such that we can apply proposition 5.1, from which it follows that the posterior beliefs about expected returns, μ, after taking into account the investor's views, are

$$\mu|\mathbf{z} \sim N(\mathbf{v}, \mathbf{Q}),$$

where

$$\mathbf{Q} = (b^{-1}\Sigma^{-1} + \mathbf{X}\Omega^{-1}\mathbf{X}')^{-1}$$

and

$$\mathbf{v} = \mathbf{Q}\left(\frac{a}{b}\mathbf{w} + \mathbf{X}\Omega^{-1}\mathbf{z}\right).$$

Moreover, given that $\tilde{\mu} \sim N(\mu, \Sigma)$, the posterior beliefs about return distributions, $\tilde{\mu}$, are

$$\tilde{\mu}|\mathbf{z} \sim N(\mathbf{v}, \Sigma + \mathbf{Q}).$$

The extra factor $\mathbf{Q}$ contributing to the covariance matrix takes into account that the uncertainty about μ increases the variance with the additional factor $\mathbf{Q}$, a similar effect to the one we saw in the example at the beginning of this section. The prior covariance matrix is $\Sigma + b\Sigma$, which is even higher.

Note that these expressions do not require knowledge of μ. The μ-vector is replaced by $\mathbf{w}$ because of the equilibrium argument. Note also that when the investor has no views, $K=0$, so the terms that include $\mathbf{X}$ vanish, the expected return collapses to $\mathbf{v} = a\Sigma\mathbf{w}$ consistent with the original CAPM.

AN EXAMPLE Consider a market with three assets and the covariance matrix

$$\Sigma = \begin{bmatrix} 0.3 & 0.2 & 0 \\ 0.2 & 0.5 & 0 \\ 0 & 0 & 0.2 \end{bmatrix}.$$

The market portfolio is $\mathbf{w} = (0.2, 0.2, 0.6)'$, the risk-aversion parameter is estimated to be $a=1$, and the uncertainty parameter is $b=0.2$. The investor has the view that the expected excess return on asset 1 is $\mu_1 \sim N(0.15, 0.25)$. We calculate the investor's posterior belief about expected returns, and the portfolio (s)he chooses.

We first note that $\mathbf{X} = (1,0,0)'$, $\mathbf{z} = 0.15$, and $\Omega = 0.25$. Furthermore, the investor's prior beliefs about expected returns are $E[\mu] = a\Sigma\mathbf{w} = (0.1, 0.14, 0.12)'$. We next calculate

$$\mathbf{Q} = \begin{bmatrix} 0.048 & 0.032 & 0 \\ 0.032 & 0.095 & 0 \\ 0 & 0 & 0.04 \end{bmatrix}$$

and posterior beliefs

$$\mathbf{v} = (0.1097, 0.1465, 0.12)'.$$

This in turn leads to the portfolio holdings

$$\mathbf{w}^p = \frac{\Sigma^{-1}\mathbf{v}}{\mathbf{1}'\Sigma^{-1}\mathbf{v}} = (0.225, 0.194, 0.581)',$$

given that the investor uses Σ as the covariance matrix. If the uncertainty associated with not knowing μ is also taken into account, implying that instead of Σ, the covariance matrix is $\Sigma + \mathbf{Q}$, the resulting portfolio becomes

$$\mathbf{w}^p = \frac{(\Sigma + \mathbf{Q})^{-1}\mathbf{v}}{\mathbf{1}'(\Sigma + \mathbf{Q})^{-1}\mathbf{v}} = (0.234, 0.192, 0.574)'.$$

In either case, the investor rebalances toward holding more of asset 1, consistent with having a more optimistic view about its expected return (15%) than the market (which believes it is 10%).

5.4 Consumption-Based Models

The model we analyze here is quite similar to the classical general equilibrium exchange economy model in microeconomics, introduced by Arrow (1951) and Debreu (1951, 1959). The main difference compared with those models is that instead of having (many) heterogeneous goods, there is only one good here but many (although a finite number of) different states. So the goods are in some sense replaced by states in this finance-oriented version of the model, and the focus here is on risk. As in the original model, there are multiple price-taking agents whose preferences may differ, and equilibrium is determined by market clearing.

We assume expected-utility-maximizing agents, a specification that implies linearity in the utility specification: $U = p_1 u(c_1) + p_2 u(c_2) + \cdots + p_M u(c_M)$. This is much more restrictive than the assumptions made in the original model of Arrow and Debreu's, where utility of the bundle of consumption goods $x_1, x_2, \ldots$, is of the form $U = u(x_1, x_2, \ldots)$. It makes the finance-oriented version of the model introduced here more straightforward to analyze than the original model.

The model is still quite abstract, and without further assumptions the results are general rather than specific. We will mainly focus on the questions of (i) existence of equilibrium, (ii) how "good" the equilibrium outcome is from an efficiency perspective, and (iii) the so-called stochastic discount factor interpretation of the equilibrium pricing relations. We will also study some examples in which we make additional assumptions, leading to further interesting results. Importantly, this is a workhorse equilibrium model that can be taken in several directions.

5.4.1 Arrow–Debreu Model

There are two dates, $t = 0, 1$, which represent "today" and "tomorrow." There are $M \geq 1$ possible tomorrow states. There is one *perishable* consumption good, meaning that it cannot be stored/saved at time 0 for consumption at time 1. Moreover, it cannot be transferred across states.

There are $K \geq 1$ agents. Agent k's utility of consuming c_0^k (of the consumption good) today and $c_{1,m}^k$ tomorrow in states $m = 1, \ldots, M$ is

$$U^k = u^k(c_0^k) + \sum_{m=1}^{M} v_m^k(c_{1,m}^k),$$

where u^k and v_m^k are smooth, strictly increasing, and strictly concave functions. Note that this specification is more general than the expected utility specification we have used so far, since here we allow the utility functions to vary for an agent across time and states, and there is no explicit personal discount rate or probabilities in the formula. Since the v_m^k variables are general, expected utility arises as a special case of this specification when $v_m^k(c_{1,m}^k) = \delta \pi_m^k u^k(c_{1,m}^k)$, where $0 < \delta \leq 1$ and $0 < \pi_m^k$, $\sum_m \pi_m^k = 1$, for all k. This then corresponds to agents with expected utility, with discount factor δ, and subjective probability estimates for different states (since π_m^k depends on agent, k). Note that we assume that all agents believe that all states may occur with strictly positive probability. If all agents agree that a state is impossible, that state is irrelevant and can be excluded from the model. If some but not all agents think the state is impossible, there can be no equilibrium. Specifically, we will allow for short-selling of assets. So without this assumption, an agent who believed some states to be impossible would be willing to short-sell an infinite amount of an asset that pays off solely in such a state, for an arbitrarily low price, whereas an agent who believed the probability to be strictly positive would have a very high demand for such a low-priced asset. It would not be possible to have an equilibrium in such a setting.

Some special cases of the expected utility formulation are

- $u^k = u^{k'}$ for all k, k': this occurs when agents have the same utility functions,
- $\pi_m^k = \pi_m^{k'}$ for all m, k, k': this occurs when agents agree on probabilities.

Our aim is not to introduce the most general version of the model, with respect to technical assumptions (smoothness of utility functions, etc.), but rather to provide a sufficiently general version that is still straightforward to analyze. To simplify the analysis, we therefore assume that the following so-called Inada conditions are satisfied for the utility functions:

$$\lim_{c\to 0}(u^k)'(c)=\infty, \quad \lim_{c\to\infty}(u^k)'(c)=0.$$

These conditions were originally imposed on production functions in macroeconomic growth theory, but are also useful for utility functions. Note that the CRRA utility functions satisfy the Inada conditions, whereas the CARA utility functions do not (at $c=0$).

Each agent receives an endowment stream of the consumption good,

$$e_0^k>0, \quad e_{1,m}^k>0.$$

This is the exchange economy part of the model. The stream could, for example, represent labor income at times 0 and 1. In the absence of financial markets, agents consume what they earn. This so-called *autarky* outcome is then

$$c_0^k=e_0^k, \quad c_{1m}^k=e_{1m}^k, \quad 1\le k\le K,\ 1\le m\le M.$$

Agents' utilities under autarky are

$$U^k=u^k(e_0^k)+\delta\sum_m u^k(e_{1,m}^k)\pi_m^k.$$

It is important to keep track of the aggregate variables in this economy. The total amount of the consumption good available in each period/state is

$$C_0=\sum_k e_0^k, \quad C_{1,m}=\sum_k e_{1,m}^k, \quad m=1,\dots,M.$$

Note that this total amount cannot be affected by any decisions the agents make, an assumption that constitutes one part of the *endowment economy* assumption. The other part is that the economy allows for *transfers*, i.e., that the good can be traded between agents at any time, in any state. In a more general version of the model, real investments at $t=0$ are allowed, allowing the total amount of the consumption to change across time and state, and thereby leading to a *production economy*.

A unit of the consumption good at time 0 is not the same as a unit at time 1, and neither is a unit in two different states at time 1. We introduce a currency that agents can use to relate the value of the consumption good at different times, in different states, and we normalize the $t=0$ price of one unit of the consumption good so that it costs \$1.

A market for *contingent claims* allows agents to trade with each other, to smooth consumption over time and states. Specifically, the *Arrow–Debreu* (AD) security, δ_m, $m=1,\dots,M$, pays a unit of the consumption good in state m at $t=1$ and 0 units in all other states. The contingent claim δ_0 pays a unit of the consumption good at time 0—or equivalently, a dollar.

Let us denote the $t=0$ price of δ_m by ψ_m. The *state-price vector* is then

$$\psi=(\psi_1,\dots,\psi_M)',$$

and we also have $\psi_0=1$.

Agents are *price takers*, so they view the supply of contingent claims as perfectly elastic. When K is large, this seems like a reasonable assumption. Such markets are called *Walrasian*. The markets for AD securities can be thought of as agents signing enforceable contracts, in which they pay using today-consumption, and then receive tomorrow-consumption in specific states (or get today-consumption and pay with tomorrow-consumption, if on the selling side).

This economy is *decentralized*, in that each agent's actions are determined by their individually optimal decisions. These decisions, in turn, determine aggregate outcomes. In equilibrium, the market-clearing condition must imply that total demand equals total supply of the consumption good at all times and in each state. It is a priori unclear what the aggregate properties of equilibrium will be like, and even whether it exists.

Consider agent k's budget constraint, given the state-price vector ψ:

$$e_0^k + \sum_m \psi_m e_{1,m}^k = W^k = c_0^k + \sum_m \psi_m c_{1,m}^k.$$

Alternatively, we can let d_m^k denote agent k's demand for the AD security δ_m, and d_0^k for δ_0 (or equivalently for the time-0 consumption good). This is the net demand, which may be negative, above and beyond the agent's endowment, e_k^m. The budget constraint can then be written

$$c_0^k = e_0^k + d_0^k, \quad c_{1,m}^k = e_{1,m}^k + d_m^k, \quad d_0^k + \sum_m d_m^k \psi_m = 0,$$

which states that the total value of the agent's change in consumption, as implemented by trading in AD securities, is zero.[3]

Agent k solves max U^k subject to the budget constraint, leading to FOC

$$\psi_m = \delta \frac{(u^k)'(c_{1m}^k)}{(u^k)'(c_0^k)} \pi_m^k, \quad m = 1, \ldots, M. \tag{5.7}$$

Strict concavity of all utility functions ensures that a solution to the FOC is a unique global maximum. Moreover, the Inada conditions imply that for any $\psi \gg \mathbf{0}$, a solution exists. A state-price vector ψ is an *equilibrium state-price vector* if all AD markets clear. An equilibrium state-price vector thus defines an equilibrium, from which all other properties of the economy can be derived. Note that if $\psi_m \leq 0$ for any state m, each agent's demand in that state would be infinite. So an equilibrium state-price vector must have $\psi \gg \mathbf{0}$. The market-clearing constraint is

$$\sum_k d_m^k = 0, \quad m = 0, \ldots, M.$$

Our first goal is to show that an equilibrium state-price vector exists. To this end, define aggregate demand for AD security δ_m, $m = 0, \ldots, M$:

$$D_m = \sum_k d_m^k.$$

As in the original AD model, *Walras' law* is helpful in proving existence of equilibrium.

Theorem 5.3 (Walras' law). *Given a state-price vector ψ, agents' demand functions are such that the sum of aggregate demand across dates and states is zero:*

$$\sum_{m=0}^{M} \psi_m D_m = 0.$$

[3] Possible free disposal of the consumption good is sometimes incorporated into the model, which would replace equalities with inequalities. Since all agents have strictly increasing utility functions, these inequalities would always bind under agent optimality, so equalities may be assumed even if free disposal is possible.

Proof. Agent k's budget constraint is

$$d_0^k \psi_0 + \sum_{m=1}^{M} d_m^k \psi_m = 0.$$

Summing over agents, we get

$$\begin{aligned} 0 &= \sum_{k=1}^{K} \left(d_0^k \psi_0 + \sum_{m=1}^{M} d_m^k \psi_m \right) \\ &= D_0 \psi_0 + \sum_{m=1}^{M} \left(\sum_{k=1}^{K} d_m^k \right) \psi_m \\ &= D_0 \psi_0 + \sum_{m=1}^{M} D_m \psi_m. \end{aligned}$$

□

Note that Walras' law holds for every strictly positive state-price vector, whether that vector defines an equilibrium or not.

We now have the following result:

Theorem 5.4 (Existence of equilibrium). *If agent utility functions are bounded, i.e.,* $u^k(\infty) < \infty$, *and at zero satisfy the conditions* $(u^k)'(0+) = \infty$, *then there exists a strictly positive equilibrium state-price vector,* $\psi \gg \mathbf{0}$.

Note that the boundedness condition at infinity is stronger than the Inada condition at infinity. For example, logarithmic utility satisfies the latter condition but not the former. The boundedness condition can be relaxed, but we are more interested in having a tractable and intuitive proof than in finding the most general equilibrium existence result, so we include it.[4]

The theorem is still very general, since few assumptions are made about utility functions and endowment streams. The theorem does not guarantee uniqueness of equilibrium. Indeed, although individual demand functions are uniquely defined given a strictly positive state-price vector, there may be multiple equilibrium state-price vectors.

Proof of existence of an equilibrium state-price vector. Proofs of equilibrium existence are often based on so-called fixed-point theorems. Here we use Brouwer's fixed-point theorem:

Definition 5.1. A set $X \subset \mathbb{R}^r$ is said to be *convex* if $x, y \in X \Rightarrow \lambda x + (1-\lambda)x \in X$, for all $\lambda \in (0,1)$.

Theorem 5.5 (Brouwer's fixed-point theorem). *Consider a closed, bounded, nonempty, convex set,* $X \subset \mathbb{R}^r$, *and a continuous function,* $f: X \to X$. *Then* f *has a fixed point,* $\mathbf{x} = f(\mathbf{x})$.

We note that the closed unit simplex, $\bar{S}^r = \{\mathbf{x} \in \mathbb{R}_+^r : \sum_{j=1}^r \mathbf{x}_j = 1\}$ is closed, nonempty, and convex. It therefore follows from Brouwer's theorem that for any $r \geq 1$, a continuous function $f: \bar{S}^r \to \bar{S}^r$ has a fixed point.

The following lemma, which is based on a similar argument to one made in Nash (1951), will be useful for us.[5]

[4] The condition $u(0) = 0$ is also an Inada condition, which is not imposed here.

[5] Nash (1951) used the argument to prove the existence of Nash equilibrium in multiplayer noncooperative games.

Lemma 5.1. *Consider a continuous function* $F\colon \bar{S}^r \to \mathbb{R}^r$. *Moreover, assume that each nonzero vector in the range* $F(S^r)$ *contains both positive and negative elements,*

$$\exists j : F(\mathbf{x})_j > 0 \;\Leftrightarrow\; \exists j' : F(\mathbf{x})_{j'} < 0, \tag{5.8}$$

and that for all $\mathbf{x} \in \bar{S}^r$,

$$\mathbf{x}_j = 0 \;\Rightarrow\; F(\mathbf{x})_j > 0. \tag{5.9}$$

Then there exists an $\mathbf{x} \in S^r$ *such that*

$$F(\mathbf{x}) = \mathbf{0}.$$

Proof. Define the function $G\colon \bar{S}^r \to \bar{S}^r$ by

$$G(\mathbf{x})_j \stackrel{\text{def}}{=} \frac{\mathbf{x}_j + \max(F(\mathbf{x})_j, 0)}{1 + \sum_{j=1}^r \max(F(\mathbf{x})_j, 0)}.$$

Also, define $C = \sum_{j=1}^r \max(F(\mathbf{x})_j, 0) \geq 0$. Since F is continuous, G is too, and therefore G has a fixed point, $\mathbf{y} \in \bar{S}^r$, by Brouwer's theorem. Because of (5.9), it follows that $\mathbf{y} \in S^r$, i.e., the fixed point cannot lie on the boundary of the unit simplex.

One way such a fixed point may arise is if $F(\mathbf{y}) = \mathbf{0}$, in which case $C = 0$, and we get

$$G(\mathbf{y})_j = \frac{\mathbf{y}_j + \max(F(\mathbf{y})_j, 0)}{1 + C} = \mathbf{y}_j.$$

In fact, this is the *only* way that $\mathbf{y}$ may define a fixed point of G. Assume, to the contrary, that there is a fixed point, $\mathbf{y} \in S^r$, such that $F(\mathbf{y}) \neq \mathbf{0}$. Then there must exist a j such that $F(\mathbf{y})_j > 0$, and a j' such that $F(\mathbf{y})_{j'} < 0$. It follows that $C > 0$. But this then implies that

$$\mathbf{y}_{j'} = G(\mathbf{y})_{j'} = \frac{\mathbf{y}_{j'} + \max(F(\mathbf{y})_{j'}, 0)}{1 + C} = \frac{\mathbf{y}_{j'}}{1 + C},$$

so $\mathbf{y}_{j'} = 0$, contradicting $\mathbf{y} \in S^r$. Thus, $F(\mathbf{y}) = \mathbf{0}$ for some $\mathbf{y} \in S^r$, as the lemma states. □

Our goal is now to apply the lemma, using the aggregate demand function $D(\psi)$. A state-price vector $\psi \gg \mathbf{0}$, such that $D(\psi) = \mathbf{0}$, will then define an equilibrium, i.e., it will make markets clear. From Walras' law it follows that $\sum_m \psi_m D(\psi)_m = 0$, so either $D(\psi) = \mathbf{0}$, or the vector contains both negative and positive elements. So (5.8) is satisfied for D. An issue with trying to use D in this proof is that it is not well defined on the boundaries when a state price tends to zero, since we expect aggregate demand to become infinite in this case. We will fix this issue later, by introducing a bounded transformation of D that preserves its important properties. For the time being, we continue to work with D.

We first focus on the individual agent's demand functions, given the state-price vector $\psi \in \mathbb{R}^M_{++}$. Because of the strict concavity of the problem, agent k will choose the consumption profile, $c_0^k, c_1^k, \ldots, c_M^k$, if the following FOCs are satisfied:

$$(u^k)'(c_0^k)\frac{\psi_m}{\delta \pi_m^k} = (u^k)'(c_m^k), \quad m = 1, \ldots, M, \tag{5.10}$$

and

$$c_0^k + \sum_{m=1}^M \psi_m c_m^k = W^k. \tag{5.11}$$

We first show that a solution to (5.10, 5.11) exists for each $\psi \gg \mathbf{0}$, defining the demand function $d^k = (c_0^k - e_0^k, c_1^k - e_1^k, \ldots, c_M^k - e_m^k)'$. Define the inverse marginal utility function, $g^k(x)$, such that $g^k((u^k)'(x)) = x$. Since $(u^k)'(x)$ is a continuously differentiable, strictly decreasing function, and satisfies the Inada conditions, it follows that g^k is also a strictly decreasing continuously differentiable function, such that $g^k(0+) = \infty$ and $g^k(\infty) = 0$.

Now assume that the agent chooses to consume x at time 0, as the optimal choice. Given that (5.10) is satisfied, the agent's consumption in state m is then

$$c_m^k = g^k\Big(\frac{(u^k)'(x)\psi_m}{\delta\pi_m^k}\Big), \quad m = 1, 2, \ldots, M,$$

leading to a demand function $d^k(x) = (x - e_0^k, c_1^k - e_1^k, \ldots, c_M^k - e_M^k)'$. The total *implied wealth* of this choice of consumption profile is

$$\widehat{W}^k(x; \psi) = x + \sum_m \psi_m g^k\Big(\frac{(u^k)'(x)\psi_m}{\delta\pi_m^k}\Big),$$

and the net wealth surplus is

$$\widehat{W}^k(x; \psi) - W^k.$$

It follows immediately that $\widehat{W}^k$ is a smooth function of both its arguments (c_0^k and ψ) in $\mathbb{R}_{++} \times \mathbb{R}_{++}^M$, strictly increasing in x for a fixed ψ, that $\lim_{x\to 0} \widehat{W}(x, \psi) = 0$ for any $\psi \in \mathbb{R}_{++}^M$, and that $\lim_{x\to\infty} \widehat{W}(x, \psi) = \infty$ for any $\psi \in \mathbb{R}_{++}^M$. Consequently (from the intermediate value theorem), for any $\psi \in \mathbb{R}_{++}^M$, there is a unique strictly positive c_0^k, such that

$$\widehat{W}(c_0^k; \psi) - W^k = 0.$$

This consumption profile will then define the agent's demand function $d^k(c_0^k)$ As a function of the state-price vector, we can write $d^k(\psi)$.

We next show that the agent's demand function depends continuously on the state-price vector. Consider a small change of the state-price vector, by $\Delta\psi = (\Delta\psi_1, \ldots, \Delta\psi_M)'$, and an associated change of c_0^k, by Δc_0^k. By a Taylor expansion, the total change of the net wealth surplus is then

$$\begin{aligned}
\Delta\widehat{W}^m - \Delta W^k &= \Delta c_0^k \underbrace{\Big(1 + \sum_m \psi_m (g^k)'\Big(\frac{(u^k)'(c_0^k)\psi_m}{\delta\pi_m^k}\Big)\frac{(u^k)''(c_0^k)\psi_m}{\delta\pi_m^k}\Big)}_{Q} \\
&\quad + \sum_m (g^k)'\Big(\frac{(u^k)'(c_0^k)\psi_m}{\delta\pi_m^k}\Big)\Delta\psi_m \\
&\quad + \sum_m \psi_m (g^k)''\Big(\frac{(u^k)'(c_0^k)\psi_m}{\delta\pi_m^k}\Big)\frac{(u^k)'(c_0^k)}{\delta\pi_m^k}\Delta\psi_m \\
&\quad - \sum_m e_m^k \Delta\psi_m + O(\Delta(c_0^k)^2, \|\Delta\psi\|^2) \\
&\stackrel{\text{def}}{=} Q\Delta c_0^k + \sum_m q_m \Delta\psi_m + O(\Delta(c_0^k)^2, \|\Delta\psi\|^2).
\end{aligned}$$

Note that $Q > 1$ since $(g^k)' < 0$ and $(u^k)'' < 0$. The inverse function theorem now implies that

$$\Delta c_0^k = -\frac{\sum_m q_m \Delta\psi_m}{Q} + O(\|\Delta\psi\|^2),$$

when

$$\Delta \widehat{W}^m - \Delta W^k = 0.$$

The consumption change at time 0, Δc_0^k, thus depends continuously on the change in the state-price vector, $\Delta\psi$, as therefore also does the demand function $d^k(\psi)$.

We have so far used the normalization $\psi_0 = 1$, and viewed the state-price vector as an M-vector. We can also include the time-0 state price ψ_0, define $\psi = (\psi_0, \psi_1, \dots, \psi_M) \in \mathbb{R}_{++}^{1+M}$, and relax the normalization assumption, so that we allow for arbitrary $\psi_0 > 0$. One verifies that agent k's optimization problem in this case,

$$U^k = u^k(c_0^k) + \delta \sum_{m=1}^{M} u_m^k(c_m^k)\pi_m^k, \tag{5.12}$$

subject to

$$W^k = \psi_0 c_0^k + \sum_{m=1}^{M} \psi_n c_m^k, \tag{5.13}$$

where the agent's wealth is

$$W^k = \psi_0 e_0 + \sum_{m=1}^{M} \psi_k e_m^k, \tag{5.14}$$

is homogeneous of degree zero in the sense that the agent's chosen consumptions for the problems with ψ and $\alpha\psi$ are the same for any $\alpha > 0$. In other words, $d^k(\alpha\psi) = d^k(\psi)$, $\alpha > 0$. Hence, the aggregate demand D is also homogeneous of degree zero. We can therefore without loss of generality assume that $\psi \in S^{1+M}$, i.e., that ψ belongs to the interior of the $(1 + M)$-dimensional unit simplex,

$$S^{1+M} = \left\{\mathbf{x} \in \mathbb{R}_{++}^{1+M} : \textstyle\sum_{m=1}^{1+M} \mathbf{x}_m = 1\right\}.$$

This alternative normalization of the state-price vector will allow us to apply lemma 5.1. Indeed, $D : S^{1+M} \Rightarrow \mathbb{R}^{1+M}$ is continuous and satisfies (5.8). To be able to apply the lemma, we introduce a modified version of D that is continuously defined on the whole of $\bar{S}^{1+M}$, that satisfies (5.9). Specifically, we define the function

$$F(\psi)_m = \Phi(D(\psi)_m), \tag{5.15}$$

where $\Phi\colon \mathbb{R} \to \mathbb{R}$ is a smooth strictly increasing, bounded, function, such that $\Phi(-\infty) = -1$, $\Phi(0) = 0$, and $\Phi(\infty) = 1$. We could, for example, choose $\Phi(x) = \frac{2}{\pi}\tan^{-1}(x)$. It then follows that $F(\psi) = \mathbf{0}$ if and only if $D(\psi) = \mathbf{0}$, and that F is continuous for $\psi \in S^{1+M}$. Also, since D satisfies (5.8), F will also satisfy (5.8) because the function Φ preserves signs (note that (5.8) only needs to be satisfied in the interior, S^{1+M}, so we do not need to check whether the condition holds on the boundary of the continuous extension).

We first show that F can be continuously extended to the whole of $\bar{S}^{1+M}$, i.e., to include state-price vectors on the boundary of the unit simplex. Note that an agent's demand for an AD security with zero price will be infinite, taking the limit of (5.10). However, $\Phi(D(\psi)_m)$ tends to 1 for such an asset with limit price 0, and thus converges and is finite for such assets. If we can also extend the function continuously for the assets with nonzero prices when some prices tend to zero, we can then define the function F on the whole of $\bar{S}^{1+M}$.

An important property of the agent's optimization problem is that it can be decomposed into subproblems, in that if it is known how much wealth the agent will spend on consumption in total in a subset of the states—say that it is known that (s)he will spend $\dot{W}$ in states $0, \ldots, r$ in total for some $r < M$—then the solution to the maximization problem over those states will coincide (that is, have the same consumption) in those states with the solution to the full problem over all $1+M$ states. In the remaining states, the solution will then coincide with the solution of the subproblem over those states, with wealth $W - \dot{W}$. So, if we can infer how much the agent will spend in the limit in states whose state prices converge to zero, we can calculate how much (s)he will consume in the other states by solving the subproblem in those states with the remaining wealth. We next show that no agent, in the limit, will spend any of their wealth on consumption in states whose state prices converge to zero.

Consider the vector $\psi \in \bar{S}^{1+M}$. Without loss of generality, we assume that $\psi_m > 0$ for $m = 0, \ldots, r$, $r \geq 0$, and $\psi_m = 0$ for $m = r+1, \ldots, M$, i.e., that the boundary points of ψ occur for the higher coordinates (otherwise one can relabel the states). Consider a sequence $\psi^\epsilon \in S^{1+M}$, $\epsilon > 0$, such that $\max_m |\psi^\epsilon_m - \psi_m| \leq \epsilon$, with the corresponding demand functions $d^k(\psi^\epsilon)$. We show that

$$\lim_{\epsilon \to 0} d^k(\psi^\epsilon)_m, \quad k = 1, \ldots, K,\ m = 0, \ldots, M,$$

exists and is independent of how the sequence ψ^ϵ is chosen (as long as it converges to ψ).

Our goal is to show that

$$\lim_{\epsilon \to 0} \psi_m c^k(\psi^\epsilon)_m = 0, \quad m = r+1, \ldots, M,$$

that is, that an agent in the limit will spend no wealth on consumption in states with state prices that tend to zero. The intuitive reason is that they can obtain very high consumption levels in such states without having to spend much, since the AD securities are so inexpensive.

This result depends specifically on the fact that the utility functions are bounded. Dropping the k superscript, since u is bounded, it follows that $\lim_{x \to \infty} u'(cx)x = 0$ for all $c > 0$. Otherwise, for a fixed $c > 0$, for any $\delta > 0$, for any $y > 0$, there exists an $x > y$, such that $u'(x)x \geq \delta$. In fact, there exists an arbitrarily large x for which this is the case, since y may be chosen arbitrarily large. Since $u(cx) = u(cy) + \int_y^x cu'(cs)\,ds \geq u(cy) + cu'(cx)\int_y^x ds = u(cy) + cu'(cx)(x-y)$, it follows that $u(cx) \geq u(cy) + cu'(cx)(x-y)$. Now define $C = u(\infty)$ and choose y sufficiently large so that $u(cy) > C - \frac{c\delta}{2}$. Moreover, choose $x \geq 2y$, so that $x - y \geq \frac{x}{2}$. It then follows that

$$u(cx) > u(cy) + cu'(cx)(x-y) > C - \frac{c\delta}{2} + c\frac{u'(cx)x}{2} \geq C - \frac{c\delta}{2} + c\frac{\delta}{2} = C = u(\infty).$$

The assumption thus leads to a contradiction since u is increasing, which means that $u(\infty) > u(cx)$. So no such $\delta > 0$ exists, and the result follows for all agent utility functions, u^k, $k = 1, \ldots, K$.

Now, the FOC (5.10), together with the fact that $c^k_0 \leq \frac{W^k}{\psi_0}$ for small ϵ (since the agent cannot spend more than total wealth on any given asset because this would need to be financed with negative consumption in some other state which would in turn imply negative infinite expected utility), imply that

$$\frac{1}{\psi^\epsilon_m}(u^k)'\left(\frac{c^k_m \psi^\epsilon_m}{\psi^\epsilon_m}\right) \geq Z, \tag{5.16}$$

where

$$Z = \frac{(u^k)'(2\frac{W^k}{\psi_0})}{\delta\psi_0\pi^k_m} > 0.$$

It follows that $\psi^\epsilon c^k_m \to 0$, since otherwise the left-hand side of (5.16) would tend to zero as $\psi^\epsilon_m \to 0$. Equivalently, $\psi^\epsilon_m d^k(\psi^\epsilon)_m \to 0$.

So, in the limit, the agent gets maximum utility in states where state prices tend to zero, and thus

$$\lim_{\epsilon \to 0} (D(\psi^\epsilon))_m = \infty, \quad m = r+1, \ldots, M,$$

but the agent does not spend any wealth on these states, rather (s)he spends all the wealth on consumption in states $0, \ldots, r$. The consumptions in these states, c_m^k, $m = 0, \ldots, r$, then converge to the solution of the $(r+1)$-dimensional optimization problem

$$\max u^k(c_0^k) + \delta \sum_{m=1}^{r} u_n^k(c_m^k)\pi_m^k, \tag{5.17}$$

subject to

$$W^k = \psi_0 c_0^k + \sum_{m=1}^{r} \psi_m c_m^k. \tag{5.18}$$

Of course, $\hat{\psi} = (\psi_0, \ldots, \psi_r) \in S^{1+r}$ lies in the interior of the $(1+r)$-dimensional unit simplex, since all these state prices are strictly positive. A $(1+r)$-dimensional version of the arguments we made before implies the existence of a continuous demand function, d_m^k, for these $1+r$ AD securities, $m = 0, \ldots, r$, for each agent, k. We denote the aggregate demand function associated with this $(1+r)$-dimensional problem by $\dot{D}(\hat{\psi}) \in \mathbb{R}^{1+r}$. It also follows that $\lim_{\epsilon \to 0}(D(\psi^\epsilon))_m \to \dot{D}(\hat{\psi})_m$, $m = 0, \ldots, r$. So it follows that the function F can be continuously extended to $\bar{S}^{1+M}$ by defining $F(\psi)_m = \Phi(\dot{D}(\hat{\psi})_m)$, $m = 0, \ldots, r$, and $F(\psi)_m = 1$, $m = r+1, \ldots, M$. Finally, note that $F(\psi)_m = 1 > 0$ when $\psi_m = 0$, so (5.9) is satisfied on the boundary as well as in the interior for this function.

So, altogether, F is continuous, defined on $\bar{S}^{1+M}$, and satisfies (5.8) in the interior, as well as (5.9) on the whole of $\bar{S}^{1+M}$. By lemma 5.1, an interior solution to the problem $F(\psi) = \mathbf{0}$ exists, $\psi \in S^{1+M}$, which because of how the function Φ is defined also satisfies $D(\psi) = \mathbf{0}$. We have shown the existence of a state-price vector that defines equilibrium! Finally, note that the M-dimensional version of the state-price vector, under the normalization $\psi_0 = 1$, is given by the vector $(\psi_1/\psi_0, \ldots, \psi_M/\psi_0)'$. □

5.4.2 Efficiency

We mentioned earlier that the equilibrium mechanism in the AD economy is inherently decentralized, and that there is no reason to believe that the equilibrium outcomes will be especially "good." The classical welfare theorems applied to the finance-focused Arrow–Debreu model imply that equilibrium outcomes are "good," as defined by efficiency. In addition to these results being important from a welfare perspective, they also suggest a powerful methodology for finding equilibria by solving a so-called *planner's problem*, which we now explore.

A *complete market* is one in which an agent can generate any consumption pattern across states. Technically, we require that for every $\mathbf{f} \in \mathbb{R}^M$, a portfolio of assets exists, for which the time-1 payoff in state m is $\mathbf{f}_m$. It follows immediately that the AD economy is complete, and that the f payoff is obtained by choosing the AD security demand $d_m = \mathbf{f}_m$.[6] Intuitively, complete markets are "good" because they allow for total unbundling of goods/payoffs, and thereby for agents to choose their own optimal mix of consumption across states and time.

[6] In the dynamic markets that we will study later on, the completeness property may be less transparent, because dynamic investment strategies may generate completeness.

Consider an economy with a *central planner*, who maximizes some linear combination of agents' utilities

$$\max \sum_k \lambda^k U^k, \quad \lambda^k > 0, \; \forall k. \tag{5.19}$$

The planner cares about all agents, $\lambda^k > 0$, but may put more weight on some agents than others. We can without loss of generality assume $\sum_k \lambda_k = 1$. The planner has dictatorial powers. (S)he can redistribute endowments freely among agents. However, the planner *cannot* change aggregate consumption in any state, but must obey the aggregate constraints:

$$\sum_k c_0^k = C_0, \quad \sum_k c_{1m}^k = C_{1m}, \quad \forall m.$$

The planner's objective function (5.19) may seem quite arbitrary. Why should it have a linear specification? The key is that the specification is such that any allocation for which one agent's utility may be increased—by a reallocation—without decreasing the utility of any other agent, cannot be a solution to the planners's problem. Therefore, the solutions to the planner's problem in the finance-oriented Arrow–Debreu economy are *Pareto efficient*, as defined in general welfare economics.

Definition 5.2. An *allocation* in the economy is defined by the vector $a \in \mathbb{R}^{K \times (1+M)} = (c_0^1, \ldots, c_{1M}^K)$, representing agent consumption in all states at all times. The associated utility of agent k is denoted $U^k(a)$.

Definition 5.3. An allocation is *feasible*, $a \in \mathcal{F}$, if

$$\sum_k c_0^k = C_0, \quad \sum_k c_{1m}^k = C_{1m}, \quad \forall m.$$

Definition 5.4. Allocation a is said to dominate b, $a \succ b$, if $U^k(a) \geq U^k(b)$ for all k, and $U^k(a) > U^k(b)$ for some k.

Definition 5.5. A feasible allocation a is *Pareto efficient* if there is no other feasible allocation b that dominates a,

$$\neg(\exists\, b \in \mathcal{F} : b \succ a).$$

Definition 5.6. The set of Pareto-efficient outcomes is denoted $\mathcal{E}$.

For the planner's problem, we use the K-dimensional unit simplex,

$$S^K = \left\{\lambda \in \mathbb{R}_{++}^K : \textstyle\sum_k \lambda^k = 1\right\},$$

and its closure $\bar{S}^K$.

Definition 5.7. Denote by $\mathcal{C}_\lambda$ the set of allocations that solve the central planner's problem with weights $\lambda \in \bar{S}^K$, and by

$$\mathcal{C} = \bigcup_{\lambda \in \bar{S}^K} \mathcal{C}_\lambda,$$

the set of all such allocations.

So far, we have assumed that all agents are allocated strictly positive endowments, which will correspond to $\lambda \in S^K$ in the planner's formulation. To also span the boundary points, we include economies in which agents with zero weights do not receive positive endowment allocations in any state at any time.

Lemma 5.2. *The set of solutions to the planner's problem is equivalent to the set of Pareto-efficient allocations,* $\mathcal{E} = \mathcal{C}$.

So the solutions to the central planner's problem cover all Pareto-efficient outcomes! We leave to proof of this result as an exercise.

We define the set of equilibrium allocations associated with initial endowments e (where $e \in \mathbb{R}_+^{(1+M)\times K}$ represents endowments of all agents at all times) by $\mathcal{M}_e$, and define $\mathcal{M} = \bigcup_e \mathcal{M}_e$, where the union is over all feasible endowments that are consistent with aggregate consumption constraints.

The first welfare theorem in this context states the following:

Theorem 5.6 (First welfare theorem). *Any equilibrium allocation is Pareto efficient in that it belongs to* $\mathcal{C}_\lambda$ *for some* $\lambda \in \bar{S}^K$, *so* $\mathcal{M} \subset \mathcal{C}$.

The second welfare theorem states the following:

Theorem 5.7 (Second welfare theorem). *Any Pareto-efficient allocation is supported by an equilibrium outcome,* $\mathcal{C} \subset \mathcal{M}$.

So these results show the equivalence between the centralized (planner's) and decentralized economy, in showing that the decentralized economy manages to implement the solution to the planner's problem, without involving the planner. The result in this context of the finance-oriented Arrow–Debreu economy is the financial market version of Adam Smith's "invisible hand." We can then summarize the equivalences in the formula

$$\mathcal{M} = \mathcal{E} = \mathcal{C}. \tag{5.20}$$

The proofs of the two welfare theorems are left as exercises.

That $\mathcal{M} = \mathcal{C}$ implies that we can find all equilibria by solving the planner's problem. This is a very useful method to find equilibria, since the planner's problem is often more straightforward to solve than finding the prices for which markets clear in all states at all times.

5.4.3 Equilibrium Stochastic Discount Factor

For simplicity, we assume that all agents agree on probabilities, $\pi_m^k = \pi_m$, for all k and m, and also have the same utility function, $u^k = u$, for all k.[7] From an agent's first-order condition, it follows that the pricing function for an AD security satisfies

$$\psi_m = \delta \frac{u'(c_{1m}^k)}{u'(c_0^k)} \pi_m, \quad \forall m. \tag{5.21}$$

We can use these prices as building blocks to calculate the price of any asset, with payoff $\widetilde{F}$ at $t = 1$,

$$p = \delta \sum_m \frac{u'(c_{1m}^k)}{u'(c_0^k)} \widetilde{F}_m \pi_m$$

[7]The argument goes through without this simplification, but needs to be agent specific in that case, which makes the interpretation less transparent.

$$= E\left[\delta \frac{u'(\tilde{c}_1^k)}{u'(c_0^k)} \tilde{F}\right]$$

$$= E[\tilde{m}\tilde{F}]. \tag{5.22}$$

The term $\tilde{m} = \delta \frac{u'(\tilde{c}_1^k)}{u'(c_0^k)}$ does not depend on k because all agents have the same FOC, up to a constant.[8] The term $\tilde{m}$ is a discount factor, but it is stochastic. It is therefore a *stochastic discount factor*, an SDF. We will return to the SDF later. The SDF is also called the *pricing kernel.*

5.4.4 Equity Premium Puzzle

The *equity premium puzzle* that arises in consumption-based asset pricing models was introduced by Mehra and Prescott (1985). It roughly says that an unreasonably high risk-aversion coefficient is needed to match the historical risk premium of stocks over the risk-free rate, $r^e = r^m - r^f$. As we discussed earlier, a risk premium of 6% or even higher is reasonable, based on historical data. A driving factor behind the puzzle is that aggregate consumption volatility in the economy has historically been very low. The equity premium puzzle pops up in many different model environments, and was originally noted in a dynamic setting. It is, however, inherently a cross-sectional phenomenon, and arises already in the Arrow–Debreu economy.

Consider an Arrow–Debreu economy with one agent, $K = 1$, who has CRRA utility,

$$U = \frac{c_0^{1-\gamma}}{1-\gamma} + \delta E\left[\frac{\tilde{c}_1^{1-\gamma}}{1-\gamma}\right]. \tag{5.23}$$

This is thus a *representative agent* environment—the agent is a representative for all the agents in the economy. One can always rewrite the AD economy with $K > 1$ agents as a representative agent economy, because of the first-order conditions that all line up for each agent in equilibrium, so they all behave in "the same" way. This argument is basically the same as the central planner's formulation of equilibrium. As shown in the exercises, in the specific case when all agents have CRRA utility with the same γ's, the representative agent also has CRRA utility with the same γ. So we may equivalently think of this example as one with many agents who all have CRRA utility and the same beliefs.

There is one unit of time-0 consumption, $C_0 = c_0 = 1$, and two possible future states with aggregate consumption,

$$C_{11} = c_{11} = 1 + \mu_0 + \sigma_0,$$

$$C_{12} = c_{12} = 1 + \mu_0 - \sigma_0,$$

which are equally likely, $\pi_1 = \pi_2 = \frac{1}{2}$. Equivalently, we can identify $C_{1,i}$ with the state ω_i, $\mathbb{P}(\omega_i) = \frac{1}{2}$, and write

$$\tilde{C}_1 = 1 + \mu_0 + \sigma_0\tilde{\theta}, \tag{5.24}$$

where $\tilde{\theta}(\omega_1) = 1$, $\tilde{\theta}(\omega_2) = -1$.

We assume that $\mu_0 = \mu\Delta t$, $\sigma_0 = \sigma\sqrt{\Delta t}$, and $\delta = 1 - \rho\Delta t$, where Δt is "small," so we may use Taylor expansions. Recall that

$$f(x + \Delta x) = f(x) + \Delta(x)f'(x) + \frac{1}{2}\Delta x^2 f''(x) + \text{h.o.t.},$$

[8] This is the main reason why the equilibrium can be characterized as a solution to the planner's problem for some planner's weights.

for a smooth function, f, where h.o.t. stands for higher-order terms, which in this context means of order Δx^3 or higher (see appendix C).

Let us calculate the risk-free rate and risk premium in this economy. From the SDF pricing formulation, we know that $u' = c^{-\gamma}$ will be important, and since $c \approx 1$, we therefore expand around $x = 0$:

$$(1+x)^{-\gamma} = 1 - \gamma x + \frac{1}{2}\gamma(\gamma+1)x^2 + \text{h.o.t.}$$

It will also be convenient to have the expansion for $1-\gamma$ rather than γ:

$$(1+x)^{1-\gamma} = 1 + (1-\gamma)x + \frac{1}{2}\gamma(\gamma-1)x^2 + \text{h.o.t.}$$

It is easy to see that $E[\widetilde{C}_1] = 1 + \mu\Delta t$, and $\text{Var}(\widetilde{C}_1) = \sigma^2\Delta t$. The state-price vector formula (5.21) now gives us

$$\begin{aligned}
\psi_1 &= \frac{1}{2}(1-\rho\Delta t)(1+\mu\Delta t + \sigma\sqrt{\Delta t})^{-\gamma} \\
&\approx \frac{1}{2}(1-\rho\Delta t)\Big(1 - \gamma(\mu\Delta t + \sigma\sqrt{\Delta t}) + \frac{1}{2}\gamma(\gamma+1)(\mu\Delta t + \sigma\sqrt{\Delta t})^2\Big) \\
&\approx \frac{1}{2}\Big(1 - \rho\Delta t - \gamma(\mu\Delta t + \sigma\sqrt{\Delta t}) + \frac{1}{2}\gamma(\gamma+1)\sigma^2\Delta t\Big), \\
\psi_2 &= \frac{1}{2}(1-\rho\Delta t)(1+\mu\Delta t - \sigma\sqrt{\Delta t})^{-\gamma} \\
&\approx \frac{1}{2}(1-\rho\Delta t)\Big(1 - \gamma(\mu\Delta t - \sigma\sqrt{\Delta t}) + \frac{1}{2}\gamma(\gamma+1)(\mu\Delta t - \sigma\sqrt{\Delta t})^2\Big) \\
&\approx \frac{1}{2}\Big(1 - \rho\Delta t - \gamma(\mu\Delta t - \sigma\sqrt{\Delta t}) + \frac{1}{2}\gamma(\gamma+1)\sigma^2\Delta t\Big).
\end{aligned}$$

Here we only kept terms up to order Δt, an approach that will be better explained later, in the continuous-time part of the text. The price of the risk-free bond, that pays 1 at time 1, is therefore, up to a first-order approximation,

$$p^f = \psi_1 + \psi_2 \approx 1 - r^f\Delta t, \quad \text{where } r^f = \rho + \gamma\mu - \frac{1}{2}\gamma(\gamma+1)\sigma^2. \tag{5.25}$$

Note that the $\sqrt{\Delta t}$ terms cancel out when summing the two state prices, which is why the expression does not contain a $\sqrt{\Delta t}$ term.

We do a similar calculation for the "stock market," which we think of as a firm that pays out aggregate consumption at $t = 1$ (more about this interpretation in the next section, when we introduce the Lucas model). We are thus looking at the stock price, right after the firm paid out the time-0 dividends of 1 unit of the consumption good, which is then according to the SDF formula (5.22),

$$\begin{aligned}
p^m &= (1-\rho\Delta t)E[\widetilde{C}_1^{-\gamma} \times \widetilde{C}_1] \\
&= (1-\rho\Delta t)E[\widetilde{C}_1^{1-\gamma}].
\end{aligned}$$

This expectation has the same form as the one for the bond, but with the parameter $-\gamma$ replaced by $1-\gamma$, so an identical argument as for the bond leads to

$$p^m \approx 1 - g\Delta t, \quad \text{where } g = \rho + (\gamma-1)\mu - \frac{1}{2}\gamma(\gamma-1)\sigma^2.$$

The expected gross return on the stock is then

$$1+r^m\Delta t=\frac{E[\widetilde{C}_1]}{P^m}\approx\frac{1+\mu\Delta t}{1-g\Delta t}\approx 1+(g+\mu)\Delta t, \tag{5.26}$$

leading to

$$r^m\approx g+\mu=\rho+\gamma\mu-\frac{1}{2}(\gamma-1)\sigma^2. \tag{5.27}$$

We arrive at the risk premium (equity premium)

$$r^m-r^f\approx\gamma\sigma^2. \tag{5.28}$$

Now, in the investor's portfolio choice problem, we used the market volatility of 15%, which together with a risk premium of 6% would correspond to an implied risk-aversion coefficient of $\frac{6\%}{(15\%)^2}\approx 2.67$. This seems quite reasonable. However, because this is a consumption-based asset pricing model, volatility should here be measured in real consumption terms, i.e., σ on the right-hand side is aggregate *consumption volatility*, which is known to be much lower than market volatility. A reasonable estimate of aggregate consumption volatility may be about $\sigma\approx 2\%$ per year, which when plugged into (5.28) gives us the implied risk-aversion coefficient

$$\gamma=\frac{6\%}{(2\%)^2}=150.$$

This is *extremely high*, which is why the equity premium puzzle is a puzzle. For example, a CRRA investor with a risk-aversion coefficient of 150 and wealth of $100,000 would not accept a bet with a 75% chance of doubling wealth, and a 25% risk of losing $1000. It seems quite unreasonable that investors in the market would be so risk averse. Indeed, Mehra and Prescott (1985) viewed any risk-aversion coefficient above 10 as unreasonably high.

Moreover, if we are willing to go with such a high risk-aversion coefficient as $\gamma=150$ to match the equity premium, this introduces a bunch of other challenges, the most immediate one being the *risk-free rate puzzle*. Specifically, the formula for the risk-free rate (5.25) is quadratic in γ, and therefore highly sensitive for high values of the parameter. If we plug in $\sigma=2\%$, $\rho=5\%$, and $\mu=1\%$, reasonable numbers for consumption volatility, personal discount rate, and the real growth rate of consumption, respectively, we end up with $r^f=-298\%$. That is an extreme value for the annualized risk-free discount rate!

For knife-edge cases of parameter values, we can get reasonable risk-free rates. For example, if we change consumption volatility to $\sigma=1.16\%$ in this example, we get $r^f\approx 2.6\%$. However, any small changes in parameters immediately lead to extreme values of r^f, either positive or negative. As a consequence, in a world where μ and σ vary over time, we would expect the discount rate—or specifically the short rate in a dynamic setting—to be extremely volatile, introducing yet another puzzle. We conclude that "solving" the equity premium puzzle by jacking up the representative investor's risk-aversion coefficient does not seem like the right approach.

5.4.5 HARA Utility and Habit Formation

A potential resolution to the equity premium puzzle may be to move away from the CRRA utility specification. Indeed, if we replace the CRRA utility function with *HARA utility* (where HARA stands for hyperbolic absolute risk aversion)

$$u(c)=\frac{(c-k)^{1-\gamma}}{1-\gamma},\quad 0<k<1,$$

things begin to look better. With the new specification, the SDF pricing relation becomes

$$p = (1-\rho\Delta t)E\Big[\Big(\frac{\widetilde{C}_1 - k}{1-k}\Big)^{-\gamma}\widetilde{F}\Big],$$

and the state prices are

$$\begin{aligned}\psi_1 &= \frac{1}{2}(1-\rho\Delta t)\Big(\frac{1+\mu\Delta t+\sigma\sqrt{\Delta t}-k}{1-k}\Big)^{-\gamma}\\ &= \frac{1}{2}(1-\rho\Delta t)\Big(1+\frac{\mu\Delta t+\sigma\sqrt{\Delta t}}{1-k}\Big)^{-\gamma}\\ &\approx \frac{1}{2}\Big(1-\rho\Delta t-\frac{\gamma}{1-k}(\mu\Delta t+\sigma\sqrt{\Delta t})+\frac{1}{2}\gamma(\gamma+1)\frac{\sigma^2}{(1-k)^2}\Delta t\Big),\\ \psi_2 &= \frac{1}{2}(1-\rho\Delta t)\Big(\frac{1+\mu\Delta t-\sigma\sqrt{\Delta t}-k}{1-k}\Big)^{-\gamma}\\ &= \frac{1}{2}(1-\rho\Delta t)\Big(1+\frac{\mu\Delta t-\sigma\sqrt{\Delta t}}{1-k}\Big)^{-\gamma}\\ &\approx \frac{1}{2}\Big(1-\rho\Delta t-\frac{\gamma}{1-k}(\mu\Delta t-\sigma\sqrt{\Delta t})+\frac{1}{2}\gamma(\gamma+1)\frac{\sigma^2}{(1-k)^2}\Delta t\Big).\end{aligned}$$

Both mean and volatility are thus magnified by a factor of $\frac{1}{1-k}$ in this case, $\mu \mapsto \frac{\mu}{1-k}$, $\sigma \mapsto \frac{\sigma}{1-k}$, in the state-price formulas. Intuitively, the agent is more risk averse than the CRRA agent, being closer to the subsistence level, k, where marginal utility becomes infinite. The formula for the risk-free rate becomes

$$r^f = \rho + \frac{\gamma}{1-k}\mu - \frac{1}{2}\gamma(\gamma+1)\frac{\sigma^2}{(1-k)^2}. \tag{5.29}$$

The price of the market is

$$\begin{aligned}P^m &= (1-\rho\Delta t)E\Big[\Big(\frac{\widetilde{C}_1-k}{1-k}\Big)^{-\gamma}\widetilde{C}_1\Big]\\ &\approx (1-\rho\Delta t)\frac{1}{2}\Big(1-\frac{\gamma}{1-k}(\mu\Delta t+\sigma\sqrt{\Delta t})+\frac{1}{2}\gamma(\gamma+1)\frac{\sigma^2}{(1-k)^2}\Delta t\Big)(1+\mu\Delta t+\sigma\sqrt{\Delta t})\\ &\quad+(1-\rho\Delta t)\frac{1}{2}\Big(1-\frac{\gamma}{1-k}(\mu\Delta t-\sigma\sqrt{\Delta t})+\frac{1}{2}\gamma(\gamma+1)\frac{\sigma^2}{(1-k)^2}\Delta t\Big)(1+\mu\Delta t-\sigma\sqrt{\Delta t})\\ &\approx 1-\underbrace{\Big(\rho+\Big(\frac{\gamma}{1-k}-1\Big)\mu-\frac{1}{2}\gamma(\gamma+1)\frac{\sigma^2}{(1-k)^2}+\frac{\gamma}{1-k}\sigma^2\Big)}_{g}\Delta t,\end{aligned}$$

and the associated expected returns

$$r^m = g+\mu \approx \rho + \frac{\gamma}{1-k}\mu + \sigma^2\Big(\frac{\gamma}{1-k}-\frac{1}{2}\gamma(\gamma+1)\frac{1}{(1-k)^2}\Big).$$

This leads us to the equity premium

$$r^m - r^f \approx \frac{\gamma}{1-k}\sigma^2.$$

So the closer k is to 1, the more the equity premium increases. If $k=\frac{14}{15}$, $\gamma=10$ is sufficient to match the equity premium with the previously used parameters.

This seems like an interesting approach, but in a dynamic environment we cannot really expect k to have a major impact in the longer run. Indeed, as the economy keeps growing, the impact of k decreases. For example, if $\widetilde{C}_0$ is 2, k's impact effectively decreases from a 15-times amplification to less than 2 times. A dynamic setup is needed to sort out the details, but the intuition for why HARA utility will not resolve the equity premium puzzle in the long run is clear already in this setting.

The idea works better in the dynamic setting if the agent increases k as C increases. For example, if we set $k(C) = k \times C$, $k > 0$, we could have the agent relatively close to the subsistence level all the time. This is in some sense the idea behind *habit formation* models; see Abel (1990) and Campbell and Cochrane (1999). Under habit formation, agents find it excessively painful to revise down consumption levels below a habit level. For example, the agent's habit level can be defined as some weighted average of recent consumption levels. One separates here between *internal habit* models, where it is the agent's own average consumption that matters for the habit level, and *external habit* models (keeping up with the Joneses preferences), where it is the aggregate average consumption that determines the habit level. Campbell and Cochrane (1999) find that the equity premium puzzle, the risk-free rate puzzle, and also countercyclical variations in risk premia can be explained by a model with an external habit specification.

5.4.6 Rare Disasters

A somewhat related explanation relies on rare catastrophic disasters, which bring the high-curvature part of the CRRA utility function close to zero into play; see Barro (2006). Let us assume the following possible consumption outcomes:

$$\widetilde{C}_1 = \begin{cases} 1 + (\mu + (1-k)\lambda)\Delta t + \sigma\sqrt{\Delta t}, & \text{with probability } \frac{1}{2}(1-\lambda\Delta t), \\ 1 + (\mu + (1-k)\lambda)\Delta t - \sigma\sqrt{\Delta t}, & \text{with probability } \frac{1}{2}(1-\lambda\Delta t), \\ k & \text{with probability } \lambda\Delta t, \end{cases}$$

where $\lambda\Delta t$ represents the risk for a catastrophe that brings consumption down to $k \ll 1$. The growth coefficient in the case of no catastrophe has been adjusted upward so that $E[\widetilde{C}_1] = 1 + \mu\Delta t$, as before. Moreover, for small Δt, we get $\text{Var}(\widetilde{C}_1) \approx (\sigma^2 + (1-k)^2\lambda)\Delta t$, unconditionally. Conditional on there being no catastrophe, $\text{Var}(\widetilde{C}_1 | \text{no catastrophe}) = \sigma^2\Delta t$. For sufficiently small λ, the unconditional and conditional volatilities are very close, allowing us to bypass the discussion of which measure an econometrician would actually use when estimating consumption volatility.

Now, the Taylor expansion argument can still be made for states 1 and 2, whereas it will not work for the catastrophic state since $k \ll 1$. This leads to the approximate state prices

$$\begin{aligned}
\psi_1 &= \frac{1}{2}(1-\lambda\Delta t)(1-\rho\Delta t)\left(1 + (\mu + (1-k)\lambda)\Delta t + \sigma\sqrt{\Delta t}\right)^{-\gamma} \\
&\approx \frac{1}{2}\left(1 - \lambda\Delta t - \rho\Delta t - \gamma\left((\mu + (1-k)\lambda)\Delta t + \sigma\sqrt{\Delta t}\right) + \frac{1}{2}\gamma(\gamma+1)\sigma^2\Delta t\right), \\
\psi_2 &= \frac{1}{2}(1-\lambda\Delta t)(1-\rho\Delta t)\left(1 + (\mu + (1-k)\lambda)\Delta t - \sigma\sqrt{\Delta t}\right)^{-\gamma} \\
&\approx \frac{1}{2}\left(1 - \lambda\Delta t - \rho\Delta t - \gamma\left((\mu + (1-k)\lambda)\Delta t - \sigma\sqrt{\Delta t}\right) + \frac{1}{2}\gamma(\gamma+1)\sigma^2\Delta t\right), \\
\psi_3 &= \lambda\Delta t(1-\rho\Delta t)k^{-\gamma} \\
&\approx \lambda k^{-\gamma}\Delta t.
\end{aligned}$$

The bond price is

$$P^f = \psi_1 + \psi_2 + \psi_3 \approx 1 - \left(\lambda + \rho + \gamma(\mu + (1-k)\lambda) - \frac{1}{2}\gamma(\gamma+1)\sigma^2 - \lambda k^{-\gamma}\right)\Delta t,$$

so the risk-free rate is

$$r^f \approx \rho + \gamma\mu - \frac{1}{2}\gamma(\gamma+1)\sigma^2 + \lambda(1 - k^{-\gamma} + \gamma(1-k)).$$

We see that the difference compared with the market without catastrophic risk (in which case $\lambda = 0$) is the term $\lambda F(k;\gamma)$, where $F(k;\gamma) = 1 - k^{-\gamma} + \gamma(1-k)$. One verifies that $F(1;\gamma) = 0$, and $F_k > 0$ (recall that $0 < k \leq 1$), so F is negative, which means that the risk-free rate is lower than in the economy with no catastrophic events. Naturally, risk-averse agents value safety higher when catastrophic risk is present. This increases the price of risk-free bonds, and thus lowers the risk-free rate.

For the price of the market, we get

$$\begin{aligned}
P^m &= (1-\rho\Delta t)E[(\widetilde{C}_1)^{-\gamma}\widetilde{C}_1] \\
&\approx (1-\rho\Delta t - \lambda\Delta)\frac{1}{2}\left(1 - \gamma\left((\mu + (1-k)\lambda)\Delta t + \sigma\sqrt{\Delta t}\right) + \frac{1}{2}\gamma(\gamma+1)\sigma^2\Delta t\right) \\
&\quad \times \left(1 + (\mu + (1-k)\lambda)\Delta t + \sigma\sqrt{\Delta t}\right) \\
&\quad + (1-\rho\Delta t - \lambda\Delta)\frac{1}{2}\left(1 - \gamma\left((\mu + (1-k)\lambda)\Delta t - \sigma\sqrt{\Delta t}\right) + \frac{1}{2}\gamma(\gamma+1)\sigma^2\Delta t\right) \\
&\quad \times \left(1 + (\mu + (1-k)\lambda)\Delta t - \sigma\sqrt{\Delta t}\right) \\
&\quad + \lambda\Delta t k^{1-\gamma} \\
&\approx 1 - \left(\lambda + \rho + (\gamma-1)(\mu + (1-k)\lambda) - \frac{1}{2}\gamma(\gamma-1)\sigma^2 - \lambda k^{1-\gamma}\right)\Delta t,
\end{aligned}$$

and the associated expected market return, taking into account that $E[\widetilde{C}_1] = 1 + \mu\Delta t$,

$$r^m \approx \lambda + \rho + \gamma\mu + \lambda(\gamma-1)(1-k) - \frac{1}{2}\gamma(\gamma-1)\sigma^2 - \lambda k^{1-\gamma}.$$

We arrive at an equity premium of

$$r^m - r^f \approx \gamma\sigma^2 + \lambda(k^{-\gamma} - 1)(1-k).$$

For example, the parameter values $\mu = 1\%$, $\rho = 6\%$, $\lambda = 0.5\%$, $k = 0.53$, $\sigma = 2\%$, $\gamma = 5$ lead under these assumptions to an equity premium of about 5.6% and a risk-free rate of about 0.1%. So adding a rare event risk of a catastrophe that cuts the size of the economy in roughly half, and that occurs on average once every 200 years, allows us to roughly match the equity premium and risk-free rate, with a relatively low risk-aversion coefficient of $\gamma = 5$. Of course, actually estimating λ and k from data will be very difficult, if such shocks only occur on average once every other century. In figure 5.2, the value of λF is shown for different values of k (x-axis) and γ (different lines), for $\lambda = 0.5\%$.

5.4.7 Incomplete Markets

Another potential "fix" for the equity premium puzzle is to deviate from the complete market assumption. If markets are incomplete, individual agents may face more risk than what is shown from aggregate variables. A modestly risk-averse agent who faces a lot of consumption risk may

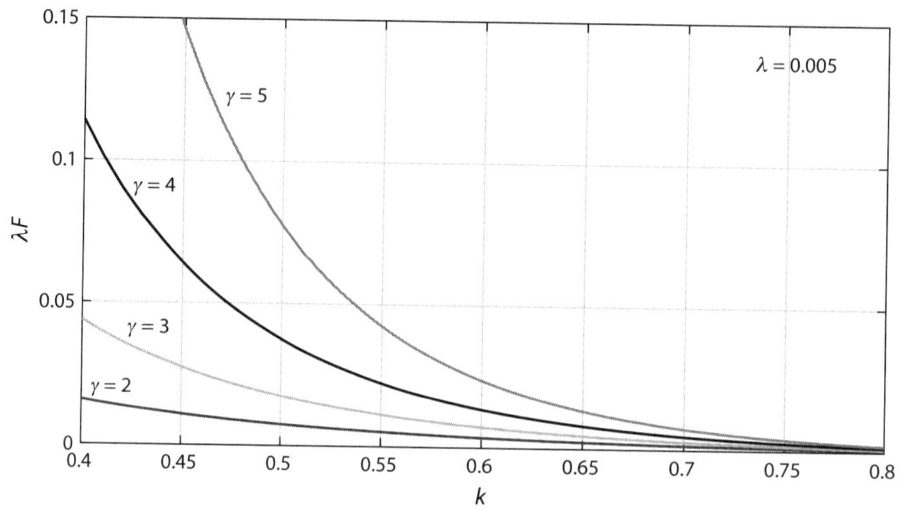

Figure 5.2: Contribution to equity premium by λF, for different k and γ.

look very risk averse when the behavior is calibrated in terms of the market's smooth aggregate consumption. This idea of using *incomplete markets* to explain pricing relations that do not fit well with the representative agent setting was analyzed in Constantinides and Duffie (1996), in a dynamic setting. They show that, with the appropriate form of individual agent shocks, any pricing kernel can be justified in terms of aggregate variables, given that some technical conditions are satisfied. We study here a simplified static version of their argument, and avoid getting into the technical details needed for the analysis to be formally justified.

The aggregate economic environment is the same as before, with aggregate consumption described by (5.24). There is a very large number of ex ante identical agents, $k \in \mathcal{K}$, each with the CRRA utility specification (5.23), and who all have the same δ and γ. Aggregate consumption is defined, in average terms, as $\widetilde{C}_t = \frac{1}{|\mathcal{K}|}\sum_{k\in\mathcal{K}} \tilde{c}_t^k$, where $\tilde{c}_t^k$ is agent k's consumption at time t. In the complete market setting, the representative agent would then also have CRRA utility, leading to the model that we studied before, with the associated equity premium puzzle. At $t=0$, each agent receives an endowment of one unit of the consumption good.

As a point of departure from the representative agent framework, let us assume that the agents are exposed to idiosyncratic endowment shocks at $t=1$, so that an agent's shock at $t=1$ is

$$e_1^k = (\tilde{\xi}^k - 1)\widetilde{C}_1.$$

We define these idiosyncratic shocks in a way that they, by the law of large numbers (LLN), exactly cancel out.[9] Now assume that

$$\tilde{\xi}^k = e^{\tilde{\eta}^k \tilde{y} - \frac{1}{2}\tilde{y}^2},$$

where $\tilde{y}$ is some random variable, common across all agents, which may or may not be related to aggregate consumption, $\widetilde{C}$. The random variables $\tilde{\eta}^k \sim N(0,1)$ are jointly independent, and independent of $\tilde{y}$.

[9]Technically, we need to assume that there are an infinite number of agents for the LLN to hold, but it may be easier to think of a very large but finite number, so the LLN approximately holds.

Note that

$$E[\tilde{\xi}^k|\tilde{y}] = E[e^{\tilde{\eta}^k\tilde{y}-\frac{1}{2}\tilde{y}^2}|\tilde{y}] = e^{-\frac{1}{2}\tilde{y}^2}E[e^{\tilde{\eta}^k\tilde{y}}|\tilde{y}] = e^{-\frac{1}{2}\tilde{y}^2} \times e^{\frac{1}{2}\tilde{y}^2} = 1,$$

regardless of the realization of $\tilde{y}$. The LLN conditional on $\tilde{y}$ then gives us

$$\frac{1}{|\mathcal{K}|}\sum_{k\in\mathcal{K}}\tilde{\xi}^k|\tilde{y} =_{\text{a.s.}} 1,$$

and as long as $\tilde{y}$ has a sufficiently thin-tailed distribution, such that unconditional expectations are well defined and the law of iterated expectations (LIE) holds, we get unconditionally

$$\frac{1}{|\mathcal{K}|}\sum_{k\in\mathcal{K}}\tilde{\xi}^k =_{\text{a.s.}} 1$$

and

$$\frac{1}{|\mathcal{K}|}\sum_{k} e_1^k =_{\text{a.s.}} 0.$$

So the endowment shocks are idiosyncratic in that they perfectly cancel out in aggregate.

Individual agents will be affected by the shocks though. Specifically, we assume that there is no market for AD securities on these shocks, so there is no way for the agents to hedge the shocks. Each agent therefore values an asset in line with his/her optimization FOCs, and since all agents are in the same position at $t=0$ (at $t=1$ they will obviously be in different situations because of the different realizations of the endowment shocks), it is natural for us to explore an equilibrium in which no trade occurs at $t=0$.

Specifically, since all agents are ex ante in the same position at $t=0$, there is no one who can provide them with another aggregate "consumption mix," should they wish to adjust because of their increased risk exposure. Instead, prices must adjust so that all agents choose not to trade. In equilibrium, agent k's consumption is therefore 1 at $t=0$, and at $t=1$ it is

$$\tilde{c}_1^k = \widetilde{C}_1 + \tilde{e}^k = \tilde{\xi}^k\widetilde{C}_1.$$

Any agent's FOC (using that $c_0^k = 1$ for all k) then leads to the pricing equation

$$\begin{aligned}
p &= E\left[\delta\frac{u'(\tilde{c}_1^k)}{u'(c_0^k)}\widetilde{F}\right]\\
&= E[\delta(\tilde{\xi}^k\widetilde{C}_1)^{-\gamma}\widetilde{F}]\\
&= E[\delta e^{-\gamma(\tilde{\eta}^k\tilde{y}-\frac{1}{2}\tilde{y}^2)}\widetilde{C}_1^{-\gamma}\widetilde{F}]\\
&= E[\delta e^{-\gamma(\tilde{\eta}^k\tilde{y}-\frac{1}{2}\tilde{y}^2)}\widetilde{C}_1^{-\gamma}\widetilde{F}]\\
&= E[E[\delta e^{-\gamma(\tilde{\eta}^k\tilde{y}-\frac{1}{2}\tilde{y}^2)}\widetilde{C}_1^{-\gamma}\widetilde{F}|\widetilde{C}_1,\tilde{y}]]\\
&= E[\delta e^{\frac{1}{2}\gamma(\gamma+1)\tilde{y}^2}\widetilde{C}_1^{-\gamma}\widetilde{F}].
\end{aligned}$$

This pricing equation must hold for all assets, $\widetilde{F}$, whose payoffs are not allowed to depend on the realization of $\tilde{\xi}^k$ risk (we do not allow $\tilde{\xi}^k$ dependence since the market is incomplete). It follows that the pricing kernel in this economy is[10]

$$\widetilde{m} = \delta e^{\frac{1}{2}\gamma(\gamma+1)\tilde{y}^2}\widetilde{C}_1^{-\gamma}.$$

In principle, we can generate *any* pricing kernel, depending on how we define $\tilde{y}$. In particular, if $\tilde{y}^2$ is high when $\widetilde{C}_1$ is low, then endowment shocks tend to be very risky exactly when agents are most risk averse because aggregate consumption is low. In this case, the pricing kernel will look "more risk averse," i.e., as if agents have higher γ's than they actually do. Indeed, if we assume $\tilde{y}^2 = A - b\ln(\widetilde{C}_1)$, where A is a positive constant, sufficiently large so that $\tilde{y}^2$ is always positive, we get

$$\widetilde{m} = \hat{\delta}\widetilde{C}_1^{-\frac{1}{2}b\gamma(\gamma+1)}\widetilde{C}_1^{-\gamma},$$

where $\hat{\delta} = \delta e^{\frac{1}{2}\gamma(\gamma+1)A}$, so the stochastic discount factor is the same as in a representative agent economy, but with associated "risk-aversion coefficient"

$$\hat{\gamma} = \gamma + \frac{1}{2}b\gamma(\gamma+1).$$

With our previous parameter values, $\sigma = 2\%$, $r^m - r^f = 6\%$, one verifies that when $b = 5$, an individual agent risk-aversion coefficient of $\gamma \approx 7.08$ leads to $\hat{\gamma} = 150$, and thus matches the equity premium.

Since any pricing kernel (satisfying the technical conditions) can be generated with this "trick," it seems like incomplete markets can be used to explain any pricing relation. However, note that the assumptions we make about $\tilde{y}^2$ are not innocent. Indeed, they map to unhedgeable risk exposure at the individual level. What may these idiosyncratic shocks represent in practice? One major source of individual risk is labor income. For the incomplete market explanation to be a good candidate for explaining asset pricing puzzles, the assumptions about $\tilde{y}^2$ should then map well to the properties of labor income shock distributions in the real economy, as discussed in Constantinides and Duffie (1996).

5.4.8 Epstein–Zin Preferences

A fourth potential explanation of the equity premium puzzle is long-run risk, in combination with Epstein–Zin preferences, as proposed in Bansal and Yaron (2005). Recall that Epstein–Zin preferences allow us to separate risk aversion from intertemporal substitution, i.e., to separate the risk-aversion coefficient γ from the EIS, ψ. This fact alone is helpful in addressing the risk-free rate puzzle, since the equilibrium risk-free rate will depend on ψ, as well as γ, whereas the risk premium only depends on γ. So one can "jack up" γ without getting extreme values of the risk-free rate.

To see what the pricing kernel looks like in the AD economy with EZ preferences, we begin with the representative agent preference specification in (3.7), here repeated,

$$U(c_0, c_1) = V^{\frac{1}{1-\rho}} = \left(c_0^{1-\rho} + \delta E[\tilde{c}_1^{1-\gamma}]^{\frac{1-\rho}{1-\gamma}}\right)^{\frac{1}{1-\rho}},$$

where $\rho = \frac{1}{\psi}$ is the EIS, and it is also convenient to define $\theta = \frac{1-\gamma}{1-\frac{1}{\psi}}$, a parameter that equals 1 in the special case of CRRA preferences, i.e. when $\gamma = \frac{1}{\psi}$. In equilibrium, the representative agent

[10]Technically, there are many different pricing kernels because the market is incomplete, a point we return to later in this text. But this is one valid pricing kernel.

chooses to consume aggregate consumption, $c_0 = C_0$ and $\tilde{c}_1 = \widetilde{C}_1$, so any additional asset, which costs 1 at $t=0$ and has returns $\widetilde{R}$ in the next period, must be in zero demand. In other words,

$$\arg\max_\epsilon U(c_0 - \epsilon, c_1 + \epsilon\widetilde{R}) = \arg\max_\epsilon \left((c_0-\epsilon)^{1-\rho} + \delta E_0[(c_1+\epsilon\widetilde{R})^{1-\gamma}]^{\frac{1-\rho}{1-\gamma}}\right)^{1/(1-\rho)}$$

is realized at $\epsilon = 0$ for any such asset, leading to the FOC

$$0 = \frac{1}{\rho} V^{1/(1-\rho)-1}\left((1-\rho)C_0^{-\rho} - \delta\frac{1-\rho}{1-\gamma} E_0[(1-\gamma)\widetilde{C}_1^{-\gamma}\widetilde{R}]E_0[\widetilde{C}_1^{1-\gamma}]^{\frac{1-\rho}{1-\gamma}-1}\right).$$

Thus,

$$C_0^{-\rho} = \delta E_0[\widetilde{C}_1^{-\gamma}\widetilde{R}]E_0[\widetilde{C}_1^{1-\gamma}]^{\frac{1-\rho}{1-\gamma}-1}, \tag{5.30}$$

in turn leading to the EZ equilibrium SDF equation

$$1 = \delta E_0\left[\left(\frac{\widetilde{C}_1}{C_0}\right)^{-\gamma}\widetilde{R}\right]E_0\left[\left(\frac{\widetilde{C}_1}{C_0}\right)^{1-\gamma}\right]^{\frac{1-\rho}{1-\gamma}-1}. \tag{5.31}$$

Now, $\widetilde{R} = \frac{\widetilde{F}}{p}$, so the EZ version of (5.22) becomes

$$\begin{aligned} p &= \delta E_0\left[\left(\frac{\widetilde{C}_1}{C_0}\right)^{-\gamma}\widetilde{F}\right]E_0\left[\left(\frac{\widetilde{C}_1}{C_0}\right)^{1-\gamma}\right]^{\frac{1-\rho}{1-\gamma}-1} \\ &= E_0[\widetilde{m}\times\widetilde{F}], \end{aligned}$$

where

$$\widetilde{m} = \delta k\left(\frac{\widetilde{C}_1}{C_0}\right)^{-\gamma}, \quad k = E_0\left[\left(\frac{\widetilde{C}_1}{C_0}\right)^{1-\gamma}\right]^{\frac{1-\rho}{1-\gamma}-1}. \tag{5.32}$$

The extra k factor is what distinguishes the SDF in the EZ case from the CRRA case.

Now consider our economy with aggregate consumption according to (5.24), with the "small" parameters $\mu_0 = \mu\Delta t$, $\sigma_0 = \sigma\sqrt{\Delta t}$, and $\delta = 1 - \hat{\rho}\Delta t$. Note that here we use $\hat{\rho}$ to define the personal discount factor, since the term ρ is already "used" in the definition of EZ preferences. A Taylor expansion, similar to what we did before, leads to

$$\begin{aligned} k &\approx 1 + \left(\frac{1-\rho}{1-\gamma} - 1\right)\left((1-\gamma)\mu - \frac{1}{2}\gamma(1-\gamma)\sigma^2\right)\Delta t \\ &= 1 - (\rho-\gamma)\left(\mu - \frac{1}{2}\gamma\sigma^2\right)\Delta t \\ &\stackrel{\text{def}}{=} 1 - q\Delta t, \end{aligned}$$

where the factor

$$q = (\rho-\gamma)\left(\mu - \frac{1}{2}\gamma\sigma^2\right)$$

has the same effect on all prices of securities that pay out at $t=1$. If $q>0$, all prices decrease, i.e., their returns increase compared with the corresponding CRRA economy. If $q<0$, prices increase so returns decrease.

Adjusting for the effect of k on the risk-free rate, we add $q\Delta t$ to the risk-free rate from the CRRA economy, to get

$$\begin{aligned} r^f &\approx q + \hat{\rho} + \gamma\mu - \frac{1}{2}\gamma(\gamma+1)\sigma^2 \\ &= \hat{\rho} + \rho\mu - \frac{1}{2}\gamma(\rho+1)\sigma^2 \\ &= \hat{\rho} + \frac{1}{\psi}\mu - \frac{1}{2}\gamma\Big(\frac{1}{\psi}+1\Big)\sigma^2. \end{aligned}$$

Since all prices change with the same factor, k, compared with the CRRA economy, the equity premium remains the same under EZ preferences in this case:

$$r^m - r^f \approx \gamma\sigma^2.$$

So, if we use the same parameters as before, $\hat{\rho} = 5\%$, $\gamma = 150$, $\sigma = 2\%$, $\mu = 1\%$, and in addition choose the "moderate" value $\psi = 1$ (we do not really have an intuition for what a reasonable value of ψ is at this point, but 1 seems moderate, at least compared to 150...), we get

$$r^f = 5\% + 1 \times 1\% - \frac{1}{2} \times 150 \times 2 \times (2\%)^2 = 0,$$

which seems quite reasonable. So the risk-free rate puzzle seems to be resolved by using EZ preferences.

However, $\gamma = 150$ is still a very large number. So far, we have seen nothing that helps resolve the equity premium puzzle by switching to EZ preferences. To appreciate the argument in Bansal and Yaron (2005), a dynamic model is needed which is right now outside the scope of our analysis. We will return to this question later, when we have introduced the dynamic model.

5.4.9 Lucas Model

Our general equilibrium approach so far has started with a given set of prices, which agents take as given (price-taking behavior), used these prices to derive individuals' demand functions, and then found prices for which all markets clear. A clever alternative approach, taken in Lucas (1978), starts with the equilibrium condition in the exchange economy, namely that demand equals supply, assumes the existence of a representative investor—which could, e.g., be guaranteed because markets are complete—so that the stochastic discount factor, i.e., the pricing relation that needs to be satisfied because of an agent's FOC (the Euler equation) is known, and then uses this formulation to calculate prices. This is the *Lucas tree economy* approach.

Following Lucas (1978), we assume an infinite horizon economy with discrete time, $t = 0, 1, 2 \ldots$. There is one consumption good, and the random aggregate supply at time t of this good is Y_t. There is also an infinitely lived (price-taking) representative agent with utility

$$U = E_0\left[\sum_{t=0}^{\infty} \delta^t u(c_t)\right].$$

Here, u is increasing, continuously differentiable, concave, bounded, and we normalize such that $u(0) = 0$. Note that these assumptions exclude some of the common utility functions we use in finance, e.g., log-utility. The variable Y_t is exogenously specified. Indeed, this is a dynamic *exchange economy*.[11]

[11] The other part of the exchange economy assumption, that the good can be transferred between agents, is needed to justify the representative agent setting if there are multiple agents in the model.

There are N firms (trees), such that

- in each period, firms produce the consumption good (the fruit),
- firm n's production is $y_{n,t}$,
- total production is

$$Y_t = \sum_n y_{n,t}.$$

In equilibrium, consumption must equal production in each period:

$$Y_t = c_t, \quad \forall t.$$

Each firm is publicly traded, with one share available in total. The consumption good is paid as a dividend to the owner, $D_{n,t} = y_{n,t}$. The price of firm n at time t is $p_{n,t}$. This price is measured in units of consumption good (at t). The total price of all firms at time t is

$$P_t = \sum_n p_{n,t}.$$

The representative agent is a price taker, who knows the price and dividend process. The number of shares in firm n owned by the representative agent at t is $z_{n,t}$. The agent's intertemporal budget constraint is then

$$c_t + \sum_n p_{n,t} z_{n,t+1} = \sum_n y_{n,t} z_{n,t} + \sum_n p_{n,t} z_{n,t}.$$

This leads us to the following optimization problem for the agent:

$$\max_{\{z_{n,t}\}_{n,t}, \{c_t\}_t} \quad E_0\left[\sum_{t=0}^{\infty} \delta^t u(c_t)\right],$$

subject to

$$c_t + \sum_n p_{n,t} z_{n,t+1} = \sum_n y_{n,t} z_{n,t} + \sum_n p_{n,t} z_{n,t}, \quad \forall t.$$

Note that (pre-consumption) wealth is $W_t = \sum_n z_{n,t}(p_{n,t} + y_{n,t})$, i.e., the right-hand side of the budget constraint above.

In the agent's maximization problem, (s)he behaves as if there is full freedom to choose consumption and investments, period by period, as long as the intertemporal budget constraint is satisfied. However, in equilibrium, prices must be such that (s)he chooses to consume $c_t = Y_t$ in each period, and demands exactly one share of each stock in each period. This leads to the following definition of equilibrium:

Definition 5.8. An equilibrium is defined by price processes, $\{p_{n,t}\}_{n,t}$, $n = 1, \dots, N$, $t = 0, 1, \dots,$ such that

- the agent's demands for financial and real goods are based on solving the optimization problem;
- markets clear, so that demand equals supply:
  - financial assets: $z_{n,t} = 1$ for all n and t,
  - real goods: $c_t = Y_t$ for all t.

This looks like a really complicated problem. The trick is to start with the equilibrium consumption and recover the pricing relations that follow from the agent's FOC that are satisfied.

Assuming an equilibrium exists, the agent's FOC between periods t and $t+1$ states that (s)he is indifferent between consuming a small amount, ϵ, more at t, and instead investing the same amount in asset n, holding on to the additional position for a period and then selling and consuming the revenues instead, i.e.,

$$u'(c_t) = E_t\left[\delta u'(c_{t+1})\frac{y_{n,t+1}+p_{n,t+1}}{p_{n,t}}\right].$$

This is the agent's intertemporal *Euler equation*. Equivalently, since $c_t \equiv Y_t$,

$$p_{n,t} = E_t\left[\delta\frac{u'(Y_{t+1})}{u'(Y_t)}(y_{n,t+1}+p_{n,t+1})\right].$$

Now we define

$$m_{t,t+\tau} = \delta^\tau\frac{u'(Y_{t+\tau})}{u'(Y_t)}, \tag{5.33}$$

and we can then write

$$p_{n,t} = E_t[m_{t,t+1}(y_{n,t+1}+p_{n,t+1})].$$

We also write m_t for $m_{t,t+1}$. It follows that

$$m_{t,t+\tau} = m_t \times m_{t+1} \times \cdots \times m_{t+\tau-1},$$

from a so-called telescoping product argument.

Now,

$$p_{n,t+1} = E_{t+1}[m_{t+1,t+2}(y_{n,t+2}+p_{n,t+2})],$$

so we can use the LIE to show that

$$\begin{aligned}
p_{n,t} &= E_t[m_{t,t+1}(y_{n,t+1}+p_{n,t+1})]\\
&= E_t\big[m_{t,t+1}\big(y_{n,t+1}+E_{t+1}[m_{t+1,t+2}(y_{n,t+2}+p_{n,t+2})]\big)\big]\\
&= E_t[m_{t,t+1}(y_{n,t+1}+m_{t+1,t+2}(y_{n,t+2}+p_{n,t+2}))]\\
&= E_t[m_{t,t+1}y_{n,t+1}+m_{t,t+2}(y_{n,t+2}+p_{n,t+2})],
\end{aligned}$$

and applying the same argument iteratively (under some technical growth conditions that ensure convergence) leads to

$$p_{n,t} = E_t\left[\sum_{s=t+1}^{\infty} m_{t,s}y_{n,s}\right].$$

This expression looks very similar to the standard net present value (NPV) investment formula, with the differences that

- $m_{t,t+\tau}$ replaces the τ-period discount factor, $\frac{1}{(1+r_{t,\tau})^\tau}$;
- $m_{t,t+\tau}$ needs to be inside the expectation operator, since $m_{t,t+\tau}$ is stochastic.

The pricing relationship holds for all assets in the market, as long as equilibrium exists. The process m_t, $t=0,1,\ldots$, is called the *stochastic discount factor* (SDF) process. Technically, it is a one-period conditional stochastic discount factor process. We will also later use a multiperiod version, M_t, defined by $M_0=1$, and $M_t = m_{0,t} = \prod_{s=1}^{t} m_{s-1,s}$, so that $m_t = \frac{M_{t+1}}{M_t}$. These different versions of the SDF are equivalent in discrete time. In continuous time, the M_t process will be more straightforward to use.

5.4.10 Existence of Equilibrium in the Lucas Model

The argument so far has been made under the assumption that equilibrium exists. Much of the analysis in Lucas (1978) concerns showing the existence of equilibrium, like we did in the Arrow–Debreu model. To show equilibrium, we need to make significantly stronger assumptions here. This is because the infinite horizon setting can "go wrong" in many more ways than the static model. Specifically, we assume that

1. $y_t \in \mathbb{R}_+^N$ follows a Markov process;
2. the transition distribution for y is defined by $F\colon E \times E \to \mathbb{R}$, where $E \subset \mathbb{R}_+^N$ is such that $\mathbf{0} \in E$, and
$$F(y', y) = \mathbb{P}(y_{t+1} \le y' | y_t = y),$$
so that
$$\int_E dF(y', y) = 1, \quad \forall\, y \in E;$$
3. the transition distribution F is a continuous function;
4. the probability that $y_{t+1} = \mathbf{0}$ is 0, i.e., $F(\mathbf{0}, y) = \mathbf{0}$ for all $y \in E$;
5. the y_t process has a unique stationary distribution:
$$\phi(y') = \int F(y', y)\, d\phi(y).$$
6. *Technical condition*: For any continuous function $f\colon E \to \mathbb{R}^N$, the function $g\colon E \to \mathbb{R}^N$, defined by $g(y) = \int f(y')\, dF(y', y)$, is continuous in y.

This setup with a Markov transition process with a unique stationary distribution leads to a natural value function formulation of the agent's maximization problem.

Definition 5.9. Given the price function $p\colon E \to \mathbb{R}_+^N$, define the associated value function $v\colon Z \times E \to \mathbb{R}_+$, as the solution to

$$v(z, y) = \max_{c \ge 0,\, x \in Z} u(c) + \delta \int v(x, y')\, dF(y', y), \tag{5.34}$$

subject to budget constraint

$$c + p(y)^T x = y^T z + p(y)^T z,$$

where $Z = [0, \bar{z}]^N$, and $\bar{z} > 1$.

This value function describes the solution to the agent's infinite horizon optimization problem, given the price function p of the financial assets. Here, the z argument denotes the initial asset holdings that the agent has at time t, given that the optimization occurs from t and forward. In equilibrium, it must be that $z = \mathbf{1}$, but the value function is defined for arbitrary $z \in Z$. The constraint $z \in Z$ is technical, to avoid having to analyze potentially arbitrarily large stock positions. The second argument in the value function is the current state, y_t. The unique stationarity assumption, together with the infinite horizon setting, make it possible for us to study the agent's optimization problem as a time-independent problem, by setting up a recursive formulation.[12]

[12] This is similar to how the linear equation $\mathbf{y} = \sum_{n=0}^{\infty} \delta^n \mathbf{A}^n \mathbf{x}$, defined by an infinite sum, can be equivalently calculated by solving $\mathbf{y} = \mathbf{x} + \delta \mathbf{A}\mathbf{y}$ (recursively) for matrices $\mathbf{A}$ that satisfy the norm condition $\delta \|\mathbf{A}\| < 1$. Also, it is similar to how the time dimension "disappears" in some continuous-time infinite horizon problems, as we will see in later chapters.

Definition 5.10. An equilibrium is defined by the pair (p, v), where p is a price function and v the associated value function, such that

- the value function v solves the maximization problem in (5.34), and
- for each $y \in E$, $v(\mathbf{1}, y)$ is attained by choosing $c = Y = \sum_n y_n$, and $x = \mathbf{1}$ in (5.34).

We now have the following general existence theorem:

Theorem 5.8. *There exists a unique equilibrium pair (p, v), where the price function $p\colon E \to \mathbb{R}^N_+$ is continuous and bounded.*

Proof. The proof of this general result uses another workhorse fixed-point theorem, namely the contraction mapping theorem:

Theorem 5.9 (Contraction mapping theorem). *Let (X, d) be a nonempty complete metric space, and consider a mapping (function) $T\colon X \to X$, such that $d(T(x), T(y)) \leq qd(x, y)$ for all $x, y \in X$, where $0 \leq q < 1$ is the* modulus *of the mapping. Then T has a unique fixed point in X, i.e., there is a unique $x^* \in X$, such that $T(x^*) = x^*$.*

Proof. The proof of the contraction mapping theorem is actually really straightforward. Consider an arbitrary element $x_1 \in X$, and define the iteration $x_{n+1} = T(x_n)$. We then have $A \overset{\text{def}}{=} d(x_1, x_2)$, and

$$d(x_2, x_3) = d(T(x_1), T(x_2)) \leq qd(x_1, x_2) = qA,$$

$$d(x_3, x_4) = d(T(x_2), T(x_3)) \leq qd(x_2, x_3) \leq q^2 A,$$

$$d(x_4, x_5) = d(T(x_3), T(x_4)) \leq qd(x_3, x_4) \leq q^3 A,$$

$$\dots$$

$$d(x_n, x_{n+1}) \leq q^{n-1} A.$$

The triangle inequality then implies, for $M \geq N$,

$$d(x_n, x_{n+m}) \leq d(x_n, x_{n+1}) + \cdots + d(x_{n+m-1}, x_{n+m}) \leq q^{n-1}(1 + q + \cdots + q^{m-n-1})A < \frac{q^{n-1}}{1-q} A,$$

which tends to zero for large n, in a way that does not depend on $m > n$, so the sequence $\{x_n\}_n$ is a Cauchy sequence, which because of the completeness of the metric space must converge to some $x^* \in X$.

Now, it follows immediately that T is a continuous mapping, since the contraction property implies that $d(T(x), T(y)) \to 0$ whenever $d(x, y) \to 0$. Recall that for a continuous mapping, if $x_n \to x^*$, then $T(x_n) \to T(x^*)$ (the continuous function theorem). Therefore,

$$x^* = \lim_{n\to\infty} x_{n+1} = \lim_{n\to\infty} T(x_n) = T\big(\lim_{n\to\infty} x_n\big) = T(x^*),$$

so x^* is a fixed point.

Finally, x^* is unique, since assume that x^* and y^* are both fixed points to T. Then, from the contraction property, $d(x^*, y^*) = d(T(x^*), T(y^*)) \leq qd(x^*, y^*) = 0$, so $d(x^*, y^*) = 0$, and thus $x^* = y^*$ from the standard properties of a metric; see appendix B. This completes the proof of the contraction mapping theorem. □

The proof of theorem 5.8, which follows Lucas (1978) closely, has two parts. First, we use the contraction mapping theorem to show that for an arbitrary continuous pricing function on E, there exist a unique well-behaved value function and associated optimal consumption and investment policies that solve (5.34). Second, we use the existence result from the first step to show that there is a unique pricing function that leads to an equilibrium, i.e., which is such that the optimal consumption and investment policies make markets clear, $c = Y$ and $z = \mathbf{1}$.

Step 1: To apply the contraction mapping theorem, we need to carefully keep track of the function spaces we work with. To this end, we define the space

$$V = \{v \colon \mathbb{R}_+^N \times E \to \mathbb{R}_+, \text{ such that } v \text{ is bounded and continuous}\}.$$

Under the supremum norm, $\|v\|_\infty = \sup_{z \in \mathbb{R}_+^N, e \in E} |v(z, e)|$, it follows that V is a Banach space, i.e., a complete metric space under the metric defined by the norm $d(u, v) = \|v - u\|_\infty$. Indeed, the space of bounded and continuous functions under this supremum norm is one of the standard Banach spaces; see, e.g., Yosida (1995, page 55).

Let us start with the agent's maximization problem, given a continuous and bounded price function $p \colon E \to \mathbb{R}_+^N$. To this end, we define the operator $T_p \colon V \to V$ by

$$T_p(v)(z, y) = \max_{c \in \mathbb{R}_+, x \in Z} \left\{ u(c) + \delta \int_E v(x, y')\, dF(y', y) \right\},$$

$$\text{s.t. } c + p(y)^T x \le y^T z + p(y)^T z.$$

An equivalent definition of the agent's value function v is then that it defines a fixed point of the operator T_p (see (5.34)).

Now, by showing that T_p is a contraction mapping on V, we will be able to conclude that there is a fixed point, $v \in V$. To show that T_p is a contraction mapping, we first note that the definition of T_p immediately implies that it maps V into V, i.e., that $T_p(v)$ is continuous and bounded. Moreover, T_p is monotone, in that when $v_2 \ge v_1$ (for all arguments, i.e., $v_2(z, e) \ge v_1(z, e)$, for all $z \in Z$ and $e \in E$), then $T_p(v_2) \ge T_p(v_1)$ (for all arguments), and it satisfies the following linearity with respect to adding a constant: $T_p(v + k) = T_p(v) + \delta k$ for any $k \in \mathbb{R}_+$.

An argument from Blackwell (1965) then implies that T_p is a contraction mapping with modulus δ. Specifically, for functions $v_1 \in V$ and $v_2 \in V$, we can write $v_2 = v_1 + (v_2 - v_1)$, and it then follows that $v_2 \le v_1 + \|v_2 - v_1\|_\infty$ (for all $(z, e) \in \mathbb{R}_+^N \times E$). Therefore, because of monotonicity and linearity, $T_p(v_2) \le T_p(v_1 + \|v_2 - v_1\|_\infty) = T_p(v_1) + \delta\|v_2 - v_1\|_\infty$, i.e., $T_p(v_2) - T_p(v_1) \le \delta\|v_2 - v_1\|_\infty$. An identical argument based on the identity $v_1 = v_2 + (v_1 - v_2)$ implies that $T_p(v_1) - T_p(v_2) \le \delta\|v_2 - v_1\|_\infty$, so $\|T_p(v_2) - T_p(v_1)\|_\infty \le \delta\|v_2 - v_1\|_\infty$ and T_p is indeed a contraction mapping with modulus δ. We conclude that T_p has a unique fixed point, $v \in V$, which is the agent's value function under the price function, p.

Step 2: We have shown that a unique value function is defined for any continuous bounded price function. To show that a price function exists such that (p, v) defines an equilibrium pair, we need to infer some further properties of v.

The definition of T_p immediately implies that $T_p(w)(z, y)$ is increasing in z for all $y \in E$, regardless of $w \in V$. Moreover, one easily shows that if v is concave in z for each $y \in E$, then $T_p(w)$ is also concave in z for each $y \in E$. Specifically, if c_1, x_1 represent optimal consumption and investment for $T_p(w)(z_1, y)$, and c_2, x_2 for $T_p(w)(z_2, y)$, then $c = \lambda c_1 + (1 - \lambda)c_2$, and $x = \lambda x_1 + (1 - \lambda)x_2$ provides a feasible consumption-investment pair when $z = \lambda z_1 + (1 - \lambda)z_2$, $0 \le \lambda \le 1$, leading to the value

$$u(c)+\delta\int_E w(x,y')\,dF(y',y)\geq \lambda u(c_1)+(1-\lambda)u(c_2)$$
$$+\int_E(\lambda w(x_1,y')+(1-\lambda)w(x_2,y'))\,dF(y',y)$$
$$=\lambda T_p(w)(x_1,y)+(1-\lambda)T_p(w)(x_2,y).$$

The value under the optimal consumption-investment pair, c^*, x^*, must be at least as high, i.e., $T_p(w)(z,y)\geq \lambda T_p(w)(x_1,y)+(1-\lambda)T_p(w)(x_2,y)$, so $T_p(w)(z,y)$ is concave in z. Now, since $v=\lim_{n\to\infty}T_p^n(w)$ for any $w\in V$, it therefore follows by induction and continuity (the limit of a sequence of concave functions is concave) that the value function v must be concave in z.

Lemma 5.3. *Given the price function, p, if the value function $v(z,y)$ is attained at optimal consumption and next period investment (c^*,x^*), where optimal consumption $c^*>0$, then v is differentiable in z, and*

$$\frac{\partial v(z,y)}{\partial z_i}=u'(c^*)(y_i+p_i(y)).$$

This is an envelope condition that states that the marginal utility benefit on the value function of owning a bit more of stock i at time 0 (left-hand side) is equal to the marginal benefit of not owning more of the stock, but instead immediately consuming the dividends and sales revenue associated with such stock ownership (right-hand side).

Proof of lemma 5.3. Given the price function, p, and associated value function, v, define

$$f(A)=\max_{c,x}\left\{u(c)+\delta\int_E v(x,y')\,dF(y',y)\right\},\quad \text{s.t. } c+p(y)^T x\leq A.$$

The parameter A thus defines a budget constraint in the agent's maximization problem. Since u is strictly concave, it follows that $c^*(A)$ is unique and continuous as a function of A. Specifically, because u is strictly increasing, the budget constraint at any maximum policy will bind, and because u is strictly concave, the average of two different optimal policies is feasible and strictly more valuable than either policy, contradicting that the policies were optimal in the first place. So optimal consumption is unique.

Also, since v is concave in x, if $c^*(A)>0$, then for small enough $h>0$,

$$f(A+h)\geq u(c^*(A)+h)+\delta\int_E v(x(A),y')\,dF=u(c^*(A)+h)-u(c^*(A))+f(A),$$

and also

$$f(A)\geq u(c^*(A+h)-h)-u(c^*(A+h))+f(A+h).$$

The first inequality represents that it is feasible for an agent with wealth $A+h$ to immediately consume all of the increased wealth (thereby consuming $c^*(A)+h$) and from then on behave as the agent with wealth A. The second inequality represents that one feasible way to behave for the agent with wealth A is to consume h less than the agent with wealth $A+h$, and from then on behave like that agent.

It thus follows that

$$\frac{u(c^*(A+h)) - u(c^*(A+h)-h)}{h} \geq \frac{f(A+h)-f(A)}{h} \geq \frac{u(c^*(A)+h) - u(c^*(A))}{h},$$

and since $c^*(A)$ is continuous in A, we get $f'(A) = u'(c^*(A))$ when h tends to zero. Plugging in $A = y^T z + p(y)^T z$, we get $f(A) = v(z, y)$ (see (5.34)), and via the chain rule,

$$\frac{\partial v}{\partial z_i} = \frac{\partial f}{\partial A}\frac{\partial A}{\partial z_i} = u'(c^*)(y_i + p_i(y)).$$

We have proved the lemma. □

Now, since v is well defined and smooth in z, it must satisfy the first-order condition

$$u'(c^*)p_i = \delta \int_E \frac{\partial v(z, y')}{\partial z_i}\, dF(y', y),$$

i.e., marginal utility associated with buying more of stock i is the same as marginal utility of using the money to consume more today (see (5.34)). Plugging in the result from the lemma above, we then get

$$u'(c^*)p_i = \delta \int_E u'(c')(y'_i + p_i(y'))\, dF(y', y).$$

In equilibrium, we must have

$$c = \sum_i y_i, \quad c' = \sum_i y'_i, \quad \sum_i x_i = 1, \quad \sum_i z_i = 1,$$

so for a candidate price function that leads to an equilibrium, it must then be that

$$u'(\mathbf{1}^T y)p_i(y) = \delta \int_E u'(\mathbf{1}^T y')(y'_i + p_i(y'))\, dF(y', y), \tag{5.35}$$

where $c = \mathbf{1}^T y$ and $c' = \mathbf{1}^T y'$ are the optimal consumptions in the current and the next period, respectively. Conversely, if a pricing function that satisfies (5.35) can be found, it will define equilibrium (together with the associated value function), since the first-order conditions being satisfied are sufficient for an optimum of a concave optimization problem.

Now let us define the function $g\colon E \to \mathbb{R}^N_+$ by

$$(g(y))_i = \delta \int_E u'(\mathbf{1}^T y')y'_i\, dF(y', y). \tag{5.36}$$

Note that $g \stackrel{\text{def}}{=} \int_E f(y')\, dF(y', y)$, where $f(y')$ is defined as $f(y') \stackrel{\text{def}}{=} \delta u'(\mathbf{1}y')y' \in \mathbb{R}^N_+$, is continuous, so per technical condition 6 on page 137, g is continuous. It also follows that g is nonnegative, since u' is positive, as are y'_i and δ. Next, note that

$$xu'(x) \leq u(x), \quad x \geq 0,$$

since

$$u(x) = u(0) + \int_0^x u'(t)\, dt \geq u(0) + \int_0^x u'(x)\, dt = u(0) + xu'(x) = xu'(x), \quad x \geq 0,$$

where we used the concavity of u, and that $u(0) = 0$. Finally, since u is bounded, say by the finite number B, we get

$$\mathbf{1}^T g(y) = \delta \int_E u'(\mathbf{1}^T y')(\mathbf{1}^T y')\, dF(y', y)$$

$$\leq \delta \int_E u(\mathbf{1}^T y')\, dF(y', y)$$
$$\leq \delta B \int_E dF(y', y)$$
$$= \delta B.$$

Thus, $\|g(y)\|_\infty \leq \delta B$, so g is bounded.

Also, define the space of price functions:

$$P = \{p\colon E \to \mathbb{R}_+^N, \text{ such that } p \text{ is bounded and continuous}\}.$$

Just like the space V, P is a Banach space under the maximum norm, $\|p\|_\infty = \sup_{y \in E} \|p(y)\|_\infty$. Moreover, define $T\colon P \to P$ by

$$(Tp)(y) = g(y) + \delta \int_E p(y')\, dF(y', y). \tag{5.37}$$

Because g is bounded and continuous, and the fact that the integral operator $f \mapsto \int_E f(y')\, dF(y', y)$ preserves boundedness and continuity (per technical condition 6 on page 137, for the continuity part), it follows that T maps P into P.

From (5.35, 5.36, 5.37) it follows that if f is a fixed point of T, then the function p, defined by

$$p_i(y) = \frac{f_i(y)}{u'(\mathbf{1}^T y)},$$

is an equilibrium price function, since

$$\begin{aligned} u'(\mathbf{1}^T y) p(y) &= f(y) \\ &= g(y) + \delta \int_E f(y')\, dF(y', y) \\ &= \delta \int_E u'(\mathbf{1}^T y') y'\, dF(y', y) + \delta \int_E u'(\mathbf{1}^T y') p(y')\, dF(y', y) \\ &= \delta \int_E u'(\mathbf{1}^T y')(y' + p(y'))\, dF(y', y), \end{aligned}$$

and therefore (5.35) is satisfied. So, if we can show that T is a contraction mapping, we know that a unique such pricing function exists, and we are done.

We have

$$\begin{aligned} \|T(f_1) - T(f_2)\|_\infty &= \left\| \delta \int_E (f_1(y') - f_2(y'))\, dF(y', y) \right\|_{n\infty} \\ &\leq \delta \sup_{y' \in E} \|f_1(y') - f_2(y')\| \int_E |\, dF(y', y)| \\ &= \delta \|f_1 - f_2\|_\infty \times 1. \end{aligned}$$

So T is a contraction mapping with modulus δ, and therefore has a unique fixed point, f, with associated unique equilibrium pricing function, p, and value function, v. We are done! □

5.4.11 More on Consumption-Based Asset Pricing

We can rewrite the SDF pricing equation in a covariance form, which looks a lot like the CAPM. Specifically, define

$$\widetilde{R}_t = 1 + \tilde{r}_t = \frac{\tilde{p}_{t+1} - p_t}{p_t},$$

for an asset that does not pay dividends. The SDF relation

$$p_t = E[m_{t,t+1}\tilde{p}_{t+1}]$$

implies that

$$1 = E[m_{t,t+1}\widetilde{R}_t]$$

for any asset (including the risk-free asset, which has returns R_t^f). This is yet another form of the Euler equation. It follows that

$$0 = E[m_{t,t+1}(\widetilde{R}_t - R_t^f)] = \delta E\Big[\frac{u'(\tilde{c}_{t+1})}{u'(c_t)}(\widetilde{R}_t - R_t^f)\Big].$$

Now recall that $E[\tilde{a}\tilde{b}] = \text{Cov}(\tilde{a}, \tilde{b}) + E[\tilde{a}]E[\tilde{b}]$ for general random variables $\tilde{a}$ and $\tilde{b}$. This in turn implies

$$\begin{aligned}0 &= \text{Cov}\Big[\frac{u'(\tilde{c}_{t+1})}{u'(c_t)}, \widetilde{R}_t - R_t^f\Big] + E\Big[\frac{u'(\tilde{c}_{t+1})}{u'(c_t)}\Big](E[\widetilde{R}_t] - R_t^f) \\ &= \text{Cov}\Big[\frac{u'(\tilde{c}_{t+1})}{u'(c_t)}, \widetilde{R}_t\Big] + E\Big[\frac{u'(\tilde{c}_{t+1})}{u'(c_t)}\Big](E[\widetilde{R}_t] - R_t^f).\end{aligned}$$

We may therefore write

$$E[\widetilde{R}_t] = R_t^f - \frac{1}{E[u'(\tilde{c}_{t+1})]} \times \text{Cov}[u'(\tilde{c}_{t+1}), \widetilde{R}_t].$$

This is the *consumption CAPM* (CCAPM); see Breeden (1979). It has a very similar form to the formula for the expected return of a risky asset in the CAPM. Instead of the return on the market portfolio, marginal utility of aggregate consumption (the SDF) is used in the covariance calculation. This makes a lot of sense. In the consumption-based model, the bad states are calculated as those where aggregate consumption is low (marginal utility is high). This is then what determines the risk premium. In the special case of quadratic utility, $u(c_t) = Ac_t - \frac{B}{2}c_t^2$, the formula simplifies even further, since marginal utility is linear in aggregate consumption in this case. We get

$$E[\widetilde{R}_t] = R_t^f + \frac{B}{A - BE[\tilde{c}_{t+1}]} \times \text{Cov}[\tilde{c}_{t+1}, R_t].$$

The same trick as we used there to arrive at the CCAPM can be applied for a general SDF. Consider the general SDF, $\{m_t\}_t$, such that $1 = E[\frac{M_{t+1}}{M_t}\widetilde{R}_t]$ for any asset (recall that $m_{t,t+1} = \frac{M_{t+1}}{M_t}$). This then implies

$$\begin{aligned}0 &= \text{Cov}\Big[\frac{M_{t+1}}{M_t}, \widetilde{R}_t - R_t^f\Big] + E\Big[\frac{M_{t+1}}{M_t}\Big](E[\widetilde{R}_t] - R_t^f) \\ &= \text{Cov}\Big[\frac{M_{t+1}}{M_t}, \widetilde{R}_t\Big] + E\Big[\frac{M_{t+1}}{M_t}\Big](E[\widetilde{R}_t] - R_t^f),\end{aligned}$$

and thus

$$\begin{aligned} E[\widetilde{R}_t] - R_t^f &= -\operatorname{Cov}\Big[\frac{M_{t+1}}{M_t}, \widetilde{R}_t\Big] \times \frac{1}{E[\frac{M_{t+1}}{M_t}]} \\ &= \underbrace{\left(\frac{\operatorname{Cov}[\frac{M_{t+1}}{M_t}, \widetilde{R}_t]}{\operatorname{Var}[\frac{M_{t+1}}{M_t}]}\right)}_{\beta_{i,M}} \times \underbrace{\left(-\frac{\operatorname{Var}[\frac{M_{t+1}}{M_t}]}{E[\frac{M_{t+1}}{M_t}]}\right)}_{\lambda_M} \\ &= \beta_{i,M}\lambda_M. \end{aligned}$$

This is the general *state-price beta model.*

Now, since

$$0 = \operatorname{Cov}\Big[\frac{M_{t+1}}{M_t}, \widetilde{R}_t\Big] + E\Big[\frac{M_{t+1}}{M_t}\Big](E[\widetilde{R}_t] - R_t^f),$$

we can write

$$-\operatorname{Cov}\Big[\frac{M_{t+1}}{M_t}, \widetilde{R}_t\Big] = E\Big[\frac{M_{t+1}}{M_t}\Big](E[\widetilde{R}_t] - R_t^f),$$

which in turn, since $\operatorname{Cov}(\tilde{a}, \tilde{b}) \leq \sigma(\tilde{a})\sigma(\tilde{b})$ for arbitrary random variables, implies

$$E\Big[\frac{M_{t+1}}{M_t}\Big] \times |E[\widetilde{R}_t] - R_t^f| \leq \sigma\Big(\frac{M_{t+1}}{M_t}\Big)\sigma(\widetilde{R}_t).$$

Reordering the terms gives us a bound on any asset's Sharpe ratio in the market:

$$|S| = \frac{|E[\widetilde{R}_t] - R_t^f|}{\sigma(\widetilde{R}_t)} \leq \frac{\sigma(\frac{M_{t+1}}{M_t})}{E[\frac{M_{t+1}}{M_t}]} = \sigma\Big(\frac{M_{t+1}}{M_t}\Big)R^f.$$

This is the famous Hansen and Jagannathan (1991) bound. It essentially states that the Sharpe ratio of any asset in the market cannot be higher than the volatility of the SDF. The equity premium puzzle can now be interpreted in light of this bound.

In our AD economy with small shocks, in section 5.4.4, one verifies that the approximate value for the volatility of the pricing kernel is $\sigma(\widetilde{M}_1) \approx \gamma\sigma$ (setting $\Delta t = 1$). Given that consumption growth is so smooth, $\sigma \approx 2\%$, to get a volatile pricing kernel, the volatility must come from a high risk-aversion coefficient, γ. Indeed, given a market Sharpe ratio of $S = 0.4$, γ needs to be at least 20. So the equity premium puzzle can equivalently be viewed as a statement about the SDF not being volatile enough to allow for the high Sharpe ratio we observe in the market.[13]

5.4.12 EZ Preferences and the Equity Premium Puzzle

Let us return to equilibrium with EZ preferences in the dynamic model, to understand how long-run risk, in the form of shock persistence, affects the equity premium under such preferences, as studied in Bansal and Yaron (2005). We first derive a recursive formula for the SDF, using the

[13] Note that the Hansen and Jagannathan version of the equity premium puzzle does not look quite as severe with this formulation, since it is sufficient to have a risk-aversion coefficient of 20 here, rather than 150, which was the number we derived before. The reason is that the Hansen–Jagannathan bound is $r^m - r^f \leq \gamma\sigma_C\sigma_m$, rather than $r^m - r^f = \gamma\sigma_C^2$. Since the market volatility, σ_m, is several times larger than consumption volatility, σ_C, this reduces the lower bound on γ.

same approach as we did before when there were only two dates. The recursive specification of the representative agent's utility is

$$U(c_t, U_{t+1}) = V^{\frac{1}{1-\rho}} = \left(c_t^{1-\rho} + \delta E_t[U_{t+1}^{1-\gamma}]^{\frac{1-\rho}{1-\gamma}}\right)^{\frac{1}{1-\rho}},$$

where, as before, $\rho = \frac{1}{\psi}$. In equilibrium, the representative agent chooses to consume aggregate consumption, $c_t = C_t$ and $\tilde{c}_{t+1} = \widetilde{C}_{t+1}$, so any asset, which costs 1 at $t = 0$ and has returns $\widetilde{R}$ in the next period, must be in zero demand. In other words,

$$\begin{aligned} 0 &= \arg\max_\epsilon U(C_t - \epsilon, U_{t+1}(C_{t+1} + \epsilon\widetilde{R}, U_{t+2})) \\ &= \arg\max_\epsilon \left((C_t - \epsilon)^{1-\rho} + \delta E_t[U_{t+1}(C_{t+1} + \epsilon\widetilde{R}, U_{t+2})^{1-\gamma}]^{\frac{1-\rho}{1-\gamma}}\right)^{1/(1-\rho)} \\ &= \arg\max_\epsilon \Big(\underbrace{(C_t - \epsilon)^{1-\rho} + \delta E_t\big[\big((C_{t+1} + \epsilon\widetilde{R})^{1-\rho} + \delta E_{t+1}[U_{t+2}^{1-\gamma}]^{\frac{1-\rho}{1-\gamma}}\big)^{\frac{1-\gamma}{1-\rho}}\big]^{\frac{1-\rho}{1-\gamma}}}_{V(\epsilon)}\Big)^{1/(1-\rho)} \end{aligned}$$

is realized at $\epsilon = 0$ for any such asset, leading to the FOC

$$0 = \frac{1}{1-\rho} V^{1/(1-\rho)-1} \times \left.\frac{\partial V}{\partial \epsilon}\right|_{\epsilon=0},$$

so it must be that $V'(0) = 0$. Now,

$$0 = V'(0) = -(1-\rho)C_t^{-\rho} + \delta(1-\rho)E_t[C_{t+1}^{-\rho}U_{t+1}^{\rho-\gamma}\widetilde{R}]E_t[\widetilde{U}_{t+1}^{1-\gamma}]^{\frac{1-\rho}{1-\gamma}-1}.$$

Here we used that $(C_{t+1}^{1-\rho} + \delta E_{t+1}[U_{t+2}^{1-\gamma}]^{\frac{1-\rho}{1-\gamma}})^{\frac{1-\gamma}{1-\rho}-1} = U_{t+1}^{\rho-\gamma}$. Therefore,

$$C_t^{-\rho} = \delta E_t[C_{t+1}^{-\rho}U_{t+1}^{\rho-\gamma}\widetilde{R}]E_t[U_{t+1}^{1-\gamma}]^{\frac{1-\rho}{1-\gamma}-1}, \tag{5.38}$$

which in turn leads to the SDF pricing equation

$$p = E_t[\widetilde{m}_t\widetilde{F}],$$

where the SDF is of the form

$$\widetilde{m}_t = \delta E_t[U_{t+1}^{1-\gamma}]^{\frac{1-\rho}{1-\gamma}-1}\left(\frac{C_{t+1}}{C_t}\right)^{-\rho} U_{t+1}^{\rho-\gamma}.$$

This can equivalently be written

$$\widetilde{m}_t = \delta k_t \left(\frac{C_{t+1}}{C_t}\right)^{-\rho}\left(\frac{U_{t+1}}{C_t}\right)^{\rho-\gamma}, \tag{5.39}$$

where

$$k_t = E_t\left[\left(\frac{U_{t+1}}{C_t}\right)^{1-\gamma}\right]^{\frac{1-\rho}{1-\gamma}-1}.$$

One verifies that when $\frac{1}{\psi} = \rho = \gamma$, one gets recursively $U_t^{1-\rho} = \sum_{s=t}^T E_t[\delta^{t-s}C_s^{1-\gamma}]$ for all t, and that the pricing kernel in this case reduces to

$$\widetilde{m}_t = \delta E_t\left[\left(\frac{U_{t+1}}{C_t}\right)^{1-\gamma}\right]^0 \left(\frac{C_{t+1}}{C_t}\right)^{-\gamma}\left(\frac{U_{t+1}}{C_t}\right)^0 = \delta\left(\frac{C_{t+1}}{C_t}\right)^{-\gamma},$$

in line with the pricing kernel under CRRA utility.

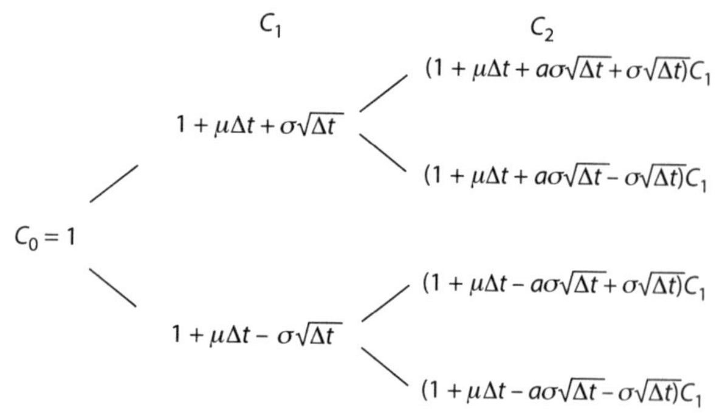

Figure 5.3: Two-period EZ model.

Now, consider the two-period (i.e., three-date, $t=0,1,2$) economy with aggregate consumption according to figure 5.3, where the probabilities for up- and down-moves are the same, $\frac{1}{2}$. The parameter a represents shock persistence in that the shock between 0 and 1 also impacts growth between 1 and 2. If $a>0$—the case we will focus on—higher than expected growth of C_1 (represented by an up-move) increases expected growth of C_2, whereas a lower than expected growth (represented by a down-move) decreases expected growth of C_2. For CRRA utility, a contingent claim that pays off at $t=1$ will not be influenced by the value of a, only the ratios of marginal utilities between $t=0$ and $t=1$, and δ matter. Let's see how this changes under EZ preferences. To use (5.39), we need to know U_1. We have, after an up-move,

$$
\begin{aligned}
U_{1u}^{1-\rho} &= \left(C_{1u}^{1-\rho} + (1-\hat{\rho}\Delta t)E_1[C_2^{1-\gamma}]^{\frac{1-\rho}{1-\gamma}}\right)^{1/(1-\rho)} \\
&\approx 2 + (2+a)(1-\rho)\sigma\sqrt{\Delta t} \\
&\quad + \left(-\hat{\rho} + \frac{1}{2}(-1+\rho)\left(-6\mu + (-2a+\gamma+(2+a(2+a))\rho)\sigma^2\right)\right)\Delta t,
\end{aligned}
$$

and after a down-move,

$$
\begin{aligned}
U_{1d}^{1-\rho} &= \left(C_{1d}^{1-\rho} + (1-\hat{\rho}\Delta t)E_1[C_2^{1-\gamma}]^{\frac{1-\rho}{1-\gamma}}\right)^{1/(1-\rho)} \\
&\approx 2 - (2+a)(1-\rho)\sigma\sqrt{\Delta t} \\
&\quad + \left(-\hat{\rho} + \frac{1}{2}(-1+\rho)\left(-6\mu + (-2a+\gamma+(2+a(2+a))\rho)\sigma^2\right)\right)\Delta t,
\end{aligned}
$$

where we use a Taylor expansion that includes terms up to order Δt in the approximation step. Here, $\delta = 1-\hat{\rho}\Delta t$ is the one-period personal discount rate. A similar Taylor expansion for the constant k_0 gives us

$$
\begin{aligned}
k_0 &= E_0[U_1^{1-\gamma}]^{\frac{1-\rho}{1-\gamma}-1} \\
&\approx \left(\frac{1}{2}\right)^{\frac{\rho-\gamma}{1-\rho}}\left(1+\frac{1}{8}(\rho-\gamma)\left(\frac{4\hat{\rho}}{1-\rho} - 12\mu + (6\gamma + a(4\gamma + a\gamma + a\rho - 4))\sigma^2\right)\right)\Delta t,
\end{aligned}
$$

and we arrive at the following values of $\widetilde{m}$ at $t=1$ after an up- and a down-move, respectively:

$$
\begin{aligned}
m_u &= 2\psi_u \approx 1 - r^f\Delta t - \left(\gamma + \frac{1}{2}a(\gamma-\rho)\right)\sigma^2\sqrt{\Delta t}, \\
m_d &= 2\psi_d \approx 1 - r^f\Delta t + \left(\gamma + \frac{1}{2}a(\gamma-\rho)\right)\sigma^2\sqrt{\Delta t},
\end{aligned}
$$

where

$$
r^f = \hat{\rho} + \rho\mu - \frac{1}{2}\left((\rho-1)\left(\gamma + \frac{1}{4}a^2(\rho-\gamma)\right) - 2\gamma - a(\gamma-\rho)\right)\sigma^2.
$$

That r^f must be the risk-free rate follows from the pricing formula for a one-period bond $P_B = E[\widetilde{m}\times 1] \approx 1 - r^f\Delta t$. Clearly, $E[\widetilde{m}] = 1 - r^f\Delta t$, so the result follows (up to the first-order approximation in Δt).

This is promising! We know that the secret to a high equity premium is a volatile SDF, from the Hansen–Jagannathan bound. Here,

$$m_u - m_d = 2\Big(\gamma + \frac{1}{2}a(\gamma - \rho)\Big)\sigma^2\sqrt{\Delta t},$$

so if $\gamma > \rho$ the volatility of the SDF increases with a, which should be helpful for the equity premium.

Now consider a claim on aggregate consumption at time 1, i.e., a claim that pays $\widetilde{C}_1$ at time 1. Its expected payoff is $E_0[\widetilde{C}_1] = 1 + \mu\Delta t$, and the time-0 price of the claim, P, is then (plugging in our formulas for m_u, m_d, C_{1u}, and C_{1d})

$$P = E_0[\widetilde{m}\widetilde{C}_1] \approx 1 - \Big(\hat{\rho} + (\rho - 1)\mu - \frac{1}{2}(\rho - 1)\Big(\gamma + \frac{1}{4}a^2(\rho - \gamma)\Big)\sigma^2\Big)\Delta t.$$

So the expected return on this consumption claim is

$$\frac{E[\widetilde{C}_1]}{P} - 1 \approx \mu\Delta t + \Big(\hat{\rho} + (\rho - 1)\mu - \frac{1}{2}(\rho - 1)\Big(\gamma + \frac{1}{4}a^2(\rho - \gamma)\Big)\sigma^2\Big)\Delta t,$$

and the expected return on a claim on time-1 aggregate consumption is then

$$r^m = \hat{\rho} + \rho\mu - \frac{1}{2}(\rho - 1)\Big(\gamma + \frac{1}{4}a^2(\rho - \gamma)\Big)\sigma^2.$$

We arrive at the equity premium

$$r^m - r^f = \Big(\gamma + \frac{1}{2}a(\gamma - \rho)\Big)\sigma^2. \tag{5.40}$$

So when $a > 0$ and $\gamma > \rho$, the risk premium is higher under EZ preferences than under CRRA preferences.

The case $\gamma > \rho$ corresponds to the agent preferring early uncertainty resolution. Intuitively, the shock persistency introduced by $a > 0$ makes the impact of the state revelation between 0 and 1 larger from that agent's perspective, since not only is the growth between 0 and 1 learned, but also whether future growth will be higher. In contrast to CRRA utility, the EZ agent's utility of consumption at 1 is affected by this revelation, increasing the difference in marginal utility across the two states at time 1 compared with the CRRA utility case. Note also that (5.40) reduces to the CRRA equity premium formula, $\gamma\sigma^2$, when $\gamma = \rho$.

To be able to match the equity premium with moderate values of γ in this example, a needs to be really large. In a many-period extension of the model, however, not only will the effect from $t = 2$ influence SDF volatility at $t = 1$, but, if the shock is persistent over many periods, there will also be impact from $t = 3, 4, \ldots$, due to the recursive way the SDF is defined here. For example, if the effect on growth of the first period shock is a at $t = 1$, and then a^s at time s, corresponding to an autoregressive (so-called AR(1)) specification of shock persistence, the cumulative effect leads to an equity premium of something like[14]

$$r^m - r^f = \Big(\gamma + \frac{1}{2}\frac{1}{1 - a}(\gamma - \rho)\Big)\sigma^2. \tag{5.41}$$

So when a is close to 1, corresponding to shocks that have long-lasting impact, the premium can be high even for moderate values of γ. For example, the parameter values $\gamma = 7$, $a = 0.98$, $\rho = 1$, $\sigma = 2\%$, lead to $r^m - r^f \approx 6.3\%$.

[14]The derivation is more subtle in this case, since the Taylor expansion is only valid close to C_0. Bansal and Yaron (2005) take a different approach, basing their argument on a log-linear approximation.

5.5 Arbitrage Pricing Theory, APT

The Ross (1976) *arbitrage pricing theory* (APT) offers another justification for using multifactor models to explain the cross section of expected returns. Recall that we showed that the CAPM with unknown market portfolio would lead to such a K-factor pricing relationship, if one knew that the market portfolio's returns lay in the span of these K factors. Ross (1976) derives a similar pricing relation in a more general setting, under weaker assumptions.

The key mechanism in the APT is based on diversification. As such, much less is needed to be known about investor preferences than in the CAPM derivation. The argument is based on an economy with many—basically an infinite number of—assets, and the pricing relations are approximate except when applied to a specific type of portfolio. As such, the model is quite abstract. In the asset pricing pyramid, the APT lies somewhere in the middle: the assumptions about investor behavior are weaker than in the CAPM, but the assumptions about the payoff/return distributions of individual assets are stronger than in no-arbitrage models. As such, the APT belongs somewhere in the middle of the asset pricing pyramid; see figure 1.1.

The general intuition here is that diversifiable risk should not be priced, i.e., such risk should not be associated with a risk premium above the risk-free rate. There are a very large number, N, of assets with a linear factor structure of returns. Specifically, we assume that

$$\widetilde{R}_n = a_n + \sum_{k=1}^{K} b_n^k \tilde{f}_k + \tilde{\epsilon}_n,$$

for the nth asset, where

$$E[\tilde{\epsilon}_n] = 0,$$

$$E[\tilde{f}_k] = 0,$$

$$E[\tilde{\epsilon}_n \tilde{f}_k] = 0,$$

$$E[\tilde{f}_k \tilde{f}_m] = 0, \quad k \neq m,$$

$$E[\tilde{f}_k^2] = 1,$$

$$E[\tilde{\epsilon}_n \tilde{\epsilon}_j] = 0, \tag{5.42}$$

$$E[\tilde{\epsilon}_n^2] = s_n^2 < S^2 < \infty. \tag{5.43}$$

Thus, a one-dollar investment in asset n is expected to pay off a_n. The payoff is potentially influenced by K risky factors, which are common to all assets and which have expected values of zero, which are pairwise uncorrelated, and which are normalized to have unit variance. The payoff is also influenced by an asset-specific, idiosyncratic, component, $\tilde{\epsilon}_n$, that is uncorrelated with the factors, as well as with all other asset-specific components, $\tilde{\epsilon}_{n'}$, $n' \neq n$. Moreover, the variances of the asset-specific risks are bounded above by some finite value $S^2 < \infty$. This is important to ensure that the diversification argument holds. A note: In practice N is of course finite. The important thing for the APT to be useful is that it is a large number, say a thousand or more (there are about 5000 stocks in the Wilshire 5000 index, for example), whereas the number of factors, K, is much smaller, say $K \leq 10$.

Of course, for an arbitrary risk structure, standard orthogonalization techniques (for example, Gram–Schmidt) can be used to define a K-factor structure. But the model's assumptions are still not innocent, because they will typically not lead to (5.42, 5.43). In the context of this model, there is a "true" K-factor structure since all residual risk is idiosyncratic.

It will be convenient to reformulate these assumptions in vector form. We introduce the N-vectors $\widetilde{\mathbf{R}}$, $\mathbf{a}$, and ϵ, the K-vector $\tilde{\mathbf{f}}$, the $N \times K$ matrix $\mathbf{B}$, with $(\mathbf{B})_{nk} = b_n^k$, leading to the relation

$$\widetilde{\mathbf{R}} = \mathbf{a} + \mathbf{B}\tilde{\mathbf{f}} + \tilde{\epsilon},$$

and

$$E[\tilde{\epsilon}] = \mathbf{0},$$

$$E[\tilde{\mathbf{f}}] = \mathbf{0}$$

$$E[\tilde{\epsilon}\tilde{\mathbf{f}}'] = \mathbf{0},$$

$$E[\tilde{\mathbf{f}}\tilde{\mathbf{f}}'] = \mathbf{I},$$

$$E[\tilde{\epsilon}\tilde{\epsilon}'] = \text{diag}(\mathbf{s}).$$

To gain an intuition, we study a couple of examples from Ingersoll (1987), which do not have $\tilde{\epsilon}$-risk, so that $s_n^2 = 0$ for all n.

5.5.1 One-Factor Model without Idiosyncratic Risk

Assume that $K = 1$, i.e., a one-factor model, and $\epsilon_i \equiv 0$, for all i. The pricing relation then becomes

$$\widetilde{R}_i = a_i + b_i \tilde{f}.$$

Our modest goal here is to find a relation between an asset's expected return, a_n, and its corresponding factor loading, b_n, with as few assumptions as possible about investor behavior. In contrast with the equilibrium models we have studied so far, we thus wish to avoid making more than minimal assumptions about investor preferences.

One such minimal assumption, which we will focus on throughout part II of these notes, is that of *no arbitrage*, which in this context states that it should not be possible to buy a portfolio of assets that costs 0, and for sure makes a strictly positive payout. Such an investment opportunity must clearly be too good to be true, since any investor with increasing utility function would have infinite demand for such a portfolio. In equilibrium, prices would then need to adjust for supply and demand to be equal. This no-arbitrage argument depends on an equilibrium concept of supply equaling demand. But no-arbitrage models are still typically viewed as partial equilibrium models, since they make such minimal assumptions about investor behavior—investors liking more over less.

We now assume that there is no arbitrage and that there exist at least two assets i, j, with different b's, so that $b_j > b_i$. We can then derive a relation between a_n and b_n as follows. We choose a (dollar) portfolio $\mathbf{v}$ with weights

$$\mathbf{v}_i = \frac{b_j}{b_j - b_i},$$

$$\mathbf{v}_j = -\frac{b_i}{b_j - b_i},$$

$$\mathbf{v}_m = 0, \quad m \neq i, j.$$

With this portfolio, we get

$$\mathbf{v}'\widetilde{\mathbf{R}} = \frac{b_j}{b_j - b_i}(a_i + b_i\tilde{f}) - \frac{b_i}{b_j - b_i}(a_j + b_j\tilde{f}) = \frac{b_j a_i - b_i a_j}{b_j - b_i} = R^f,$$

i.e., the portfolio weights are chosen so that the portfolio's factor loading is zero, and since $\tilde{\epsilon}_n \equiv 0$, it is therefore risk-free. We can rewrite this as

$$\frac{a_i - R^f}{b_i} = \frac{a_j - R^f}{b_j} \stackrel{\text{def}}{=} \lambda,$$

and the same argument can now be made with any other asset, n (with $b_n \neq 0$), leading to

$$\frac{a_n - R^f}{b_n} = \lambda, \quad \forall n.$$

So we end up with the pricing equation

$$E[\widetilde{R}_n] = a_n = R^f + b_n\lambda \tag{5.44}$$

(which obviously also needs to hold when $b_n = 0$, because of no arbitrage). So λ is the risk premium associated with $\tilde{f}$-risk, and the one-factor pricing formula (5.44) perfectly captures the cross section of expected returns in this special case.

5.5.2 Two-Factor Model without Idiosyncratic Risk

Now assume that $K = 2$, and there is no idiosyncratic risk: $\tilde{\epsilon}_n \equiv 0$, for all n. This leads to the two-factor relation $\widetilde{R}_n = a_n + b_n^1\tilde{f}_1 + b_n^2\tilde{f}_2$. A similar argument to before leads to

$$E[\widetilde{R}_n] = a_n = R^f + b_n^1\lambda_1 + b_n^2\lambda_2.$$

To show this, let us define the vectors $\mathbf{b}^1 = (b_1^1, b_2^1, \ldots, b_N^1)'$, $\mathbf{b}^2 = (b_1^2, b_2^2, \ldots, b_N^2)'$. Note that if $\mathbf{b}^1$ and $\mathbf{b}^2$ are linearly dependent, such that $\mathbf{b}^1 = k\mathbf{b}^2$, then this is really a one-factor model, with the factor $\tilde{f} = \frac{1}{\sqrt{1+k^2}}(\tilde{f}_1 + k\tilde{f}_2)$, and the previous result implies the pricing relation. So we can focus on the case for which $\mathbf{b}^1$ and $\mathbf{b}^2$ are linearly independent, in which case there must be two assets with linearly independent factor loadings. Let us without loss of generality assume that $(b_1^1, b_2^1)'$ and $(b_1^2, b_2^2)'$ are linearly independent (otherwise, we can simply relabel assets).

We study the returns of the portfolio $\mathbf{v} = (w_1, w_2, w_3, 0, 0, \ldots, 0)'$,

$$\widetilde{R}_p = \sum_{i=1}^{3} w_i a_i + \left(\sum_{i=1}^{3} w_i b_i^1\right)\tilde{f}_1 + \left(\sum_{i=1}^{3} w_i b_i^2\right)\tilde{f}_2.$$

Now we can choose w_1, w_2, and w_3, such that

$$w_1 + w_2 + w_3 \neq 0,$$

$$w_1 b_1^1 + w_2 b_2^1 + w_3 b_3^1 = 0, \tag{5.45}$$

$$w_1 b_1^2 + w_2 b_2^2 + w_3 b_3^2 - 0, \tag{5.46}$$

i.e., such that $\mathbf{v} \not\perp \mathbf{1}$, $\mathbf{v} \perp \mathbf{b}^1$, and $\mathbf{v} \perp \mathbf{b}^2$. In this case,

$$\widetilde{R}_p \equiv \sum_{i=1}^{3} w_i a_i \stackrel{\text{def}}{=} R^f\left(\sum_{i=1}^{3} w_i\right). \tag{5.47}$$

We can write equations (5.45, 5.46, 5.47) in matrix form as

$$\mathbf{A}\mathbf{v} = \mathbf{0},$$

where the matrix $\mathbf{A}$ is defined as

$$\mathbf{A} = \begin{bmatrix} a_1 - R^f & a_2 - R^f & a_3 - R^f \\ b_1^1 & b_2^1 & b_3^1 \\ b_1^2 & b_2^2 & b_3^2 \end{bmatrix}.$$

So $\mathbf{A}$ must be a singular matrix, since $\mathbf{v} \neq \mathbf{0}$, and therefore

$$\begin{bmatrix} a_1 - R^f \\ a_2 - R^f \\ a_3 - R^f \end{bmatrix} = \lambda_1 \begin{bmatrix} b_1^1 \\ b_2^1 \\ b_3^1 \end{bmatrix} + \lambda_2 \begin{bmatrix} b_1^2 \\ b_2^2 \\ b_3^2 \end{bmatrix},$$

for some unique constants, λ_1 and λ_2 (unique, because the factor loadings are linearly independent), i.e.,

$$a_i = R^f + \lambda_1 b_i^1 + \lambda_2 b_i^2, \quad i \in \{1, 2, 3\}.$$

Now, for an arbitrary asset $j > 3$, repeat the argument with assets 1, 2, j, to get

$$a_i = R^f + \hat{\lambda}_1 b_i^1 + \hat{\lambda}_2 b_i^2, \quad i \in \{1, 2, j\}.$$

Clearly, for this equation to hold for assets 1 and 2, it must be that $\hat{\lambda}_1 = \lambda_1$, and $\hat{\lambda}_2 = \lambda_2$. Since j was arbitrary, the pricing relation therefore holds for all i.

5.5.3 Factor Pricing with Idiosyncratic Risk

It is straightforward to show that with K factors and no idiosyncratic (ϵ) risk, the pricing relations become

$$E[\widetilde{R}_n] = a_n = R^f + \sum_{k=1}^{K} b_n^k \lambda_k. \tag{5.48}$$

We wish to derive a similar pricing relation, even when idiosyncratic risk is present. The argument is similar to what we did in the previous examples, namely that if assets' returns would deviate from the K-factor relationship, it should be possible to trade in a portfolio of assets and create a "free lunch," an *arbitrary opportunity*, by taking advantage of deviations from the K-factor prices. Any agent with increasing utility functions would love such an opportunity and demand an infinite amount of such a portfolio. It would therefore never exist in equilibrium, just like negative state prices could never be an equilibrium outcome in the Arrow–Debreu model.

This argument is straightforward when there are no idiosyncratic $\tilde{\epsilon}$-terms. However, when idiosyncratic risk is present, such arbitrages will not exist, since any nonzero portfolio loads up on $\tilde{\epsilon}$-risks. The insight from APT is that with sufficiently many assets, $\tilde{\epsilon}$-risk can basically be diversified away, effectively allowing an investor to be exposed only to the K systematic factors in many different ways, by holding large portfolios. The prices and returns of these large portfolios then need to be closely aligned for an approximate arbitrage to be ruled out. We make this argument solid by introducing the concept of asymptotic arbitrage opportunity.

Definition 5.11. An *asymptotic arbitrage opportunity* (AAO) is a sequence of portfolios $\{\mathbf{v}^n\}$, $n = 1, 2, \ldots$, where $\mathbf{v}^n \in \mathbb{R}^n$, such that

$$\sum_{i=1}^{n} \mathbf{v}_i^n = 0, \quad \forall\, n, \tag{5.49}$$

$$\sum_{i=1}^{n} \mathbf{v}_i^n a_i \geq \delta > 0, \quad \forall\, n, \tag{5.50}$$

$$\sum_{i=1}^{n}\sum_{j=1}^{n} \mathbf{v}_i^n \mathbf{v}_j^n \sigma_{ij} \to 0 \quad \text{as } n \to \infty. \tag{5.51}$$

Here, $E[\widetilde{R}_i] = a_i$, and $\mathrm{Cov}(\widetilde{R}_i, \widetilde{R}_j) = \sigma_{ij}$.

The following result shows that if there is an asymptotic arbitrage opportunity, then a zero-cost portfolio exists that has very high expected payoff and very low variance:

Proposition 5.2. *If an AAO exists, then there exists a sequence of investment portfolios $\{\mathbf{v}^n\}$, each with zero price, $\sum_j \mathbf{v}_j^n = 0$ for all n, such that the payoff $\widetilde{R}_p^n = \sum_j \mathbf{v}_j^n \widetilde{R}_j$ tends to infinity in that for all $R > 0$, there exists n_0 such that $\mathbb{P}(\widetilde{R}_p^n < R) \leq \frac{1}{R^2}$, for all $n > n_0$, and the portfolio variance tends to zero,* $\mathrm{Var}(\widetilde{R}_p^n) \to 0$.

Proof. The proof has two parts: (i) scaling the sequence of portfolios in the AAO, such that the expected payoff increases and tends to infinity in the limit, while ensuring that the variances of the returns still tend to zero, and (ii) using Chebyshev's inequality from probability theory to infer bounds on the tail probability from the bounds on variances of the sequences.

(i) Let us define the scaled portfolios, $\mathbf{z}^n = \gamma_n \mathbf{v}^n$ with associated portfolio returns $\widetilde{R}_p^n = (\mathbf{z}^n)'\widetilde{R}$, where $\gamma_n = ((\mathbf{v}^n)'\Sigma\mathbf{v}^n)^{-1/4}$. It follows that $\gamma_n \to \infty$ when n tends to infinity, and that $((\mathbf{v}^n)'\Sigma\mathbf{v}^n) = \gamma_n^{-4}$, that for sufficiently large n,

$$E[\widetilde{R}_p^n] \geq \gamma_n \delta,$$

which tends to infinity as n tends to infinity. Also, since the portfolios $\mathbf{v}^n$ have zero cost, so do the portfolios $\mathbf{z}^n$. Moreover,

$$\mathrm{Var}(\widetilde{R}_p^n) = \gamma_n^2((\mathbf{v}^n)'\Sigma\mathbf{v}^n) = \gamma_n^{-2} \to 0,$$

as n tends to infinity.

(ii) Recall Chebyshev's inequality from probability theory:

Lemma 5.4 (Chebyshev's inequality). *Consider a random variable $\tilde{x}$ with mean $\mu = E[\tilde{x}]$ and finite variance $\sigma^2 = \mathrm{Var}(\tilde{x})$. Then, for any $L > 0$,*

$$\mathbb{P}(|\tilde{x} - \mu| \geq L\sigma) \leq \frac{1}{L^2}.$$

From the vanishing variance and increasing expectation of $\widetilde{R}_p^n$, defining $\mu_n = E[\widetilde{R}_p^n]$, $\sigma_n = \mathrm{Var}(\widetilde{R}_p^n) \leq \gamma_n \delta$, $Q = \frac{\gamma_n \delta}{2}$, and $L = \gamma_n Q = \frac{\gamma_n^2 \delta}{2}$, we can use Chebyshev's inequality to derive the following bound:

$$\begin{aligned}
\mathbb{P}\left(\widetilde{R}_p^n \leq \frac{\gamma_n \delta}{2}\right) &- \mathbb{P}\left(\widetilde{R}_p^n - \mu_n \leq \frac{\gamma_n \delta}{2} - \mu_n\right) \\
&\leq \mathbb{P}\left(\widetilde{R}_p^n - \mu_n \leq -\frac{\gamma_n \delta}{2}\right) \\
&\leq \mathbb{P}\left(|\widetilde{R}_p^n - \mu_n| \geq \frac{\gamma_n \delta}{2}\right)
\end{aligned}$$

$$
\begin{aligned}
&= \mathbb{P}(|\widetilde{R}_p^n - \mu_n| \geq L\sigma_n) \\
&\leq \frac{1}{L^2} \\
&= \frac{1}{\gamma_n^2 Q^2} \\
&\leq \frac{1}{Q^2},
\end{aligned}
$$

so the result follows. □

The proposition makes clear the way through which an asymptotic arbitrage allows an investor to get an extremely good deal, from the viewpoint of a portfolio's expected returns and volatility, and therefore also Sharpe ratio. Indeed, portfolios with arbitrarily high Sharpe ratios exist in a market that allows for asymptotic arbitrage. This may be viewed as too good to be true in any real market, and we may therefore wish to rule out such asymptotic arbitrage opportunities.

The following result shows that if asymptotic arbitrage opportunities are ruled out, then there exists an approximate K-factor pricing relation:

Theorem 5.10 (Arbitrage pricing theorem). *In the K-factor model, if there are no asymptotic arbitrage opportunities, then there exists an approximate K-factor pricing relation (dependent on the market, n), $\lambda_0, \ldots, \lambda_K$, such that the pricing error,*

$$z_i = a_i - \lambda_0 - \sum_{k=1}^{K} b_i^k \lambda_k,$$

vanishes asymptotically:

$$\lim_{n\to\infty} \sum_{i=1}^{n} \frac{1}{n} z_i^2 = 0. \tag{5.52}$$

In other words, the theorem says that absence of an AAO implies the approximate K-factor pricing relation

$$a_i \approx \lambda_0 + \sum_{k=1}^{K} b_i^k \lambda_k. \tag{5.53}$$

This pricing relation, although very good "on average" as specified by (5.52), can be far off for individual assets.

Proof of theorem 5.10. We use a proof-by-contradiction approach. Specifically, for a fixed market, n, with n assets, we construct λ's for all assets that minimize pricing errors in a least squares sense. This boils down to a standard regression problem. Given those λ's, we then assume that (5.52) does *not* hold, and show that this implies that there is an asymptotic arbitrage opportunity. It follows that if there is *no* asymptotic arbitrage opportunity, (5.52) must hold under the constructed λ factors.

We suppress the n superscript in the proof, for notational convenience. Consider the minimization problem

$$\min_{\lambda_0,\lambda_1,\ldots,\lambda_K} \sum_i \left(a_i - \lambda_0 - \sum_{k=1}^{K} b_i^k \lambda_k\right)^2.$$

Define the matrix $\widehat{\mathbf{B}} = [\mathbf{1}, \mathbf{B}] = [\mathbf{1}, \mathbf{b}^1, \ldots, \mathbf{b}^K]$, where $\mathbf{b}^k = (b_1^k, b_2^k, \ldots, b_n^k)'$, $k = 1, \ldots, K$, $\bar{\mathbf{a}} = (a_1, \ldots, a_n)'$, and $\bar{\lambda} = (\lambda_0, \ldots, \lambda_K)'$. The coefficient vector, $\bar{\lambda}$, is then

$$\bar{\lambda} = (\widehat{\mathbf{B}}'\widehat{\mathbf{B}})^{-1}\widehat{\mathbf{B}}'\bar{\mathbf{a}},$$

which follows from the standard multivariate regression formula.

The vector of estimated a-coefficients is then

$$\hat{\mathbf{a}} = \widehat{\mathbf{B}}\bar{\lambda},$$

and the estimation error is $\mathbf{z} = \bar{\mathbf{a}} - \hat{\mathbf{a}}$. Equivalently,

$$\bar{\mathbf{a}} = \mathbf{z} + \hat{\mathbf{a}} = \mathbf{z} + \widehat{\mathbf{B}}\bar{\lambda}.$$

Now, from standard properties of regressions, the estimation error is orthogonal to the column vectors of $\widehat{\mathbf{B}}$, i.e., $\mathbf{z}'\mathbf{1} = 0$, $\mathbf{z}'\mathbf{b}^k = 0$, $k = 1, \ldots, K$.

Our goal is not to choose a portfolio $\mathbf{v}$ that maximizes the opportunity for excess return from the factor pricing errors. Intuitively, higher portfolio weights should be put on assets that deviate a lot from the factor part of the expected returns.

We choose

$$\mathbf{v} = \frac{1}{\sqrt{n}} \frac{\mathbf{z}}{\|\mathbf{z}\|_2},$$

where $\|\mathbf{z}\|_2 = (\sum_i \mathbf{z}_i^2)^{1/2}$ is the standard ℓ^2 norm. Note that since $\mathbf{z}'\mathbf{1} = 0$, this portfolio satisfies the first condition of an asymptotic arbitrage opportunity, namely that it does not cost anything.

We then get

$$\begin{aligned}
\widetilde{R}_p = \mathbf{v}'\widetilde{\mathbf{R}} &= \frac{1}{\sqrt{n}\|\mathbf{z}\|_2}\mathbf{z}'(\bar{\mathbf{a}} + \mathbf{B}\tilde{\mathbf{f}} + \tilde{\epsilon}) \\
&= \frac{1}{\sqrt{n}\|\mathbf{z}\|_2}\mathbf{z}'(\bar{\mathbf{a}} + \tilde{\epsilon}) \\
&= \frac{1}{\sqrt{n}\|\mathbf{z}\|_2}\mathbf{z}'(\mathbf{z} + \widehat{\mathbf{B}}\bar{\lambda} + \tilde{\epsilon}) \\
&= \frac{1}{\sqrt{n}\|\mathbf{z}\|_2}\mathbf{z}'(\mathbf{z} + \tilde{\epsilon}).
\end{aligned}$$

Here we use the fact that $\mathbf{z}'\mathbf{b}^k = 0$. Now, since $E[\tilde{\epsilon}] = \mathbf{0}$, it follows that

$$\begin{aligned}
E[\widetilde{R}_p] &= \frac{\mathbf{z}'\mathbf{z}}{\sqrt{n}\|\mathbf{z}\|_2} \\
&= \frac{1}{\sqrt{n}}\|\mathbf{z}\|_2.
\end{aligned}$$

Note that this term tends to zero if and only if (5.52) is satisfied. Thus, if (5.52) is *not* satisfied, the second condition for an asymptotic arbitrage opportunity is satisfied.

It remains to be shown that the third condition for an asymptotic arbitrage opportunity is satisfied by this portfolio. It is straightforward to show that the covariance matrix of the assets is

$$\Sigma = \text{diag}(\mathbf{s}) + \sum_{k=1}^{K} \mathbf{b}^k(\mathbf{b}^k)'.$$

We then have

$$\begin{aligned}\mathrm{Var}(\widetilde{R}_p) &= \mathbf{v}'\Sigma\mathbf{v}\\ &= \frac{1}{\sqrt{n}\|\mathbf{z}\|_2}\mathbf{z}'\left(\mathrm{diag}(\mathbf{s}) + \sum_{k=1}^{K}\mathbf{b}^k(\mathbf{b}^k)'\right)\frac{1}{\sqrt{n}\|\mathbf{z}\|_2}\mathbf{z}\\ &= \frac{1}{\sqrt{n}\|\mathbf{z}\|_2}\mathbf{z}'\,\mathrm{diag}(\mathbf{s})\frac{1}{\sqrt{n}\|\mathbf{z}\|_2}\mathbf{z}\\ &= \frac{1}{n}\frac{\sum_i \mathbf{z}_i^2\mathbf{s}_i^2}{\sum_i \mathbf{z}_i^2}\\ &\le \frac{1}{n}\frac{\sum_i \mathbf{z}_i^2 S^2}{\sum_i \mathbf{z}_i^2}\\ &= \frac{1}{n}S^2,\end{aligned}$$

which tends to zero as $n \to \infty$. The result therefore follows. □

For a so-called fully diversified portfolio, the pricing error will be zero, as shown below.

Definition 5.12. A *fully diversified portfolio*, is a sequence of portfolios $\{\mathbf{w}^n\}$, $n = 1, 2, \ldots$, such that $\mathbf{1}'\mathbf{w}^n = 1$ for all n, which for all n satisfies the boundedness condition

$$n\sum_{i=1}^{n}(\mathbf{w}_i^n)^2 \le C < \infty.$$

Because of the scaling with n in the boundedness condition, portfolio holdings in each individual asset will become vanishingly small as n grows, as will then also the impact of individual assets' pricing errors. The following result therefore follows almost immediately:

Theorem 5.11. *If there are no asymptotic arbitrage opportunities, any fully diversified portfolio is correctly priced by the K-factor pricing relation, in that*

$$\lim_{n\to\infty} E[\widetilde{R}_p^n] - \left(\lambda_0 + \sum_{k=1}^{K} b_p^{n,k}\lambda_k\right) = 0,$$

where $\widetilde{R}_p^n = \widetilde{\mathbf{R}}'\mathbf{w}^n$, *and* $b_p^{n,k} = \sum_{i=1}^{n} b_i^k \mathbf{w}_i^n$, $n = 1, 2, \ldots, k = 1, \ldots, K$.

Proof. Using the same notation as in the proof of theorem 5.10, we can write

$$\begin{aligned}E[\widetilde{R}_p^n] &= (\mathbf{w}^n)'\mathbf{a}\\ &= (\mathbf{w}^n)'(\mathbf{z} + \widehat{\mathbf{B}}\bar{\lambda})\\ &= \lambda_0 + \sum_{k=1}^{K} b_p^{n,k}\lambda_k + e^n,\end{aligned}$$

where the error term $e^n = \sum_{i=1}^{n} \mathbf{w}_i^n z_i$. Via the Cauchy–Schwarz inequality, it follows that

$$e^n \le \sqrt{n\sum_{i=1}^{n}(\mathbf{w}_i^n)^2} \times \sqrt{\frac{1}{n}\sum_{i=1}^{n} z_i^2}.$$

The leftmost term in this expression is bounded since the portfolio is fully diversified, and the rightmost term tends to zero since there exists no AAO, so the error term tends to zero, and the result therefore follows. □

If a fully diversified portfolio $\{\mathbf{w}^n\}$ exists that generates a risk-free return,[15] i.e., such that $(\mathbf{w}^n)'\widetilde{\mathbf{R}} \to_{\text{a.s.}} R^f$, then the pricing formula, which is exact in this case due to the theorem, gives us

$$(\mathbf{w}^n)'(\lambda_0\mathbf{1} + \mathbf{b}^1\lambda_1 + \cdots + \mathbf{b}^K\lambda_K + \mathbf{B}\tilde{\mathbf{f}} + \tilde{\epsilon}) \to_{\text{a.s.}} R^f.$$

Now, because there is no residual risk, it must be that $(\mathbf{w}^n)'\mathbf{b}^k \to 0$, $k = 1, \ldots, K$, and, moreover, since the portfolio is fully diversified, $(\mathbf{w}^n)'\tilde{\epsilon} \to_{\text{a.s.}} 0$. Therefore,

$$(\mathbf{w}^n)'\widetilde{\mathbf{R}} \to_{\text{a.s.}} (\mathbf{w}^n)'\lambda_0\mathbf{1} = \lambda_0,$$

and it follows that $\lambda_0 = R^f$ in (5.53) in this case, in line with the intuition in the no-arbitrage case without idiosyncratic risk (5.48).

A natural follow-up question is under what conditions one can conclude that there are no asymptotic arbitrage opportunities. It is straightforward to show that when the factor pricing formula is exact, asymptotic arbitrage opportunities cannot exist.

Proposition 5.3. *If the factor pricing formula is exact,*

$$a_n = R_f + \sum_{k=1}^{K} b_n^k \lambda_k, \quad \forall\, n,$$

there exist no asymptotic arbitrage opportunities.

Proof. Consider a candidate AAO, $\{\mathbf{v}^n\}_n$. Condition (5.49) implies that $\mathbf{1}'\mathbf{v}^n = 0$. Moreover, (5.50) implies that

$$E[(\mathbf{v}^n)'\widetilde{\mathbf{R}}] = (\mathbf{v}^n)'\mathbf{1}R_f + \sum_{k=1}^{K}(\mathbf{v}^n)'\mathbf{b}^k\lambda_k \geq \delta > 0,$$

and since $(\mathbf{v}^n)'\mathbf{1} = 0$, this means that $(\mathbf{v}^n)'\mathbf{b}^k \geq \frac{\delta}{K\lambda_k}$ for some k.

It follows that (5.51) cannot be satisfied, since

$$(\mathbf{v}^n)'\Sigma(\mathbf{v}^n) \geq (\mathbf{v}^n)'(\mathbf{b}^k(\mathbf{b}^k)')\mathbf{v}^n \geq \left(\frac{\delta}{K\lambda_k}\right)^2,$$

which does not converge to zero as $n \to \infty$. So it is not possible to satisfy all three AAO conditions simultaneously, and thus an AAO does not exist. □

5.6 Exercises

1. *General equilibrium*: Consider an economy with M CARA investors, each with risk-aversion coefficient γ, and a fixed risk/free rate of R^f. There is a supply of S shares in a firm. Each share pays a normally distributed liquidating dividend at time 1,

$$\widetilde{D} \sim N(a, b^2).$$

   (a) Derive an expression for the time-0 market-clearing price, P_0, of the asset.

[15] Without further restrictions on the factor loadings, we cannot guarantee that such a portfolio exists.

(b) What is the asset's risk premium, $\mu^e = E[\tilde{\mu}] - R^f$? Explain intuitively how the risk premium depends on the different variables.

2. *Arrow–Debreu economy*: There are $M > 1$ agents with CRRA utility

$$U = \frac{c_0^{1-\gamma}}{1-\gamma} + \delta E\left[\frac{\tilde{c}_1^{1-\gamma}}{1-\gamma}\right],$$

and $N > 1$ possible future states. All agents agree on probabilities, $\pi_n^m = \pi_n$ for all m.

Define agent m's consumption share in state n as

$$\frac{c_{1n}^m}{C_{1n}}.$$

How do equilibrium consumption shares vary across states, n, for an agent? You may assume that there is no aggregate uncertainty, $C_{1,n} = C_1$ for all n.

3. *CAPM*: In a market, in which the CAPM holds, the expected return on the market is $r^m = 10\%$ per year, the risk-free rate is $r^f = 4\%$ per year, and the market volatility is $\sigma^m = 15\%$ per year. What is the highest obtainable Sharpe ratio in this market?

4. *CAPM from market clearance*: Consider a market with two companies, each paying liquidating dividends $\tilde{D}_n \sim N(a_n, \sigma_n^2)$, $n = 1, 2$, at $t = 1$. Define the vector $\tilde{\mathbf{D}} = (\tilde{D}_1, \tilde{D}_2)'$, with covariance matrix Σ, and $\mathbf{a} = (a_1, a_2)$. Moreover, assume that the risk-free rate is R^f and that there are M CARA investors in the market, each with risk-aversion coefficient γ. The total supply of stocks is $\mathbf{S} = (S_1, S_2)'$. The parameter values are

$$\Sigma = \begin{bmatrix} 0.45 & 0 \\ 0 & 0.45 \end{bmatrix}, \quad \mathbf{a} = \begin{bmatrix} 1.1 \\ 1.1 \end{bmatrix}, \quad \mathbf{S} = \begin{bmatrix} 1 \\ 1 \end{bmatrix},$$

$$R^f = 1.04, \qquad \gamma = 1, \qquad M = 5.$$

(a) What are the equilibrium prices of the two stocks in this market?

(b) Assume there is a new entrant, so that there are now three companies in the market, with $a_3 = 1.1$, $S_3 = 3$, $\sigma(\tilde{D}_3) = 0.45$, $\text{Cov}(\tilde{D}_1, \tilde{D}_3) = 0.1$, $\text{Cov}(\tilde{D}_2, \tilde{D}_3) = -0.1$. No new competition arises in the product market between the companies, so the dividend distributions of the initial two companies remain the same. Calculate the prices of existing companies, 1 and 2, when the new entrant is present. Why are they different compared with (a), even though there is no new competition in the product market?

5. *CAPM with human capital risk*: Assume that there are two publicly traded companies in the whole market, each worth \$500 million, with independent returns $\tilde{\mu}_i$, $i \in \{1, 2\}$. The risk-free rate is $r^f = 10\%$. Assume that $E[\tilde{\mu}_1] = E[\tilde{\mu}_2] = 20\%$ and $\sigma(\tilde{\mu}_1) = \sigma(\tilde{\mu}_2) = 30\%$.

(a) Assume that the CAPM holds. What is the variance and expected return on the market portfolio, $\tilde{r}^m$?

(b) What is the beta of each of the two companies, β_i, $i \in \{1, 2\}$?

(c) Assume that a third company purchases half of the operations of each of firms 1 and 2, and becomes publicly traded as company $i = 3$, with returns $\tilde{\mu}_3$.

We can think of this as each of the original firms having two identical factories. Each of a firm's factories generates identical cash flows. The third firm then purchases one factory from each company. Each of the original firms therefore becomes smaller but the total size of the market remains the same.

Calculate company 3's value, expected returns $E[\tilde{\mu}_3]$, standard deviation $\sigma(\tilde{\mu}_3)$, and beta, β_3.

(d) Now assume that the investors in the market turn company 1 into a private company. The investors still receive the cash flows generated from this company, so in real terms nothing has changed, but the *stock market* portfolio now consists of only companies 2 and 3. Since "the market" is usually thought of as the stock market when estimating the CAPM, this portfolio of the stocks of companies 2 and 3 would then be used.

There are several possible interpretations of this new situation. One could be that the cash flows generated by company 1 actually represent the labor income investors receive. If these are risky, they should be taken into account when making investment decisions. The stock market portfolio is then a strict subset of the total market for risk, and $\tilde{r}^{\text{total}} \neq \tilde{r}^m$, in general. Intuitively, investors should take *all* their risky positions into account, suggesting that the CAPM will hold with respect to $\tilde{r}^{\text{total}}$, but no longer with respect to $\tilde{r}^m$.

Calculate the betas, β_i^m, of the publicly traded companies 2 and 3, based on the stock market portfolio, $\tilde{r}^m$. Does the CAPM relation

$$E[\tilde{\mu}_i] = \beta_i^m (E[\tilde{r}^m] - r^f) + r^f,$$

hold in this case?

(e) What lessons can we learn from this exercise, about whether the CAPM holds?

6. *Arrow–Debreu economy*: Consider an Arrow–Debreu economy with two dates, $t = 0, 1$, one state, $N = 1$, and two agents, $M = 2$, with log-utility

$$U^m = \log(c_0^m) + \log(c_{11}^m), \quad m = 1, 2.$$

Agent 1 receives the endowment stream $e_0^1 = 1$, $e_{11}^1 = 1$, and agent 2 the stream $e_0^2 = 1$, $e_{11}^2 = 2$. Derive expressions for the equilibrium price of the Arrow–Debreu security, p_1, and the consumption of the two agents, c_0^1, c_0^2, c_{11}^1, and c_{11}^2.

7. *Arrow–Debreu economy*: There are two agents, $M = 2$, each with log-utility

$$U^m = \log(c_0^m) + E[\log(\tilde{c}_1^m)].$$

There are two possible future states, $N = 2$. Each agent gets one unit of consumption good at each time in each state, $e_0^m = e_{1,n}^m = 1$, $m = 1, 2$, $n = 1, 2$. There is thus no aggregate risk in the economy: $C_0 = C_{1,n} = 2$. Agents disagree about the probabilities, $\pi_{1,1}^1 = 1 - \pi_{1,1}^2 \in (0, \frac{1}{2}]$. Derive the equilibrium consumption, and also the welfare for the two agents in terms of a subjective certainty equivalent for each agent. Compare the welfare in the market equilibrium and in the autarky. Has risk decreased? Are both agents better off?

8. *Arbitrage pricing theory*: Consider a sequence of portfolio investments, $\mathbf{v}^1, \mathbf{v}^2, \ldots, \mathbf{v}^n \in \mathbb{R}^n$, with associated returns $\widetilde{R}_p^n$, such that $\sum_i \mathbf{v}_i^n = 0$ for all n, $\mu_n = E[\tilde{R}_p^n] = 3n$, for all n, and $\sigma_n^2 = \text{Var}(\widetilde{r}_p^n) = 12$, for all n.

(a) Show that this sequence does not constitute an AAO.

(b) Does there exist an AAO in this economy?

9. *Arbitrage pricing theory*: Consider a sequence of portfolio investments, $\mathbf{v}^1, \mathbf{v}^2, \ldots, \mathbf{v}^n \in \mathbb{R}^n$, with associated returns $\widetilde{R}_p^n$, such that $\sum_i \mathbf{v}_i^n = 0$ for all n, and

$$\tilde{r}_p^n = \begin{cases} 1 - n + \ln(n), & \text{with probability } n^{-3}, \\ 1 + n + \ln(n), & \text{with probability } n^{-3}, \\ 1 + \ln(n), & \text{with probability } 1 - 2n^{-3}. \end{cases}$$

   (a) Does this constitute an AAO?
   (b) What would a CARA investor's expected utility be in the limit, $\lim_{n\to\infty} E[u(\tilde{r}_p^n)]$? Would the investor appreciate this investment opportunity?

10. *Arbitrage pricing theory*: The returns of assets in an economy with an infinite number of assets are given by

$$\widetilde{R}_1 \equiv 1,$$

$$\widetilde{R}_n = \frac{11}{10} + \epsilon_n, \quad n \geq 2,$$

where $\text{Var}(\epsilon_n) = 1$ for all n. Consider the sequence of portfolios $\{\mathbf{v}^n\}$, $n = 1, \ldots$, where $\mathbf{v}^n$ contains n assets:

$$(\mathbf{v}^n)_i = \begin{cases} -n + 1, & i = 1, \\ 1, & 2 \leq i \leq n, \\ 0, & i > n. \end{cases}$$

   (a) Is there a portfolio, $\mathbf{v}^n$, for some specific n that constitutes a (pure) arbitrage opportunity?
   (b) Show that the sequence $\{\mathbf{v}^n\}$, $n = 1, \ldots$, does *not* constitute an asymptotic arbitrage opportunity.
   (c) Construct a modified sequence of portfolios, $\{\mathbf{y}^n\}$, such that $\mathbf{y}^n = \gamma_n \mathbf{v}^n$, where $\{\gamma_n\}_n$ is a sequence of positive numbers, such that the sequence $\{\mathbf{y}^n\}$, $n = 1, \ldots$, *does* constitute an asymptotic arbitrage opportunity.

11. *CAPM and the size distribution of firms*: Consider a one-period market, $t \in \{0, 1\}$, in which there is a price-taking representative CARA investor, maximizing expected utility

$$U = E[-e^{-\gamma \widetilde{W}_1}].$$

The gross risk-free rate in the economy is $R^f = 1$, and there are N publicly traded firms. The terminal dividend paid by firm n is

$$\widetilde{D}_n = s_n(1 + a_n \tilde{\xi}_0 + \sqrt{1 - a_n^2} \tilde{\xi}_n), \quad n = 1, \ldots, N,$$

where ξ_n, $n = 0, \ldots, N$, are i.i.d. normally distributed random variables, $\xi_n \sim N(0, 1)$. We can think of this as one share of each stock being available, $n = 1, 2, \ldots, N$, each paying the dividend, $\widetilde{D}_n$. The vector $\mathbf{s} = (s_1, s_n, \ldots, s_N)'$ then defines the sizes of the firms' expected dividends, since $E[\widetilde{D}_n] = s_n$. Moreover, the vector $\mathbf{a} = (a_1, a_2, \ldots, a_N)'$ determines the firms' exposures to systemic and firm-specific risk. Note that $\text{Var}(\widetilde{D}_n) = s_n^2$ and $\text{Cov}(\widetilde{D}_n, \widetilde{D}_m) = s_n s_m a_n a_m$. We assume that $0 < a_n < 1$ for all n, and that size distributions are normalized such that $\sum_n s_n = 1$. Furthermore, we make the technical assumption that $\sum_n \frac{a_n^2}{1 - a_n^2} \neq 1$.

The assets' prices at time 0 are determined by market clearing. We also define the price vector, $\mathbf{P}=(P_1,P_2,\ldots,P_N)'$, where P_n denotes the price at time 0 of firm n.

(a) Derive an expression for the equilibrium price vector, $\mathbf{P}$, that only depends on γ, $\mathbf{s}$, and $\mathbf{a}$ (and that does not contain expectations).

(b) Discuss the expression for the price discount, $\frac{P_n}{s_n}$, given your answer in (a). How should we interpret the dependence of this discount on $\mathbf{s}$ and $\mathbf{a}$? Will a_n or s_n be most important for the discount?

(c) Derive an expression for the market risk premium in the economy. Show that, given $\mathbf{a}$, the market risk premium is minimized when the size distribution is such that

$$s_n = C\left(\frac{1}{1-a_n^2} - \frac{1}{1+\sum_k \frac{a_k^2}{1-a_k^2}}\left(\sum_k \frac{a_k}{1-a_k^2}\right)\frac{a_n}{1-a_n^2}\right),$$

where C is a normalization constant, chosen such that $1=\sum_n s_n$. For what size distribution(s) is the market risk premium maximized?

(d) Does the CAPM hold in this economy?

(e) Can this model explain the size effect mentioned in section 5.2.3?

(f) In this question, you may assume that $a_n=0.5$ for all n. The size distribution of firms in the US economy has been extensively analyzed, and it has been proposed that it is very heavy tailed. Assuming that a so-called Zipf law holds for firm dividends, the relationship of the sizes of the largest and the nth largest firm dividends would be approximately $s_n=\frac{s_1}{n}$. Compare this with a market with more thin-tailed firm dividend distribution (exponentially distributed), in which the relation is $s_n = s_1 - c\ln(n), c>0$. How is the market risk premium associated with the size distribution of dividends across firms?

Hint: The following matrix inverse relationship holds for vectors $\mathbf{a}=(a_1,\ldots,a_N)'$ and $\mathbf{b}=(b_1,\ldots,b_N)'$:

$$(\Lambda_{\mathbf{b}}+\mathbf{aa}')^{-1}=\Lambda_{\mathbf{b}}^{-1}-\frac{1}{1+t}\Lambda_{\mathbf{b}}^{-1}(\mathbf{aa}')\Lambda_{\mathbf{b}}^{-1}.$$

Here, $\Lambda_{\mathbf{b}}=\operatorname{diag}(\mathbf{b})$ and $t=\mathbf{a}'\Lambda_{\mathbf{b}}^{-1}\mathbf{a}=\sum_n \frac{a_n^2}{b_n}$. The formula holds as long as $t\neq -1$ and $b_n\neq 0$ for all n.

12. *Lucas tree economy*: Consider the one-tree economy with equilibrium stochastic discount factor $M_{0,t}=e^{-\rho t-\gamma v_t}$, $v_t\sim N(\mu t,\sigma^2 t)$, $\mu>0$, $\sigma>0$. Let us assume that the time-0 dividend ("fruit") is $Y_0=1$.

(a) Consider a so-called digital option, which pays out 1 at the given time, $T>0$, if (and only if) the price of the economy's stock (tree) $p_t>Z$, for some $Z>0$. Thus, if $p_T>Z$, the owner of the option gets 1 at time T, and if $p_T<Z$, the owner gets nothing.

Denote the price at time t of the option by D_t. Using what you know about SDFs, derive an expression for the value of the option at time 0, D_0.

(b) Now consider an asset that pays p_T at time T. What is the value of this asset at time 0?

PART II

No-Arbitrage Pricing and Derivatives

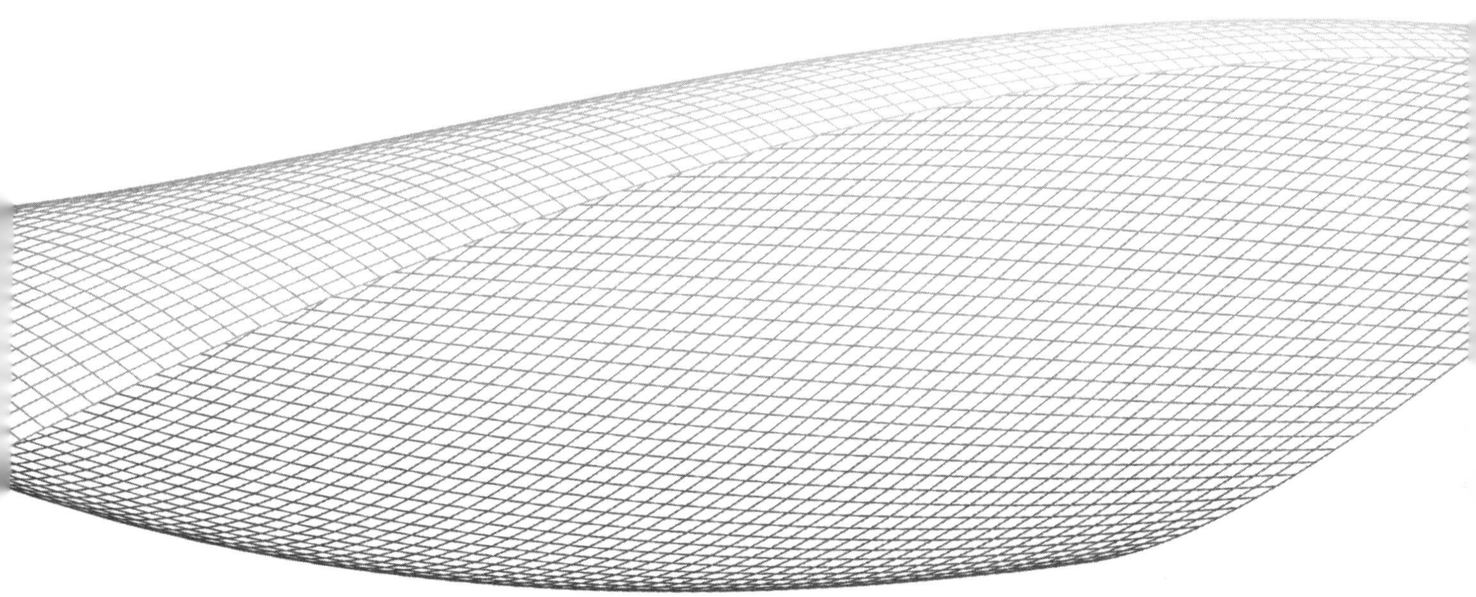

CHAPTER 6 Introduction to No-Arbitrage Pricing

The explosive development of derivatives markets is arguably the most important innovation in financial markets in the last fifty years. The number and types of derivative contracts have grown exponentially, as these contracts have been widely adopted in capital markets.

The celebrated Black–Scholes option pricing formula, also called the Black–Scholes–Merton formula, that was introduced in the early 1970s is one of the most successful formulas in the economic sciences, as acknowledged when Robert Merton and Myron Scholes obtained the Sveriges Riksbank Prize in Economic Sciences in Memory of Alfred Nobel (the "Nobel prize in Economics"), in 1997. The formula and its many variations has led to the development of a whole new field, *financial engineering*, which occupies tens of thousands of employees at financial institutions and also faculty at universities around the world. Part II of this text covers some of the theory behind these classical formulas, in a self-contained format.

We cover no-arbitrage theory, stochastic calculus with focus on Brownian motion, Itô integrals and calculus (Itô's lemma), the martingale representation theorem, change of measure (Girsanov's theorem), and links to partial differential equations (Feynman–Kac's theorem and the Kolmogorov equations for diffusion processes), as well as applications to derivative pricing and fixed income markets. Several fundamental tools and concepts are introduced: self-financing portfolios, no-arbitrage pricing, risk-neutral measures, hedging, and partial differential equations for pricing of assets. This toolbox is then used to derive the famous Black–Scholes formula, as well as valuation formulas for many other securities.

The organization of this part is as follows: After introducing some notation in section 7.1 and briefly discussing capital markets in section 7.2, we begin with the static one-period model in sections 7.3–7.8. This is the simplest possible setting and, as we will see, much of the economic intuition of the subsequent more advanced chapters can be understood within this setting. It is natural to first develop the static model of trading and pricing, using standard mathematical structures from linear algebra (linear vector spaces, matrices, and vectors). A nice intuition for the asset pricing results is provided by a tight link between these results and classical results in linear algebra. The purpose of chapter 7 is thus mainly to provide a simple setting that allows us to develop a good intuition for the results in subsequent more advanced environments in later chapters.

The next step in generalizing the analysis is taken in chapter 8, where we move from one-period to multiperiod models with finite state spaces. We first develop the binomial model. This model, which has been widely used in practice, is theoretically a special case of the general multiperiod model. As we will see, much of the intuition from the static model carries over to the multiperiod setting. Specifically, the multiperiod model can in many ways be interpreted as a sequence of one-period economies over time and states. The results on no arbitrage, existence of martingale measures, and the links between these concepts are therefore basically identical to those in the one-period model. The two concepts that do not arise in the static setting, but that are fundamental in the multiperiod setting, are (i) the power of dynamic trading strategies to drastically increase the types of payoffs that can be generated, and (ii) the modeling of gradual diffusion of information into prices over time. We will spend some effort on these new concepts.

Chapter 9 introduces the continuous-time model in a sequence of steps. As a lead-in, the end of chapter 8 studies the convergence of the binomial method when we let the number of time periods tend to infinity, following the approach in Cox, Ross, and Rubinstein (1979). Here we carefully choose the parameters in the model to match the moments of a real-world security. The goal of this exercise is twofold: First it moves us from the theory of asset prices in abstract markets to pricing in real markets, by allowing for calibration to real data. Second, it allows us to take a first cut at deriving the Black–Scholes pricing formula for a European call option and, especially, to informally understand the steps of going from the discrete to the continuous-time setting, before introducing the full-blown continuous-time theory.

Sections 9.1 and 9.2 discuss Brownian motion, stochastic integration, and diffusion processes—concepts that are then used when introducing the continuous-time portfolio model in section 9.3. In section 9.4 we discuss the fundamental link between diffusion processes and partial differential equations (PDEs), via the Kolmogorov equations. In Section 9.5, we use this relation to derive the Black–Scholes PDE and the Black–Scholes pricing formula. We derive the results with both a replicating portfolio argument and a risk-neutral pricing argument to provide as much intuition as possible for these fundamental results.

In section 9.6, we introduce measure transformations and Girsanov's theorem, and in chapter 10 we apply our theory to some specific asset pricing problems, including options on stocks that pay dividends and barrier options. Finally, in chapter 11, we discuss some classical numerical methods in derivatives pricing.

CHAPTER 7 One-Period Model

7.1 Preliminary Notation

In this part, we mainly use bold lowercase Latin letters for vectors and bold uppercase Latin letters for matrices. In some cases we use non-bold (i.e., normal) Greek letters (e.g., the expected return vector μ and the covariance matrix Σ), in line with the literature. The transpose of a vector, $\mathbf{v}$, is $\mathbf{v}^T$, where we also use the notation $\mathbf{v}'$. Specifically, if $\mathbf{v}$ is an $N \times 1$ column vector, then $\mathbf{v}^T$ is a $1 \times N$ row vector. We use MATLAB matrix notation, i.e., $[\mathbf{A}, \mathbf{B}]$ denotes column concatenation and $[\mathbf{A}; \mathbf{B}]$ row concatenation of the matrices $\mathbf{A}$ and $\mathbf{B}$, respectively. So, for example, $\mathbf{A} = [1, 2, 3]$ and $\mathbf{B} = [4, 5, 6]$ concatenate to

$$\mathbf{C} = [\mathbf{A}; \mathbf{B}] = \begin{bmatrix} 1 & 2 & 3 \\ 4 & 5 & 6 \end{bmatrix}.$$

The $N \times N$ identity matrix, $\mathbf{I}$ (or $\mathbf{I}_N$, if we want to emphasize its dimensionality), is defined as the matrix with 1's on the diagonal, and 0's as off-diagonal elements, e.g.,

$$\mathbf{I}_3 = \begin{bmatrix} 1 & 0 & 0 \\ 0 & 1 & 0 \\ 0 & 0 & 1 \end{bmatrix}.$$

If $\mathbf{v}$ is an N-vector, then $\Lambda = \text{diag}(\mathbf{v})$ is the $N \times N$ diagonal matrix with $\mathbf{v}$'s elements on its diagonal, e.g.,

$$\text{diag}((1, 2, 3)^T) = \begin{bmatrix} 1 & 0 & 0 \\ 0 & 2 & 0 \\ 0 & 0 & 3 \end{bmatrix}.$$

The ith element of vector $\mathbf{a}$ is $(\mathbf{a})_i$, or if there can be no confusion, $\mathbf{a}_i$. Similarly, the element on the ith row and jth column of the matrix $\mathbf{A}$ is $(\mathbf{A})_{ij}$, or $\mathbf{A}_{ij}$.

For a vector $\mathbf{a}$, we write $\mathbf{a} \geq \mathbf{0}$, if all elements are nonnegative, $\mathbf{a} > \mathbf{0}$ if at least one element is strictly positive, and $\mathbf{a} \gg \mathbf{0}$ if all elements are strictly positive, with similar definitions for $\leq$, $<$, and $\ll$.

We use the following set-theoretic notation: The complement of a set, A, is $A^c = \{b \in \Omega : b \notin A\}$. Here, it is assumed that $A \subset \Omega$ for some universal set Ω. The union of A and B is $A \cup B$, and the intersection is $A \cap B$.

We expand on these and other concepts in appendixes A and B.

7.2 Capital Markets

We are interested in the pricing of assets that are traded in capital markets. Examples of such assets are stocks, bonds, and derivative contracts. A stock gives the owner an ownership share in a publicly traded firm. Specifically, the firm has many stakeholders, e.g., its workers, its lenders, and also its shareholders. The firm generates cash flows over time. After the other stakeholders have been paid off, i.e., workers have received their salaries, interest on loans has been paid to the bank, etc., shareholders capture the residual cash flows, e.g., when the stock makes a *dividend payment.* The buyer of a stock share pays a price, S, today to get the rights to such future payments.

The action of buying a stock leads to a transfer of money from the present (at which point money is paid) to the future (at which point it is received), either via dividend payments, or by selling the stock. In addition to this time dimension of the transfer, there is also a risk dimension, in that once the price is determined, the cash flow in the present is known, whereas the future dividend/sales price is not; it is *random.*

A simpler asset, which only involves the time dimension of the transaction, is the risk-free bond. Here, the buyer pays a price today and ensures a future payment which is determined by the so-called *face value* of the bond. For example, the bond contract may have a face value of USD 100, to be paid one year into the future, and trade at the current price of $B =$ USD 97.5. The difference between today's price and the payment in a year represents the *time value of money.* Government bonds are usually considered approximately risk-free, although they can never completely be, since there are always some calamitous events under which payments will not be made. Another thing to note is that the risk-freeness is with respect to the number of dollars to be paid. Under other metrics, e.g., the value of the payments in terms of British pounds sterling (GBP), or in terms of the number of Big Mac hamburgers one can buy, the future payments are *not* risk-free. We discussed stocks and bonds in part I.

A third example is a so-called *call option.* In the simplest case, the buyer of such an option has the right, but not the obligation, to purchase a share of a stock at a future date, e.g., three months from today, for a price, K, that is agreed upon today, and that is called the option's *strike price.* For example, IBM stocks may be trading at a price of USD 90 right now, and a call option on IBM may give the owner of the option the right to purchase one IBM share from the seller at the price $K =$ USD 135 on the *exercise date* in three months. Now, on that date, this right is only valuable if IBM's stock price is higher than USD 135, in which case the owner chooses to *exercise* the option, and buys the stock at a discount. On the other hand, if IBM's stock price is below USD 135 on that date, in which case we say that the option expires *out of the money*, the option is worthless since the owner will never buy the stock for USD 135 when (s)he can purchase it for a lower price in the market.

Now, one may believe that the chance that the option will expire in the money three months from today is low. Indeed, IBM's stock price would have to increase by 50%, an event that is quite unlikely to happen. Thus, the market value, C, of the option today, i.e., the value of the contract that gives the owner this right to purchase the stock, may be very low. However, the point is that since the owner of the option always has the right *not* to exercise it, there is never any downside of owning it. As long as there is some chance, albeit very small, that the option will expire in the money, it will have a positive value today. We will discuss these contracts and others in more detail later on.

What determines the price of an asset, e.g., a stock, bond, or derivative contract, in the capital market? Capital markets operate much like any other market: potential buyers and sellers get together and agree on a price at which a trade occurs. These potential buyers and sellers in the market determine prices through their willingness to purchase and sell the assets, and it therefore seems that we would need to know what is going on in the brain of each and every individual to be able to answer this question.

Our goal is to answer this general question, by making simple and reasonable assumptions about how agents, markets, and assets behave. Technically, we develop a *model*, within which we can make strong statements about asset prices. It is important to always remember that the whole point of a model is to be a simplification of the very complex real world. As such, the model will never be able to exactly replicate the real world. The aim is thus to capture as much as possible of the real world in a model based on as simple as possible assumptions, introducing two dimensions that need to be balanced.[1]

7.3 Modeling the Market

Our general goal is thus to introduce a model based on a minimal set of assumptions, within which as strong as possible quantitative statements about the prices of assets can be made. No-arbitrage theory provides such a set of assumptions and, in addition, provides a useful framework for how to think about capital markets. For some asset classes and markets (e.g., certain types of derivative and fixed income contracts) it works really well in the quantitative dimension. For others (e.g., stocks), stronger assumptions are usually needed to be able to say much about prices, as discussed in part I. We note the tension here: weaker model assumptions allow more general assets to be covered, and make results fairly robust, but also lead to weaker predictions.

So which components do we need in our model? Given that prices are ultimately decided by the traders in the market, we obviously need traders and assets! Traders typically invest in more than one asset, i.e., they hold *portfolios*. The future value of a trader's portfolio depends on the performance of the portfolio's *constituents* (the assets in the portfolio), which in turn is uncertain. Specifically, we would expect random events, like oil-price shocks, unforeseen weather patterns, and future unemployment rates, to impact the future value of an asset and a portfolio.

A good set of base assumptions turn out to be those of a *static, friction-free market*, in which investors *agree on the state space*. Let us discuss each of these:

1. *Static*: Initially, we assume that there are only two points in time: "today," $t = 0$, and "tomorrow," $t = 1$. This is of course a quite drastic deviation compared with the real world that progresses continuously—or in a sequence of extremely small discrete time increments, if one takes quantum physics into account. The assumption simplifies the analysis a lot

[1] My thesis adviser, Jon Ingersoll, stressed that the only asset pricing model that prices all assets perfectly is the real-world itself, a "model" that fails spectacularly in the second dimension.

and, as it turns out, many results can be generalized to a richer setting. We will see this in subsequent chapters when we analyze *dynamic* markets.

2. *Friction-free*: In physics the resistance an object encounters when moving on another object, or through a medium like water, is a friction. In an idealized world without frictions, based on Newtonian mechanics, a ball put in motion on a flat surface would continue to roll at the same speed perpetually. In practice, it loses speed over time. Similarly, frictions in models of financial economics represent deviations from an idealized world, which is based on perfect competition among agents, no transaction costs, and no informational asymmetries. The term *friction* in this context thus rules out a plethora of effects that are present in real-world markets. Our explicit assumptions in this part are those of (i) no transaction costs, i.e., of there being no fees associated with trading in an asset, and (ii) perfectly elastic supply curves, i.e., no matter what the demand is for an asset, the price per unit of the asset remains the same. We also used the concept of friction-free (perfect) markets in chapter 7.3.
3. *Agreement on the state space*: We discussed there being assets for which there is uncertainty about the "tomorrow" value, i.e., for which there are multiple possible values, depending on what happens in the economy. We allow agents to disagree about how likely different outcomes may be. For example, one agent may believe that there is a 10% chance that IBM's stock price will increase to USD 110 tomorrow, whereas another may believe that there is only a 5% chance. However, we require all agents to agree on what the set of *possible* outcomes are, i.e., the set of outcomes that occur with strictly positive probability.

Technically, we proceed as follows. We assume that all agents agree that here are M different potential *outcomes*, or *states*. Formally, we define the *sample space* (or state space), which is the set of possible outcomes, $\Omega = \{\omega_1, \omega_2, \ldots, \omega_M\}$. For the time being, we do not associate probabilities with these outcomes, but we do assume that all traders agree that there is a strictly positive chance for each to occur (see point 3 above). An interpretation is that we "throw away" all impossible states, since these should not influence asset prices anyway.

There are N *assets* traded in a *financial market*, enumerated by $n = 1, \ldots, N$. The price of asset n at time $t \in \{0, 1\}$ is S_n^t, and all the prices can be represented by the vectors $\mathbf{s}^t = (S_1^t, \ldots, S_N^t)^T \in \mathbb{R}^N$. We will also use the term *value* at $t = 0, 1$, and *payoff* for the price at $t = 1$.

Since the outcome, $\omega \in \Omega$, is not known at $t = 0$, $\mathbf{s}^1$ is a *random variable*, i.e., it is a function of the (currently unknown) state of the world at $t = 1$. We can write this ω-dependence in functional form as $\mathbf{s}^1(\omega)$. Furthermore, the dependence can be conveniently summarized by the matrix $\mathbf{D} = [\mathbf{s}^1(\omega_1), \mathbf{s}^1(\omega_2), \ldots, \mathbf{s}^1(\omega_M)] \in \mathbb{R}^{N \times M}$. Here, the element $(\mathbf{D})_{nm}$ of the matrix represents the payoff of one unit of asset n in state m. We will work with the augmented matrix $\bar{\mathbf{D}} = [-\mathbf{s}^0, \mathbf{D}] \in \mathbb{R}^{N \times (1+M)}$, which conveniently summarizes all information about the prices of all assets, in all states of the world, at all points in time. Our third assumption above can then be formalized as the assumption that all investors agree on the state space, Ω, and that the probability for each element in Ω to occur is greater than zero.

Example 7.1. Consider a market in which there are three assets: a risky stock, a risk-free bond making a payment of 3 in each state, and a call option with strike price of $K = 4$. There are four possible future states, $\Omega = \{\omega_1, \omega_2, \omega_3, \omega_4\}$. The stock price in these states is 1, 3, 4, and 5, respectively. The three assets' current (time $t = 0$) prices are $S = 3.5$, $B = 2.5$, and $C = 0.5$. Using the matrix notation, with the assets in the same order as introduced above, this leads to the $\bar{\mathbf{D}}$-matrix

$$\bar{\mathbf{D}} = \begin{bmatrix} -3.5 & 1 & 3 & 4 & 5 \\ -2.5 & 3 & 3 & 3 & 3 \\ -0.5 & 0 & 0 & 0 & 1 \end{bmatrix}.$$

You should verify that this is indeed the matrix that represents the economy just defined.

Example 7.2. The following example also shows an economy with four states and three assets, but with different payout structures:

$$\bar{\mathbf{D}} = \begin{bmatrix} -1 & 1 & 2 & 2 & 2 \\ -\frac{1}{2} & 1 & 2 & 2 & 2 \\ 1 & 1 & 0 & 0 & 0 \end{bmatrix}.$$

The first asset has a time $t=0$ price of $S_1^0 = 1$, a future payoff of 1 in state ω_1, and a payoff of 2 in all other states. The second asset has the same payoffs as asset 1, but only costs $\frac{1}{2}$. Finally, the third asset has a negative price, since it generates a positive time-0 cash flow when purchased. It pays off 1 in ω_1 and nothing in the other three states.

For example, an asset with time-0 price $S^0 = 1$, and time-1 price $S^1 = R$ in all states of the world for some constant, $R > 1$, can be viewed as a fixed-rate bank deposit, paying a one-period net interest rate of $r = R - 1$: the price today is 1, and at $t = 1$, the asset is worth $1 + r$, so the interest paid is r. We note that the elements of $\bar{\mathbf{D}}$ need not be positive. For example, an asset with $S^0 = -1$, and $S^1 = -R$ in all states, can be interpreted as a fixed-rate *loan*, where the "price" at $t=0$ of -1 corresponds to receiving a dollar at $t=0$, and the $t=1$ "payoff" of $-R$ corresponds to paying back R to the lender at $t=1$. It is natural to call an asset with $S^1(\omega_m) = R$ for some constant R, for all $m = 1, \ldots, M$, a *risk-free* asset.[2] Note that so far we are making no restrictions on the elements of $\bar{\mathbf{D}}$.

We next formalize the concept of the market being friction-free (perfect):

- Fractional holdings of assets are possible, as is short-selling, i.e., negative asset holdings, and there is no bound on how many assets can be purchased (or sold). In summary, it is possible to purchase any number $c \in \mathbb{R}$ of any asset.
- Linearity: The price and payoff of a portfolio (bundle) of different assets is the sum of the prices and payoffs of the individual assets: the price of purchasing c_i units of asset i and c_j units of asset j is $c_i S_i^0 + c_j S_j^0$, and the future payoff is $c_i S_i^1 + c_j S_j^1$ in all states. This implies lack of transaction costs or bid-ask spreads in that
  - (price linearity:) the cost of c units of an asset is c times the cost of one unit, $c \in \mathbb{R}$;
  - (payoff linearity:) the payoff of c units of an assets is c times the payoff of one unit, $c \in \mathbb{R}$.

These assumptions are typically *never* satisfied in practice but can be viewed as good approximations in liquid markets.

We also make (minimal) behavioral assumptions on the traders in the market, namely that all investors prefer more to less, and that they are rational in that they understand markets and how to trade in them to reach their objective of earning as much as possible. This, for example,

[2] In part I, we used the notation R^f for the risk-free rate.

means that the trader would be happier to purchase an asset at the price of 1, than at the price of 2. However, it does *not* mean that all agents will do the same thing. First, agents may disagree in their beliefs about probabilities and second, agents may be different in their attitude toward risk as well as toward the trade-off between spending a lot today and saving for the future. Later on we will make stronger assumptions, about the probabilities for different outcomes, and about investors' preferences.

A *portfolio* of assets can now be represented by a vector $\mathbf{h} \in \mathbb{R}^N$,[3] and given the assumption of no frictions, it is clear that the value of the portfolio is $V^0 = \mathbf{h}^T \mathbf{s}^0$, and the payoff at $t=1$ can be represented by the row vector $\mathbf{V}^1 = \mathbf{h}^T \mathbf{D}$, where the mth element of the $1 \times M$-vector $\mathbf{V}^1$ represents the value of the portfolio at $t=1$ if the mth state occurs. It also follows immediately that

$$[-V^0, \mathbf{V}^1] = \mathbf{h}^T \bar{\mathbf{D}}. \tag{7.1}$$

We can think of a portfolio as a new—*derived*—asset (i.e., derivative), with payoffs $\mathbf{V}^1 = \mathbf{h}^T \mathbf{D}$ and price $V^0 = \mathbf{h}^T \mathbf{s}^0$. The derived assets are thus constructed by the N *primitive* assets. Given these assumptions, it is thus clear that the *price system* is completely summarized by $\bar{\mathbf{D}}$.

Example 7.3. Consider a portfolio $\mathbf{h} = [1, -1, -1]^T$, in the market of Example 7.1. We have

$$\begin{aligned}
[-V^0, \mathbf{V}^1] &= \mathbf{h}^T \bar{\mathbf{D}} \\
&= [1, -1, -1] \begin{bmatrix} -1 & 1 & 2 & 2 & 2 \\ -\frac{1}{2} & 1 & 2 & 2 & 2 \\ 1 & 1 & 0 & 0 & 0 \end{bmatrix} \\
&= [-\tfrac{3}{2}, -1, 0, 0, 0].
\end{aligned}$$

So the portfolio's price at $t=0$ is $\frac{3}{2}$, and it pays off -1 in state 1 and 0 in all other states at $t=1$.

We are now in the position to make additional assumptions that allow us to rule out some price systems. Informally, an *arbitrage portfolio* is a portfolio that either has a negative price today and in no state of the world makes a negative payment tomorrow, or that has a nonpositive price today, in no state of the world makes a negative payout, and in at least one state makes a positive payout. If there exists an arbitrage portfolio in an economy, we say that there is an *arbitrage opportunity*. Otherwise, we say that the economy is *arbitrage-free*. An informal term for an arbitrage portfolio is a *free lunch*, capturing the economic interpretation that the buyer of an arbitrage portfolio get something valuable for free. Formally, we define these concepts as follows:

Definition 7.1. An *arbitrage portfolio*, $\mathbf{h}$, is a portfolio for which $\bar{\mathbf{D}}^T \mathbf{h} > \mathbf{0}$. A market is said to be *arbitrage-free* (free of arbitrage) if no arbitrage portfolio exists.

We have thus taken an economically intuitive term—the concept of a "free lunch"—and given it a precise meaning by introducing a formal definition that is based on linear algebra. This allows us to analyze the exact implications of having or not having free lunches in the market.

Note that although the definition of an arbitrage portfolio seems reasonable, it is a priori not clear that it is the "right" one. In fact, we could have considered several other definitions that may seem equally plausible. For example, we could have required the payments in all states to be

[3] The relation with the notation in part I, chapter 4, is that $\mathbf{h}_i \mathbf{s}_i^0 = a_i$ represents the dollar investment in asset i.

strictly positive: $\bar{\mathbf{D}}^T\mathbf{h} \gg \mathbf{0}$. This alternative definition is not equivalent to the one we have chosen, and would not be "quite as good" for the type of results we wish to obtain.

An arbitrage opportunity may be classified as being of type I or type II, or both. A type-I arbitrage is one for which $(\bar{\mathbf{D}}^T\mathbf{h})_i > 0$ for some $i \geq 2$, and $(\bar{\mathbf{D}}^T\mathbf{h})_1 \geq 0$. A type-II arbitrage is one for which $(\bar{\mathbf{D}}^T\mathbf{h})_1 > 0$ and $(\bar{\mathbf{D}}^T\mathbf{h})_i \geq 0$, for all $i \geq 2$. So a type-I arbitrage is one which generates strictly positive cash flows in the future in some state, whereas a type-II arbitrage is one that generates strictly positive cash flows immediately. An arbitrage opportunity that generates strictly positive cash flows both immediately and in some future state is both of type I and of type II.

The following example shows how one can verify whether a portfolio is an arbitrage portfolio within our economic environment:

Example 7.4. The portfolio $\mathbf{h} = [-1, 1, 0]^T$, in the market of Example 7.1 is an arbitrage portfolio. We verify that it has a negative price of $-\frac{1}{2}$ and generates zero payoffs in all states at time 1, thus satisfying the conditions for being an arbitrage portfolio:

$$\begin{aligned}
\mathbf{h}^T\bar{\mathbf{D}} &= [-1, -1, 0]\begin{bmatrix} -1 & 1 & 2 & 2 & 2 \\ -\frac{1}{2} & 1 & 2 & 2 & 2 \\ 1 & 1 & 0 & 0 & 0 \end{bmatrix} \\
&= [\tfrac{1}{2}, 0, 0, 0, 0] \\
&> \mathbf{0}^T.
\end{aligned}$$

Now, it seems reasonable to assume that in a "normal" market, no arbitrage opportunities will exist, since any such opportunity would allow an investor to make an arbitrarily large amount of money for free. Specifically, since we are assuming that investments are scalable, if an investor can make one dollar without investing anything (remember that in no state, including today, does the arbitrage portfolio require any capital from the investor) by buying one unit of the portfolio, then it is possible to make a trillion dollars by buying a trillion units. Such a market would, of course, be absolutely fantastic for everyone, but not realistic. This is a strong argument against the presence of arbitrage in real-world markets.

Some people argue, however, that there exist real-world examples of what seem to be arbitrage opportunities in markets. One such example is the carve-out of Palm from the company 3Com in the early 2000s; see Lamont and Thaler (2003). The examples are often supported by observations of irrational behavior by some investors in the market, together with frictions that hinder other investors from taking advantage of the arbitrage opportunities.

A weaker argument in favor of the no-arbitrage assumption is that if and when arbitrage opportunities arise, *arbitrageurs*—rational investors who see the opportunities and are ready to step in and profit from them—step in and trade aggressively, and prices then adjust very quickly so that the market becomes free of arbitrage. Under the weaker argument, arbitrage opportunities may exist, but only rarely and temporarily.

Whether one subscribes to the weak or strong argument against arbitrage, the no-arbitrage assumption is a good first-order approximation for the behavior of markets. No-arbitrage theory only fails completely in a market where there are so strong frictions and/or so many agents who behave irrationally that the weak argument against arbitrage is invalid.

Note that the probabilities for different outcomes are not relevant for the definition of arbitrage, as long as they are strictly positive for all states. An arbitrage opportunity therefore constitutes a very strong form of mispricing in the market, since all investors will agree on its existence, regardless of their assessment of probabilities. For example, in a market with two states, one investor might believe that the probability for the first state is 99.9% and that the probability for the other is 0.1%. Another investor may have the reverse assessment. Even with these hugely different views, both investors will agree about whether a portfolio constitutes a free lunch or not (since all investors agree on the state space and that the probability for any state occurring is greater than zero). This makes the arbitrage concept nonparametric with respect to probability distributions.

A weaker mispricing concept is that of *statistical arbitrage*, which should not be confused with pure arbitrage. A statistical arbitrage opportunity represents "too high" payoffs and returns, compared with what one would expect in the market. It thus relates the *expected* returns of a portfolio to some type of benchmark. For example, the momentum and size anomalies discussed in part I may be viewed as allowing for statistical arbitrage, as may so-called pairs-trading strategies.

Whether a statistical arbitrage opportunity exists or not then depends on the probabilities for different outcomes, and which model is chosen to define the benchmark. Therefore, statistical arbitrage is a much weaker concept (depending on stronger assumptions about the market) than pure arbitrage.

A natural question is now under what conditions one can rule out arbitrage opportunities. It turns out that there are very natural such conditions—as given by the so-called *fundamental theorem of asset pricing*—that both are technically well defined and have a sound economic interpretation.[4]

To formulate and derive the fundamental theorem, which is actually an umbrella term for several results, we use the nice linear algebraic structure that defines the financial market. Indeed, the payoffs of portfolios are defined by a linear operation on the portfolio weights, by (7.1), and whether this payoff constitutes an arbitrage is defined by whether it lies in the (strictly) positive orthant of $\mathbb{R}^{1+M}$, as expressed by Definition 7.1. Concepts from linear algebra will be helpful here.[5] To formulate and derive the fundamental theorem, which is actually an umbrella term for several results, we use the nice linear algebraic structure that defines the financial market. Indeed, the payoffs of portfolios are defined by a linear operation on the portfolio weights, by (7.1), and whether this payoff constitutes an arbitrage is defined by whether it lies in the (strictly) positive orthant of $\mathbb{R}^{1+M}$, as expressed by Definition 7.1.

To this end, we define the *reachable payoff space*, $\mathcal{R}$, to be the row space of $\mathbf{D}$, $\mathcal{R}=\{\mathbf{D}^T\mathbf{h} : \mathbf{h}\in\mathbb{R}^N\}\subset\mathbb{R}^M$. This space is also called the *asset span* and *marketed space*. If the reachable payoff space is the whole of $\mathbb{R}^M$, then the market is said to be *complete*. Intuitively, this means that any payoff pattern across future states of the world can be generated. Completeness is equivalent to the condition that each of the M so-called *Arrow–Debreu* securities δ_i, $i=1,\ldots,M$, belongs to $\mathcal{R}$. Here, the ith Arrow–Debreu security pays 1 if state i occurs, and 0 in all other states. We also define the asset δ_0, which pays 1 at time 0 and 0 in all future states.

It will also be useful to define an augmented payoff space, that includes time-0 cash flows:

Definition 7.2. The augmented payoff space, is defined as $\overline{\mathcal{R}}=\{\overline{\mathbf{D}}^T\mathbf{h}:\mathbf{h}\in\mathbb{R}^N\}$.

[4] Cox and Ross (1976) derived initial results, which were later generalized by Harrison and Kreps (1979) and Harrison and Pliska (1981).

[5] See appendix B for a brief summary of notation and some results from linear algebra.

The first coordinate of an element in the augmented payoff space thus represents the cash flow associated with buying a portfolio at time 0 (which is minus the price of the portfolio), and the rest of the coordinates represent the portfolio's state contingent payoffs at $t=1$.

Now, $\mathbf{x}\in\overline{\mathcal{R}} \Leftrightarrow \mathbf{x}=\bar{\mathbf{D}}^T\mathbf{h}$ for some $\mathbf{h}\in\mathbb{R}^N$ and, furthermore, for any invertible $N\times N$ matrix, $\mathbf{A}$, we have

$$\mathbf{x}=\bar{\mathbf{D}}^T(\mathbf{A}^{-1}\mathbf{A})^T\mathbf{h}=\bar{\mathbf{D}}^T\mathbf{A}^T\mathbf{A}^{-T}\mathbf{h}=(\mathbf{A}\bar{\mathbf{D}})^T(\mathbf{A}^{-T}\mathbf{h})=(\mathbf{A}\bar{\mathbf{D}})^T\hat{\mathbf{h}},$$

where $\hat{\mathbf{h}}=\mathbf{A}^{-T}\mathbf{h}$. In other words, $\overline{\mathcal{R}}$ is invariant to multiplying $\bar{\mathbf{D}}$ by arbitrary invertible square matrices, $\mathbf{A}$, in the sense that $\bar{\mathbf{D}}$ and $\mathbf{A}\bar{\mathbf{D}}$ have exactly the same payoff space for any invertible matrix, $\mathbf{A}\in\mathbb{R}^{N\times N}$. Economically, such matrix multiplication defines new assets from portfolios of old assets. As long as the old assets can be reconstructed (i.e., as long as $\mathbf{A}$ is invertible), the asset span will not change. For example, by choosing $\mathbf{A}=\Lambda=\mathrm{diag}(\lambda)$, $\lambda\gg\mathbf{0}$, $\lambda\in\mathbb{R}^N$, the new assets are scaled versions of the old ones.

We define the *positive orthant*, $\mathcal{S}$, in $\mathbb{R}^{1+M}$: $\mathcal{S}=\{\mathbf{x}\in\mathbb{R}^{1+M}:\mathbf{x}_i\geq 0,\ i=1,\ldots,M+1\}$. This is a generalization of the concept of the positive quadrant in the plane. With this definition, we arrive at the following formulation of what constitutes an arbitrage-free market:

Definition 7.3. A market is said to be arbitrage-free if

$$\overline{\mathcal{R}}\cap\mathcal{S}=\{\mathbf{0}\}. \tag{7.2}$$

This definition is thus equivalent to the previous one in Definition 7.1. We also provide a third definition. First, we define the closed unit simplex $\bar{\mathbb{S}}=\{\mathbf{x}\in\mathbb{R}^{1+M}:\mathbf{x}_i\geq 0,\ i=1,\ldots, M+1,\ \sum_{i=1}^{M+1}\mathbf{x}_i=1\}$. Of course, $\bar{\mathbb{S}}\subset\mathcal{S}$, and $\mathbf{0}\notin\bar{\mathbb{S}}$, so in an arbitrage-free market, $\overline{\mathcal{R}}\cap\bar{\mathbb{S}}=\overline{\mathcal{R}}\cap(\mathcal{S}\cap\bar{\mathbb{S}})=(\overline{\mathcal{R}}\cap\mathcal{S})\cap\bar{\mathbb{S}}=\{\mathbf{0}\}\cap\bar{\mathbb{S}}=\emptyset$ (note the difference between the calligraphic-style orthant $\mathcal{S}$, and the unit simplex $\bar{\mathbb{S}}$, as well as between the zero vector, $\mathbf{0}$, and the empty set, $\emptyset$). However, $\overline{\mathcal{R}}\cap\bar{\mathbb{S}}=\emptyset$ also implies no arbitrage, since assume to the contrary that there is an arbitrage opportunity, i.e., a vector $\mathbf{x}>\mathbf{0}$ such that $\mathbf{x}\in\overline{\mathcal{R}}\cap\mathcal{S}$. Then $\lambda\mathbf{x}\in\bar{\mathbb{S}}$, where $\lambda=\frac{1}{\sum_i\mathbf{x}_i}$, and since $\overline{\mathcal{R}}$ is a subspace of $\mathbb{R}^{1+M}$, it follows that $\lambda\mathbf{x}\in\overline{\mathcal{R}}$, in turn implying that $\lambda\mathbf{x}\in\overline{\mathcal{R}}\cap\bar{\mathbb{S}}$, i.e., that $\overline{\mathcal{R}}\cap\bar{\mathbb{S}}$ is nonempty. Thus, $\overline{\mathcal{R}}\cap\bar{\mathbb{S}}=\emptyset$ indeed implies no arbitrage. We therefore have another equivalent definition of an arbitrage-free market:

Lemma 7.1. *A market is arbitrage-free if and only if*

$$\overline{\mathcal{R}}\cap\bar{\mathbb{S}}=\emptyset. \tag{7.3}$$

To summarize, we now have three equivalent definitions of what it means for a market to be arbitrage-free. In addition to our original definition based on not being able to find an arbitrage portfolio, as given in Definition 7.1, we have two definitions based on the intersection of the reachable payoff space with appropriate sets (Definition 7.3 and Lemma 7.1).

A *state-price vector* (SPV) is a vector $\psi\in\mathbb{R}^M$ that, when acting as a linear operator through the standard inner product operation on $\mathbb{R}^M$, prices all payoffs in the reachable payoff space correctly, i.e., for all $[-V^0,\mathbf{V}^1]^T\in\overline{\mathcal{R}}$,

$$V^0=\mathbf{V}^1\psi=\langle\mathbf{V}^1,\psi\rangle=\sum_m(V^1)_m\psi_m. \tag{7.4}$$

Equivalently, the pricing relationship can be written as

$$[-V^0,\mathbf{V}^1][1;\psi]=0. \tag{7.5}$$

Clearly, having a state-price vector is very convenient. It basically provides the ultimate solution to the question of how to price assets—not only for the individual assets, but for any portfolios.[6]

Define the null space $\mathcal{N}=\overline{\mathcal{R}}^{\perp}=\{\mathbf{x}:\bar{\mathbf{D}}\mathbf{x}=\mathbf{0}\}$, and since $0=[-V^0,\mathbf{V}^1][1;\psi]=\mathbf{h}^T\bar{\mathbf{D}}[1;\psi]$ for all $\mathbf{h}$, it follows that the set of state-price vectors can be defined as $\Lambda=\{\psi:[1;\psi]\in\mathcal{N}\}$ and, furthermore, that the decomposition

$$\mathbb{R}^{1+M}=\overline{\mathcal{R}}\oplus\mathcal{N} \tag{7.6}$$

therefore relates the space of state prices to the span of asset payoffs.[7]

We also note that a state-price vector can be defined by only focusing on the N primitive assets in the economy, i.e., one does not need the whole reachable space. Specifically, a state-price vector can be defined as a vector that satisfies

$$\mathbf{s}_0=\mathbf{D}\psi, \tag{7.7}$$

since for such a ψ and an arbitrary portfolio, $\mathbf{h}$, we have $V_0=\mathbf{h}^T\mathbf{s}_0=\mathbf{h}^T(\mathbf{D}\psi)=(\mathbf{h}^T\mathbf{D})\psi=\langle\mathbf{V}^1,\psi\rangle$, so (7.4) is satisfied. We will use versions of this equivalent definition in the multiperiod and continuous-time versions of the model.

The decomposition in (7.6) provides a "tension" between the possible size of the set of state-price vectors and the size of the reachable payoff space. The total dimensionality of the two spaces is $1+M$, so the larger the augmented reachable space is (which basically tells us how "close" to complete the market is), the smaller the space of state-price vectors will be. This is intuitive: the larger $\overline{\mathcal{R}}$ is, the more restrictions are imposed on state-price vectors—since they need to price more portfolios correctly—and the fewer state-price vectors will therefore exist.

As an example, consider a market with one asset and two states, such that $\mathbf{s}^0=1$ and $\mathbf{D}=[1,1]$. Any vector of the form $\psi=(c,1-c)'$, $c\in\mathbb{R}$, then satisfies $\mathbf{s}^0=\mathbf{D}\psi$ and is therefore a valid state-price vector. If there is also an AD security on state 2 that costs $\frac{1}{2}$, such that $\mathbf{s}^0=(1,\frac{1}{2})'$ and

$$\mathbf{D}=\begin{bmatrix}1 & 1\\ 0 & 1\end{bmatrix},$$

then the set of possible state-price vectors shrinks to $\psi=(\frac{1}{2},\frac{1}{2})'$.

7.4 The Fundamental Theorems

7.4.1 The First Fundamental Theorem

We now have the machinery to define, discuss, and prove the fundamental theorems of asset pricing. These theorems link absence of arbitrage in a market with the existence of a strictly positive state-price vector.

Theorem 7.1 (First fundamental theorem of asset pricing). *The market is arbitrage-free if and only if there exists a strictly positive state-price vector, $\psi\gg\mathbf{0}$.*

The first fundamental theorem of asset pricing thus shows that no arbitrage in a market is completely equivalent to the existence of a state-price vector. We now prove this theorem.

[6] We introduced the state-price vector concept in the Arrow–Debreu model in part I. The general equilibrium environment in that model was quite different from the no-arbitrage environment here, though.

[7] Since $\overline{\mathcal{R}}$ and $\mathcal{N}$ are orthogonal spaces, they provide an orthogonal decomposition of $\mathbb{R}^{1+M}$, and the direct sum of $\overline{\mathcal{R}}$ and $\mathcal{N}$ is $\overline{\mathcal{R}}\oplus\mathcal{N}=\{r+n:r\in\overline{\mathcal{R}},\ n\in\mathcal{N}\}$.

Proof of the first fundamental theorem. The easy part of the proof is to show that the existence of a state-price vector ensures that the market is free of arbitrage ($\Leftarrow$), so we begin with this part. Proofs in textbooks are often void of intuition. This does not mean that one does not need intuition to come up with proofs. On the contrary, proving a new theorem usually starts with an informal, often quite vague, intuition for why the result should hold, an intuition that then provides crucial guidance throughout the process of actually showing the result. In the final mathematical write-up of the proof, the underlying intuition may not be very transparent. We put some effort into understanding the underlying intuition when working through this proof.

In this case, the intuition is quite simple. A positive state-price vector provides consistent prices at time 0 of payoffs in a state at time 1. For example, if $\psi_3 = 2$, this means that a portfolio that generates payoffs of $c > 0$ in state ω_3 must have a total price that is consistent with a price of $2c$ for the state 3 payoff alone. More generally, a portfolio that generates time-1 payoffs of $\mathbf{r} \in \mathcal{R}$ must have a time-0 price of $\sum_{i=1}^{M} \mathbf{r}_i \psi_i$. But, since all elements of ψ are strictly positive, if all $\mathbf{r}_i \geq 0$, and at least one $\mathbf{r}_i$ is strictly positive, then $\sum_{i=1}^{M} \mathbf{r}_i \psi_i$ must also be strictly positive, i.e., the price of such a portfolio must be strictly positive, thereby not constituting an arbitrage opportunity. So a strictly positive state-price vector must rule out any arbitrage opportunity for which at least one $\mathbf{r}_i$ is strictly positive.

The only remaining potential arbitrage portfolio is one for which the payoff at $t = 1$ is 0 in each state, and the time-0 price is strictly negative. However, if the payoff is 0 in all states, then the price must also be 0 if ψ is a state-price vector, since $-V^0 = \sum_{i=1}^{M} \mathbf{r}_i \psi_i = \sum_{i=1}^{M} 0\psi_i = 0$. Thus, with strictly positive state prices, strictly positive (or nonnegative) payoffs at time 1 must always be associated with strictly positive (or nonnegative) prices at time 0, ruling out arbitrage opportunities.

The above argument is very intuitive, but quite lengthy and informal, which is why a standard textbook proof may use the following formulation instead: *Consider a portfolio with augmented payoffs $\mathbf{r}_a \in \overline{\mathcal{R}}$. By Definitions 7.1 and 7.2, for the portfolio to be an arbitrage portfolio it must be that $\mathbf{r}_a > \mathbf{0}$, in turn implying that $\mathbf{r}_a^T[1; \psi] > 0$ (given that $\psi \gg \mathbf{0}$). By (7.6), however, $\mathbf{r}_a^T[1; \psi] = 0$, so no such arbitrage portfolio exists.* With some practice one can learn to "see" the intuition behind mathematical proofs.

We next turn to the reverse direction of the proof ($\Rightarrow$), i.e., showing that no arbitrage implies the existence of (at least one) strictly positive state-price vector. This direction is trickier. Often some intuition can be generated by looking at a special case. We study the special case when the market is complete, i.e., $\mathcal{R} = \mathbb{R}^M$. Clearly, the M Arrow–Debreu securities, δ_i, $i = 1, \ldots, M$, belong to $\mathcal{R}$, and we choose their prices, $p_1, \ldots, p_M$, as candidates for a strictly positive state-price vector, $\psi_i = p_i$.

In general, there could, of course be multiple possible prices of any Arrow–Debreu security, but under no arbitrage in the complete market setting, $\psi_1, \ldots, \psi_M$ must be unique, since otherwise it would be possible to create an arbitrage by simply buying one unit of the less expensive AD security and selling one unit of the more expensive one. Also, under no arbitrage, it must be that $\psi_i > 0$ for all i, since an arbitrage would be created by buying any AD security with a negative price. Thus, $\psi \gg \mathbf{0}$.

Now, the price of c units of AD security δ_i is $c\psi_i$, so the state-price vector can be used to price any number of individual AD securities, and because of linearity of pricing over portfolio formation, also to price portfolios of AD securities, i.e., the price of a portfolio of c_i units of AD security i, $i = 1, \ldots, M$, is $\sum_i c_i \psi_i$, so the proposed state-price vector indeed prices portfolios of AD securities correctly. We note that this also shows that no other state-price vector could exist, since any $\hat{\psi}_i \neq \psi_i$ would misprice the ith AD security. This fact will be further discussed in the second fundamental theorem.

Finally, we need to check that ψ also works for all other portfolios of assets, not only the AD securities. However, this must indeed be the case, since assume that there is a portfolio that generates payoffs $\mathbf{r} \in \mathcal{R}$, for which the price is *not* $\sum_i r_i \psi_i$. Then the same payoff, state by state, can be generated by a portfolio of the AD securities, which *will* have that price, again immediately leading to an arbitrage opportunity, by selling the higher-priced portfolio and buying the lower-priced portfolio, a version of the so-called "buy low, sell high," strategy.

The previous argument is *constructive*, i.e., it not only shows the existence of a strictly positive state-price vector, but actually constructs one. Constructive proofs usually provide a lot of intuition. The drawback with the previous argument is that it only shows the result in a complete market. Let us recapitulate the steps taken: first look at some specifically simple securities (the AD securities, which are possibly derived securities) which allow a well-informed conjecture for the state-price vector, and then show that if this state-price vector does not work in pricing all securities, there must be an arbitrage opportunity because of the linearity of the price system.

It is not immediately clear how we would extend the above argument to incomplete markets. When the market is incomplete, we are not guaranteed the existence of AD securities (in fact, it is trivial to show that there cannot be a complete set of AD securities in an incomplete market), so we will not be able to use the previous argument to construct a candidate state-price vector. Nevertheless, our intuition tells us that, if anything, it should be *easier* to construct a state-price vector in this case, since the smaller the asset span, the fewer constraints are imposed on the state-price vector. Because of this, guaranteeing the existence of a state-price vector should be most challenging in a complete market.

In principle, we could build upon this intuition and view an incomplete market as a complete one, in which some assets have been "deleted." A state-price vector that works in a complete market will of course also work when some assets are "deleted"—since it still prices the remaining ones correctly. This approach would, in principle, work, but it risks becoming quite involved, which one sees upon further reflection. The issue is that one would need to ensure that any incomplete market in which there is no arbitrage can be extended to a complete market in which there is no arbitrage, and this is not trivial. It *is* trivial that an incomplete market can be extended to a complete one (just add AD securities), but not that absence of arbitrage can be kept.

When setting out to prove a result, one often runs into these types of hurdles. Fortunately, proofs that do not work—or do not cover the most general case—usually provide good intuition for alternative approaches that may work. In this case, it turns out that the relation (7.6) provides a good starting point for a general proof. According to that formulation of the theorem, no arbitrage implies that we can find a vector, $[1; \psi]$, where ψ is strictly positive, which is orthogonal to $\overline{\mathcal{R}}$. Now, of course, the existence of such a vector is equivalent to the existence of a vector $\mathbf{z} \gg \mathbf{0}$, which is orthogonal to $\overline{\mathcal{R}}$, since such a vector can always be rescaled so that its first coordinate equals unity, while still being kept orthogonal to $\overline{\mathcal{R}}$. Thus, given Definition 7.3 of no arbitrage, what we wish to prove—in compact notation—is, equivalently,

$$\overline{\mathcal{R}} \cap \mathcal{S} = \{\mathbf{0}\} \;\Rightarrow\; \exists \mathbf{z} \gg \mathbf{0} : \mathbf{z} \perp \overline{\mathcal{R}}.$$

This result has a geometric interpretation, visualized in two dimensions in figure 7.1. Here, $\mathcal{S}$ is the positive quadrant, $\overline{\mathcal{R}}$ is a line, which means that there is always a line, Z, which is perpendicular (orthogonal) to $\overline{\mathcal{R}}$. The vector $\mathbf{z} \gg (0,0)^T$ will then lie on this line. Now, if $\overline{\mathcal{R}} \cap \mathcal{S} = \{\mathbf{0}\}$, then $\overline{\mathcal{R}}$ has no points in the positive quadrant, except for $\mathbf{0}$. It must therefore go through the second and fourth quadrants. However, this means that Z, being perpendicular, will go through the first (and third) quadrant, so it will indeed be possible to choose a $\mathbf{z} \gg \mathbf{0}$ which is orthogonal to $\overline{\mathcal{R}}$. Moreover, there is clearly a specific element in Z that will be of the form $[1; \psi]$, which will therefore have ψ as a state-price vector.

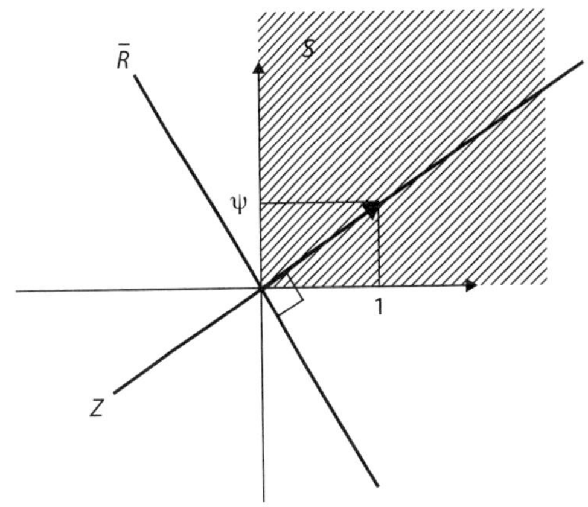

Figure 7.1: Existence of a state-price vector when $M = 1$.

So in the special case when $M = 1$, we are done. More importantly, this argument actually works in the general case. Let us go over the argument again, but in the terminology of linear algebra instead of geometry, which will allow for generalization to arbitrary M: We have a true (1-dimensional) subspace, $\overline{\mathcal{R}}$, of $\mathbb{R}^2$, which only overlaps with the positive quadrant, $\mathcal{S}$, at the origin, $(0,0)^T$. In this case, the orthogonal complement of $\overline{\mathcal{R}}$, Z, must contain a strictly positive element, $\mathbf{z} \gg (0,0)^T$.

The so-called *separating hyperplane theorem* allows us to make such an argument for general $M \geq 2$. It is stated in appendix B, and is repeated below for convenience:

Theorem 7.2 (Separating hyperplane theorem). *Suppose A and B are convex subsets of $\mathbb{R}^n$ with no interior point in common. Then there exists a nonzero vector $\mathbf{x} \in \mathbb{R}^n$ and a constant, c, such that $\mathbf{x}^T\mathbf{a} \leq c$ for all $\mathbf{a} \in A$, and $\mathbf{x}^T\mathbf{b} \geq c$ for all $\mathbf{b} \in B$. If A is closed and B is compact (i.e., closed and bounded) and A and B are disjoint, the inequalities can be made strict.*

At first sight, the separating hyperplane theorem may seem quite unrelated to our previous argument. It is not! We choose the set A in the theorem to be our augmented payoff space, $\overline{\mathcal{R}}$. This clearly works, since a subspace of $\mathbb{R}^{1+M}$ is always closed and convex. Furthermore, we choose the set B to be $\mathcal{S}$, which is indeed convex. Since $A \cap B = \{\mathbf{0}\}$ (because of no arbitrage), and $\{\mathbf{0}\}$ does not belong to the interior of A, the conditions of the separating hyperplane theorem are satisfied, so there is an $\mathbf{x}$, such that $\mathbf{x}^T\mathbf{a} \leq \mathbf{x}^T\mathbf{b}$, for all $\mathbf{a} \in A$, for all $\mathbf{b} \in B$. Now, since A is a subspace of $\mathbb{R}^n$, it must then be that $\mathbf{x}^T\mathbf{a} = 0$ for all $\mathbf{a} \in A$, because any element for which $\mathbf{x}^T\mathbf{a} \neq 0$ could be scaled to arbitrary sizes (in a linear space, if $\mathbf{a} \in A$, then $\lambda\mathbf{a} \in A$ for arbitrary $\lambda \in \mathbb{R}$). But this is equivalent to saying that $\mathbf{x} \perp A$. The theorem therefore implies that $\mathbf{x}^T\mathbf{b} \geq 0$ for all $\mathbf{b} \in B$, and since $\delta_i \in B$ for $i = 1, \ldots, M$, it must then be that each coordinate of $\mathbf{x}$ is nonnegative.

This application of the separating hyperplane theorem seems pretty close to our previous argument in $\mathbb{R}^2$, with the additional power of holding for arbitrary dimensions M. However, it is not quite what we need, since there is no guarantee that $\mathbf{x}$ is *strictly* positive. This is troublesome, especially if $\mathbf{x}_1 = 0$, in which case there is no way to scale $\mathbf{x}$ so that it takes the form $[1; \psi]$. Even if $\mathbf{x}_1 > 0$, and we can scale, we are not guaranteed that all elements of ψ are strictly positive, only that they are nonnegative.

The final insight that allows us to nail down the proof of the theorem is that by replacing $\mathcal{S}$ by the unit simplex, $\bar{\mathbb{S}}$, we can use the strict version of the separating hyperplane theorem, which then implies that $\mathbf{x} \gg \mathbf{0}$. Recall that by Definition 7.3, no arbitrage is equivalent to $\overline{\mathcal{R}} \cap \bar{\mathbb{S}} = \emptyset$. Now we instead choose the set B to be $\bar{\mathbb{S}}$. Clearly, $\bar{\mathbb{S}}$ is compact (closed and bounded). Moreover, because of no arbitrage, A and B are disjoint. So, by the strict version of the separating hyperplane theorem, there is an $\mathbf{x}$, so that $\mathbf{x}^T\mathbf{a} < \mathbf{x}^T\mathbf{b}$ for all $\mathbf{a} \in A$ and $\mathbf{b} \in B$. A similar argument to when we used the weak version of the theorem then implies that $\mathbf{x} \perp A$ and, furthermore, the strictness of the theorem implies that $\mathbf{x}^T\mathbf{b} > 0$ for all $\mathbf{b} \in B$, and especially for $\mathbf{b} = \delta_i$, $i = 1, \ldots, M+1$. Thus, $\mathbf{x} \gg \mathbf{0}$. We can now rescale with $\frac{1}{\mathbf{x}_1}$, and define $\psi = (\frac{\mathbf{x}_2}{\mathbf{x}_1}, \frac{\mathbf{x}_3}{\mathbf{x}_1}, \ldots, \frac{\mathbf{x}_{M+1}}{\mathbf{x}_1})^T$. It then follows that $\psi \gg \mathbf{0}$, and that $[1; \psi] \perp \overline{\mathcal{R}}$, i.e., $[1; \psi] \in \mathcal{N}$. So ψ *is a state-price vector*. We have proved the reverse part of the theorem!

This argument became quite lengthy, because we wanted to understand the intuition behind the result. A shorter (but less intuitively clear) proof proceeds along the following lines:

1. $\overline{\mathcal{R}}$ is a linear subspace of $\mathbb{R}^{1+M}$, and therefore closed and convex. Furthermore, the unit simplex $\bar{S} = \{\mathbf{x} \in \mathbb{R}^{1+M} : \mathbf{x} \geq \mathbf{0}, \ \sum_i (\mathbf{x})_i = 1\}$ is convex and compact. No arbitrage, by lemma 7.1, can be stated as $\overline{\mathcal{R}} \cap \bar{S} = \emptyset$.
2. The separating hyperplane theorem, with $A \stackrel{\text{def}}{=} \overline{\mathcal{R}}$, $B \stackrel{\text{def}}{=} \bar{S}$, states that no arbitrage implies the existence of a vector, $\mathbf{z} \in \mathbb{R}^{1+M}$, such that for all $\mathbf{r} \in \overline{\mathcal{R}}$, for all $\mathbf{s} \in S$, $\mathbf{r}^T\mathbf{z} < \mathbf{s}^T\mathbf{z}$.
3. Since $\overline{\mathcal{R}}$ is a linear subspace, it must be that for $\mathbf{r} \in \overline{\mathcal{R}}$, $\mathbf{z}^T\mathbf{r} = 0$, and since the inequality in point 2 above is strict, and $\delta_i \in S$, it follows that $\mathbf{z}^T\delta_i > 0$, so $(\mathbf{z})_i > 0$, i.e., $\mathbf{z} \gg \mathbf{0}$.
4. Defining $\psi \in \mathbb{R}^M = (\frac{\mathbf{z}_2}{\mathbf{z}_1}, \ldots, \frac{\mathbf{z}_{M+1}}{\mathbf{z}_1})^T$, it follows that $\psi \gg \mathbf{0}$, and $[1; \psi] \perp \overline{\mathcal{R}}$, i.e., ψ is a strictly positive state-price vector, as defined by (7.5). □

7.4.2 The Second Fundamental Theorem

The first fundamental theorem tells us about the existence, but provides no information about how many such vectors there are in a market with no arbitrage. The second fundamental theorem addresses that question:

Theorem 7.3 (Second fundamental theorem of asset pricing). *Given a market that admits no arbitrage, the state-price vector is unique if and only if the market is complete.*

Proof of the second fundamental theorem. Completeness implies uniqueness:

1. If the market is complete, then $\mathcal{R}$ has dimension M, and therefore $\overline{\mathcal{R}}$ has dimension either M or $M+1$, i.e., $\overline{\mathcal{R}}^\perp$ has dimension either 1 or 0. This follows from the rank theorem (see appendix B), $\dim(\overline{\mathcal{R}}) + \dim(\overline{\mathcal{R}}^\perp) = M + 1$.
2. Any state-price vector must satisfy $[1; \psi] \in \overline{\mathcal{R}}^\perp = \mathcal{N}$.
3. Since there is no arbitrage, there is a strictly positive state-price vector (from the first fundamental theorem), so $[1; \psi] \in \overline{\mathcal{R}}^\perp$. Thus, $\overline{\mathcal{R}}^\perp$ has dimension 1 and there is exactly one vector of the form $[1; \psi] \in \overline{\mathcal{R}}^\perp$.
4. The state-price vector is thus unique.

Uniqueness implies completeness:

1. If the state-price vector is unique, then $\overline{\mathcal{R}}^\perp$ has dimension 1, so the rank theorem implies that $\dim(\overline{\mathcal{R}}) = M$, i.e., that $\text{rank}(\bar{\mathbf{D}}) = M$.
2. Since $[1; \psi] \in \mathcal{N}$, it follows that $\bar{\mathbf{D}}[1; \psi] = 0$, and therefore $\mathbf{s}_0 = \mathbf{D}\psi$. Thus, $\mathbf{s}_0$ is within the column space of $\mathbf{D}$ and deleting it from $\bar{\mathbf{D}}$ will thus not reduce its rank, so $\text{rank}(\mathbf{D}) = M$, i.e., $\dim(\mathcal{R}) = M$. In other words the market is complete. □

Note that in a complete market, the unique state prices, $\psi_1, \ldots, \psi_M$, are the prices of Arrow–Debreu securities that pay off one dollar in one state of the world, $P[\delta_1] = \psi_1, P[\delta_2] = \psi_2, \ldots, P[\delta_M] = \psi_M$. This is discussed in the proof of the first fundamental theorem.

7.4.3 The Law of One Price, LOOP

A weaker condition than no arbitrage is the *law of one price* (LOOP). The law of one price is said to hold if the price today of two portfolios that make the same future payoff in all states must be the same, i.e., if

$$\mathbf{h}_1^T\mathbf{D} = \mathbf{h}_2^T\mathbf{D} \;\Rightarrow\; \mathbf{h}_1^T\mathbf{s}^0 = \mathbf{h}_2^T\mathbf{s}^0.$$

Clearly, if the LOOP fails, there is an arbitrage, since if $\mathbf{h}_1^T\mathbf{s}^0 - \mathbf{h}_2^T\mathbf{s}^0 = z \neq 0$, the portfolio $-\frac{1}{z}(\mathbf{h}_1 - \mathbf{h}_2)$ gives an immediate payoff of 1 and has $\mathbf{0}$ payoff in the future. Equivalently stated, if the LOOP fails,

$$\delta_0 \in \overline{\mathcal{R}}.$$

But, of course, if $\delta_0 \in \overline{\mathcal{R}}$, then there is an $\mathbf{h}_1$ such that $\mathbf{h}_1^T\mathbf{D} = \mathbf{0}$ and $\mathbf{h}_1^T\mathbf{s}^0 = 1$, and by choosing $\mathbf{h}_2 = \mathbf{0}$, we get $\mathbf{h}_1^T\mathbf{D} = \mathbf{h}_2^T\mathbf{D}$ and $\mathbf{h}_1^T\mathbf{s}^0 \neq \mathbf{h}_2^T\mathbf{s}^0$ so the LOOP fails. Therefore, an equivalent definition of the LOOP is

$$\delta_0 \notin \overline{\mathcal{R}}.$$

Here, $\overline{\mathcal{R}} \subset \mathbb{R}^{1+M}$, where the first coordinate represents time-0 cash flows associated with an asset. The AD securities, δ_i, then have their $(i+1)$st coefficient equal to 1 in $\overline{\mathcal{R}}$, although they have their ith coefficient equal to 1 in $\mathcal{R}$. The security δ_0 has its first coefficient equal to 1 in $\overline{\mathcal{R}}$, $(\delta_0)_1 = 1$.

We are now ready to show the following result:

Theorem 7.4 (Law of one price theorem, LOOP). *The law of one price holds if and only if there exists a state-price vector, ψ.*

Proof. ($\Rightarrow$)

1. If the LOOP holds, since $\delta_0 \notin \overline{\mathcal{R}}$, it must be that there is a nonzero $\mathbf{n} \in \mathcal{N}$ such that $\langle \mathbf{n}, \delta_0 \rangle \neq 0$, since otherwise $\langle \mathbf{n}, \delta_0 \rangle = 0$ for all $\mathbf{n} \in \mathcal{N}$, which leads to the contradiction that $\delta_0 \in \mathcal{N}^\perp = \overline{\mathcal{R}}$. Thus, $(\mathbf{n})_1 \neq 0$ for some $\mathbf{n} \in \mathcal{N}$.
2. Now, since $\mathbf{n}_1 \neq 0$, we can define $\psi \in \mathbb{R}^M = (\frac{\mathbf{n}_2}{\mathbf{n}_1}, \ldots, \frac{\mathbf{n}_{M+1}}{\mathbf{n}_1})^T$ to be a state-price vector since it immediately satisfies $V^0 = \overline{V}^{1}\psi$ for all payoffs, $[-V^0, \overline{V}^1] \in \overline{\mathcal{R}}$, and thus $[1; \psi] \in \mathcal{N}$.

($\Leftarrow$) follows immediately, since if there is a (not necessarily positive) state-price vector ψ, which prices all time-1 payoffs, it follows that $\mathbf{0}^T\psi = 0$, so $\delta_0 \notin \overline{\mathcal{R}}$. □

7.4.4 Discussion and Examples

We note the LOOP theorem highlights that LOOP is a weaker concept than no arbitrage, since the state-price vector does not need to be strictly positive under the LOOP, but must be under no arbitrage. The LOOP thus holds even though there is an arbitrage opportunity, when there are only state-price vectors that have some nonpositive elements.

We here have an example of the trade-off we discussed earlier. By making stronger assumptions, we get stronger results, but at the same time we decrease the number of situations in which the results hold. Figure 7.2, which is repeated from part I, shows this trade-off in a pyramid. The higher up we are in the pyramid, the stronger the assumptions and results, but the more narrow the applicability. LOOP and no arbitrage are far down in the pyramid: broadly applicable, but for many asset classes too generic to allow for much to be said. At the top of the pyramid, on the other hand, we have equilibrium models, in which we make strong assumptions about how agents behave, about the distribution of risk, and about markets. An example here is the capital asset pricing model (CAPM) that we discussed in part I.

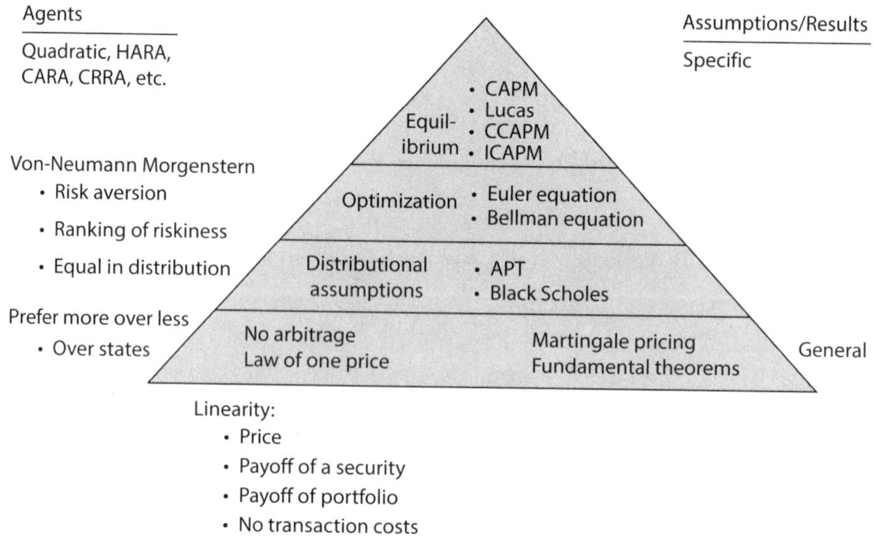

Figure 7.2: The asset pricing pyramid—again.

Example 7.5. Consider a market with M assets and M-dimensional asset span. Such a market is complete if and only if $\mathbf{D}$ is invertible. In this case, the unique state-price vector is $\psi = \mathbf{D}^{-1}\mathbf{s}^0$, so the LOOP must hold. If $\psi \gg \mathbf{0}$, then the market is arbitrage-free.

Example 7.6 (Binomial model—first encounter)**.** There are two states ($M=2$), and two assets ($N=2$)—one risky and one risk-free—where the price of each asset is normalized to unity. We have

$$\bar{\mathbf{D}} = \begin{bmatrix} -1 & u & d \\ -1 & R & R \end{bmatrix}.$$

Without loss of generality we can assume that $d \leq u$ (otherwise, we just switch the names of the two states). We are interested in the following cases:

(a) $d < R < u$,
(b) $d = R = u$,
(c) $d < u$.

Note that (a) implies (c), and that (b) and (c) cannot be satisfied simultaneously. It is straightforward to show that absence of arbitrage is equivalent to either (a) or (b) being satisfied, whereas market completeness is equivalent to (c) being satisfied, see exercise 7.10 at the end of this chapter.

Our next objective is to introduce a probabilistic formulation of no-arbitrage theory. Specifically, an implication of the linearity and no-arbitrage results in section 7.4 is that the pricing equation given by the state-price vector can be interpreted as an expectation. This formulation allows for additional intuition, and in more advanced settings (continuous time), it allows for powerful methods from probability theory and stochastic calculus to be used. We first go over some probability concepts, and then introduce the so-called risk-neutral formulation of the pricing equation.

7.5 Probability Theory I

Modern dynamic asset pricing is often developed in a measure-theoretic framework. In this introduction to asset pricing, we will not dig very deep into the theory, but it is useful to introduce some concepts and terminology, which will be especially helpful in our subsequent study of the dynamic model.

Let Ω be a sample space. A *partition* of $\Omega=\{\omega_1,\omega_2,\ldots,\omega_M\}$ is a set of subsets of Ω, $P=\{p_1,p_2,\ldots,p_m\}$, where $p_i\subset\Omega$ satisfies $i\neq j \Rightarrow p_i\cap p_j=\emptyset$, and $\bigcup_i p_i=\Omega$. The finest partition of Ω is $P=\{\{\omega_1\},\{\omega_2\},\ldots,\{\omega_M\}\}$. The coarsest partition is $P=\{\Omega\}$. Given a partition, the *sigma-algebra* (σ-algebra, also called a σ-field) generated by P is the set of all unions of sets in P, $\mathcal{F}_P=\{q: q=p_{i_1}\cup p_{i_2}\cup\cdots\cup p_{i_k}$ for some sequence $i_1,\ldots,i_k,\ k\geq 0\}$. We call the elements in the original partition the *components* of the partition. They are also called the *atoms* of the sigma-algebra.[8] Conversely, given a sigma-algebra, $\mathcal{F}$, a partition $P_{\mathcal{F}}$ is generated by taking the set of all atoms of $\mathcal{F}$. The *power set* of Ω, 2^Ω, is the set of all subsets of Ω. It is also the sigma-algebra generated by the finest partition of Ω in this finite setting. It is easy to show that

1. $\emptyset\in\mathcal{F}$,
2. $A\in\mathcal{F} \Rightarrow A^c\in\mathcal{F}$,
3. $A_i\in\mathcal{F},\ i=1,2,\ldots, \Rightarrow \bigcup_i A_i\in\mathcal{F}$,
4. $A_i\in\mathcal{F},\ i=1,2,\ldots, \Rightarrow \bigcap_i A_i\in\mathcal{F}$.

Conditions 1 to 4 above are usually taken as the definition of a sigma-algebra, with the advantage of also working when the state space is infinite, $|\Omega|=\infty$. In the infinite case, we allow unions and intersections to be (countably) infinite. The advantage of basing the definition on partitions in the finite case is that it is a lot more intuitive.

We next introduce the concept of a probability space. A (finite) *probability space* is a triplet $(\Omega,\mathcal{F},\mathbb{P})$, where Ω is the sample space, $\mathcal{F}$ is a sigma-algebra, and $\mathbb{P}\colon \mathcal{F}\to[0,1]$ is a *probability measure*, satisfying the following so-called *Kolmogorov axioms*:

1. $\mathbb{P}(\emptyset)=0$,
2. $\mathbb{P}(\Omega)=1$,
3. $A,B\in\mathcal{F},\ A\cap B=\emptyset \Rightarrow \mathbb{P}(A\cup B)=\mathbb{P}(A)+\mathbb{P}(B)$.

Elements in $\mathcal{F}$ are called *events* and the interpretation is that $\mathbb{P}(A)$ is the probability that an event A occurs. We say that elements in $\mathcal{F}$ are *measurable* (with respect to $\mathcal{F}$), and $\mathbb{P}(A)$ is A's ($\mathbb{P}$-) probability. One can easily show that the axioms imply that $\mathbb{P}(A^c)=1-\mathbb{P}(A)$.

Note that we do not require all events to occur with strictly positive probability in the general treatment, i.e., there may be some events, $A\neq\emptyset$, such that $\mathbb{P}(A)=0$. This is in contrast to the previous section, where we assumed that all such events had been excluded from the state space. For the time being, we assume that $\mathcal{F}$ is the finest sigma-algebra, i.e., $\mathcal{F}=2^\Omega$. In this case, a representation of the probability measure, $\mathbb{P}$, is given by $(p_1,\ldots,p_M)$, and we can (with some slight abuse of notation) write $\mathbb{P}(\omega_i)$ instead of $\mathbb{P}(\{\omega_i\})$.

[8] For the time being, we are dealing with sigma-algebras of finite size, for which there will always be atoms. In this finite case, a sigma-algebra is equivalent to an *algebra*. The situation is quite different when there are an infinite number of sets, in which case a sigma-algebra may be *nonatomic*, i.e., it may not have smallest elements, no atoms. There are algebras that are not sigma-algebras in the infinite case.

At this point it is fair to ask why we need to introduce the probability space notation. In fact, many readers may feel that they have acquired a good notion of how probability theory works without ever knowing anything about probability spaces. A reason why it is useful here is that we will have more than one probability measure acting on the same sample space. Specifically, we will have the probability measure $\mathbb{P}$ representing true probabilities, and also an "artificial" measure, $\mathbb{Q}$, which will be very convenient for pricing purposes. The probability space formulation underlines that this is just a mathematical construct that satisfies certain axioms. It may or may not be associated with real probabilities, but as long as it satisfies the Kolmogorov axioms, all the mathematical properties of true probabilities also hold for artificial probabilities.

A random variable (r.v.) is a function, $X\colon \Omega \to \mathbb{R}$. The expectation and variance of a random variable are

1. $E^{\mathbb{P}}[X] = \sum_i X(\omega_i)\mathbb{P}(\omega_i)$,
2. $\mathrm{Var}^{\mathbb{P}}[X] = E^{\mathbb{P}}[(X - E^{\mathbb{P}}[X])^2] = \sum_i (X(\omega_i) - E^{\mathbb{P}}[X])^2\mathbb{P}(\omega_i)$.

We only use the $\mathbb{P}$-superscript when there may be ambiguity about the probability space. We have the useful relationship

$$\mathrm{Var}[X] = E[X^2] - E[X]^2. \tag{7.8}$$

Now consider the case where we have probability measures, $\mathbb{P}$ and $\mathbb{Q}$, defined over the same sample space. We say that $\mathbb{P}$ and $\mathbb{Q}$ are *equivalent*, $\mathbb{P} \sim \mathbb{Q}$, if for any event, $A \in \mathcal{F}$, $\mathbb{P}(A) = 0 \Leftrightarrow \mathbb{Q}(A) = 0$. Under the weaker condition that $A \in \mathcal{F}$, $\mathbb{P}(A) = 0 \Rightarrow \mathbb{Q}(A) = 0$, we say that $\mathbb{Q}$ is *absolutely continuous* with respect to $\mathbb{P}$, $\mathbb{Q} \ll \mathbb{P}$. Equivalence between probability measures captures the intuitive idea discussed earlier that even though different probability measures may take different "stands" on what the probability for a specific event is, they "agree" upon which events are possible.

If $\mathbb{Q} \ll \mathbb{P}$, we can define the *Radon–Nikodym* derivative of $\mathbb{Q}$ with respect to $\mathbb{P}$, $\frac{d\mathbb{Q}}{d\mathbb{P}}$, such that for all events $A \in \mathcal{F}$, such that $\mathbb{P}(A) > 0$, $L = \frac{d\mathbb{Q}}{d\mathbb{P}} \overset{\text{def}}{=} \frac{\mathbb{Q}(A)}{\mathbb{P}(A)}$. We also call L the *likelihood ratio* of $\mathbb{Q}$ with respect to $\mathbb{P}$. We may also think of L as a function $L\colon \Omega \to [0, 1]$, defined by $L(\omega_i) = \frac{q_i}{p_i}$. For events of ($\mathbb{P}$-) measure zero, we can formally define $\frac{d\mathbb{Q}}{d\mathbb{P}} = \infty$ (or any other number). We then have

(i) $E^{\mathbb{P}}[LX] = E^{\mathbb{Q}}[X]$, for any random variable, X,
(ii) and a special case of the above formula is given by $E^{\mathbb{P}}[L] = 1$.

Exercise 7.1. Verify the two properties (i) and (ii) of the likelihood ratio above.

The likelihood ratio, $L(A)$, represents how well the two probability measures agree on the probability for the event A. If $L(A) = 1$, they completely agree. If $L(A) > 1$, the $\mathbb{Q}$ probability is higher than the $\mathbb{P}$ probability, and if $L(A) < 1$ it is lower. Note that $L(\omega_i)$ cannot be greater than 1 for all i (nor less than 1), since the q_i and p_i both sum to 1.

7.6 Risk-Neutral Pricing and the Stochastic Discount Factor

In the one-period setting, we will work with the probability space $(\Omega, 2^{\Omega}, \mathbb{Q})$, i.e., with the sigma-algebra generated by the finest partition of the sample space and with general probability measures.

These measures may or may not represent "true" probabilities. We stress again that in this case the measure-theoretic approach with partitions and sigma-algebras is not really needed; an intuitive approach that simply associates probabilities with every state in Ω would work equally well. We choose the more advanced setup because we will use it in the dynamic setting, and it will be nice to be able to draw parallels with the one-period case then.

We wish to define a risk-free gross discount rate, R: If there is a risk-free asset, i.e., if $\mathbf{1} \in \mathcal{R}$, then clearly $V^0 = \frac{1}{R}$, so R has the interpretation of being the gross discount rate. If there is not a risk-free asset, $\frac{1}{R}$ is defined as a *consistent* price for a hypothetical risk-free asset, *if such an asset existed*, i.e., it is a price (out of possibly several such prices) that would not generate arbitrage opportunities. Such a hypothetical risk-free rate can of course always be defined.

For a state-price vector, define $\hat{\psi} = \sum_i \psi_i$, $R = \frac{1}{\hat{\psi}}$, and

$$q_i = \frac{\psi_i}{\hat{\psi}}, \quad i = 1, \ldots, M.$$

Then it follows immediately that today's price, V^0, for an asset that pays $\mathbf{V}^1 \in \mathcal{R}$ in the next period is

$$V^0 = \sum_i \psi_i \mathbf{V}_i^1 = \frac{1}{R} \sum_i q_i \widetilde{V}_i^1 = \frac{1}{R} E^{\mathbb{Q}}[\widetilde{V}^1]. \tag{7.9}$$

Here we interpret $\widetilde{V}^1$ as the random variable defined by $\widetilde{V}^1(\omega_i) = (\mathbf{V}^1)_i$.

The last identity in (7.9) emphasizes that the summation over the q's has an interpretation of a discounted "expectation." This is true, since it is easy to check that the q_i's are nonnegative and sum to 1. Thus, $(\Omega, \mathcal{F}, \mathbb{Q})$ represents a probability space, where $\mathbb{Q}$ is generated from the atoms, $\mathbb{Q}(\{\omega_i\}) = q_i$. The $\mathbb{Q}$ measure is called the *risk-neutral measure*, or the *equivalent martingale measure* (EMM). Of course, it has absolutely nothing to do with true probabilities. It just offers a convenient notation for the linear pricing formula that we know must exist from the fundamental theorem.

Another way of writing (7.9) is to use the Radon–Nikodym derivative of $\mathbb{Q}$ with respect to $\mathbb{P}$, scaled with $\frac{1}{R}$, $M_i \stackrel{\text{def}}{=} \frac{1}{R}\frac{q_i}{p_i} = \frac{1}{R}L_i$, where $L_i = \frac{q_i}{p_i}$ (i.e., $L = \frac{d\mathbb{Q}}{d\mathbb{P}}$). We then get

$$V^0 = \frac{1}{R} E^{\mathbb{Q}}[\widetilde{V}^1] = \frac{1}{R} E^{\mathbb{P}}[L\widetilde{V}^1] = E^{\mathbb{P}}\left[\frac{M_1}{M_0}\widetilde{V}^1\right], \tag{7.10}$$

where we define $M_0 = 1$ (we will see later that the rightmost expression has a natural generalization in multiple periods). Here, $\mathbb{P}$ represents the *objective* (physical, true) probability distribution. Of course, since all states are possible, and the no-arbitrage theorem ensures that all state prices are positive, it is trivially the case that $\mathbb{Q}$ and $\mathbb{P}$ are equivalent.

The true expectation can thus be used as shown in (7.10), but the "discount factor," M, is no longer deterministic—it is a *stochastic discount factor* that needs to be moved inside the expectations operator.[9]

The existence of a state-price vector, ψ, can now equivalently be formulated using the risk-neutral terminology leading to the following version of the fundamental theorem:

[9] This is the same "object" that we defined in an equilibrium context in section 5.4.3. Here, the argument is based on absence of arbitrage, which typically imposes fewer constraints on the stochastic discount factor than in the earlier equilibrium context.

Theorem 7.5 ((Risk-neutral) first fundamental theorem of asset pricing). *The market is arbitrage-free if and only if there exist an equivalent martingale measure, $\mathbb{Q}$, and risk-free rate, R, such that the price of any asset in $\mathcal{R}$ is given by* (7.10).

Theorem 7.6 ((Risk-neutral) second fundamental theorem of asset pricing). *Given a market that is arbitrage-free, the equivalent martingale measure is unique if and only if the market is complete.*

We will from here on usually assume that there is a risk-free asset within $\mathcal{R}$, so that the risk-free rate is indeed unique. Moreover, we will typically assume that $R \geq 1$.

The four equivalent pricing representations we have introduced are summarized as follows:

$$\begin{aligned}
V^0 &= \mathbf{V}^1\psi \\
&= \frac{1}{R}E^{\mathbb{Q}}[\tilde{V}^1], \qquad q_i = \frac{\psi_i}{\hat{\psi}},\ R = \frac{1}{\hat{\psi}}, \\
&= \frac{1}{R}E^{\mathbb{P}}[L\tilde{V}^1], \qquad L_i = \frac{q_i}{p_i}, \\
&= E^{\mathbb{P}}\left[\frac{M_1}{M_0}\tilde{V}^1\right], \qquad (M_1)_i = \frac{L_i}{R},\ M_0 = 1.
\end{aligned} \tag{7.11}$$

7.7 More on Derivative Contracts

We mentioned stocks, bonds, and call options in section 7.2. Call options define a type of *derivative* contract. Specifically, a derivative is a security whose payoff *derives* from the value of another asset or security. Examples of derivatives include *forwards*, *swaps*, *futures*, and *options*. A call option gives the buyer the right but not the obligation to buy an underlying asset at a specific price, whereas a put option gives the buyer the right but not the obligation to sell such an underlying asset. Options can further be divided into *American* options, which give the buyer the right to exercise the contract on, or any time before, the so-called *expiration date*, and *European* options, which give the buyer the right to exercise the option only *on* the expiration date.

A European option is therefore more restricted than an American option from the buyer's perspective. Equivalently, the seller of an American option provides a higher degree of flexibility to the buyer than a seller of a European option.

Since the payoffs of options are closely related to the prices of the underlying assets, no-arbitrage techniques tend to be very powerful for options, as we will explore. We begin by showing some classical relationships. In these examples, we assume that the underlying asset pays no dividends between now and expiration, and that there are no costs associated with owning it.[10]

Other examples of derivative contracts include forwards, swaps, and futures. A forward contract specifies an agreement where the buyer agrees to purchase a specific quantity of a commodity or financial asset at a set price on a fixed date. Forward contracts are written directly between two counterparties "over-the-counter" (OTC), as opposed to being traded on an exchange.

[10] If the underlying is a real asset, e.g., a barrel of oil, there may be storage costs associated with owning it, which affects the analysis.

A swap specifies a series of forward transactions at different points in time. At each point in time, a fixed quantity of the commodity/asset is exchanged for a fixed price. Examples of swaps include interest rate swaps, where a fixed interest rate is swapped for a floating rate, and currency swaps, where payments in one currency are swapped for payments in another. It is easy to see how the latter contract allows two counterparties to *hedge* risks.

Consider company A, which mainly operates in a eurozone country, but which has some operations in the United States. Company A has received a large order from a US customer, and payments in dollars, USD, are expected in a sequence of installments every 30 days over the next 6 months. The payments are very welcome, because company A has some major bills it needs to pay over the same time period—denominated in euros, EUR. The one concern for company A is what happens if the dollar happens to depreciate significantly against the euro over this time period. If this happens, the payments may not be sufficient to cover what is due, leading to a liquidity crisis where company A will be forced to take out a costly short-term loan. The USD/EUR exchange rate is not *expected* to move drastically over the next 6 months, but there is some risk that it will. Company A would ideally like to hedge this risk.

Now, fortunately, another company, the US-based company B, is in the same situation but with a sequence of EUR-denominated payments expected over the next 6 months, and USD-denominated bills. By entering into a currency swap, *both* companies can avoid the risk associated with being paid in the wrong currency! This is a prime example of how a derivative contract, although it is a zero-sum game where in retrospect one party will be a "winner" and the other a "loser," actually is ex ante valuable for both parties by providing insurance.

Another potential role of derivatives is to allow for *speculation*, i.e., to allow a party that believes it is better informed than its counterparty to bet on the outcome. The value of derivative markets in allowing for speculation is harder to justify, which has led some, e.g., the investor Warren Buffet, to argue that derivative markets are dangerous "financial weapons of mass destruction." A detailed discussion of arguments for and against derivative markets is outside the scope of this text.

A third example of a derivative contract is the future contract. A future contract is similar to a forward contract, but is typically more standardized, which allows it to be traded on an exchange. Standardization allows a market to be more liquid: it is easier to find a counterparty when trading in a standardized product. Compare the market for IBM shares, which is standardized and very liquid, with the market for houses, which is less standardized and often less liquid. Another difference between an exchange and an OTC market is that whereas the counterparties in an OTC market "know" each other and can therefore establish a degree of trust, exchanges are anonymous in that buyers and sellers do not know each other. To avoid a situation where the counterparty runs off instead of making the payment, so-called *margin requirements* are usually imposed, in the form of collateral that a counterparty must hold in a separate account, as a guarantee. Moreover, changes in a contract's value are typically settled on a regular, e.g., daily, basis, so that no more than one day's price movement is at risk at any time.

We derive three classical forward and option pricing results.

1. *Forward pricing*: Assume that a forward contract states that, at time T, the owner of the contract will (i.e., has both the right and the obligation) to buy an underlying asset at the price F. The price of the underlying asset over time is S_t, $0 \le t \le T$. The discount rate between now ($t = 0$) and T is R, i.e., if you deposit one dollar today, you will have R dollars

at T. To calculate the price of this asset, we note that the payoff of owning the contract at time T is $S_T - F$, where S_T is the price of the underlying asset at time T. Now, that payoff can be replicated by buying the asset today, at price S_0, and short-selling $\frac{F}{R}$ in the risk-free asset. By the law of one price, the price of this strategy is

$$S_0 - \frac{F}{R},$$

which is thus the value of the contract. Initially, the forward price, F, is usually set so that the contract is worth zero, leading to the forward price formula

$$F = S_0 R.$$

The forward rate is thus set as if the underlying asset is appreciating in value at the risk-free rate, even though it is a risky asset!

2. *Option bounds*: We use the following notation: $C_t^{\text{Euro},K,T}$ is the time-t price of a European call option with strike price K, and exercise date T, and $P_t^{\text{Euro},K,T}$ is the price of a European put option. Similarly, for American options we have $C_t^{\text{Amer},K,T}$ and $P_t^{\text{Amer},K,T}$. It follows immediately that

   - $C_t^{\text{Amer},K,T} \geq C_t^{\text{Euro},K,T}$,
   - $P_t^{\text{Amer},K,T} \geq P_t^{\text{Euro},K,T}$,

   since the owner of an American option can always choose to exercise on the expiration date. At expiration, the payoffs of the contracts are obviously

   - $C_T^{K,T} = \max(S_T - K, 0)$,
   - $P_T^{K,T} = \max(K - S_T, 0)$,

   where, since the payoffs of an American and a European option are the same on the actual expiration date, if the American option is still "alive" at that point, we do not need to specify whether the option is American or European. Furthermore, since the options give their owners the right *but not the obligation* to exercise, they will be worth at least as much as forward contracts, which *do* come with the obligation. Also, since the buyer of an option can never be forced to exercise, the value can never be negative. We therefore have

   - $C_0^{\text{Euro},K,T} \geq \max(S_0 - \frac{K}{R}, 0)$,
   - $P_0^{\text{Euro},K,T} \geq \max(\frac{K}{R} - S_0, 0)$.

   Now, since an American call option, if exercised at time 0, generates the payoff $S_0 - K$, and

$$C_0^{\text{Amer},K,T} \geq C_0^{\text{Euro},K,T} \geq \max(S_0 - \tfrac{K}{R}, 0) \geq S_0 - \tfrac{K}{R} \geq S_0 - K,$$

   it can never be optimal to exercise an American call option at time 0 (recall that we are assuming that $R \geq 1$). In fact, the same argument holds at *any* time $0 \leq t < T$, so the American option must always be worth at least as much if kept alive as if exercised. But this means that the option of exercising early is not worth anything, so the American call option must be worth the same as the European call option,

   - $C_t^{\text{Amer},K,T} = C_t^{\text{Euro},K,T}$.

   This argument typically does not hold for an American put option. Furthermore, recall that we are assuming that the option does not pay dividends: American call options on dividend-paying assets may be worth strictly more than their respective European counterparts.

3. *Put-call parity*: The following relations hold immediately for any $a \in \mathbb{R}$:

$$\max(a, 0) = -\min(-a, 0),$$
$$\max(a, 0) = a - \min(a, 0),$$
$$\min(a, 0) = a - \max(a, 0).$$

The payoff at expiration of a portfolio containing one share of the underlying asset, one put option, and $-\frac{K}{R}$ in the risk-free asset is therefore

$$\begin{aligned} S_T + \max(K - S_T, 0) - K &= S_T - \min(S_T - K, 0) - K \\ &= S_T - ((S_T - K) - \max(S_T - K, 0)) - K \\ &= \max(S_T - K, 0), \end{aligned}$$

i.e., the same as the payoff of a call option with the same strike price. The time-0 price of this portfolio is $S_0 + P_0^{\text{Euro},K,T} - \frac{K}{R}$. In absence of arbitrage, it must therefore be that

- $C_0^{\text{Euro},K,T} = S_0 + P_0^{\text{Euro},K,T} - \frac{K}{R}$.

This is the famous so-called *put-call parity* relationship; see Stoll (1969).

We next focus on a complete market with the same number of assets as states.

Example 7.7 (State prices from option prices). Recall the state-price equation (7.7):

$$\mathbf{s}_0 = \mathbf{D}\psi.$$

In a complete market with the same number of assets as states, N, $\mathbf{D} \in \mathbb{R}^{N \times N}$ is an invertible matrix, so the state price is

$$\psi = \mathbf{D}^{-1}\mathbf{s}_0.$$

Now consider a market in which the states represent the possible prices of a stock at $t = 1$: $S_1 = a + 1, S_2 = a + 2, S_3 = a + 3, \ldots, S_N = a + N$, and asset i is a call option on the stock with strike price

$$K_i = a + (i - 1), \quad 1, \ldots, N.$$

It follows that the matrix $\mathbf{D}$ has elements

$$\mathbf{D}_{ij} = \max(S_j - K_i, 0) = \max(1 + j - i, 0).$$

We thus exclude the stock itself from the assets included in the $\mathbf{D}$ matrix (the stock is a redundant asset when the options are available, so it is not needed for calculating the state prices). An example with five states is given below, leading to the matrix

$$\mathbf{D} = \begin{bmatrix} 1 & 2 & 3 & 4 & 5 \\ 0 & 1 & 2 & 3 & 4 \\ 0 & 0 & 1 & 2 & 3 \\ 0 & 0 & 0 & 1 & 2 \\ 0 & 0 & 0 & 0 & 1 \end{bmatrix}.$$

The price vector is $\mathbf{s}_0 = (C_a, C_{a+1}, \ldots, C_{a+N-1})'$, where C_K is the price of a call option with strike price K.

To calculate the inverse of $\mathbf{D}$, we note that

$$\mathbf{D} = \mathbf{B}^2,$$

where $\mathbf{B}$ is an upper triangular matrix defined by $\mathbf{B}_{i,j} = 1$ if $j - i \geq 0$, and $\mathbf{B}_{i,j} = 0$ otherwise. It follows that $\mathbf{D}^{-1} = \mathbf{B}^{-2}$. One verifies that $\mathbf{B}^{-1}$ is an upper triangular matrix with $\mathbf{B}_{i,i} = 1$, $\mathbf{B}_{i,i+1} = -1$, and $\mathbf{B}_{i,j} = 0$ otherwise,

$$\mathbf{B}^{-1} = \begin{bmatrix} 1 & -1 & 0 & 0 & 0 \\ 0 & 1 & -1 & 0 & 0 \\ 0 & 0 & 1 & -1 & 0 \\ 0 & 0 & 0 & 1 & -1 \\ 0 & 0 & 0 & 0 & 1 \end{bmatrix},$$

in turn leading to $\mathbf{B}^{-2}_{i,i} = 1$, $\mathbf{B}^{-2}_{i,i+1} = -2$, $\mathbf{B}^{-2}_{i,i+2} = 1$, and $\mathbf{B}^{-2}_{i,j} = 0$ otherwise,

$$\mathbf{B}^{-2} = \begin{bmatrix} 1 & -2 & 1 & 0 & 0 \\ 0 & 1 & -2 & 1 & 0 \\ 0 & 0 & 1 & -2 & 1 \\ 0 & 0 & 0 & 1 & -2 \\ 0 & 0 & 0 & 0 & 1 \end{bmatrix}.$$

Calculating $\psi = \mathbf{D}^{-1}\mathbf{s}_0$ now gives us, using the notation $\psi^{S=a+N+1-j}$ for the state ψ_j,

$$\psi^{S=K} = C_{K+1} - 2C_K + C_{K-1}, \quad K = a+1, \ldots, a+N-2.$$

This is the discrete version of the state-price formula derived in Breeden and Litzenberger (1978), which we will discuss later.

The derived relationships in this section are very general, because they are model-free: they only depend on absence of arbitrage. By making further assumptions about the state space, we will be able to derive stronger pricing formulas.

7.8 Price Bounds in Incomplete Markets

Recall the one-period binomial model from section 7.4,

$$\bar{\mathbf{D}} = \begin{bmatrix} -1 & u & d \\ -1 & R & R \end{bmatrix},$$

as shown in figure 7.3. Here, the first asset represents a risky stock, and the second asset a risk-free bond. When $d < R < u$, we know from Example 7.6 that the market is complete and arbitrage-free, so any derivative can be priced in this market.

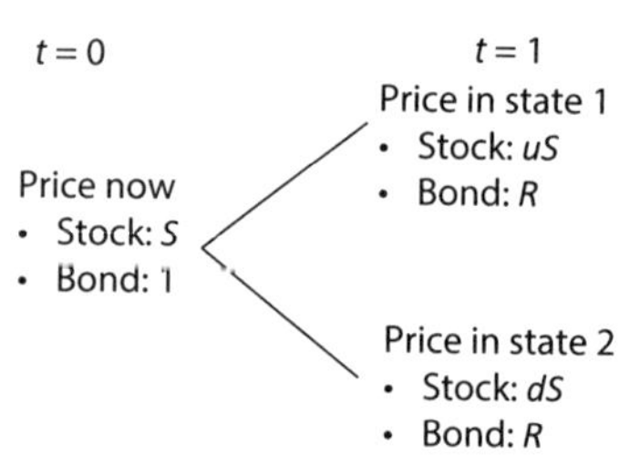

Figure 7.3: One-period binomial model: Complete market.

Exercise 7.2. Consider the one-period binomial model above:

1. Let q denote the risk-neutral probability for an up-move. Verify that the expression for q is
$$q = \frac{R-d}{u-d}.$$

Figure 7.4: One-period model: Incomplete market.

2. Derive the following expression for the price, C_0, of a general option, with payoffs C_u and C_d in the up- and down-states, respectively:

$$C_0 = \frac{1}{R}(qC_u + (1-q)C_d).$$

3. Derive the following expressions for the portfolio weights, $\mathbf{h} = (\Delta, B)^T$, that replicate the option's payoff

$$\Delta = \frac{C_u - C_d}{(u-d)S}, \quad B = \frac{uC_d - dC_u}{(u-d)R}.$$

Here, Δ denotes the number of shares purchased of the stock, and B the number of dollars invested in the risk-free asset.

In complete markets we can price any derivative, because the state-price vector is unique. In an incomplete market, the exact price can typically not be nailed down, but we may still have valuable information that can be used to derive bounds on the option price. Specifically, assume that the market is arbitrage-free and that we observe the price of N assets, but we do not know the price of asset $N+1$ traded in the market. We can define a set of state-price vectors, Ψ^N, such that all $\psi \in \Psi^N$ are consistent with the (no-arbitrage) prices of the first N assets.[11]

Now, the true state-price vector(s) must also be consistent with the unobserved price of asset $N+1$, in addition to the prices of the other N assets, so the set of pricing kernels that are consistent with the prices of all $N+1$ assets is $\Psi^{N+1} \subset \Psi^N$. The price of the $(N+1)$th asset, S^0_{N+1}, must therefore be $S^0_{N+1} = \mathbf{x}^T\psi$ for any $\psi \in \Psi^{N+1}$, where $\mathbf{x} = (S^1_{N+1}(\omega_1), \ldots, S^1_{N+1}(\omega_M))'$. If we knew the set Ψ^{N+1}, this would of course imply a unique price of S_0^{N+1}. However, the point is that we do not know Ψ^{N+1}, but we do know that it is a subset of Ψ^N, so by studying all the prices that would arise for different state-price vectors in Ψ^N, $\{\mathbf{x}^T\psi : \psi \in \Psi^N\}$, we get a whole range of potential prices that are consistent with no arbitrage. We call this an *arbitrage pricing interval*; see El Karoui and Quenez (1995) and Bizid and Jouini (1995) for applications and further discussion.

The idea is easiest shown in an example. Consider the model with a stock and a bond, so that $N=2$. The stock price can take on four different values at $t=1$, and the interest rate is $r=21\%$. We are interested in finding arbitrage pricing bounds on a call option on the stock with strike price $K=100$. The market is shown in figure 7.4, and is summarized by the price system

$$\bar{\mathbf{D}} = \begin{bmatrix} -100 & 150 & 100 & 96 & 64 \\ -1 & 1.21 & 1.21 & 1.21 & 1.21 \end{bmatrix}.$$

[11] We prefer the current formulation to the one where we introduce a new asset into a market with N assets. The reason is that adding a new asset may potentially change the prices of all the existing assets, and thereby change the state-price vector. Indeed, in equilibrium models of a market, this often happens. In that case, the analysis needs to be based on the "new" state-price vectors, i.e., the ones that correctly price the assets, once the new asset has been introduced.

What are the highest and lowest possible prices of the option in this market, $C_0^{\min}$ and $C_0^{\max}$? Since the option only makes a payment in state 1, and it pays 50 in that state, it is clear that its price is $C_0 = 50\psi_1$. Absence of arbitrage implies that $\psi_1 > 0$, so it follows that $C_0 > 0$. Moreover, the price of the stock is $100 = 150\psi_1 + 100\psi_2 + 96\psi_3 + 64\psi_4$, immediately implying that $150\psi_1 < 100$, i.e., $\psi_1 < \frac{2}{3}$. Thus, $C_0 = 50\psi_1 < 33.33$. The argument so far therefore leads to the bounds

$$0 < C_0 < 33.33,$$

by introducing the restrictions $0 < \psi_1 < \frac{2}{3}$ on the possible state-price vector.

We want to take a more structured approach. Define the strictly positive orthant $\mathcal{S} = \{\mathbf{x} \in \mathbb{R}^4 : \mathbf{x} \gg 0\}$, and the linear space

$$B = \left\{\psi \in \mathbb{R}^4 : 1.21(\psi_1 + \psi_2 + \psi_3 + \psi_4) = 1 \text{ and } 150\psi_1 + 100\psi_2 + 96\psi_3 + 64\psi_4 = 100\right\}.$$

The set of state-price vectors that are consistent with the bond and stock prices is then

$$\Psi^{B,S} = B \cap \mathcal{S}.$$

Since $C_0 = 50\psi_1$, it follows that $C^{\max} = 50 \sup_{\psi \in \Psi^{B,S}} \psi_1$, and $C^{\min} = 50 \inf_{\psi \in \Psi^{B,S}} \psi_1$, so we find the arbitrage pricing interval by finding the largest and smallest ψ_1 in $\Psi^{B,S}$.

From linear algebra, we know that B is a subspace of $\mathbb{R}^4$, of dimension 2, and that its elements $\mathbf{b} \in B$ can be written in the form

$$\mathbf{b} = \left(\frac{2}{3025}(525 + 121\psi_3 + 1089\psi_4), \frac{1}{3025}(1450 - 3267\psi_3 - 5203\psi_4), \psi_3, \psi_4\right)^T, \quad \psi_3, \psi_4 \in \mathbb{R}.$$

To find the maximal ψ_1, we should thus solve the linear programming problem,

$$\begin{aligned} &\max \frac{2}{3025}(525 + 121\psi_3 + 1089\psi_4), \\ &\text{s.t. } 0 \le 1450 - 3267\psi_3 - 5203\psi_4, \\ &0 \le \psi_3, \\ &0 \le \psi_4. \end{aligned} \tag{7.12}$$

In general, this problem can be solved by using standard techniques, e.g., the so-called simplex method. In this case it is also straightforward to solve it by hand. Specifically, it follows immediately from (7.12) that to make ψ_1 as large as possible, we want to make ψ_3 and ψ_4 as large as possible. However, from the positiveness restriction on ψ_2, a tension is introduced in that the more positive ψ_3 is, the less positive can ψ_4 be. Since the constraints are linear, it follows that to obtain the optimal solution, all weight should be put either on ψ_3 or on ψ_4. We therefore compare the two ψ_1's we get when we make either of ψ_3 and ψ_4 as large as possible.

The maximum ψ_3 consistent with ψ_2 being nonnegative is $\psi_3 = \frac{1450}{3267}$, leading to $\psi_4 = 0$, and

$$\psi_1 = \frac{2}{3025}\left(525 + 121\frac{1450}{3267}\right) \approx 0.3826.$$

The maximum ψ_4 is $\psi_4 = \frac{1450}{5203}$, leading to

$$\psi_1 = \frac{2}{3025}\left(525 + 1089\frac{1450}{5203}\right) \approx 0.5478.$$

It is clear that choosing ψ_4 as large as possible makes ψ_1 as large as possible. Now, remember that although we only imposed weak positivity when solving the problem, no arbitrage requires each state price to be strictly positive, so we arrive at $\psi < 0.5478$, leading to $C_0 < C_0^{\max} = 50 \times 0.5478 = 27.38$.

The minimum price, $C_0^{\min}$ is calculated with an identical approach, but minimizing ψ_1 instead, leading to

$$\psi_1 > \frac{2}{3025}525 \approx 0.3471,$$

$C_0 > C_0^{\min} = 50 \times 0.3471 = 17.36$. Altogether,[12]

$$17.36 < C_0 < 27.38.$$

Let us also consider an alternative approach, namely constructing dominating portfolios. Specifically, assume that a portfolio of h_1 stocks and h_2 bonds costs P, pays at least 50 in state 1 and in no other states makes a negative payment. Then, clearly, it must be that $C_0 \leq P$, since otherwise purchasing the $(h_1, h_2)^T$ portfolio and short-selling the option would generate an arbitrage opportunity. The argument immediately implies that

$$C_0 \leq \min_{h_1, h_2} 100h_1 + h_2, \tag{7.13}$$

$$\text{s.t. } 50 \leq 150h_1 + 1.21h_2, \tag{7.14}$$

$$0 \leq 100h_1 + 1.21h_2, \tag{7.15}$$

$$0 \leq 96h_1 + 1.21h_2, \tag{7.16}$$

$$0 \leq 64h_1 + 1.21h_2. \tag{7.17}$$

Finding the solution to this linear programming problem is a bit trickier than solving the programming problem associated with the state-price vector, but we can proceed as follows: We note that for the payment to be strictly positive in state 1, it must be that at least one of the portfolio weights h_1 and h_2 is strictly positive. Assume that it is h_1 that is positive. In this case, given h_1, we want to choose h_2 as low as possible so that the four constraints at $t = 0$ are satisfied. Clearly, given that constraint (7.17) is satisfied, it must be the case that constraints (7.15, 7.16) are also satisfied. Under the assumption that $h_1 \geq 0$, we can thus equivalently study the reduced problem

$$\mathop{min}_{h_1 \geq 0, h_2} \quad 100h_1 + h_2,$$

$$\text{s.t. } 50 \leq 150h_1 + 1.21h_2,$$

$$0 \leq 64h_1 + 1.21h_2.$$

[12]The arbitrage pricing interval may be too large in practice. Additional assumptions may then be needed to decrease the size of this interval; see Bizid and Jouini (1995) and Cvitanic, Pham, and Touzi (1999).

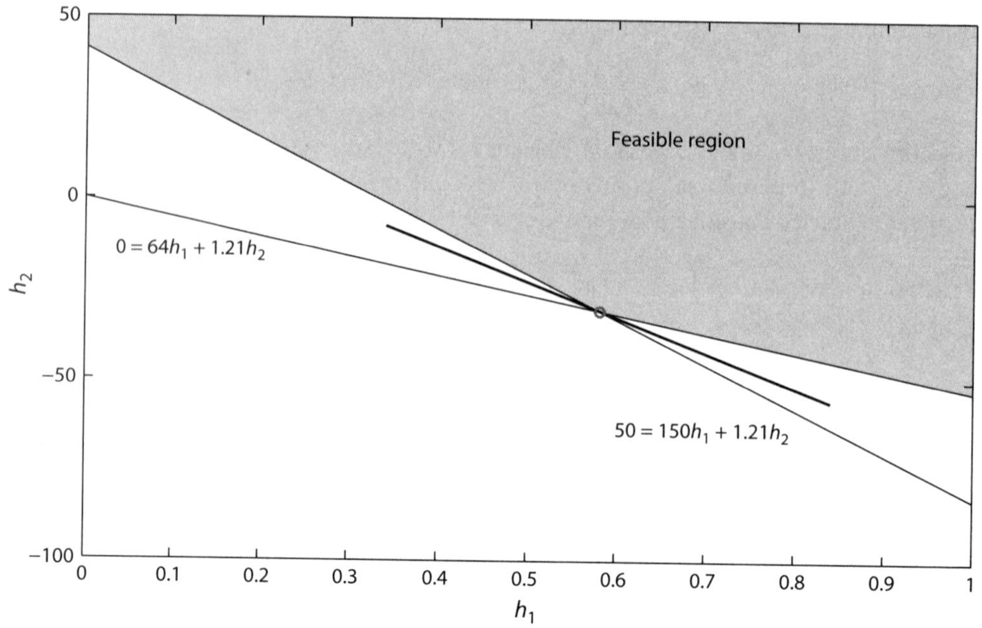

Figure 7.5: Incomplete market: The thick line shows a hyperplane that separates higher from lower prices of portfolios. The feasible region consists of the portfolios that pay at least as much as the option in all states. The circle shows the portfolio with the lowest price in the feasible region, corresponding to $h_1 = \frac{50}{86}$, $h_2 = -\frac{40}{1.21}$.

Solving the latter two equations under equality yields $h_1 = \frac{50}{86}$ and $h_2 = -\frac{40}{1.21}$, and the price of $100h_1 + h_2 = 27.38$. This is the same price we arrived at when using the set of state-price vectors! We see in figure 7.5 that this is indeed the portfolio with the lowest price. A similar analysis for the region $h_1 \leq 0$ shows that this is the lowest price that can be obtained for *any* h_1. Moreover, an identical analysis of the problem

$$C_0 \geq \max_{h_1,h_2} 100h_1 + h_2, \tag{7.18}$$

$$\text{s.t. } 50 \geq 150h_1 + 1.21h_2, \tag{7.19}$$

$$0 \geq 100h_1 + 1.21h_2, \tag{7.20}$$

$$0 \geq 96h_1 + 1.21h_2, \tag{7.21}$$

$$0 \geq 64h_1 + 1.21h_2, \tag{7.22}$$

allows one to derive the lower bound $C_0 \geq 17.36$, altogether again leading to the arbitrage pricing interval

$$17.36 < C_0 < 27.38.$$

The two approaches thus yield the same result. This should not come as a surprise, given how we defined the state-price vector and our derivation of the fundamental theorems. Specifically, the underlying argument is always that we assume absence of arbitrage, which leads to restrictions on asset prices, in this case in the form of an arbitrage pricing interval within which the derivative's price must lie. If the price lay outside the interval, an arbitrage opportunity would exist. In the case of a too high price, for example, a dominating portfolio would exist that had higher cash flows in all states at $t=1$, and a lower price at $t=0$. Now, it is exactly these restrictions we use when determining the bound using the set of state-price vectors!

The two problems are dual: The state-price vectors are defined by the implied absence of arbitrage, summarizing the implications of this assumption in Ψ. Which approach is the easiest depends on the specific problem. In this case it was more straightforward to study the set of state-price vectors. In other problems—especially when the space of state-price vectors is large—it may be more straightforward to study the dominating portfolios directly.

The state-price vector approach could of course have been formulated using risk-neutral terminology, in which case the pricing implications would be formulated as constraints on (risk-neutral) expectations.

7.9 Exercises

1. *One-period model*: Consider the following one-period market, with the state space $\Omega=\{\omega_1,\omega_2,\omega_3\}$:

$$\mathbf{D}=\begin{bmatrix}0&1&1\\1&0&1\\1&1&0\\1&1&1\end{bmatrix},\quad \mathbf{s}^0=\begin{bmatrix}0.5\\0.5\\0.5\\0.75\end{bmatrix}.$$

   (a) Is this market arbitrage-free?
   (b) Is this market complete?
   (c) What is the risk-free rate ($R=1+r$) in this market?
   (d) What is the value of a derivative contract that pays out 1 in state ω_1, 2 in state ω_2, and 3 in state ω_3?

2. Consider the following one-period market, with the state space $\Omega=\{\omega_1,\omega_2,\omega_3\}$:

$$\mathbf{D}=\begin{bmatrix}1&1&1\\0&1&2\\0&0&10\end{bmatrix},\quad \mathbf{s}^0=\begin{bmatrix}0.8\\0.5\\0.2\end{bmatrix}.$$

   The probabilities for different events are $\mathbb{P}(\omega_1)=0.2$, $\mathbb{P}(\omega_2)=0.3$, $\mathbb{P}(\omega_3)=0.5$.

   (a) Is there a risk-free rate ($R=1+r$) in this market? If so, what is it?
   (b) Is the market complete?
   (c) Brian Debt (who has just started a hedge fund) claims that prices are clearly nonsensical in this market, and that there exists an arbitrage opportunity because asset 3 is underpriced. Is he correct?
   (d) Define a stochastic discount factor, M (i.e., M_1), in this economy.

3. Consider the market represented by the state space $\Omega=\{\omega_1,\omega_2,\omega_3\}$, and the price system

$$\bar{\mathbf{D}}=\begin{bmatrix}-100&50&100&150\\-100&100&100&100\end{bmatrix}.$$

The first asset is a stock, with time-0 price $S = 100$, and the second is a risk-free bond, with the same time-0 price, $B = 100$.

(a) Does this market permit arbitrage?
(b) Is the market complete?
(c) Consider an *at-the-money* call option on the stock, thus with the strike price $K = S = 100$, with time-0 price C in this market. Derive upper and lower bounds on C. Clearly state the assumptions you are making.

4. Consider the following one-period market, with the state space $\Omega = \{\omega_1, \omega_2, \omega_3, \omega_4\}$:

$$\mathbf{D} = \begin{bmatrix} 1 & 1.2 & 0 & 0 \\ 1.1 & 1.1 & 0 & 0 \\ 0 & 0 & 1 & 1.3 \\ 0 & 0 & 1.1 & 1.1 \end{bmatrix}, \quad \mathbf{s}^0 = \begin{bmatrix} 0.5 \\ 0.5 \\ 0.5 \\ 0.5 \end{bmatrix}.$$

(a) Is this market arbitrage-free?
(b) Is this market complete?
(c) What is the risk-free rate ($R = 1 + r$) in this market?
(d) Define an equivalent martingale measure (EMM) for this market.

5. *One-period model*: Consider the following one-period market, with the state space $\Omega = \{\omega_1, \omega_2, \omega_3, \omega_4, \omega_5\}$ and six assets:

$$\mathbf{D} = \begin{bmatrix} 1 & 2 & 3 & 4 & 6 \\ 1 & 0 & 0 & 0 & 0 \\ 0 & 1 & 0 & 0 & 0 \\ 0 & 0 & 1 & 0 & 0 \\ 0 & 0 & 0 & 2 & 0 \\ 0 & 0 & 0 & 0 & 3 \end{bmatrix}, \quad \mathbf{s}^0 = \begin{bmatrix} 10 \\ 1 \\ 1 \\ 1 \\ 1 \\ 1 \end{bmatrix},$$

where $\mathbf{D}_{ij}$ is the time-1 price of asset i in state ω_j, and $\mathbf{s}_i^0$ is the time-0 price of asset i.

(a) Does this market permit arbitrage? If so, which type(s) of arbitrage? Also, is the law of one price satisfied?
(b) Is the market complete?
(c) What is the market price of a call option on asset 1, with strike price $K = 3$?
(d) What is the risk-free rate, R?
(e) What is the risk-neutral probability, $\mathbb{Q}(\omega_4)$?

6. Consider the market defined by $\mathbf{D} = [0, 1, 1, 1, 2]$, $\mathbf{s}^0 = [1]$.

(a) Define the set of state-price vectors that are consistent with the law of one price.
(b) Define the set of state-price vectors that are consistent with no arbitrage.
(c) Given that the market permits no arbitrage, derive an upper bound on the price (at $t = 0$) of a derivative which at time 1 pays off 2 in state 4, 3 in state 5, and 0 in all other states, i.e., $V^1 = (0, 0, 0, 2, 3)$.

7. Consider the market defined by $\mathbf{D} = [0]$, $\mathbf{s}^0 = [1]$.

(a) Does the LOOP hold in this market?
(b) Is there an arbitrage opportunity?

(c) Is there a Type I arbitrage opportunity?
(d) Is there a Type II arbitrage opportunity?

Next consider the market defined by $\mathbf{D} = [1, 1]$, $\mathbf{s}^0 = [0]$.

(e) Does the LOOP hold in this market?
(f) Is there an arbitrage opportunity?
(g) Is there a Type I arbitrage opportunity?
(h) Is there a Type II arbitrage opportunity?

8. Consider the economy

$$\mathbf{s}^0 = \begin{bmatrix} 1 \\ 1 \end{bmatrix}, \quad \mathbf{D} = \begin{bmatrix} 5 & 5 & 5 & 5 & 5 \\ 3 & 3 & 3 & 3 & 7 \end{bmatrix}.$$

(a) Is the market complete?
(b) Is there an arbitrage opportunity?
(c) Is there a strictly positive state-price vector?

9. Consider the economy

$$\mathbf{s}^0 = \begin{bmatrix} 1 \\ 2 \\ 3 \\ 4 \\ 5 \end{bmatrix}, \quad \mathbf{D} = \begin{bmatrix} 5 & 5 \\ 6 & 9 \\ 8 & 11 \\ 9 & 10 \\ 11 & 6 \end{bmatrix}.$$

(a) Is the market complete?
(b) Is there an arbitrage opportunity?
(c) Is there a strictly positive state-price vector?

10. Verify the following conditions in Example 7.6:

(a) If (a) or (b) is satisfied then there is no arbitrage. Otherwise there is arbitrage.
(b) If (c) is satisfied, then the market is complete. Otherwise it is incomplete.

So the market admits no arbitrage and is complete if (a) is satisfied.

11. Consider an economy with three assets and three states, which has the time-0 price vector $\mathbf{s}^0 = (1, 1, 1)^T$, and time-1 payoff matrix

$$\mathbf{D} = \begin{bmatrix} 3 & 0 & 0 \\ 0 & 1 & 1 \\ 0 & 1 & -1 \end{bmatrix}.$$

(a) What is the risk-free rate, R^f, in this economy?
(b) Is there an arbitrage opportunity in this economy?

12. Consider the market defined by

$$\mathbf{D} = \begin{bmatrix} 1 & 3 & 5 \\ 5 & -1 & -5 \end{bmatrix}, \quad \mathbf{s}^0 = \begin{bmatrix} 1 \\ 1 \end{bmatrix}.$$

Here, $\mathbf{s}^0 = (S_1(0), S_2(0))'$ denotes the time-0 prices of assets 1 and 2, and $\mathbf{D}$ their prices in different states at $t = 1$. Assume that there is no arbitrage.

(a) What can you say about the price of a European put option on asset 1, with strike price $K = 4$ (and expiration at $t = 1$)?

(b) What can you say about the risk-free rate, R?

CHAPTER 8 Multiperiod Model

We extend the model to multiple time periods. Intuitively, this should be fairly straightforward. As an example, the two-period binomial model has the structure shown in figure 8.1. Here we have made specific assumptions about the size of up- and down-moves, and the prices of assets in different states.

In principle, one may think that this model should be very similar to the one in figure 7.4. Indeed, we have two assets in both cases (the stock and the bond), and four final states with the same values of the stock and bond in each state, in both examples. However, there are two *fundamental* differences between the two models:

- *Dynamic replication*: Investors in the two-period model can change their portfolio holdings at $t = \frac{1}{2}$. This will greatly expand the asset span compared with the model in figure 7.4. Indeed, whereas the market in the model of figure 7.4 is incomplete (four states and two assets), the market in the two-period binomial model will typically be complete! A consequence is that no-arbitrage pricing becomes much more powerful in the multiperiod model—recall that the more complete the market is, the more restrictions no-arbitrage pricing imposes.
- *Information*: We will need to keep track of how information evolves over time in the multiperiod market with a so-called information structure. Specifically, in the one-period model, the information structure is trivial: at $t = 0$, the investor knows nothing about which state will occur, and at $t = 1$, the investor knows exactly which state occurred. Compare this with the model in figure 8.1. At $t = 0$ and $t = 1$, the situations correspond to the one-period model. However, at $t = \frac{1}{2}$, the investor has some, but not complete, information. If the stock moved up, then clearly it is impossible for the economy to end up in either du or dd at $t = 1$. However, it may end up in either uu or ud.

To address these new challenges we introduce some more concepts from probability theory and the theory of stochastic processes. We begin by further exploring the example in figure 8.1, to better understand the concepts of dynamic replication and information structures.

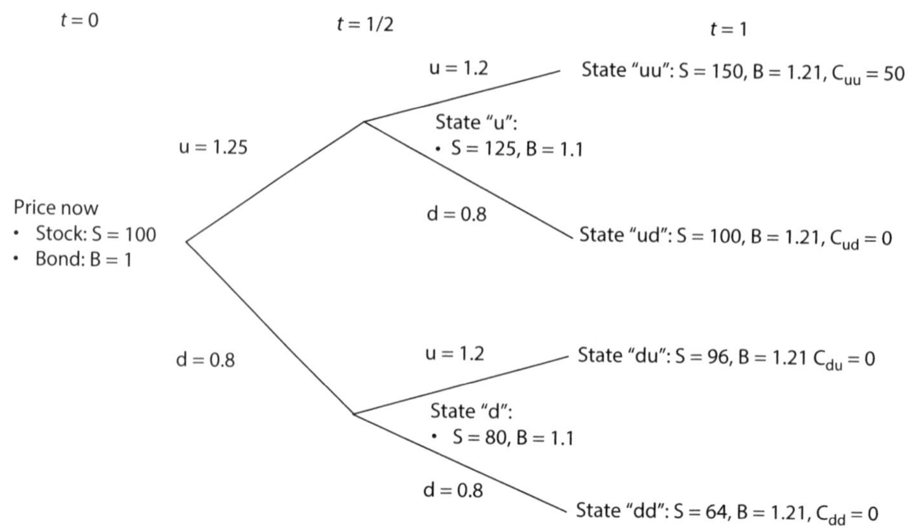

Figure 8.1: Two-period binomial model.

8.1 An Example with Two Periods

Consider the two-period example in figure 8.1. As mentioned, the distinction between this example and the one we studied in the previous section is that the investor is allowed to trade the asset at $t=\frac{1}{2}$. At that point some, but not all, information has been revealed. Specifically, let us denote the state space by $\Omega=\{uu, ud, du, dd\}$. At $t=1$, it is known which state occurred. However, at $t=\frac{1}{2}$, what is known after an up-move is that either *uu* or *ud* will occur. Similarly, after a down-move it is known that either *du* or *dd* will occur.

A convenient way to represent this information structure at $t=0$, $t=\frac{1}{2}$, and $t=1$ is to use three partitions: At $t=0$, we use the roughest partition, $P_0=\{\Omega\}$. At $t=\frac{1}{2}$, we use the partition $P_{1/2}=\{\{uu, ud\}, \{du, dd\}\}$, and at $t=1$ we use the finest partition, $P_1=\{\{uu\}, \{ud\}, \{du\}, \{dd\}\}$. The idea here is thus that the investor's information at any time, t, is such that they know which *set* in the partition the economy is in, but not the specific *element* in that set. In fact, we could even take the $\{uu, ud\}$ set as the definition of an up-move, since the two conditions "the stock went up," and "at $t=1$, the stock price will either have gone up twice or have first gone up and then down," are equivalent. The three partitions P_0, P_1, P_2, jointly describe the *information structure* in the market.

We mentioned that partitions and sigma-algebras are equivalent in the case with a finite number of states. So we could of course equivalently have represented the information structure by the three sigma-algebras $\mathcal{F}_0 \stackrel{\text{def}}{=} \{\emptyset, \Omega\}$, $\mathcal{F}_{1/2} \stackrel{\text{def}}{=} \{\emptyset, \{uu, ud\}, \{du, dd\}, \Omega\}$, and $\mathcal{F}_1 \stackrel{\text{def}}{=} 2^{\Omega}$. This is the standard approach, and it also works when state spaces are infinite and there is no finest partition (no atoms). We use the partition approach for the time being since it is simpler.

We next move to the second major change compared with the one-period model, namely that of dynamic replication. As we recall from the previous section, without trading at $t=\frac{1}{2}$, the option price could not be completely nailed down; we had to settle for an arbitrage pricing bound. With trading allowed at $t=\frac{1}{2}$ we may be more optimistic about finding a price. Specifically, figure 8.1 suggests that the "tree" from $t=0$ to $t=1$ can be decomposed into three one-period subtrees—one from $t=0$ to $t=\frac{1}{2}$, one from $t=\frac{1}{2}$ to $t=1$ after an up-move, and one from $t=\frac{1}{2}$ to $t=1$ after a down-move—and since the market in each of these subtrees is complete, it seems like the whole market may be complete.

Against this intuition stands the fact that there are only two assets in a market with four states. This is where the power of dynamic trading comes in: by *rebalancing* the portfolio at $t=\frac{1}{2}$, conditioned on whether the stock went up or down, the market becomes *dynamically complete*. We show how this works by *replicating* the payoffs of the option in the previous example, using a *replicating portfolio*. Specifically, we want to find a trading strategy that leads to payments at $t=1$ of $C_{uu}=50$ after two up-moves, and $C_{ud}=C_{du}=C_{dd}=0$ in all other states.

We begin with the dynamics from $t=\frac{1}{2}$ to $t=1$ after an up-move. The return of the stock and bond are then represented by the following **s** vector and **D** matrix:

$$\mathbf{s}=\begin{bmatrix}1\\1\end{bmatrix},\qquad \mathbf{D}=\begin{bmatrix}1.2 & 0.8\\1.1 & 1.1\end{bmatrix}.$$

We have thus rescaled so that we are studying returns on one dollar of investments. For example, the element $\mathbf{D}_{11}=\frac{150}{125}=1.2$ represents the return on the stock if the price moves up again. Similarly, $R=1.1$ represents the per-period risk-free rate. Using the formulas in the one-period model derived in exercise 7.2, noting that $u=1.2$ and $d=0.8$ in this period, we then get

$$q_u=\frac{R-d}{u-d}=\frac{3}{4},$$

$$C_u=\frac{1}{R}(q_uC_{uu}+(1-q_u)C_{ud})=34.1,$$

$$\Delta_u=\frac{C_{uu}-C_{ud}}{(u-d)S}=\frac{50}{0.4\times 125}=1,$$

$$B_u=\frac{uC_{ud}-dC_{uu}}{(u-d)R}=\frac{-0.8\times 50}{0.4\times 1.1}=-90.91.$$

Thus, the value of the option at $t=\frac{1}{2}$ is 34.1.

Doing the same calculation after a down-move, in which case **s** and **D** are the same as after an up-move, leads to

$$q_d=\frac{R-d}{u-d}=\frac{3}{4},$$

$$C_d=0,$$

$$\Delta_d=0,$$

$$B_d=0.$$

Not surprisingly, the value of the option, C_d, is zero in this case, since it will expire out of the money after both an up- and a down-move between $t=\frac{1}{2}$ and $t=1$.

Finally, the returns between $t=0$ and $t=\frac{1}{2}$ are described by

$$\mathbf{s}=\begin{bmatrix}1\\1\end{bmatrix},\qquad \mathbf{D}=\begin{bmatrix}1.25 & 0.8\\1.1 & 1.1\end{bmatrix},$$

i.e., we have $u=1.25=\frac{125}{100}$ and $d=0.8=\frac{80}{100}$, leading to

$$q=\frac{R-d}{u-d}=\frac{2}{3},$$

$$C=\frac{1}{R}(qC_u+(1-q)C_d)=\frac{1}{1.1}\left(\frac{2}{3}\times 34.091+\frac{1}{3}\times 0\right)=20.66,$$

$$\Delta=\frac{34.1}{0.45\times 100}=0.7578,$$

$$B=\frac{-0.8\times 34.1}{0.45\times 1.1}=-55.1.$$

Thus, the value of the option at time 0 is unambiguously determined:

$$C=20.66.$$

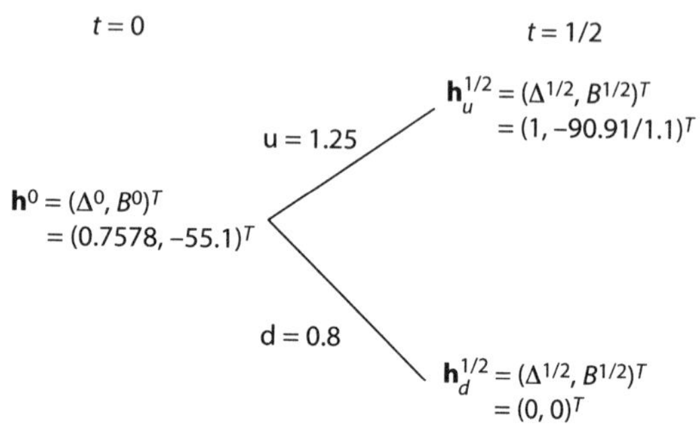

Figure 8.2: Dynamic trading in the two-period binomial model.

By rebalancing the portfolio positions, it is thus possible for the investor to replicate any cash flows in the four states, *without having to infuse or withdraw additional capital at* $t=\frac{1}{2}$, i.e., the portfolio trading strategy is self-financed. We summarize the portfolio holdings at different times and in different states in figure 8.2 (at $t=1$, the portfolio is liquidated to generate the cash flows, which is not shown in the figure). At $t=0$, the investor purchased 0.7578 stocks and borrows 55.1, paying a total price of 20.66. Now consider the situation at $t=\frac{1}{2}$ after an up-move, just before the portfolio is rebalanced. At this point, the stock price has increased to 125, and the loan has also appreciated by 10%.

The total value of the portfolio is thus $0.7578\times 125-55.1\times 1.1=34.1$. The investor now rebalances to the new position, holding 1 stock and borrowing 90.9 (which corresponds to selling $\frac{90.9}{1.1}$ units of the bond which is now worth 1.1). The total value of this investment strategy is $125-90.9=34.1$, i.e., it is the same and no additional cash is needed at $t=\frac{1}{2}$! Finally, the payoff at $t=1$ after another up-move is $1\times 150-\frac{90.9}{1.1}\times 1.1^2=50$, and after a down-move it is $1\times 100-\frac{90.9}{1.1}\times 1.1^2=0$. So the payoffs of the option are replicated. Similarly, after a down-move between $t=0$ and $t=\frac{1}{2}$, the portfolio's value is $0.7578\times 80-55.1\times 1.1=0$, the portfolio is liquidated, and the cash flows of zero are realized at $t=1$, both after an up-move and after another down-move.

This example shows how powerful the mechanism of replicating payoffs through dynamic trading is in multiperiod markets!

8.2 Probability Theory II

We assume a sample space $\Omega=\{\omega_1,\ldots,\omega_M\}$. A set of nonempty events, $\{B_1,\ldots,B_m\}$, forms a *partition* of Ω if $\bigcup_i B_i=\Omega$ and $B_i\cap B_j=\emptyset$ when $i\neq j$. An example is given by the state space $\Omega=\{\omega_1,\omega_2,\omega_3,\omega_4,\omega_5,\omega_6\}$, with partition $B_1=\{\omega_1,\omega_2,\omega_3\}$, $B_2=\{\omega_4,\omega_5,\omega_6\}$. As before, we will be somewhat sloppy with notation, sometimes writing $\mathbb{P}(\omega_i)$ instead of $\mathbb{P}(\{\omega_i\})$.

We recall the following results from probability theory:

- *Conditional probability*: The conditional probability for the event A to occur given that B has occurred, $\mathbb{P}(A|B)$, where $\mathbb{P}(B)>0$, is

$$\mathbb{P}(A|B)\stackrel{\text{def}}{=}\frac{\mathbb{P}(A\cap B)}{\mathbb{P}(B)}.$$

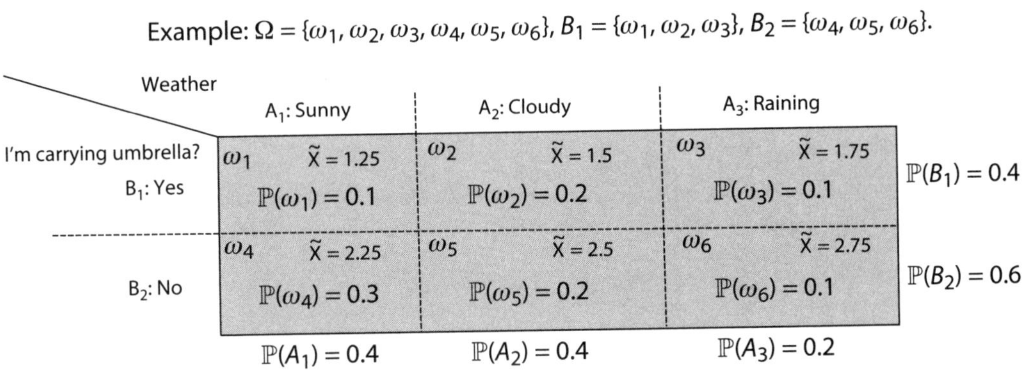

Figure 8.3: Basic probability theory: Umbrella example.

- *Law of total probability*: Let $\{B_1, \ldots, B_m\}$ be a partition of Ω. Then for any event A, $\mathbb{P}(A) = \sum_j \mathbb{P}(A \cap B_j) = \sum_j \mathbb{P}(A|B_j)\mathbb{P}(B_j)$.
- *Conditional expectation*: The conditional expectation $E[\widetilde{X}|B]$ is

$$E[\widetilde{X}|B] \stackrel{\text{def}}{=} \sum_{i=1}^{M} \mathbb{P}(\omega_i|B)\widetilde{X}(\omega_i).$$

- *Bayes' rule*: Let A and B be two events, with $\mathbb{P}(B) > 0$. Then $\mathbb{P}(A|B) = \frac{\mathbb{P}(B|A)\mathbb{P}(A)}{\mathbb{P}(B)}$.
- *Law of iterated expectations* (LIE): Let $\widetilde{X}$ be a random variable. Then $E[E[\widetilde{X}|B]] = E[\widetilde{X}]$.

Example 8.1. Let us assume the following probability space, as shown in figure 8.3, where different events correspond to different combinations of the weather and whether (!) I am carrying an umbrella. Note that each ω corresponds to a combination of the weather and umbrella. For example, ω_1 represents the state in which it is sunny and I carry an umbrella, i.e., $\{\omega_1\} = A_1 \cap B_1$.

- The conditional probability that it is sunny if I am carrying an umbrella is

$$\mathbb{P}(A_1|B_1) = \frac{\mathbb{P}(A_1 \cap B_1)}{\mathbb{P}(B_1)} = \frac{10\%}{40\%} = 25\%.$$

Now, this makes perfect sense: I am carrying an umbrella in states ω_1, ω_2, and ω_3, and the total probability for these three states is $10\% + 20\% + 10\% = 40\%$. Half of the time that I am carrying an umbrella (20% out of the 40%) it is cloudy, 25% of the time it is raining (10% out of the 40%) and, similarly, 25% of the time it is sunny.

In figure 8.4, a tree representation of the same example is shown. The conditional probabilities correspond to the probabilities of different branches in the second level of the tree. For example, the conditional probability that it is sunny if I wear an umbrella, $\mathbb{P}(\{\omega_1\}|B_1) = 25\%$, would correspond to the probability for the uppermost branch in the second level of the tree, given that the first branch is the up-branch. The unconditional probability is then

$$\mathbb{P}(\omega_1) = \mathbb{P}(B_1) \times \mathbb{P}(\{\omega_1\}|B_1) = 40\% \times 25\% = 10\%.$$

So individual branch probabilities correspond to conditional probabilities, and unconditional probabilities can be calculated by multiplying together conditional probabilities. This intuition will be helpful later on.

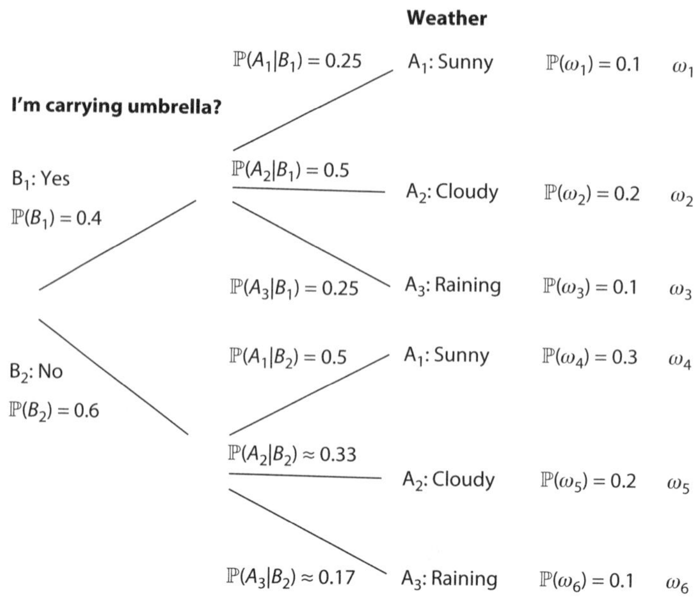

Figure 8.4: Basic probability theory: The same umbrella example, with tree representation.

- The total probability for it being sunny is 40%=10%+30%, since there is a 10% chance that it is sunny and I carry an umbrella, and there is a 30% that it is sunny and I do not, $\mathbb{P}(A_1) = \mathbb{P}(A_1 \cap B_1) + \mathbb{P}(A_1 \cap B_2)$.
- The conditional expectation, $E[\widetilde{X}|B_1]$, is

$$E[\widetilde{X}|B_1] = \mathbb{P}(A_1|B_1) \times 1.25 + \mathbb{P}(A_2|B_1) \times 1.5 + \mathbb{P}(A_3|B_1) \times 1.75,$$

  where we do not include the events A_4, A_5, and A_6 in the sum, since they all have zero conditional probabilities, given B_1.
- Let us consider Bayes' rule. The probability that it is sunny if I am not holding an umbrella is

$$\mathbb{P}(A_1|B_2) = \frac{\mathbb{P}(A_1 \cap B_2)}{\mathbb{P}(B_2)} = \frac{30\%}{60\%} = 50\%.$$

  According to Bayes' rule, this is the same as the probability that I am not holding an umbrella if it is sunny, multiplied by the probability that it is sunny, divided by the probability that I am not holding an umbrella. The probability that I am not holding an umbrella if it is sunny is

$$\mathbb{P}(B_2|A_1) = \frac{\mathbb{P}(A_1 \cap B_2)}{\mathbb{P}(A_1)} = \frac{30\%}{40\%} = 75\%.$$

  The probability that I am not holding an umbrella is $\mathbb{P}(B_2) = 60\%$, and the probability that it is sunny is $\mathbb{P}(A_1) = 40\%$. So, indeed,

$$50\% = \mathbb{P}(A_1|B_2) = \frac{\mathbb{P}(B_2|A_1) \times \mathbb{P}(A_1)}{\mathbb{P}(B_2)} = \frac{75\% \times 40\%}{60\%} = 50\%.$$

- Finally, let us verify the law of iterated expectations, $E[E[\widetilde{X}|B]] = E[\widetilde{X}]$. We have

$$\begin{aligned}E[\widetilde{X}|B_1] &= \mathbb{P}(A_1|B_1) \times 1.25 + \mathbb{P}(A_2|B_1) \times 1.5 + \mathbb{P}(A_3|B_1) \times 1.75\\ &= 25\% \times 1.25 + 50\% \times 1.25 + 25\% \times 1.75 = 1.5,\\ E[\widetilde{X}|B_2] &= \mathbb{P}(A_1|B_2) \times 2.25 + \mathbb{P}(A_2|B_2) \times 2.5 + \mathbb{P}(A_3|B_2) \times 2.75\\ &= 50\% \times 2.25 + 33.33\% \times 2.5 + 16.67\% \times 2.75 = 2.417.\end{aligned}$$

So, since $\mathbb{P}(B_1) = 40\%$, and $\mathbb{P}(B_2) = 60\%$, we get

$$\begin{aligned}E[E[\widetilde{X}|B]] &= 40\% \times 1.5 + 60\% \times 2.417\\ &= 2.05.\end{aligned}$$

The right-hand side of the relationship yields

$$\begin{aligned}E[\widetilde{X}] &= 10\% \times 1.25 + 20\% \times 1.5 + 10\% \times 1.75 + 30\% \times 2.25 + 20\% \times 2.5 + 10\% \times 2.75\\ &= 2.05.\end{aligned}$$

So, indeed, the two are the same. Mathematically, the relationship follows directly from the relationship

$$\begin{aligned}E[E[\widetilde{X}|B]] &= \sum_j \mathbb{P}(B_j)E[\widetilde{X}|B_j]\\ &= \sum_j \mathbb{P}(B_j)\left(\sum_i \mathbb{P}(A_i|B_j)\widetilde{X}(A_i \cap B_j)\right)\\ &= \sum_j \mathbb{P}(B_j)\left(\sum_i \frac{\mathbb{P}(A_i \cap B_j)}{\mathbb{P}(B_j)}\widetilde{X}(A_i \cap B_j)\right)\\ &= \sum_{i,j} \mathbb{P}(A_i \cap B_j)\widetilde{X}(A_i \cap B_j)\\ &= E[\widetilde{X}].\end{aligned}$$

Consider a partition, denoted by $B_1, \ldots, B_k$, which is not necessarily the finest one. If this partition is a coarser partition than the finest one, then the corresponding sigma-algebra will not be the power set, $\mathcal{F} \neq 2^{\Omega}$. In this case, there will be some subsets of Ω for which the probability is not defined.

For a general probability space $(\Omega, \mathcal{F}, \mathbb{P})$, where $\Omega = \{\omega_1, \ldots, \omega_M\}$ is a finite sample space, the sigma-algebra, $\mathcal{F}$, is constructed by taking unions of the elements of a partition of Ω. We assume that $\mathbb{P}(B_i) > 0$, $i = 1, \ldots, K$, i.e., that all events in the partition occur with positive probability. Note that the conditional probability $\mathbb{P}(A|B)$ can be defined along similar lines to before, for all $A, B \in \mathcal{F}$ (since $A \cap B \in \mathcal{F}$ because $\mathcal{F}$ is a sigma-algebra).

The case $\mathcal{F} = 2^{\Omega}$ arises when the finest partition is chosen, $P = \{\{\omega_1\}, \ldots, \{\omega_M\}\}$, or with a slight abuse of notation, $P = \Omega$. We write $\mathcal{F} = \sigma(P)$, as the sigma-algebra generated by an arbitrary partition, P.

In Example 8.1,

$$\sigma(\{B_1, B_2\}) = \left\{\emptyset, \{\omega_1, \omega_2, \omega_3\}, \{\omega_4, \omega_5, \omega_6\}, \Omega\right\}.$$

A set $A \subset \Omega$ is said to be $\mathcal{F}$-measurable if $A \in \mathcal{F}$. A random variable, $\widetilde{X}$, is said to be $\mathcal{F}$-*measurable* if $\widetilde{X}^{-1}(I) \in \mathcal{F}$ for every interval, $I \subset \mathbb{R}$. Equivalently, for finite sample spaces, $\widetilde{X}$ is $\mathcal{F}$-measurable if $\widetilde{X}$ is constant (takes on the same value) for all elements in B_i, for all $i = 1, \ldots, K$, where $\mathcal{F} = \sigma(\{B_1, \ldots, B_K\})$. This means that for all i, j, k, if $\omega_i \in B_k$, and $\omega_j \in B_k$, then $\widetilde{X}(\omega_i) = \widetilde{X}(\omega_j)$.

For an $\mathcal{F}$-measurable random variable, $\widetilde{X}$, the conditional expectation $E[\widetilde{X}|Z]$, for $Z \in \mathcal{F}$, can now be defined as

$$E[\widetilde{X}|Z] \stackrel{\text{def}}{=} \sum_{k=1}^{K} \mathbb{P}(B_k|Z)\widetilde{X}(\omega_i), \quad \omega_i \in B_k.$$

We can define this conditional expectation for all $Z \in \mathcal{F}$. We therefore write $E[\widetilde{X}|\mathcal{F}]$ for this expectation. Of course, if $\mathcal{G} \subset \mathcal{F}$, i.e., $\mathcal{G}$ is a coarser sigma-algebra than $\mathcal{F}$, we can restrict our attention to $E[\widetilde{X}|Z]$ for $Z \in \mathcal{G}$. Indeed, $\mathcal{G}$ will be generated by a partition $P_Z = \{Z_1, \ldots, Z_{K'}\}$, $K' \leq K$, and we can define a function $\widetilde{Y}: \Omega \to \mathbb{R}$, such that $\widetilde{Y}(\omega_i) = E[\widetilde{X}|Z_k]$, where $\omega_i \in Z_k$. Obviously, $\widetilde{Y}$ is $\mathcal{G}$-measurable. Furthermore, for $Z \in \mathcal{G}$, we have

$$\begin{aligned}
E[\widetilde{Y}|Z] &= \sum_{k'=1}^{K'} \mathbb{P}(Z_{k'}|Z)E[\widetilde{X}|Z_{k'}] \\
&= \sum_{k':Z_{k'} \subset Z} \mathbb{P}(Z_{k'}|Z)E[\widetilde{X}|Z_{k'}] \\
&= \frac{1}{\mathbb{P}(Z)} \sum_{k':Z_{k'} \subset Z} \mathbb{P}(Z_{k'} \cap Z)E[\widetilde{X}|Z_{k'}] \\
&= \frac{1}{\mathbb{P}(Z)} \sum_{k':Z_{k'} \subset Z} \mathbb{P}(Z_{k'})E[\widetilde{X}|Z_{k'}] \\
&= \frac{1}{\mathbb{P}(Z)} \sum_{k':Z_{k'} \subset Z} \mathbb{P}(Z_{k'}) \sum_{k:B_k \subset Z_{k'}} \frac{\mathbb{P}(B_k \cap Z_{k'})}{\mathbb{P}(Z_{k'})}\widetilde{X}(\omega_i), \quad \omega_i \in B_k \\
&= \frac{1}{\mathbb{P}(Z)} \sum_{k':Z_{k'} \subset Z} \sum_{k:B_k \subset Z_{k'}} \mathbb{P}(B_k \cap Z_{k'})\widetilde{X}(\omega_i), \quad \omega_i \in B_k \\
&= \frac{1}{\mathbb{P}(Z)} \sum_{s:B_s \subset Z} \mathbb{P}(B_s \cap Z)\widetilde{X}(\omega_i), \quad \omega_i \in B_s \\
&= \sum_{s=1}^{K} \mathbb{P}(B_s|Z)\widetilde{X}(\omega_i), \quad \omega_i \in B_s \\
&= E[\widetilde{X}|Z].
\end{aligned}$$

So $E[\widetilde{X}|\mathcal{F}]$ offers a "refined" version of the expectation, $E[\widetilde{Y}|\mathcal{G}]$, that is the same for elements in $\mathcal{G}$. This gives us the law of iterated expectations in measure-theoretic form,

$$E\big[E[\widetilde{X}|\mathcal{F}]\big|\mathcal{G}\big] = E[\widetilde{X}|\mathcal{G}], \quad \mathcal{G} \subset \mathcal{F}.$$

We also introduce notation for Bernoulli and binomially distributed random variables. A random variable, $\widetilde{X} \in \{0, 1\}$, has a *Bernoulli distribution*, $\widetilde{X} \sim \text{Ber}(q)$, if $\mathbb{P}(\widetilde{X} = 1) = q$, $\mathbb{P}(\widetilde{X} = 0) =$

$1-q$. The sum of n independent and identically distributed (i.i.d.) Bernoulli distributed random variables, $\widetilde{Y} = \sum_{i=1}^{n} \widetilde{X}_i$, has a *binomial distribution*, $\widetilde{Y} \sim \text{Bin}(n, q)$. Here,

$$\mathbb{P}(\widetilde{Y} = k) = f(k; n, q) \stackrel{\text{def}}{=} \binom{n}{k} q^k (1-q)^{n-k}, \quad k = 0, \ldots, n,$$

and $\binom{n}{k} = \frac{n!}{(n-k)!k!}$ is the n choose k (combinations) function. We have

$$E[\widetilde{Y}] = nq, \tag{8.1}$$

$$\text{Var}[\widetilde{Y}] = nq(1-q). \tag{8.2}$$

8.3 More Probability Theory and Stochastic Processes

Given a probability space $(\Omega, \mathcal{F}, \mathbb{P})$, a *random variable* (r.v.) is a function $X\colon \Omega \to \mathbb{R}$. For a measurable random variable on a continuous state space, we write $E[X] = \int_{\Omega} X \, d\mathbb{P}$.

For an event, $A \subset \Omega$, the *indicator function* 1_A is the random variable

$$1_A(\omega) = \begin{cases} 1, & \omega \in A, \\ 0, & \omega \notin A. \end{cases}$$

For a (measurable) event, A, $\mathbb{P}(A) = E[1_A] = \int_A d\mathbb{P}$. An event, A, is said to hold *almost surely* (a.s.) if $\mathbb{P}(A) = 1$. When there are events that are nonmeasurable, a more general definition is $A^c \subset B$, where $\mathbb{P}(B) = 0$, i.e., if the events for which A fails are a subset of a measurable set of events, with measure zero.

The *cumulative distribution function* (c.d.f.) of a (measurable) r.v., X, is the function $F_X\colon \mathbb{R} \to [0, 1]$ defined by

$$F_X(x) = \mathbb{P}(\{\omega \in \Omega : X(\omega) \leq x\}) = \mathbb{P}(X \leq x).$$

We then have $E[X] = \int_{\Omega} X \, d\mathbb{P} = \int_{\mathbb{R}} x \, dF$.

The *normal distribution* plays an important role in continuous-time finance. For a random variable, X, we write $X \sim N(0, 1)$ if X has a standard normal distribution. Then X has the following properties:

1. Its probability density function (p.d.f.) is $f_X(x) = \varphi(x) \stackrel{\text{def}}{=} \frac{1}{\sqrt{2\pi}} e^{-\frac{x^2}{2}}$.
2. Its cumulative distribution function (c.d.f.) is $\Phi(x) \stackrel{\text{def}}{=} \int_{-\infty}^{x} \varphi(s) \, ds$.

If X has a standard normal distribution, then $Y = \mu + \sigma X$, $\sigma > 0$, has a normal distribution, $Y \sim N(\mu, \sigma^2)$, with p.d.f.

$$f_Y(x) = \frac{1}{\sqrt{2\pi\sigma^2}} e^{-\frac{(x-\mu)^2}{2\sigma^2}}.$$

The distribution of the sum of two independent normally distributed random variables, $Y_1 \sim N(\mu_1, \sigma_1^2)$, $Y_2 \sim N(\mu_2, \sigma_2^2)$ is

$$Y_1 + Y_2 \sim N(\mu_1 + \mu_2, \sigma_1^2 + \sigma_2^2).$$

We will use the *central limit theorem* (CLT), which states that a scaled average of many i.i.d. random variables in the limit converges to a normal distribution.

Theorem 8.1 (Central limit theorem). *If $\tilde{\mu}_i$, $i=1,2,\ldots$, are i.i.d. random variables with $E[\tilde{\mu}_i]=\mu$ and $\mathrm{Var}(\tilde{\mu}_i)=\sigma^2$, then*

$$\frac{\sum_{i=1}^{n}\tilde{\mu}_i - n\mu}{\sigma\sqrt{n}} \xrightarrow{d} N(0,1), \qquad \text{as } n\to\infty.$$

Here, $\xrightarrow{d}$ denotes convergence in distribution, which means that the distribution functions of the random variables on the left-hand-side converge to the standard normal distribution function, as n tends to infinity.

We also define the k-dimensional multivariate normal distribution: $Z\sim N(\mu,\Sigma)\in\mathbb{R}^k$. Here, $Z\in\mathbb{R}^k$, $\mu\in\mathbb{R}^k$, and $\Sigma\in\mathbb{R}^{k\times k}$ is a symmetric positive definite matrix. The p.d.f. of Z is then

$$f_Z(\mathbf{x}) = \frac{1}{(2\pi)^{k/2}|\Sigma|^{1/2}} e^{-\frac{1}{2}(\mathbf{x}-\mu)'\Sigma^{-1}(\mathbf{x}-\mu)},$$

and it follows that

- $E[Z]=\mu$,
- $E[(Z_n-\mu_n)(Z_{n'}-\mu_{n'})]=\Sigma_{nn'}$ (so $\mathrm{Var}(Z_n)=\Sigma_{nn'}$).

Here, $|Z|$ is the determinant of Z, which is positive since Z is invertible and positive definite.

A special case of independent standard normals arises when $\mu=\mathbf{0}$ and $\Sigma=\mathbf{I}$. Assume that $Z\sim N(\mu,\Sigma)$. Then it follows that the multivariate random variable $Y=\mathbf{c}+\mathbf{B}\mu$, $\mathbf{B}\in\mathbb{R}^{k\times k}$, where $\mathbf{B}$ is invertible, has the distribution

$$Y\sim\mathbf{c}+\mathbf{B}Z\sim N(\mathbf{c}+\mathbf{B}\mu,\mathbf{B}\Sigma\mathbf{B}^T).$$

In fact, this can be taken as the definition of a multivariate normal distribution, starting with i.i.d. standard normal random variables, $Z\sim N(\mathbf{0},\mathbf{I})$, and then defining $Y=\mathbf{c}+\mathbf{B}\mu$. This also works when $\mathbf{B}$ is singular or not square. In that case, the p.d.f. will only be nonzero on a subspace of $\mathbb{R}^k$.

One can also reverse the argument and construct Z from a multivariate k-dimensional normal distribution Y, so that $Y=\mu+\mathbf{G}Z$, where $Z\sim N(\mathbf{0},\mathbf{I})$, and $\Sigma=\mathbf{G}\mathbf{G}^T$. This factorization can be done in many ways, for example,

- defining $\mathbf{G}$ as a lower triangular matrix obtained by Cholesky factorization,
- defining $\mathbf{G}$ as a symmetric positive definite matrix obtained by orthogonalization, $\Sigma=\mathbf{Q}\Lambda\mathbf{Q}^T$, $\mathbf{G}=\mathbf{Q}\Lambda^{1/2}\mathbf{Q}^T$, $\mathbf{Q}^{-1}=\mathbf{Q}^T$, $\Lambda=\mathrm{diag}(\lambda_1,\ldots,\lambda_k)$.

If Z is multivariate normal, and $\mathrm{Cov}(Z_i,Z_j)=0$, then Z_i and Z_j are independent. This is in general only true for normal distributions, although the reverse implication is true in general. A special case is when Y_1 and Y_2 are independent, in which case it follows that Y_1+Y_2 and Y_1-Y_2 are independent.

8.3.1 Sigma-Algebras

We next move to *sigma-algebras* (σ-algebras) over infinite sets. Given an infinite state space, Ω, a sigma-algebra is a set $\mathcal{F}\subset 2^{\Omega}$, such that

1. $\emptyset\in\mathcal{F}$,
2. $A\in\mathcal{F}\ \Rightarrow\ A^c\in\mathcal{F}$,
3. $A_i\in\mathcal{F},\ i=1,2,\ldots,\ \Rightarrow\ \bigcup_i A_i\in\mathcal{F}$,
4. $A_i\in\mathcal{F},\ i=1,2,\ldots,\ \Rightarrow\ \bigcap_i A_i\in\mathcal{F}$.

Here, $\bigcup_i$ and $\bigcap_i$ denote countable unions and intersections. For infinite state spaces, the general equivalence between a sigma-algebra and its smallest partition is no longer valid. For example, the so-called Borel sigma-algebra, $\mathcal{B}$, is generated by all intervals $[a, b]$, $a, b \in \mathbb{R}$, i.e., it is the smallest sigma-algebra that contains the set of such intervals. In general, for a set of sets, A, $\sigma(A)$ denotes the smallest sigma-algebra $\mathcal{F}$, such that $A \subset \mathcal{F}$, and we call this the sigma-algebra generated by A. It is easy to show that for every $a \in \mathbb{R}$, the singleton set $\{a\}$ is in $\mathcal{B}$, and we can of course also generate the sigma-algebra $\sigma(\{a\}_{a\in\mathbb{R}})$.

For finite sets, the finest partition is sufficient to generate the sigma-algebra, and the partition characterization is therefore equivalent to the sigma-algebra. However, that is in general not the case for sigma-algebras over infinite sets. The crux is that an interval $[a, b]$, $a < b$, cannot be written as a countable union of numbers (there are uncountably many numbers in any interval), so $[a, b] \in \mathcal{B}$ but $[a, b] \notin \sigma(\{\{a\} : a \in \mathbb{R}\})$. In the infinite case, the equivalence between partitions and sigma-algebras therefore breaks down: there are sigma-algebras that are not generated by partitions.

8.3.2 Stochastic Processes

Consider a probability space $(\Omega, \mathcal{F}, \mathbb{P})$. A continuous-time *stochastic process* on $[0, \infty)$ is a function $X\colon [0, \infty) \times \Omega$. A *filtration* is a nondecreasing family of σ-algebras, $\{\mathcal{F}_t\}$, $\mathcal{F}_s \subset \mathcal{F}_t$, $s < t$, such that $\mathcal{F}_t \subset \mathcal{F}$ for all t.

A stochastic process is said to be *adapted* if X_t is $\mathcal{F}_t$-measurable for all t. Sometimes the terminology *progressively measurable* is used, which is stronger than being adapted. The difference is related to the measurability of so-called stopping times. A stochastic process is a *martingale* if for all $s < t$, $E[X_t|\mathcal{F}_s] = X_s$.

8.4 Information Refinement over Time

Sigma-algebras offer a convenient way to represent how information is refined over time. Basically, the sigma-algebra at any point in time describes how much information we have about which ultimate state we are in. For example, in figure 8.1 we could represent the four states by the state space $\Omega = \{uu, ud, du, dd\}$. At $t = 1$, we know which state we are in, which we can represent by the finest sigma-algebra: $\mathcal{F}_1 = \sigma(\{uu\}, \{ud\}, \{du\}, \{dd\})$. In contrast, at $t = 0$, all four states are possible, represented by the sigma-algebra $\mathcal{F}_0 = \{\emptyset, \Omega\}$. Finally, at $t = \frac{1}{2}$ we have intermediate information. We know whether we are in either of uu and ud, or in either of du or dd. This can be represented by the sigma-algebra $\mathcal{F}_{1/2} = \{\emptyset, \{uu, ud\}, \{du, dd\}, \Omega\}$. We now push this idea further in the general multiperiod model with discrete time, $t = 0, 1, \ldots, T$.

- A *filtration*, $\underline{\mathcal{F}}$, on the probability space $(\Omega, \mathcal{F}, \mathbb{P})$ is an increasing sequence of σ-algebras, $\mathcal{F}_0 \subset \cdots \subset \mathcal{F}_T \subset \mathcal{F}$.
- An $\underline{\mathcal{F}}$-*adapted* process, $X\colon \mathcal{T} \times \Omega \to \mathbb{R}$, where $\mathcal{T} = \{0, 1, \ldots, T\}$, is a process such that X_t is $\mathcal{F}_t$-measurable for all t.[1] Intuitively, this definition takes into account that X_t can only depend on the information that is available at time t.
- An important example of an $\underline{\mathcal{F}}$-adapted process is the expectation, $Y_t = E[Y_T|\mathcal{F}_t]$, $t = 0, \ldots, T$, where Y_T is an $\mathcal{F}_T$-measurable r.v.

[1] Here, X_t represents the value of X at time t. We will use this notation when there is no confusion. We may also write $X(t)$, or $X(t, \omega)$.

- An $\underline{\mathcal{F}}$-*martingale* is an adapted process, m, such that for all $0 \leq s \leq t$, $E[m_t|\mathcal{F}_s] = m_s$.
- It follows immediately from the law of iterated expectations that Y_t defined above is an $\underline{\mathcal{F}}$-martingale.

8.5 General Multiperiod Model

The general multiperiod model is now defined as follows: Assume we are given a probability space $(\Omega, \mathcal{F}, \mathbb{P})$, a filtration, $\underline{\mathcal{F}} = (\mathcal{F}_0, \ldots, \mathcal{F}_T)$, with $\mathcal{F}_0 = \{\emptyset, \Omega\}$, $\mathcal{F}_T = 2^{\Omega}$, and a market with N traded assets:

- Each security is a claim to an adapted *dividend process*. Formally, define the vector-valued adapted process, $\delta_t \in \mathbb{R}^N$, where $(\delta_t)_i$ represents the dividends paid by asset i at time t. We refer to δ_t as the (*security*) *dividend process*.
- Each security is associated with an adapted *price process*, representing the price of the security right after the dividend is paid (*ex dividend*). Formally, define the vector-valued adapted process, $\mathbf{s}_t \in \mathbb{R}^N$, where $(\mathbf{s}_t)_i$ represents the price of asset i at time t, just after dividends have been paid (ex dividend). We refer to $\mathbf{s}_t$ as the (*security*) *price process*.

The market is summarized by the dividend–price pair $(\delta, \mathbf{s})$. Also, the before-dividend (*cum dividend*) price process is $\mathbf{s}_t + \delta_t$. These processes characterize the dynamic behavior of the individual assets in the economy.

We next introduce trading into the model:

Definition 8.1. A *trading strategy* is a vector-valued adapted process, $\mathbf{h}\colon \{-1, 0, \ldots, T\} \times \Omega \to \mathbb{R}^N$, where $\mathbf{h}_{-1} = \mathbf{0}$, by convention.

Here, the assumption that the trading strategy is adapted ensures that investors cannot trade on future information. The *payout process* (or, more specifically, the *portfolio payout process*) generated by a trading strategy, $\delta_t^{\mathbf{h}} \in \mathbb{R}$, is an adapted process defined by

$$\delta_t^{\mathbf{h}} = \mathbf{h}_{t-1}'(\mathbf{s}_t + \delta_t) - \mathbf{h}_t'\mathbf{s}_t. \tag{8.3}$$

Here, Δ_- denotes the finite difference operator, $\Delta_- \mathbf{x}_t \stackrel{\text{def}}{=} \mathbf{x}_t - \mathbf{x}_{t-1}$, for an arbitrary vector process, $\{\mathbf{x}_t\}_t$. Similarly, $\Delta_+ \mathbf{x}_t \stackrel{\text{def}}{=} \mathbf{x}_{t+1} - \mathbf{x}_t$. Of course, we have the immediate relations

$$\mathbf{x}_t = \mathbf{x}_{t-1} + \Delta_- \mathbf{x}_t, \quad \mathbf{x}_t = \mathbf{x}_{t-1} + \Delta_+ \mathbf{x}_{t-1},$$

which in turn lead to

$$\mathbf{x}_T - \mathbf{x}_0 = \sum_{t=1}^{T} \Delta_- \mathbf{x}_t = \sum_{t=0}^{T-1} \Delta_+ \mathbf{x}_t. \tag{8.4}$$

We note that in the case of assets that do not pay dividends, $\delta_t = \mathbf{0}$, (8.3) reduces to

$$\delta_t^{\mathbf{h}} = (\mathbf{h}_{t-1} - \mathbf{h}_t)'\mathbf{s}_t = -(\Delta_- \mathbf{h}_t)'\mathbf{s}_t. \tag{8.5}$$

The left-hand side of (8.3) is the dollar amount the portfolio pays out at time t, generated by both dividends and portfolio rebalancing. A negative value means that capital was invested into the portfolio.

The *value process* of a trading strategy is

$$V_t^{\mathbf{h}} = \mathbf{h}_t'\mathbf{s}_t. \tag{8.6}$$

Figure 8.5: Sequencing in the multiperiod model.

Given an adapted *consumption process*, c_t, a trading strategy is said to be *self-financed* (self-financing) if

$$\delta^{\mathbf{h}}_t = c_t, \quad \text{for } t = 1, \ldots, T. \tag{8.7}$$

In most cases we consider, the consumption process is 0 for $t \leq T$. A trading strategy is self-financed in this case if $\delta^{\mathbf{h}}_t = 0$, $t = 1, 2, \ldots, T-1$, which means that all dividends are reinvested into the portfolio for $0 < t < T$.

You should convince yourself that the relationship (8.3) makes sense. Indeed, it captures several assumptions about how trades and payouts are sequenced over time, as shown in figure 8.5. At $t-1$ (the left-hand part of the figure), we are immediately after the assets paid their dividends (*ex dividend*). The portfolio $\mathbf{h}_{t-1}$ is held and has value $\mathbf{h}'_{t-1}\mathbf{s}_{t-1}$. At t (the right-hand part of the figure), the prices have changed to $\mathbf{s}_t$, and the assets generate dividends δ_t. Before any portfolio readjustments are made, the value of the stock portfolio is $\mathbf{h}'_{t-1}\mathbf{s}_t$, and the total dividends are $\mathbf{h}'_{t-1}\delta_t$. If no portfolio readjustments are made, (8.3) reduces to $\delta^{\mathbf{h}}_t = \mathbf{h}'_{t-1}\delta_t$, i.e., the payouts of the portfolio are generated solely by asset dividends. Otherwise,

$$\delta^{\mathbf{h}}_t = \mathbf{h}'_{t-1}\delta_t + (\mathbf{h}_{t-1} - \mathbf{h}_t)'\mathbf{s}_t \tag{8.8}$$

(which is an equivalent way of writing (8.3)), i.e., the payout also depends on rebalancing.

We stress that the rebalancing only occurs *after* the prices of assets have changed and dividends have been paid. In the right-hand part of figure 8.5, first prices change, as does the total (cum dividend) value of the portfolio, based on the $\mathbf{h}_{t-1}$ portfolio position. Then dividends are paid, still based on that position. Finally, after that, the investor is allowed to rebalance from $\mathbf{h}_{t-1}$ to $\mathbf{h}_t$, reaching the position furthest to the right in the figure. Any other sequencing (e.g., replacing $\mathbf{h}'_{t-1}$ with $\mathbf{h}'_t$ in the first term on the right-hand side in (8.8), or replacing $\mathbf{s}_t$ with $\mathbf{s}_{t-1}$ in the second term on the right-hand side in the same equation) would allow the investor to trade on future information, and the value process would then not be adapted.

We note two other equivalent formulations of (8.3):

$$\delta^{\mathbf{h}}_t = \mathbf{h}'_{t-1}(\Delta_-\mathbf{s}_t) - \Delta_- V_t + \mathbf{h}'_{t-1}\delta_t, \tag{8.9}$$

$$\Delta_- V_t = \mathbf{h}'_{t-1}\Delta_-\mathbf{s}_t + \Delta_-\mathbf{h}'_t(\mathbf{s}_{t-1} + \Delta_-\mathbf{s}_t). \tag{8.10}$$

You should convince yourself that these formulas are valid. We can now formulate the multiperiod version of the no-arbitrage pricing formulas:

Definition 8.2. A trading strategy, $\mathbf{h}$, provides an *arbitrage opportunity*, if $\delta^{\mathbf{h}}_t \geq 0$ for all t, for all $\omega \in \Omega$, $\delta^{\mathbf{h}}_t > 0$ for some t and $\omega \in \Omega$, and $\mathbf{h}_T = \mathbf{0}$.

Naturally, there are consistency relations that need to be satisfied between the trading strategy, $\mathbf{h}_t$, the generated portfolio payout process, $\delta^{\mathbf{h}}_t$, and the value process, $V^{\mathbf{h}}_t$. Otherwise, an investor could freely choose both a high value process, V_t, and payout process, δ_t, at all points in time, which would imply arbitrage. For consistency, the following must hold:

- Given $\mathbf{h}_t$, the portfolio payout process and the value process are uniquely defined through (8.3) and (8.6).
- Given a value process, V_t, there are typically many trading strategies that can generate that value process, being consistent with (8.6). Each such trading strategy leads to a unique portfolio payout process through (8.3).
  - If there is an asset that always has strictly positive value (e.g., a risk-free asset), *any* trading strategy can be chosen for the other $N-1$ assets, and the value processes can be matched by rebalancing in this Nth asset. That is, any adapted value process, V_t, and trading strategy in the $N-1$ other assets, $(\mathbf{h}_t)_i$, $i=1,\ldots,N-1$, can be supported in the economy by choosing $(\mathbf{h}_t)_N$ appropriately.
- Given a portfolio payout process, δ_t, there are typically many trading strategies that can generate that portfolio payout process, in that they are consistent with (8.3). Each such trading strategy leads to a unique value process through (8.6).
  - Similarly, if there is an asset that always has strictly positive value, *any* trading strategy can be chosen for the other $N-1$ assets, and the portfolio payout processes can be matched by rebalancing in this Nth asset. That is, any adapted portfolio payout process, δ_t, and trading strategy in the $N-1$ other assets, $(\mathbf{h}_t)_i$, $i=1,\ldots,N-1$, can be supported in the economy by choosing $(\mathbf{h}_t)_N$ appropriately.

We define $\bar{L}$, the (augmented) space of adapted processes, Θ, the space of trading strategies, $\Theta=\{\mathbf{h}:\mathbf{h}\text{ is a trading strategy}\}$, and $\overline{\mathcal{R}}$, the augmented marketed (reachable payoff) space, $\overline{\mathcal{R}}=\{\delta^{\mathbf{h}}:\mathbf{h}\in\Theta\}$. Then we have the natural embedding

$$\overline{\mathcal{R}}\subset\bar{L}\subset\mathbb{R}^{\mathcal{T}\times\Omega},$$

where $\mathcal{T}=\{0,1,\ldots,T\}$. Similarly, we define the space of adapted processes between $t=1$ and $t=T$,

$$L=\left\{\ell_t\colon\{1,\ldots,T\}\times\Omega\to\mathbb{R}:\ell_t=y_t,\ t=1,\ldots,T,\ \text{for some } y\in\bar{L}\right\},$$

and the marketed space

$$\mathcal{R}=\left\{m_t\colon\{1,\ldots,T\}\times\Omega\to\mathbb{R}:m_t=y_t,\ t=1,\ldots,T,\ \text{for some } y\in\overline{\mathcal{R}}\right\},$$

with the natural embedding

$$\mathcal{R}\subset L\subset\mathbb{R}^{\{1,\ldots,T\}\times\Omega}.$$

Definition 8.3. The market is said to be *complete* if $\mathcal{R}=L$.

Definition 8.4. A *stochastic discount factor (SDF)*, M_t, is a strictly positive adaptive process, such that for all assets, $i=1,\ldots,N$,

$$(\mathbf{s}_t)_i=\frac{1}{M_t}E_t^{\mathbb{P}}\left[\sum_{k=t+1}^{T}M_k(\delta_k)_i+M_T(\mathbf{s}_T)_i\right],\quad t=0,1,\ldots,T-1. \tag{8.11}$$

As in the one-period model, we normalize so that $M_0=1$. For the risk-neutral pricing formulas, we will not use the most general form, in that we assume the presence of a short-term risk-free asset at every point in time.

Assumption 8.1. For all $t=0,1,\ldots,T-1$, for all states, there exists a one-period trading strategy, $\mathbf{h}\in\mathbb{R}^N$, which invests 1 at t and receives the payout R_t at $t+1$, where R_t is $\mathcal{F}_t$-measurable. The process $\{R_t\}_t$ defines the *short-rate process*.

The value of R_t is thus known at t, so a one-period risk-free investment exists at all times, and the process is adapted, but R_t may still change over time and vary across states. In a complete market, assumption 8.1 is always satisfied. In an incomplete market, there may in general exist multiple short-rate processes that are consistent with asset prices. The assumption rules out such situations.

The n-period gross (risk-free) return is then defined as

$$R_{t,t+n} = R_t R_{t+1} \cdots R_{t+n-1}, \tag{8.12}$$

and is $\mathcal{F}_{t+n-1}$-adapted.

Definition 8.5. An *equivalent martingale measure*, $\mathbb{Q}$, satisfies

$$(\mathbf{s}_t)_i = E_t^{\mathbb{Q}}\left[\sum_{k=t+1}^{T} \frac{(\delta_k)_i}{R_{t,k}} + \frac{(\mathbf{s}_T)_i}{R_{t,T}} \middle| \mathcal{F}_t \right], \quad t = 0, 1, \ldots, T-1, \tag{8.13}$$

for all assets, $i = 1, \ldots, N$.

We note that, as when analyzing the one-period model, we here define the stochastic discount factor risk-neutral expectation with respect to the N primitive assets only. As in the one-period model, it follows that the pricing relations then hold for all elements in the marketed space, $\mathcal{R}$.

Example 8.2. Consider the example of a three-period economy, given in figure 8.6. There are 11 possible states, and we do not find out the actual state until $t = 3$. Note that there are two nodes in the tree with three branches, so the possible moves in these branches are up (u), mid (m), and down (d). The filtration that captures the gradual resolution of information is

- $\mathcal{F}_0 = \sigma(\{\Omega\})$,
- $\mathcal{F}_1 = \sigma(\{u, d\})$,
- $\mathcal{F}_2 = \sigma(\{uu, um, ud, du, dd\})$,
- $\mathcal{F}_3 = 2^{\Omega}$.

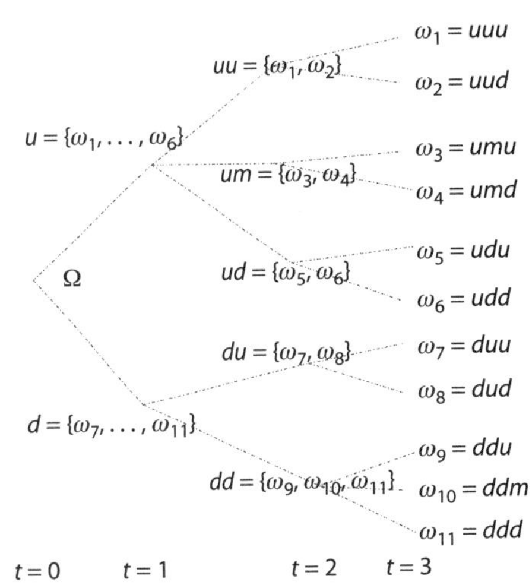

Figure 8.6: Three-period example.

In line with the definition of a filtration, we have $\mathcal{F}_0 \subset \mathcal{F}_1 \subset \mathcal{F}_2 \subset \mathcal{F}_3$. Moreover, any trading strategy must be adapted. So, for example, at $t = 2$, a trading strategy cannot be different for ω_3 and ω_4, since it would then not be $\mathcal{F}_2$-measurable.

In this economy, we have that $\bar{L}$ is a 19-dimensional subspace of the 44-dimensional space $\mathbb{R}^{\{0,1,2,3\}\times\Omega}$. Specifically, we have 1 distinct (distinguishable, measurable) event at $t = 0$, 2 events at $t = 1$, 5 events at $t = 2$, and 11 events at $t = 3$. A basis for $\bar{L}$ in $\mathbb{R}^{\{0,1,2,3\}\times\Omega}$ is given by basis functions that are 1 for elements in the set B_t^k of the partition $\{B_t^1, \ldots, B_t^K\}$ that generates $\mathcal{F}_t$, and 0 for all other elements. The space $\bar{\mathcal{L}}$ can also be identified with the nodes in the tree in figure 8.6.

Once we have taken into account the additional payoff space that dynamic trading strategies generate, the analysis is identical to that in the one-period model, but with each partition set B_t^k treated as a state. Note that the state prices of these states can easily be inferred from the stochastic discount factor and probability measure. For example, the state price ψ_{ud}^2, representing the time-0 price of an AD security that pays 1 at time 2 in state ud (i.e., after an upmove in the first period and a downmove in the second period) is

$$\psi_{ud}^2 = \frac{1}{M_0} E_{\mathbb{P}}^0[M_k(ud)] = M_k(ud)\mathbb{P}(ud).$$

8.6 Multiperiod Fundamental Theorems

We can now state the multiperiod versions of the fundamental theorems of asset pricing:

Theorem 8.2 (First fundamental theorem). *The market admits no arbitrage if and only if there exists a stochastic discount factor.*

Theorem 8.3 (Risk-neutral first fundamental theorem). *The market admits no arbitrage if and only if there exists an equivalent martingale measure.*

Theorem 8.4 (Second fundamental theorem). *Given a market that admits no arbitrage, the market is complete if and only if the stochastic discount factor is unique.*

Theorem 8.5 (Risk-neutral second fundamental theorem). *Given a market that admits no arbitrage, the market is complete if and only if the equivalent martingale measure is unique.*

How can we see whether there is an arbitrage opportunity in the (discrete) multiperiod model? Given the increased dimensionality introduced by dynamic trading strategies (e.g., increasing the dimensionality from 11 states to 19 state–time events in the example above), one may conjecture that checking for arbitrage would be difficult. Fortunately, it is relatively straightforward. Indeed, we can study one-period trading strategies that are zero except for in one node of the tree In other words, a one-period trading strategy only allows the investor to trade at one point in time, and only in one of the distinguishable events at that point. For example, such a trading strategy may be one where the investor invests at $t = 2$ in state dd, and then liquidates the portfolio at $t = 3$. The time-t price of such a strategy is then $\mathbf{h}_t'\mathbf{s}_t$, and the payoff is $\mathbf{h}_t'(\mathbf{s}_{t+1} + \delta_{t+1})$.

Focusing on such one-period trading strategies basically allows us to decompose the dynamic market into many one-period submarkets. The only way for an arbitrage opportunity to arise in the dynamic market is for there to be an arbitrage opportunity in at least one of the submarkets, as shown by the following result:

Theorem 8.6. *A multiperiod market contains an arbitrage opportunity if and only if there exists an arbitrage opportunity among the possible one-period trading strategies.*

Proof. Sufficiency is easily seen, since a one-period arbitrage opportunity can be embedded in the dynamic model to generate an arbitrage in that model. Specifically, assume that a one-period arbitrage opportunity exists at time t, for the partition set, B_t^k, i.e., there is a trading strategy at t, $\mathbf{h}_t(B_t^k)$, in the state represented by B_t^k that has nonnegative cost and generates nonnegative payouts in all feasible states at $t+1$, $B_{t+1}^{j_1}, \ldots, B_{t+1}^{j_m}$, when the portfolio is liquidated at $t+1$, and strictly positive payouts in a least one state at one point in time. That strategy can be embedded in a dynamic strategy according to Definition 8.1, by setting the portfolio weights to $\mathbf{h}_s = \mathbf{0}$ in all other states at all other times, which then immediately defines an arbitrage opportunity in terms of Definition 8.2.

For necessity, we show that absence of arbitrage in the multiperiod model is inconsistent with there being no arbitrage in each one-period submarket. The idea here is to show that a positive payout in one B_k^t will have to lead to a negative payout in some other B_m^s if all one-period submarkets are arbitrage-free. The following properties follow immediately from the absence of arbitrage in all the one-period submarkets, for any trading strategy **h**:

- If $V_t(B_t^k) \leq 0$ and $V_{t+1}(B_{t+1}^m) + \delta_{t+1}^{\mathbf{h}}(B_{t+1}^m) > 0$ for some $B_{t+1}^m \subset B_k^t$, $B_t^k \in \mathcal{F}_t$, $B_{t+1}^m \in \mathcal{F}_{t+1}$, then $V_{t+1}(B_{t+1}^{m'}) + \delta_{t+1}^{\mathbf{h}}(B_{t+1}^{m'}) < 0$ for some $B_{t+1}^{m'} \in \mathcal{F}_{t+1}$.
- If $V_t(B_t^k) < 0$ and $V_{t+1}(B_{t+1}^m) + \delta_{t+1}^{\mathbf{h}}(B_{t+1}^m) > 0$ for some $B_t^k \in \mathcal{F}_t$, then $V_{t+1}(B_{t+1}^{m'}) + \delta_{t+1}^{\mathbf{h}}(B_{t+1}^{m'}) < 0$ for some $B_{t+1}^{m'} \in \mathcal{F}_{t+1}$.

These properties formalize the one-period no-arbitrage conditions: a nonpositive value at t cannot turn into a strictly positive value at $t+1$, and a negative value at t must remain negative at $t+1$ in some state.

Now, it is easy to see that the second property implies that if $V_t(B_t^k) < 0$ for some t and B_t^k, then $\delta_s^{\mathbf{h}} < 0$ in some state for some $s > t$. Indeed, $V_{t+1}(B_{t+1}^{m'}) + \delta_{t+1}^{\mathbf{h}}(B_{t+1}^{m'}) < 0$, so either $\delta_{t+1}^{\mathbf{h}}(B_{t+1}^{m'}) < 0$ or $V_{t+1}(B_{t+1}^{m'})$ (or both). Therefore, a negative value at t with a nonnegative payout at $t+1$ will "push" the negative value forward to $t+1$ in some state, and in extension to any future time period, $s > t$. At $s = T$, the portfolio is liquidated, and $V_T = 0$, so at that point it must be that the payout is strictly negative in some state. As a consequence, an arbitrage strategy may never have $V_t < 0$ at any point.

At $t = 0$, it must be that $V_t = 0$ for **h** to be a candidate arbitrage opportunity, since if $V_0 > 0$ it must be that $\delta^{\mathbf{h}} < 0$ because the one-period submarket at $t = 0$ is free of arbitrage. Consider a trading strategy, **h**, associated with an arbitrage opportunity. Define t, B_t^k as the first point in time and state when $\delta_t^{\mathbf{h}} > 0$ (if there are multiple states, pick one). It must then be that $V_t(B_t^k) \geq 0$, since otherwise the trading strategy does not define an arbitrage opportunity, per the discussion above. It must also be that $V_{t-1} \geq 0$, for the same reason.

Now, if $V_{t-1} = 0$, then, per the first property above, it must be that $V_{t+1}(B_{t+1}^{m'}) + \delta_{t+1}^{\mathbf{h}}(B_{t+1}^{m'}) < 0$ for some m' state, which is not consistent with absence of arbitrage, per the previous discussion. So it must be that $V_{t-1} > 0$. However, since $V_0 = 0$, there must be some $s < t$, such that $V_s > 0$, and $V_{s-1} = 0$ (again, $V_s < 0$ is inconsistent with arbitrage). But, since $\delta^{\mathbf{h}} = 0$ (remember, t was the first time with a positive payout), because of the first property above, there must also be an event $B_s^{m''}$, such that $V(B_s^{m''}) < 0$.

Altogether, we have shown that a positive payout, $\delta^{\mathbf{h}} > 0$, in some state at some point in time must be associated with a negative payout in some state at some other point in time, when all the one-period submarkets are free of arbitrage. An arbitrage opportunity must therefore necessarily be associated with a one-period arbitrage opportunity in one of the submarkets. □

8.7 Limit of the Binomial Model

We next study the n-period binomial model for an option, where we assume that R, q, u, and d are the same in each step. We choose the values of these parameters to match the expected return of the underlying stock and the risk-free rate in the market. The risk-neutral asset pricing formula, together with the fact that the number of up-moves in the model is binomially distributed, then leads to

$$C(0) = \frac{1}{R^n} \sum_{k=0}^{n} \binom{n}{k} q^k (1-q)^{n-k} C(n,k), \tag{8.14}$$

where $C(n,k) = F(Su^k d^{n-k})$, and F is the payoff function. For example, $F(x) = \max(x - K, 0)$ for the European call option.

We want to take the limit of this formula as the number of steps tends to infinity, $n \to \infty$, in such a way that the limiting dynamics of the stock movements is in line with what we observe in practice. Our hope is that the option price formula will converge to a convenient expression.

Now, assume that the risk-free rate is constant per period, so that over any time period between t and T, the value of a risk-free asset increases from $B(t)$ to $e^{r(T-t)}B(t)$. This is a standard continuous compounding formula with a constant interest rate. If we divide the total time period, $T-t$, into n small time periods, each of length Δt,

$$\Delta t = \frac{T-t}{n}, \tag{8.15}$$

it then follows that the return on the risk-free asset over one time period is $e^{r\Delta t}$. The correct choice of R in each period is therefore

$$R = e^{r\Delta t}. \tag{8.16}$$

Next, assume that the change in the log-stock price between t and T has expectation and variance

$$E\left[\log\left(\frac{S_T}{S_t}\right)\right] = \mu(T-t) \tag{8.17}$$

and

$$\mathrm{Var}\left[\log\left(\frac{S_T}{S_t}\right)\right] = \sigma^2(T-t), \tag{8.18}$$

respectively, and that the stock price changes are the product of very many small i.i.d. random changes. Specifically, let us assume that over the time period $[t, t+\Delta t]$, the stock dynamics is $S((k+1)\Delta t) = S(k\Delta t)\tilde{\mu}_k$, where $\tilde{\mu}_k$ are i.i.d. across k. It then follows that $\log(\frac{S_T}{S_t}) = \log(S_T) - \log(S_t) = \log(\prod_{k=1}^{n} \tilde{\mu}_k) = \sum_k \log(\tilde{\mu}_k)$. For i.i.d. $\tilde{\mu}_k$'s, it must then be that

$$E[\log(\tilde{\mu}_k)] = \mu\Delta t \tag{8.19}$$

and

$$\mathrm{Var}[\log(\tilde{\mu}_k)] = \sigma^2\Delta t. \tag{8.20}$$

Assume that we choose a two-point distribution, $\tilde{\eta}_k$, to approximate $\tilde{\mu}_k$:

$$\tilde{\eta}_k = \begin{cases} u & \text{with probability } p, \\ d & \text{with probability } 1-p, \end{cases}$$

with associated approximated stock price dynamics $\widehat{S}(t+\Delta t) = \tilde{\eta}_k \widehat{S}(t)$. This means that $\widehat{S}$ will evolve in line with a binomial (tree) model. We choose parameter values

$$u = \frac{1}{d} = e^{\sigma\sqrt{\Delta t}} \tag{8.21}$$

and

$$p = \frac{1}{2}\left(1 + \frac{\mu}{\sigma}\sqrt{\frac{T}{n}}\right).$$

One can verify that

$$E[\log(\tilde{\eta}_k)] = \mu\Delta t$$

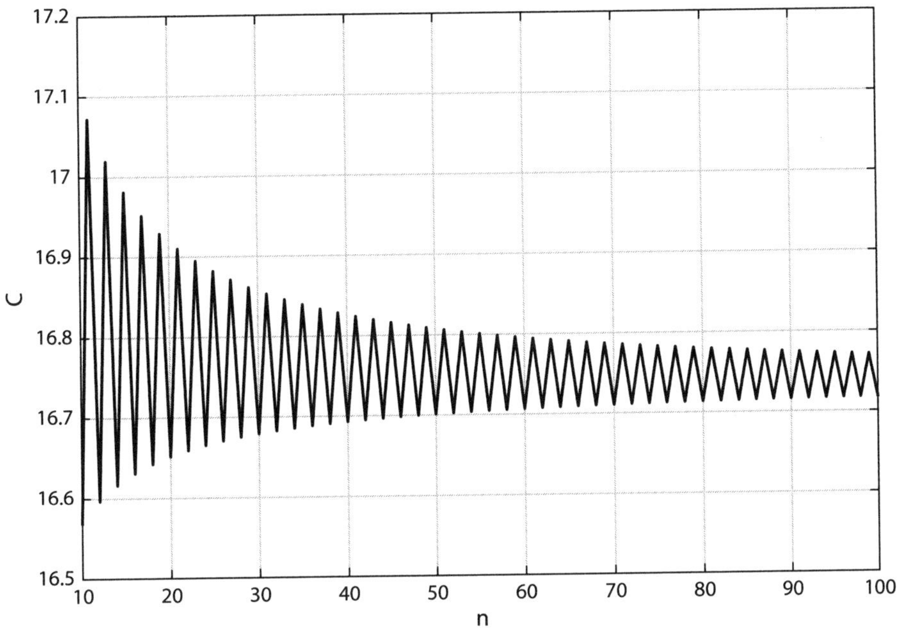

Figure 8.7: Calculated option value as a function of the number of steps in the binomial method. Parameters: $S = 100$, $K = 100$, $T = 1$, $r = 0.1$, and $\sigma = 0.3$.

and

$$\mathrm{Var}[\log(\tilde{\eta}_k)] = \left(1 - \frac{\mu^2}{\sigma^2}\frac{T}{n}\right)\sigma^2(T - t).$$

Summing all the n changes then (where $\tilde{\eta}_k$ are chosen to be i.i.d.), via (8.1, 8.2), gives us

$$E\left[\log\left(\frac{\widehat{S}_T}{\widehat{S}_t}\right)\right] = \mu(T - t) \tag{8.22}$$

and

$$\mathrm{Var}\left[\log\left(\frac{\widehat{S}_T}{\widehat{S}_t}\right)\right] = \left(1 - \frac{\mu^2}{\sigma^2}\frac{T}{n}\right)\sigma^2 T. \tag{8.23}$$

Thus, the expectation perfectly matches the expectation of the log-stock return. The variance formula is not a perfect match, but note that when n becomes large the difference becomes negligible, i.e., $\mathrm{Var}[\log(\frac{\widehat{S}_T}{\widehat{S}_t})]$ converges to $\sigma^2(T - t)$ when n tends to infinity. So, by choosing R, u, and d according to (8.15, 8.16, 8.21), we match the important moments of the stock and bond dynamics in the binomial tree method. As before, we define

$$q = \frac{R - d}{u - d}.$$

This is the approach taken in Cox, Ross, and Rubinstein (1979).

We next study what happens to (8.14) when n grows. We choose parameter values $S = 100$, $K = 100$, $T = 1$, $r = 0.1$, and $\sigma = 0.3$. The calculated option value as a function of the number of steps, shown in figure 8.7, indeed seems to approach a limit somewhere between 16.7 and 16.8.

In Cox, Ross, and Rubinstein (1979), the following result is derived:

Theorem 8.7 (Black–Scholes formula for a European call option)**.** *As the number of steps, n, in the binomial model tends to infinity, where R, u, and d are chosen according to* (8.16) *and* (8.21)*, the price of a European call option with strike price K converges to*

$$C = SN(x) - Ke^{-rT}N(x - \sigma\sqrt{T}), \tag{8.24}$$

where $x = \frac{\ln(\frac{S}{K}) + (r + \frac{\sigma^2}{2})T}{\sigma\sqrt{T}}$ *and $N(\cdot)$ is the cumulative distribution function of the standard normal distribution.*

This is the Black–Scholes option pricing formula, which here will be derived without advanced continuous-time stochastic calculus or partial differential equations, in contrast to our forthcoming derivation in Chapter 9! Indeed, the proof of the theorem uses nothing more advanced than the central limit theorem and Taylor's theorem. We use the notation $C = \mathcal{BS}(S, K, r, \sigma, T)$ for the formula defined by (8.24).

Proof of theorem 8.7. We want to show the convergence of (8.14) to (8.24) as n grows. Using the definitions of q, R, u, d, we rewrite (8.14) as

$$C(0) = \frac{1}{e^{rT}} \sum_{k=0}^{n} \binom{n}{k} q^k (1-q)^{n-k} \max(0, Sd^{n-k}u^k - K).$$

We first determine the point at which $Sd^{n-k}u^k - K$ becomes positive. Once we know it, we can get rid of the max operator and simply sum over k above that point. It is easy to show that $Sd^{n-k}u^k - K > 0$ is equivalent to $k > \frac{\ln(K/S) - n\ln(d)}{\ln(u/d)}$, so we define

$$a = \text{Int}\left(\frac{\ln(\frac{K}{S}) - n\ln(d)}{\ln(\frac{u}{d})}\right) = \frac{\ln(\frac{K}{S}) - n\ln(d)}{\ln(\frac{u}{d})} - \xi, \quad 0 \le \xi \le 1,$$

where $\text{Int}(x)$ represents the integer part of the real number x, so that, for example, $\text{Int}(2.53) = 2$. We then have

$$C(0) = \frac{1}{e^{rT}}\left(S\sum_{k=a}^{n}\binom{n}{k} q^k(1-q)^{n-k}u^k d^{n-k} - K\sum_{k=a}^{n}\binom{n}{k} q^k(1-q)^{n-k}\right).$$

We rewrite this as

$$C(0) = S\sum_{k=a}^{n}\binom{n}{k}(que^{-rT/n})^k((1-q)de^{-rT/n})^{n-k} - Ke^{-rT}\sum_{k=a}^{n}\binom{n}{k}q^k(1-q)^{n-k},$$

and note that since $q = \frac{e^{rT/n} - d}{u-d}$, it follows that $(1 - que^{-rT/n}) = (1-q)de^{-rT/n}$. Therefore, if we define $q' = que^{-rT/n}$, it follows that $(1 - q') = (1-q)de^{-rT/n}$, so we can write

$$C(0) = S\sum_{k=a}^{n}\binom{n}{k}(q')^k(1-q')^{n-k} - Ke^{-rT}\sum_{k=a}^{n}\binom{n}{k}q^k(1-q)^{n-k}.$$

This is nice, since it means that the first term also has the form of a binomial probability distribution, albeit with a modified probability, q', and therefore that we can use standard probability formulas to represent the first term.

We define the cumulative complementary binomial distribution function $\Psi(a, n, q) = \sum_{k=a}^{n}\binom{n}{k}q^k(1-q)^{n-k}$, and can then rewrite the option price as

$$C(0) = S\Psi(a, n, q') - Ke^{-rT}\Psi(a, n, q).$$

This formula is indeed looking pretty similar to the ultimate formula we wish to derive, and we have a good hunch that what is needed is the central limit theorem, to get convergence from the distribution function Ψ to the standard normal distribution function N.

We use the definition of q to get

$$q = \frac{e^{rT/n} - e^{-\sigma/\sqrt{n}}}{e^{\sigma\sqrt{n} - e^{-\sigma/\sqrt{n}}}},$$

and use a Taylor expansion for large n to get

$$q = \frac{1}{2}\left(1 + \frac{rT - \sigma^2 T/2}{\sigma\sqrt{T}\sqrt{n}}\right) + \text{h.o.t.}, \tag{8.25}$$

close to $\frac{1}{2}$ for large n. Here, h.o.t. means "higher-order terms."[2]

We next study the behavior of Ψ for large n. If $Z_k^q \sim \text{Ber}(q)$ (i.i.d.), then $W = \sum_{k=1}^n Z_k^q \sim \text{Bin}(n, q)$, and by the definition of the cumulative complementary binomial distribution it follows that $\mathbb{P}(W < a) = 1 - \Psi(a, n, q)$. We want to use the CLT to imply that

$$\frac{W - nq}{\sqrt{n}\sqrt{q(1-q)}} \xrightarrow{d} Y \sim N(0,1), \tag{8.26}$$

in which case we will be able to replace Ψ with N. A potential complication is that q varies with n. This means that the standard CLT will not work, which fixes the distribution and then increases n. By using a more general version of the CLT, we get around this issue:

Lemma 8.1 (Triangular array CLT with Lyapunov condition). *Consider a double sequence of random variables Y_k^n, $k = 1, \ldots, n$, $n = 1, 2, \ldots$, with expectations $\mu_k^n = E[Y_k^n]$ and variances $\sigma_{nk}^2 = \text{Var}(Y_t^n) < \infty$, such that for each n, $\{Y^n\}_{k=1,\ldots,n}$ is independent. Define the sums $T_n = \sum_{k=1}^n Y_k^n - \mu_k^n$, and $s_n^2 = \sum_{k=1}^n \sigma_{nk}^2$. If for some $\delta > 0$,*

$$\frac{1}{s_n^{2+\delta}} \sum_{k=1}^n E(|Y_k^n - \mu_k^n|^{2+\delta}) \to 0, \quad \text{as } n \to \infty,$$

then $\frac{T_n}{s_n} \xrightarrow{d} N(0,1)$ as $n \to \infty$.

It follows immediately that if we choose $Y_k^n = Z_k$ in the n step model, $n = 1, 2, \ldots$, that $\sigma_{nk}^2 \to \frac{1}{4}$, which in turn implies that $\frac{s_n}{\sqrt{n}} \to \frac{1}{2}$. Moreover, $E[|Z_k^n - E[Z_k^n]|^3] = q(1-q)^3 + (1-q)q^3 \leq 1$. Thus, by choosing $\delta = 1$, we get

$$\frac{1}{s_n^{2+\delta}} \sum_{k=1}^n E(|Y_k^n - \mu_k^n|^{2+\delta}) \leq \frac{9}{n^{3/2}} \times n \to 0$$

for large n. The condition of the lemma is therefore satisfied, so (8.26) holds. We note that for the condition in the lemma *not* to be satisfied, the sequence of expectations $E(|Y_k^n - \mu_k^n|^{2+\delta})$ needs to "misbehave" in the sense that it grows fast enough to not be more than offset by $s_n^{2+\delta}$. For example, if σ_{nk} stays roughly constant as n grows, then $s_n^{2+\delta}$ will roughly grow as $n^{1+\delta/2}$. Now, if $E(|Y_k^n - \mu_k^n|^{2+\delta})$ is roughly constant across k, for any given n, this means that $E(|Y_k^n - \mu_k^n|^{2+\delta})$ must grow at least at the rate of $n^{\delta/2}$ to offset $s_n^{2+\delta}$. Such growth of a higher-order moment (the $2+\delta$-moment)

[2]We are a bit "sloppy" here, in that we do not keep track of these higher-order terms. Strictly speaking, we should keep track of these higher-order terms to ensure that there isn't anything that makes them blow up (there isn't).

relative to the variance means that the random variables in some sense are becoming more and more heavy tailed as n grows. This is obviously not an issue for our random variables, which are all Bernoulli distributed with almost constant q.

Now we are almost done, since we have

$$1-\Psi(a,n,q)=\mathbb{P}(W<a)=\mathbb{P}\Big(\frac{W-nq}{\sqrt{n}\sqrt{q(1-q)}}<\frac{a-nq}{\sqrt{n}\sqrt{q(1-q)}}\Big)$$
$$\to \mathbb{P}\Big(Y<\frac{a-nq}{\sqrt{n}\sqrt{q(1-q)}}\Big)=N\Big(\frac{a-nq}{\sqrt{n}\sqrt{q(1-q)}}\Big).$$

Plugging in a defined earlier, it follows that

$$\frac{a-nq}{\sqrt{n}\sqrt{q(1-q)}}=\frac{\frac{\ln(\frac{K}{S})-n\ln(d)}{\ln(u/d)}-\xi-nq}{\sqrt{n}\sqrt{q(1-q)}}$$
$$=\frac{\frac{\ln(\frac{K}{S})+n\sigma\frac{T}{\sqrt{n}}}{2\sigma\frac{T}{\sqrt{n}}}-\xi-nq}{\sqrt{n}\sqrt{q(1-q)}}$$
$$=\frac{\ln(\frac{K}{S})}{2\sigma T\sqrt{q(1-q)}}+\frac{n(\frac{1}{2}-q)}{\sqrt{n}\sqrt{q(1-q)}}-\frac{\xi}{\sqrt{n}\sqrt{q(1-q)}}$$
$$=\frac{\ln(\frac{K}{S})}{2\sigma T\sqrt{q(1-q)}}-\frac{\frac{1}{2}n(\frac{rT-\sigma^2T/2}{\sigma\sqrt{T}\sqrt{n}}+\text{h.o.t.})}{\sqrt{n}\sqrt{q(1-q)}}-\frac{\xi}{\sqrt{n}\sqrt{q(1-q)}}$$
$$=\frac{\ln(\frac{K}{S})}{2\sigma T\sqrt{q(1-q)}}-\frac{rT-\frac{\sigma^2T}{2}}{2\sigma\sqrt{T}\sqrt{q(1-q)}}+\text{h.o.t.}$$
$$\to\frac{\ln(\frac{K}{S})-(rT-\frac{\sigma^2T}{2})}{\sigma\sqrt{T}}=-(x-\sigma\sqrt{T})$$

as n tends to infinity. An identical argument implies that $\frac{a-nq'}{\sqrt{n}\sqrt{q(1-q)}}\to -x$ as n tends to infinity.

So we have arrived at the formula

$$C(0)\to S(1-N(-x))-Ke^{-rT}\big(1-N(-(x-\sigma\sqrt{T}))\big),\quad \text{as } n\to\infty.$$

Finally, using the symmetry of the standard normal distribution function, $N(-y)=1-N(y)$, we get

$$C(0)\to SN(x)-Ke^{-rT}N(x-\sigma\sqrt{T}),\quad \text{as } n\to\infty.$$

We are done! □

We can now use either put-call parity or a similar argument to the previous proof to derive the following formula for a put option:

Theorem 8.8 (Black–Scholes formula for a European put option). *As the number of steps, n, in the binomial model tends to infinity, where R, u, and d are chosen according to (8.16) and (8.21), the price of a European put option with strike price K converges to*

$$P=Ke^{-rT}[1-N(x-\sigma\sqrt{T})]-S[1-N(x)],$$

where $x = \frac{\ln(\frac{S}{K})+(r+\frac{\sigma^2}{2})T}{\sigma\sqrt{T}}$ *and* $N(\cdot)$ *is the cumulative distribution function of the standard normal distribution.*

Note that in deriving this formula, we have moved up in the asset pricing pyramid (see figure 7.2) compared with the general no-arbitrage model, since we are making quite specific distributional assumptions about the evolution of states, defined by u, d, and R. This will also be the case in the continuous-time model in the forthcoming chapters, in which asset prices will be characterized by so-called diffusion processes. Diffusion processes allow for more general dynamics than assumed here, but also exclude many interesting processes, e.g., those that allow for instantaneous jumps in asset prices.

8.8 Exercises

1. Consider the following tree representation of a two-period (three-date) market with two assets, with prices $S(t)$ and $X(t)$, respectively, $t = 0, 1, 2$:

$t=0$		$t=1$		$t=2$	State
				$S(2)=1.8, X(2)=0.6$	ω_1
			$\nearrow$		
		$S(1)=1, X(1)=1$	$\longrightarrow$	$S(2)=1.6, X(2)=1.2$	ω_2
	$\nearrow$		$\searrow$		
$S(0)=1, X(0)=0.8$				$S(2)=1.2, X(2)=2.4$	ω_3
	$\searrow$				
		$S(1)=1.5, X(1)=1$	$\longrightarrow$	$S(2)=1, X(2)=1.2$	ω_4
			$\searrow$		
				$S(2)=3, X(2)=1.2$	ω_5

   (a) Is the market complete?
   (b) Is there a risk-free rate process? If so, what is it? If not, why not?
   (c) Define the filtration associated with the market.
   (d) What is the $t=0$ price of an Arrow–Debreu security that pays out 1 at time 2 in state ω_5?

2. Consider the binomial tree model, with a stock and a risk-free bond, as described in the diagram below. The (dollar) prices of the stock and the bond at time 0 are $S_0 = S$ and $B_0 = 1$, respectively, and in each period the stock's price may move from S_t to $S_{t+1} = uS_t$ or $S_{t+1} = dS_t$, whereas the bond's return is always R, $B_{t+1} = RB_t$. The stock pays no dividend and the bond makes no coupon payments, and we also assume that

$$u > R > 1 > d.$$

   The probability, p, for an up-move in each period is 50% (which is thus also the probability for a down-move). We initially, in questions (a)–(c), assume that the model lasts until $T = 3$, as in the diagram.

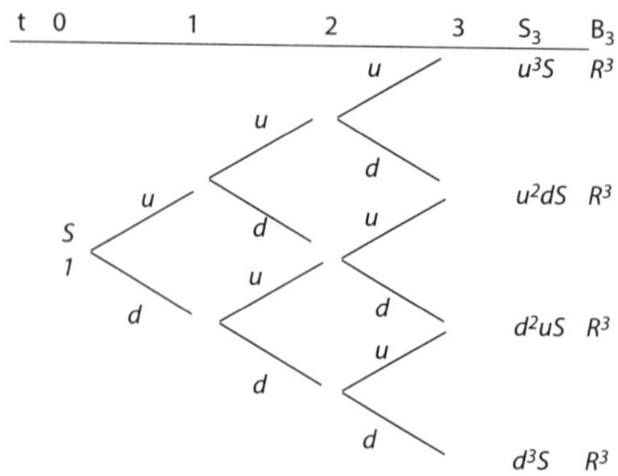

(a) Define a state space and filtration that are consistent with the information diffusion of the model for $0 \leq t \leq 3$.

(b) What is the likelihood process $L = \frac{d\mathbb{Q}}{d\mathbb{P}}$ in this market?

(c) Mr. Rando Nidokym "does not like the state u^2d," and he therefore decides to introduce a derivative into the market that pays a dollar in each state of the world at $t = 3$, *except in the* state u^2d, in which it pays 0. What is the price at $t = 0$ of such a derivative?

In questions (d)–(f), we assume that the binomial tree model lasts for many periods. Specifically, we assume that T is so large that $T = \infty$ is a reasonable approximation, which we use.

(d) Mr. Nidokym next decides that he wants to "celebrate up-moves" by introducing a derivative that pays a dollar at the first point in time that the market experiences an up-move. Thus, if the stock moves up in the first period (which it does for all $u \cdots$ paths), the derivative will pay 1 at $t = 1$ and then cease to exist, whereas if the stock moves down for four periods followed by an up-move in period five (which it does for all $ddddu \cdots$ paths), the derivative will pay 1 at $t = 5$ and then cease to exist, etc. What is the price at $t = 0$ of such a derivative?

(e) Mr. Nidokym decides also to introduce another derivative that is similar to the derivative in (d) in that it makes a terminal payment after the first up-move in the market, but instead of making a payment of one dollar, the stock price is paid that point. Thus, with the $u \cdots$ path the derivative would pay uS at $t = 1$, and with the $ddddu \cdots$ price path it would pay d^4uS at $t = 5$. What is the price at $t = 0$ of such a derivative?

(f) Describe a trading strategy that only uses the primitive assets (the stock and the bond) to replicate the payoff of the derivative in (e).

3. The diagram below shows the possible price dynamics of a stock (S) (that pays no dividends) and a call option (C), in a two-period market, $t = 0, 1, 2$. The state space is $\Omega = \{uu, ud, du, dd\}$.

   (a) What is the short risk-free rate process, R_t, $t = 0, 1$?

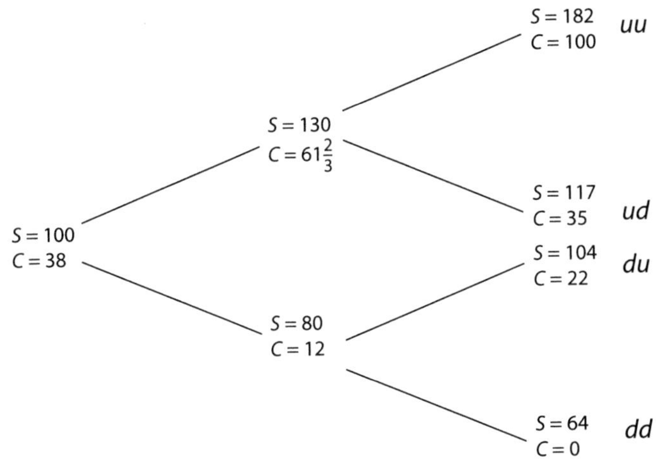

(b) What is the price of a path-dependent derivative that pays out \$1 at time 2 in state *ud*, i.e., if the stock moves up in the first period and down in the second period?

(c) Is the market complete?

4. Consider the complete market as shown in the diagram below.

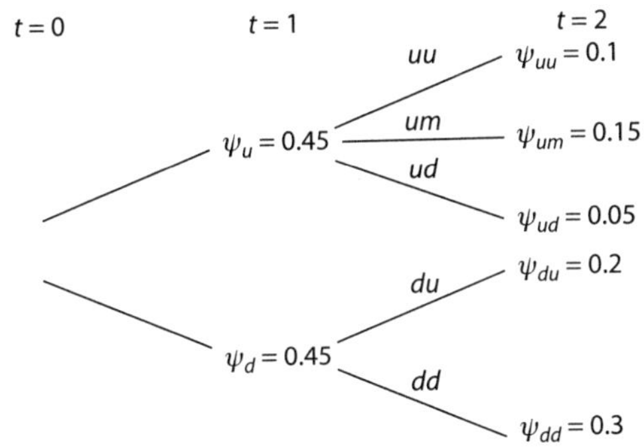

The state prices are all in time $t=0$ terms, so that, for example, $\psi_{uu}=0.1$ represents the $t=0$ price of an AD security that pays out \$1 at $t=2$ after two consecutive up-moves. The (objective) probabilities for up- and down-moves $t=0$ are the same, $p_u=p_d=\frac{1}{2}$, as are the conditional probabilities at $t=1$, $p_{uu}=p_{um}=p_{ud}=\frac{1}{3}$, $p_{du}=p_{dd}=\frac{1}{2}$.

(a) Define the filtration associated with this economy, $\underline{\mathcal{F}}=(\mathcal{F}_0,\mathcal{F}_1,\mathcal{F}_2)$.

(b) What is the risk-free rate at $t=1$, after an up-move, $R_{1,u}$?

(c) Define the SDF process, $\{M_t\}_t$.

5. Consider a two-period binomial tree model, with parameters $u=1.3$, $d=0.8$, and $R=1.1$. The current stock price is $S_0=100$. Consider a two-period European call option with strike price $K=110$, $t=0,1,2$, expiring at $T=2$. The option's current price is C_0.

(a) What is the value of the call option at time 0?

(b) What is the time-0 value of an Arrow–Debreu security, δ_{dd}, that pays \$1 at $t=2$, if the stock moves down twice.

6. Consider a two-period model with a stock and a bond, in which no arbitrage opportunities exist. The stock dynamics are shown in the diagram below over the three dates, $t = 0, 1, 2$. The one-period risk-free rate at time 0 is $R_0 = 1.2$. At time 1, the one-period risk-free rate is $R_u = 1.25$ after an up-move of the stock, and $R_d = 1.1$ after a down-move.

   (a) What is the price at $t = 0$ of a two-period risk-free bond, that pays 10 at $t = 2$?
   (b) What is the trading strategy, $\mathbf{h}_t$, $t = 0, 1$, that replicates the payoff of the bond in (a)?

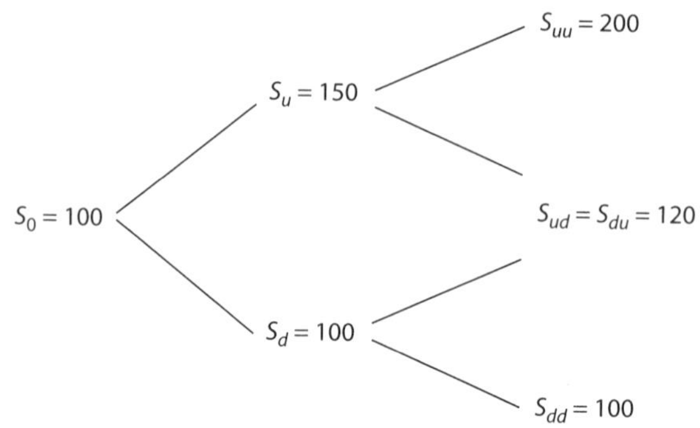

CHAPTER 9 Continuous-Time Model

We have shown the Black–Scholes formula without any advanced continuous-time mathematics, like Itô calculus, and one could argue that there is no need to push any further—that the limit argument in the previous chapter already covers it all. An issue with the limit argument though is that it is not very convenient. Indeed, what if the payoff of the option at maturity is something more complicated than that of a plain vanilla option? Or if the interest rate and/or volatility vary over time, or with the state? Every time we encounter a new situation, we would in principle have to do a full re-derivation.

Approaching the problem directly in continuous time is actually often more straightforward, once the theory has been developed. An analogy may be the comparison of sums with integrals: Although the sum $\sum_{k=1}^{\infty} x^{-2}$ is quite easy to interpret, actually deriving that the sum is equal to $\frac{\pi^2}{6}$ (as shown by Leonhard Euler in 1735) is quite tricky. Moreover, if we want to calculate $\sum_{k=1}^{\infty} x^{-4}$, we have to start all over again. Compare this with the simple and general formula $\int_1^{\infty} x^{-t}\,dx = \frac{1}{t-1}$, for all $t > 1$. Although there is some effort in developing the concept of an integral (we will discuss integrals later), once defined and understood, integrals are often more convenient to work with than sums.

9.1 Brownian Motion

The continuous-time model fundamentally depends on the concept of Brownian motion:

Definition 9.1 (Standardized Brownian motion). A stochastic process, $W\colon \mathbb{R}_+ \to \mathbb{R}$, is said to be a *standard Brownian motion* (a *Wiener process*), if it satisfies the following four properties:

1. Starts at the origin: $W_0 = 0$.
2. Independent increments: For all $r < s \leq t < u$, $W_u - W_t$ is independent of $W_s - W_r$.
3. Gaussian distribution of increments: For all $s < t$, $W_t - W_s \sim N(0, t-s)$.
4. Continuous sample paths: W_t is a continuous function of t (almost surely).

Of course, it is a priori unclear whether such a process can actually be constructed. We could for example define a set of all functions

$$A = \{f\colon \mathbb{R} \to \mathbb{R},\ f \text{ is continuous and } f \text{ is discontinuous}\},$$

which is a valid definition, but the set is obviously empty. The mathematical construction of Brownian motions dates back to 1923, when it was introduced by Norbert Wiener. However, the idea had been used earlier, notably by Albert Einstein in 1905 to explain pollen grain movements in water by random collisions with water molecules, and by Louis Bachelier in 1900 to explain random stock price movements. The name originates from the botanist Robert Brown, who in 1827 observed such irregular pollen grain movements that Einstein later explained.

Definition 9.2 (Brownian motion). A stochastic process $X\colon \mathbb{R}_+ \to \mathbb{R}$ is called a *Brownian motion* (also called an *arithmetic Brownian motion*) if $X_t = y_0 + \mu t + \sigma W_t$, where y_0, μ, and σ are constants, $\sigma > 0$, and W_t is a Wiener process.

Wiener's original proof of the existence of the Wiener process was fairly complicated. However, there are simpler, constructive approaches. We sketch how a Wiener process on the interval $[0, 1]$ can be constructed by so-called dyadic interpolation. Once the process is constructed on an interval, it is straightforward to extend it to the whole of $\mathbb{R}_+$ by "gluing" together many such intervals. We first note that the "naïve" way of creating a Brownian motion, by taking a sequence of random draws at points $t_k = \frac{k}{n}$, $k = 0, \ldots, n$, similar to how we constructed the n-step binomial tree model, and then increasing n, is not going to work. Indeed, every time we increase n we will get a new random draw of numbers, and there will in general be no convergence to a specific function as n increases. We therefore need to construct the refinements in a more clever way.

The construction starts with the following standard (special case of) the *projection theorem* for normally distributed random variables:

Theorem 9.1 (Projection theorem). *If $y_1 = y_0 + x_1$, $y_2 = y_1 + x_2$, where $x_1, x_2 \sim N(0, \tau^2)$ are independent, then given y_2 and y_0, $y_1 \sim N(\frac{y_0+y_2}{2}, \frac{\tau^2}{2})$.*

A more general version of this theorem is introduced in chapter 15.

We now proceed as follows:

1. Assume that we want to construct a stochastic process, Z_t, such that Z_t is a Wiener process. Assume that we know the value of Z_t at two endpoints, a and b. We can then "fill in a hole" at $c = \frac{a+b}{2}$.
   - Assume $a < b$, and that $Z_a \sim N(0, a)$, $Z_b = Z_a + \eta\sqrt{b-a}$, where $\eta \sim N(0, 1)$ is independent of Z_a. It must of course be this way for Z_t to be a Wiener process.
   - Assume that we know Z_a, and Z_b. Define $c = \frac{a+b}{2}$ and

$$Z_c = \frac{Z_a + Z_b}{2} + \frac{\sqrt{b-a}}{2}\xi = Z_a + \frac{\sqrt{b-a}}{2}\eta + \frac{\sqrt{b-a}}{2}\xi,$$

   where $\xi \sim N(0, 1)$ is independent of Z_a and η.
   - It then follows that $Z_b - Z_c = \frac{\sqrt{b-a}}{2}\eta - \frac{\sqrt{b-a}}{2}\xi$ is independent of $Z_c - Z_a = \frac{\sqrt{b-a}}{2}\eta + \frac{\sqrt{b-a}}{2}\xi$, and normally distributed, $Z_b - Z_c \sim N(0, \frac{b-2}{2})$, $Z_c - Z_a \sim N(0, \frac{b-2}{2})$.
2. We have thus filled in a midpoint between a and b, as seen in figure 9.1, in a way that is consistent with Z being a Wiener process evaluated at discrete points. Since a and b were

arbitrary, we can do this recursively on the unit interval [0, 1], starting with $Z_0 = 0$ (property 1 of the Wiener process) and $Z_1 \sim N(0, 1)$:

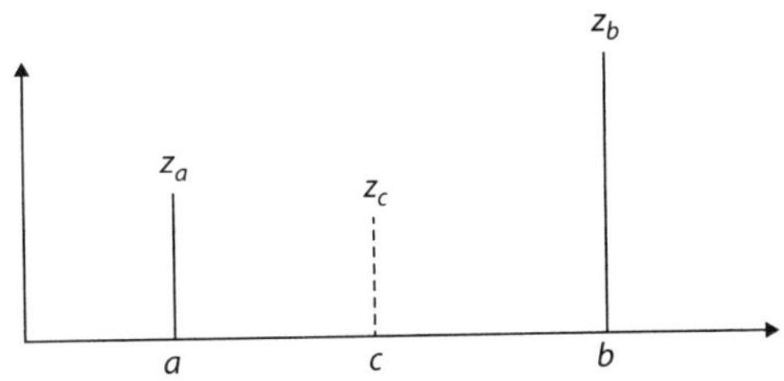

Figure 9.1: Filling in a hole.

- We get $Z_{1/2}$ from Z_0 and Z_1.
- We get $Z_{1/4}$ from Z_0 and $Z_{1/2}$, and we get $Z_{3/4}$ from $Z_{1/2}$ and Z_1.
- Similarly, we get $(Z_0, Z_{1/4}) \rightarrow Z_{1/8}$, $(Z_{1/4}, Z_{1/2}) \rightarrow Z_{3/8}$, $(Z_{1/2}, Z_{3/4}) \rightarrow Z_{5/8}$, $(Z_{3/4}, Z_1) \rightarrow Z_{7/8}$.
- We repeat the procedure, so that Z_t is defined for all dyadic rational points in [0,1], $t = 2^{-j}k$, $0 \leq k \leq 2^j$. By construction, in each step we keep the independence of increments, so all increments are indeed independent (property 2), with the appropriate distribution (property 3) at the dyadic points.

3. We next define the function Z^J in the dyadic decomposition with 2^J points to be the continuous function defined on [0, 1], by linearly interpolating between points. For example, the function Z^3, which is continuous and piecewise linear on $[k2^{-3}, (k+1)2^{-3}]$, $k = 0, \ldots, 7$, is shown in figure 9.2.

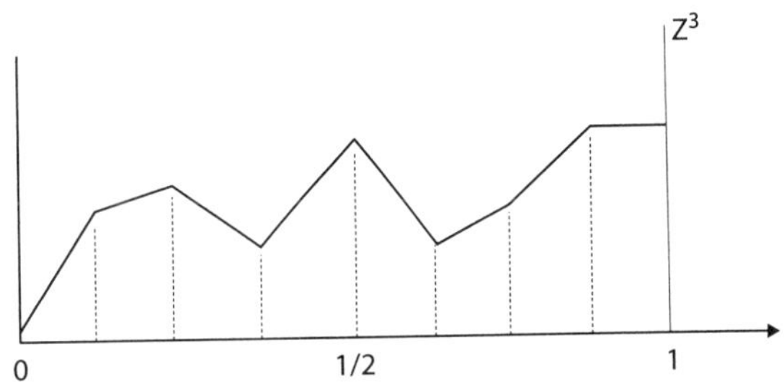

Figure 9.2: The function Z^3.

4. We note that $Z^K(t) = Z^J(t)$ for $K \geq J$, $t = k2^{-J}$, $k = 0, \ldots, 2^J$, so the sequence of functions "fixes" more and more points as J increases. Indeed, we can say something stronger: $\lim_{J\to\infty} Z^J$ converges to a continuous function as $J \to \infty$. To show this, we use the result on uniform convergence (see appendix C) that if a sequence of continuous functions, Z^J, converges *uniformly* to a function Z, then that function is continuous. It is now fairly straightforward to show (although we will not do it here) that almost surely, for all $\epsilon > 0$, there is a J, such that

$$\sup_{t\in[0,1],J'>J} |Z^{J'}(t) - Z^J(t)| < \epsilon,$$

i.e., almost surely $\{Z^J\}_J$ converges uniformly to a function Z. That function is therefore (almost surely) continuous (property 4).

5. The continuity now immediately implies that properties 2 and 3 can be extended to all t (not only dyadic points). Specifically, $Z(t_2) - Z(t_1) = \lim_{J\to\infty} Z(t_2^J) - Z(t_1^J)$ (a.s.) for a sequence of dyadic points, $t_2^J \rightarrow t_2$ and $t_1^J \rightarrow t_1$, $Z(t_2^J) - Z(t_1^J) \xrightarrow{d} N(0, t_2 - t_1)$, and since a.s. convergence implies convergence in distribution, it follows that $Z(t_2) - Z(t_1) \sim N(0, t_2 - t_1)$. Similarly, the independence of increments can be extended to all t.

In appendix E, MATLAB code is provided that shows how to create sample paths of a Wiener process in dyadic points.

The sample paths of Brownian motions are continuous but not very smooth. In fact, they are very "wiggly." For example, almost surely, the sample path W_t of a Brownian motion is nowhere differentiable. To further explore the regularity of Brownian motions, we introduce a refinement of the continuity concept.

Definition 9.3. A function, f, is locally Hölder continuous with exponent $\alpha \in [0, 1]$ at t, if

$$\frac{|f(t+h)-f(t)|}{|h|^\alpha} \leq C_H < \infty, \tag{9.1}$$

for any $H < \infty$, $h \in [-H, H]$.

Note that the larger α is, the stronger this condition is. It follows immediately that any locally Hölder continuous function with exponent $\alpha > 0$ is continuous. Moreover, any continuously differentiable function is locally Hölder continuous with exponent $\alpha = 1$ (and thereby with any exponent $\alpha < 1$). Indeed, note that (9.1) with $\alpha = 1$ is close to the condition that f is differentiable at t, but somewhat weaker. Under differentiability,

$$\left|\frac{f(t+h)-f(t)}{h}\right| = a + o(1), \tag{9.2}$$

whereas under (9.1),

$$\left|\frac{f(t+h)-f(t)}{h}\right| = O(1). \tag{9.3}$$

Under differentiability, convergence is obtained, whereas under the Hölder continuity condition only boundedness is ensured.

Theorem 9.2. *Almost surely, for all t, the sample path of a Wiener process satisfies*

- *for any* $\alpha < \frac{1}{2}$, W_t *is locally Hölder continuous with exponent* α,
- *for any* $\alpha \geq \frac{1}{2}$, W_t *is* not *locally Hölder continuous with exponent* α.

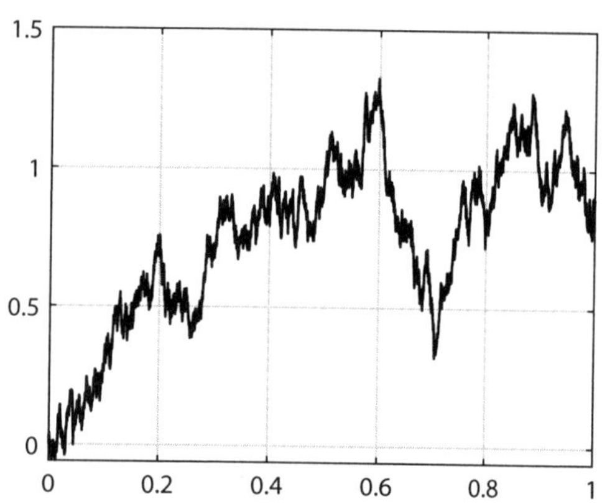

Figure 9.3: Example of Brownian motion.

The threshold for Hölder continuity is thus $\frac{1}{2}$ for a Brownian motion, so it wiggles way too much to be differentiable *anywhere*. On the other hand, it is quite far away from being discontinuous (at which point it would not be Hölder continuous for any coefficient $\alpha > 0$). The coefficient $\alpha = \frac{1}{2}$ in some sense corresponds to the Brownian motion being "one-half times differentiable" at any point. We show an example of a Brownian motion sample path in figure 9.3.

Another way of measuring regularity is through a function's *variation*. The variation of a Brownian motion is different from that of standard smooth functions.

Definition 9.4. The *mth variation* between a and b of a function, X, $V^m = \mathcal{V}^m[X]$, is

$$V^m(a,b) = \lim_{t_{k+1}-t_k \to 0} \sum_{a \leq t_k \leq b} |X_{t_{k+1}} - X_{t_k}|^m.$$

If $a = 0$, we write $V^m(b)$, and V^2 is called the *quadratic variation*. If $V^1(a, b) < \infty$ for a function X, X is said to be of *bounded variation*. Smooth functions are of bounded variation and have zero higher variation. For a smooth function, $V^1(a, b)$ is the total distance traveled vertically when going from $X(a)$ to $X(b)$.

Theorem 9.3. *Almost surely, the sample path of a Wiener process*

1. *is of infinite variation,* $V^1(t) = \mathcal{V}^1[W]$ *satisfies* $V(t) = \infty$ *for all* $t > 0$;
2. *has finite quadratic variation:* $V^2(t) = t$;
3. *has zero higher-order variations:* $V^m(t) = 0$, $m > 2$.

There are several further implications of the high "wiggliness" of a Wiener process: First, if we define the zero set $A(t) = |\{s \in [0, t] : W_s = 0\}|$, then, almost surely, $A(t) = \infty$ for all $t > 0$. Second, if we define the set of local maxima, $B = \{t : \exists h > 0,\ W_s \leq W_t,\ \forall s \in [t-h, t+h]\}$, then, almost surely,

- B is dense in $[0, \infty)$, i.e., for any t, W_s has local maximum for an s arbitrarily close to t,
- B is countable, so that for almost every t, $W_t \notin B$.

We have the following additional properties of Wiener processes: If W_t is a Wiener process, then so is V_t^i, $i = 1, 2, 3$, where

- $V_t^1 \stackrel{\text{def}}{=} W_{t+c} - W_c$, $c > 0$;
- $V_t^2 \stackrel{\text{def}}{=} \sqrt{c} W_{t/c}$, $c > 0$;
- $V_t^3 \stackrel{\text{def}}{=} t W_{1/t}$, $t > 0$, $V_0^3 \stackrel{\text{def}}{=} 0$.

It is natural to ask what the probability space $(\Omega, \mathcal{F}, \mathbb{P})$, and filtration, $\{\mathcal{F}_t\}$, for a Brownian motion are. There are many ways of defining Ω, since it is basically a question of "naming" states. Furthermore, since we always have the possibility of putting zero probability on some events, it does not matter if we choose Ω to be a bit "too large." Neither does it matter if we "leave out" some events, as long as they altogether occur with probability zero (for example, sample paths with discontinuities). For example, we can identify Ω with the space of continuous functions, $C([0, \infty))$. We could also identify Ω with the sequence of real numbers, $(\xi_0^1, \xi_0^2, \xi_1^2, \ldots)$, representing the realization of random numbers used in the constructive approach of defining Brownian motions. If we want to use numbers between 0 and 1, instead of real numbers, we could instead identify Ω with a sequence of numbers in $[0, 1]$, representing the cumulative distribution function, $N(\xi^k)$, of the random variable's realization in the constructive approach.

Concerning the filtration, it is clear that $\mathcal{F}$ and $\{\mathcal{F}_t\}_t$ will be "large complicated objects." A lot of work is needed to ensure measurability, etc., and the analysis is outside the scope of this text. However, intuitively, it is quite clear how one may proceed. One can choose the filtration as the smallest filtration such that $W_t \in \mathcal{F}_t$ for all t,[1] $\mathcal{F}_t = \sigma(\{W_s : s \leq t\})$. Intuitively, $\mathcal{F}_t$ contains all information about W_s up until t, just like in the discrete case, and $\mathcal{F}_s \subset \mathcal{F}_t$, when $s \leq t$. Then we can construct $\mathcal{F} = \bigcup_{t \geq 0} \{\mathcal{F}_t\}$.

Just like multivariate normally distributed random variables, we can introduce the multivariate version of Brownian motion:

Definition 9.5. Given a k-vector of independent standard Brownian motions, $\mathbf{W}_t = (W_t^1, \ldots, W_t^k)^T$, and vectors, $\mu \in \mathbb{R}^k$, and $\Sigma = \sigma\sigma^T$, where $\sigma \in \mathbb{R}^{k \times k}$ is invertible,

- the process $\mathbf{Z}_t = \mathbf{Z}_0 + \mu t + \sigma \mathbf{W}_t$ is a k-dimensional Brownian motion;
- $\mathbf{Z}_t \sim N(\mu t, \Sigma t)$;
- the process $\mathbf{Y}_t = (Y_t^1, \ldots, Y_t^k)^T$, where $Y_t^i = e^{(\mathbf{Z}_t)_i}$, is a k-dimensional geometric Brownian motion.

[1] Here, one can use the result that if $\mathcal{F}_i$ are sigma-algebras, $i \in \mathcal{I}$, then so is their intersection, $\bigcap_{i \in \mathcal{I}} \mathcal{F}_i$. This is a standard way of constructing a smallest sigma-algebra, satisfying some condition, which works as long as there is at least one sigma-algebra that does satisfy the condition (in this case $\mathcal{F} = 2^\Omega$).

NAME	FUNCTION	RELATION	DIFFERENTIAL FORM
Chain rule	$g(t)=f(h(t))$	$g'(t)=f'(h(t))h'(t)$	$dg=f'\,dh$
Leibniz' rule	$g(t)=f(t)h(t)$	$g'(t)=f(t)h'(t)+h(t)f'(t)$	$dg=f\,dh+h\,df$
Fundamental theorem of calculus	$g'(t)=f(t)$	$g(t)-g(0)=\int_0^t f(s)\,ds$	$dg=f\,dt$
Gradient rule	$g=g(t,s)$		$dg=g_t\,dt+g_s\,ds$

Table 9.1: Classical differential calculus.

9.2 Stochastic Integrals

We will develop a model for portfolio trading in continuous time. Brownian motions will be used for modeling asset dynamics and, because they are so "wiggly," the formulas—that is, the *calculus*—are going to be different from under standard calculus. We first give a quick recap of classical calculus formulas for derivatives and integration, so that we can later appreciate the difference.

9.2.1 Classical Calculus

Consider a function, $g(t)$, which we for simplicity assume is defined for all $t \in \mathbb{R}$. The function is said to be differentiable at t if

$$\lim_{h\to 0} \frac{g(t+h)-g(t)}{h} = c$$

exists and is finite, and we then write $g'(t)=c$. If the function g' is continuous (as a function of t), we say that g is continuously differentiable. We also write $\frac{dg}{dt}$, and say that g is smooth. Smoothness is not a very precise concept in that it is usually context dependent, meaning sufficiently continuously differentiable (one, twice, thrice, etc.) for a specific formula to hold.

We also write, in differential form, $dg=g'(t)\,dt$, which represents the limit case of the Taylor expansion, $g(t+\Delta t)=g(t)+g'(t)\Delta t+o(\Delta t)$.[2] For multidimensional functions, $g(s,t)$, we define the partial derivatives $g_t=\frac{\partial g}{\partial t}$ and $g_s=\frac{\partial g}{\partial s}$.

Consider smooth functions, f and h. We recall the differentiation formulas from calculus given in table 9.1.

From the gradient rule and the chain rule, it follows that if $Y(t)=g(t,X(t))$, where X is a smooth function, then $dY=g_t\,dt+g_X\,dX(t)$, where $dX(t)=X'\,dt$, and from the fundamental theorem of calculus, it then follows that

$$Y(T)-Y(0)=\int_0^T g_t\,dt+\int_0^T g_X\,dX(t). \tag{9.4}$$

The pathwise integration of equation (9.4) is shown in figure 9.4. Here, the integral $\int_0^T g_X\,dX(t)$ should be interpreted as a Riemann–Stieltjes integral, which we will cover in the next section.

[2] Here, "little-o," $a(\Delta t)$, is defined as follows: The function a satisfies $a(\Delta t)=o(f(\Delta t))$ as Δt tends to 0 if $\lim_{\Delta t\to 0} a(\Delta t)/f(\Delta t)=0$. We discuss this concept in more detail in chapter 11, on numerical methods.

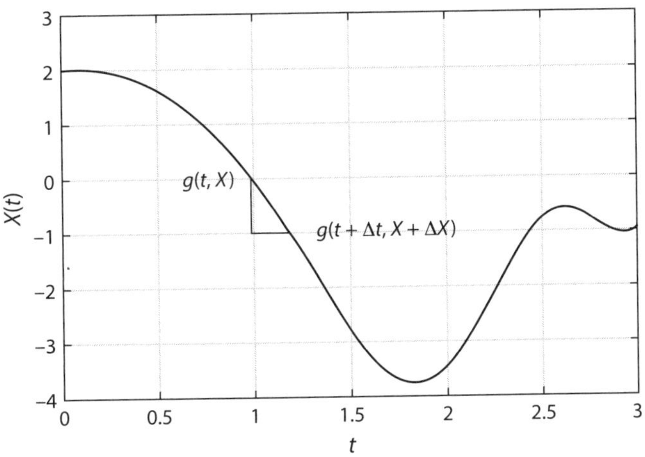

Figure 9.4: Pathwise integral: Since $g(t+\Delta t, X+\Delta X) \approx g_t \Delta t + g_X \Delta X$, it follows that $Y(T) = Y(0) + \int_0^T Y'\,dt = g(0, X(0)) + \int_0^T g_t\,dt + \int_0^T g_X\,dX$.

9.2.2 Portfolio Investing in Continuous Time

Let us study what portfolio rebalancing in continuous time might look like. We begin with the discrete formula for a self-financed portfolio,

$$c_t = \mathbf{h}'_{t-1}(\Delta_- \mathbf{s}_t) - \Delta_- V_t + \mathbf{h}_{t-1}\delta_t,$$

see (8.9), where the self-financing assumption implies that $c_t = \delta_t^{\mathbf{h}}$. If the asset does not pay dividends, this leads to

$$\Delta_- V_t = \mathbf{h}'_{t-1}(\Delta_- \mathbf{s}_t) - c_t.$$

Let us modify this discrete trading model to a continuous-time setting. We assume that there is a natural small time-step, which divides the time period $[0, T]$ into n subperiods of length $\Delta t = \frac{T}{n}$, so we have $t_k = k\Delta t$, and that consumption at t_k can be written as $c_{t_k} = c_k \Delta t$. We therefore rewrite this as

$$\Delta_- V_{k\Delta t} = \mathbf{h}'_{(k-1)\Delta t} \Delta_- \mathbf{s}_{k\Delta t} - c_{k\Delta t}\Delta t.$$

Summing the differences, we now arrive at

$$V_T - V_0 = \sum_{k=1}^{n} \Delta_- V_{k\Delta t} = \sum_{k=1}^{n} \mathbf{h}'_{(k-1)\Delta t} \Delta_- \mathbf{s}_{k\Delta t} - \sum_{k=1}^{n} c_{k\Delta t}\Delta t. \tag{9.5}$$

The idea is now that we would like to take limits $\Delta t \to 0$, and be able to rewrite

$$V_T - V_0 = \int_{t=0}^{T} dV_t = \int_{t=0}^{T} \mathbf{h}'_t\, d\mathbf{s}_t - \int_{t=0}^{T} c_t\, dt. \tag{9.6}$$

To allow for such a representation of the value process, we will need to introduce the Itô integral. The Itô integral is designed for our continuous-time stochastic environment, and to really appreciate its properties it is helpful to first recall the definition of the Riemann–Stieltjes integral from classical (nonstochastic) calculus.

9.2.3 Riemann–Stieltjes Integral

We define and discuss some fundamental properties of the Riemann–Stieltjes (RS) integral. A more extensive treatment is, e.g., given in Rudin (1976). Assume a bounded function, $f\colon [a, b] \to \mathbb{R}$.

A partition (or more specifically an interval partition) of $[a, b]$, $\mathcal{P}$, is given by a finite sequence of points, $\{x_i\}_{i=0,\dots,n}$, such that $a = x_0 \le x_1 \le x_2 \le \cdots \le x_n = b$, and associated intervals $\{[x_i, x_{i+1})\}_{i=0,\dots,n-1}$.

Also assume a function $\alpha\colon [a, b] \to \mathbb{R}$, and define $\Delta\alpha_i = \alpha(x_i) - \alpha(x_{i-1})$. The function α is said to be of *bounded variation* on $[a, b]$, if $T(\alpha, a, b) \stackrel{\text{def}}{=} \sup_{\{P\}} \sum_i |\Delta\alpha_i| < \infty$, and $T(\alpha, a, b)$ is then α's *total variation* on $[a, b]$ (this is the same concept as the first variation discussed when we introduced Brownian motions, in section 9.1). If α is of bounded variation, it is of course then also bounded. The following property of a function of bounded variation is useful:

Lemma 9.1. *A function of bounded variation is the difference of two nondecreasing functions.*

Proof (Riesz and Nagy, 1990). The function $T(\alpha, a, x)$ is nondecreasing in x. Clearly, $T(\alpha, a, y) = T(\alpha, a, x) + T(\alpha, x, y)$ for all $a \le x < y$. Also, clearly, $|\alpha(y) - \alpha(x)| \le T(\alpha, x, y)$ for all $x < y$, with equality if and only if α is monotone. Now, this implies that $T(\alpha, a, x) - \alpha(x)$ is nondecreasing in x, since for $x < y$,

$$\begin{aligned}\alpha(y) - \alpha(x) &\le |\alpha(y) - \alpha(x)| \\ &\le T(\alpha, x, y) \\ &= T(\alpha, a, y) - T(\alpha, a, x),\end{aligned}$$

and therefore

$$T(\alpha, a, x) - \alpha(x) \le T(\alpha, a, y) - \alpha(y).$$

Finally, since $\alpha(x) = T(\alpha, a, x) - (T(\alpha, a, x) - \alpha(x))$, the function is indeed the difference between two nondecreasing functions. □

For a given partition, define $M_i = \sup_{x_{i-1} \le x \le x_i} f(x)$ and $m_i = \inf_{x_{i-1} \le x \le x_i} f(x)$, $i = 1, \dots, n$. Furthermore, define the upper and lower sums, $U(P, f) = \sum_i M_i \Delta\alpha_i$ and $L(P, f) = \sum_i m_i \Delta\alpha_i$. Finally, define the upper and lower Riemann–Stieltjes integrals:

$$\overline{\int_a^b} f\, d\alpha = \inf_P U(P, f, \alpha)$$

and

$$\underline{\int_a^b} f\, d\alpha = \sup_P L(P, f, \alpha).$$

The following two properties of the upper and lower Riemann–Stieltjes integrals are important:

Lemma 9.2. $\overline{\int_a^b} f\, d\alpha$ *and* $\underline{\int_a^b} f\, d\alpha$ *are finite.*

Proof. Follows immediately from the boundedness of f and bounded variation of α. □

Lemma 9.3. $\underline{\int_a^b} f\, d\alpha \le \overline{\int_a^b} f\, d\alpha$.

Proof. The result may seem trivial because the upper Riemann–Stieltjes integral uses the supremum, and the lower Riemann–Stieltjes integral uses the infimum. The challenge is that the two integrals are not guaranteed to use the *same* partition. Indeed, for the same partition, it is of course the case that $L(P, f, \alpha) \le U(P, f, \alpha)$, but here, different partitions may be used in the lower and upper Riemann integrals.

We find a way of using common partitions for L and U that converge to the upper and lower Riemann–Stieltjes integrals. Let P_n^1, P_n^2 be sequences such that $\lim_{n\to\infty} L(P_n^1, f, \alpha)$ converges to the lower integral and $\lim_{n\to\infty} U(P_n^2, f, \alpha)$ converges to the upper integral. Then define P_n^* as the common refinement of the two partitions, using the partition formed by the union of the points defining the two partitions, $\bigcup_i\{x_i^1\} \cup \bigcup_i\{x_i^2\}$. Clearly,

$$L(P_n^1, f, \alpha) \le L(P_n^*, f, \alpha) \le U(P_n^*, f, \alpha) \le U(P_n^2, f, \alpha).$$

The first and third inequalities follow because taking the supremum and infimum over a refined partition must always tighten the bound. The second inequality is also straightforward, since infima and suprema are now taken over the same partition intervals. Finally, it must be that $L(P_n^*, f, \alpha)$ converges to the lower integral, since otherwise it would be larger than the limit of $L(P_n^1, f, \alpha)$, contradicting that $L(P_n^1, f, \alpha)$ converges to the supremum. A similar argument holds for $U(P_n^*, f, \alpha)$, and thus the inequality follows. □

We now have the machinery to define the Riemann–Stieltjes integral:

Definition 9.6. If $\underline{\int_a^b} f\, d\alpha = \overline{\int_a^b} f\, d\alpha$ then we say that $f \in \mathcal{R}(\alpha)$ and define the *Riemann–Stieltjes integral* as $\int_a^b f\, d\alpha = \underline{\int_a^b} f\, d\alpha = \overline{\int_a^b} f\, d\alpha$.

We next explore some properties of the Riemann–Stieltjes integral, and also define the Riemann integral as a special case:

Lemma 9.4. *The Riemann–Stieltjes integral is defined if and only if there is a sequence of partitions, $\{\mathcal{P}_n\}$, such that $U(\mathcal{P}_n, f, \alpha) - L(\mathcal{P}_n, f, \alpha)$ converges to zero.*

Proof. For $\Rightarrow$, take the common refinement; $\Leftarrow$ is immediate since $L \le U$. □

Equivalently, the RS integral is defined if and only if there is a sequence of partitions such that the sum $\sum_i f(y_i^n)\Delta\alpha_i^n$ converges to the same value (as n tends to infinity) regardless of which $y_i^n \in [x_i^n, x_{i+1}^n]$ is chosen.

When the function $\alpha(x)$ is the identity function, the Riemann–Stieltjes reduces to the classical Riemann integral:

Definition 9.7. When $\alpha(x) \equiv x$, the *Riemann integral*, is obtained. In this case we use the notation $f \in \mathcal{R}$ and $\int_a^b f\, dx$.

Lemma 9.5 (Fundamental theorem of calculus). *If $f \in \mathcal{R}$ and $f = F'$ for some differentiable function, F, then $\int_a^b f\, dx = F(b) - F(a)$.*

Lemma 9.6. *If f is continuous and α is of bounded variation, then $f \in \mathcal{R}(\alpha)$.*

The Riemann integral is also well defined, $f \in \mathcal{R}$, when f is continuous except for at a finite (or even countably infinite) number of points.

Lemma 9.7. *If f is of bounded variation and α is continuous, then $f \in \mathcal{R}(\alpha)$.*

Lemma 9.8. *If f is continuous, and α is of bounded variation, then it is sufficient to consider a sequence of uniform partitions when defining the Riemann–Stieltjes integral, i.e., $x_i = a + \frac{b-a}{N} i$ will converge as $N \to \infty$.*

Lemma 9.9. *If α is differentiable, $\alpha' \in \mathcal{R}$ (e.g., if α' is continuous), and $f \in \mathcal{R}(\alpha)$, then $\int f\, d\alpha = \int f\alpha'\, dx$.*

Corollary 9.1. *Under the conditions of lemma 9.9, $\int_a^b \alpha\, d\alpha = [\frac{\alpha(x)}{2}]_a^b = \frac{\alpha(b)^2}{2} - \frac{\alpha(a)^2}{2}$.*

Proof. From the lemma it follows that $\int \alpha \, d\alpha = \int \alpha\alpha' \, dx$, and from the chain rule, $\alpha\alpha' = \frac{(\alpha^2)'}{2}$, so the result follows from the fundamental theorem of calculus. □

Lemma 9.10 (Integration by parts). *If f and α are continuously differentiable, then*

$$\int_a^b f \, d\alpha = f(b)\alpha(b) - f(a)\alpha(a) - \int_a^b \alpha \, df.$$

Proof. The result follows from the chain rule, $d(f\alpha) = fd\alpha + \alpha \, df$, and the fundamental theorem of calculus. □

Lemma 9.10 provides the precise interpretation of the integration formula (9.4) we saw earlier in this chapter.

Lemma 9.11 (Young 1936). *If $f \in C^\alpha$, and $g \in C^\beta$, i.e., if f and g are Hölder continuous with exponents α and β, respectively, such that $\alpha + \beta > 1$, then $\int f \, d\alpha$ exists.*

9.2.4 Integral of a Wiggly Function

Now let us see what happens if we use the Riemann–Stieltjes approach to the portfolio trading formulas (9.5, 9.6), where the functions involved are "wiggly." Let us use the following discrete model with a stock, S, and a bond, B, where $S(0) = 0$, $B(0) = 1$:

$$S_{(k+1)\Delta t} = S_{k\Delta t} + \sqrt{\Delta t}\xi_{k\Delta t}, \tag{9.7}$$

$$B_{(k+1)\Delta t} = B_{k\Delta t}. \tag{9.8}$$

Here, $\xi_k = 1$ are i.i.d., $\xi_k \sim N(0, 1)$, so

$$S_{k\Delta t} \sim N(0, k\Delta t),$$

$$B_{k\Delta t} = 1.$$

Indeed, we may view $S_{k\Delta t}$ as the values of a Wiener process, evaluated at discrete points, $S_{k\Delta t} = W(k\Delta t)$. Neither the stock, nor the bond, makes any dividend payments, so $\delta_t \equiv 0$.

We study the behavior of a self-financed portfolio where h_t is invested in the stock, and c_t consumed at t. Let us first look at the second part of the evolution in (9.5),

$$\sum_{k=1}^{n} c_{k\Delta t}\Delta t.$$

Clearly, as long as c_t is nicely behaved, e.g., if $c_t = c(t)$, where $c\colon [0, 1] \to \mathbb{R}$ is continuous except at a finite number of points, the sum will converge to the standard Riemann integral,

$$\lim_{n\to\infty} \sum_{k=1}^{n} c_{k\Delta t}\Delta t = \underbrace{\int_0^T c(t) \, dt}_{\text{Riemann}}.$$

In fact, let us from here on assume that consumption is zero, so that this term vanishes.

With $c \equiv 0$, we arrive at

$$V_{k\Delta t} = V_{(k-1)\Delta t} + \mathbf{h}'_{(k-1)\Delta t}\Delta_{-}\mathbf{s}_{k\Delta t}, \tag{9.9}$$

$$V_T - V_0 = \sum_{k=1}^{n} \mathbf{h}'_{(k-1)\Delta t}\Delta_{-}\mathbf{s}_{k\Delta t}, \tag{9.10}$$

where $\mathbf{h}_{(k-1)\Delta t} = (h_{(k-1)\Delta t}, y_{(k-1)\Delta t})'$. Because the bond satisfies $\Delta_- B = 0$, this reduces to

$$V_T - V_0 = \sum_{k=1}^{n} h_{(k-1)\Delta t} \Delta_- S_{k\Delta t}. \tag{9.11}$$

Here, $y_{(k-1)\Delta t}$ is the amount invested in the bond that matches a consumption of 0 (recall from the discrete model that we can freely choose a portfolio dividend process—0 in this case since consumption is 0 and the trading strategy is self-financed). These choices will then determine the investments needed in the risk-free asset, and also the value process. Finally, we choose a trading strategy that has $y_0 = 0$, i.e., no initial bond investments.

Let us study what happens to the sum in (9.11), as $n \to \infty$, for a couple of choices of h_t. First, let us assume that h_t is constant, $h_t = a$. In this case we have

$$V_T - V_0 = \sum_{k=1}^{n} h'_{(k-1)\Delta t} \Delta_- S_{k\Delta t} = \sum_{k=1}^{n} a \Delta_- S_{k\Delta t} = aW(T).$$

This is indeed what we would expect to get when replacing the sum by the integral

$$\int_0^T a\, dW_t = aW(T), \tag{9.12}$$

so for this choice of h_t, a standard Riemann–Stieltjes interpretation of the integral is valid.

AN INCORRECT APPROACH FOR A DIFFERENT CHOICE OF h_t Now let us consider another strategy, namely $h_t = S_t = W(t)$. This strategy corresponds to one where the investor scales up the investment in the risky asset in some time periods, so that a lot of capital is invested when S_t is either very high or very low. The value of the stock part of the portfolio at time t is $W(t) \times W(t) = W(t)^2$, which is indeed high when $|W(t)|$ is high. Given our positive experience with a constant portfolio, where we could immediately go from a sum to an integral in (9.12), we may hope that such an approach will work in this case.

The total value process (including the risk-free asset and consumption) in this case is

$$V_T - V_0 = \sum_{k=1}^{n} h'_{(k-1)\Delta t} \Delta_- S_{k\Delta t} = \sum_{k=1}^{n} S_{(k-1)\Delta t} \Delta_- S_{k\Delta t} = \sum_{k=1}^{n} W_{(k-1)\Delta t} \Delta_- W_{k\Delta t}, \tag{9.13}$$

and since $h_0 = W(0) = 0$, $y_0 = 0$, it follows that $V_0 = 0$. Moreover, from (8.5) (remember that neither of the assets pays dividends, and the portfolio is self-financed) it follows that

$$y_{k\Delta t} - y_{(k-1)\Delta t} = -(h_{(k-1)\Delta t} - h_{k\Delta t}) S_{k\Delta t} = -W_{k\Delta t} \Delta_- W_{k\Delta t}. \tag{9.14}$$

This relationship simply expresses the budget constraint that any rebalancing of the portfolio position in the stock (the right-hand side) needs to be financed by rebalancing in the bond (the left-hand side), since the portfolio is self-financed. Now, summing over all the changes, we get

$$y(T) - y(0) = \sum_k (y_{k\Delta t} - y_{(k-1)\Delta t}) = -\sum_k W_{k\Delta t} \Delta_- W_{k\Delta t}. \tag{9.15}$$

We next naïvely replace the sums in (9.13) and (9.15) with integrals, letting $n \to \infty$, to get

$$V_T = \int_0^T W_t\, dW_t,$$

$$y_T = -\int_0^T W_t\, dW_t.$$

The reason this approach is naïve is of course that W_t does *not* have bounded variation, so we do not a priori know whether the integral is defined. Finally, using lemma 9.9—again not formally allowed since W_t is not differentiable—we arrive at the conjectured solution:

$$V_T = \frac{1}{2} W(T)^2, \tag{9.16}$$

$$y_T = -\frac{1}{2} W(T)^2. \tag{9.17}$$

A warning: this approach is wrong! We now explore why. A priori, one may think that (9.16) and (9.17) look reasonable. Indeed, since we know that the value of the stock part of the portfolio at time T is $h_T S_T = W(T)^2$, the relationship seems to satisfy the budget constraint

$$V_T = h_T S_T - y_T = W_T^2 - \frac{1}{2} W_T^2 = \frac{1}{2} W_T^2,$$

as expected. However, upon further reflection, we can conclude there is something *very* weird with these formulas. Specifically, recall that the portfolio is self-financed, and that its initial value is 0. If (9.16) is correct, the value at T is (almost surely) positive, i.e., the trading strategy would constitute an arbitrage opportunity! This is very surprising, since the economy in (9.7, 9.8) does not seem to provide any arbitrage opportunities.

In fact, at each point in time, the expected change in the stock price is 0, so it is highly unclear how such an arbitrage could be created. The mystery deepens when we note that (9.9) implies that the expected change in the value process between $(k-1)\Delta t$ and $k\Delta t$ is always 0, since

$$E_{(k-1)\Delta t}[V_{k\Delta t}] = V_{(k-1)\Delta t} + \mathbf{h}'_{(k-1)\Delta t} E_{(k-1)\Delta t}[\Delta_{-}\mathbf{s}_{k\Delta t}],$$

and clearly $E_{(k-1)\Delta t}[\Delta_{-}\mathbf{s}_{k\Delta t}] = 0$, since all increments in the stock price are random and the bond price is constant. So, between any two time periods, the expected increment in the portfolio's value is 0, i.e., the value process is a martingale. How can it then at T be almost surely strictly positive if the portfolio value starts at 0?!? We conclude that (9.16) must be wrong!

THE CORRECT APPROACH Now let us *carefully* calculate what happens to (9.13) and (9.15) when the number of steps n tends to infinity. First, let us focus on $V_T - V_0$, and calculate

$$\lim_{n\to\infty} \sum_{k=1}^{n} W_{(k-1)\Delta t}(W_{k\Delta t} - W_{(k-1)\Delta t}).$$

We use the algebraic relation

$$z(x-z) = \frac{1}{2}(x^2 - z^2 - (x-z)^2)$$

to rewrite

$$\sum_{k=1}^{n} W_{(k-1)\Delta t}(W_{k\Delta t} - W_{(k-1)\Delta t}) = \frac{1}{2}\sum_{k=1}^{n}(W_{k\Delta t}^2 - W_{(k-1)\Delta t}^2) - \frac{1}{2}\sum_{k=1}^{n}(W_{k\Delta t} - W_{(k-1)\Delta t})^2. \tag{9.18}$$

The first term on the right-hand side is identically equal to $\frac{1}{2}W(T)^2$ (which follows from (8.4)). The second term is just one-half times the quadratic variation; see Definition 9.4. From theorem 9.3, we know that the quadratic variation of a Brownian motion is (a.s.) equal to T, for any given T. We can check that this is indeed the case here, since

$$\sum_{k=1}^{n}(W_{k\Delta t}-W_{(k-1)\Delta t})^2=\frac{1}{2}\sum_{k=1}^{n}(\sqrt{\Delta t}\xi_{(k-1)\Delta t})^2=\frac{\Delta t}{2}\sum_{k=1}^{n}\frac{\xi^2_{(k-1)\Delta t}}{n}.$$

Now, $E[\xi^2_{\Delta t}]=\text{Var}(\xi_{\Delta t})+E[\xi_{\Delta t}]^2=1+0=1$ (from (7.8)), and all ξ's are i.i.d., so by the law of large numbers, the sum a.s. converges to $\frac{T}{2}$ as $n\to\infty$. Thus, a.s.,

$$V_T=\lim_{n\to\infty}\sum_{k=1}^{n}W_{(k-1)\Delta t}(W_{k\Delta t}-W_{(k-1)\Delta t})=\frac{1}{2}W(T)^2-\frac{T}{2}. \tag{9.19}$$

So there is an extra $-\frac{T}{2}$ term compared with what our naïve—and incorrect—application of the Riemann–Stieltjes formula suggested!

Again, the RS argument breaks down because corollary 9.1 depends on α being differentiable, which it is not in this case (W_t is only "one-half times" differentiable). Moreover, the RS integral is only guaranteed to be defined for dS functions of bounded variation (lemmas 9.6 and 9.8), which the Wiener process was shown not to be. Young's result (lemma 9.11) shows that $\int W\,dW$ is close to being defined in the Riemann–Stieltjes sense here, since the sample path $W_t\in C^\alpha$ for $\alpha<\frac{1}{2}$, but the lemma is not quite sufficient: in the context of the lemma, $\alpha+\beta=1-2\epsilon$, for any $\epsilon>0$, which is just below 1.

Indeed, the Riemann–Stieltjes integral is not defined in this case, i.e., $W\notin\mathcal{R}(W)$ (a.s.). The reason is that the sum in (9.19) depends on the choice of the left endpoint, $W_{(k-1)\Delta t}$, in the sum, whereas for the Riemann–Stieltjes integral to hold, the sum should converge to the same number regardless of which point is chosen in the partition interval, captured by the suprema and infima in the upper and lower sums. Using the same argument as before, it is easy to check that for any $q\in[0,1]$, a.s.,

$$\lim_{n\to\infty}\sum_{k=1}^{n}W_{(k-1+q)\Delta t}(W_{k\Delta t}-W_{(k-1)\Delta t})=\frac{1}{2}W(T)^2+\frac{T}{2}(2q-1). \tag{9.20}$$

Previously, we chose $q=0$, but by, e.g., choosing the midpoint, $q=\frac{1}{2}$, we get the form that we would have expected from the naïve Riemann–Stieltjes formulation, $\frac{W(T)^2}{2}$, and by choosing $q=1$, we would have gotten a third expression, $\frac{W(T)^2}{2}+\frac{T}{2}$. We can use this third case to derive the expression for y_T-y_0:

$$y(T)=-\sum_{k}W_{k\Delta t}\Delta_-W_{k\Delta t}=-\frac{1}{2}W(T)^2-\frac{T}{2}. \tag{9.21}$$

We note that the inconsistencies of the previous approach disappear with the new formulas (9.19, 9.21). It is still the case that the total value of the portfolio, $V_T=\frac{1}{2}W(T)^2-\frac{T}{2}$, is made up of the value of stock investments, $W(T)^2$, and the value of bond investments, $y_T=-\frac{1}{2}W(T)^2-\frac{T}{2}$. But in contrast to the previous "derivation," the value of the portfolio can be negative. Indeed,

$$E_0[V_T]=\frac{1}{2}E_0[W(T)^2]-\frac{T}{2}=\frac{T}{2}-\frac{T}{2}=0, \tag{9.22}$$

reflecting the fact that the stock's expected returns at each point in time are zero. Another way of stating this is that by choosing $q=0$ in (9.14), we do not let an investor "peek" into the future when making their portfolio choice. In contrast, by choosing $q=\frac{1}{2}$—which would lead to the inconsistent formula in the previous section—we would let an investor "peek" a small period ($\frac{\Delta t}{2}$)

into the future, and choose a slightly larger portfolio position when the stock will move up, and a slightly smaller one when the stock will move down. Although the difference is very marginal in each time period, there are enough periods for it to make a difference when all the time periods are added up.

So we can conclude that when the *alpha* function wiggles as much as it does for a Brownian motion, it is crucial how we choose the points in our summation when defining the integral—in contrast to the standard Riemann–Stieltjes situation.[3] For trading strategies to be adapted, we have to choose the *left* endpoint—any other choice would allow an investor to "peek" into the future.

We next formalize this correct approach by introducing the stochastic Itô integral.

9.2.5 The Itô Integral

We say that $a_t \in L^2([0,T])$ for the stochastic process $\{a_t\}_t$, if $E[\int_0^T a_t^2\,dt] < \infty$. This motivates the following definition of the Itô integral:

Definition 9.8 (Itô integral)**.** Assume that W_t is a Brownian motion, and $a_t \in L^2([0,T])$ is an adapted process with a.s. continuous sample paths. Then the Itô integral is defined as

$$\int_{t=0}^{T} a_t\,dW \stackrel{\text{def}}{=} \lim_{n\to\infty} \sum_{k=1}^{n} a_{(k-1)\Delta t}(W_{k\Delta t} - W_{(k-1)\Delta t}) = \sum_{k=1}^{n} a_{(k-1)\Delta t}\Delta_- W_{k\Delta t}, \tag{9.23}$$

where $\Delta t = \frac{T}{n}$. If we want to stress that this is the Itô version of the integral, we write $\oint$.

From the previous argument, it thus follows that

$$\oint_0^T W_t\,dW_t = \frac{1}{2}W^2(T) - \frac{T}{2}. \tag{9.24}$$

The following properties of the Itô integral are fundamentally important:

$$E\left[\oint_0^T a_t\,dW_t\right] = 0, \qquad \text{martingale property,}$$

$$E\left[\left(\oint_0^T a_t\,dW_t\right)^2\right] = \int_0^T E[a_t^2]\,dt, \qquad \text{Itô isometry.}$$

The first part follows from taking the expectation for all partitions in (9.23), noting that since a_t is adapted, the conditional expectation $E_t[a_t(W_{t+\Delta t} - W_t)] = 0$, which by the LIE implies that $E_0[a_t(W_{t+\Delta t} - W_t)] = 0$. Similarly, for the second part, $a_t\Delta_- W_t \sim N(0, a_t^2\Delta t)$, and since innovations are i.i.d., $E_0[(\sum a_t\Delta_- W_t)(\sum a_t\Delta_- W_t)] = E_0[\sum a_t^2(\Delta_- W_t)^2] \to E_0[\int_0^T a_t^2\,dt] = \int_0^T E_0[a_t^2]\,dt$.

To extend the concept to include integrals over time ("*dt* integrals"), we have the following definition:

Definition 9.9 (Itô process)**.** Assume that W_t is a Brownian motion. An *Itô process* (*stochastic integral*) is a stochastic process (which is adapted), $F : [0,\infty) \times \Omega$, of the form

$$F(T) = F(0) + \oint_0^t u(t,\omega)\,dt + \oint_0^T v(t,\omega)\,dW_t = \oint_0^T (u(t,\omega)\,dt + v(t,\omega)\,dW_t), \tag{9.25}$$

[3] The reader familiar with measure theory may ask whether moving to the (more general) Lebesgue–Stieltjes formulation would also mitigate the issue with the Stieltjes approach. As discussed in appendix D, it would not.

where u and v are adapted processes, such that $\mathbb{P}[\int_0^t v(s,\omega)^2\, ds < \infty \text{ for all } t \geq 0] = 1$, and $\mathbb{P}[\int_0^t |u(s,\omega)|\, ds < \infty \text{ for all } t \geq 0] = 1$.

Remark 9.1. Note that we have here replaced $a_t \in L^2([0,T])$ with the weaker probabilistic bound on v; see Oksendahl (1998, page 44) for a discussion. The martingale property and Itô isometry might not hold under this extended definition.

We have seen that the dW_t part of a stochastic integral satisfies the martingale property, and therefore a pure dW_t integral will define a martingale. One can show that under appropriate technical conditions, a martingale process can always be represented by such a stochastic integral:

Theorem 9.4 (Martingale representation theorem). *Assume that the process* $\{\xi_t\}_t$

- *is adapted with respect to the filtration generated by the Wiener process* W_t,
- *is a martingale,* $E[\xi_s|\mathcal{F}_t] = \xi_t$, $s > t$,
- *satisfies the boundedness condition* $E[|\xi_t|^2] < \infty$ *for all* $t > 0$.

Then ξ_t *has the stochastic integral representation*

$$\xi_t = \xi_0 + \int_0^t g_t\, dW_t,$$

for a unique adapted process $g_t \in L^2([0,t])$.

9.2.6 A Deterministic Example

The issues of integrability associated with Brownian motions are not fundamentally driven by the random realizations of these processes. It is therefore instructive to study a deterministic example. We use a similar approach to section 9.1, but instead of "filling in the holes" with random variables, we deterministically alternate between choosing the realizations $+1$ and -1 in the dyadic interpolations.

Specifically, we introduce a sequence of continuous functions, $f_J\colon [0,1] \to \mathbb{R}$, $J = 1, 2, 3, \ldots$, that converges to a function, f. For $J = 1$, we define

$$f_1(t) = t.$$

Also, let us associate with f_1, the dyadic points $t_0 = 0$, $t_1 = \frac{1}{2}$, $t_2 = 1$, the set $X^1 = \{t_0, t_1, t_2\}$, and the partition of the interval into $[t_0, t_1)$ and $[t_1, t_2)$. Note that f_1 is a linear function on each of the subintervals in the partition (being a linear function on the whole of $[0,1]$). More generally, for $J \geq 1$, we define $N = 2^J$, the set $X^J = \{t_0, t_1, \ldots, t_N\} = \{0, 2^{-J}, 2 \times 2^{-J}, 3 \times 2^{-J}, \ldots, 1\}$, and the partition of the interval into subintervals, $\mathcal{P}^J = \{[t_0, t_1), [t_1, t_2), \ldots, [t_{N-1}, t_N)\}$. The set of dyadic points is $X = \bigcup_{J=1}^{\infty} X^J$, which is dense in $[0,1]$ (see appendix B.1).

We now define the function f_{J+1} from f_J in such a way that

- $f_{J+1}(t) = f_J(t)$ for all $t \in X^J$, that is, the value of $f_{J'}(t)$ never changes in the dyadic points $t \in X^J$, as J' grows,
- f_J is continuous for all J and linear on each of the subintervals in $\mathcal{P}^J$,
- f_J converges to a continuous function $f\colon [0,1] \to \mathbb{R}$ as J tends to infinity.

We proceed as follows: To define f_2, we keep the values $f_2(t) = f_1(t)$ at the points $t \in X^1 = \{0, \frac{1}{2}, 1\}$, but we modify the values in $X^2 \backslash X^1 = \{\frac{1}{4}, \frac{3}{4}\}$, so that

$$f_2(\tfrac{1}{4}) = f_1(\tfrac{1}{4}) - \frac{1}{\sqrt{8}} = \frac{f_1(0) + f_1(\frac{1}{2})}{2} - \frac{1}{\sqrt{8}} = \frac{1}{4} - \frac{1}{\sqrt{8}} \approx -0.1036$$

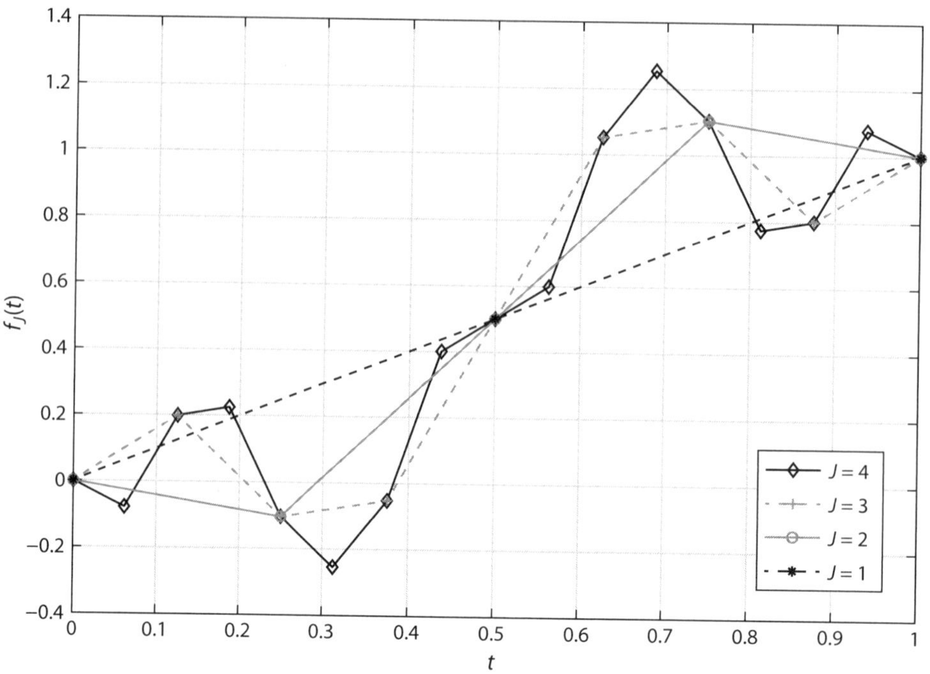

Figure 9.5: Functions f_1, f_2, f_3, and f_4.

and

$$f_2(\tfrac{3}{4}) = f_1(\tfrac{3}{4}) + \frac{1}{\sqrt{8}} = \frac{f_1(\frac{1}{2}) + f_1(1)}{2} + \frac{1}{\sqrt{8}} = \frac{3}{4} + \frac{1}{\sqrt{8}} \approx 1.1036.$$

Thus, f_2 is now defined for all elements of X^2. To extend f_2 to the whole of $[0, 1]$, we simply make it linear on each of the intervals in $\mathcal{P}^2 = \{[0, 0.25), [0.25, 0.5), [0.5, 0.75), [0.75, 1)\}$, so that it is continuous on the whole of $[0, 1]$, i.e., we connect the endpoints with straight lines.

We repeat this procedure to define functions $f_J \colon [0, 1] \to \mathbb{R}$ for $J > 2$. Specifically, given the continuous function f_J that is piecewise linear on each interval in $\mathcal{P}^J$ (and therefore completely defined by its values in X^J), we first define $f_{J+1}(t) = f_J(t)$ for all $t \in X^J$. For $t = (2k-1)2^{-(J+1)} \in X^{J+1} \setminus X^J$, $k = 1, \ldots, 2^J$, we moreover define $f_{J+1}(t) = f_J(t) + (-1)^{k+J} 2^{-J/2-1}$. Finally, we extend the definition of f_{J+1} from X^{J+1} to the whole of $[0, 1]$, by connecting the endpoints with straight lines, thus making it continuous and piecewise linear. The functions f_1, f_2, f_3, f_4 are shown in figure 9.5, and in figure 9.6 the procedure has been further repeated for $J = 4, \ldots, 12$.

You should take some time to make yourself comfortable with the properties of these functions and the methodology used to construct them. Specifically, convince yourself that each function is continuous and piecewise linear on X^J, and that $f_J(t) = f_{J'}(t)$ for all $t \in X^J$ and $J' > J$. Furthermore, note from figure 9.5 that as J grows, f_J converges to a function f that "wiggles" a lot but looks like it is continuous.

We analyze the smoothness properties of f. We begin by showing convergence of f_J to f. Recall that the space of continuous functions from $[0, 1]$ to $\mathbb{R}$, $C([0, 1], \mathbb{R})$, is a Banach space under the supremum norm

$$\|f\| = \sup_{t \in [0,1]} |f(t)|;$$

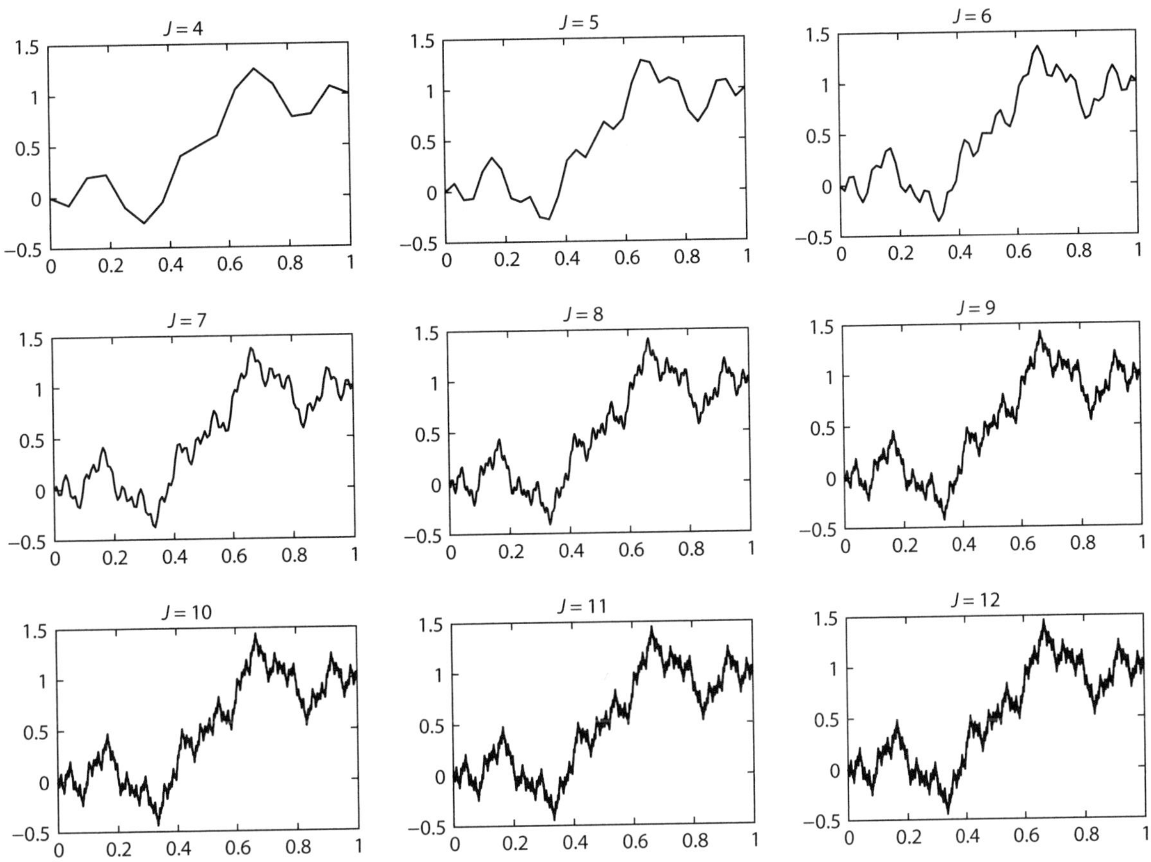

Figure 9.6: Functions f_J, $J = 4, \ldots, 12$.

see appendix B.1. It now follows that the sequence $f_1, f_2, \ldots,$ converges to a continuous function, $f\colon [0,1] \to \mathbb{R}$, since one can show that it is a Cauchy sequence in supremum norm.

The limit function is thus continuous, but it "wiggles" a lot. Indeed, recalling the definition of Hölder continuity, $f \in C^\alpha([0,1], \mathbb{R})$ if

$$\sup_{x,y \neq x} \frac{|f(x) - f(y)|}{|x-y|^\alpha} < \infty, \qquad 0 < \alpha \leq 1,$$

it is straightforward to show that $f \notin C^\alpha([0,1], \mathbb{R})$ for any $\alpha \geq \frac{1}{2}$, just like for a Wiener process.

Since for a function to be differentiable at a point, it must be locally Hölder continuous of degree $\alpha = 1$ at that point, it follows that f is not differentiable anywhere. Since f is continuous, it follows immediately that the function is Riemann integrable, i.e., that $\int_0^1 f(t)\, dt$ exists. Indeed, one can show that $\int_0^1 f(t)\, dt = \frac{1}{2}$ (do this as an exercise).

Now although f's nonsmoothness is not an issue for Riemann integration, it *is* for the Riemann–Stieltjes integral. Consider, for example, the integral $\int_0^t f(t)\, df(t)$. The result in Young (1936) implies that if $f \in C^\alpha$ for $\alpha > \frac{1}{2}$, then the integral $\int f\, df$ is defined, but since f's Hölder regularity in this case is just short of $\alpha = \frac{1}{2}$, Young's result cannot be applied.

Recall that for the Riemann–Stieltjes integral to be defined, it must be that for any sequence of finer and finer partitions of [0, 1], the upper and lower sums converge to the same number. Now consider the two sums

$$I_L^J = \sum_{k=0}^{2^J-1} f(k2^{-J})\big(f((k+1)2^{-J}) - f(k2^{-J})\big)$$
$$= \sum_{k=0}^{2^J-1} f_J(k2^{-J})\big(f_J((k+1)2^{-J}) - f_J(k2^{-J})\big)$$

and

$$I_R^J = \sum_{k=0}^{2^J-1} f((k+1)2^{-J})\big(f((k+1)2^{-J}) - f(k2^{-J})\big)$$
$$= \sum_{k=0}^{2^J-1} f_J((k+1)2^{-J})\big(f_J((k+1)2^{-J}) - f_J(k2^{-J})\big).$$

Here, "L" corresponds to left, "R" to right, and I_L^J will correspond to the Itô integral as J tends to infinity. A necessary condition for the Riemann–Stieltjes integral $\int f\, df$ to exist is then that $\lim_{J\to\infty} I_L^J = \lim_{J\to\infty} I_R^J$ (or equivalently that $\lim_{J\to\infty} I_R^J - I_L^J = 0$), since the I_L^J corresponds to a Riemann–Stieltjes sum over the partition X^J when the left-hand endpoint of each interval is chosen to evaluate f, and I_R^J is the sum when the right-hand endpoint of each interval is chosen.[4]

From the above relations, it follows that

$$I_R^J - I_L^J = \sum_{k=0}^{2^J-1} \big(f_J((k+1)2^{-J}) - f_J(k2^{-J})\big)^2.$$

One can use the above relationship to show that $I_R^J - I_L^J = 1 - 2^{-J}$, and thus that $\lim_{J\to\infty} I_R^J - I_L^J = I_R - I_L = 1$ (do this as an exercise).

So it follows that the Riemann–Stieltjes integral is *not* defined for f! In fact, one can show that $\lim_{J\to\infty} I_L^J = 0$ and $\lim_{J\to\infty} I_R^J = 1$ (do this as an exercise). An intuition for why the sum is higher when the right-hand endpoint is used to evaluate f is as follows: When $f((k+1)2^{-J}) > f(k2^{-J})$, df is positive, and should be multiplied by as large a number as possible to increase the sum, i.e., by the right-hand endpoint. Similarly, when $f((k+1)2^{-J}) < f(k2^{-J})$, df is negative and a small number should be used to make the sum large. Again, the right-hand endpoint achieves this objective.

The above argument for how to make $\int g\, dg$ large also holds when g is a smooth differentiable function, but when the partition becomes fine enough in that case, the difference between using the left- or right-hand endpoint becomes marginal, which is why the integral exists. Specifically, since $|g(t+\Delta t) - g(t)| \le C|\Delta t|$ for a smooth function, it follows that each term $(g_J((k+1)2^{-J}) - g_J(k2^{-J}))^2 \le C2^{-2J}$, and since there are 2^J such terms to be summed, their sum is bounded by $C2^{-2J}2^J = C2^{-J}$, which in turn converges to 0 for large J. For f on the other hand, $|f(t+\Delta t) - f(t)| \sim C\sqrt{\Delta t}$, and thus $(f_J((k+1)2^{-J}) - f_J(k2^{-J}))^2 \sim C2^{-J}$. Summing 2^J such square terms thus leads to $I_R - I_L$ being of order 1.

[4] For the Riemann–Stieltjes integral to exist, the sums should converge to the same number for *any* point within each subinterval chosen to evaluate f, so of course they must converge to the same number in the special case when the endpoints are chosen.

This example gets to the core of why Itô calculus is needed in continuous-time finance, using a function that is not stochastic!

9.2.7 Differential Formulas

Next we want to develop a calculus for Itô integrals. Specifically, we would like to write differential formulas of general adapted processes, such that

$$F(T) - F(0) = \oint_0^T dF. \tag{9.26}$$

Here, there will be *no* classical interpretation of $\frac{dF}{dt}$ as a "derivative." The correct interpretation of "dF" is through the stochastic process it defines via (9.25): for the pair (u, v), the function $F(T)$ is defined through (9.25), and the differential notation for this relation is

$$\text{“}dF = u\,dt + v\,dW.\text{”}$$

The closest to a differential notation we can get is that for small Δt,

$$F(t + \Delta t) - F(t) \tag{9.27}$$

is close to $N(u\Delta t, v^2\Delta t)$ distributed.

For example, given our previous derivation, with $F(T) = W_T^2$, we have

$$W^2(T) - W^2(0) = \left(2\oint_0^T W_t\,dW_t\right) + T = \oint_0^T (2W_t\,dW_t + dt) = \oint_0^T d(W_t^2). \tag{9.28}$$

The interpretation here is that the leftmost equality follows from the definition of the Itô integral, and the middle equality from the fact that the Itô integral coincides with the standard integral for standard functions, so $T = \int_0^T dt$. The rightmost equality is now a purely definitional one: our notation of "dF" (in this case $d(W_t^2)$) represents the fact that "dF" defines the formula that obtains $\oint_0^T dF = F(T) - F(0)$. Thus, with this interpretation, we formally have

$$d(W_t^2) = 2W_t\,dW_t + dt. \tag{9.29}$$

Note that this rule differs from the chain rule in classical calculus, which is valid for smooth functions,

$$\frac{d(f(t)^2)}{dt} = 2f\frac{df}{dt} \quad \Rightarrow \quad d(f^2) = 2f\,df, \tag{9.30}$$

where the right-hand side of $\Rightarrow$ is the differential formula used in the Riemann–Stieltjes integral to achieve $\int_0^T 2f\,df = f(T)^2 - f(0)^2$ (see corollary 9.1). Our goal is now to derive a general rule for how to construct the differential of an adapted process, in the sense of the Itô integral (9.25, 9.26).

9.2.8 Itô's Lemma

Assume that X_t is an Itô process, with $dX_t = u\,dt + v\,dW_t$, and that $Y_t = g(t, X_t)$ for some smooth function $g\colon [0, \infty) \times \mathbb{R}$. Here the drift and volatility coefficients may vary stochastically over time, $\mu = \mu_t = \mu(t, \omega)$, $v = v_t = v(t, \omega)$. What can we say about dY_t? Recall that dY_t is defined such that $g(t, X_t) - g(0, X_0) = \oint_0^t dY_s$ for all t.

Theorem 9.5 (Itô's lemma). *Let X_t be an Itô process given by*

$$dX_t = u\,dt + v\,dW_t.$$

Let $g(t,x) \in C^2([0,\infty] \times \mathbb{R})$. Then $g(t,X_t)$ is an Itô process, and

$$dY_t = g_t\,dt + g_x\,dX_t + \frac{1}{2}g_{xx}(dX_t)^2. \tag{9.31}$$

Here, $(dX_t)^2$ is computed according to the following rules: $dt \cdot dt = 0$, $dt \cdot dW_t = 0$, $dW_t \cdot dW_t = dt$, leading to $(dX_t)^2 = v^2\,dt$.

Sketch of proof of Itô's lemma.

1. Write $g(T,X_T) = g(0,X_0) + \sum_{k=1}^{n} \Delta_- g(k\Delta t, X_{k\Delta t})$.
2. For each term, Taylor expand g around $(k-1)\Delta t$:

$$g(k\Delta t, X_{k\Delta t}) = g((k-1)\Delta t, X_{(k-1)\Delta t}) + g_t\Delta t + g_x\Delta_- X_{k\Delta t} + \frac{1}{2}g_{xx}(\Delta_- X_{k\Delta t})^2 + o(\Delta t).$$

3. So $\Delta_- g(k\Delta t, X_{k\Delta t}) = g_t\Delta t + g_x\Delta_- X_{k\Delta t} + \frac{1}{2}g_{xx}(\Delta_- X_{k\Delta t})^2 + o(\Delta t)$.
4. Further, $(\Delta_- X_{k\Delta t})^2 = v^2_{(k-1)\Delta t}(\Delta_- W_{k\Delta t})^2 + o(\Delta t)$.
5. In total, $\sum_k \Delta_- g(k\Delta t, X_{k\Delta t}) = \sum_k (g_t\Delta t + g_x\Delta_- X_{k\Delta t} + \frac{1}{2}g_{xx}v^2(\Delta_- W_{k\Delta t})^2) + o(\Delta t)$.
6. The first two terms in 5 convergence to $\oint_0^T (g_t\,dt + g_x\,dX)$.
7. For the third term, we need the following generalization of the quadratic variation result we studied earlier for Brownian motions:

Lemma 9.12. *Assume that $f\colon [0,\infty) \times \Omega$ is a continuous adapted process. Then*

$$\lim_{\substack{n\to\infty \\ \Delta t = T/n}} \sum_{k=1}^{n} f((k-1)\Delta t, \omega)(W_{k\Delta t} - W_{(k-1)\Delta t})^2 = \int_0^T f(t,\omega)\,dt,$$

almost surely. Also, the convergence occurs in L^2, $\lim_{n\to\infty} E[\int_0^T (G_n(t,\omega) - f(t,\omega))^2\,dt] = 0$, where $G_n(t,\omega) = \sum_{k=1}^{n} f((k-1)\Delta t, \omega)(W_{k\Delta t} - W_{(k-1)\Delta t})^2$, $\Delta t = \frac{t}{n}$.

The quadratic variation result is obtained when $f \equiv 1$. We therefore get, for the third term above, $\int_0^T \frac{1}{2}g_{xx}v^2\,dt$, and Itô's lemma follows. □

Remark 9.2. For a complete proof, one needs to be more careful with the $o(\Delta t)$ term above.

We stress again that the interpretation of dY_t here is via (9.26), i.e., the differential formula is only defined in the sense of integration.

Example 9.1. Let $X_t = 2 + t + e^{W_t}$. In this case, $dX_t = (1 + \frac{1}{2}e^{W_t})\,dt + e^{W_t}\,dW_t$.

Example 9.2. We see that $Y_t = W_t^2$ leads to $dY_t = 2W_t\,dW_t + dt$, so $W_T^2 = \oint_0^T (2W_t\,dW_t + dt)$, in line with what we previously showed.

Example 9.3. We calculate $\oint_0^T t\,dW_t$. If the integral was evaluated in the classical Riemann–Stieltjes sense, we may expect from lemma 9.10 that $\oint_0^T t\,dW_t = TW_T - \int_0^T W_t\,dt$. Define $Y_t = tW_t$, and use Itô' s lemma to get $dY_t = W_t\,dt + t\,dW_t + 0\,dt$, i.e., $TW_T - 0W_0 = \oint_0^T W_t\,dt + \oint_0^T t\,dW_t$. This implies that the same result holds in the Itô sense as in the classical sense. The key here is that $(tW_t)_{tt} = 0$, so the extra Itô term vanishes.

Example 9.4 (Arithmetic Brownian motion). Define $X_t = \mu t + \sigma W_t$. We can use Itô's lemma to get

$$dX_t = \mu\,dt + \sigma\,dW_t.$$

Example 9.5 (*Geometric Brownian motion* (GBM)). Define $Y_t = e^{X_t}$, where X_t is an arithmetic Brownian motion. Thus, at t, Y_t has a log-normal distribution. Let's derive $E[e^{Y_t}]$ using Itô's lemma: $dY_t = e^{X_t}\,dX_t + \frac{\sigma^2}{2} X_t\,dt = Y_t((\mu + \frac{\sigma^2}{2})\,dt + \sigma\,dW_t) \stackrel{\text{def}}{=} Y_t(\hat{\mu}\,dt + \sigma\,dW_t)$, implying

$$\frac{dY_t}{Y_t} = \hat{\mu}\,dt + \sigma\,dW_t, \quad \hat{\mu} = \mu + \frac{\sigma^2}{2}. \tag{9.32}$$

We have $E[Y_T] = E[\oint_0^T dY_t\,dt] = \hat{\mu}E[\oint_0^T Y_t\,dt]$ (where we used the martingale property). Defining $z_T = E[Y_T]$, differentiating, and using the fundamental theorem of calculus, we get $z'_T = \hat{\mu} z_T$, and using $z_0 = 1$, solving this ordinary differential equation (for more on ODEs, see section 9.4.1), we get $z_T = e^{\hat{\mu}T}$, which is indeed the formula for the expectation of a log-normally distributed random variable.

MULTIDIMENSIONAL ITÔ LEMMA Just like there are multivariate versions of Taylor expansions (see appendix C), there are multivariate versions of Itô's lemma.

Lemma 9.13 (Multidimensional Itô, uncorrelated form). *Let $\mathbf{X}_t$ be a k-dimensional Itô process given by*

$$d\mathbf{X}_t = \mu\,dt + \sigma\,d\mathbf{W}_t,$$

where $\mu = \mu(t,\omega) \in \mathbb{R}^k$, $\sigma = \sigma(t,\omega) \in \mathbb{R}^{k\times k}$, and we define $\Sigma = \sigma\sigma^T$, $\sigma^i = (\sigma_{i,1}, \ldots, \sigma_{i,k})$, $i = 1, \ldots, k$, and where $\mathbf{W}_t$ is a standardized, k-dimensional Brownian motion. Let $g(t,x) \in C^2([0,\infty] \times \mathbb{R}^k)$. Then $Y_t = g(t, \mathbf{X}_t)$ is an Itô process, and

$$dY_t = \left(g_t + \sum_i g_{x_i}\mu_i + \frac{1}{2}\sum_{i,j} g_{x_i x_j}\Sigma_{ij}\right) dt + \sum_i g_{x_i}\sigma^i d(\mathbf{W}_t)_i.$$

The lemma can also be expressed in correlated form:

Lemma 9.14 (Multidimensional Itô, correlated form). *Let $\mathbf{X}_t = (X_t^1, \ldots, X_t^k)^T$ be a k-dimensional Itô process given by*

$$dX_t^i = \mu_i\,dt + \sigma_i\,dV_t^i,$$

where V_t^i are standard univariate Brownian motions, so $\mu_i = \mu_i(t,\omega) \in \mathbb{R}$ and $\sigma_i = \sigma_i(t,\omega) \in \mathbb{R}$, $i = 1, \ldots, k$, $\mathrm{Cov}(dV_t^i, dV_t^j) = \rho_{ij}\,dt$, and $\sigma_{ij} = \sigma_i\sigma_j\rho_{ij}$. Let $g(t,x) \in C^2([0,\infty] \times \mathbb{R}^k)$. Then $Y_t = g(t, \mathbf{X}_t)$ is an Itô process, and

$$\begin{aligned} dY_t &= \left(g_t + \sum_i g_{x_i}\mu_i + \frac{1}{2}\sum_{i,j} g_{x_i x_j}\sigma_{ij}\right) dt + \sum_i g_{x_i}\sigma_i\,dV_t^i \\ &= g_t\,dt + \sum_i g_{x_i}\,dX_t^i + \frac{1}{2}\sum_{i,j} g_{x_i x_j}\,dX_t^i\,dX_t^j. \end{aligned}$$

ITÔ VERSION OF THE PRODUCT RULE From calculus, we have the product rule (Leibniz' formula) for smooth functions: $(fg)' = fg' + gf'$, or in differential form, $d(fg) = f\,dg + g\,df$, or in integral form $f(t)g(t) - f(0)g(0) = \int f\,dg + \int g\,df$. We want a similar rule for Itô processes, for diffusion processes $dX = \mu_X\,dt + \sigma_X\,dV_X$ and $dY = \mu_Y\,dt + \sigma_Y\,dV_Y$, where the instantaneous correlation between their two Wiener processes is ρ_{XY}, so that $dV_X\,dV_Y = \rho_{XY}\,dt$. Thus, we want to be able to calculate

$$X(t)Y(t) - X(0)Y(0) = \int_0^t d(XY).$$

Define the *quadratic covariance* of two Itô processes,

$$\langle X, Y\rangle_t = \lim_{\Delta t_k \to 0} \sum_{0 \le t_k \le t} (X_{t_k} - X_{t_{k-1}})(Y_{t_k} - Y_{t_{k-1}}).$$

We have $\langle X, Y\rangle_t = \int (dX\, dY)$, where $dX\, dY = \sigma_X \sigma_Y \rho_{XY}\, dt$, for Itô processes written in correlated form.

The Itô version of the product rule can now be written in the following forms:

- Integral formula: $X_t Y_t - X_0 Y_0 = \int X\, dY + \int Y\, dX + \langle X, Y\rangle_t$.
- Differential formula: $d(XY) = X\, dY + Y\, dX + dX\, dY$.

So, in contrast to the classical product rule, in the Itô version of the rule the product of the differentials also needs to be included.

9.3 Continuous-Time Portfolios

With the insight generated from the previous section, we are now ready to introduce the continuous-time trading model. We assume that stock prices are described by a vector diffusion process, $\mathbf{s}_t$, and the cumulative dividends paid up until t by the vector diffusion process, Θ_t. The instantaneous dividends generated at time t are thus $d\Theta_t$. A trading strategy, $\mathbf{h}_t$, is an adapted process, and for the time being we restrict our study to strategies that are continuous.

We define the cumulative payouts generated by a trading strategy from 0 to t as $F_t^{\mathbf{h}}$, and the so-called gain process, $G_t = \mathbf{s}_t + \Theta_t$ (again a vector process), which describes the cumulative value of buying one share in an asset—including both asset value and cumulative cash flows generated from dividends. Here, $dF_t^{\mathbf{h}}$ corresponds to $\delta_t^{\mathbf{h}}$—the instantaneous portfolio dividend generated by a trading strategy in the discrete model. Moreover, dG_t corresponds to $\Delta_- \mathbf{s}_t + \delta_t$ in the discrete model. For a self-financing trading strategy (with no consumption), $dF_t^{\mathbf{h}} = 0$.

The value process is, of course, again

$$V_t = \mathbf{h}_t' \mathbf{s}_t.$$

Using the Itô version of the product rule, we get

$$dV_t = \mathbf{h}_t'\, d\mathbf{s} + d\mathbf{h}_t'\, \mathbf{s}_t + d\mathbf{h}_t'\, d\mathbf{s}_t = \mathbf{h}_t'\, d\mathbf{s}_t + d\mathbf{h}_t'(\mathbf{s}_t + d\mathbf{s}_t). \tag{9.33}$$

This is the continuous-time version of (8.10).

We next move to the continuous-time version of (8.9), which reads

$$dF_t^{\mathbf{h}} = \mathbf{h}_t'\, d\mathbf{s} - dV_t + \mathbf{h}_t'\, d\Theta = \mathbf{h}_t'\, dG - dV_t. \tag{9.34}$$

From these two relationships, it immediately follows that

$$dF_t^{\mathbf{h}} = -d\mathbf{h}_t'(\mathbf{s}_t + d\mathbf{s}_t) + \mathbf{h}_t'\, d\Theta_t, \tag{9.35}$$

which is the continuous-time version of (8.3).

We have the following special cases: If the stocks pay no dividends, so that $d\Theta_t = \mathbf{0}$,

$$dF_t^{\mathbf{h}} = -d\mathbf{h}_t'(\mathbf{s}_t + d\mathbf{s}_t).$$

Moreover, if the stocks pay no dividends, then the trading strategy is self-financed (with no consumption) if and only if the following equivalent conditions hold:

$$(d\mathbf{h}_t)' \mathbf{s}_t = -(d\mathbf{h}_t)'\, d\mathbf{s}_t, \tag{9.36}$$

$$dV_t = \mathbf{h}_t'\, d\mathbf{s}_t. \tag{9.37}$$

The restrictions imposed by these conditions are strong. For example, the right-hand side of (9.36) includes only terms of order dt, whereas we would expect the left-hand side for a general stochastic trading strategy, $\mathbf{h}_t$, to include dW_t-terms. These terms therefore need to cancel out at each point in time for the strategy to be self-financed, an idea we will use when we derive the Black–Scholes formula later in this chapter.

9.4 ODEs, SDEs, and PDEs

Ordinary differential equations (ODEs), *stochastic differential equations*, (SDEs) and *partial differential equations* (PDEs) provide fundamental tools in the theory of continuous-time asset pricing, as we will see. A general process for stock dynamics that we would like to consider may look something like

$$dS_t = \mu(t, S_t)\, dt + \sigma(t, S_t)\, d\omega. \tag{9.38}$$

Here we allow the drift and volatility terms of the stock price to depend on both time and the stock price itself (for example, we have seen that the geometric Brownian motion is a special case of this formula, with $\mu(t, S_t) = \mu S_t$, $\sigma(t, S_t) = \sigma S_t$ for constants, μ and $\sigma > 0$). Moreover, from our previous discussions, we expect that the current price of an asset may be viewed as some type of risk-neutral expectation of its future value, similar to (8.13),

$$S_0 = E_0^{\mathbb{Q}}\left[\frac{S_T}{R_T}\right], \tag{9.39}$$

for some discount factor R_T and risk-neutral expectation. We would therefore also like to be able to calculate expectations of the future value of stochastic processes. We will see that this can be done by solving a partial differential equation.

Consider first the stochastic differential equation (SDE)

$$dX = \mu(t, X)\, dt + \sigma(t, X)\, dW_t.$$

As before, this differential formula really represents the integral form of a process X that satisfies

$$X_T = X_0 + \int_0^T \mu(t, X_t)\, dt + \int_0^T \sigma(t, X_t)\, dW_t.$$

What can we say about this process? Well, this equation is fundamentally different compared with the one we had when defining the Itô integral. Specifically, the coefficients, μ and σ, in this case depend on X in contrast to when defining the Itô process, where the dependence was

$$dX_t = \mu(t, \omega)\, dt + \sigma(t, \omega)\, dW_t, \quad \omega \in \Omega.$$

This means that in the current case we have a process that feeds back into itself. Such self-dependence also arises in deterministic systems for ODEs, and has been extensively studied in that context. We provide a brief summary of the deterministic theory, since the stochastic results build upon it.

9.4.1 A Primer on Ordinary Differential Equations (ODEs)

Starting with linear algebra, consider the equation

$$\mathbf{y} = \mathbf{A}\mathbf{f}, \tag{9.40}$$

where $\mathbf{A} \in \mathbb{R}^{N\times N}$ and $\mathbf{f} \in \mathbb{R}^N$. Given $\mathbf{A}$ and $\mathbf{f}$, the solution $\mathbf{y}$ is easily obtained by evaluating a matrix–vector multiplication. Now consider the equation

$$\mathbf{y} = \mathbf{A}(\mathbf{f} + \mathbf{y}) \tag{9.41}$$

instead. This equation is more subtle, because $\mathbf{y}$ enters implicitly on the right-hand side. In other words, the equation has a feedback loop, as shown in figure 9.7.

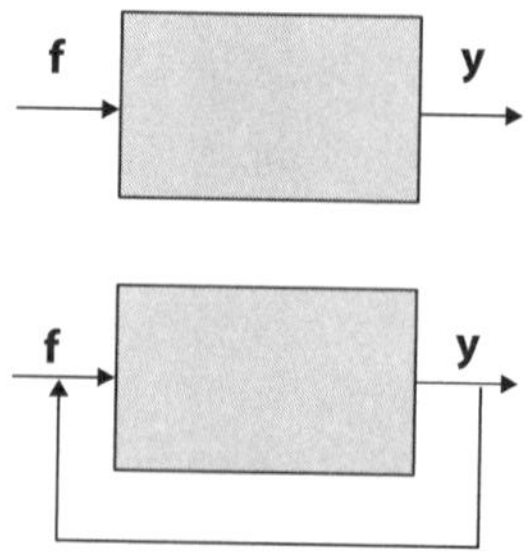

Figure 9.7: Feedback loop.

Now, for this second equation, a unique solution is only guaranteed if the matrix $\mathbf{I} - \mathbf{A}$ is invertible. Otherwise, the equation may have no solution, or many solutions, depending on whether $\mathbf{f}$ lies within the span of $\mathbf{I} - \mathbf{A}$ or not.

A similar situation arises in the continuous (deterministic) setting. The equation

$$\frac{dy}{dt} = f(t), \tag{9.42}$$

corresponding to (9.40), has a solution

$$y(T) = y(0) + \int_0^T f(t)\, dt \tag{9.43}$$

under very general conditions, as long as $f(t)$ does not have an extremely irregular behavior, so that an integral can be defined. The equation

$$\frac{dy}{dt} = f(t, y), \tag{9.44}$$

on the other hand, is different since it has y on the right-hand side. This is a classical first-order (nonlinear) ordinary differential equation. Consider the following two examples:

- The equation $\frac{dy}{dt} = y^2, y(0) = 1$. It has a unique solution, $y(t) = \frac{1}{1-t}$, for $y < 1$. However, the solution blows up as t approaches 1, and the solution is not defined for $t \geq 1$. Intuitively, as y grows, so does its derivative through the feedback, which causes the solution to blow up as y approaches 1.
- The equation $\frac{dy}{dt} = \sqrt{y}, y(0) = 0$, has a solution defined for all $y \geq 0$, but the solution is not unique. In fact, for any $s \geq 0$,

$$y(t) = \frac{1}{4}(t - s)_+^2$$

is a solution, where $(x)_+ = \max(x, 0)$.

Picard's theorem (also called Picard–Lindelöf's theorem) provides sufficient conditions for the existence of a unique solution to an ODE in a neighborhood of a point. It states the following:

Theorem 9.6 (Picard's theorem). *Consider the first-order ODE*

$$\frac{dy}{dt} = f(t, y(t)),$$

$y(t_0) = y_0$. *Given that f is Lipschitz continuous in a neighborhood of y and continuous in t, then there exists a unique solution to the ODE in a neighborhood of t_0.*

Lipschitz continuity is similar to Hölder continuity with exponent $\alpha = 1$, i.e., a bit less restrictive than differentiability, as discussed before.

The theorem can be generalized to systems of ODEs,

$$\frac{d\mathbf{y}}{dt} = f(t, \mathbf{y}), \quad \mathbf{y} \in \mathbb{R}^k, \ \mathbf{y}(t_0) = \mathbf{y}_0.$$

A special case, where we have an explicit expression for the solution, is given by a linear first-order ODE:

Proposition 9.1 (First-order linear ODE). *Consider the linear first-order ODE*

$$\frac{dy}{dt}+p(t)y=q(t).$$

Define the primitive function $P(t)=\int_0^t p(s)\,ds$. *The general solution to the ODE is then*

$$y(T)=e^{-P(T)}\left(\int_0^T e^{P(t)}q(t)\,dt+y(0)\right).$$

Proof. The trick is to define $z(t)=e^{P(t)}y(t)$, so that $z'=e^{P(t)}(y'+p(t)y)$. This follows from the chain rule and the product rule. We multiply both the left- and right-hand sides of the ODE with $e^{P(t)}$ to get

$$e^{P(t)}(y'+p(t)y)=e^{P(t)}q(t),$$

and therefore the trick together with the fundamental theorem of calculus gives us

$$[e^{P(s)}y(s)]_0^t=e^{P(t)}y(t)-y(0)=\int_0^t e^{P(s)}q(s)\,ds,$$

and thus

$$y(t)=e^{-P(t)}\left(\int_0^t e^{P(s)}q(s)\,ds+y(0)\right).$$ □

Example 9.6. An even more special case is given by the above first-order linear ODE with $p(t)=\alpha$, $q(t)=0$, in which case the equation is a first-order constant-coefficient ODE,

$$\frac{dy}{dt}+\alpha y=0,$$

with solution

$$y_T=e^{-\alpha t}y_0.$$

In general, there is no simple trick to find a closed-form solution to the second-order linear ODE, but there are many cases for which such solutions are known. We have the following general existence and uniqueness result:

Proposition 9.2 (Existence of a solution to a second-order linear ODE). *Consider the linear second-order ODE*

$$\frac{d^2y}{dt^2}+p(t)\frac{dy}{dt}+q(t)y(t)=r(t), \tag{9.45}$$

where p, q, and r are continuous functions, together with the initial conditions $y(0)=y_0$, $y'(0)=y_0'$. *There is a unique solution to this ODE.*

Proof. See Simmons (1988). □

The second-order linear ODE is called *homogeneous* if $r(t)\equiv 0$. Solutions to homogeneous linear ODEs satisfy the *superposition principle*, that is, if $y_1(t)$ and $y_2(t)$ are solutions, then $Ay_1(t)+By_2(t)$ are also solutions, for arbitrary constants A and B. More generally, consider the ODE (9.45) without caring about the initial conditions, and assume that $y_1(t)$ and $y_2(t)$ are solutions to the homogeneous version of the ODE, which you get if you set $r(t)\equiv 0$. Moreover, assume that y_p is a *particular solution* to the ODE, i.e., it is a solution to (9.45) without bothering about the initial conditions. Then *any* solution to (9.45), including the one that satisfies the initial conditions, is of the form

$$y(t) = Ay_1(t) + By_2(t) + y_p(t), \quad A, B \in \mathbb{R}.$$

So a good way of solving (9.45), including initial conditions, is to find the three functions y_1, y_2, and y_p, and then choose the constants A and B so that the initial conditions are satisfied.

In the special case with constant coefficients, the solutions to the homogeneous ODE are known:

Proposition 9.3 (Homogeneous, constant-coefficient second-order ODE). *Consider the constant-coefficient second-order ODE*

$$\frac{d^2y}{dt^2} + p\frac{dy}{dt} + qy(t) = 0, \quad p, q \in \mathbb{R}. \tag{9.46}$$

Define the characteristic equation

$$r^2 + pr + q = 0,$$

with roots

$$r_\pm = -\frac{p}{2} \pm \sqrt{\frac{p^2}{4} - q}.$$

- *If the roots r_+ and r_- are real and distinct (because $p^2 - 4q > 0$), the solution to (9.46) is of the form*
$$y(t) = Ae^{r_+ t} + Be^{r_- t}, \quad A, B \in \mathbb{R}.$$
- *If the roots are the same, $r_+ = r_- = r$ (because $p^2 - 4q = 0$), and $p \neq 0$, the solution to (9.46) is of the form*
$$y(t) = Ae^{rt} + Bte^{rt}, \quad A, B \in \mathbb{R}.$$
- *If the roots are complex numbers, $r_+ = \alpha + i\beta$, $r_- = \alpha - i\beta$ (because $p^2 - 4q < 0$), the solution to (9.46) is of the form*
$$y(t) = Ae^{\alpha t}\cos(\beta t) + Be^{\alpha t}\sin(\beta t), \quad A, B \in \mathbb{R}.$$

Proof. For each of the cases, one verifies that the postulated solution satisfies the ODE. □

Another type of ODE which often arises in finance is the *Riccati equation*, which is a nonlinear first-order ODE with a quadratic term. The following transformation turns the Riccati equation into a linear second-order equation:

Proposition 9.4 (Riccati equation). *Consider the Riccati equation*

$$\frac{dy}{dt} = q_0(t) + q_1(t)y(t) + q_2(t)y(t)^2,$$

with $q_2(t) \neq 0$, and with initial condition

$$y(0) = y_0.$$

Define

$$u(t) = e^{-\int_0^t y(s)q_2(s)\,ds}.$$

Then u satisfies the second-order linear ODE

$$\frac{d^2u}{dt^2} + p(t)\frac{du}{dt} + r(t)u = 0,$$

where $p = -q_1 - \frac{q_2'}{q_2}$, and $r = q_0 q_2$.

Proof. Use the definition of u to calculate u' and u'', using standard calculus, and plug into the ODE for u, resulting in

$$q_2(-y' + y^2 q_2 + q_1 y + q_0) = 0,$$

which is satisfied if and only if y satisfies the Riccati equation. □

The mapping from u to y is then

$$y = -\frac{1}{q_2}\frac{u'}{u},$$

where y is a solution to the Riccati equation. The initial condition implies that any solution u, such that $u'(0) = q_2(0)y(0)u(0)$, will give the right solution, y.

Yet another important first-order nonlinear equation is the *Bernoulli differential equation*, which is of the form

$$\frac{dy}{dt} + p(t)y(t) = q(t)y(t)^{\alpha}, \quad \alpha \in \mathbb{R}\backslash\{0,1\}. \tag{9.47}$$

Note that when $\alpha = 2$, this equation coincides with a special case of the Riccati equation, with $q_0 \equiv 0$. In other cases, the equations are different. The following result provides a method for solving the Bernoulli equation:

Proposition 9.5 (Bernoulli differential equation). *Consider the Bernoulli differential equation* (9.47). *If u solves the linear ODE*

$$\frac{du}{dt} + (1-\alpha)p(t)u - (1-\alpha)q(t) = 0, \tag{9.48}$$

then y solves (9.47), *where $y = u^{1/(1-\alpha)}$ (i.e., $u = y^{1-\alpha}$).*

Proof. Use the chain rule to calculate $u' = (1-\alpha)y'y^{-\alpha}$, which when plugged into (9.48) leads to

$$(1-\alpha)y'y^{-\alpha} + (1-\alpha)p(t)y^{1-\alpha} - (1-\alpha)q(t) = 0.$$

This is in turn equivalent to

$$(1-\alpha)y^{-\alpha}(y' + p(t)y - q(t)y^{\alpha}) = 0.$$

So y satisfies the Bernoulli differential equation. □

9.4.2 Stochastic Differential Equations (SDEs)

Just like Picard's theorem for ODEs, we would like to have a general existence theorem for SDEs. The following general existence theorem holds (see Björk 2009):

Theorem 9.7 (Existence theorem for stochastic ODEs). *Consider the linear first-order SDE*

$$d\mathbf{X} = \mu(t,\mathbf{X})\,dt + \sigma(t,\mathbf{X})\,d\mathbf{W}_t, \quad \mathbf{X}_0 = \mathbf{x},$$

where $\mathbf{W}_t$ is a k-dimensional Wiener process, $\mathbf{X}_t \in \mathbb{R}^n$, $\mu\colon \mathbb{R}_+ \times \mathbb{R}^n \to \mathbb{R}^n$, $\sigma : \mathbb{R}_+ \times \mathbb{R}^n \to \mathbb{R}^{n\times k}$. Assume that there is constant, K, such that for all $\mathbf{x}$, for all $\mathbf{y}$, for all t,

1. $\|\mu(t,\mathbf{x}) - \mu(t,\mathbf{y})\| + \|\sigma(t,\mathbf{x}) - \sigma(t,\mathbf{y})\| \leq K\|\mathbf{x}-\mathbf{y}\|$,
2. $\|\mu(t,\mathbf{x})\| + \|\sigma(t,\mathbf{x})\| \leq K(1+\|\mathbf{x}\|)$.

Then the SDE has a unique solution, $\mathbf{X}$. *This solution*

- *is $\mathcal{F}_t^W$-adapted,*
- *has continuous trajectories,*
- *is a Markov process,*

- *satisfies the following growth bound, for some constant, K':*

$$E[\|\mathbf{X}\|^2] \le K' e^{K't}(1+\|\mathbf{x}\|^2).$$

Note that the first condition in the existence theorem corresponds to the Lipschitz continuity in Picard's theorem. However, in contrast to Picard's theorem, here we have a *global* condition, i.e., it is not sufficient for the condition to be satisfied in a neighborhood of any y to get a local existence result. At second thought, this is not surprising since the stochastic nature of Brownian motions is such that they can move very far over a very short time period, albeit with very low probability. This makes the stochastic ODE global in a way that a deterministic ODE is not.

The ODE $y' = y^2$ that we discussed earlier is an interesting example, with solution $\frac{1}{1-t}$. Now, at $t = 1$, this solution blows up and ceases to exist. However, Picard's theorem still applies since for any time $0 \le s < t$, there is indeed a neighborhood over which the solution is defined—it is just that the neighborhood has to be chosen smaller and smaller the closer s is to 1. For a stochastic ODE, however, such an argument does not hold.

The conditions in t are also much stronger for the SDE, with continuity sufficient for the ODE but a linear growth condition similar to the global Lipschitz condition in x is needed over time too.

Example 9.7. Define $Y_t = e^{X_t}$, where $X_t = \mu t + \sigma W_t$ is a Brownian motion, i.e., Y_t is a geometric Brownian motion. The SDE for X_t is $dX_t = \mu_t\, dt + \sigma\, dW_t$, and the Brownian motion is thus the unique solution to this SDE.

One verifies that the SDE for Y_t is

$$\frac{dY_t}{Y_t} = \hat{\mu}\, dt + \sigma\, dW_t, \quad \hat{\mu} = \mu + \frac{\sigma^2}{2},$$

just like in (9.32), and that this SDE satisfies the conditions of theorem 9.7. This implies that the GBM solution to the SDE is unique.

Example 9.8. Consider the SDE

$$dX = \kappa(\theta - X_t)\, dt + \sigma\, dW_t, \quad X_0 = x \in \mathbb{R}.$$

The solution to this SDE is the *Ornstein–Uhlenbeck process*. It is mean reverting toward θ and has a long-term stationary distribution, in contrast to the Brownian motion and GBM. Specifically, given the initial value, X_0, the distribution of X_t is

$$X_t \sim N\Big(\theta + e^{-\kappa t}(X_0 - \theta), \frac{\sigma^2}{2\kappa}(1 - e^{-2\kappa t})\Big).$$

There is no general solution method for SDEs that always works. Moreover, only in very rare cases are explicit solutions available. However, it is straightforward to simulate solutions, as we will discuss in chapter 11.

We next show some analytical methods that can be used to characterize the distributional properties of the solution to an SDE. Specifically, the Kolmogorov equations can be used for such characterizations, by analyzing related partial differential equations, PDEs. There are two such equations: The Kolmogorov backward equation is in turn closely related to the immensely important Feynman–Kac equation, which is useful in describing the expectation of the solution to an SDE. The Kolmogorov forward equation in turn, also called the Fokker–Planck equation, characterizes the evolution of the distribution of the solution!

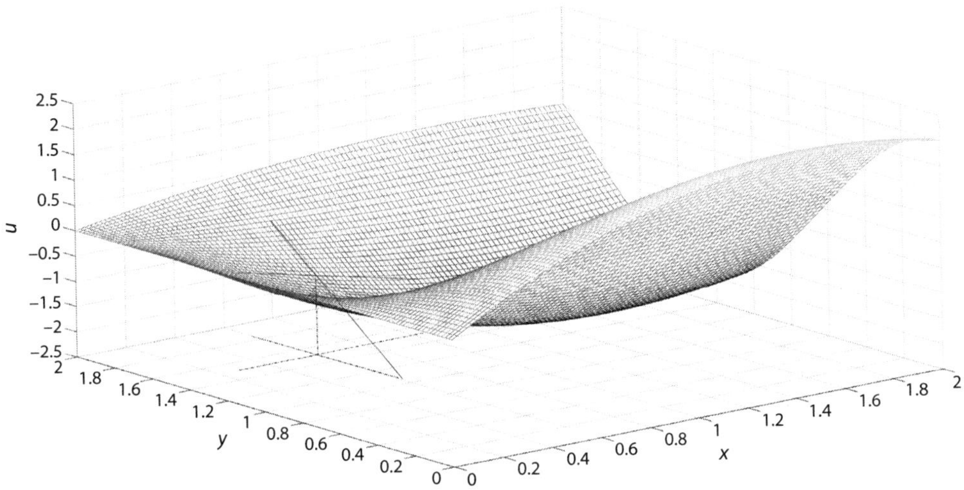

Figure 9.8: The constraints imposed by a PDE.

9.4.3 Partial Differential Equations (PDEs)

Partial differential equations provide a key analysis tool in the study of natural, as well as social, sciences. Specifically, a PDE provides a *law of motion* in a continuous setting that characterizes the local behavior of a dynamic system. The PDE could represent as widely different processes as the flow of fluids, traffic, electromagnetic waves, the spread of rumors or viruses in a population, or the dynamics of the price of a contingent claim. A PDE is similar to an ODE, involving a function and its derivatives. But, in contrast to an ODE, the PDE includes derivatives in multiple directions; it is the multivariate version of an ODE.

A *well-posed* PDE, including appropriately specified *boundary conditions*, completely determines the dynamics of a system. PDEs have been extensively analyzed and there are many solution techniques available, both analytical and numerical. They provide an extremely powerful tool. The most famous PDE in social sciences is the Black–Scholes PDE, which we will discuss extensively!

A standard classification of PDEs is into *hyperbolic*, *elliptic*, and *parabolic*, analogous to how bivariate quadratic equations are characterized. Most (but not all) interesting PDEs fall within these three classes or a combination thereof. As we will see, the Black–Scholes PDE is parabolic.

The *wave equation*,

$$\frac{\partial^2 u}{\partial x^2} = \frac{\partial^2 u}{\partial y^2}, \tag{9.49}$$

is an example of a hyperbolic PDE. Here, $u(x, y)$, is a two-dimensional function over some domain, $(x, y) \in E \subset \mathbb{R}^2$. In the simplest case the domain has no boundaries, $E = \mathbb{R}^2$, which defines a so-called *Cauchy problem*.

Equation (9.49) relates the second-order partial derivative of u in the x-direction, u_{xx}, with that in the y-direction, u_{yy}, as shown in figure 9.8. It may come as a surprise that this simple PDE relation is so powerful as to be informative about what the function u looks like. Indeed, it looks like just one equation, whereas u is defined over the whole set E. The key here is that (9.49) must hold *for all* x and y in E. It therefore represents an infinite number of equations.

We have seen this before, for ODEs. For example, the simple equation $y' = y$ represents a relation that needs to hold for *all* t for the function $y(t)$. The only functions that satisfy the relation for all x are $y(t)=ce^t$, $c\in\mathbb{R}$. To get a unique solution for the ODE, we also need to know the value of y at some t, so that the constant c can be nailed down. Similarly, for a PDE we will need additional constraints on u to ensure uniqueness.

The *Laplace equation*,

$$\frac{\partial^2 u}{\partial x^2}=-\frac{\partial^2 u}{\partial y^2}, \tag{9.50}$$

is an example of an *elliptic equation*. Note that the only difference compared with the wave equation is the sign shift on the right-hand side. This little difference completely changes the characteristics of the solutions to the PDE, just like the solutions to the quadratic equation $x^2=c^2$, $c\in\mathbb{R}$, are very different from solutions to $x^2=-c^2$. The former solutions are real numbers whereas the latter solutions are imaginary numbers.

Finally, the *heat equation*,

$$\frac{\partial u}{\partial t}=\frac{\partial^2 u}{\partial x^2}, \tag{9.51}$$

is an example of a parabolic equation. Here, the partial derivative on the left-hand side is only first order. Note that we use the variable name t for the first-order derivative since it usually represents time. As mentioned, the Black–Scholes PDE belongs to this class of PDEs.

The additional information needed to ensure that there is a unique solution, i.e., to make the problem well posed,[5] is almost always expressed in terms of boundary conditions and initial/terminal conditions (if there is a time dimension). Let us first consider an even simpler hyperbolic PDE than the wave equation:

$$\frac{\partial u}{\partial t}=-a\frac{\partial u}{\partial x},\qquad a\in\mathbb{R}. \tag{9.52}$$

Here we choose to interpret one of the dimensions as time (t), and the other as a space dimension (x), as we did for the heat equation. This PDE is known as the *convection equation*. We first study the Cauchy problem, which in this case takes the form $t\geq 0$, $x\in\mathbb{R}$, $u=u(t,x)$. The initial condition that makes the problem well posed is

$$u(0,x)=g(x),$$

i.e., we need to specify the solution at the "beginning," when $t=0$. The general solution is then of the form

$$u(t,x)=g(x-at),\qquad t\geq 0,\ x\in\mathbb{R},$$

where g is a continuously differentiable function. This can be verified by taking the partial derivatives of the conjectured solution in both directions, and verifying that they satisfy the PDE, as well as that the solution satisfies the initial condition $u(0,x)=g(x-a0)=g(x)$. So whenever $x-at=C$, for a constant C, the solution is the same. In other words, the value of u at time t, at the point $x+at$, is the same as the value of u at time 0, at the point x: $u(t,x+at)=u(0,x)$. So

[5]In addition to ensuring that the solution is unique, well-posedness requires that the solution depends continuously on initial and boundary conditions. Otherwise, arbitrarily small measurement errors may generate completely different solutions, corresponding to having a very ill-conditioned problem. An example of a generically ill-posed problem (i.e., not well-posed) is the backward heat equation, $u_t=-u_{xx}$, $t\geq 0$, $u(0,x)=g(x)$. The backward heat equation is thus like the regular heat equation, but with the sign in front of the u_{xx} coefficient negative instead of positive. One can show that arbitrarily small perturbations of the initial condition $g(x)$ have dramatic effects on the solution to the backward heat equation.

the solution moves at speed $|a|$, to the right (to higher x) when $a > 0$, and to the left (to lower x) when $a < 0$. This behavior of the solution "traveling" in the domain at a finite speed, similar to a wave in a liquid, is a characterizing feature of solutions to hyperbolic PDEs. The lines $x - at = C$, $C \in \mathbb{R}$, are called characteristic lines. They determine the flow of information about the solution.

We next study the convection equation on a semibounded domain. Specifically, we assume that the solution, u, is only defined for nonnegative x, $t \geq 0$, $x \geq 0$. The initial condition is the same as before, $u(0, x) = g(x)$, but now g is only defined for $x \geq 0$. The domain the solution is defined over is shown in figure 9.9.

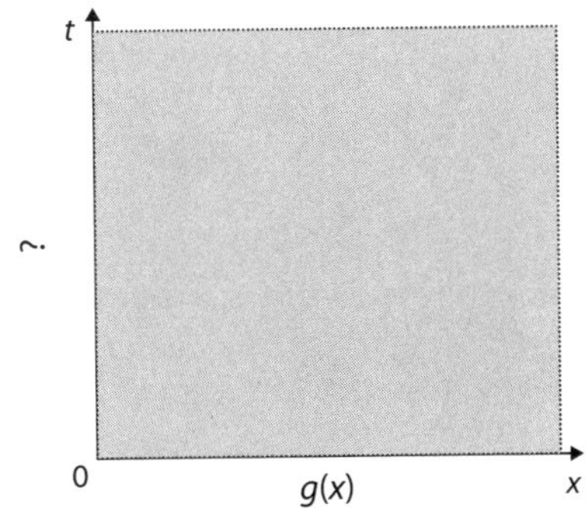

Figure 9.9: Domain for the convection equation with boundary at $x = 0$.

On the x-axis, the initial condition is specified by $g(x)$. Do we need to provide any information about u at the new boundary, $x = 0$? The answer is that it depends on the sign of a. If $a > 0$, then the solution is moving to the right, and there will gradually be more and more information missing about the solution. In other words, the characteristic lines have positive slope in this case, and therefore the information at $t = 0$ is not sufficient to cover the whole domain with characteristic lines.

If $a < 0$, on the other hand, the characteristic lines have negative slope and therefore those that go through the $t = 0$ boundary provide enough information to completely determine the solution. The two different situations are shown in figure 9.10. In the left-hand panel, $a = 1$, the characteristic lines have positive slope, and the additional boundary condition $u(t, 0) = h(t)$ is needed to make the PDE well posed. In this case, information about the solution flows in at the $x = 0$ boundary, which is called an *inflow boundary*. In the right-hand panel, the characteristic lines have negative slope, and the characteristic lines originating at $x = 0$ are sufficient to fill the whole of $E = \mathbb{R}_+ \times \mathbb{R}_+$. The boundary at $x = 0$ in this case is an *outflow boundary*.

Example 9.9. The following convection equation with an inflow boundary at $x = 0$ has the solution shown in figure 9.11:

$$
\begin{aligned}
u_t &= u_x, \\
u(0, x) &= \sin(5x) + e^{-2500(x-0.5)^2}, \\
u(t, 0) &= -\frac{t}{1 + 3t}, \\
x &\in [0, 1], \\
t &\geq 0.
\end{aligned}
$$

Note that the solution is only defined in the region $0 \leq x \leq 1$. Since the $x = 1$ boundary is an outflow boundary, no additional information is needed at that boundary.

As mentioned, solutions to elliptic PDEs behave quite differently from solutions to hyperbolic PDEs. For elliptic PDEs, a change in one part of the domain, for example, at a boundary, affects the solution globally, contrary to the finite speed of information shown by solutions to hyperbolic PDEs. Also, more boundary conditions need to be specified. For the convection equation in a "box" domain, $(x, t) \in [0, 1] \times [0, 1]$, regardless of the sign of a, only two boundaries of the box need to be specified: the initial condition boundary, $t = 0$, and one of the boundaries $x = 0$ and $x = 1$, depending on the sign of a. For the elliptic PDE, the Laplace equation, all four boundaries

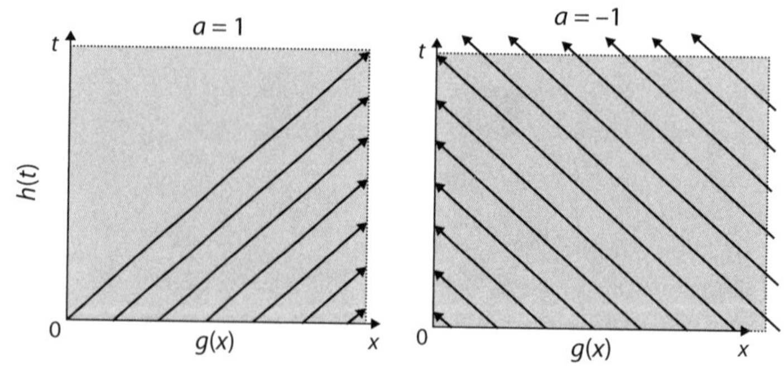

Figure 9.10: Characteristic lines for the convection equation with boundary at $x=0$. Left panel: inflow boundary. Right panel: outflow boundary.

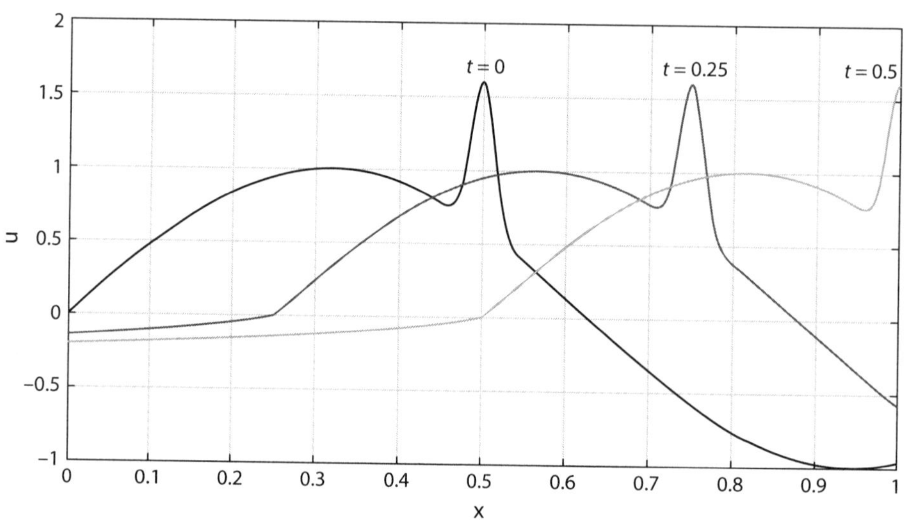

Figure 9.11: Solution to the convection equation.

need to be specified ($x=0$, $x=1$, $t=0$, $t=1$) for the PDE to be well posed. Finally, for the heat equation, in the box, the initial condition at $t=0$, and the boundary conditions at both $x=0$ and $x=1$, are needed for the PDE to be well posed, but no condition at $t=1$ should be specified.

How do we characterize the type of a PDE in the general case? For linear PDEs, which just as for linear ODEs are characterized by their linear dependence on all (partial) derivatives, it is the terms of highest order and the sign in front of their coefficients that determine the type of PDE. A general form here is

$$a(x,y)u_{xx}+b(x,y)u_{yy}+c(x,y)u_x+d(x,y)u_y+f(x,y)u+g(x,y)=0.$$

If $a(x,y)>0$, and $b(x,y)>0$ for all x and y, this PDE is elliptic. If $a(x,y)>0$ and $b(x,y)<0$ for all x and y, the PDE is hyperbolic. If $a(x,y)=0$, $c(x,y)<0$, and $b(x,y)>0$ for all x and y, then the PDE is parabolic.[6]

[6]The classification is straightforward to generalize to higher dimensions, e.g., t, x, and y, as well as to having nonlinearities in the lower-order terms. Also, a term of the form $q(x,y)u_{xy}$ can be introduced. However, when there are nonlinearities

A parabolic PDE that will be very important for us is

$$F_t + \mu(t,x)F_x + \frac{1}{2}\sigma^2(t,x)F_{xx} - r(t,x)F + g(t,x) = 0,$$

where $\sigma(t,x) > 0$, as we will now see.

9.4.4 Feynman–Kac's Theorem and the Kolmogorov Equations

Assume that we want to calculate $E[X_T]$ at $t=0$, for some diffusion process, X, satisfying

$$dX = \mu(t,X)\,dt + \sigma(t,X)\,dW_t.$$

Let us define

$$F(t,x) = E_t[X_T | X_t = x]. \tag{9.53}$$

Thus, $F(t,x)$ is the time-t expectation of what X_T is going to be. We use Itô's lemma to derive a law of motion for F. Assuming that F is a smooth function (it is—it is actually infinitely differentiable), we get

$$F(t+dt, X_{t+dt}) = F(t,X_t) + F_t\,dt + F_x(\mu\,dt + \sigma\,dW) + \frac{\sigma^2}{2}F_{xx}\,dt, \tag{9.54}$$

$$dF = F_t\,dt + F_x(\mu\,dt + \sigma\,dW) + \frac{\sigma^2}{2}F_{xx}\,dt. \tag{9.55}$$

We now take the expectation of (9.55). The law of iterated expectations gives us

$$E_t[F_{t+dt}] = E_t[E_{t+dt}[X_T]] = E_t[X_T] = F(t,X_t), \tag{9.56}$$

so $E[dF_t] = 0$, which we can use for the left-hand side of (9.55). For the expectation of the right-hand side of (9.55), we use the fact that $E[dW_t] = 0$, so all in all we get

$$0 = \left(F_t + F_x\mu + \frac{\sigma^2}{2}F_{xx}\right)dt. \tag{9.57}$$

Thus, F satisfies the PDE

$$0 = F_t + \mu F_x + \frac{\sigma^2}{2}F_{xx}. \tag{9.58}$$

Equation (9.58) provides a remarkable link between SDEs and PDEs! This derivation was heuristic, but the result is correct, as shown by *Feynman–Kac's theorem*, which provides a more general relationship.

Consider the PDE

$$F_t + \mu(t,x)F_x + \frac{1}{2}\sigma^2(t,x)F_{xx} - r(t,x)F + g(t,x) = 0, \tag{9.59}$$

$$F(T,x) = \Phi(x), \tag{9.60}$$

$$t \le T, \tag{9.61}$$

$$x \in \mathbb{R}, \tag{9.62}$$

$$\sigma(t,x) > 0. \tag{9.63}$$

---

in the highest-order terms, all bets are usually off. One example of such a nonlinear equation is the inviscid Burgers' equation, $u_t + uu_x = 0$, which has the intriguing property of generating discontinuous solutions over time, even when initial conditions are very smooth.

We then have the following result:

Theorem 9.8 (Feynman–Kac). *Assume that $F(t,x)$ solves the PDE (9.59–9.63), and that F, g, and Φ satisfy some regularity and growth conditions. Then*

$$F(t,x) = E_t\left[e^{-\int_t^T r(s,X_s)\,ds}\Phi(X_T) + \int_t^T g(s,X_s)e^{-\int_t^s r(u,X_u)\,du}\,ds \middle| X_t = x\right],$$

where X_t is the solution to the SDE

$$dX_s = \mu(s,X_s)\,ds + \sigma(s,X_s)\,dW_s, \quad X_t = x.$$

The Feynman–Kac theorem is more general than we showed in our heuristic derivation, in that it allows for discounting (via the function r), general terminal conditions (as defined by the function Φ), and a flow (the function g).

Example 9.10. A useful application of Feynman–Kac's theorem is as follows: Consider Feynman–Kac's formula with $r=0$, $g=0$, so that

$$F(t,x) = E_t[\Phi(X_T)|X_t = x],$$

and consider the function $\Phi(X_T) = \chi_{X_T \in A}$ for some (measurable) set $A \subset \mathbb{R}$. Here, $\chi_{X_T \in A}$ is the indicator function on A. As mentioned earlier, $E_t[\Phi(X_T)|X_t = x] = \mathbb{P}(X_T \in A|X_t = x)$, and specifically, if $A = [y, \infty)$, for some y,

$$E_t[\Phi(X_T)|X_t = x] = \mathbb{P}(X_T \geq y|X_t = x) = 1 - Z(y),$$

where $Z(y)$ is the c.d.f. for the random variable $X_T|X_t = x$. Let us apply this to the Brownian motion

$$dX = \mu\,dt + \sigma\,dW.$$

We have

$$\begin{aligned} F(t,x) \stackrel{\text{def}}{=} E_t[\Phi(X_T)|X_t = x] &= 1 - N\left(\frac{y - x - \mu(T-t)}{\sigma\sqrt{T-t}}\right) \\ &= N\left(\frac{x - y + \mu(T-t)}{\sigma\sqrt{T-t}}\right), \end{aligned} \tag{9.64}$$

where $N(x)$ is the c.d.f. of the standard normal distribution. Feynman–Kac's theorem then implies that (9.64) is the solution to the PDE

$$F_t + \mu F_x + \frac{\sigma^2}{2}F_{xx} = 0,$$
$$F(T,x) = \chi_{x \geq y}.$$

Example 9.11. Define $Y = e^x$, where x is the process in the previous example (equivalently, $x = \ln(Y)$). As we know from before,

$$dY = \hat{\mu}Y\,dt + \sigma Y\,dW.$$

Moreover,

$$\begin{aligned} \mathbb{P}(Y_T \geq e^y) &= \mathbb{P}(X_t \geq y) \\ &= 1 - N\left(\frac{y - x - \mu(T-t)}{\sigma\sqrt{T-t}}\right) \end{aligned}$$

$$= 1 - N\left(\frac{\ln(\frac{K}{Y_t}) - (\hat{\mu} - \frac{\sigma^2}{2})(T-t)}{\sigma\sqrt{T-t}}\right)$$

$$= N\left(\frac{\ln(\frac{Y_t}{K}) + (\hat{\mu} - \frac{\sigma^2}{2})(T-t)}{\sigma\sqrt{T-t}}\right), \quad \text{where } K = e^y. \tag{9.65}$$

Another application of Feynman–Kac's theorem implies that (9.65) is the solution to the PDE

$$F_t + \hat{\mu} Y F_Y + \frac{\sigma^2}{2} Y^2 F_{YY} = 0,$$

$$F(T, S) = \chi_{Y \geq K}.$$

Let us return to the relation $E_t[\Phi(X_T)|X_t = x] = \mathbb{P}(X_T \in A|X_t = x)$ when $\Phi(X_T) = \chi_{X_T \in A}$. Consider the probability density function $p(T, y|t, x)$, which describes the probability of $X_T = y$ given that $X_t = x$ at an earlier point in time $t < T$. It can be shown that diffusion processes have smooth such probability density functions, and therefore

$$p(T, y|t, x) = \lim_{\epsilon \searrow 0} \frac{1}{\epsilon} \mathbb{P}(X_T \in A_\epsilon | X_t = x), \quad \text{where } A_\epsilon = [y - \tfrac{\epsilon}{2}, y + \tfrac{\epsilon}{2}]$$

$$= \lim_{\epsilon \searrow 0} \frac{1}{\epsilon} E_t[\Phi_\epsilon(X_T)|X_t = x], \quad \text{where } \Phi_\epsilon(y) = \chi_{y \in A_\epsilon}. \tag{9.66}$$

Now we can formally define the so-called Dirac distribution (also called the δ-distribution) as

$$\delta_y = \lim_{\epsilon \searrow 0} \frac{1}{\epsilon} \Phi_\epsilon(y). \tag{9.67}$$

The defining properties of the Dirac distribution are

$$\delta_y(x) = 0, \quad \text{when } x \neq y, \tag{9.68}$$

$$\int_{-\infty}^{\infty} \delta_y(x)\, dx = 1. \tag{9.69}$$

Clearly, δ_y cannot be defined as a regular function since the only point at which it may be nonzero is y, and it is impossible for such a function to have a nonzero integral, as required by (9.69). It would have to be so massively infinite at y to have a positive integral at that point.

Regular functions cannot be massively infinite. Rather, δ_y is defined through a weak functional relation. For an arbitrary integrable function $f\colon \mathbb{R} \to \mathbb{R}$, we can define the operation

$$\mathcal{F}_f(\phi) = \int_{-\infty}^{\infty} f(x)\phi(x)\, dx, \tag{9.70}$$

for any smooth positive function, $\phi\colon \mathbb{R} \to \mathbb{R}$ with compact nontrivial support, i.e., such that $\phi(x) = 0$ when $|x| > M$ for some finite M. Such an operation, $\mathcal{F}_f$, is a *functional*, in that it takes a function (ϕ) as an argument and maps it to a number.

Now, for a regular smooth function, f, we can essentially recover the function from the behavior of the functional, $\mathcal{F}_f$. Specifically, by choosing a ϕ with support close to y, such that $\phi(x) = 0$ when $|x - y| > \epsilon$, we will get

$$\frac{\mathcal{F}_f(\phi)}{\int \phi(x)\, dx} = f(y) + o(1),$$

at any point x where f is continuous. In a weak sense, the functional $\mathcal{F}_f$ and the function f are then equivalent.

The great thing with this approach is that such functionals may also include those that do not arise from integrals of the form (9.70). Consider, for example, the functional

$$\mathcal{F}:\phi \mapsto \phi(y), \quad y \in \mathbb{R}, \tag{9.71}$$

i.e., the functional value is the value of its argument, the function, ϕ, at some point, $y \in \mathbb{R}$. How would we think of a function f that would be consistent with this functional through the integral (9.70)? Such a function, δ_y, would have

$$\int \delta_y(x)\phi(x)\,dx = \phi(y), \quad \forall \phi, \tag{9.72}$$

so it would need to satisfy (9.68, 9.69). As noted, this is impossible for a function, which is why we need to think of δ_y as a functional.

The theory of Dirac distributions goes beyond what we can cover in any detail in this text; for a thorough treatment, see Hörmander (2003). For us, it is sufficient to think of δ_y as defined via (9.67), implying (9.71), which is heuristically equivalent to (9.72).

Returning to where we were before diving into the theory of Dirac distributions, we can now rewrite (9.66) as

$$p(T,y|t,x) = E_t[\delta_y(X_T)|X_t = x],$$

and by defining the function $f(t,x) = p(T,y|t,x)$, the following *Kolmogorov backward equation* then follows from Feynman–Kac's theorem:

Theorem 9.9 (Kolmogorov backward equation). *Consider the diffusion process*

$$dX_t = \mu(t,X_t)\,dt + \sigma(t,X_t)\,dW_t,$$

with the transition probability density function, $p(t,y|s,x)$. Define $f(t,x) = p(T,y|t,x)$, as the probability density of $X_T = y$ (y and T treated as constants), given that $X_t = x$, $t < T$. Then f is the solution to the PDE

$$f_t + \mathcal{A}_t f = 0, \qquad t < T,\ x \in \mathbb{R},$$

$$f(t,x) \to \delta_y(x), \quad t \nearrow T.$$

Here, $\mathcal{A}_t$ is the infinitesimal generator, $(\mathcal{A}_t f)(t,x) = \mu(t,x)f_x(t,x) + \frac{1}{2}\sigma^2(t,x)f_{xx}(t,x)$.

We also have the following Kolmogorov forward equation, which is also known as the *Fokker–Planck equation*:

Theorem 9.10 (Kolmogorov forward equation). *Consider the diffusion process $dX_t = \mu(t,X_t)\,dt + \sigma(t,X_t)\,dW_t$, with the transition probability density function, $p(t,y|s,x)$. Define $g(t,y) = p(t,y|s,x)$, $t > s$, as the density of X being at y at time $t > s$, given that $X_s = x$ (x, s treated as constants). Then g is the solution to the PDE*

$$g_t = \mathcal{A}_t^* g, \qquad t > s,\ y \in \mathbb{R},$$

$$g(t,y) \to \delta_x(y), \quad t \searrow s.$$

Here, $\mathcal{A}^*$ is the adjoint operator to $\mathcal{A}$, $(\mathcal{A}^* g)(t,y) = -\frac{d}{dy}(\mu(t,y)g(t,y)) + \frac{1}{2}\frac{d^2}{dy^2}(\sigma^2(t,y)g(t,y))$.

The Kolmogorov forward equation is the adjoint of the Kolmogorov backward equation.[7]

[7] Formally, $\langle f, \mathcal{A}g\rangle = \langle \mathcal{A}^* f\rangle$ for smooth functions, $f \in L^2$ and $g \in L^2$, where the inner product on L^2 is defined by $\langle f, g\rangle = \int f(x)g(x)\,dx$; see appendix B. An intuition for the adjointness relation between the Kolmogorov forward and backward equations for the discrete Markov process versions of these equations is also provided in appendix B.

9.5 No-Arbitrage Pricing in Continuous Time

We now have all the machinery needed to apply no-arbitrage arguments in the continuous-time setting. Specifically, we will study a Black–Scholes economy with one risk-free and one risky asset, and derive the Black–Scholes option pricing formula directly in the continuous-time economy.[8]

We assume the following stochastic processes for the bond and the stock:

$$\frac{dB}{B} = r(t, S)\, dt, \tag{9.73}$$

$$\frac{dS}{S} = \hat{\mu}(t, S)\, dt + \sigma(t, S)\, dW, \quad \sigma > 0. \tag{9.74}$$

Thus, we allow general time- and state-varying processes, assuming that the conditions in theorem 9.7 hold. Moreover, we assume that neither asset pays any dividends, $d\Theta = (0, 0)'$.

We need to define what an arbitrage opportunity means in the continuous-time setting.

Definition 9.10. A self-financed (no consumption) trading strategy constitutes an *arbitrage opportunity* if for some $T > 0$, the corresponding value process satisfies

$$V_0^{\mathbf{h}} = 0,$$

$$V_T^{\mathbf{h}} \geq 0,$$

$$\mathbb{P}(V_T^{\mathbf{h}} > 0) > 0.$$

A market in which there is no arbitrage is said to be *arbitrage-free*.[9]

We are interested in pricing derivatives on the underlying assets, B and S. We focus on assets that do not pay any intermediate dividends, and whose payoffs only depend on the value of the stock at expiration, S_T. To this end, we introduce the concept of a *simple contingent claim*, which is one that pays off $\Phi(S_T)$ at time T, for some payoff function $\Phi: \mathbb{R} \to \mathbb{R}$. For example, European call and put options are simple contingent claims with payoffs

$$\Phi(S_T) = (S_T - K)_+$$

and

$$\Phi(S_T) = (K - S_T)_+,$$

for a call and put, respectively, where $(x)_+ = \max(x, 0)$.

9.5.1 Black–Scholes' PDE and Formula

Assuming no arbitrage, we now have the following fundamental pricing relationship:

Theorem 9.11 (Black–Scholes PDE). *The value of any simple contingent claim with payout function $C_T = \Phi(S(T))$ satisfies the PDE*

$$C_t + rSC_S + \frac{1}{2}\sigma^2 C_{SS} S^2 - rC = 0, \tag{9.75}$$

$$C(S, T) = \Phi(S).$$

[8]We have already derived the formulas, in section 8.7, by taking the limit of the binomial model.

[9]There are also some technical restrictions needed on the allowed trading strategies. We do not discuss these restrictions.

In the special case when r and σ are constant, and the payout function is that of a European call option, this PDE leads us to the classical Black–Scholes formula (again).

Theorem 9.12 (Black–Scholes formula). *The time-0 price of a European call option with strike price K and expiration date T in the Black–Scholes economy with constant r and σ is*

$$C = SN(x) - Ke^{-rT}N(x - \sigma\sqrt{T}). \tag{9.76}$$

Here, $x = \frac{\ln(\frac{S}{K})+(r+\frac{\sigma^2}{2})T}{\sigma\sqrt{T}}$.

Proof. Note that the payoff function can be written

$$\Phi(S) = \max(S-K, 0) = (S-K)\chi_{S\geq K} = S\chi_{S\geq K} - K\chi_{S\geq K}.$$

Thus, the payoff function looks quite similar to what we analyzed in Example 9.11, suggesting that we should take that example as a starting point. We postulate that the pricing function can be written in the form

$$C(t,S) = SF(t,S) - Ke^{-r(T-t)}G(t,S),$$

where the functions F and G are smooth, and such that $F(T,S) = G(T,S) = \chi_{S\geq K}$. Such a decomposition will clearly satisfy the terminal condition $SF(T,S) - Ke^{r(T-T)}G(T,S) = (S-K)\chi_{S\geq K} = \Phi(S)$.

We next rewrite the Black–Scholes PDE under the decomposition, using the chain rule to calculate partial derivatives. Specifically, we have

$$(SF)_S = F + SF_S,$$

$$(SF)_{SS} = 2F_S + SF_{SS},$$

$$(Ke^{-r(T-t)}G)_t = Ke^{-r(T-t)}G_t + Kre^{-r(T-t)}G,$$

which when applied to $C = SF - Ke^{-r(T-t)}G$ yields

$$C_t = SF_t - Ke^{-r(T-t)}G_t - Kre^{-r(T-t)}G,$$

$$C_S = F + SF_S - Ke^{-r(T-t)}G_S,$$

$$C_{SS} = 2F_S + SF_{SS} - Ke^{-r(T-t)}G_{SS}.$$

We plug these expressions into the PDE (9.75), and collect the F and G terms separately, to arrive at

$$F_t + (r+\sigma^2)SF_S + \frac{\sigma^2}{2}F_{SS} = 0,$$

$$G_t + rSG_S + \frac{\sigma^2}{2}G_{SS} = 0,$$

which together with the two terminal conditions, $F(T,S) = \chi_{S\geq K}$, $G(T,S) = \chi_{S\geq K}$, via Example 9.12, leads to

$$F(t,S) = N\left(\frac{\ln(\frac{S}{K}) + (r+\frac{\sigma^2}{2})(T-t)}{\sigma\sqrt{T-t}}\right),$$

$$G(t,S) = N\left(\frac{\ln(\frac{S}{K}) + (r-\frac{\sigma^2}{2})(T-t)}{\sigma\sqrt{T-t}}\right),$$

and thus to $C_0 = S_0F(0,S_0) - Ke^{-rT}G(0,S_0)$ of the form (9.76). We are done. □

The trick to rewrite $C = SF - Ke^{-r(T-t)}G$ may seem almost magical, but as we will see when analyzing multidimensional Black–Scholes, these types of decompositions are quite common when the terminal conditions have particularly simple forms. A key property of the Black–Scholes PDE which we used in this decomposition is that it is linear, so that the sum of two solutions to the PDE is also a solution to the PDE (the superposition principle again, which is also valid for linear PDEs).

Since the probability of ending up at one given price is zero in the continuous model, we cannot think of a state price as the price of a contingent claim that pays 1 in such a state. The price of any such claim will be zero. Rather, we define the state price as that of an asset that pays δ_S, i.e., that has the Dirac distribution as a payoff.

Definition 9.11. The state price ψ_S^T is the price of an asset that pays $\delta_S(S_T)$ at time T.

We can use the same argument to calculate state prices in the continuous-time model. The argument is based on the following result:

Proposition 9.6. *If the smooth function F, satisfies the PDE*

$$F_t + \mathcal{A}F = 0,$$

$$F(T, S) = \Phi(S),$$

then, defining the derivatives $f = \frac{\partial F}{\partial S}$, $\phi = \frac{d\Phi}{dS}$, *the function* f *satisfies the PDE*

$$f_t + \mathcal{A}f = 0,$$

$$f(T, S) = \phi(S).$$

This follows from the linearity properties of the PDE and the differential operator. Now consider the call and put option prices C_K^T, P_K^T for different strike prices K of options that mature at T. These could be consistent with classical Black–Scholes, giving the closed-form solutions, or could more generally be calculated by solving the Black–Scholes PDE using the risk-free rate and volatility coefficients defined in (9.73, 9.74), and with payoff functions

$$\Phi^C(S-K) = (S-K)_+,$$

$$\Phi^P(S-K) = (K-S)_+.$$

We have

$$\delta_K = \frac{\partial^2 \Phi^C(S-K)}{\partial S^2} = \frac{\partial^2 \Phi^C(S-K)}{\partial K^2} = \frac{\partial^2 \Phi^P(S-K)}{\partial S^2} = \frac{\partial^2 \Phi^P(S-K)}{\partial K^2},$$

i.e., all of these second-order partial derivatives correspond to the Dirac distribution. Together with proposition 9.6, it follows that

$$\psi_K^T = \frac{\partial^2 C_K^T}{\partial K^2} = \frac{\partial^2 P_K^T}{\partial K^2}.$$

So the state prices can be inferred from the prices of plain vanilla options with different strike prices, if these are available. In practice, such prices are only available for discrete strike prices, $K - \Delta K, K, K + \Delta K, \ldots$, in which case one can use the approximations

$$\psi_K^T \approx \frac{C_{K+\Delta K}^T - 2C_K^T + C_{K-\Delta K}^T}{(\Delta K)^2} \tag{9.77}$$

$$\approx \frac{P_{K+\Delta K}^T - 2P_K^T + P_{K-\Delta K}^T}{(\Delta K)^2}. \tag{9.78}$$

This argument was originally made in Breeden and Litzenberger (1978). Formula (9.77) can also be understood through the context of the discrete analysis in Example 7.7 earlier.

9.5.2 Proving the Black–Scholes PDE Formula

A thorough proof of the theorem requires keeping track of higher-order terms, just as when we took the limit of the binomial model for the call option. As before, we avoid this part of the analysis and sketch the proof. We first look at a proof that follows the original steps of Black and Scholes (1973).

Sketch of steps in the original derivation.

1. First it is argued that if a self-financed trading strategy leads to a locally risk-free value process, $dV^{\mathbf{h}} = k(t, S_t)V^{\mathbf{h}}\, dt$, then it must be that $k(t, S_t) \equiv r(t, S_t)$. This is natural, since otherwise there would be two risk-free rates at some point in time, which suggests an arbitrage opportunity.
2. Next it is assumed that $C_t = C(t, S_t)$ is a smooth function (can be verified once C_t has been constructed). Then Itô's lemma implies that $dC = (C_t + \hat{\mu}SC_S + \frac{1}{2}\sigma^2 C_{SS}S^2)\, dt + \sigma SC_S\, dW$.
3. Finally, one looks at the instantaneous dynamics of a portfolio that is long one share of contingent claim and short C_S shares of stock:
   - Value: $V = C - C_S S$.
   - Dynamics: $dV = dC - C_S\, dS$

$$= \left(C_t + \hat{\mu}SC_S + \frac{1}{2}\sigma^2 C_{SS}S^2 - C_S\hat{\mu}S\right) dt + (\sigma SC_S - \sigma SC_S)\, dW$$

$$= \left(C_t + \frac{1}{2}\sigma^2 C_{SS}S^2\right) dt.$$

Since this portfolio is locally risk-free, it must be that $dV = rV\, dt$ (see above) so

$$\left(C_t + \frac{1}{2}\sigma^2 C_{SS}S^2\right) = r(C - C_S S),$$

i.e.,

$$C_t + rSC_S + \frac{1}{2}\sigma^2 C_{SS}S^2 - rC = 0.$$

Thus, indeed, the Black–Scholes PDE must hold, otherwise there would be an arbitrage opportunity. □

There are some weaknesses with the above argument—most notably the smoothness properties of the pricing function, which are assumed rather than proved. The issue is that the call option—the price of which we a priori know nothing about—is used in the arbitrage strategy. A more modern approach, which is more in line with our previous no-arbitrage model—is to replicate the payoff of the option by trading in the stock and the bond, and then use the no-arbitrage argument to nail down the price of the option as that of the portfolio. The key result that allows this alternative approach is the following theorem, which shows that the value of any self-financing portfolio must satisfy the Black–Scholes PDE:

Theorem 9.13 (Black–Scholes PDE for a self-financing trading strategy). *In the Black–Scholes economy, the value process $V = V^{\mathbf{h}}$ of any self-financing portfolio process $\mathbf{h}_t$, where $\mathbf{h} = \mathbf{h}(t, S)$ is a smooth function, satisfies the Black–Scholes PDE*

$$V_t + rSV_S + \frac{1}{2}\sigma^2 V_{SS}S^2 - rV = 0.$$

A self-financing trading strategy is said to *replicate* the simple contingent claim, with payoff $\Phi(S(T))$, if $V^{\mathbf{h}}(T) = \Phi(S(T))$, a.s. Moreover, a market is said to be complete with respect to simple contingent claims if any simple contingent claim can be replicated.

The following theorem shows that the Black–Scholes economy is complete with respect to simple contingent claims, and how the solution to the Black–Scholes PDE allows the construction of a replicating portfolio for any simple payoff function.

Theorem 9.14. *Consider a simple contingent claim with time-T payoff $\Phi(S(T))$. Define $F(t, S)$ as the solution to the PDE*

$$F_t + rSF_S + \frac{1}{2}\sigma^2 F_{SS}S^2 - rF = 0,$$

$$F(T, S) = \Phi(S).$$

Then the contingent claim can be replicated by a self-financed portfolio with time-t value $V^{\mathbf{h}}(t, S_t) = F(t, S_t)$. The self-financed replicating portfolio trading strategy is defined as $\mathbf{h}_t = (h^B, h^S)' = (\frac{F - SF_S}{B}, F_S)'$.

It immediately follows that the time-0 value of the asset is $F(0, S_0)$.

Sketch of proof in modern derivation.

1. It is immediately clear that $\mathbf{h}_t$ is an adapted process, since it only depends on t and S_t.
2. It also follows immediately that $V_t = F(t, S_t)$ (and therefore specifically that $V_T = \Phi(S_T)$), since $\mathbf{h}_t'(B_t, S_t)' = (\frac{F-SF_S}{B}, F_S)(B_t, S_t)' = F - SF_S + F_S S = F$.
3. It remains to show that $\mathbf{h}_t$ is self-financed, which from (9.37) follows if $dV_t^{\mathbf{h}} = \mathbf{h}'\, ds = \mathbf{h}'(dB, dS)$. We have
   - $dV_t^{\mathbf{h}} = F_t\, dt + F_S\, dS + \frac{1}{2}F_{SS}(dS)^2 = F_t\, dt + F_S\, dS + \frac{\sigma^2}{2}S^2 F_{SS}\, dt,$
   - $\mathbf{h}_t'\, d(B, S)' = \frac{F-SF_S}{B} Br\, dt + F_S\, dS = (F - SF_S)r\, dt + F_S\, dS,$
   - so $dV_t^{\mathbf{h}} - \mathbf{h}_t'\, d(B, S)' = (F_t + \frac{\sigma^2}{2}S^2 F_{SS} - Fr + rSF_S)\, dt = 0 \times dt$ (because F satisfies Black–Scholes' PDE) and indeed the trading strategy is self-financed. □

So, because of the possibility of dynamic portfolio rebalancing, the stock and the bond are sufficient for the market to be complete with respect to simple contingent claims, even though there are an infinite number of possible states at T. This is in contrast to the one-period model, where there could be no more than two states for the market to be complete. In continuous time with diffusion processes, the market is typically complete if and only if the number of Brownian motions that affect asset prices is the same as the number of risky assets. A more detailed discussion of the proof of the Black–Scholes formula is found in Björk (2009).

Another way of deriving the Black–Scholes PDE (not just the pricing formula for the call option, which we did before) is as the limit of the binomial tree model, just as we derived the Black–Scholes formula via such a limit. Indeed, a step in the binomial tree model provides a law of motion, just like a PDE does. The law of motion in the binomial tree model is

$$C(t,S) = \frac{1}{R}(qC(t+\Delta t, uS) + (1-q)C(t+\Delta t, dS)),$$

or, using the definition of $q = \frac{R-d}{u-d}$,

$$C(t,S)R(u-d) = (R-d)C(t+\Delta t, uS) + (u-R)C(t+\Delta t, dS). \tag{9.79}$$

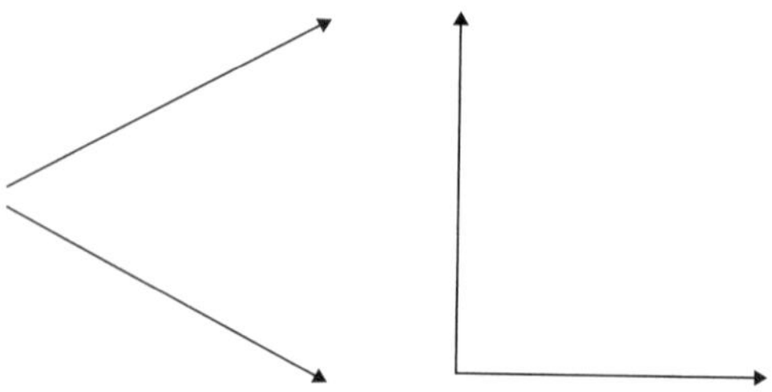

Figure 9.12: Different coordinates. Left: Binomial tree model. Right: Cartesian.

The binomial method corresponds to the left-hand panel in figure 9.12, in which $C(t,S)$ is calculated from values where both t (x-axis) and S have changes (y-axis). The right-hand panel corresponds to the PDE approach, where derivatives with respect to t and S are used, i.e., the coordinates are rectangular (Cartesian). However, using Taylor expansions, we can rewrite the law of motion in the binomial method in Cartesian coordinates. We use the Taylor expansion around $x=0$:

$$e^x = 1 + x + \frac{x^2}{2} + \text{h.o.t.},$$

where h.o.t. denotes higher-order terms.

Recalling that $u = e^{\sigma\sqrt{\Delta t}}$, $d = e^{-\sigma\sqrt{\Delta t}}$, we can write $uS = S(1+\sigma\sqrt{\Delta t} + \sigma^2\frac{\Delta t}{2}) + \text{h.o.t.}$ and $dS = S(1-\sigma\sqrt{\Delta t}+\sigma^2\frac{\Delta t}{2}) + \text{h.o.t.}$ Moreover, $R = e^{r\Delta t} = 1 + r\Delta t + \text{h.o.t.}$ We use this to expand the left-hand side of (9.79) and get

$$C(t,S)R(u-d) = C(1+r\Delta t)2\sigma\sqrt{\Delta t} + \text{h.o.t.}$$

For the right-hand side of (9.79), we have

$$\begin{aligned}
\text{R.H.S.} &= (R-d)C(t+\Delta t, uS) + (u-R)C(t+\Delta t, dS)\\
&= (-r\Delta t + \sigma\sqrt{\Delta t} + \sigma^2\tfrac{\Delta t}{2})\\
&\quad \times \left(C + C_t\Delta t + S(-\sigma\sqrt{\Delta t} + \sigma^2\tfrac{\Delta t}{2})C_S + S^2\sigma^2\tfrac{\Delta t C_{SS}}{2}\right)\\
&\quad + (r\Delta t + \sigma\sqrt{\Delta t} - \sigma^2\tfrac{\Delta t}{2})\\
&\qquad \times \left(C + C_t\Delta t + S(\sigma\sqrt{\Delta t} + \sigma^2\tfrac{\Delta t}{2})C_S + S^2\sigma^2\tfrac{\Delta t C_{SS}}{2}\right) + \text{h.o.t.},
\end{aligned}$$

which after some algebra reduces to

$$\text{R.H.S.} = \sigma\sqrt{\Delta t}(2rS\Delta t C_S + S^2\Delta t\sigma^2 C_{SS} + 2C + 2C_t\Delta t) + \text{h.o.t.}$$

Neglecting higher-order terms, it must therefore be that

$$C(1+r\Delta t)2\sigma\sqrt{\Delta t} = \sigma\sqrt{\Delta t}(2rS\Delta t C_S + S^2\Delta t\sigma^2 C_{SS} + 2C + 2C_t\Delta t),$$

and by dividing both sides by $2\sigma\sqrt{\Delta t}$, we get

$$C(1+r\Delta t) = rS\Delta t C_S + S^2\Delta t\frac{\sigma^2}{2}C_{SS} + C + C_t\Delta t,$$

and subtracting C, then dividing by Δt on both sides, finally gives us

$$rC = rSC_S + S^2\frac{\sigma^2}{2}C_{SS} + C_t,$$

i.e.,

$$C_t + rSC_S + S^2\frac{\sigma^2}{2}C_{SS} - rC = 0.$$

Again, we arrive at Black–Scholes' PDE, this time from the law of motion associated with the binomial model!

9.5.3 Risk-Neutral Formulation

Once we know that the option price satisfies the Black–Scholes PDE (with constant coefficients), we can also use Feynman–Kac to derive an explicit solution for the price. Specifically, from theorems 9.8 and 9.11, it is clear that the price of an option can be written *as if* it would be the discounted expectation of the payoff,

$$F(t,s) = e^{-r(T-t)} E_t^{\mathbb{Q}}[\Phi(S(T))|S(t)=s], \tag{9.80}$$

given that the underlying assets follow the stochastic processes

$$\frac{dB}{B} = r\,dt, \tag{9.81}$$

$$\frac{dS}{S} = r\,dt + \sigma\,dW^{Q}, \tag{9.82}$$

for some Wiener process, W_t^{Q}. For the time being, we do not discuss further how to interpret this Wiener process—although we set $\mathbb{Q}$ as a superscript as if it is a "risk-neutral" process, with associated $\mathbb{Q}$ measure. The interpretation for now is the following:

1. The price is the solution to the PDE (9.11).
2. Feynman–Kac's theorem tells us that the solution to that PDE can be found by looking up the formula for the expectation of a stochastic process.

Feynman–Kac's theorem thus provides us with a powerful "solution machine," where solutions to PDEs can be found by checking out statistical expectations. Technically, the key difference between the "risk-neutral expectation" PDE and the PDE based on true stock price dynamics is that $\hat{\mu}$ in (9.74) is replaced by r in (9.82).

The Black–Scholes formula for the call option in theorem 9.11 can now be calculated via (9.80). Indeed,

$$C = e^{-rT} E^{\mathbb{Q}}[(S_T - K)_+].$$

The following steps lead to the Black–Scholes option pricing formula:

1. Define $N(x)$ as the cumulative normal distribution, $N(x) = \int_{-\infty}^{x} \varphi(y)\,dy$, where $\varphi(y) = \frac{1}{\sqrt{2\pi}} e^{-\frac{y^2}{2}}$. Then it follows that if we define $\varphi_{\mu,\sigma}(y) = \frac{1}{\sqrt{2\pi\sigma^2}} e^{-\frac{(y-\mu)^2}{2}}$, we have $\int_{-\infty}^{x} \varphi_{\mu,\sigma}(y)\,dy = N(\frac{x-\mu}{\sigma})$.
2. Moreover, since $N(\infty) = 1$, and $N(-x) = 1 - N(x)$, we have $\int_{x}^{\infty} \varphi_{\mu,\sigma}(y)\,dy = 1 - N(\frac{x-\mu}{\sigma}) = N(\frac{\mu-x}{\sigma})$.
3. We want to calculate

   $$C = e^{-rT} E^{\mathbb{Q}}[(S_T - K)_+] = e^{-rT} E^{\mathbb{Q}}[(Se^{y} - K)_+],$$

   where $y = \log(\frac{S_T}{S}) \sim N((r - \frac{\sigma^2}{2})T, \sigma^2 T) = N(\hat{\mu}, \hat{\sigma}^2)$.
4. Thus,

   $$C = e^{-rT} \int_{-\infty}^{\infty} (Se^{y} - K)_+ \varphi_{\hat{\mu},\hat{\sigma}}(y)\,dy = e^{-rT} \int_{y=\ln(\frac{K}{S})}^{\infty} (\underbrace{Se^{y}}_{(i)} - \underbrace{K}_{(ii)}) \varphi_{\hat{\mu},\hat{\sigma}}(y)\,dy.$$

5. To evaluate the second term, (ii), we write

$$-Ke^{-rT}\int_{y=\ln(\frac{K}{S})}^{\infty}\varphi_{\hat{\mu},\hat{\sigma}}(y)\,dy = -Ke^{-rT}N\Big(\frac{\hat{\mu}-\ln(\frac{K}{S})}{\hat{\sigma}}\Big) = -Ke^{-rT}N(x-\sigma\sqrt{T}).$$

6. The first term, (i), is

$$S\int_{y=\ln(\frac{K}{S})}^{\infty}e^{y-rT}\varphi_{\hat{\mu},\hat{\sigma}}(y)\,dy = S\frac{1}{\sqrt{2\pi\hat{\sigma}^2}}\int_{y=\ln(\frac{K}{S})}^{\infty}e^{y-rT}e^{-\frac{(y-\hat{\mu})^2}{2\hat{\sigma}^2}}\,dy.$$

(a) We rewrite the first term as

$$S\frac{1}{\sqrt{2\pi\hat{\sigma}^2}}\int_{y=\ln(\frac{K}{S})}^{\infty}e^{-\frac{1}{2\hat{\sigma}^2}(2rT\hat{\sigma}^2-2y\hat{\sigma}^2+(y-\hat{\mu})^2)}\,dy.$$

(b) We rewrite the term in the exponent as

$$\begin{aligned}
&2rT\hat{\sigma}^2 - 2y\hat{\sigma}^2 + (y-\hat{\mu})^2\\
&= 2rT\hat{\sigma}^2 - 2y\hat{\sigma}^2 + y^2 + \hat{\mu}^2 - 2\hat{\mu}y\\
&= y^2 - 2y(\hat{\mu}+\hat{\sigma}^2) + (\hat{\mu}+\hat{\sigma}^2)^2 - (\hat{\mu}+\hat{\sigma}^2)^2 + 2rT\hat{\sigma}^2 + \hat{\mu}^2\\
&= (y-\hat{\sigma}^2-\hat{\mu})^2 - (\hat{\mu}+\hat{\sigma}^2)^2 + 2rT\hat{\sigma}^2 + \hat{\mu}^2\\
&= (y-\hat{\sigma}^2-\hat{\mu})^2 - \hat{\mu}^2 - \hat{\sigma}^4 - 2\hat{\mu}\hat{\sigma}^2 + 2rT\hat{\sigma}^2 + \hat{\mu}^2\\
&= (y-\hat{\sigma}^2-\hat{\mu})^2 - \hat{\sigma}^2(\hat{\sigma}^2 + 2\hat{\mu} - 2rT)\\
&= (y-\hat{\sigma}^2-\hat{\mu})^2 - \hat{\sigma}^2\Big(\sigma^2T + 2\Big(rT - \frac{\sigma^2}{2}T\Big) - 2rT\Big)\\
&= (y-\hat{\sigma}^2-\hat{\mu})^2.
\end{aligned}$$

(c) Thus, the first term is

$$S\frac{1}{\sqrt{2\pi\hat{\sigma}^2}}\int_{y=\ln(\frac{K}{S})}^{\infty}e^{-\frac{(y-\hat{\sigma}^2-\hat{\mu})^2}{2\hat{\sigma}^2}}\,dz = S\frac{1}{\sqrt{2\pi\hat{\sigma}^2}}\int_{z=\ln(\frac{K}{S})-\hat{\sigma}^2}^{\infty}e^{-\frac{(z-\hat{\mu})^2}{2\hat{\sigma}^2}}\,dz,$$

where $z = y - \hat{\sigma}^2$.

(d) We therefore get that the first term equals

$$SN\Big(\frac{\hat{\mu}-(\ln(\frac{K}{S})-\hat{\sigma}^2)}{\hat{\sigma}^2}\Big) = SN\Big(\frac{(r-\frac{\sigma^2}{2})T - \ln(\frac{K}{S}) + \sigma^2T}{\sigma\sqrt{T}}\Big) = SN(x).$$

7. Thus, putting the first and second steps together we get the call option formula

$$C = SN(x) - Ke^{-rT}N(x-\sigma\sqrt{T}),$$

where $x = \frac{\ln(\frac{S}{K})+(r+\frac{\sigma^2}{2})T}{\sigma\sqrt{T}}$. □

We have arrived at the risk-neutral pricing formula:

Theorem 9.15 (Risk-neutral Black–Scholes pricing formula)**.** *Consider a simple contingent claim with time-T payoff $\Phi(S(T))$. Then the value of the claim at t is*

$$V_t = e^{-r(T-t)}E_t^{\mathbb{Q}}[\Phi(S(T))|S(t)=s],$$

where, under the $\mathbb{Q}$ measure, S satisfies the dynamics $\frac{dS}{S} = r\,dt + \sigma\,dW^{\mathbb{Q}}$.

9.5.4 Varying Volatility and Interest Rates

The Black–Scholes argument is also valid when the volatility and interest rate vary. Indeed, since the replicating portfolio argument is completely local, it can also be applied when the instantaneous values of the short rate and volatility are $r_t = r(t, S_t)$ and $\sigma_t = \sigma(t, S_t)$, to get the PDE formulation:

Theorem 9.16 (Black–Scholes PDE—variable coefficients). *Consider a simple contingent claim with time-T payoff $\Phi(S(T))$. Define $F(t,S)$ as the solution to the PDE*

$$F_t + r(t,S)SF_S + \frac{1}{2}\sigma(t,S)^2 F_{SS}S^2 - r(t,S)F = 0,$$
$$F(T,S) = \Phi(S).$$

Then the contingent claim can be replicated by a self-financed portfolio with time-t value $V^{\mathbf{h}}(t,S_t) = F(t,S_t)$. The self-financed replicating portfolio trading strategy is defined as $\mathbf{h}_t = (h^B, h^S)' = (\frac{F-SF_S}{B}, F_S)'$.

Similarly, when the volatility and interest rate vary, we get the corresponding risk-neutral formulation:

Theorem 9.17 (Risk-neutral Black–Scholes—variable coefficients). *Consider a simple contingent claim with time-T payoff $\Phi(S(T))$. Then the value of the claim at t is*

$$V_t = E_t^{\mathbb{Q}}\left[e^{-\int_0^T r_s\,ds}\Phi(S(T))\right],$$

where under the $\mathbb{Q}$ measure, S satisfies the dynamics $\frac{dS}{S} = r_t\,dt + \sigma_t\,dW^{\mathbb{Q}}$.

Note that the discount factor $e^{-\int_0^T r_s\,ds}$ needs to go inside the expectation operator in this case, since it stochastic. Indeed, although the short rate, r_t, is known at t (the bond is indeed risk-free in the very short run), future values of r_s are not. So the value at time t of a bond that pays \$1 at T, $\Phi(B(T)) \equiv 1$, is, according to the theorem,

$$B_{t,T} = E_t^{\mathbb{Q}}\left[e^{-\int_0^T r_s\,ds}\right].$$

The value of the short rate, r_t, is not sufficient to determine $B_{t,T}$. We will consider additional assumptions needed to price bonds later, in section 10.3.

Consider the value of buying a short-term bond at t and instantaneously rolling it over, reinvesting the proceeds in short-term bonds at $t + dt, t + 2\,dt, \ldots,$ until T. The instantaneous return on this strategy is then $r_t\,dt$, and the total gross return over the period is

$$R_{t,T} = e^{\int_t^T r_s\,ds}.$$

This is the continuous-time version of the return formula we introduced in the multiperiod model, in chapter 8; see (8.12). We also write $R_T = R_{0,T}$. The risk-neutral pricing formula can then equivalently be written as

$$V_t = E_t^{\mathbb{Q}}[R_{t,T}^{-1}\Phi(S(T))].$$

9.6 Girsanov's Theorem

As discussed in the previous section, the Feynman–Kac theorem allows us to reformulate the Black–Scholes PDE for a simple contingent claim—which arises via a portfolio replication

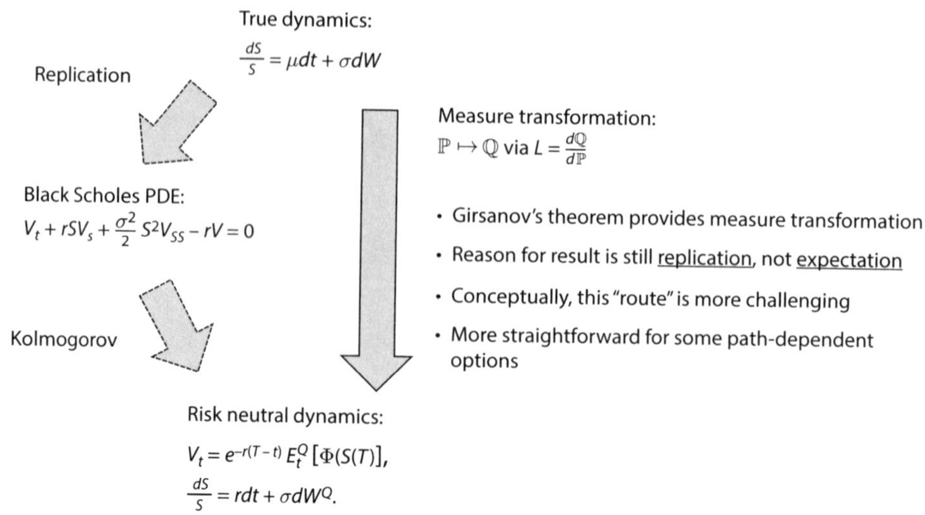

Figure 9.13: Risk-neutral pricing via measure transformation.

argument—with a formulation of the price as a discounted expectation where the dynamics of the stock price is artificial (risk-neutral) instead of true, since r replaces $\hat{\mu}$. This argument works well with simple contingent claims, but there are other claims, e.g., with path dependence, for which the PDE formulation is not as straightforward (although with some extra work it is often possible to take the PDE approach for such claims too). We will therefore use another approach to define a risk-neutral pricing formula: a measure transformation.

Recall from the one-period model that by multiplying by a likelihood ratio, $L = \frac{d\mathbb{Q}}{d\mathbb{P}}$, we could transform from one probability measure to another. We used this trick to define $\mathbb{Q}$ probabilities with which prices could be expressed as discounted expectations. This is exactly the approach we will take now. We will construct an appropriate $\mathbb{Q}$ measure by using *Girsanov's theorem*, which provides a general method for generating equivalent measure transformations for diffusion processes. Once the risk-neutral measure is constructed, it can be used to price general contingent claims, not only simple ones. The situation is thus as in figure 9.13. Our approach so far has been to take the left "route" and obtain a risk-neutral formulation via a replication argument, leading to Black–Scholes' PDE, and then to use Feynman–Kac's theorem to do an "as if" risk-neutral argument. Our new approach is to go directly to the risk-neutral formulation via a measure transformation, i.e., to take the "route" to the right in the figure.

Before discussing Girsanov's theorem, we need to think about what makes $\mathbb{Q}$ an appropriate risk-neutral measure. A risk-neutral measure should be such that for any self-financed portfolio with value V_t, $0 \leq t \leq T$, the pricing formula

$$V_t = E_t^{\mathbb{Q}}[R_{t,T}^{-1} V_T]$$

holds. It turns out that it is actually sufficient to study a small subset of all portfolios to ensure that $\mathbb{Q}$ is the risk-neutral measure.

Let us study the following market, in which there is a risk-free asset with associated short-rate process, $\{r_s\}_s$, where $\int_0^t |r_s|\, ds < \infty$ a.s.,

$$\frac{dB_t}{B_t} = r_t\, dt.$$

As before, we define the gross return process $R_{t,T} = e^{\int_t^T r(s)\,ds} < \infty$ a.s., and $R_T = R_{0,T}$. We also use the notation S_t^0 for the bond process ($S_t^0 \equiv B_t$). Note that $dR_t = r_t R_t\,dt$, so the gross return process is locally risk-free (i.e., it contains no Brownian term), just like the short-term bond.

There are N risky assets with true ($\mathbb{P}$) price dynamics

$$\frac{dS_t^i}{S_t^i} = \hat{\mu}_t^i\,dt + \sigma_t^i\,dV_t^i, \quad i = 1, \dots, N, \tag{9.83}$$

written in correlated form, where $\mathrm{Cov}(dV_t^i, dV_t^j) = \rho_t^{ij}\,dt$. We assume that no assets pay dividends (this assumptions is straightforward to relax). The total price system of these assets is then $\mathbf{s}_t = (S_t^0, S_t^1, \dots, S_t^N)'$.

An equivalent martingale measure (EMM) is now defined as follows:

Definition 9.12 (EMM). The probability measure $\mathbb{Q}$ is an equivalent martingale measure if $\mathbb{Q} \sim \mathbb{P}$, and $S_t^i = E_t^{\mathbb{Q}}[R_{t,T}^{-1} S_T^i]$, for $i = 1, \dots, N$.

The definition of an EMM thus requires that the measure is equivalent to the true measure, and that it prices the N primitive assets correctly (the risk-free asset is per definition priced correctly) when using the risk-neutral pricing formula. The equivalent differential version of the EMM formula is

$$\frac{dS_t^i}{S_t^i} = r_t\,dt + \sigma_t^i\,dV_t^{\mathbb{Q},i}, \quad i = 1, \dots, N.$$

This looks reasonable, except that it does not seem to ensure that the EMM also prices the payoffs that can be generated through dynamic portfolio strategies. Recall that we want to be able to calculate the price of any contingent claim within the asset span, e.g., the price of a call option on stock n, $1 \le n \le N$. The following result shows that as long as the measure is an EMM in the sense defined above, it also prices payoffs generated by a self-financed dynamic trading strategy correctly.

Proposition 9.7. *Assume that $\mathbb{Q}$ is an EMM, and that $\mathbf{h}_t$ is a self-financed trading strategy (which needs to satisfy some technical well-behavedness conditions). Then*

$$V_0^{\mathbf{h}} = \mathbf{h}_0' \mathbf{s}_0 = E_0^{\mathbb{Q}}[R_T^{-1} V_T^{\mathbf{h}}]. \tag{9.84}$$

Sketch of proof. Define $\mathbf{v}_t = R_t^{-1}\mathbf{s}_t$. The numeraire invariance principle, see section 10.5, implies that $\mathbf{h}_t$ is also self-financed with respect to $\mathbf{v}$. We have $V_0^{\mathbf{h}} = \mathbf{h}_0'\mathbf{v}_0$. Furthermore, define $\xi_t = E_t^{\mathbb{P}}[\xi_T]$, for the Radon–Nikodym derivative, ξ_T, which satisfies $E_t^{\mathbb{Q}}[X] = E_t^{\mathbb{P}}[\xi_T X]$ for random variables, X. Note that $\xi_0 = 1$. We study

$$E_0^{\mathbb{Q}}[\mathbf{h}_T'\mathbf{v}_T] = E_0^{\mathbb{P}}[\xi_T(\mathbf{h}_T'\mathbf{v}_T)] = \xi_0(\mathbf{h}_0'\mathbf{v}_0) + E^{\mathbb{P}}\left[\int_0^T d(\xi_t\mathbf{h}_t'\mathbf{v}_t)\right] = \mathbf{h}_0\mathbf{s}_0 + E^{\mathbb{P}}\left[\int_0^T d(\xi_t\mathbf{h}_t'\mathbf{v}_t)\right].$$

Thus, if we can show that $E_0^{\mathbb{P}}[\int_0^T d(\xi_0\mathbf{h}_0'\mathbf{v}_0)] = 0$, we are done. We have

$$d(\xi_t\mathbf{h}_t'\mathbf{v}_t) = \mathbf{h}_t'\,d(\xi_t\mathbf{v}_t) + d\mathbf{h}_t'(\xi_t\mathbf{v}_t + d(\xi_t\mathbf{v}_t)).$$

Since $\xi_t\mathbf{v}_t$ is a martingale under the $\mathbb{P}$ measure, $E_0^{\mathbb{P}}[\int_0^T \mathbf{h}_t'\,d(\xi_t'\mathbf{v}_t)] = 0$, by the martingale property, so the first term vanishes. Furthermore, the differentials in the second and third terms can be written as $d\mathbf{h}_t'(\mathbf{v}_t + d\mathbf{v}_t)(\xi_t + d\xi_t)$, and since the portfolio is self-financed, $d\mathbf{h}_t'(\mathbf{v}_t + d\mathbf{v}_t) \equiv 0$ for all t, see (9.36), so the second term also vanishes. Therefore the result follows. □

Remark 9.3. A more stringent proof would use the martingale representation theorem.

Remark 9.4. A consequence of the proposition is that $E_t^{\mathbb{Q}}[dV_t^{\mathbf{h}}] = r_t V_t^{\mathbf{h}}\, dt$ for any self-financed trading strategy. Indeed, this is the differential version of the EMM pricing formula (9.84).

The theorem can also be generalized to trading strategies that are not self-financed. Recall that $dF_t^{\mathbf{h}}$ represents the instantaneous dividends generated by a general trading strategy. In the general case, the pricing relation becomes

$$V_0^{\mathbf{h}} = \mathbf{h}_0' \mathbf{s}_0 = E_0^{\mathbb{Q}}\left[\int_0^T R_t^{-1}\, dF_t^{\mathbf{h}} + R_T^{-1} V_T^{\mathbf{h}}\right]. \tag{9.85}$$

Note that neither proposition 9.7 nor equation (9.85) assumes that the payoff function, $V_T^{\mathbf{h}}$, is simple. In general, $V_T^{\mathbf{h}}$, as well as $dF_t^{\mathbf{h}}$, can have a complicated path-dependent behavior.

So does this mean that the price of any option within the asset span of the primitive asset is completely nailed down by the EMM? Well, we are not quite there yet. Recall that in the static model we also needed to make a no-arbitrage assumption. Without such an assumption, there is nothing that links the price of the asset with the value of the trading strategy that generates the same payoff. The fundamental theorem in the static case, furthermore, ensures that when the no-arbitrage assumption is satisfied, the EMM exists.

Ideally, we would like to carry out exactly the same argument in the continuous setting, i.e., assume no arbitrage and show that the EMM must exist. The situation is a lot trickier in the continuous-time setting though:

- The allowed dynamic portfolio strategies need to be restricted to rule out so-called doubling strategies, which otherwise would allow an investor to create arbitrages in markets that we would like to view as being arbitrage-free.
- It is quite straightforward to show that the existence of a risk-neutral measure that prices *all* assets (not just the primitive ones) implies that there is no arbitrage in the market.
- It is much more challenging to ensure that no arbitrage implies the existence of a risk-neutral measure that prices all such assets. Indeed, under the standard definition of no arbitrage, the existence of such a measure is *not* ensured. It is therefore necessary to weaken the definition of what constitutes an arbitrage, so that fewer markets are free from arbitrage (namely, exactly those for which no risk-neutral measure exists). It is shown in Delbaen and Schachermayer (1994), that the correct definition is that of a so-called *no free lunch with vanishing risk* (NFLVR), which makes equivalence hold.

The interested reader is referred to Björk (2009, chapter 10). Important contributions in the theory of risk-neutral pricing are made in Cox and Ross (1976), Harrison and Kreps (1979), Harrison and Pliska (1981), and Delbaen and Schachermayer (1994, 1998). Going forward, we assume that the NFLVR condition is satisfied, so that an equivalent martingale measure exists, and we now explore how it can be constructed.

9.6.1 An Insightful Example

We start with an example that shows how, given an arithmetic Brownian motion, X_t, with drift, μ, under the true $\mathbb{P}$ measure, we can construct another probability measure, $\mathbb{Q}$, under which the drift of X_t is 0, i.e., under which X_t is a martingale. We have

$$dX_t = \mu\, dt + \sigma\, dW_t,$$

and equivalently,

$$X_t = \mu t + \sigma W_t, \quad t \le T.$$

We define the variable

$$W_t^{\mathbb{Q}} = \frac{\mu}{\sigma} t + W_t = \lambda t + W_t,$$

and it then follows that

$$dX_t = \sigma \, dW_t^{\mathbb{Q}},$$

so if we can find a probability measure, $\mathbb{Q}$, under which $W_t^{\mathbb{Q}}$ is a Wiener process, then X_t is a martingale under the new probability measure (in the probability space $(\Omega, \mathcal{F}_T, \mathbb{Q})$). This follows from the martingale property.

Remember that the way to construct a new equivalent measure in the static case is to multiply the $\mathbb{P}$ probabilities by a Radon–Nikodym derivative, a likelihood ratio. Similarly, for the multi-period model we multiplied by a likelihood process. Following this approach, we want to find a likelihood process, ξ_t, such that the $\mathbb{Q}$ measure defined as $E_0^{\mathbb{Q}}[Z_t] = E_0^P[\xi_t Z_t]$ has the property that $W_t^{\mathbb{Q}}$ is a Wiener process under $\mathbb{Q}$. In other words, we want $\xi_t W_t^{\mathbb{Q}} \sim N(0, t)$.

Also, recall that the $\mathbb{P}$ probability density function of $W_t^{\mathbb{Q}}$, $\mathbb{P}(W_t^{\mathbb{Q}} = \lambda t + x) = \mathbb{P}(W_t = x)$, is[10]

$$\mathbb{P}(W_t = x) = \frac{1}{\sqrt{2\pi t}} e^{-\frac{x^2}{2t}} \, dx.$$

We choose $\xi_t = e^{-\lambda W_t - \lambda^2 \frac{t}{2}}$, so

$$\mathbb{Q}(W_t^{\mathbb{Q}} = \lambda t + x) = e^{-\lambda x - \lambda^2 \frac{t}{2}} \frac{1}{\sqrt{2\pi t}} e^{-\frac{x^2}{2t}} \, dx = \frac{1}{\sqrt{2\pi t}} e^{-\frac{(\lambda t + x)^2}{2t}} \, dx.$$

The $\mathbb{Q}$ distribution of $W_t^{\mathbb{Q}}$ is then that of a Wiener process! The other properties of the Wiener process in $\mathbb{Q}$-space can also be verified.

Now, this may seem confusing. How can it be that both

$$dX_t = \mu \, dt + \sigma \, dW_t \quad \text{and} \quad dX_t = \sigma \, dW_t^{\mathbb{Q}},$$

where both W_t and $W_t^{\mathbb{Q}}$ are Wiener processes? Note that, just as in the static case, we are working with abstract probability spaces, for which the only restrictions are that they need to satisfy some axioms. The Brownian motion, W_t, may indeed be a Wiener process in the "true" physical sense. The differential formula for the other process, $W_t^{\mathbb{Q}}$, however, $dX_t = \sigma \, dW_t^{\mathbb{Q}}$, is really just a convenient way of expressing the "probability" associated with different observed sample paths of X_t by the abstract measure $\mathbb{Q}$. It does *not* express the true dynamics of a Wiener process.

The idea is shown in figures 9.14 and 9.15. Here we have simulated some possible realized sample paths of X_t, $0 \le t \le T$, where $T = 100$, using the true dynamics, with $\mu > 0$, as shown in the first figure. The line represents the expected value of X_t over time, and naturally the realized sample paths are centered around that line, with a few outliers.

Figure 9.15 shows the probability distributions the two measures associate with ending up at a specific point at $t = T$. The $\mathbb{Q}$ measure treats X_t as if it is a martingale, and "expects it" to stay around 0. When an observed sample path of X_t which ends up somewhere close to μT at time T is observed, the $\mathbb{P}$ measure will not be "surprised" since this is what is expected. The $\mathbb{Q}$ measure on the other hand will treat this as a very unlikely sample path that went far above what was expected (when $\mu > 0$). Both measures, of course, agree on the observed X_t dynamics.

[10] Here we use infinitesimal notation and write $\mathbb{P}(W_t = x)$ as shorthand for $\mathbb{P}(W_t \in [x, x + dx])$.

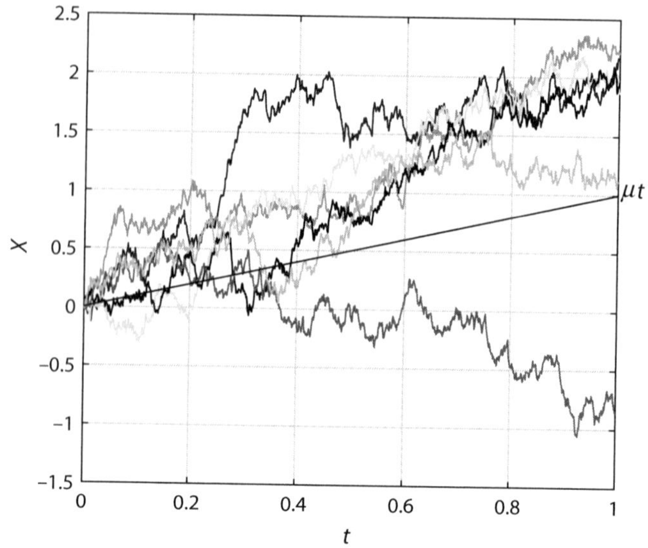

Figure 9.14: Some possible realized sample paths of X_t.

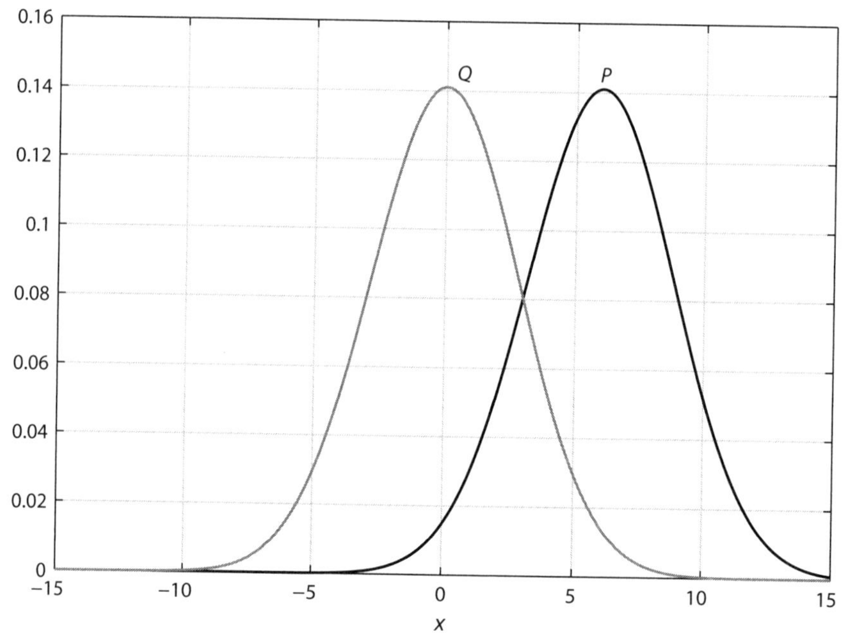

Figure 9.15: Associated probabilities with different outcomes.

This is the only interpretation we are allowed to have of the formula $dX_t = \sigma \, dW_t^{\mathbb{Q}}$: it is a convenient way of expressing the numbers (probabilities) that the $\mathbb{Q}$ measure associates with specific sample paths of X_t. These numbers do not represent true probabilities, but may be useful for other purposes, e.g., for expressing the price of an asset as a discounted expectation.

The example above captures much of the intuition behind how Girsanov's theorem works. We use a constructive approach to go from one probability measure to another by multiplying by a strictly positive likelihood ratio. The multiplication changes the drift term (in this case from μ to 0), but does not affect the volatility, σ. That σ does not change should not come as a surprise upon some reflection. Since the quadratic variation of X over any time period, $[t_1, t_2]$, is almost surely $\sigma^2(t_2 - t_1)$, it is impossible to change it by multiplying the sample paths by some finite likelihood function. Moreover, since quadratic variation and volatility are directly linked via σ, this also means that σ cannot be changed by a likelihood transformation.

Note that the disagreement between the two measures about the drift terms of the two processes, W_t and $W_t^{\mathbb{Q}}$, is $\lambda = \frac{\mu}{\sigma}$, i.e., in the $\mathbb{P}$ measure W_t is a Wiener process, whereas $W_t^{\mathbb{Q}}$ has drift term $-\lambda$. In the $\mathbb{Q}$ measure, $W_t^{\mathbb{Q}}$ is a Wiener process, whereas W_t has drift term λ. The generalization Girsanov's theorem provides is to allow the same type of measure transformation for adapted diffusion processes with variable coefficients (as long as they satisfy some growth conditions).

Theorem 9.18 (Girsanov's theorem). *Assume that θ_t, $0 \le t \le T$, is an adapted process that satisfies* Novikov's condition: $E_0^{\mathbb{P}}[e^{\frac{1}{2}\int_0^T \theta_s^2\, ds}] < \infty$. *Define*

- *the process* $\xi_t = e^{-\int_0^t \theta_s\, dW_s - \frac{1}{2}\int_0^t \theta_s^2\, ds}$,
- *the process* $W_t^{\mathbb{Q}} = W_t + \int_0^t \theta_s\, ds$, *(i.e.,* $dW_t^{\mathbb{Q}} = dW_t + \theta_t\, dt$*),*
- *and the equivalent measure,* $\mathbb{Q} \sim \mathbb{P}$*, defined via the likelihood process, such that* $E_0^{\mathbb{Q}}[Z_T] = E_0^{\mathbb{P}}[\xi_T Z_T]$*, for arbitrary r.v.'s* Z_T.

Then $W_t^{\mathbb{Q}}$ *is a Wiener process under the* $\mathbb{Q}$ *measure.*

We see that the constant drift term in the insightful example above, $\lambda = \frac{\mu}{\sigma}$, is replaced by the general adapted process θ_t in Girsanov's theorem.

We make several observations. First, from Itô's lemma,

$$d\xi_t = -\xi_t \theta_t\, dW_t.$$

Second, from the martingale property, ξ_t is therefore a $\mathbb{P}$-martingale: $\xi_t = E_t^P[\xi_T | \mathcal{F}_t]$. Specifically, $E_0^P[\xi_T] = 1$. The construction of $\mathbb{Q}$ is therefore justified. Third, it follows that

$$E_t^{\mathbb{Q}}[Z_T] = E_t^{\mathbb{P}}\left[\frac{\xi_T}{\xi_t} Z_T\right], \quad 0 \le t \le T.$$

We thus have a powerful method to create $\mathbb{Q}$ probabilities from $\mathbb{P}$ probabilities, and associated $\mathbb{Q}$ Wiener processes from $\mathbb{P}$ Wiener processes. Indeed, we can use Girsanov to construct a transformation to any drift term, not only to 0. This is helpful for us, since to satisfy the EMM conditions we will typically want to transform an asset's drift term from $\hat{\mu}$ to r. This is because it is the *discounted* asset price process that should be a martingale under the EMM condition.

We achieve the general drift transformation from the following result:

Proposition 9.8. *Let X_t be an Itô process:*

$$dX_t = \mu_t\, dt + \sigma_t\, dW_t.$$

For some adapted process v_t (in L^1), define

$$\theta_t = \frac{\mu_t - v_t}{\sigma_t}.$$

If θ_t satisfies Novikov's condition, then X_t is also an Itô process with respect to the $\mathbb{Q}$ measure introduced by Girsanov's theorem, and

$$dX_t = v_t\, dt + \sigma_t\, dW_t^{\mathbb{Q}}.$$

The proposition thus shows that the drift term can be changed arbitrarily by varying v_t, whereas the volatility, σ_t, stays the same.

Example 9.12. We use Girsanov's theorem to derive the risk-neutral asset dynamics, pricing formula, and stochastic discount factor in the Black–Scholes economy,

$$\frac{dB}{B} = r\,dt,$$
$$\frac{dS}{S} = \hat{\mu}\,dt + \sigma\,dW.$$

We want to find the measure transformation that leads to the risk-neutral stock dynamics

$$\frac{dS}{S} = r\,dt + \sigma\,dW.$$

It follows that we should define

$$\theta_t = \frac{\hat{\mu}S_t - rS_t}{\sigma S_t} = \frac{\hat{\mu} - r}{\sigma},$$

with associated likelihood function

$$\xi_t = e^{-\int_0^t \theta_s\,dW_s - \frac{1}{2}\int_0^t \theta_s^2\,ds} = e^{-\frac{\hat{\mu}-r}{\sigma}W_t - \frac{t}{2}\left(\frac{\hat{\mu}-r}{\sigma}\right)^2}.$$

We next state the multidimensional version of Girsanov's theorem:

Theorem 9.19 (Girsanov's theorem in multiple dimensions). *Assume that θ_t is a k-dimensional adapted process, $\theta\colon [0,T]\times\Omega \to \mathbb{R}^k$, on a k-dimensional Wiener process, $\mathbf{W}_t$, and that θ_t satisfies* Novikov's condition: $E_0^{\mathbb{P}}[e^{\frac{1}{2}\int_0^t \theta_s'\theta_s\,ds}] < \infty$, $0 \le t \le T$. *Define*

- *the process* $\xi_t = e^{-\int_0^t \theta_s'\,d\mathbf{W}_s - \frac{1}{2}\int_0^t \theta_s'\theta_s\,ds}$,
- *the process* $\mathbf{W}_t^{\mathbb{Q}} = \mathbf{W}_t + \int_0^t \theta_s\,ds$ *(i.e.,* $d\mathbf{W}_t^{\mathbb{Q}} = d\mathbf{W}_t + \theta_t\,dt$*),*
- *and the equivalent measure,* $\mathbb{Q}\sim\mathbb{P}$, *via the likelihood process* $E_0^{\mathbb{Q}}[Z_T] = E_0^{\mathbb{P}}[\xi_T Z_T]$, *for arbitrary r.v.* Z_T.

Then $\mathbf{W}_t^{\mathbb{Q}}$ *is a k-dimensional Wiener process under the* $\mathbb{Q}$ *measure.*

The arbitrary drift transformation can then be carried out in multiple dimensions, as follows: Let X_t be an N-dimensional Itô process:

$$d\mathbf{X}_t = \mu_t\,dt + \sigma_t\,d\mathbf{W}_t.$$

For some adapted process $\mathbf{v}_t$ (in L^1), define

$$\theta_t = \sigma_t^{-1}(\mu_t - \mathbf{v}_t).$$

If θ_t satisfies Novikov's condition, then $\mathbf{X}_t$ is also an Itô process with respect to the $\mathbb{Q}$ measure introduced by Girsanov's theorem, and

$$d\mathbf{X}_t = \mathbf{v}_t\,dt + \sigma_t\,d\mathbf{W}_t^{\mathbb{Q}}.$$

Furthermore, Itô's lemma implies that $d\xi_t = -\xi_t\theta_t'\,d\mathbf{W}_t$.

We use theorem 9.19 to create an EMM in the multi-asset market. In uncorrelated form (9.83) can be written as

$$d\mathbf{z}_t = \Lambda_{\mathbf{z}_t}\hat{\mu}_t\,dt + \Lambda_{\mathbf{z}_t}\sigma_t\,d\mathbf{W}_t, \tag{9.86}$$

where $\mathbf{z}_t = (S_t^1, S_t^2, \ldots, S_t^N)'$ and $\Lambda_{\mathbf{z}_t} = \text{diag}(\mathbf{z}_t)$. By choosing $\mathbf{v}_t = r_t\mathbf{z}_t$ in the drift transformation, we get $\theta_t = \sigma_t^{-1}(\hat{\mu}_t - r_t\mathbf{1})$, and from theorem 9.19 the likelihood ratio process ξ_t and associated $\mathbb{Q}$ measure, such that

$$d\mathbf{z}_t = r_t\mathbf{z}_t\, dt + \Lambda_{\mathbf{z}_t}\sigma_t\, d\mathbf{W}_t^{\mathbb{Q}}.$$

The $\mathbb{Q}$ measure is therefore an EMM.

We also define the *stochastic discount factor* process

$$M_t = \frac{\xi_t}{R_t}.$$

From Itô's lemma,

$$\frac{dM_t}{M_t} = -r_t\, dt + \theta_t'\, d\mathbf{W}_t,$$

and from the martingale property,

$$E_t^{\mathbb{P}}\left[\frac{dM_t}{M_t}\right] = -r_t\, dt.$$

For any self-financed trading strategy, we then have the following three equivalent continuous-time pricing relations (compare with (7.11) in the one-period model):

$$\begin{aligned} V_t^{\mathbf{h}} &= E_t^{\mathbb{Q}}\left[\frac{1}{R_{t,T}} V_T^{\mathbf{h}}\right] \\ &= E_t^{\mathbb{P}}\left[\frac{1}{R_{t,T}}\frac{\xi_T}{\xi_t} V_T^{\mathbf{h}}\right] \\ &= E_t^{\mathbb{P}}\left[\frac{M_T}{M_t} V_T^{\mathbf{h}}\right]. \end{aligned} \tag{9.87}$$

Note that the $M_t V_t^{\mathbf{h}}$ process is a $\mathbb{P}$-martingale for any self-financed trading strategy. The Itô version of the product rule implies that

$$E_t^{\mathbb{P}}\left[\frac{dV_t^{\mathbf{h}}}{V_t^{\mathbf{h}}}\right] = r_t\, dt - \left(\frac{dM_t}{M_t}\right)\left(\frac{dV_t^{\mathbf{h}}}{V_t^{\mathbf{h}}}\right).$$

This is the continuous-time version of the general SDF pricing formula we saw in section 5.4.11, showing how the risk-premium depends on the covariation between the SDF and the asset's return.

9.7 Exercises

1. *Itô processes and Itô's lemma*: Assume that W_t is a Wiener process.

   (a) Consider the Itô process $X_t = t\sin(W_t)$. Calculate the Itô differential of X_t, dX_t.
   (b) Use Itô's lemma to prove that $\int_0^t W_s^2\, dW_s = \frac{1}{3}W_t^3 - \int_0^t W_s\, ds$.
   (c) Assume that $X_t = \int_0^t v^2\, dW_v$. Calculate the variance of X_{t+s}, given the information known at t, i.e., $\text{Var}(X_{t+s}|\mathcal{F}_t)$.

2. *Product rule*: Consider the diffusion processes X_t and Y_t,

$$dX_t = \mu_X\, dt + \sigma_X\, dV_X,$$

$$dY_t = \mu_Y\, dt + \sigma_Y\, dV_Y,$$

   with $\text{Cov}(dV_X, dV_Y) = \rho\, dt$.

Calculate $d(e^X e^Y)$. Verify that the result is the same as what you get when you define $Z = X + Y$ and calculate $d(e^Z)$.

3. *Itô processes and Itô's lemma*: Assume that W_t is a Wiener process.

   (a) Consider the Itô process $X_t = e^{W_t^2}$. Calculate the Itô differential of X_t, dX_t.
   (b) Assume that $dX_t = (2W_t - t)(t\, dW_t - W_t\, dt)$, $X_0 = 0$. Calculate $\int_0^T dX_t$.

4. Consider a market with one stock with GBM dynamics for prices and constant dividend yield, α. Also, there is a risk-free asset with constant returns. So the asset price dynamics are

$$\frac{dS}{S} = \hat{\mu}\, dt + \sigma\, dW, \quad S_0 = 1,$$
$$\frac{dB}{B} = r\, dt, \quad B_0 = 1,$$
$$d\Theta = (\alpha S\, dt, 0)^T,$$

$\alpha > 0$, $\hat{\mu}$ and σ constant.

Calculate V_t and $F_t^{\mathbf{h}}$ for the following three trading strategies:

- $\mathbf{h}_t = (0, e^{-rt})^T$,
- $\mathbf{h}_t = (e^{\alpha t}, 0)^T$,
- $\mathbf{h}_t = (\frac{1}{\sigma S_t}, -\frac{1}{\sigma B_t})^T$, assuming $\alpha = 0$.

5. *Itô calculus*: Let W_t, $t \geq 0$, be a Wiener process.

   (a) Derive an expression for the stochastic integral $F(T) \stackrel{\text{def}}{=} \int_0^T W_t^3 t^4\, dW_t$ of the form $F(T) = h(T, W_T) + \int_0^T g(t, W_t)\, dt$, where the right-hand side of the expression uses the standard Riemann integral.
   (b) Use your result in (a), and the fact that $E_0[W_t^2] = t$, to derive an expression for $E_0[W_T^4]$, without using any further known properties of normal distributions.

6. *Continuous-time model:* Consider an economy with one stock with GBM dynamics for prices, and one risk-free asset with constant returns:

$$\frac{dS}{S} = \hat{\mu}\, dt + \sigma\, dW,$$
$$\frac{dB}{B} = r\, dt,$$

$\hat{\mu}$, r, and $\sigma > 0$ constants. The bond makes no dividend payments, but the stock makes instantaneous payments proportional to the stock price. Thus, $d\Theta_t = (\alpha S_t\, dt, 0)$ is the instantaneous dividend process of the two assets, where $\alpha > 0$ is a constant.

Consider the trading strategy

$$\mathbf{h}_t = (h_t^S, h_t^B)' = \left(2e^{(r+\sigma^2-2\alpha)(T-t)} S_t, -e^{(r+\sigma^2-2\alpha)(T-t)} \frac{S_t^2}{B_t}\right)', \quad T > 0.$$

   (a) What is the value process, $V_t^{\mathbf{h}}$, for this trading strategy?
   (b) What is the cumulative dividend processes, $F_t^{\mathbf{h}}$, of this trading strategy?
   (c) What asset pricing conclusions can be drawn from your results in (a) evaluated at $t = 0$ and $t = T$, and (b)?

7. Consider the Ornstein–Uhlenbeck SDE

$$dX = \kappa(\theta - X_t)\,dt + \sigma\,dW_t, \quad X_0 = x \in \mathbb{R}.$$

The solution is the classical Ornstein–Uhlenbeck process. Using stochastic integration, derive an expression for the solution, X_t, and its distribution.

Hint: It may be useful to define the process $Y_t = e^{\kappa t}X_t \stackrel{\text{def}}{=} g(t, X_t)$.

8. *Fokker–Planck's equation*: Derive the Fokker–Planck equation for the Ornstein–Uhlenbeck process and verify that the asymptotic long-term distribution, implied from the distribution derived in exercise 7, is consistent with the ODE obtained when the time derivative in the Fokker–Planck equation is set to zero.

9. *SDEs*:

(a) Consider the stochastic differential equation

$$dX_t = \frac{X_t}{2}\,dt + \sqrt{1 + X_t^2}\,dW_t, \quad X_0 = 0,$$

where W_t is a Wiener process. What can we say about the general existence and uniqueness of solution(s) to this SDE?

(b) Recall the calculus of hyperbolic functions: $\cosh^2(x) - \sinh^2(x) = 1$, $\sinh'(x) = \cosh(x)$, $\cosh'(x) = \sinh(x)$, where $\sinh(x) = \frac{e^x - e^{-x}}{2}$ and $\cosh(x) = \frac{e^x + e^{-x}}{2}$. Use these relations to conjecture and verify a solution to the SDE in (a).

10. *Kolmogorov equations:* Consider the PDE

$$\begin{aligned} F_t + a(b - x)F_x + cF_{xx} &= 0, \\ F(T, x) &= x, \\ t &\geq 0, \\ x &\in \mathbb{R}. \end{aligned}$$

(a) What is the solution $F(t, x)$, $0 \leq t \leq T$, $x \in \mathbb{R}$, to this PDE?

(b) How does the solution in (a), via Feynman–Kac's theorem, relate to properties of the Ornstein–Uhlenbeck process

$$dX = \kappa(\theta - X)\,dt + \sigma\,dW?$$

11. *Binary options and Girsanov*: Consider an economy in which there are two indices that evolve as Brownian motions:

$$dz_1 = \frac{1}{5}\,dt + dW_1,$$

$$dz_2 = \frac{2}{5}\,dt + 2\,dW_2,$$

where $z_1(0) = z_2(0) = 0$, and W_1 and W_2 are independent Wiener processes. The market is complete. Specifically, there is a risk-free asset with constant returns, and two stocks,

$$\frac{dB}{B} = \frac{1}{5}\,dt, \qquad B(0) = 1,$$

$$\frac{dS_1}{S_1} = \frac{1}{5}\,dt + \frac{1}{3}\,dz_1 + \frac{2}{3}\,dz_2, \quad S_1(0) = 1,$$

$$\frac{dS_2}{S_2} = \frac{8}{15}\,dt + \frac{2}{3}\,dz_1 + \frac{1}{2}\,dz_2, \quad S_2(0) = 1.$$

Use Girsanov's theorem to calculate the price of a digital index insurance contract that pays out a thousand dollars at $T = 1$ if $z_1 < 0$,

$$\Phi(z_1(T)) = 1000 \times (1_{z_1 < 0}).$$

12. *Stochastic discount factors and net present value*: In the market

$$\frac{dB}{B} = 0.01\,dt,$$

$$\frac{dS_1}{S_1} = 0.09\,dt + 0.5\,dW_1 + 0.3\,dW_2,$$

$$\frac{dS_2}{S_2} = 0.10\,dt + 0.5\,dW_1 + 0.6\,dW_2,$$

where W_1 and W_2 are independent Wiener processes, a real investment opportunity—an "investment project"—requires an immediate investment of 300 (measured in million dollars), and will at $T = 3$ generate cash flows $\widetilde{\text{CF}} = e^{2W_1(T)}$ (also measured in million dollars).

(a) What are the expected cash flows associated with the investment at $T = 3$, $E_0[\widetilde{\text{CF}}]$?
(b) If discounted at the risk-free rate, what would be the net present value (NPV) of the project?
(c) What is the true NPV of the project?

CHAPTER 10 Applications

In this section we consider various applications and extensions of the Black–Scholes economy introduced in the previous chapter.

10.1 Dividends

We first analyze the Black–Scholes economy,

$$\frac{dB_t}{B_t} = r_t\,dt,$$

$$\frac{dS_t}{S_t} = \hat{\mu}_t\,dt + \sigma\,dW,$$

in which the stock makes dividend payments. We assume that the stock makes instantaneous payments, which at each point in time are proportional to the current stock price, so that

$$d\Theta_t = \theta_t S_t\,dt.$$

This is a constant dividend yield assumption.

So dividends are paid out as a flow in this model, rather than in discrete installments. This is a very convenient model assumption, which over longer horizons can be viewed as a reasonable approximation of the discrete dividend payments made by an asset in practice. For example, over a 20-year period, quarterly dividends paid by a company may well be approximated by a dividend flow. Over a short horizon, say a year, the assumption is less appealing.

To understand what the implications for our pricing methodology are when assets pay dividends, the simplest approach may be to transform the problem into one with "artificial" assets that do not pay dividends. Specifically, in exercise 4 in chapter 9 we studied a dynamic trading strategy that reinvests all dividends. The value process of this trading strategy is then one of an asset that does not pay any dividends, and all our previous results will then hold for this value process.

The general investment strategy is

$$\mathbf{h}_t = (0, e^{\int_0^t \theta_s\,ds})',$$

for which it is easy to verify that $dF_t^{\mathbf{h}} = 0$, so the trading strategy is self-financed (it makes no portfolio payouts and requires no additional investments beyond $t = 0$). The value process of this trading strategy, $V_t = e^{\int_0^t \theta_s\, ds} S_t$, then satisfies

$$\frac{dV_t}{V_t} = (\hat{\mu}_t + \theta_t)\, dt + \sigma\, dW.$$

This is the process that determines the risk-neutral measure, in line with our previous arguments, and it therefore follows that

$$\begin{aligned} \frac{dB_t}{B_t} &= r_t\, dt, \\ \frac{dV_t}{V_t} &= r_t\, dt + \sigma_t\, dW^Q, \\ \frac{dS_t}{S_t} &= (r_t - \theta_t)\, dt + \sigma_t\, dW^Q. \end{aligned}$$

Intuitively, in the risk-neutral measure, the dividend-paying stock will have a drift term that is below the risk-free rate, since part of the value of owning the stock is obtained by the dividend payments, rather than by stock appreciation alone.

From a replicating portfolio argument, the following general result follows:

Theorem 10.1. *Consider a generalized simple contingent claim with time-T payoff $\Phi(S(T))$, and the flow of payouts*

$$dF^{\mathbf{h}} = \delta(t, S)\, dt = \delta_t\, dt.$$

Here, the bond and stock in the Black–Scholes economy follow the dynamics

$$\begin{aligned} \frac{dB_t}{B_t} &= r_t\, dt, \\ \frac{dS_t}{S_t} &= \hat{\mu}_t\, dt + \sigma_t\, dW, \\ d\Theta_t &= \theta_t S_t\, dt. \end{aligned} \tag{10.1}$$

Define $G(t, S)$ as the solution to the PDE

$$G_t + (r_t - \theta_t) S G_S + \frac{1}{2}\sigma_t^2 G_{SS} S^2 - r_t G + \delta_t = 0,$$
$$G(T, S) = \Phi(S).$$

Then the contingent claim with dividends can be replicated by a trading strategy with time-t value $V^{\mathbf{h}}(t, S_t) = G(t, S_t)$. The replicating portfolio trading strategy is defined as $\mathbf{h}_t = (h^B, h^S)' = (\frac{G - SG_S}{B}, G_S)'$.

Proof. The argument is identical to that in the proof of theorem 9.14. □

A direct implication of theorem 10.1 is that the Black–Scholes PDE for a simple contingent claim on a stock that pays continuous dividends is

$$G_t + (r_t - \theta_t) S G_S + \frac{1}{2}\sigma_t^2 G_{SS} S^2 - r_t G = 0,$$
$$G(T, S) = \Phi(S). \tag{10.2}$$

It is straightforward to verify that when the theorem is applied to the European call option with a dividend-paying underlying asset, the following result is obtained:

Theorem 10.2 (Black–Scholes for a European call option on stock that pays dividends). *The time-0 price of a European call option with strike price K, constant dividend yield θ, and expiration date T in the Black–Scholes economy with constant r and σ, is*

$$C = Se^{-\theta T}N(x) - Ke^{-rT}N(x - \sigma\sqrt{T}).$$

Here, $x = \frac{\ln(\frac{S}{K}) + (r - \theta + \frac{\sigma^2}{2})T}{\sigma\sqrt{T}}$.

10.2 Barrier Options

Barrier options are a specific type of *path-dependent* options, for which the terminal payoffs depend on whether the price of the underlying asset reached a barrier between 0 and T or not. The following are some standard types of barrier options:

- Knock-in option, payoff function $\Phi(S_T)$, but only if $S_t = b$ for some $t \in [0, T]$:
  - high barrier, $S_0 < b$: up-and-in option;
  - low barrier, $S_0 > b$: down-and-in option.
- Knock-out option, payoff function $\Phi(S_T)$, but only if $S_t \neq b$ for all $t \in [0, T]$:
  - high barrier, $S_0 < b$: up-and-out option;
  - low barrier, $S_0 > b$: down-and-out option.

As an example, consider the high barrier knock-in option in figure 10.1. The knock-in barrier level is at $S = b$. The solid line sample path reaches b at some $t < T$, and therefore makes the payment $\Phi(S_T)$ at time T. The thin line sample path, on the other hand, never crosses the line $S_t = b$, and is therefore never "knocked in." Its terminal payment for this sample path is zero.

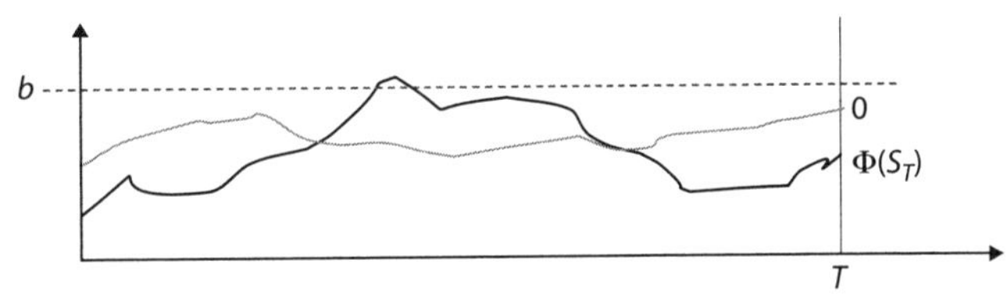

Figure 10.1: High barrier knock-in option (up-and-in option).

We want to develop a methodology to price barrier options, but these options are not simple contingent claims. Their path dependence makes a risk-neutral approach natural.[1]

AN INSIGHTFUL EXAMPLE Consider the Black–Scholes economy,

$$\frac{dB}{B} = r\,dt,$$

$$\frac{dS}{S} = r\,dt + \sigma\,dW^Q.$$

We wish to price a *digital* knock-in option, defined by the payoff function $\Phi(S_T) \equiv 1$, so that the risk-neutral pricing formula becomes

$$P = e^{-rT}E^Q[1_{\tau_b \leq T}] = e^{-rT}\mathbb{Q}(\tau_b \leq T).$$

[1]Because of the simple structure of the path dependence, it is quite straightforward to use the PDE approach for these barrier options too, but not quite as straightforward as the risk-neutral approach.

Here, τ_b is the so-called *hitting time* (also called the *stopping time* in this context)

$$\tau_b = \inf\{t : S_t \geq b\},$$

denoting the first point in time that the stock price, S_t, reaches the barrier b, and $1_{\tau_b \leq T}$ is the indicator function on the event $\tau_b \leq T$, i.e., a function that takes the value 1 if S_t reaches b before or at T, and 0 otherwise. We thus need to find $\mathbb{Q}(\tau_b \leq T)$.

How do we find the price of this digital option? Let us first rewrite $S_T = S_0 e^{y_T}$, where y_t is an arithmetic Brownian motion with distribution $y_t \sim N((r - \frac{\sigma^2}{2})t, \sigma^2 t)$, $0 \leq t \leq T$. We next define

$$\tau_x^y = \inf\{t : y_t \geq x\},$$

and note that $\tau_x^y \equiv \tau_b$, for $x = \ln(\frac{b}{S_0})$. This reformulation allows us to work with arithmetic Brownian motions, in log-coordinates, as opposed to geometric Brownian motions. The transformation is particularly simple for the stopping time, since the event of reaching b is equally easily formulated in S and y coordinates. Thus, with this alternative formulation, our objective is to calculate

$$\mathbb{Q}(\tau_x^y \leq T), \quad x = \ln(\tfrac{b}{S_0}). \tag{10.3}$$

So how do we find $\mathbb{Q}(\tau_x^y \leq T)$? One way is to look up the formula for the distribution of the hitting time in a book, for example in Borodin and Salminen (2000), but it is more insightful to actually derive the formula. We use the so-called *reflection principle*, initially focusing on the case when the drift of y_t is 0. The following argument is especially helpful, because it basically carries over line by line to the general case with nonzero drift. First, we use the law of total probability to divide the event $\tau_x^y \leq T$ into two disjoint subevents, conditioned on whether $y_T < x$ or $y_T \geq x$. In words, there are two ways for τ_x^y to be less than or equal to T. Either y_t reaches x for some $t \leq T$ and then ends up below x, or it reaches x before T and ends up above x.

The total probability is thus

$$\mathbb{Q}(\tau_x^y \leq T) = \mathbb{Q}(\tau_x^y \leq T \cap y_T \geq x) + \mathbb{Q}(\tau_x^y \leq T \cap y_T < x).$$

The first term on the right-hand side is easy to evaluate, since the event $y_T \geq x$ already implies that $\tau_x^y \leq T$ (recall that the Brownian motion a.s. has continuous sample paths, so if it ends above x, it must have passed through x at some earlier point). Thus,

$$\mathbb{Q}(\tau_x^y \leq T \cap y_T \geq x) = \mathbb{Q}(y_T \geq x),$$

which we know how to calculate.

The second term is a bit trickier, and this is where the reflection principle is useful. The reflection principle is based on the idea that if V_t is a Brownian motion with zero drift, then so is $-V_t$. Therefore, at any point in time, s, one can switch from the Brownian motion V to the reflected Brownian motion $\widehat{V}_t$, which is the same as V until time s, but then is defined as $\widehat{V}_t = V_s + (V_s - V_t) = 2V_s - V_t$ for $t \geq s$, and the distributional properties of the reflected Brownian motion, $\widehat{V}_t$, are exactly the same as those of V_t.

An immediate implication is that whenever y reaches x, from that point on, the probability is exactly $\frac{1}{2}$ that y will end up above x and $\frac{1}{2}$ that it will end up below x, since any path has an equal probability to occur as the reflected path associated with it. But this then implies that

$$\mathbb{Q}(\tau_x^y \leq T \cap y_T < x) = \frac{1}{2}\mathbb{Q}(\tau_x^y \leq T),$$

and in total we therefore have

$$\begin{aligned}\mathbb{Q}(\tau_x^y \le T) &= \mathbb{Q}(\tau_x^y \le T \cap y_T \ge x) + \mathbb{Q}(\tau_x^y \le T \cap y_T < x)\\ &= \mathbb{Q}(y_T \ge x) + \mathbb{Q}(\tau_x^y \le T \cap y_T < x)\\ &= \mathbb{Q}(y_T \ge x) + \frac{1}{2}\mathbb{Q}(\tau_x^y \le T),\end{aligned}$$

in turn leading to

$$\mathbb{Q}(\tau_x^y \le T) = 2\mathbb{Q}(y_T \ge x) = 2\Big(1 - N\Big(\frac{x}{\sigma\sqrt{T}}\Big)\Big),$$

and the associated pricing formula,

$$P = 2e^{-rT}\Big(1 - N\Big(\frac{x}{\sigma\sqrt{T}}\Big)\Big). \tag{10.4}$$

THE GENERAL CASE We are now ready to derive the formula in the general case, when y's drift is nonzero (in the $\mathbb{Q}$ measure), $y_t \sim N(\mu t, \sigma^2 t)$. We begin with same argument as before to define

$$\begin{aligned}\mathbb{Q}(\tau_x^y \le T) &= \mathbb{Q}(\tau_x^y \le T \cap y_T \ge x) + \mathbb{Q}(\tau_x^y \le T \cap y_T < x)\\ &= \mathbb{Q}(y_T \ge x) + \mathbb{Q}(\tau_x^y \le T \cap y_T < x).\end{aligned}$$

The first term on the right-hand side is straightforward: $\mathbb{Q}(y_T \ge x) = 1 - N(\frac{x-\mu T}{\sigma\sqrt{T}})$.

For the second term, however, the reflection principle is not immediately applicable since the drift term is not zero. The idea is now to use Girsanov's theorem to transform to a new measure, $\mathbb{Q}'$, under which the drift of y is zero, and then use what we know about the zero-drift case. We set $\lambda = \frac{\mu}{\sigma}$, $W_t^{\mathbb{Q}'} = W_t^{\mathbb{Q}} + \lambda t$, $\xi_t = e^{-\lambda W_t^{\mathbb{Q}} - \lambda^2 \frac{t}{2}}$, and then get $E^{\mathbb{Q}'}[X_T] = E^{\mathbb{Q}}[\xi_T X_T]$ for an arbitrary random variable, X_T.

It follows from Girsanov's theorem that $y_T = \sigma W_T^{\mathbb{Q}'} \sim N(0, \sigma^2 T)$ under the $\mathbb{Q}'$ measure. Moreover, since y_t has zero drift under the $\mathbb{Q}'$ measure, the reflection principle implies, for $z < x$,

$$\mathbb{Q}'(\tau_x^y \le T \cap y_T = z) = \mathbb{Q}'(\tau_x^y \le T \cap y_T = 2x - z) = \mathbb{Q}'(y_T = 2x - z) = \frac{1}{\sqrt{2\pi\sigma^2 T}} e^{-\frac{(z-2x)^2}{2\sigma^2 T}}\, dz.$$

We now transform this back to the $\mathbb{Q}$ measure, using the Girsanov transformation from $\mathbb{Q}'$ to $\mathbb{Q}$:

$$\begin{aligned}\mathbb{Q}(\tau_x^y \le T \cap y_T = z) &= \xi_T^{-1}\mathbb{Q}'(\tau_x^y \le T \cap y_T = z)\\ &= e^{\lambda W_T^{\mathbb{Q}} + \lambda^2 \frac{T}{2}}\mathbb{Q}'(y_T = 2x - z)\\ &= e^{\lambda(W_T^{\mathbb{Q}'} - \lambda T) + \lambda^2 \frac{T}{2}}\mathbb{Q}'(y_T = 2x - z)\\ &= e^{\lambda W_T^{\mathbb{Q}'} - \lambda^2 \frac{T}{2}}\mathbb{Q}'(y_T = 2x - z)\\ &= e^{\lambda \frac{y_T}{\sigma} - \lambda^2 \frac{T}{2}}\mathbb{Q}'(y_T = 2x - z)\\ &= \frac{1}{\sqrt{2\pi\sigma^2 T}} e^{\lambda \frac{z}{\sigma} - \lambda^2 \frac{T}{2} - \frac{(z-2x)^2}{2\sigma^2 T}}\, dz\end{aligned}$$

$$= \frac{1}{\sqrt{2\pi\sigma^2 T}} e^{-\frac{1}{2\sigma^2 T}(-2\mu z T + \mu^2 T^2 + (z-2x)^2)}\, dz$$

$$= \frac{1}{\sqrt{2\pi\sigma^2 T}} e^{2\frac{\mu x}{\sigma^2}} e^{-\frac{(z-2x-\mu T)^2}{2\sigma^2 T}}\, dz,$$

ending up with $\mathbb{Q}(\tau_x^y \leq T \cap y_T \leq x) = e^{2\frac{\mu x}{\sigma^2}} N(\frac{x-2x-\mu T}{\sigma\sqrt{T}}) = e^{2\frac{\mu x}{\sigma^2}} N(\frac{-x-\mu T}{\sigma\sqrt{T}})$.

So the price of the digital option is

$$P = e^{-rT}\Big(1 - N\Big(\frac{x-\mu T}{\sigma\sqrt{T}}\Big) + e^{\frac{2\mu x}{\sigma^2}} N\Big(\frac{-x-\mu T}{\sigma\sqrt{T}}\Big)\Big),$$

where $\mu = r - \frac{\sigma^2}{2}$ and $x = \ln(\frac{b}{S})$, i.e.,

$$P = e^{-rT}\Bigg(1 - N\Bigg(\frac{\ln(\frac{b}{S}) - (r - \frac{\sigma^2}{2})T}{\sigma\sqrt{T}}\Bigg) + \Big(\frac{b}{S}\Big)^{\frac{2r-\sigma^2}{\sigma^2}} N\Bigg(\frac{\ln(\frac{S}{b}) - (r - \frac{\sigma^2}{2})T}{\sigma\sqrt{T}}\Bigg)\Bigg)$$

$$= e^{-rT}\Bigg(N\Bigg(\frac{\ln(\frac{S}{b}) + (r - \frac{\sigma^2}{2})T}{\sigma\sqrt{T}}\Bigg) + \Big(\frac{b}{S}\Big)^{\frac{2r-\sigma^2}{\sigma^2}} N\Bigg(\frac{\ln(\frac{S}{b}) - (r - \frac{\sigma^2}{2})T}{\sigma\sqrt{T}}\Bigg)\Bigg)$$

$$= e^{-rT}\Bigg(N\Bigg(\frac{\ln(\frac{S}{b}) + (r - \frac{\sigma^2}{2})T}{\sigma\sqrt{T}}\Bigg) + \Big(\frac{b}{S}\Big)^{2\frac{r-\frac{\sigma^2}{2}}{\sigma^2}} \Bigg(1 - N\Bigg(\frac{\ln(\frac{b^2/S}{b}) + (r - \frac{\sigma^2}{2})T}{\sigma\sqrt{T}}\Bigg)\Bigg)\Bigg).$$

Exactly the same approach for the general up-and-in claim formula with arbitrary payoff function, $\Phi(S_T)$, can be used to derive the following formula:

Theorem 10.3 (Price of up-and-in claim). *In the standard Black–Scholes setting, consider a simple up-and-in contingent claim with time-T payoff,*

$$\Phi(S_T; L) = \begin{cases} \Phi(S_T), & \tau_L \leq T, \\ 0 & \text{otherwise.} \end{cases}$$

The $t = 0$ value of the contract is then

$$F^I(S; L, \Phi) = \begin{cases} F(S; \Phi_L) + \left(\frac{L}{S}\right)^{2\frac{r-\frac{\sigma^2}{2}}{\sigma^2}} F\left(\frac{L^2}{S}; \Phi^L\right), & S < L, \\ F(S; \Phi), & S \geq L, \end{cases}$$

where $F(S; \Phi)$ is the value of a standard (not barrier) simple contingent claim, with payout function Φ at current stock price S, $\Phi_L(x) = \Phi(x) \times 1_{x \geq L}$, and $\Phi^L(x) = \Phi(x) \times 1_{x \leq L}$.

The same approach can also be used to calculate the prices of down-and-in contracts, and up-and-out and down-and-out contracts.

10.3 Bond Pricing in Continuous Time

In this section we focus on pricing of risk-free bonds. The only bond we have covered so far in the continuous-time part of the text is the short bond, where we have often used the constant rate of return dynamics

$$\frac{dB}{B} = r\,dt, \quad r \in \mathbb{R},$$

leading to a bond price of

$$B_T = e^{r(T-t)} B_t.$$

Equivalently,

$$B_t = e^{-r(T-t)} B_T, \quad t < T.$$

In this setting, this pricing formula is valid for any finitely lived bond that does not make coupon payments. Specifically, consider a generic *T-bond*, which makes a terminal principal payment of \$1 at T and then ceases to exist. Its price at time $t < T$ is then

$$p(t, T) = e^{-r(T-t)}.$$

The formula is straightforward to generalize to varying but deterministic short interest rates. Consider the bond with dynamics

$$\frac{dB_t}{B_t} = r_t \, dt, \tag{10.5}$$

where r_t is the short rate at t, which is a deterministic function. The ODE associated with B_t is

$$B' = r_t B,$$

with solution

$$B_T = e^{\int_t^T r_s \, ds} B_t,$$

which implies the following pricing formula for a T-bond:

$$p(t, T) = e^{-\int_t^T r_s \, ds}.$$

The *yield* of the bond, $y_{t,T}$, is defined such that

$$p(t, T) = e^{-(T-t) y_{t,T}},$$

i.e.,

$$y_{t,T} = -\frac{1}{T-t} \ln(p(t, T)). \tag{10.6}$$

When $t = 0$, we write $y_t = y_{0,T}$. The yield can be calculated regardless of whether short interest rates are deterministic or not. When they are deterministic, yields are also deterministic, and will be given by the average short rate between t and T:

$$y_{t,T} = \frac{1}{T-t} \int_t^T r_s \, ds.$$

The T-bonds are great building blocks for determining the pricing of coupon bonds. For example, consider a five-year, 5% coupon bond, issued at time 0, which makes periodic coupon payments and also a principal payment of \$100 upon maturity. Coupon payments are measured as a fraction of principal payments, so this means that the bond will pay \$5 at $t = 1, 2, 3, 4$, and 5, in addition to the principal \$100 payment at $T = 5$. Consequently, the price of this coupon bond at $t = 0$ is

$$P = 5(p_{0,1} + p_{0,2} + p_{0,3} + p_{0,4} + p_{0,5}) + 100 p_{0,5}.$$

Alternatively, using the yield formulation, we have

$$P = 5(e^{-y_1 \times 1} + e^{-y_2 \times 2} + e^{-y_3 \times 3} + e^{-y_4 \times 4} + e^{-y_5 \times 5}) + 100 e^{-y_5 \times 5}.$$

This methodology for building the price of an arbitrary bond follows from no arbitrage, regardless of what assumptions we make about the discount rate. For a coupon bond, the yield $\hat{y}$ is again defined as the average interest rate that will price the bond correctly, e.g., in the example above so that

$$P = 5(e^{-\hat{y}\times 1} + e^{-\hat{y}\times 2} + e^{-\hat{y}\times 3} + e^{-\hat{y}\times 4} + e^{-\hat{y}\times 5}) + 100e^{-\hat{y}\times 5},$$

for the bond above. When interest rates vary, the yields of coupon bonds are in general different from those of T-bonds.

What will the pricing formula be if r_t is not deterministic? Risk-neutral pricing tells us that

$$p(t,T) = E^{\mathbb{Q}}[e^{-\int_t^T r_s\,ds}].$$

What can we infer from this formula without making additional assumptions beyond those we have done so far?

Consider what is maybe the simplest possible continuous-time setting with a stochastic short interest rate:

$$dr = \sigma\,dW_t.$$

Here, W_t is a Wiener process in the physical (i.e., not in the risk-neutral) measure. In our previous analysis, all randomness has occurred for the other risky assets, i.e., for the stocks. We assume that this new Wiener process is linearly independent from the other processes associated with the stocks (although it could be correlated).

What does it even mean that the risk-free rate is stochastic when the bond is supposed to be risk-free? The idea here is that over a very short time period, the investor may achieve risk-free returns by purchasing the bond at price B, with the dynamics

$$\frac{dB_t}{B_t} = r_t\,dt. \tag{10.7}$$

Using infinitesimal notation,

$$B_{t+dt} = e^{r_t\,dt}B_t = (1 + r_t\,dt)B_t.$$

So, in the short run, the bond guarantees the (per unit time) return r_t. In the next instant, the short rate will have changed though, to $r_{t+dt} = r_t + \sigma\,dW_t$, as will then the promised return over the next instantaneous period. As a consequence, the dynamics of the price, B_t, is now random beyond the next dt period, but not between 0 and dt. It follows that the quadratic variation of B_t is 0, in contrast to that of the stock, i.e., $(dB_t)^2 = 0$.

An alternative interpretation of the dynamics of B_t is that it corresponds to a trading strategy that consistently rolls over investments into very short-term bonds that pay a dollar dt into the future, with current price $p_{t,t+dt}$. Such short-term bonds are the only assets that (10.7) immediately prices. It is therefore unclear what inferences we can draw from (10.7) about the prices of other T-bonds, $p_{t,T}$, $T > t$.

A SIMPLE EXAMPLE Let us consider a specific example to gain some intuition. Assume that $W_t^Q = W_t$, so that the risk-neutral and objective measures are the same. As we mentioned before, this is a situation that we would expect if investors are risk neutral, for example. Thus, we have

$$dr = \sigma\,dW_t^Q.$$

Moreover, assume that $r_0 = 0$, i.e., that the short rate at $t = 0$ is 0.

We study the bond that pays \$1 at $T = 1$, with price dynamics $P_t = p_{t,1}$. Of course, $P_1 \equiv 1$. First, note that r_t is a martingale, so $E_0[r_t] = r_0 = 0$ for all $t > 0$. So the short rate is expected to be 0 at every future point in time. We calculate P_0 using the risk-neutral pricing formula. Specifically, we define

$$\widetilde{Y}_T = \int_0^T r_s\, ds = \sigma \int_0^T W_s\, ds = \sigma\left(TW_t - \int_0^T s\, dW_s\right) = \sigma \int_0^T (T-s)\, dW_s,$$

where we used the integration by parts rule previously discussed in Example 9.3.

What is the distribution of $\widetilde{Y}_T$? Because of the martingale property for stochastic integrals, $E_0[\widetilde{Y}_T] = 0$. Moreover, we can use Itô isometry to infer that $\text{Var}(\widetilde{Y}_T) = \frac{\sigma^2 T^3}{3}$, and since $\widetilde{Y}_T$ is made up of a deterministically weighted sum/integral of normally distributed increments, $\widetilde{Y}_T$ also has a normal distribution: $\widetilde{Y}_T \sim N(0, \sigma^2 \frac{T^3}{3})$, in both the risk-neutral and the physical measures. We therefore have

$$P_0 = E_0^{\mathbb{Q}}[e^{-\widetilde{Y}_1}] = e^{\frac{\sigma^2}{6}},$$

where we used the expectation formula for log-normal distributions.

Note that $P_0 > 1$, although $P_1 = 1$, which is obviously possible if interest rates may be negative. However, there is still something surprising with this price formula. Specifically, the expected return on the bond is

$$E_0\left[\frac{P_1 - P_0}{P_0}\right] = e^{-\frac{\sigma^2}{6}} - 1 \neq 0.$$

Actually, the expectation operator is not needed since P_1 is not random. What may seem surprising here is that this expected return is not zero, even though the interest rate is expected to be zero between 0 and 1. This "puzzle" is resolved by realizing that there is a Jensen's inequality at play here, in that

$$1 = e^{E_0[-\widetilde{Y}_1]} < E_0[e^{-\widetilde{Y}_1}] = e^{\frac{\sigma^2}{6}}.$$

The distinction between the "exponential of the expectation" and the "expectation of the exponential" originally caused some confusion during the early days of the continuous-time term structure literature when the so-called *expectations hypothesis* was analyzed; see Cox, Ingersoll, and Ross (1981).

This example was based on the strong assumption that the risk-neutral and physical measures coincide. What if the two measures are different? Can we still use no-arbitrage arguments to price the T-bonds? We now study a more general setting, making some further assumptions. Specifically, we assume

- at each point in time, there are zero-coupon bonds of all maturities traded in the market, with prices $p_{t,T}$;
- the objective dynamics of the short rate, r_t, follow a diffusion process:

$$dr_t = \mu(t, r_t)\, dt + \sigma(t, r_t)\, dW_t; \tag{10.8}$$

- only t, T, and $\{W_s\}_{s \leq t}$ influence bond prices;
- the prices of T-bonds are of the form $p_{t,T} = F(t, T, r_t)$; we also write $p_{t,T} = F^T(t, r_t) = p(t, T|r_t)$;
- for any $T > t$, $F(t, T, r_t)$ is a smooth function of its arguments.

Note that in contrast to the Black–Scholes model we just studied, these are assumptions that are not derived from first principles. Also, note that we just introduced a whole lot of new assets. There are infinitely many T-bonds traded at any point in time!

How far does this take us? It turns out that it does not take us all the way to a no-arbitrage price. This should come as no surprise. Indeed, if we go back to our previous example, Girsanov suggests that we could in general be in a situation where

$$dr = \mu \, dt + \sigma \, dW_t^P, \quad dr = \sigma \, dW_t^Q,$$

where $\mu \neq 0$. In this case, the $\mathbb{Q}$ pricing formula we discussed earlier still holds, but we would not be able to infer it by studying the physical measure. So, in general, no arbitrage will not take us all the way here, in contrast to the options we studied earlier.

Although there are a huge number of new assets, there is essentially just one common degree of freedom across these assets for the wedge between the $\mathbb{P}$ and $\mathbb{Q}$ measures, as shown by the following result:

Theorem 10.4. *In an arbitrage-free market, given the previous one-factor assumptions, the price at time t of a T-bond, is $p(t, T|r) = F^T(t, r)$, where F^T satisfies the PDE*

$$F_t^T + (\mu_t - \theta_t\sigma_t)F_r^T + \frac{1}{2}\sigma_t^2 F_{rr}^T - r_t F^T = 0,$$

$$F^T(T, r) = 1.$$

Here, θ_t is the market price of risk *process, which is the same regardless of the maturity date, T. Equivalently, F^T has the risk-neutral representation*

$$F^T(t, r_t) = E_t^{\mathbb{Q}}[e^{-\int_t^T r_s \, ds}],$$

where $dr_s = (\mu_s - \theta_s\sigma_s)\, dt + \sigma \, dW_s^Q$.

Proof. The proof is based on finding the "gap" between the $\mathbb{P}$- and $\mathbb{Q}$-dynamics, in line with what proposition 9.8 did when applying Girsanov's theorem. The approach is similar to the classical Black–Scholes no-arbitrage argument, but here using two bonds of different maturities, specifically an S-bond and a T-bond. Since S and T are arbitrary, this will then imply the result.

First, consider the T-bond, which per assumption satisfies the price relation $p(t, T|r_t) = F^T(t, r_t)$, where F^T is a smooth function. Itô's lemma then gives us

$$\begin{aligned} dF^T &= F_t^T \, dt + F_r^T \, dr + \frac{1}{2} F_{rr}^T (dr)^2 \\ &= F_t^T \, dt + F_r^T(\mu_t \, dt + \sigma_t \, dW^P) + \frac{\sigma_t^2}{2} F_{rr}^T \, dt \\ &= \left(F_t^T + F_r^T \mu_t + \frac{\sigma_t^2}{2} F_{rr}^T\right) dt + F_r^t \sigma_t \, dW^P, \end{aligned}$$

where we used $dr = \mu_t \, dt + \sigma_t \, dW^P$, $dr^2 = \sigma_t^2 \, dt$. An identical formula holds for dF_t^S, of course.

Now, following a similar approach to the Black–Scholes argument, consider a portfolio where the investor holds $\frac{u_T}{F^T}$ T-bonds and $\frac{u_T}{F^T}$ S-bonds, for some trading strategy $\mathbf{h} = (u_T, u_S)'$. The value of this portfolio is then $V = \mathbf{h}'(F^T, F^S)' = u_T + u_S$. Moreover, its local return dynamic is

$$\begin{aligned} dV = u_T \frac{F_t^T + F_r^T \mu_t + \frac{\sigma_t^2}{2} F_{rr}^T}{F^T} \, dt + u_S \frac{F_t^S + F_r^S \mu_t + \frac{\sigma_t^2}{2} F_{rr}^S}{F^S} \, dt \\ + \left(u_T \frac{F_r^T}{F^T} \sigma_t + u_S \frac{F_r^S}{F^S} \sigma_t\right) dW^P \\ \stackrel{\text{def}}{=} (u_T \alpha_T + u_S \alpha_S) \, dt + (u_T \sigma_T + u_S \sigma_S) \, dW^P, \end{aligned}$$

where

$$\alpha_T = \frac{F_t^T + F_r^T \mu_t + \frac{\sigma_t^2}{2} F_{rr}^T}{F^T},$$

$$\alpha_S = \frac{F_t^S + F_r^S \mu_t + \frac{\sigma_t^2}{2} F_{rr}^S}{F^S},$$

$$\sigma_T = \frac{F_r^T}{F^T} \sigma_t,$$

$$\sigma_S = \frac{F_r^S}{F^S} \sigma_t.$$

Note that α_T, α_S, σ_T, and σ_S will in general vary over time, i.e., they are random processes, but for notational convenience we suppress this dependence. To make this portfolio instantaneously risk-free, we choose u_T and u_S such that $u_T\sigma_T + u_S\sigma_S = 0$, i.e., $u_S = -u_T\frac{\sigma_T}{\sigma_S}$. By no arbitrage, we then have

$$dV = (u_T\alpha_T + u_S\alpha_S)\, dt = rV\, dt = r(u_T + u_S)\, dt,$$

which in turn leads to

$$u_T(\alpha_T - r) = -u_S(\alpha_S - r) = u_T\frac{\sigma_T}{\sigma_S}(\alpha_S - r),$$

and finally,

$$\frac{\alpha_S - r}{\sigma_S} = \frac{\alpha_T - r}{\sigma_T}.$$

Since S and T were arbitrary, the instantaneous Sharpe ratios of any two bonds must then be the same. In other words, if we define the Sharpe ratio process

$$\theta_t \stackrel{\text{def}}{=} \frac{\alpha_S(t) - r(t)}{\sigma_S(t)},$$

all bonds have this same instantaneous Sharpe ratio.

By plugging in the definitions of α_S and σ_S for an arbitrary S-bond, we then get

$$\theta_t = \frac{\frac{F_t^S + F_r^S \mu_t + \frac{\sigma_t^2}{2} F_{rr}^S}{F^S} - r_t}{\frac{F_r^S}{F^S}\sigma_t},$$

and thus

$$F_t^S + (\mu_t - \theta_t\sigma_t)F_r^S + \frac{\sigma_t^2}{2}F_{rr}^S - r_t F^S = 0,$$

which is the PDE in the proposition. The same argument also holds with a different maturity (an S' and a T bond), so the process θ_t is the same for all maturities. Obviously, the S-bond must also satisfy the boundary condition, and via Feynman–Kac's theorem we know that the risk-neutral formulation also holds. This completes the proof. □

An identical argument for other contingent claims with payouts at T that depend on r_T, i.e., that are not risk-free, leads to the same PDE, but replacing the terminal condition with the payoff function, $\Phi(r(T))$.

Now, instead of specifying the short-rate process in the $\mathbb{P}$ measure, which makes it necessary to take a stand on the θ_t process, we can specify $\mathbb{Q}$-dynamics directly. We thus assume

$$dr = \mu_t\, dt + \sigma_t\, dW^{\mathbb{Q}},$$

i.e., the μ_t here is what we previously called $\mu_t - \theta_t \sigma_t$. This is a one-factor continuous-time *term structure of interest rates* model, implying the pricing formula

$$p(t,T) = E_t^{\mathbb{Q}}[e^{-\int_t^T r_s\,ds}].$$

More generally, it allows the pricing of any simple contingent claims, including other types of interest rate derivatives:

$$V(t) = E_t^{\mathbb{Q}}[e^{-\int_t^T r_s\,ds}\Phi(r(T))].$$

A number of classical models fall within this one-factor setting:

- Vasicek: $dr = (b - ar)\,dt + \sigma\,dW^{\mathrm{Q}}$, $a > 0$ (Ornstein–Uhlenbeck process).
- Cox–Ingersoll–Ross (CIR): $dr = a(b - r)\,dt + \sigma\sqrt{r}\,dW^{\mathrm{Q}}$ (square-root process).
- Merton–Ho–Lee: $dr = \Theta(t)\,dt + \sigma\,dW^{\mathrm{Q}}$.
- Hull–White: $dr = (\Theta(t) - a(t)r)\,dt + \sigma(t)\,dW^{\mathrm{Q}}$.
- Black–Derman–Toy: $dr = \Theta(t)r\,dt + \sigma(t)r\,dW^{\mathrm{Q}}$.

Note that the cost of switching from the objective to the risk-neutral measure is that only limited inferences can be drawn about bond prices from knowing or estimating actual interest rate dynamics. Rather, the unknown functions μ_t and σ_t in the risk-neutral formulation need to be inferred from actual bond prices, $\{p_{t,T}\}_{t,T}$. The exercise then becomes to draw inferences about these functions from observed bond prices.

When choosing specific functional forms of μ and σ, our goal should then be to allow for (i) simple formulas for calculating bond prices (and ideally no need to solve complicated PDEs), (ii) a general enough specification so that actual bond prices and yields can be well approximated, and (iii) good out-of-sample performance.

So-called *affine term structure models* have prices of T-bonds that can be written as $p(t, T|r_t) = e^{A(t,T)-B(t,T)r_t}$. Remember that r_t is the short rate at time t. In this specification, the functions $A(\cdot)$ and $B(\cdot)$ do *not* depend on r_t. Since $p(T, T|r_t) \equiv 1$, it must be that $A(T,T) = B(T,T) = 0$. So, with this specification, the T-yield is linear in short rate, r, because $p(0,T) = e^{-y_{0,T}T}$ so that

$$y_{t,T} = -\frac{\ln(p(t,T))}{T-t} = \frac{B(t,T)}{T}r_t - \frac{A(t,T)}{T-t}.$$

Note, however, that the yield is typically *not* linear in t. Specifically, if we define the *yield curve* at t as the graph $(T-t, y_{t,T})$, $T > t$, i.e., by plotting $T-t$ on the positive x-axis and $y_{t,T}$ on the y-axis, then this function is typically not linear.

When μ and σ^2 in (10.8) are affine functions, then the price function can be found by solving a system of two ODEs, as shown by the following proposition:

Proposition 10.1. *Assume that the short rate follows*

$$dr_t = (\alpha r + \beta)\,dt + \sqrt{\gamma r + \delta}\,dW_t^{\mathrm{Q}}, \tag{10.9}$$

where α, β, γ, and δ are constants. Then the price of a T-bond at time t is

$$p(t,T) = e^{A(T-t)-B(T-t)r_t}, \tag{10.10}$$

where A and B satisfy the ODEs

$$B' = \alpha B - \frac{\gamma}{2}B^2 + 1, \tag{10.11}$$

$$A' = -\beta B + \frac{\delta}{2}B^2, \tag{10.12}$$

with boundary conditions $A(0) = 0$, $B(0) = 0$.

Here we have for simplicity assumed that the coefficients for μ and σ do not depend on time. The generalization to time-dependent coefficients is straightforward.

Proof. Assume that the prices of the T-bonds satisfy (10.10). Of course, given the notation, $F = F^T(t, r) = p(t, T)$, so taking partial derivatives, we get

$$\begin{aligned} F_r &= -BF, \\ F_{rr} &= B^2F, \\ F_t &= (-A' + B'r)F. \end{aligned}$$

Now, by (10.9) and theorem 10.4, we have

$$F_t + (\alpha r + \beta)F_r + \frac{\gamma r + \delta}{2}F_{rr} - rF = 0,$$

and plugging in these partial derivatives, we get

$$(-A' + B'r)F + (\alpha r + \beta)(-BF) + \frac{\gamma r + \delta}{2}B^2F - rF = 0.$$

Note that these relations must hold for all r and for all $t < T$, and also that $F > 0$. It must therefore be that

$$\begin{aligned} B' - \alpha B + \frac{\gamma}{2}B^2 - 1 &= 0, \\ -A' - \beta B + \frac{\delta}{2}B^2 &= 0, \end{aligned}$$

i.e., the ODEs in the proposition must hold. The initial conditions $A(0) = B(0) = 0$, are moreover needed to satisfy the terminal condition $p(T, T) = 1$ regardless of r. □

Note that the yield curve in the affine term structure model is

$$y_t = \frac{1}{T}(B(t)r_0 - A(t)).$$

Also, note that the second ODE, (10.12), actually contains no A term, so if B is known it can be calculated by integration (via the fundamental theorem of calculus).

10.3.1 A Generalized Example

Recall our example with $dr = \sigma\, dW^Q$. This is of course a special case of the affine term structure model, with $\alpha = \beta = \gamma = 0$, and $\delta = \sigma^2$. The corresponding system of ODEs is then, as a function of $\tau = T - t$,

$$\begin{aligned} B' &= 1, \\ A' &= \frac{\sigma^2}{2}B^2, \end{aligned}$$

$A(0) = B(0) = 0$. The first ODE (for B) has the solution $B(\tau) = \tau$, and when plugging this solution into the second ODE, we get

$$A' = \frac{\sigma^2}{2}\tau^2,$$

which together with the initial condition gives us

$$A(\tau) = \frac{\sigma^2 \tau^3}{6}.$$

The price function is then

$$p(t, T|r) = e^{\sigma^2 \frac{(T-t)^3}{6} - (T-t)r},$$

which when $t = 0$, $T = 1$, and $r_0 = 0$, collapses to $p(0, 1|0) = e^{\frac{\sigma^2}{6}}$, i.e., our previous expression. The yield curve for general t, T, and r is

$$y_{t,T} = r - \frac{\sigma^2}{2}(T-t)^2.$$

10.3.2 Example—Vasicek Model

Another example is the *Vasicek model*, in which the short-rate dynamics follow an Ornstein–Uhlenbeck process:

$$dr = (b - ar)\, dt + \sigma\, dW^Q, \quad a > 0.$$

In this case the parameters are $\beta = b$, $\alpha = -a$, $\gamma = 0$, and $\delta = \sigma^2$.

The ODE for B is then

$$B' = -aB + 1, \quad B(0) = 0,$$

which via proposition 9.1 gives us the solution

$$B(\tau) = \frac{1}{a}(1 - e^{-a\tau}).$$

The ODE for A then becomes

$$A' = -\frac{b}{a}(1 - e^{-a\tau}) + \frac{\sigma^2}{2a^2}(1 - e^{-a\tau})^2 = \frac{b}{a}(e^{-a\tau} - 1) + \frac{\sigma^2}{2a^2}(1 - 2e^{-a\tau} + e^{-2a\tau}).$$

By integrating the right-hand side, we arrive at

$$A(\tau) = \int_0^\tau A'(s)\, ds = \int_0^\tau \left(\frac{b}{a}(e^{-as} - 1) + \frac{\sigma^2}{2a^2}(1 - 2e^{-as} + e^{-2as})\right) ds$$
$$= c_0 + c_1\tau + c_2 e^{-a\tau} - c_3 e^{-2a\tau},$$

where

$$c_0 = \frac{b}{a^2} + \frac{\sigma^2}{4a^3} - \frac{\sigma^2}{a^3},$$
$$c_1 = \frac{\sigma^2}{2a^2} - \frac{b}{a},$$
$$c_2 = \frac{\sigma^2}{a^3} - \frac{b}{a^2},$$
$$c_3 = \frac{\sigma^2}{4a^3}.$$

10.3.3 Example–Cox–Ingersoll–Ross (CIR) Model

The famous *Cox–Ingersoll–Ross* model also belongs to the class of affine term structure models. The risk-neutral dynamics for the short rate is

$$dr = a(b-r)\,dt + \sigma\sqrt{r}\,dW^Q.$$

The corresponding ODEs are then

$$B' = -aB - \frac{\sigma^2}{2}B^2 + 1, \tag{10.13}$$

$$A' = -abB, \tag{10.14}$$

with initial conditions $A(0)=0$, $B(0)=0$. Focusing first on the ODE for B, we see that it is a Riccati equation. An application of proposition 9.4 yields the following constant-coefficient ODE for u:

$$u'' + au' - \frac{\sigma^2}{2}u = 0,$$

and the solution that satisfies the initial condition $u'(0)=0$ is then

$$u(t) = e^{r_+ t} + Ke^{r_- t},$$

with

$$K = \frac{z-a}{z+a}, \quad z = \sqrt{a^2 + 2\sigma^2},$$

and

$$r_\pm = \frac{1}{2}(-a \pm z).$$

This leads to the solution

$$\begin{aligned}
B(t) = \frac{2}{\sigma^2}\left(\frac{u'}{u}\right) &= \frac{2}{\sigma^2}\left(\frac{r_+ e^{r_+ t} + Kr_- e^{r_- t}}{e^{r_+ t} + Ke^{r_- t}}\right) \\
&= \frac{2}{\sigma^2}\left(\frac{r_+ e^{(r_+ - r_-)t} + Kr_-}{e^{(r_+ - r_-)t} + K}\right) \\
&= \frac{2}{\sigma^2}\left(\frac{(\frac{1}{2}(-a+z))e^{zt} + K(\frac{1}{2}(-a-z))}{e^{zt} + K}\right) \\
&= \frac{z-a}{\sigma^2} \times \frac{(e^{zt}-1)}{e^{zt} + \frac{z-a}{z+a}} \\
&= \frac{(z+a)(z-a)}{\sigma^2} \times \frac{(e^{zt}-1)}{(z+a)e^{zt} + (z-a)} \\
&= \frac{z^2 - a^2}{\sigma^2} \times \frac{(e^{zt}-1)}{(z+a)(e^{zt}-1) + 2z} \\
&= 2\frac{(e^{zt}-1)}{(z+a)(e^{zt}-1) + 2z},
\end{aligned}$$

where we used $z^2 - a^2 = a^2 + 2\sigma^2 - a^2 = 2\sigma^2$.

For $A(t)$, we have

$$A(t) = -ab\int_0^t B(s)\,ds,$$

so if we can find the primitive function of B, we are done. One verifies that the function

$$A(t) = \frac{2ab}{\sigma^2} \ln\Big(\frac{2ze^{(a+z)\frac{t}{2}}}{(z+a)(e^{zt}-1)+2z}\Big)$$

satisfies

$$A' = -abB, \quad A(0) = 0,$$

so this is the functional form of A, altogether leading to the bond price

$$P(t) = \Big(\frac{2ze^{(a+z)\frac{t}{2}}}{(z+a)(e^{zt}-1)+2z}\Big)^{\frac{2ab}{\sigma^2}} e^{-B(t)t}.$$

10.4 Multidimensional Black–Scholes

The multidimensional versions of the Black–Scholes PDE and risk-neutral pricing formula are similar to the multidimensional versions of Itô's lemma, the Kolmogorov equations, and Feynman–Kac's theorem.

Theorem 10.5 (Black–Scholes PDE in multiple dimensions). *In the standard Black–Scholes economy with N stocks and one risk-free asset, here written in correlated form,*

$$\frac{dB}{B} = r\,dt,$$
$$\frac{dS_i}{S_i} = \hat{\mu}_i\,dt + \sigma_i\,dV_i, \quad i = 1, \ldots, N,$$

the price, F, of a simple contingent claim with time-T payoff $\Phi(S_1, \ldots, S_N)$ is the solution to the N-dimensional PDE

$$F_t + r\sum_i S_i F_{S_i} + \frac{1}{2}\sum_{i,j} F_{S_iS_j} S_i S_j \sigma_{ij} - rF = 0,$$
$$F(T, S_1, \ldots, S_N) = \Phi(S_1, \ldots, S_N),$$
$$t \in [0, T],$$
$$S_i \geq 0.$$

Here, $\sigma_{ij} = \sigma_i\sigma_j\rho_{ij}$, where $\rho_{ij}\,dt = \mathrm{Cov}(dV_i, dV_j)$. The replicating portfolio is $\mathbf{h}_t = (h^B, h^{S_1}, \ldots, h^{S_N})'$, with $h^{S_i} = F_{S_i}$, and $h^B = (F - \sum_i S_i F_{S_i})/B$.

Theorem 10.6 (Multidimensional risk-neutral pricing). *In the standard Black–Scholes economy with N stocks and one risk-free asset, here written in correlated form,*

$$\frac{dB}{B} = r\,dt,$$
$$\frac{dS_i}{S_i} = \hat{\mu}_i\,dt + \sigma_i\,dW_i, \quad i = 1, \ldots, N,$$

the price, F, of a simple contingent claim with time-T payoff $\Phi(S_1, \ldots, S_N)$ satisfies the risk-neutral expectations formula

$$F(t, S_1, \ldots, S_N) = e^{-r(T-t)} E_t^{\mathbb{Q}}[\Phi(T, S_1, \ldots, S_N)],$$

where the risk-neutral dynamics of the assets are

$$\frac{dB}{B} = r\,dt,$$
$$\frac{dS_i}{S_i} = r\,dt + \sigma_i\,dW_i^Q, \quad i = 1, \ldots, N.$$

Here, $\rho_{ij}\,dt = \mathrm{Cov}(dW_i, dW_j) = \mathrm{Cov}(dW_i^Q, dW_j^Q)$.

10.4.1 Exchange Option Example

A two-dimensional example is given by a so-called *exchange option*. Consider a Black–Scholes economy with two stocks and a risk-free asset:

$$\frac{dB}{B} = r\,dt,$$
$$\frac{dS_1}{S_1} = \hat{\mu}_1\,dt + \sigma_1\,dV_1,$$
$$\frac{dS_2}{S_2} = \hat{\mu}_2\,dt + \sigma_2\,dV_1,$$

with $\sigma_{12} = \rho_{12}\sigma_1\sigma_2$, and $(dV_1)(dV_2) = \rho_{12}\,dt$. The exchange option has the payout

$$\Phi(S_1(T), S_2(T)) = \max(S_1(T) - S_2(T), 0).$$

The payoff can be thought of as a contract that gives the owner the right (but not the obligation) to exchange one share of asset 2 for asset 1 at T. If $S_1(T) > S_2(T)$, this option will be exercised, adding the difference in value $S_1(T) - S_2(T)$ to the portfolio. If $S_1(T) < S_2(T)$, the option will not be exercised and its value is then 0. Hence the name exchange option.

We see that the payout function depends on the values of both S_1 and S_2 at expiration, and therefore the two-dimensional Black–Scholes PDE is appropriate here, leading to

$$F_t + r(S_1F_1 + S_2F_2) + \frac{1}{2}(\sigma_1^2S_1^2F_{11} + \sigma_2^2S_2^2F_{22} + 2\sigma_{12}S_1S_2F_{12}) - rF = 0,$$
$$F(S_1, S_2, T) = \Phi(S_1, S_2).$$

Now, we do not know what the solution to this PDE is. In general, two-dimensional PDEs are *much* more difficult to solve than one-dimensional PDEs. For this PDE, however, we can apply a trick, and infer the solution by solving a one-dimensional PDE, using a so-called *dimensionality reduction* technique.

Specifically, when the payoff function is homogeneous of degree one, in that

$$\Phi(\alpha S_1, \alpha S_2) = \alpha\Phi(S_1, S_2), \quad \forall \alpha > 0,$$

one can define

$$F(t, S_1, S_2) = S_2G(t, x), \tag{10.15}$$

where $x = \frac{S_1}{S_2}$, and solve a one-dimensional PDE for G, as a function of t and x. The value of F can then be calculated using (10.15). One verifies that Φ is homogeneous of degree one, so the trick applies in this case.

Under the ansatz, $F(S_1, S_2, t) = S_2G(x, t)$, where $x = \frac{S_1}{S_2}$, using the product rule and the chain rule (both in classical form for the function F, since we are solving PDEs, not calculating the dynamics of stochastic processes), we get the partial derivatives

$$
\begin{aligned}
\frac{\partial G}{\partial S_2} &= -\frac{S_1}{S_2^2} G_x, \\
\frac{\partial G}{\partial S_2} &= \frac{1}{S_2} G_x, \\
F_t &= S_2 G_t, \\
F_1 &= G_x, \\
F_2 &= G - \frac{S_1}{S_2} G_x, \\
F_{11} &= \frac{1}{S_2} G_{xx}, \\
F_{12} &= -\frac{S_1}{S_2^2} G_{xx}, \\
F_{22} &= \frac{S_1^2}{S_2^3} G_{xx}.
\end{aligned}
$$

When we plug these partial derivatives into the two-dimensional PDE for F, we get

$$
\begin{aligned}
0 &= S_2 G_t + r\Big(S_1 G_x + S_2\Big(G - \frac{S_1}{S_2} G_x\Big)\Big) + \frac{S_2}{2}\Big(\sigma_1^2 \frac{S_1^2}{S_2^2} G_{xx} + \sigma_2^2 \frac{S_1^2}{S_2^2} G_{xx} - 2\sigma_{12} \frac{S_1^2}{S_2^2} G_{xx}\Big) \\
&\quad - r S_2 G \\
&= S_2\Big(G_t + \frac{\hat{\sigma}^2}{2} x^2 G_{xx}\Big), \quad \hat{\sigma}^2 = \sigma_1^2 + \sigma_2^2 - 2\sigma_{12},
\end{aligned}
$$

with terminal condition

$$
S_2 G(t, x) = S_2 \max(x - 1, 0)
$$

(this is where the homogeneity condition is needed). Indeed, the PDE for G is therefore

$$
\begin{aligned}
G_t + \frac{\hat{\sigma}^2}{2} G_{xx} &= 0, \\
G(x, T) &= \max(x - 1, 0),
\end{aligned}
$$

which is actually in the standard one-dimensional Black–Scholes PDE form, with interest rate $r = 0$, and variance $\hat{\sigma}^2$. The solution is therefore

$$
G(x, t) = \mathcal{BS}(x_0 = 1, K = 1, r = 0, \hat{\sigma}, T),
$$

and the option value is

$$
F(S_1, S_2, t) = S_2 G\Big(\frac{S_1}{S_2}, t\Big).
$$

In summary, we have found a closed-form solution of the two-dimensional problem, based on our knowledge of the closed-form solution of the one-dimensional problem.

10.5 Change of Numeraire

So far we have thought of payoffs and values in terms of "dollars." What if we were to express these in some other currency or unit? Some examples:

- the number of bonds the portfolio is worth
- the number of shares of a specific stock one could buy
- some other currency with a random strictly positive exchange rate

This takes us to the general concept of a numeraire.

Definition 10.1. A *numeraire* (*deflator*) is any strictly positive adapted Itô process, P_t. The value of an asset in the P_t-numeraire is

$$S_t^* = \frac{S_t}{P_t}.$$

Here, P_t thus provides the exchange rate between the value measures, S_t and S_t^*, so that if $P_t > 1$, then the price is lower in the new numeraire, and when $P_t < 1$, the price is higher.

Intuitively, the fundamental properties of the market should not change just because we change the way value is measured. Indeed, one can show the following invariance properties:

- *Numeraire invariance property*: Suppose $\mathbf{h}_t$ is a self-financed strategy. Then $\mathbf{h}_t$ is also self-financed in the P_t-numeraire.
- *Arbitrage invariance property* (1): Suppose the trading strategy $\mathbf{h}_t$ constitutes an arbitrage. Then it also constitutes an arbitrage in the P_t-numeraire.
- *Arbitrage invariance property* (2): Suppose a market is arbitrage-free. Then it is also arbitrage-free in the P_t-numeraire.
- *Risk-neutral measure invariance*: Suppose an EMM exists. Then an EMM also exists under the P_t-numeraire.
- *Replicating portfolio*: Suppose the self-financed portfolio $\mathbf{h}_t$ replicates the payoff function $\Phi(S_T)$. Then $\mathbf{h}_t$ replicates the payoff

$$\frac{1}{P_T}\Phi(S_T^* P_T)$$

  in the P_t-numeraire.

Now, the fact that the market's fundamental properties remain the same regardless of the choice of numeraire, often allows one to pick a numeraire in which a problem can be more conveniently solved. We show how this works by revisiting the exchange option from the previous section. In risk-neutral dynamics, the problem is to find the exchange option price, $C(t, S_1, S_2)$, where

$$\begin{aligned}
\frac{dB}{B} &= r\,dt, \\
\frac{dS_1}{S_1} &= r\,dt + \sigma_1\,dV_1^Q, \\
\frac{dS_2}{S_2} &= r\,dt + \sigma_2\,dV_2^Q, \\
\rho\,dt &= \text{Cov}(dV_1^Q, dV_2^Q),
\end{aligned}$$

$$\sigma_{12} = \rho\sigma_1\sigma_2,$$
$$C(T, S_1, S_2) = \max(S_1(T) - S_2(T), 0).$$

We rewrite this problem, using the dollar price of stock 2, S_2, as numeraire, i.e., at each point in time we express the value of the option in terms of how many shares of S_2 it is worth. Thus, in the new numeraire,

$$B_t^* = \frac{B_t}{S_{2t}},$$
$$S_{1t}^* = \frac{S_{1t}}{S_{2t}},$$
$$S_{2t}^* = 1.$$

So, in the new numeraire, the bond is no longer risk-free, because the number of bonds you will be able to buy for one unit of stock 2 in the future is not deterministic, whereas stock 2 *is* risk-free. In this numeraire, the discount rate is $r^* = 0$, since there is no appreciation associated with owning stock 2—if you buy one share at time 0, you will still have one share at time T.

In the new numeraire, the payout function of the exchange option at expiration is

$$C^*(T, S_1^*, S_2^*) = \max(S_1^* - 1, 0). \tag{10.16}$$

Indeed, as long as the price of stock 1 is below that of stock 2, the option expires out of the money with a payout of 0, and if $S_1(T) > S_2(T)$, so that $S_1^*(T) > 1$ in the new numeraire, the payout is $S_1^*(T) - 1$ in that numeraire, corresponding to $S_2(T)(S_1^*(T) - 1) = S_1(T) - S_2(T)$ in the dollar numeraire.

Using Itô calculus to calculate the dynamics of the three assets in the new numeraire, we get

$$\frac{dB^*}{B^*} = \sigma_1^2\,dt - \sigma_2\,dV_2^Q,$$
$$\frac{dS_1^*}{S_1^*} = (\sigma_2^2 - \sigma_{12})\,dt + \sigma_1\,dV_1^Q - \sigma_2\,dV_2^Q,$$
$$\frac{dS_2^*}{S_2^*} = 0.$$

Note that the standard properties of multivariate Brownian motions imply that $\sigma_1\,dV^Q - \sigma\,dV^Q = \hat{\sigma}\,dV_*^Q$, where $\hat{\sigma}^2 = \sigma_1^2 + \sigma_2^2 - 2\sigma_{12}$. So we can write the dynamics as

$$\frac{dB^*}{B^*} = \sigma_1^2\,dt - \sigma_2\,dV_2^Q,$$
$$\frac{dS_1^*}{S_1^*} = (\sigma_2^2 - \sigma_{12})\,dt + \hat{\sigma}\,dV_*^Q,$$
$$\frac{dS_2^*}{S_2^*} = 0.$$

From the no-arbitrage principle applied in the new numeraire, we know that the risk-neutral pricing in this numeraire takes the form

$$\frac{dB^*}{B^*} = 0\,dt - \sigma_2\,dV_2^{Q^*}, \tag{10.17}$$

$$\frac{dS_1^*}{S_1^*} = 0\,dt + \hat{\sigma}\,dV^{Q^*}, \tag{10.18}$$

$$\frac{dS_2^*}{S_2^*} = 0. \tag{10.19}$$

At this point, we may now use what we know about option pricing when the dynamics of the risky and risk-free assets are (10.18, 10.19), and the payout function is (10.16), leading to

$$C_0^* = \mathcal{BS}\Big(\frac{S_1(0)}{S_2(0)},\ K=1,\ r=0,\ \hat{\sigma},\ T\Big).$$

The value in the dollar numeraire is then $S_2(0)C_0^*$, which is the same formula that we derived using dimensionality reduction. Specifically, $C_0 = S_{10}C_0^*$, where $C_0^* = S_{0T}^* N(x) - N(x - \sigma_* \sqrt{T})$, and

- $x = \dfrac{\ln(\frac{S_{20}^*}{1}) + (0 + \frac{\sigma_*^2}{2})T}{\sigma_* \sqrt{T}}$,
- $\sigma_*^2 = \sigma_1^2 + \sigma_2^2 - 2\sigma_{12}$.

10.6 Forward and Futures Contracts in Continuous Time

In section 7.7, we mentioned forward contracts in the static setting. In continuous time, the same argument as before holds for a forward contract on a financial asset that does not make any dividend payments before T. Specifically, consider the forward (transaction) price $G_{0,T}$, which the buyer and seller agree upon at time 0, where the price is set so that neither party needs compensation at that point.

Assuming that the price at $t=0$ of a risk-free bond that pays 1 at T is $B_{0,T} = e^{-rT}$, where $r = r_{0,T}$ is the appropriate yield between 0 and T, the risk-neutral pricing formula becomes

$$0 = E_0^{\mathbb{Q}}[e^{-\int_0^T r_s\,ds}(S_T - G_{0,T})] = S_0 - B_{0,T}G_{0,T},$$

and thus

$$G_{0,T} = \frac{1}{B_{0,T}} S_T = e^{rT} S_0. \tag{10.20}$$

Note that if the risk-free rate is constant, we have the bond price formula

$$B_{t,T} = e^{-r(T-t)},$$

for some constant r, for all t and $T > t$. When interest rates are varying, and possibly even stochastic, the pricing formula becomes

$$B_{t,T} = E^{\mathbb{Q}}[e^{-\int_t^T r_s\,ds}].$$

Formula (10.20) is very general, and holds outside the strong diffusion process assumptions we have made so far. The reason why it is so general is that there is a *static* trading strategy that replicates the payoff of the forward contract, under very general conditions.

Specifically, consider the following trading strategy, which is equivalent to entering into the forward agreement: Purchase the asset now (at price S_0), and finance the purchase by selling a T-period (risk-free) bond, i.e., by borrowing S_0. That is, the portfolio position is

$$\mathbf{h}^G = \Big(1, -\frac{S_0}{B_{0,T}}\Big)',$$

with value $S_0 - \frac{S_0}{B_{0,T}} B_{0,T} = 0$, given that the time-0 bond price is $B_{0,T}$, and that the time-T bond price is 1. At time T, the value of this position will be

$$S_T - \frac{S_0}{B_{0,T}} = S_T - G_{0,T},$$

i.e., the same as after buying the forward contract, under the risk-neutral pricing formula above. In other words, the payoff of the forward position is within the asset span of the stock and a T-period risk-free bond under very general conditions.

Note that the forward price is *not* the price of a traded asset. Rather, it is a contractual property of the forward contract that makes the contract worth 0 at time 0. In this respect, the forward price is similar to the strike price K of a call option, which is also a contractual property of the call option.

The value of the forward contract, $V_t^G = V_{t,T}^G$, although 0 at time 0, will typically vary randomly between 0 and T. Indeed, since the value of the contract corresponds to the static portfolio $\mathbf{h}^G$, we have

$$V_t^G = S_t - \frac{S_0}{B_{0,T}} B_{t,T},$$

and thus

$$dV_t^G = dS_t - \frac{S_0}{B_{0,T}} \, dB_{t,T},$$

and

$$E^{\mathbb{Q}}[dV_t^G] = E^{\mathbb{Q}}\left[dS_t - \frac{S_0}{B_{0,T}} \, dB_{t,T}\right] = rS_t \, dt - r\frac{S_0}{B_{0,T}} B_{t,T} \, dt = rV_t^G \, dt,$$

in line with the risk-neutral return expectation of any self-financed trading strategy; see proposition 9.7.

On the other hand, the forward price is $G_t = G_{t,T} = \frac{S_t}{B_{t,T}}$. When the discount rate is constant, $B_{t,T} = e^{-r(T-t)}$, this gives us

$$G_t = e^{r(T-t)} S_t,$$

and therefore

$$dG_t = -rG_t \, dt + G_t \frac{dS_t}{S_t}.$$

So

$$E_t^{\mathbb{Q}}[dG_t] = -rG_t \, dt + rG_t \, dt = 0.$$

We see that the risk-neutral return expectation just mentioned does not apply to G_t. This is, again, because the forward price is *not* the price of a traded asset.

A *futures contract* is similar to a forward contract, but with two main exceptions:

- While forward contracts are arranged by dealers in the *over-the-counter* (OTC) markets, futures contracts are typically traded on *exchanges*, so futures contracts are typically more standardized and more liquid.
- Futures contracts are *marked to market*. This means that while the forward contract gain $G_{T,T} - G_{0,T}$ is only settled on the delivery (maturity) date, futures contracts are settled daily. At the end of every trading day, say day s, the holder of a long futures position receives the amount $H_{s,T} - H_{s-1,T}$ from the holder of the short position, where the futures price for a contract written at t is $H_{t,T}$. We also write $H_t = H_{t,T}$.

The mark-to-market property of the futures contract limits exposure to credit risk. The most widely traded futures contracts are futures on interest rates, futures on the S&P 500 index, and currency/foreign exchange (FX) futures.

Futures and forwards are very similar, but when the interest rate is stochastic, they are not exactly the same, i.e., in general,

$$G_{t,T} \neq H_{t,T}.$$

Specifically, futures contracts generate a flow of intermediate cash flows, between 0 and T, whereas forward contracts do not. When the sizes of these cash flows are related to interest rates, this creates a wedge between the two contracts. Of course, at $t = T$, we have the relation

$$G_{T,T} = H_{T,T} = S_T.$$

In general, finding the futures rate is trickier than finding the forward rate, because of the stochastic cash flows over time. When settlements occur instantaneously, i.e., after each infinitesimal time increment, dt, the analysis simplifies somewhat though. Consider a futures contract that is marked to market at $t + dt$. The cash flow at $t + dt$ is then

$$H_{t+dt} - H_t = dH_t,$$

and it follows from the risk-neutral pricing formula that

$$0 = E_t^{\mathbb{Q}}[e^{-r_t\,dt}\,dH_t].$$

So $E_t^{\mathbb{Q}}[dH_t] = 0$, and by the law of iterated expectations, $E_t^{\mathbb{Q}}[dH_s] = 0$ for all $s \geq t$. It follows that $H_{t,T}$ follows a $\mathbb{Q}$-martingale process. Moreover, since $H_{T,T} = S_T$, it follows that

$$H_{0,T} = E_0^{\mathbb{Q}}[S_T].$$

Compare this with

$$G_{0,T} = e^{r_{0,T}T} S_0.$$

In the special case when r is constant, it follows immediately that $G_t = H_t$. When the short rate, r_t, is stochastic we can write

$$\begin{aligned}
G_{0,T} &= e^{r_{0,T}T} S_0 \\
&= e^{r_{0,T}T} E_0^{\mathbb{Q}}[e^{-\int_0^T r_s\,ds} S_T] \\
&= e^{r_{0,T}T}\left(E_0^{\mathbb{Q}}[e^{-\int_0^T r_s\,ds}] E_0^{\mathbb{Q}}[S_T] + \mathrm{Cov}_0^{\mathbb{Q}}(e^{-\int_0^T r_s\,ds}, S_T)\right) \\
&= H_{0,T} + e^{r_{0,T}T}\,\mathrm{Cov}_0^{\mathbb{Q}}(e^{-\int_0^T r_s\,ds}, S_T).
\end{aligned}$$

It follows that the difference between the forward and the futures prices depends on the term

$$\mathrm{Cov}_0^{\mathbb{Q}}(R_{0,T}^{-1}, S_T),$$

where $R_{0,T} = e^{\int_0^T r_s\,ds}$ is the realized return between 0 and T on a portfolio that invests in short-term bonds and rolls over the investment in each period. Therefore, the difference between the forward and the futures rates depends on how the underlying asset's return is related to the short interest rate (in the $\mathbb{Q}$ measure).

If S_T tends to be high when $\{r_s\}_{s\in[0,T]}$ is high, then the covariance between S_T and $R_{t,T}^{-1}$ is negative, and the forward price will be lower than the futures price. Indeed, in this case, the time value of money is high, so there is a lot of value in realizing cash flows early, which is what the futures contract does. On the other hand, if S_T tends to be high when $\{r_s\}_{s\in[0,T]}$ is low, the forward price will be higher than the futures price.

10.7 Exercises

1. Show that in the special case when r, σ, and θ are constants, G in the solution of (10.2) can be expressed as the solution to the PDE

$$G_t + rSG_S + \frac{1}{2}\sigma^2 G_{SS}S^2 - rG = 0,$$
$$G(T,S) = \Phi(Se^{-\theta T}).$$

2. *Black–Scholes*: Consider the standard Black–Scholes economy where the stock (which does not pay dividends) and bond follow the dynamics

$$\frac{dB}{B} = r\,dt, \quad r > 0,$$
$$\frac{dS}{S} = \hat{\mu}\,dt + \sigma\,dW.$$

Here, $\hat{\mu}$, σ, and r are all constant. Consider a call option with the payoff function $\Phi(T) = (3S - K)_+$. What is the time-0 value of this option?

3. *Time transformation*: Consider the generalized Black–Scholes economy where the stock (which does not pay dividends) and bond follow the dynamics

$$\frac{dB}{B} = \frac{r}{(1+t)^2}\,dt, \quad r > 0,$$
$$\frac{dS}{S} = \hat{\mu}\,dt + \frac{\sigma}{1+t}\,dW.$$

Here, $\hat{\mu}$, σ, and r are all constant, and the market operates between $t = 0$ and $t = T$.

(a) Is this market arbitrage-free?
(b) Is this market complete?
(c) Consider a European call option on the stock, with exercise date T and strike price K. What is the time-0 price of this option?

Hint: Consider the diffusion process $dX = \mu(X)\,dt + \sigma(X)\,dW_t$. Define the process $Y_t = X(\tau(t))$, where $\tau(t)$ is a smooth, strictly increasing function of t. Then Y satisfies the diffusion process

$$dY = \mu(Y)\tau'(t)\,dt + \sigma(Y)\sqrt{\tau'(t)}\,dV_t,$$

where V_t is a Wiener process.

4. *Stop-loss start-gain strategy*: Consider the standard Black–Scholes model with zero risk-free rate:

$$\frac{dB}{B} = 0, \quad B_0 = 1,$$
$$\frac{dS}{S} = \hat{\mu}\,dt + \sigma\,dW,$$

$\hat{\mu} > 0$, $\sigma > 0$ constants. Further, assume that a European call option on the stock with strike price $K > S_0$ and maturity T is traded in the market. A portfolio $\mathbf{h} = (b, s, c)'$ thus consists of b bonds, s shares of the stock, and c shares of the option. Consider the following trading strategy:

$$\mathbf{h}_t = \begin{cases} (-K, 1, -1)', & S_t \geq K, \\ (0, 0, -1)', & S_t < K. \end{cases}$$

Since $S_0 < K$, the strategy has a negative initial cost, as long as $C_0 > 0$. Also, the value of the portfolio at $t = T$ is always 0. Further, since any rebalancing occurs at a price of $S = K$, the portfolio is self-financed. Thus, this strategy seems to lead to an arbitrage opportunity. Can you explain this apparent contradiction by finding a violation of the assumptions we made when deriving the Black–Scholes pricing formulas?

5. *Barrier options*: Prove the formula for the general up-and-in claim.

6. *Barrier options*: Use the general formula for the up-and-in option to derive the price of a knock-in European put option on a stock that does not pay dividends, where the knock-in barrier is the same as the exercise price, K, and the current price is $S < K$.

7. *The yesterday options of Mr. Rando Nidokym*: After having been introduced to continuous-time finance and also inspired by an old Beatles song, Mr. Rando Nidokym is exploring new options.

   In the classical Black–Scholes economy,

$$\frac{dB}{B} = r\,dt,$$

$$\frac{dS}{S} = \hat{\mu}\,dt + \sigma\,dW,$$

   Mr. Nidokym is exploring several derivatives whose payoffs depend on the stock price at earlier points in time:

   (a) The first derivative Mr. Nidokym is considering is a "yesterday derivative" that pays $S_{T-1/365}$ at time T. That is, since T is measured in years, the derivative will at time T pay out the stock price one day before maturity. Derive an expression for the value at $t = 0$ of this yesterday derivative.

   (b) Mr. Nidokym decides that the derivative in (a) is too limited, because it has no option feature. He therefore next considers allowing the owner of the claim to decide whether to base the payout on the current or the previous day's stock price. Specifically, the time-T payoff would be $\max(S_T, S_{T-1/365})$. Derive an expression for the value at $t = 0$ of this yesterday option.

   Hint: It may be helpful to write $S_T = S_{T-1/365}e^y$, where $y = \log(\frac{S_T}{S_{T-1/365}})$ is independent of $S_{T-1/365}$.

   (c) "Still not cool enough," Mr. Nidokym concludes about the option in (b). "It needs to be American." Mr. Nidokym determines that the owner of the option should get the right to decide when to exercise, i.e., to pick a time, $0 \leq t \leq T$, at which point the payoff will be $\max(S_t, S_{t-1/365})$. Moreover, Mr. Nidokym decides to make the option perpetual, i.e., to set $T = \infty$. What is the time-0 value of this perpetual American yesterday option?

8. *Fund raising, idiosyncratic risk, and barriers:* A nonprofit organization is launching a major fundraising initiative, at $t = 0$. The dollar value of the cumulative donations (net operating

costs) over time to the fund are well approximated by the geometric Brownian motion

$$\frac{dF}{F} = \hat{\mu}\, dt + \sigma\, dW,$$

$F(0) = 10{,}000$, and the initiative will last until $T > 0$, at which point the fund is liquidated and pays off $F(T)$. Here, $F(t)$ thus represents the total (net) donations up until time t, and W is a Wiener process. The risk associated with the initiative is idiosyncratic, suggesting that the $\mathbb{P}$ measure and the $\mathbb{Q}$ measure associated with dW risk coincide. The continuously compounded risk-free rate is r.

(a) Derive a formula for the time-t value, V_t, of the claim to the future payoff, $F(T)$, $0 \le t < T$.

(b) A philanthropist has promised to provide a matching donation if the (net) donations at any point in time $0 < t \le T$ reach the threshold level $\bar{F} > 10{,}000$. Specifically, at time T the philanthropist will pay $\bar{F}$ if the threshold was hit at any point in time before T. Derive a formula for the time-0 value of the philanthropist's promise.

9. *Value-line index derivatives*: Consider an $N+1$ asset economy with a risk-free bond,

$$\frac{dB}{B} = r\, dt,$$

and N stocks,

$$\frac{dS_n}{S_n} = r\, dt + \sigma_n\, dV_n^{\mathbb{Q}}, \quad n = 1, \ldots, N,$$

where $\text{Cov}(dV_n^{\mathbb{Q}}, dV_m^{\mathbb{Q}}) = \rho_{nm}\, dt$, $r > 0$, $\sigma_1, \ldots, \sigma_N$ are scalars, and $V_1^{\mathbb{Q}}, \ldots, V_N^{\mathbb{Q}}$ are Wiener processes. We define the covariance matrix Σ with elements $\Sigma_{nm} = \sigma_n \sigma_m \rho_{nm}$, which we assume is nonsingular, and the average covariance $c = \frac{1}{N^2}\mathbf{1}'\Sigma\mathbf{1} > 0$, where $\mathbf{1} \in \mathbb{R}^N$ is a vector of 1s, $\mathbf{1} = (1, 1, \ldots, 1)'$ (i.e., c is the average of all the covariance terms). The *value-line index* in the market is defined as the geometric average of the stock prices:

$$Y = (S_1 \times S_2 \times \cdots \times S_{N-1} \times S_N)^{\frac{1}{N}} = \left(\prod_{i=1}^{N} S_i\right)^{\frac{1}{N}}.$$

(a) Use Itô calculus to derive a formula for the dynamics of the value-line index of the form

$$\frac{dY}{Y} = a\, dt + b\, dV^{\mathbb{Q}},$$

where a and b are appropriately defined constants (define them!) and $dV^{\mathbb{Q}}$ is an appropriately defined Wiener process in terms of $V_1^{\mathbb{Q}}, \ldots, V_N^{\mathbb{Q}}$ (define it!).

(b) Use your result in (a) to derive a formula for the time-0 price, P, of a contingent claim that pays $Y(T)$ at time T.

(c) Use your result in (a) to derive a formula for the time-0 price, Z, of a value-line call option with strike price K, which at time T pays

$$\max(Y(T) - K, 0).$$

(d) Assume that $S_1(0) = S_2(0) = \cdots = S_N(0)$, and that $\sigma_n = \sigma$ for all n, i.e., that all stock variances are the same. How does the value of the option in (c), Z, compare with the value of a plain vanilla call option on S_1, which at T pays

$$\max(S_1(T) - K, 0).$$

10. *Mr. Rando Nidokym's very exotic basket option*: Mr. Rando Nidokym, an immensely wealthy trader with a soft spot for inventing novel—albeit not always very useful—derivatives, has decided to introduce a "very exotic basket option," to celebrate his birthday. In the classical (constant-coefficient) Black–Scholes economy with two stocks,

$$\frac{dB}{B} = r\,dt,$$

$$\frac{dS_1}{S_1} = r\,dt + \sigma_1\,dV_1^Q,$$

$$\frac{dS_2}{S_2} = r\,dt + \sigma_2\,dV_2^Q,$$

where V_1 and V_2 are Wiener processes with covariance $\mathrm{Cov}(dV_1^Q, dV_2^Q) = \rho\,dt$, Mr. Nidokym's basket option is a simple contingent claim with payoff function at time T:

$$\Phi(S_1(T), S_2(T)) = \sqrt{S_1(T)S_2(T)}\left(\ln\left(\frac{S_1(T)}{S_2(T)}\right)\right)^4.$$

(a) Consider the variable coefficient PDE

$$w_t + ax^2 w_{xx} = 0, \quad a > 0,$$

$$w(T,x) = R(x),$$

$$x \geq 0,$$

$$t \leq T.$$

Show that the solution to this PDE, w, can be written as $w(t,x) = \sqrt{x}e^{-a\frac{(T-t)}{4}}u(t,z)$, where $z = \ln(x)$, and where u is the solution to the constant-coefficient PDE

$$u_t + au_{zz} = 0,$$

$$u(T,z) = \Psi(z), \quad \text{where } \Psi(z) = e^{-\frac{z}{2}}R(e^z),$$

$$z \in \mathbb{R},$$

$$t \leq T.$$

(b) Show that for $\Psi(z) = z^4$, the solution to the PDE in (a) is

$$u(t,z) = z^4 + 12a(T-t)z^2 + 12a^2(T-t)^2.$$

(c) Denote the price of Mr. Nidokym's very exotic basket option, as a function of time and the two stock prices, by $F(t, S_1(t), S_2(t))$. What PDE in t, S_1, and S_2, will F satisfy?

(d) Use dimensionality reduction techniques to derive a one-dimensional (in space) PDE, the solution of which can be used to calculate F.

(e) Use the results in (a)–(d) to derive a closed-form solution for the price of Mr. Nidokym's derivative, $F(t, S_1(t), S_2(t))$.

CHAPTER 11 Numerical Methods

In many cases, problems within asset pricing do not have closed-form solutions, and one therefore needs to rely on numerical methods to calculate approximate solutions. We have already seen examples of such numerical methods when analyzing the binomial tree method. We approximated the solution to the Black–Scholes option pricing problem by solving a discrete binomial tree model, and as we let the number of steps in the tree tend to infinity, our approximate solution converged to the Black–Scholes formula. Specifically, the N-step binomial tree method gave us an approximate option price, $\widehat{P}_N$, that converged to the true price, P, for large N:

$$\lim_{N\to\infty} \widehat{P}_N = P.$$

Binomial trees belong to the large class of so-called lattice methods for numerical option pricing. The two other major classes are PDE-based methods—especially finite difference methods, and Monte Carlo methods. We discuss these three classes. Binomial tree methods and finite difference methods have a lot of similarities, and are both based on the law of motion implied by the Black–Scholes PDE. Monte Carlo methods are different. They are based on the risk-neutral formulation of the option pricing problem.

To evaluate the performance of a numerical method, we need to answer the following two questions:

(a) How large does the number of steps, N, have to be for the approximation to be close to the true solution?

(b) How computationally challenging is it to calculate $\widehat{P}_N$?

We will use concepts from *numerical analysis* to answer these questions.

Consider the general option pricing problem of finding the price $P = P(0, S_0)$ of a contingent claim that expires at time T. This could be a simple contingent claim, making the payment $\Phi(S_T)$ at time T. But it could also be a more general claim, which makes payments that depend on the whole price path $\{S_t\}_{t\in[0,T]}$. The payments could also depend on the realization of multiple factors, for example on the realization of the stochastic interest rate in addition to the terminal price of the underlying asset.

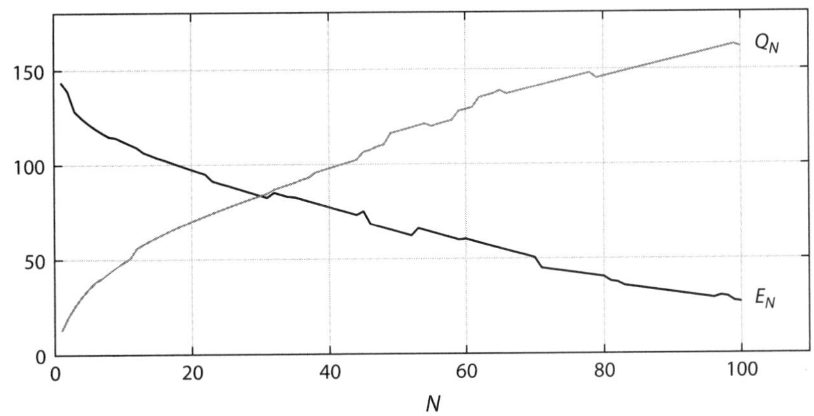

Figure 11.1: Error and number of computations as functions of N; conceptual example.

A numerical method is used to approximate the price by $\widehat{P}_N$, where $N \in \mathbb{N}$ is some parameter representing the number of steps in the numerical method, or more generally, how "refined" the approximation is. The exact measure of the number of steps will be different for different types of methods but, in general, the measure is defined such that the higher N is, the closer $\widehat{P}_N$ will be to P—or at least the closer it will *tend* to be. We define the *approximation error*,

$$E_N = E(N) = |\widehat{P}_N - P|.$$

Refining the approximation typically requires more computational work. We let $Q_N = Q(N)$ represent the "number of computations" needed to calculate $\widehat{P}_N$. Again, we avoid a precise definition. Intuitively, we aim for a measure that is proportional to the time it takes to solve the problem on a computer, when the method is implemented efficiently. An important quantity is the combined measure $E(Q^{-1}(x))$, a performance measure that shows how the approximation error depends on the number of computations, x. This measure is invariant to how the "number of steps," N, is defined.[1]

An example of what the error function and number of computations may look like is shown in figure 11.1. Note that the functions may be nonmonotone, and nonsmooth. In fact, both these features are common.

Finding the exact form of E_N and Q_N is challenging, since P is the unknown entity we wish to approximate. Instead of calculating the exact value, one is therefore usually content with finding bounds on how large E_N may be. The following concepts of *order of convergence*, from numerical analysis, are useful here:

Definition 11.1. The convergence $\widehat{P}_N \to P$ is said to be of order

[1] For example, for a problem that requires a two-dimensional version of the Black–Scholes equation, like a basket option that depends on two underlying assets, N could represent the number of pairwise realizations of the two stocks in a two-dimensional binomial tree approximation of the continuous-time problem. It could also represent the number of different realizations of one of the underlying assets. The former is the square of the latter, so the measure depends on the definition. But the measure of how many computations, x, are needed to get an approximation error of $E = 10^{-3}$ does not depend on how the number of steps is defined.

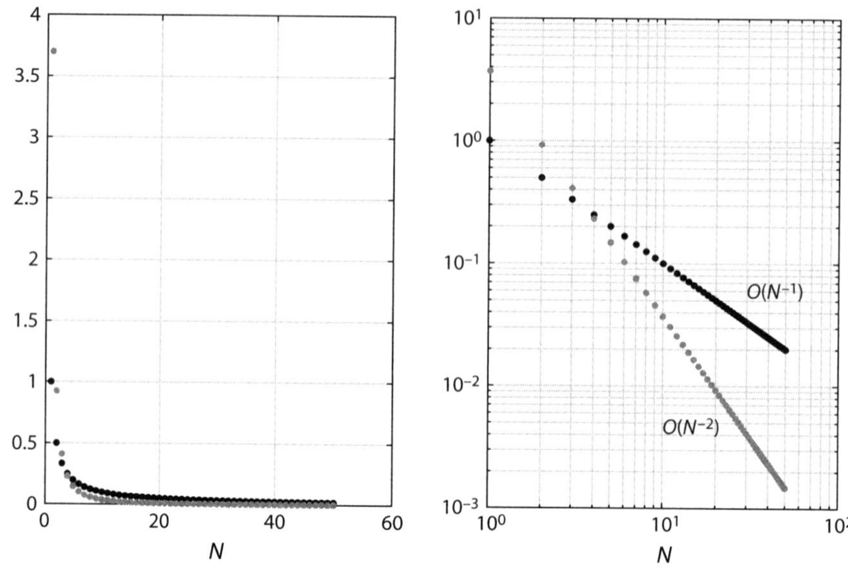

Figure 11.2: Example: Error function and order of convergence.

(a) $O(F(N))$ (denoted "big-O of $F(N)$"), where $F(N)$ is typically decreasing in N, if there exists a constant $C > 0$, such that

$$E_N \leq C \times F(N)$$

for all N, or equivalently,

$$\limsup_{N\to\infty} \frac{E_N}{F(N)} < \infty,$$

(b) $o(F(N))$ (denoted "little-o of $F(N)$"), if

$$\lim_{N\to\infty} \frac{E_N}{F(N)} = 0.$$

One can use similar definitions for $Q(N)$, which will typically be increasing in N. In figure 11.2, we show an example of the error as a function of N for two convergence orders, $E_N = O(N^{-1})$ (black points) and $E_N = O(N^{-2})$ (gray points). The left-hand panel shows the actual error, which is indeed decreasing in N. Except for $N = 1, 2, 3$, the gray points lie below the black points in line with the idea that $O(N^{-2})$ should represent faster converge than $O(N^{-1})$.

The behavior of the two error functions is more easily seen in the right-hand panel of the figure, which shows the logarithm of the (absolute) error on the y-axis. Convergence of order $O(N^{-p})$ shows up as a straight line with slope $-p$ in this panel, following from the fact that when $y = C \times N^{-p}$, then $\ln(y) = \ln(C) - p\ln(N)$. Thus, the more negative the slope, the higher the order of convergence.

There are a couple of things to note about the big-O concept. First, even though $O(N^{-2})$ implies a smaller error bound than $O(N^{-1})$ in the limit, it does not mean that the error is smaller for all N. Indeed, the definition does not nail down the constant C, which could potentially be extremely large. We see in the figure that for low N, the error is actually smaller for the function with $O(N^{-1})$ convergence. This is because it has a smaller constant. For any fixed N, the method

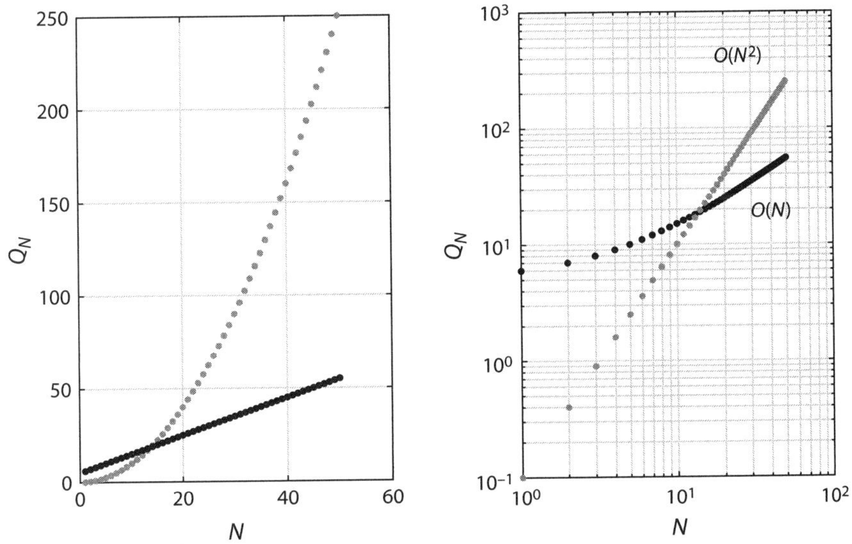

Figure 11.3: Example: Number of computations and order of convergence.

with the higher order of convergence may still have a larger error if its constant, C, is much larger than the constant of the method with the lower order of convergence.

Second, the big-O concept provides an upper bound on the error; the relationship is an inequality. This means that a convergence of order $O(N^{-2})$ is also convergence of order $O(N^{-1})$. Usually, one is interested in the best possible bound. It also means that one cannot expect the error function to be as monotone as in the examples we have just shown. Indeed, errors may be locally oscillating, so that the error $E_{N+1} \gg E_N$ for some N. This is why we have used the limit superior in the definition. To graphically find the order of convergence may therefore be "messier" than what is shown in the figure.

In figure 11.3, we show an example of the number of computations as a function of N. The function typically has a positive slope, and the slower it increases, the better. The function that grows at the first order, of $O(N)$ (black points), is therefore asymptotically to be preferred over the function that grows at the second order, $O(N^2)$ (gray points), although for low N, the function with second-order growth is faster.

We will mainly use the big-O concept. The difference between big-O and little-o is very small—in some sense arbitrarily small—and is more important for mathematical analysis than for understanding errors and number of computations in practice. Little-o is a tiny bit stronger than big-O, and it is always the case that $o(F(N))$ convergence implies $O(F(N))$ convergence. For example, if the error is $O(1)$, then it stays bounded as a function of N, which is not very impressive. It could even be increasing: for example, the function $E_N = \frac{N}{N+1} = O(1)$. If $E_N = o(1)$, on the other hand, then the error must tend to zero as N grows. The crux is that the convergence can be arbitrarily slow. For example, the error function $E_N = \frac{1}{1+\ln(1+\ln(1+\ln(1+N)))} = o(1)$ has $E_{10^{100}} \approx 0.349$, which for numerical purposes is indistinguishable from $O(1)$ convergence.

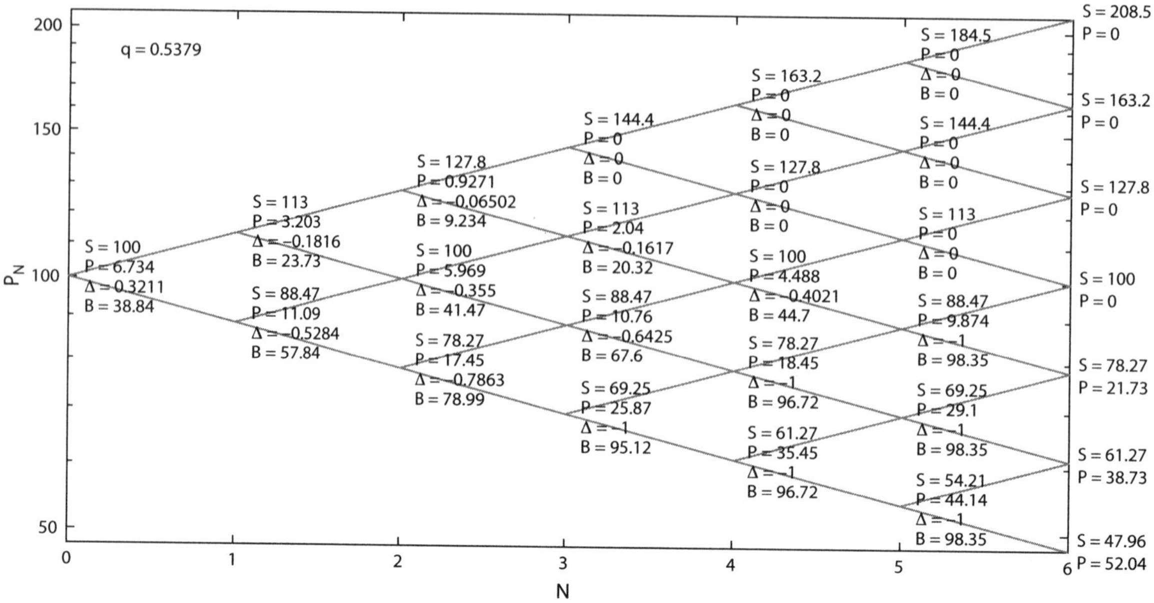

Figure 11.4: Binomial tree for the European put option.

11.1 Binomial Tree Method

We analyze the binomial tree method for a plain vanilla European put option, using our newly introduced order of convergence concepts. Consider the put option with $S=100$, $K=100$, $r=0.1$, $T=1$, $\sigma=0.4$. The correct price of the put is $P=7.2179$. The binomial tree solution with $N=6$ steps is shown in figure 11.4. The approximate solution is $\widehat{P}_6=6.734$, and the error is $E_6=|6.734-7.2179|=0.4839$. Recall that the binomial tree method starts at step N, in the right-hand part of the figure, and then systematically steps backward in time by backward induction, in each iteration calculating the solution at step $n-1$ from the solution at step n.

We first analyze how the number of computations depends on N. We show the MATLAB code for the binomial tree algorithm in algorithm 1. The function takes the five parameters needed as input to calculate the option price, P_N, which is returned by the function. The initial three lines define Δt, R, u, d, q, $1-q$, and the payoff at expiration. The price at $t=0$ is then calculated via the law of motion, using a "for loop."

Note that vector notation is used inside the loop. Specifically, `W(2:i+1)` is a vector with the elements $(W_2, W_3, \ldots, W_{i+1})$. The number of calculations in one step of the loop is therefore proportional to i. Since the variable i counts down from N to 1, we therefore get

$$Q_N = C_0 + C_1 \times (N+(N-1)+(N-2)+\cdots+2+1) = O(N^2).$$

On the last line, W—which is now not a vector but a scalar since $i=1$—is multiplied by e^{-rT}, to take the discounting into account. We could also have multiplied by $e^{-r\Delta t}$ in each step inside the loop, as we did when we introduced the multistep binomial tree method. However, this would increase the number of such multiplications from 1 to of order N^2, while leading to the same result. It is common that such computational improvements make the implementation of the algorithm look quite different from how it was originally defined.

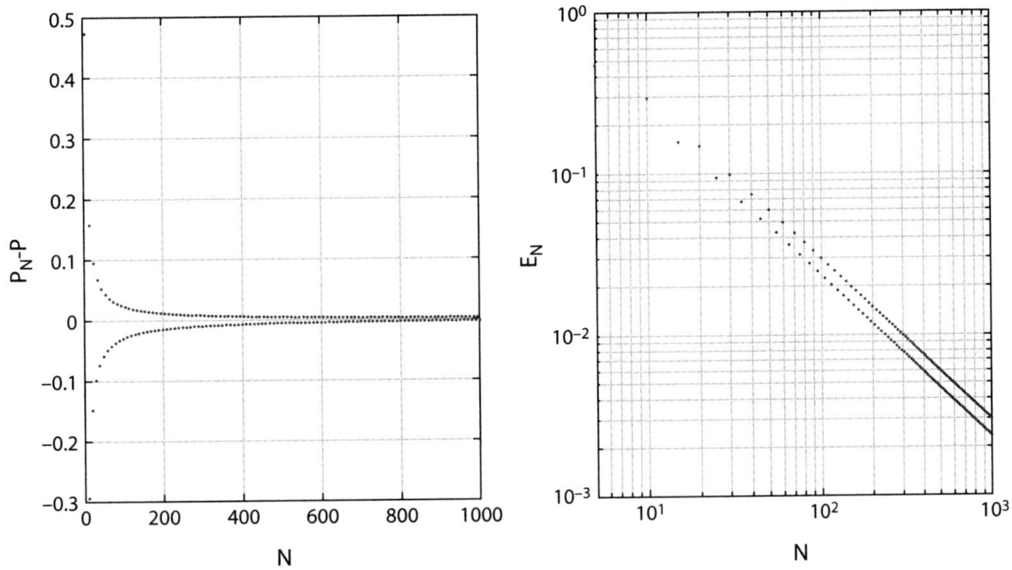

Figure 11.5: Error: Binomial tree for the European put option.

Algorithm 1 (Binomial tree method).

```
function PN=BinomialPut(S,K,r,T,sigma,N)
  dt=T/N;R=exp(r*T/N);u=exp(sigma*sqrt(T/N));d=1/u;
  qu=(R-d)/(u-d);qd=1-qu;
  PT=max(K-S*d.^([N:-1:0]').*u.^([0:N]'),0); W=PT;
  for i=N:-1:1
    W=qu*W(2:i+1) + qd*W(1:i);
  end
  PN=exp(-r*T)*W;
```

We do not do a formal error analysis of the binomial tree method. Rather, we plot the error and estimate the slope in a log-linear diagram, in figure 11.5. The left-hand part of the figure shows that the error oscillates between positive and negative for odd and even N, but decreases toward zero as N increases. This is common behavior for the binomial tree method. The right-hand part shows that the decrease of the log-error has a slope of -1, implying that the convergence is $O(N^{-1})$. The figure suggests that for the error of the option price to be 2–3 cents, about $N=100$ points are needed. The number of calculations for this error is then of the order of $100^2 = 10{,}000$ times some constant.

For the European option, we can actually improve the performance significantly. Recall that when we proved the convergence to the Black–Scholes solution, we used the unconditional risk-neutral expectation

$$P = e^{-rT} E^{\mathbb{Q}}[\Phi(S_T)] = e^{-rT} \sum_{k=0}^{N} \binom{N}{k} q^k (1-q)^{N-k} \Phi(u^k d^{N-k} S_0).$$

Note that this formula only involves $O(N)$ computations, i.e., the number of computations increases linearly in N. For this simple contingent claim, for which there is a closed-form expression for the risk-neutral distribution at T, we can therefore calculate the approximate price with $O(N)$ computations. Algorithm 2 below uses the unconditional distribution:

Algorithm 2 (Binomial tree algorithm, unconditional).

```
function PN=BinomialPut2(S,K,r,T,sigma,N);
  dt=T/N;R=exp(r*T/N);u=exp(sigma*sqrt(T/N));d=1/u;
  qu=(R-d)/(u-d);qd=1-qu;PN=0;
  PT=max(K-S*d.^([N:-1:0]').*u.^([0:N]'),0);
  for i=0:N
    PN=PN+qu^i*qd^(N-i)*nchoosek(N,i)*PT(i+1);
  end
  PN=exp(-r*T)*PN;
```

We next consider the American put option problem. The binomial tree method—that is, the first version of the algorithm—is very easy to adapt to the American option problem. Algorithm 3 shows the binomial tree method for the American put option. We note that the only difference from the European option algorithm is that in each node the value is calculated as the maximum of exercising and keeping the option alive, instead of just as the value of keeping the option alive. The fast, unconditional, version of the algorithm is not feasible for the American option though, since the value doesn't only depend on the stock price at time T. Rather, to calculate the value of the American put option, one needs to traverse through the whole tree. Therefore, $O(N^2)$ computations are needed.

Algorithm 3 (Binomial tree method, American option).

```
function PN=BinomialPutAm(S,K,r,T,sigma,N);
  dt=T/N;R=exp(r*T/N);u=exp(sigma*sqrt(T/N));d=1/u;
  qu=(R-d)/(u-d);qd=1-qu;
  PT=max(K-S*d.^([N:-1:0]').*u.^([0:N]'),0); W=PT;
  for i=N:-1:1
    W=(qu*W(2:i+1) + qd*W(1:i))/R;
    W=max(W,K-S*d.^([i-1:-1:0]').*u.^([0:i-1]'));
  end
  PN=W;
```

11.1.1 A Two-Dimensional Problem

The binomial tree method can be generalized to multidimensional problems. A rainbow option is a contingent claim with a payout that depends on the value at expiration of multiple underlying assets, i.e., the payout is of the form

$$F(T, S_1, \ldots, S_N) = \Phi(S_1, \ldots, S_N).$$

As we saw in section 10.4, a multidimensional version of the Black–Scholes formula and the risk-neutral valuation formula holds in this case. The dimensionality of the binomial tree will match that of the Black–Scholes PDE. As an example, consider the exchange option from that section, which gives the holder the option to switch asset 2 for asset 1 at expiration. If $S_1 > S_2$, the value of this option is then $S_1 - S_2$, i.e., the difference between the values of the two assets. If $S_1 \leq S_2$, the

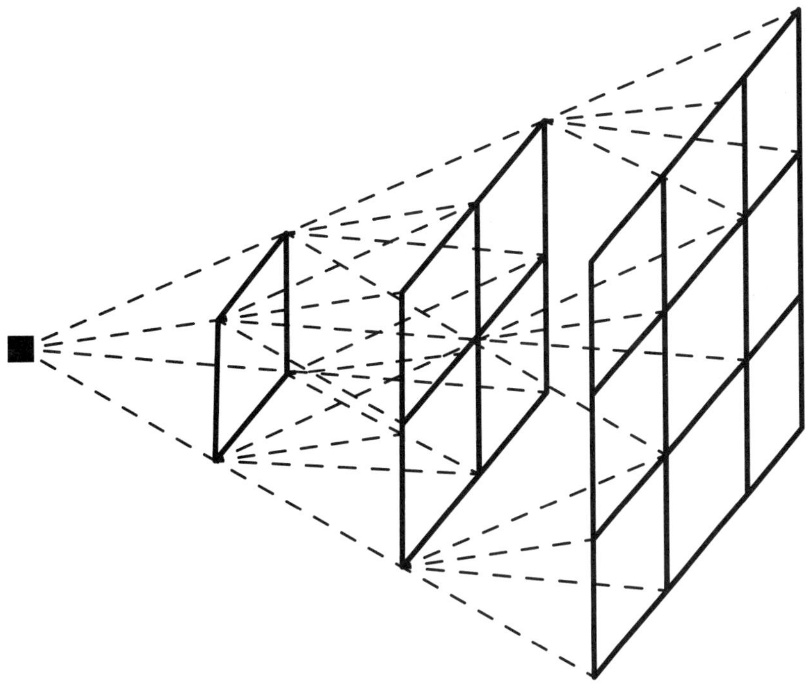

Figure 11.6: Two-dimensional binomial tree.

option is worthless at expiration. The payoff function is then

$$\Phi(S_1, S_2) = \max(S_1 - S_2, 0).$$

This payoff function is thus similar to that of a plain vanilla call option, but the strike price is no longer constant.

The two-dimensional binomial tree for this problem is shown in figure 11.6. As seen from the figure, four risk-neutral transition probabilities are needed for each step in the tree, $q^{u_1u_2}$, $q^{u_1d_2}$, $q^{d_1u_2}$, and $q^{d_1d_2}$. Formulas for calculating these probabilities for the general K-dimensional problem, as well as the appropriate sizes of the up- and down-moves of the assets, in this case u_1, u_2, d_1, and d_2, are provided in Kamrad and Ritchken (1991).

Unsurprisingly, for those who have read the section on multidimensional Itô calculus, the two assets' volatilities σ_1, σ_2, their covariance $\sigma_{12} = \rho_{12}\sigma_1\sigma_2$, and the risk-free rate r, are needed for these calculations. Algorithm 4 implements the binomial tree method for the exchange option.

Algorithm 4 (Binomial tree method, exchange option).

```
function PN=BinomialExchange(S1,S2,r,T,sigma1,sigma2,sigma12,N)
  mu1=r-sigma1^2/2;mu2=r-sigma2^2/2;rho=sigma12/(sigma1*sigma2);
  dt=T/N; sqdt=sqrt(dt);
  puu=1/4*(1+sqdt*(mu1/sigma1+mu2/sigma2)+rho);
  pud=1/4*(1+sqdt*(mu1/sigma1-mu2/sigma2)-rho);
  pdd=1/4*(1+sqdt*(-mu1/sigma1-mu2/sigma2)+rho);
  pdu=1/4*(1+sqdt*(-mu1/sigma1+mu2/sigma2)-rho);
  u1=exp(sigma1*sqdt);d1=1/u1;
```

```
u2=exp(sigma2*sqdt);d2=1/u2;
W1=zeros(N+1,1); W2=zeros(N+1,1);
W1(1)=S1; W2(1)=S2; W=zeros(N+1,N+1);
% Asset prices at time T
for i=1:N
  for n=i:-1:1
    W1(n+1)=u1*W1(n); W2(n+1)=u2*W2(n);
  end
  W1(1)=d1*W1(1); W2(1)=d2*W2(1);
end;
% Option values at time T
for n1=1:N+1
  for n2=1:N+1
    W(n1,n2)=max([W1(n1)-W2(n2),0]);
  end
end
% Calculate option value at time 0
for i=N:-1:1
  for n1=1:i
    for n2=1:i
      W(n1,n2)=exp(-r*dt)*(puu*W(n1+1,n2+1) + pud*W(n1+1,n2)+pdu*W(n1,n2+1) ...
      + pdd*W(n1,n2));
    end;
  end;
end;
PN=W(1,1);
```

We see that the code for the two-dimensional problem is a lot more extensive than the code for the one-dimensional problem. Also, it is computationally more intense. Indeed, $O(N^3)$ computations are needed to run this algorithm. Since the option is European, it is also possible to define an unconditional algorithm, which will need $O(N^2)$ calculations. In general, for the M-dimensional problem, the standard algorithm requires $O(N^{M+1})$ and the unconditional algorithm $O(N^M)$ calculations.

11.2 Finite Difference Method for ODEs

The finite difference method is the oldest numerical method for solving differential equations. We will use the finite difference method to solve the Black–Scholes PDE, but let us first develop some intuition for the method by studying the simplest ordinary differential equation, which was covered in section 9.4.1,

$$y' = ay, \quad y(0) = c.$$

We know from that section that the unique solution to this ODE is

$$y(t) = ce^{at}, \quad t \geq 0.$$

The numerical approximation is now based on solving a discrete finite difference equation that mimics the continuous ODE. To that end, we consider the function $y\colon \mathbb{N} \to \mathbb{R}$, defined by the recursive relations

$$y_1 = c,$$
$$y_{n+1} = ay_n, \quad n = 1, 2, \ldots .$$

This is an example of a first-order linear difference equation It follows that

$$y_2 = ay_1 = ac,$$
$$y_3 = ay_2 = a^2c,$$
$$\ldots$$
$$y_n = a^{n-1}c.$$

More generally, the kth-order linear difference equation is defined by

$$y_{n+k} + a_{k-1}y_{n+k-1} + \cdots + a_0y_n = 0, \tag{11.1}$$

$$y_0 = c_0, \ y_1 = c_1, \ \ldots, \ y_{k-1} = c_{k-1}. \tag{11.2}$$

Just like the binomial tree method, the equation provides a law of motion by (11.1), and initial conditions by (11.2).

Now, returning to the simplest ODE, consider replacing the exact derivative/slope on the left-hand side with an approximation by a secant line,

$$y'(x) \approx \frac{y(x+h) - y(x)}{h}.$$

If we use this approximation for y' in the ODE at x, we get

$$\frac{y(x+h) - y(x)}{h} = ay(x),$$

leading to

$$y(x+h) = y(x)(1 + ah).$$

Here we choose some small $0 < h \ll 1$, so that the approximation error introduced by replacing the derivative with the secant line is small when h is small. Since we know that $y(0) = c$, we can thus calculate

$$y(h) = y(0)(1 + ah),$$

and use the formula iteratively to calculate

$$y((n+1)h) = y(nh)(1 + ah) = \cdots = y(0)(1 + ah)^{n+1}.$$

Another interpretation of this iterative relation is that we have defined a difference equation, with $y_n = y(nh)$, defined by

$$y_{n+1} = y_n(1 + ah),$$
$$y_0 = c.$$

How good is this approximation? That we have convergence when $h \to 0$, follows by a classical result from calculus:

$$\lim_{h \to 0} (1 + h)^{\frac{1}{h}} = e \approx 2.718\ldots,$$

which in turn implies

$$\lim_{h \to 0} (1 + ah)^{\frac{x}{h}} = \lim_{h \to 0} ((1 + ah)^{\frac{1}{ah}})^{ax} = e^{ax}.$$

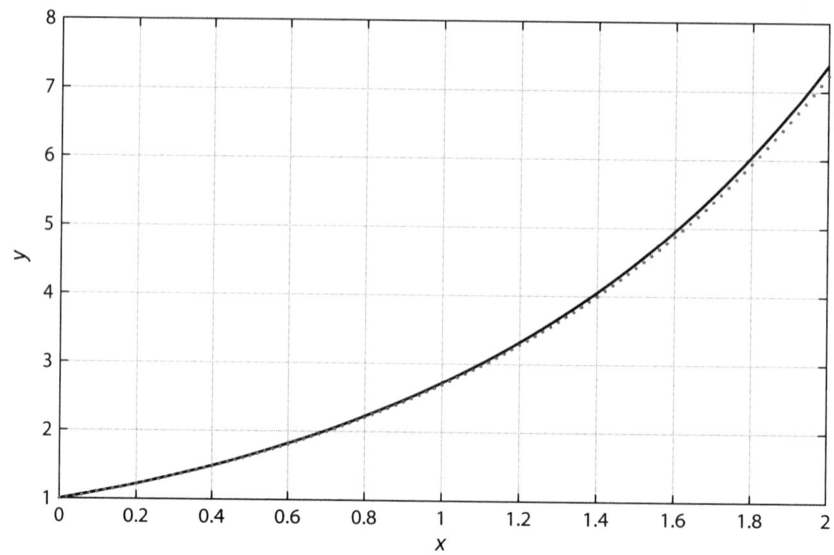

Figure 11.7: Actual and approximated solutions to the ODE $y' = ay$, $h = 0.02$, $a = 1$, $y(0) = 1$.

So, for fixed x, letting $n \to \infty$, and defining $h = \frac{x}{n}$ which converges to zero,

$$y_n = c(1 + ah)^{\frac{x}{h}} \to ce^{ax} = y(x),$$

i.e., the numerical approximation from the difference equation converges to the solution of the ODE. In figure 11.7, we show the true (solid line) and approximated (dotted line) solutions to the ODE, when $h = 0.02$.

The finite difference method for the Black–Scholes PDE is basically a multidimensional version of the method just described.

11.3 Finite Difference Method for the Black–Scholes Equation

The finite difference method starts with a law of motion for the option's price, just like the binomial tree method does. However, the law of motion is the Black–Scholes PDE, i.e., a continuous time law of motion:

$$P_t + rSP_S + \frac{\sigma^2}{2} S^2 P_{SS} - rP = 0.$$

To interpret this as a law of motion, we can informally write $P_t = \frac{P(t+dt)-P(t)}{dt}$, which then leads to

$$\frac{P(t+dt) - P(t)}{dt} = -\left(rSP_S + \frac{\sigma^2}{2} S^2 P_{SS} - rP\right),$$

and therefore

$$P(t) = P(t+dt) + dt\left(rSP_S + \frac{\sigma^2}{2} S^2 P_{SS} - rP\right). \tag{11.3}$$

Equation (11.3) provides the intuition that the price at time t depends on the price at $t + dt$ and the first and second derivatives of the price function, P_S and P_{SS}, at any point. Mathematically, the equation does not quite make sense, since infinitesimal dt operations are strictly speaking not defined. However, if we replace the dt with a Δt, where Δt is a small positive number, we can define a valid law of motion, which will lead to an approximate solution just like the binomial tree method does. This is the idea behind the finite difference method.[2]

Before we define the finite difference method, it is useful to transform the Black–Scholes PDE into a somewhat different version. We change the stock-price coordinates to log-prices by defining $x = \log(S)$, and reflect the time coordinates by defining $s = T - t$. We have $V(s, x) = P(t, S) = P(T - s, e^x)$. It is straightforward to show that in the new coordinates the Black–Scholes PDE becomes

$$\begin{aligned} V_s &= \underbrace{\left(r - \frac{\sigma^2}{2}\right)}_{a} V_x + \underbrace{\frac{\sigma^2}{2}}_{b} V_{xx} \underbrace{-r}_{c} V \\ &= aV_x + bV_{xx} + cV, \\ V(T, x) &= \Phi(e^x). \end{aligned} \tag{11.4}$$

The main advantage of the PDE for V is that the coefficients in front of the spatial derivatives (x) are constant, whereas they depend on S for the standard Black–Scholes PDE. A minor second advantage is that the time reflection puts the PDE in a form similar to the standard heat equation, $u_s = u_{xx}$. This equation is specified as an initial value problem, with initial condition $u(0, x) = u_0(x)$ and time moving forward, and the dynamic behavior of its solution is very well known.

The key result from mathematics we use for the finite difference method is Taylor's theorem (see appendix C):

Theorem 11.1 (Taylor's theorem). *Consider a $k + 1 \geq 1$ times differentiable function in a neighborhood of x. Then*

$$f(y) = f(x) + (y - x)f'(x) + \frac{1}{2}(y - x)^2 f''(x) + \cdots + \frac{1}{k!}(y - x)^k f^{(k)}(x) + O((y - x)^{k+1}).$$

We can use this theorem to approximately differentiate smooth functions. For example, for the approximation of the first derivative, we can write

$$\begin{aligned} \frac{f(x + \Delta x) - f(x - \Delta x)}{2\Delta x} &= \frac{1}{2\Delta x}\Big(\Big(f(x) + \Delta x f'(x) + \frac{1}{2}\Delta x^2 f''(x) + O(\Delta x^3)\Big) \\ &\quad - \Big(f(x) - \Delta x f'(x) + \frac{1}{2}\Delta x^2 f''(x) + O(\Delta x^3)\Big)\Big) \\ &= f'(x) + O(\Delta x^2). \end{aligned}$$

Thus, a second-order approximation of $f'(x)$, in Δx, is obtained from two discrete values: $f(x + \Delta x)$ and $f(x - \Delta x)$. We can now define a discrete *grid function*, $w = (w_0, w_1, w_2, \ldots, w_N)$, where $w_n = f(n \times \Delta x)$. The approximation of f' at the nth grid point is then calculated using the grid points w_{n+1} and w_{n-1}. This dependence on the points around the nth point is summarized by the *finite difference stencil* $(1, 0, 1)$, and the actual operator by the *finite difference coefficients* $\frac{1}{2\Delta x}(-1, 0, 1)$. Other approximations also exist. We have the following standard approximations of the first derivative of a function:

[2]Historically, the finite difference method was the first numerical method for solving differential equations, both ordinary and partial differential equations. Indeed, one can argue that the finite difference method actually precedes ODEs and PDEs, since the method actually specifies a difference equation, and difference equations were studied long before the mathematical concept of the derivative was introduced by Newton and Leibniz in the 17th century. For example, the Fibonacci number sequence was studied by Leonardo Fibonacci in the early 13th century.

- $\frac{dF}{dx}\Big|_{x=x_n}$ approximated by $\frac{1}{\Delta x}(w_{n+1} - w_n) = D_+ w(n)$, by D_+ operator $\frac{1}{\Delta x}(-1, 1)$,
- $\frac{dF}{dx}\Big|_{x=x_n}$ approximated by $\frac{1}{\Delta x}(w_n - w_{n-1}) = D_- w(n)$, by D_- operator $\frac{1}{\Delta x}(-1, 1)$,
- $\frac{dF}{dx}\Big|_{x=x_n}$ approximated by $\frac{1}{2\Delta x}(w_{n+1} - w_{n-1}) = D_0 w(n)$, by D_0 operator $\frac{1}{2\Delta x}(-1, 0, 1)$.

The D_+ and D_- operators are first-order approximations, whereas D_0 is a second-order approximation. For the second derivative, we have

- $\frac{d^2F}{dx^2}\Big|_{x=x_n}$ approximated by $\frac{1}{\Delta x^2}(w_{n+1} - 2w_n + w_{n-1}) = D_+ D_- w(n)$, by $D_+ D_-$ operator $\frac{1}{\Delta x^2}(1, -2, 1)$.

This is a second-order approximation: $\left|\frac{d^2F}{dx^2} - D_+ D_- w\right| = O(\Delta x^2)$. This use of Taylor's theorem to approximate derivatives on grids provides a systematic approach compared with the ad hoc method we previously used for the ODE.

Now, the function V depends on two variables, s and x, so we need a two-dimensional grid function for the approximation, $w_n^m \approx V(m\Delta s, n\Delta x)$. The discrete approximation to the Black–Scholes PDE in reflected log-coordinates then becomes

$$\frac{w_n^{m+1} - w_n^m}{\Delta s} = a\frac{w_{n+1}^m - w_{n-1}^m}{2\Delta x} + b\frac{w_{n+1}^m - 2w_n^m + w_{n-1}^m}{\Delta x^2} + cw_n^m. \tag{11.5}$$

Here, $N \propto \Delta x^{-1}$ measures the discretization refinement in space. There is also the time discretization, $M \propto \Delta s^{-1}$. We can now reformulate (11.5) as a discrete law of motion:

$$w_n^{m+1} = w_n^m + \frac{\Delta s}{\Delta x}\left(a\frac{w_{n+1}^m - w_{n-1}^m}{2} + b\frac{w_{n+1}^m - 2w_n^m + w_{n-1}^m}{\Delta x} + cw_n^m\right). \tag{11.6}$$

In contrast to the infinitesimal dt argument before, (11.6) provides a well-defined law of motion on a grid function, that allows w^{m+1} to be calculated from w_{n-1}^m, w_n^m, and w_{n+1}^m.

Let us summarize what we have done so far:

- We have introduced a grid function to approximate the continuous problem.
- We have approximated partial derivatives by a finite difference operators on the grid function. Each finite difference operator is defined by
  - a finite difference stencil, and the associated
  - finite difference coefficients.
- The resulting law of motion provides an algorithm that maps $(w_{n-1}^m, w_n^m, w_{n+1}^m)$ to w_n^{m+1}, for all m and n.

This is a good start, and the resulting law of motion looks very similar to that of the binomial tree method, except that our new law of motion corresponds to a trinomial tree, since three values are needed to calculate w_n^m in (11.6). We hope that when Δx becomes small, the approximation error of the solution will also become small, and that having a high-order discrete approximation of the derivatives—giving a low local approximation error—will carry over to a high convergence order to the solution.

However, finite difference methods are trickier than binomial tree methods, because the solution may actually not converge to the true solution even if the approximation order is high. This issue arises because of so-called *instability*: convergence only occurs if the finite difference method is *stable*. A general result when using finite difference methods for solving PDEs is that if a finite difference method has a high approximation order and the method is stable, then the order of convergence to the actual solution is also high. The condition for stability turns out to be defined in

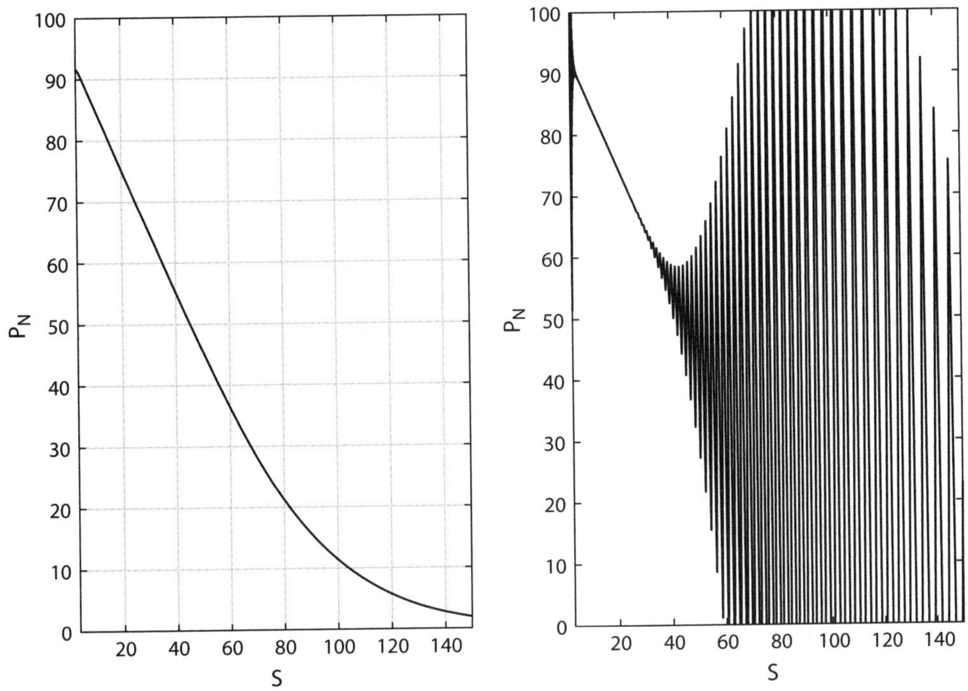

Figure 11.8: Stable and unstable finite difference methods.

terms of a uniform restriction on the growth of the approximate solution, defined in an appropriate norm.

The stability constraint of the finite difference method (11.6) for the logarithmic Black–Scholes PDE is

$$\frac{\Delta s}{\Delta x^2} \leq \frac{1}{2b}.$$

The constraint thus says that the step length in time (Δs) needs to decrease quadratically as a function of the step length in space (Δx). To illustrate that stability is crucial, we use the finite difference method for the put option (with parameters $K = 100$, $r = 0.1$, $T = 0.5$, $\sigma = 0.5$, $N = 500$). We calculate the approximate price, as a function of S, with $\frac{\Delta s}{\Delta x^2}$ just below the stability bound, and also just above the bound.

The results are shown in figure 11.8. In the left-hand panel, in which grid points are chosen so that they satisfy the stability constraint, the approximate solution has the familiar hockey stick shape. In the right-hand panel, the solution oscillates wildly and is not close to the actual solution for most values of S. In fact, when N increases for the unstable calculations, the approximate solution blows up and diverges, rather than converges to the true solution.

The finite difference method (11.6) is shown in algorithm 5:

Algorithm 5 (Finite difference method).

```
function PN=FDPut(S,K,r,T,sigma,Nx)
  Nx=2*floor(Nx/2);Max=sqrt(Nx)/2; dx=2*Max/Nx;
  k=1/sigma^2-0.01; dt=k*dx^2; Nt=floor(T/dt+1E-10);
  x=log(S)+(-Max:dx:Max);
```

```
a=r-sigma^2/2;b=sigma^2/2;c=-r;
V0=max(K-exp(x),0);Vn=zeros(1,Nx+1);
for m=1:Nt-1
  for n=2:Nx
    Vn(n)=V(n)+dt*(c*V(n)+a*(V(n+1)-V(n-1))/ ...
      (2*dx)+b*(V(n+1)-2*V(n)+V(n-1))/(dx*dx));
  end;
  V=Vn;
end;
PN=V(Nx/2+1);
```

11.3.1 More on Stability

Proving stability of finite difference methods requires some numerical analysis skills, and some work. Since the behavior of an unstable method is usually self-evident, one can often be pragmatic and not worry about stability as long as the approximate solution does not blow up.

For instructional purposes, we show what the stability analysis looks like for the finite difference method defined by (11.6). Recall that stability is defined by a growth constraint on the approximated solution in some appropriate norm. In this case, an appropriate norm is the supremum norm, and the growth constraint, as we will see, is that the solution stays bounded as $N \to \infty$. Let us show this.

Denote $a = r - \frac{\sigma^2}{2}$ and $b = \frac{\sigma^2}{2}$. Using the finite difference scheme

$$D_{+s}V = aD_{0x}V + bD_{+x}D_{-x}V - rV \tag{11.7}$$

on the grid function $V = \{V_n^m\}_{m,n}$ gives

$$\frac{V_n^{m+1} - V_n^m}{\Delta s} = a\frac{V_{n+1}^m - V_{n-1}^m}{2\Delta x} + b\frac{V_{n+1}^m - 2V_n^m + V_{n-1}^m}{\Delta x^2} - rV_n^m,$$

where $m = 0, 1, \ldots, M-1$, $n = 1, 2, \ldots, N-1$. Let $k = \frac{\Delta s}{\Delta x^2}$. Rearranging both sides of the above equation gives the following form of the law of motion:

$$V_n^{m+1} = \left[1 - \left(r + \frac{2b}{\Delta x^2}\right)\Delta s\right]V_n^m + \left(\frac{b}{\Delta x^2} - \frac{a}{2\Delta x}\right)\Delta s V_{n-1}^m + \left(\frac{a}{2\Delta x} + \frac{b}{\Delta x^2}\right)\Delta s V_{n+1}^m.$$

Let

$$\alpha = -\frac{a}{2\Delta x} + \frac{b}{\Delta x^2},$$

$$\beta = \frac{a}{2\Delta x} + \frac{b}{\Delta x^2},$$

and note that $\alpha > 0$ and $\beta > 0$ for small Δx, since $b = \frac{\sigma^2}{2} > 0$. We can now write the law of motion in the form

$$V_n^{m+1} = [1 - (r + \alpha + \beta)\Delta s]V_n^m + \alpha \Delta s V_{n-1}^m + \beta \Delta s V_{n+1}^m. \tag{11.8}$$

Moreover, we can view the evaluation of (11.8) as applying a linear operator, $\mathcal{F}$, on a one-dimensional grid function (in the x-dimension) that steps forward one period in time,

$$V^{m+1} = \mathcal{F}[V^m], \quad \text{where } V^m = (V_1^m, \ldots, V_{N-1}^m) \in \mathbb{R}^{N-1}.$$

We wish to find a bound on the operator $\mathcal{F}$ in the maximum norm. Recall that

$$\|V^m\|_\infty \stackrel{\text{def}}{=} \max_{1\le n\le N-1} |V_n^m|,$$

and the maximum norm of the operator $\mathcal{F}$ is

$$\sup_{V\neq \mathbf{0}} \frac{\|\mathcal{F}[V]\|_\infty}{\|V\|_\infty};$$

see appendix B.

It then follows from (11.8) that

$$|V_n^{m+1}| \le |V_n^m| \times |1-(r+\alpha+\beta)\Delta s| + \alpha\Delta s \times |V_{n-1}^m| + \beta\Delta s \times |V_{n+1}^m|,$$

in turn implying

$$\|\mathcal{F}[V^m]\|_\infty \le \|V^m\|_\infty \times \big(|1-(r+\alpha+\beta)\Delta s| + \alpha\Delta s + \beta\Delta s\big)$$
$$\stackrel{\text{def}}{=} K \times \|V^m\|_\infty,$$

so $\|F\|_\infty \le K$, which follows because of the subalgebraic property of the infinity norm, $\|AB\|_\infty \le \|A\|_\infty \times \|B\|_\infty$ for two operators, A and B. Since $V^m = \mathcal{F}^m[V^0]$, it therefore follows that $\|V^m\|_\infty \le K^m \|V^0\|_\infty$. So, as long as $K \le 1$, V^m does not blow up regardless of m.

To ensure that $K \le 1$, we note that when $1-(r+\alpha+\beta)\Delta s \ge 0$,

$$\begin{aligned} K = |1-(r+\alpha+\beta)\Delta s| + \alpha\Delta s + \beta\Delta s &= 1-(r+\alpha+\beta)\Delta s + \alpha\Delta s + \beta\Delta s \\ &= 1 - r\Delta s \\ &\nearrow 1, \end{aligned}$$

as $\Delta s \searrow 0$.

But

$$1-(r+\alpha+\beta)\Delta s \ge 0$$

is equivalent to

$$\Delta s \le \frac{1}{\alpha+\beta+r} = \left(r + \frac{2b}{\Delta x^2}\right)^{-1} = \frac{\Delta x^2}{r(\Delta x)^2 + \sigma^2}, \tag{11.9}$$

an inequality that holds for small enough positive Δx if and only if the stability constraint

$$\frac{\Delta s}{\Delta x^2} < \frac{1}{2b} = \frac{1}{\sigma^2} \tag{11.10}$$

is satisfied. It then follows that $\|V^m\|_\infty \le \|V^0\|_\infty \le \max_{x\in A} |\Phi(x)| = \|\Phi\|_\infty$, where the continuous maximum norm for the derivative's payout function, Φ, is used on the domain. Putting it all together, we arrive at the result that $|V_n^m|$ is bounded by $\|\Phi\|_\infty$ regardless of m and n, as long as (11.10) is satisfied.

We next show that if the stability bound is satisfied, then the method yields second-order convergence in Δx to the true solution, i.e., the error between the approximate and true solutions $|P_N - P| = O(N^{-2})$. The local truncation error introduced by $\mathcal{F}$ is defined by

$$T_n^{m+1} = \widehat{V}_n^{m+1} - (\mathcal{F}[\widehat{V}^m])_n,$$

i.e., it is the error introduced when applying $\mathcal{F}$ to the exact solution of the PDE, $\widehat{V}^m = \{V(m\Delta t, n\Delta x)\}_n$. We note that (11.7) implies that

$$\mathcal{F}[\widehat{V}^m] = \widehat{V}^m + \Delta s(aD_{0x} + bD_{+x}D_{-x} - r)V^m,$$

and since D_{0x} and $D_{+x}D_{-x}$ are second-order approximations of the first- and second-order differential operators, a Taylor expansion yields

$$\begin{aligned} T_n^{m+1} &= \widehat{V}_n^{m+1} - (\mathcal{F}[\widehat{V}^m])_n \\ &= \widehat{V}_n^{m+1} - \widehat{V}_n^m - \Delta s(a(\widehat{V}_x)_n^m + b(\widehat{V}_{xx})_n^m - r\widehat{V}_n^m + C_1\Delta x^2) \\ &= (\widehat{V}_t)_n^m \Delta s + C_2(\Delta s^2) - \Delta s(a(\widehat{V}_x)_n^m + b(\widehat{V}_{xx})_n^m - r\widehat{V}_n^m + +C_1\Delta x^2) \\ &= C_2(\Delta s^2) - C_1(\Delta s \Delta x^2). \end{aligned}$$

Here, $(\widehat{V}_t)_n^m = V_t(m\Delta s, n\Delta x)$, $(\widehat{V}_x)_n^m = V_x(m\Delta s, n\Delta x)$, and $(\widehat{V}_{xx})_n^m = V_{xx}(m\Delta s, n\Delta x)$ represent the partial derivatives of the exact solution evaluated at $s = m\Delta s$, $x = n\Delta x$. We use the fact that $\widehat{V}$ is the solution to the PDE (11.4), and

$$\begin{aligned} |C_1| \le K_1 &\stackrel{\text{def}}{=} \sup_{x\in A, s\in(0,T]} \frac{1}{6}|V_{xxx}(s,x)| + \sup_{x\in A, s\in(0,T]} \frac{1}{12}|V_{xxxx}(s,x)|, \\ |C_2| \le K_2 &\stackrel{\text{def}}{=} \sup_{x\in A, s\in(0,T]} \frac{1}{2}|V_{tt}(s,x)|. \end{aligned}$$

So $|T_n^{m+1}| \le C\Delta s(\Delta s + \Delta x^2)$, where $C = K_1 + K_2$.

We can now expand

$$\begin{aligned} &\widehat{V}^1 = \mathcal{F}[\widehat{V}^0] + T^1, \\ &\widehat{V}^2 = \mathcal{F}[\widehat{V}^1] + T^2 = \mathcal{F}^2[\widehat{V}^0] + \mathcal{F}[T^1] + T^2, \\ &\widehat{V}^3 = \mathcal{F}[\widehat{V}^2] + T^3 = \mathcal{F}^3[\widehat{V}^0] + \mathcal{F}^2[T^1] + \mathcal{F}[T^2] + T^3, \\ &\dots \\ &\widehat{V}^m = \mathcal{F}^m[\widehat{V}^0] + \sum_{k=1}^{m} \mathcal{F}^{M-k}[T^k] = V^m + \sum_{k=1}^{m} \mathcal{F}^{M-k}[T^k], \end{aligned}$$

arriving at

$$\begin{aligned} \|\widehat{V}^m - V^m\|_\infty &= \left\| \sum_{k=1}^{m} \mathcal{F}^{M-k}[T^k] \right\|_{n\infty} \\ &\le \sum_{k=1}^{m} \|\mathcal{F}\|_\infty^{M-k} \|T^k\|_\infty \\ &\le \sum_{k=1}^{m} K^{M-k} C\Delta s(\Delta s + \Delta x^2) \\ &\le Cm\Delta s(\Delta s + \Delta x^2). \end{aligned}$$

When plugging in $m = \frac{T}{\Delta s}$, this leads to the ultimate bound

$$|\widehat{V}_n^{T/\Delta s} - V_n^{T/\Delta s}| \le C\frac{T}{\Delta s}\Delta s(\Delta s + \Delta x^2) = C_T(\Delta x^2),$$

where $C_T = CT(1+k)$, and $k = \frac{\Delta s}{\Delta x^2}$. We have shown second-order convergence of the approximate solution in the maximum norm. Note that the fact that $\|\mathcal{F}\|_\infty = K \le 1$, which was needed to show stability before, was crucial in the final steps of this derivation.

To conclude, altogether we have shown that stability and second-order approximation together imply second-order convergence for the finite difference method (11.6). Without stability, the behavior of $\|\mathcal{F}\|_\infty^M$ may explode when $\Delta x \to 0$, such that $M \to \infty$, which leads to blowup of the approximate solution.

11.4 Monte Carlo Method

The Monte Carlo method is based on the risk-neutral formulation of the option pricing problem. For a simple contingent claim, we have the following formula for the value at t:

$$V_t = e^{-r(T-t)} E_t^{\mathbb{Q}}[\Phi(S(T))|S(t) = s],$$

where, under the $\mathbb{Q}$ measure, the price of the underlying asset, S_t, satisfies the dynamics $\frac{dS_t}{S_t} = r\,dt + \sigma\,dW^{\mathbb{Q}}$. The idea is now simple: we simulate many, $M \gg 1$, risk-neutral price sample paths and calculate the option payoff for each path. The average of these payoffs will be close to the expected payoff (because of the law of large numbers), and the discounted average will be close to the option's price, in line with the risk-neutral fundamental theorem. Specifically, the dynamics of the log-price of the underlying is

- $dy^m = (r - \frac{\sigma^2}{2})\,dt + \sigma\,dW^{\mathbb{Q}}$, so that
- $y_t^m \sim N((r - \sigma^2)T, \sigma^2 T)$.

The implied approximate option price is then

$$V_0 \approx e^{-rT} \frac{1}{M} \sum_{m=1}^{M} \Phi(S_0 e^{y_T^m}).$$

The speed of convergence of the approximate value as M grows will be governed by the central limit theorem, so it is not surprising that it will typically be of order $M^{-1/2}$. In contrast to the previous methods, the convergence is random, as captured by the subscript p in the following big-O formula:

$$E_M \sim O_p(M^{-\frac{1}{2}}).$$

The random convergence rate could be viewed as a weakness of the Monte Carlo method compared with each of the other two methods, for which convergence is deterministic.

Algorithm 6 implements the Monte Carlo method for the plain vanilla call option.

Algorithm 6 (Monte Carlo method).

```
function PM=MonteCarloPut(S,K,r,T,sigma,M)
  Y=T*(r-sigma^2/2)+sqrt(T)*sigma*randn(M,1);
  P=exp(-r*T)*max(K-S*exp(Y),0);
  PM=sum(P)/M;
```

Note that the algorithm is very easy to implement (the code is really short). Moreover, the general structure of the code will be the same for many other options: take the code for the payoff of one sample path, loop over this code M times, and approximate the option's value by calculating the discounted average payoff of all these paths. The only thing that needs to be changed is the payoff function.

Another strength of the Monte Carlo method is its ability to handle Asian options, with payoffs that are based on the whole sample path. These options are typically not easy to handle with binomial tree methods or finite difference methods. In algorithm 7, we provide the code for approximating the option value of an option that makes a payoff based on the average price of the underlying asset between 0 and T. We see that the code is almost as simple as for the plain vanilla option. It is a priori unclear how the binomial tree or finite difference methods would be adjusted to handle this option, since it is not possible to infer the average option price from the value of S_T.

Algorithm 7 (Monte Carlo method, Asian option).

```
function PM=MonteCarloPutAsian(S,K,r,T,sigma,M)
  dt=T/M;sqdt=sqrt(dt);
  SAverage=S*ones(M,1);
  St=S*ones(M,1);
  for j=1:M
    St=St.*exp(dt*(r-sigma^2/2)+sqdt*sigma*randn(M,1));
    SAverage=(j*SAverage+St)/(j+1);
  end;
  P=exp(-r*T)*max(K-SAverage,0);
  PM=sum(P)/M;
```

We also mention that the convergence can often be improved by simulating so-called antithetic sample paths. For each price path based on the realization $\{W_t^Q\}_t$, the price based on the realization $\{-W_t^Q\}_t$ is included in the simulation. Algorithm 8 shows the Monte Carlo method with antithetic sample paths.

Algorithm 8 (Monte Carlo method with antithetic sample paths).

```
function PM=MonteCarloAntithetic(S,K,r,T,sigma,M)
  R=sqrt(T)*sigma*randn(M,1);
  Y=T*(r-sigma^2/2)+R;
  YM=T*(r-sigma^2/2)-R;
  P=exp(-r*T)*(max(K-S*exp(Y),0)+max(K-S*exp(YM),0))/2;
  PM=sum(P)/M;
```

Another strength of the Monte Carlo method is that order of convergence, as a function of the number of sample paths, typically does not depend on the dimensionality of the problem. In higher dimensions, this becomes a major advantage compared with the binomial tree and finite difference methods, which both tend to be very slow for high-dimensional problems. The reason is that the Monte Carlo method naturally focuses on the region of the state space that is most likely to occur, whereas the lattice methods spends a lot of effort calculating payoffs for sample paths that are very unlikely to happen (close to "corners" of the state space).

Another weakness of the Monte Carlo method is that it does not readily handle American options. This is in contrast to the binomial and finite difference methods, for which the backward induction setup makes it straightforward to keep track of the option to exercise. For the Monte Carlo method, such inferences can typically not be drawn when following an individual sample path.

PART III

Advanced Topics

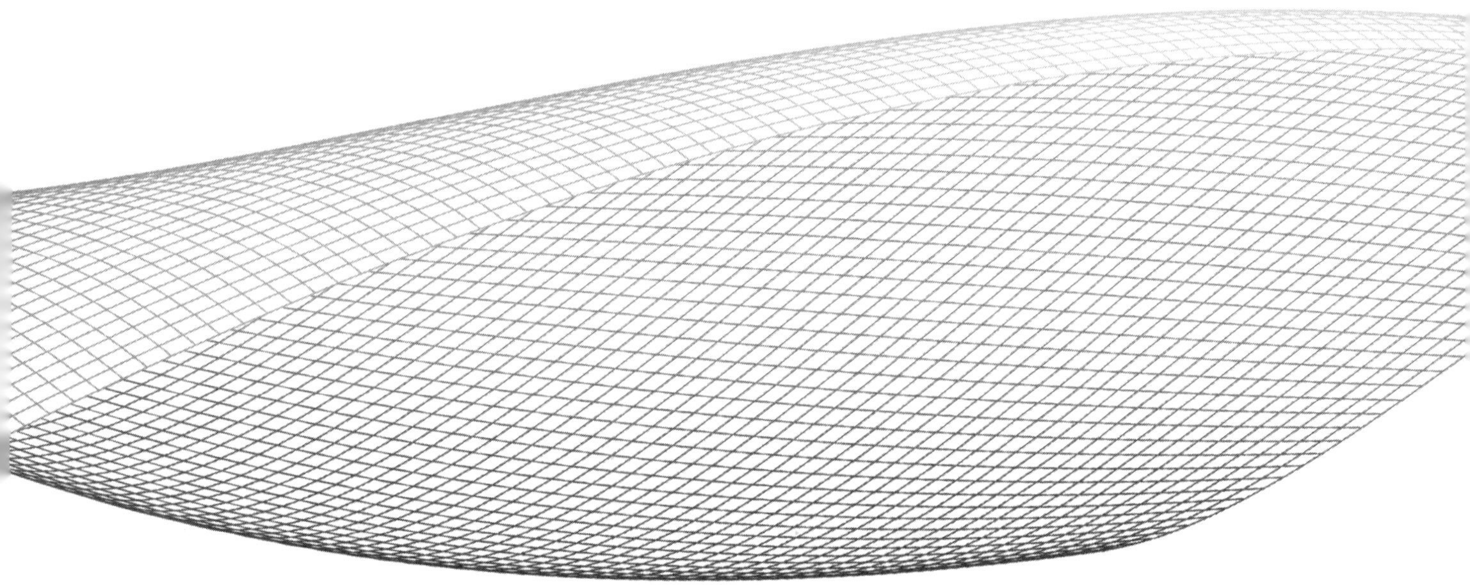

CHAPTER 12 Portfolio Choice and Equilibrium in Continuous Time

12.1 Portfolio Choice in Continuous Time

In chapter 4, we studied portfolio choice in a one-period setting, as well as some discrete dynamic portfolio choice problems. Here we study portfolio choice in continuous time. Let us begin with the portfolio choice problem of a CRRA investor, between a risk-free and a risky asset, a problem studied in Merton (1969). The investor lives between times 0 and T (for simplicity, we assume that the investor knows when (s)he will "die") with expected utility of consumption

$$U_0 = E_0\left[\int_0^T e^{-\rho t} u(c_t)\, dt\right].$$

There are two assets in the market: one risk-free bond offering a constant rate of return

$$\frac{dB}{B} = r\, dt,$$

and a risky stock with returns

$$\frac{dS}{S} = \hat{\mu}\, dt + \sigma\, d\omega,$$

so S_t is a GBM.[1]

At t, the investor has wealth W_t, invests the fraction α_t in the risky asset, and the rest in the risk-free asset. The investor also consumes at the rate c_t per unit time, i.e., between t and $t + dt$, the consumption is $c_t dt$. The instantaneous budget constraint is then

$$W_{t+dt} = W_t(1 + r\, dt + \alpha_t(\hat{\mu} - r)\, dt + \alpha_t \sigma\, d\omega_t) - c_t\, dt,$$

or in differential form,

$$dW_t = W_{t+dt} - W_t = \big(W_t(r + \alpha_t(\hat{\mu} - r)) - c_t\big)\, dt + W_t \alpha_t \sigma\, d\omega_t. \tag{12.1}$$

[1] In this section we use the symbol ω for the Wiener process, because wealth will be denoted by W.

From the martingale property, it follows that the expected change in wealth is

$$E[dW_t] = \big(W_t(r + \alpha_t(\hat{\mu} - r)) - c_t\big)\, dt.$$

The so-called Bellman principle states that the optimal solution to the investor's problem, $\max U_0$, must at any $t > 0$ solve the optimization problem from t and forward, $\max U_t$. So at each point in time the investor maximizes expected utility of future consumption,

$$J(W_t, t) = \max_{\{\alpha_s\}_s, \{c_s\}_s} \int_t^T e^{-\rho(s-t)} E_t[u(c_s)]\, ds.$$

Here, J is the derived utility function (see chapter 4) and $\{\alpha_s\}_s$ and $\{c_s\}_s$ represent the future investment and consumption at all future dates. The investor is not allowed to have any debt at the terminal date T, so the maximization is subject to the budget constraint $W_T \geq 0$. We can now rewrite

$$\begin{aligned} J(W_t, t) &= \max_{\{\alpha_s\}_s, \{c_s\}_s} \left(u(c_t)\, dt + e^{-\rho\, dt} \int_{t+dt}^T e^{-\rho(s-t)} E_t[u(c_s)]\, ds \right) \\ &= \max_{\alpha_t, c_t} (u(c_t)\, dt + e^{-\rho\, dt} E_t[J(W_{t+dt}, t + dt)]). \end{aligned}$$

Assuming the function J is smooth, we may apply Itô's lemma:

$$J(W_{t+dt}, t + dt) = J(W_t, t) + J_t\, dt + J_W\, dW + \frac{1}{2} J_{WW}(dW)^2,$$

i.e., in differential form,

$$dJ = J_t\, dt + J_W\, dW + \frac{1}{2} J_{WW}(dW)^2.$$

It also follows that

$$e^{-\rho\, dt} E_t[J(W_{t+dt}, t + dt)] = J - \rho J\, dt + E[dJ],$$

for such a smooth direct utility function, so we can rewrite the maximization problem as

$$\begin{aligned} 0 &= \max_{\alpha_t, c_t} (u(c_t)\, dt - \rho J\, dt + E[dJ]) \\ &= \max_{\alpha_t, c_t} \left(u(c_t) - \rho J + J_t + J_W \big(W(r + \alpha_t(\hat{\mu} - r)) - c_t\big) + \frac{1}{2} J_{WW} W^2 \alpha^2 \sigma^2 \right). \end{aligned} \tag{12.2}$$

This is the *Bellman equation* for the portfolio choice problem. Note that the equation contains two parts. First, it states that at the instantaneously optimal choices of α_t and c_t, the value of the right-hand side is zero, when using the derived utility function, which in turn is based on optimal choices in the future. Second, it determines the law of motion for the derived utility function, as a PDE in t and W, given those optimal choices of $\{\alpha_t\}_t$ and $\{c_t\}_t$.

Focusing on the first part, the first-order conditions on α_t and c_t are

$$\frac{\partial J}{\partial \alpha_t} : J_W W(\hat{\mu} - r) + \alpha_t J_{WW} W^2 \sigma^2 = 0, \tag{12.3}$$

$$\frac{\partial J}{\partial c_t} : u'(c_t) = J_W. \tag{12.4}$$

The second condition is intuitive: it states that the marginal contribution to total utility U of consuming a bit more right now (left-hand side) needs to be the same as the marginal losses of forsaken future utility (right-hand side), in terms of lowering current wealth and thereby future (optimal) consumption. If this condition would not be satisfied, the investor could increase total utility by either consuming more or less right now, which would not be consistent with a maximum.

The first condition, on $\frac{\partial J}{\partial \alpha_t}$, looks very much like the mean–variance trade-off we saw in the static model, and can be rewritten as

$$\alpha_t = -\frac{J_W}{WJ_{WW}}\left(\frac{\hat{\mu}-r}{\sigma^2}\right). \tag{12.5}$$

Indeed, instantaneously, the portfolio part of the problem (i.e., the choice of α_t) is a mean–variance problem, regardless of the investor's utility function. This is because of the wonderful property of a diffusion process that it very locally behaves like a normal distribution. We know that in the normally distributed case, only mean and variance matter for the expected utility maximizers in the static model. This carries over to the continuous-time setting. The investor's future attitudes to risk are summarized in the indirect utility function, and it is therefore quite natural that J_W and J_{WW} enter into the trade-off, just like u' and u'' did in the static model.

Plugging (12.5) into (12.2) leads to

$$0 = u(c_t) - \rho J + J_t + J_W(Wr - c_t) - \frac{1}{2}\frac{J_W^2}{J_{WW}}\left(\frac{\hat{\mu}-r}{\sigma}\right)^2. \tag{12.6}$$

This nonlinear PDE looks pretty challenging to solve, because of the rightmost term. Moreover, equation (12.4) is also "nasty" in general. We would like to use the equation to gain insight about $u(c_t)$ and c_t, but for general utility functions the mapping between these terms and J_W will be complicated, leading to even worse nonlinearities. So, in general, we do not expect to be able to solve (12.6) in closed form.

Merton (1969) shows that when the agent has CRRA utility, a closed-form solution does exist. Specifically, assume

$$u(c) = \begin{cases} \frac{c^{1-\gamma}}{1-\gamma}, & \gamma \neq 1, \\ \ln(c), & \gamma = 1, \end{cases}$$

so that $u'(c) = c^{-\gamma}$. The FOC (12.4) now gives us

$$c^{-\gamma} = J_W \;\Rightarrow\; c = J_W^{-\frac{1}{\gamma}}, \quad \text{and} \quad u(c) = \frac{J_W^{1-\frac{1}{\gamma}}}{1-\gamma}.$$

Plugging this into (12.6) then leads to

$$0 = \frac{\gamma}{1-\gamma} J_W^{1-\frac{1}{\gamma}} - \rho J + J_t + rWJ_W - \frac{1}{2}\frac{J_W^2}{J_{WW}} \times \frac{(\hat{\mu}-r)^2}{\sigma^2}. \tag{12.7}$$

The terminal condition is

$$J(W,T) = 0.$$

This took care of the "nasty" $u(c)$ term, but the resulting PDE is still highly nonlinear. What is our next step?

We conjecture that the indirect utility function is of the form

$$J(W,t) = A(t)\frac{W^{1-\gamma}}{1-\gamma}.$$

This assumption should not come as a complete surprise at this point. We know that the CRRA utility functions are homogeneous in wealth, so that an agent with wealth kW has utility scaled by a factor of $k^{1-\gamma}$ (when $\gamma \neq 1$). Now consider such an agent whose optimal policy under wealth

W_s is $\{\alpha_t\}_t$, $\{c_t\}_t$, $t \in [s, T]$, leading to indirect utility $J(W, s)$. If the wealth is now instead kW, then the policy $\{\alpha_t\}_t$, $\{kc_t\}_t$ is feasible, leading to utility $k^{1-\gamma}J(W, s)$. Moreover, if the original policy under wealth W_s satisfies the first-order conditions, then the revised policy also satisfies the first-order conditions, and by the LIE and backward induction, at any earlier point. So it must be that $J(kW, s) = k^{1-\gamma}J(W, s)$, justifying our conjecture.

Mathematically, we verify this intuition, like we have done several times before, by plugging the conjectured functional form into the original PDE and verifying that the PDE itself and the boundary conditions reduce to a new form that is consistent with the conjecture. We have

$$J_W = A(t)W^{-\gamma},$$

$$J_{WW} = -\gamma A(t)W^{-\gamma-1},$$

$$J_t = A'(t)\frac{W^{1-\gamma}}{1-\gamma},$$

which leads to

$$\frac{J_W^2}{J_{WW}} = -\frac{1}{\gamma}A(t)W^{-\gamma} \quad \text{and} \quad c_t = J_W^{-\frac{1}{\gamma}} = A(t)^{-\frac{1}{\gamma}}W.$$

We plug all this into (12.7) to get

$$0 = \frac{\gamma}{1-\gamma}(AW^{-\gamma})^{\frac{\gamma-1}{\gamma}} - \rho A\frac{W^{1-\gamma}}{1-\gamma} + \frac{dA}{dt} \times \frac{W^{1-\gamma}}{1-\gamma} + rAW^{1-\gamma} + \frac{1}{2}\frac{A}{\gamma} \times \frac{(\hat{\mu}-r)^2}{\sigma^2}W^{1-\gamma},$$

and after some simplification (dividing by $W^{1-\gamma}$ and collecting terms), we rewrite this as

$$0 = \frac{dA}{dt} + \gamma(A^{1-\frac{1}{\gamma}} - aA), \tag{12.8}$$

where

$$a = \frac{1}{\gamma}\left(\rho - (1-\gamma)r - \frac{1}{2}\frac{1-\gamma}{\gamma} \times \frac{(\hat{\mu}-r)^2}{\sigma^2}\right). \tag{12.9}$$

This is a first-order nonlinear ODE in $A(t)$, a *huge* simplification compared with what we started with. Moreover, the terminal condition $J(W, T) = 0$ implies that $A(T) = 0$.

For the special case when $a = 0$, one verifies that $A(t) = (T-t)^{\gamma}$ is the solution, leading to

$$c_t = \frac{1}{T-t}W_t.$$

When $a \neq 0$, (12.8) is a Bernoulli differential equation, which is covered by proposition 9.5. Using the transformation in that proposition and the terminal condition $A(T-t) = 0$, this leads to a first-order linear ODE in the variable $u = A^{\frac{1}{\gamma}}$, which in turn can be solved by using proposition 9.1. We finally arrive at

$$A(t) = \left(\frac{1-e^{-a(T-t)}}{a}\right)^{\gamma}. \tag{12.10}$$

We now have a complete characterization of the agent's behavior. Consumption is

$$c_t = J_W^{-\frac{1}{\gamma}} = \frac{1}{A^{\frac{1}{\gamma}}}W_t = \frac{a}{1-e^{-a(T-t)}}W_t. \tag{12.11}$$

So the agent ramps up the consumption rate as time T approaches, just running out of wealth at the terminal date, T. The speed with which this occurs depends on a—specifically, the larger a is, the higher the rate at any point in time at which the agent consumes is. So let us study the components of this derived parameter, defined in (12.9).

Note that (12.10) is well defined regardless of the sign of a, for finite T. However, in the limit, as $T \to \infty$, $A(t)$ is only well defined when $a > 0$, and tends to infinity when $a < 0$. So the solution in the infinite horizon economy is only defined when $a > 0$. What happens when $a < 0$ and $T \to \infty$? We explore why a may be negative in (12.9). When $\gamma > 1$, as long as $r > 0$, a is always positive (since all terms on the right-hand side of (12.9) are positive), so the limit of the solution is defined. For r sufficiently negative though, a may become negative. One can show that in this case, the indirect utility function $J(W, 0|T)$ tends to negative infinity when T grows. The reason is that the investor worries about the scenario in which wealth will be very low in the future for a long time. Indeed, for a highly risk-averse investor, this fear dominates all other concerns, and there is no way to hedge the concern in the risk-free asset when r is negative. Expected utility therefore tends to negative infinity as the horizon grows.

When $\gamma < 1$, the argument for why a may be negative is different. In this case, high enough r, and/or Sharpe ratio $\widehat{S}$, are sufficient for a to become negative. In this case, a negative value of a means that the investment environment is so good that the investor's indirect utility tends to (positive) infinity as $T \to \infty$. In the infinite horizon economy, the investor reaches *nirvana*. The breakdown in this environment occurs in the limit, as $T \to \infty$. In other environments, it may also occur for finite T, as we will see in the next section.

A higher personal discount rate, ρ, increases a, which is natural: the more impatient the agent is, the faster (s)he consumes. There is also a classical life-cycle dimension in the solution, in that it is the agent's total wealth, W_t, that determines how (s)he chooses to consume over time. Optimal life-cycle patterns were studied by Friedman (1957), who discussed agents' consumption smoothing incentives. What is novel in Merton (1969) is the continuous-time setting, and the presence of a risky asset. So let us focus on the terms that depend on r, $\hat{\mu}$, and σ^2.

First, note that the effect of an increase in r depends on whether γ is less than 1 or greater than 1. If γ is less than 1, a higher r leads to a lower a, so the agent delays consumption. If γ is higher than 1, a higher r makes the agent increase consumption. This is similar to what we saw before in the two-date model with savings, where the intertemporal substitution coefficient, $\psi = \frac{1}{\gamma}$, determined the direction of the effect.

Moving on to $\hat{\mu}$ and σ^2, we see that it is the Sharpe ratio $\widehat{S} = \frac{\hat{\mu}-r}{\sigma}$, that determines the effect on the consumption rate. This should be unsurprising since the budget constraint is such that any change in $\hat{\mu} - r$ and σ in tandem that keeps $\widehat{S}$ unchanged can be "undone" by changing α_t accordingly; see (12.1). Again, the effect of an increase in $\widehat{S}$ depends on the size of γ. For low γ the increase leads to a decrease in the consumption rate, whereas for high γ it leads to an increase in the consumption rate. The intuition from the two-date model therefore carries over to the continuous-time model here too.

With respect to the investment in the risky asset, we see that

$$\alpha_t = -\frac{J_W}{WJ_{WW}}\left(\frac{\hat{\mu} - r}{\sigma^2}\right) = \frac{\hat{\mu} - r}{\gamma\sigma^2}. \tag{12.12}$$

So, at each point in time, the investor chooses the same portfolio, i.e., α_t depends neither on time, nor on wealth. This justifies the assumption we made of a fixed α over time when discussing growth optimal portfolios, in section 4.7.1.[2] That problem did not include consumption, but it is straightforward to show that the same result applies when the agent maximizes expected utility of terminal wealth, $E[e^{-\rho T}u(W_T)]$. The Bellman equation in this case becomes

$$0 = \max_{\alpha_t}\Big(-\rho J + J_t + J_W\big(W(r + \alpha_t(\hat{\mu} - r))\big) + \frac{1}{2}J_{WW}W^2\alpha^2\sigma^2\Big), \tag{12.13}$$

with terminal condition

$$J(W, T) = \frac{W^{1-\gamma}}{1-\gamma}.$$

The FOC in α again becomes

$$J_W W(\hat{\mu} - r) + \alpha_t J_{WW} W^2\sigma^2 = 0$$

(there is no FOC in c_t since there is no consumption), and the same conjecture as before,

$$J(W, t) = A(t)\frac{W^{1-\gamma}}{1-\gamma},$$

but with terminal condition $A(T) = 1$ this time leads to the PDE

$$\frac{dA}{dt} = \gamma a A, \tag{12.14}$$

with solution (assuming $a \neq 0$)

$$A(t) = e^{\gamma a(T-t)}.$$

Again, (12.12) describes the agent's portfolio choice.[3]

12.1.1 Varying Investment Opportunity Set

The previous example with GBM returns and CRRA utility worked out beautifully, allowing us to derive a closed-form solution. Are there other settings in which closed-form solutions exist? The answer is yes, but they are very rare. Kim and Omberg (1996) study a setting with time-varying expected returns of the risky asset. As in Merton (1969), the economy operates until T, and the risk-free rate is constant, r.

There is one stock, with return dynamics

$$\frac{dS_t}{S_t} = (r + \sigma X_t)\,dt + \sigma\,dV_t^1, \tag{12.15}$$

where X_t is stochastic. The excess expected return over the risk-free rate is thus no longer constant. It will also be a diffusion process governed by X_t, which is actually the asset's Sharpe ratio, since $\hat{\mu}\,dt \stackrel{\text{def}}{=} E[\frac{dS}{S}] = (r + \sigma X_t)\,dt$, so $\frac{\hat{\mu}-r}{\sigma} = \frac{r+\sigma X_t - r}{\sigma} = X_t$.[4]

---

[2]One can show that (12.10, 12.11, 12.12) also describe the agent's behavior when $\gamma = 1$, though our analysis does not cover the log-utility case.

[3]The discounting in the utility $E[e^{-\rho T}u(W_T)]$ can be left out, corresponding to setting $\rho = 0$. As is easily checked, this affects the indirect utility function so that $\hat{J}(W, t) = e^{\rho(T-t)}J(W, t)$, the parameter a, and the PDE (the $-\rho J$ term vanishes), but does not impact the investor's portfolio choice (12.12).

[4]Kim and Omberg (1996) actually allow volatility to vary, so that σ is replaced by σ_t in (12.15). However, from our previous analysis we know that only the Sharpe ratio matters in the portfolio choice problem, so we may equivalently assume a constant σ. Indeed, under the time-varying specification, consider the instantaneous portfolio $\mathbf{h} = (\#B, \#S)'$, defined by $\mathbf{h} = ((1 - \alpha_t)S_t, \alpha_t S_t)'$, that invests in the stock and bond. The instantaneous return on this portfolio is $d(\mathbf{h}'(B_t, S_t)) = S_t((r + \alpha_t\sigma_t X_t)\,dt + \alpha_t\sigma_t\,dW_t)$. So, by choosing $\alpha_t = \sigma/\sigma_t$, we arrive at our constant σ specification. Indeed, by choosing $\sigma = 1$, one can further normalize to the stochastic return process with unit instantaneous volatility, $dR_t = R_t((r + X_t)\,dt + dV^1)$.

We assume an Ornstein–Uhlenbeck process for X_t:

$$dX_t = \lambda(\bar{X} - X_t)\,dt + \sigma_X\,dV_t^2. \tag{12.16}$$

Here we allow V^1 and V^2 to be correlated: $\langle dV^1, dV^2\rangle = \rho_{SX}\,dt$, $-1 \le \rho_{SX} \le 1$.

Since there are two sources of risk but only one risky asset, we expect this market to be incomplete. This matters for asset pricing, but less so for the portfolio choice problem. Indeed, we may set up the Bellman equation, which in this environment will lead to a PDE with two space dimensions, S and X. The problem with intermediate consumption is out of reach in this environment, at least if we want closed-form solutions, so we focus on the portfolio choice problem of maximizing expected utility of terminal wealth, $E[u(W_T)]$. Note that we have chosen the personal discount factor $\rho = 0$. Footnote 3 in this chapter provides a justification for this.

The indirect utility function is

$$J(W, X, t) = \max_{\{\alpha_s\}_s} E_t[u(W_T)],$$

subject to

$$dW_t = W_t(r + \alpha_t(\hat{\mu} - r))\,dt + W_t\alpha_t\sigma\,dV_t^1, \tag{12.17}$$

and the same argument as in the previous section leads to the Bellman equation

$$0 = \max_{\alpha_t}\Big(J_t + J_W W(r + \alpha_t\sigma X) + J_X\lambda(\bar{X} - X) + \frac{1}{2}(J_{WW}W^2\alpha_t^2\sigma^2 + 2J_{WX}W\alpha_t\sigma\sigma_X\rho_{SX} + J_{XX}\sigma_X^2)\Big).$$

The FOC for α gives us

$$\alpha = -\frac{1}{W}\Big(\frac{J_W}{J_{WW}}\frac{X}{\sigma} + \frac{J_{WX}}{J_{WW}}\frac{\sigma_X\rho_{SX}}{\sigma}\Big), \tag{12.18}$$

which when plugged into the Bellman equation leads to the PDE

$$0 = J_t + J_W Wr + J_X\lambda(\bar{X} - X) + \frac{1}{2}J_{XX}\sigma_X^2 - \frac{1}{2}J_{WW}W^2\sigma^2\alpha^2. \tag{12.19}$$

The terminal condition is

$$J(W, X, T) = u(W).$$

The PDE (12.19) looks quite nice but, of course, there is a lot hidden in the α variable, and we do not expect to find a solution for general utility functions. Kim and Omberg (1996) assume HARA utility (see theorem 4.5) which leads to risk tolerance (defined in section 3.4)

$$T(W_T) = \begin{cases} \gamma(W_T - W_*), & \gamma > 0,\ W_* \in \mathbb{R}, \\ T_0 > 0, & \gamma = 0. \end{cases} \tag{12.20}$$

We focus on the case $\gamma \ne \{0, 1\}$, i.e., we exclude the constant risk tolerance case and that with logarithmic utility (Kim and Omberg (1996) also cover these cases), so the utility function is of the form

$$u(W) = \frac{(W - W_*)^{1-\gamma}}{1-\gamma}.$$

The special case $W_* = 0$ then leads to power utility.

The next step is to make an ansatz, which we are quite used to at this point. This time, we postulate a solution of the form

$$J(W,X,\tau)=\Phi(X,\tau)u(e^{r\tau}W), \quad \tau=T-t, \tag{12.21}$$

$$\Phi(X,\tau)=e^{Z(\tau,X)}=e^{A(\tau)+B(\tau)X+C(\tau)X^2/2}, \tag{12.22}$$

$$0=A(0)=B(0)=C(0).$$

Here we have redefined the indirect utility function in terms of the time remaining to the terminal date, $\tau=T-t$. Clearly, this specification satisfies the terminal condition. As in the previous section, the separation of the solution—if it works—into wealth-dependent and time-dependent parts is extremely convenient, because it handles the partial derivatives $J_W=\frac{(1-\gamma)e^{r\tau}}{e^{r\tau}W-W_*}J$ and $J_{WW}=\frac{-\gamma(1-\gamma)e^{2r\tau}}{(e^{r\tau}W-W_*)^2}J$, and thereby their ratios. It also leads to nice expressions for

$$J_X=Z_XJ=(B(\tau)+C(\tau)X)J,$$

$$J_{XX}=(Z_{XX}+Z_X^2)J=\big(C(\tau)+(B(\tau)+C(\tau)X)^2\big)J,$$

and the cross derivative

$$J_{WX}=\frac{e^{r\tau}(1-\gamma)}{e^{r\tau}W-W_*}Z_XJ=\frac{e^{r\tau}(1-\gamma)}{e^{r\tau}W-W_*}(B(\tau)+C(\tau)X)J.$$

It follows that

$$\begin{aligned}\alpha&=\frac{e^{r\tau}W-W_*}{\gamma e^{r\tau}W}\Big(\frac{X}{\sigma}+\frac{\sigma_X\rho_{SX}}{\sigma}Z_X\Big)\\&=\frac{e^{r\tau}W-W_*}{\gamma e^{r\tau}W}\Big(\frac{X}{\sigma}+\frac{\sigma_X\rho_{SX}}{\sigma}(B(\tau)+C(\tau)X)\Big).\end{aligned} \tag{12.23}$$

Also, note that

$$\begin{aligned}J_\tau=-J_t&=\Big(Z_t+\frac{(1-\gamma)re^{r\tau}W}{e^{r\tau}W-W_*}\Big)J\\&=\Big(A'(\tau)+B'(\tau)X+C'(\tau)\frac{X^2}{2}+\frac{(1-\gamma)re^{r\tau}W}{e^{r\tau}W-W_*}\Big)J.\end{aligned} \tag{12.24}$$

Plugging these partial derivatives into the PDE (12.19) gives us

$$\begin{aligned}\Big(Z_t+\frac{(1-\gamma)re^{r\tau}W}{e^{r\tau}W-W_*}\Big)J=&\frac{(1-\gamma)e^{r\tau}}{e^{r\tau}W-W_*}WrJ+\lambda(\bar{X}-X)Z_XJ\\&+\frac{1}{2}\sigma_X^2(Z_{XX}+Z_X^2)J\\&+\frac{1}{2}\frac{1-\gamma}{\gamma}(X+\sigma_X\rho_{SX}Z_X)^2J,\end{aligned}$$

which reduces to

$$Z_t=\lambda(\bar{X}-X)Z_X+\frac{1}{2}\sigma_X^2(Z_{XX}+Z_X^2)+\frac{1}{2}\frac{1-\gamma}{\gamma}(X+\sigma_X\rho_{SX}Z_X)^2. \tag{12.25}$$

We use that $Z_t=A'(\tau)+B'(\tau)X+C'(\tau)\frac{X^2}{2}$, $Z_X=B(\tau)+C(\tau)X$, and $Z_{XX}=C(\tau)$, and along similar lines to when deriving the affine term structure model, we plug this into (12.25) and see what restrictions it implies for the functions A, B, and C. We get

$$\begin{aligned}A'(\tau)+B'(\tau)X+C'(\tau)\frac{X^2}{2} &= \lambda(\bar{X}-X)(B(\tau)+C(\tau)X)\\ &\quad+\frac{1}{2}\sigma_X^2(C(\tau)+B(\tau)^2+C(\tau)^2X^2+2B(\tau)C(\tau)X)\\ &\quad+\frac{1}{2}\frac{1-\gamma}{\gamma}\left(X+\sigma_X\rho_{SX}(B(\tau)+C(\tau)X)\right)^2. \qquad (12.26)\end{aligned}$$

Similar to what we did with the affine term structure models, we use the fact that this relation must hold for all values of X to find three ODEs from this relation, collecting terms that do not depend on X, those that depend linearly on X, and those that depend quadratically on X. Altogether, we get

$$\begin{aligned}A'(\tau)&=\lambda\bar{X}B(\tau)+\frac{1}{2}\sigma_X^2(C(\tau)+B(\tau)^2)+\frac{1}{2}\frac{1-\gamma}{\gamma}(\sigma_X\rho_{SX}B(\tau))^2,\\ B'(\tau)&=\lambda\bar{X}C(\tau)-\lambda B(\tau)+\sigma_X^2B(\tau)C(\tau)+\frac{1-\gamma}{\gamma}(B(\tau)\sigma_X\rho_{SX}+C(\tau)B(\tau)\sigma_X^2\rho_{SX}^2),\\ C'(\tau)&=\sigma_X^2C(\tau)^2-2\lambda C(\tau)+\frac{1-\gamma}{\gamma}(1+C(\tau)\sigma_X\rho_{SX})^2.\end{aligned}$$

Defining the terms

$$\begin{aligned}a^*&=\frac{1-\gamma}{\gamma},\\ b^*&=2(a^*\rho_{SX}\sigma_X-\lambda),\\ c^*&=\sigma_X^2(1+a^*\rho_{SX}^2),\end{aligned}$$

this system of ODEs can be written as

$$\begin{aligned}A'&=\frac{c^*}{2}B^2+\frac{\sigma_X^2}{2}C+\lambda\bar{X}B,\\ B'&=c^*BC+\frac{b^*}{2}B+\lambda\bar{X}C,\\ C'&=a^*+b^*C+c^*C^2,\end{aligned}$$

with initial conditions $A(0)=0$, $B(0)=0$, $C(0)=0$.[5]

This system of three ODEs looks quite demanding. The trick to solving it is to observe that the ODE for C does not contain any A or B terms. It is actually a Riccati equation with constant coefficients, so we can use proposition 9.4 to solve it. The corresponding second-order linear ODE in u is

$$u''-b^*u'+a^*c^*u=0.$$

The initial condition $C(0)=0$ implies $u'(0)=a^*c^*u(0)C(0)=0$. So we can use the initial condition $u'(0)=0$. Also, any strictly positive value of $u(0)$ will lead to the same function $C(\tau)$. This ODE for u has constant coefficients, so we can apply proposition 9.3.

[5] In Kim and Omberg (1996), γ represents risk tolerance, what we call T, where $T=\frac{1}{\gamma}$. To stay consistent with the notation we have used in the rest of this text, γ here denotes the risk-aversion coefficient. In T-terms, we have $a^*=\frac{1}{\gamma}-1=T-1$, which is consistent with their formula.

The characteristic equation for the ODE is

$$r^2 - b^* r + a^* c^* = 0.$$

We know from the proposition that the sign of the so-called discriminant, $z \stackrel{\text{def}}{=} (b^*)^2 - 4a^*c^*$, is fundamental for determining the behavior of the solution. We focus on the *normal solution*, which occurs when $z > 0$. In this case, the solution is of the form $u(\tau) = k_1 e^{r_+\tau} + k_2 e^{r_-\tau}$, with

$$r_\pm = \frac{1}{2}(b^* \pm \eta).$$

This follows from proposition 9.3, where we have conveniently defined $\eta = \sqrt{z}$.

The condition $u'(0) = 0$ implies that $k_1 r_+ + k_2 r_- = 0$, so choosing $k_1 = -r_-$ and $k_2 = r_+$ leads to a solution of the form

$$u(\tau) = r_+ e^{r_-\tau} - r_- e^{r_+\tau},$$

which satisfies $u(0) > 0$, since $r_+ > r_-$. The transformation back to C now becomes

$$\begin{aligned} C(\tau) &= -\frac{1}{c^*}\frac{u'(\tau)}{u(\tau)} \\ &= -\frac{r_+ r_-}{c^*} \times \frac{e^{r_-\tau} - e^{r_+\tau}}{r_+ e^{r_-\tau} - r_- e^{r_+\tau}} \\ &= -\frac{1}{4}\frac{(b^*)^2 - z}{c^*} \times \frac{e^{(r_- - r_+)\tau} - 1}{r_+ e^{(r_- - r_+)\tau} - r_-} \\ &= -\frac{1}{4}\frac{4a^*c^*}{c^*} \times \frac{e^{-\eta\tau} - 1}{r_+ e^{-\eta\tau} - r_-} \\ &= \frac{a^*(1 - e^{-\eta\tau})}{r_+(e^{-\eta\tau} - 1) + r_+ - r_-} \\ &= \frac{a^*(1 - e^{-\eta\tau})}{\eta - \frac{1}{2}(b^* + \eta)(1 - e^{-\eta\tau})}. \end{aligned} \tag{12.27}$$

Now that we have $C(\tau)$, we can solve the ODE for $B(\tau)$, which, given $C(\tau)$, reduces to the first-order linear ODE

$$B' - \left(c^* C + \frac{b^*}{2}\right) B = \lambda \bar{X} C.$$

We can use proposition 9.1 to solve this ODE. First, one verifies that

$$\int_0^\tau C(s)\, ds = -\frac{2a^*}{b^* + \eta}\tau - \frac{1}{c^*}\ln\left(\frac{b^* + \eta - (b^* - \eta)e^{\eta\tau}}{2\eta}\right) \stackrel{\text{def}}{=} Q(\tau), \quad \tau < \frac{1}{\eta}\ln\left(\frac{b^* + \eta}{b^* - \eta}\right).$$

The proposition now implies that the solution is of the form

$$B(\tau) = \lambda \bar{X} e^{-P(\tau)} \int_0^\tau e^{P(s)} C(s)\, ds,$$

where

$$\begin{aligned} P(\tau) &= -c^* Q(\tau) - \frac{b^*}{2}\tau \\ &= \left(\frac{2a^*c^*}{b^* + \eta} - \frac{b^*}{2}\right)\tau + \ln\left(\frac{b^* + \eta - (b^* - \eta)e^{\eta\tau}}{2\eta}\right) \end{aligned}$$

$$= \frac{1}{2}\Big(\frac{(b^*)^2-\eta^2}{b^*-\eta} - b^*\Big)\tau + \ln\Big(\frac{b^*+\eta-(b^*-\eta)e^{\eta\tau}}{2\eta}\Big)$$
$$= -\frac{\eta}{2}\tau + \ln\Big(\frac{b^*+\eta-(b^*-\eta)e^{\eta\tau}}{2\eta}\Big).$$

Note that $P(0)=0$. We can write

$$B(\tau) = -\frac{\lambda\bar{X}}{c^*}e^{-P(\tau)}\int_0^\tau e^{P(s)}\Big(-c^*C(s) - \frac{b^*}{2} + \frac{b^*}{2}\Big)\,ds$$
$$= -\frac{\lambda\bar{X}}{c^*}e^{-P(\tau)}\int_0^\tau \Big(\frac{de^{P(s)}}{ds} + \frac{b^*}{2}\Big)\,ds$$
$$= -\frac{\lambda\bar{X}}{c^*}e^{-P(\tau)}\Big(e^{P(\tau)} - e^{P(0)} + \frac{b^*}{2}\int_0^\tau e^{P(s)}\,ds\Big)$$
$$= -\frac{\lambda\bar{X}}{c^*}\Big(1 - e^{-P(\tau)} + \frac{b^*}{2}e^{-P(\tau)}\int_0^\tau e^{P(s)}\,ds\Big).$$

Also, note that

$$e^{-P(\tau)} = \frac{2\eta}{b^*+\eta-(b^*-\eta)e^{\eta\tau}}e^{\frac{\eta}{2}\tau}$$
$$= \frac{2\eta}{2\eta-(b^*+\eta)(1-e^{-\eta\tau})}e^{-\frac{\eta}{2}\tau}.$$

One verifies that

$$\int_0^\tau e^{P(s)}\,ds = \frac{2b^*-(b^*-\eta)e^{\frac{\eta}{2}\tau}-(b^*+\eta)e^{-\frac{\eta}{2}\tau}}{\eta^2}.$$

Altogether, we get

$$B(\tau) = -\frac{\lambda\bar{X}}{c^*}e^{-P(\tau)}\Big(e^{P(\tau)} - 1 + \frac{b^*}{2}\times\frac{2b^*-(b^*-\eta)e^{\frac{\eta}{2}\tau}-(b^*+\eta)e^{-\frac{\eta}{2}\tau}}{\eta^2}\Big)$$
$$= -\frac{\lambda\bar{X}}{c^*}e^{-P(\tau)}\Big(\frac{2\eta-(b^*+\eta)(1-e^{-\eta\tau})}{2\eta}e^{\frac{\eta}{2}\tau} - 1$$
$$+ \frac{b^*}{2}\times\frac{2b^*-(b^*-\eta)e^{\frac{\eta}{2}\tau}-(b^*+\eta)e^{-\frac{\eta}{2}\tau}}{\eta^2}\Big)$$
$$= -\frac{\lambda\bar{X}}{2\eta^2c^*}e^{-P(\tau)}\big(\eta(2\eta-(b^*+\eta)(1-e^{-\eta\tau}))e^{\frac{\eta}{2}\tau} - 2\eta^2$$
$$+ b^*(2b^*-(b^*-\eta)e^{\frac{\eta}{2}\tau}-(b^*+\eta)e^{-\frac{\eta}{2}\tau})\big)$$
$$= \frac{2\lambda\bar{X}a^*}{\eta^2((b^*)^2-\eta^2)}e^{-P(\tau)}(1-e^{-\frac{\eta}{2}\tau})^2((b^*)^2-\eta^2)e^{\frac{\eta}{2}\tau}$$
$$= \frac{2\lambda\bar{X}a^*}{\eta^2}\Big(\frac{2\eta}{2\eta-(b^*+\eta)(1-e^{-\eta\tau})}e^{-\frac{\eta}{2}\tau}\Big)(1-e^{-\frac{\eta}{2}\tau})^2e^{\frac{\eta}{2}\tau}$$
$$= 4\lambda\bar{X}a^*\frac{(1-e^{-\frac{\eta}{2}\tau})^2}{\eta(2\eta-(b^*+\eta)(1-e^{-\eta\tau}))}. \tag{12.28}$$

Finally, we have the ODE for A,

$$A' = \frac{c^*}{2}B^2 + \frac{\sigma_X^2}{2}C + \lambda\bar{X}B,$$

which from the fundamental theorem of calculus is really about calculating the indefinite integral

$$A(\tau) = \int_0^\tau A'(s)\,ds = \frac{c^*}{2}\int_0^\tau B(s)^2\,ds + \frac{\sigma_X^2}{2}\int_0^\tau C(s)\,ds + \lambda\bar{X}\int_0^\tau B(s)\,ds.$$

We have already calculated $\int_0^\tau C(s)\,ds$. Similar calculations for B and B^2 lead us to the following expression:

$$\begin{aligned} A(\tau) = a^*\left(\frac{2\lambda^2\bar{X}^2}{\eta^2} - \frac{\sigma_X^2}{b^* - \eta}\right)\tau \\ + \frac{4a^*\lambda^2\bar{X}^2}{\eta^3} \times \frac{(2b^* + \eta)e^{-\eta\tau} - 4b^* e^{-\frac{\eta}{2}\tau} + 2b^* - \eta}{2\eta - (b^* + \eta)(1 - e^{-\eta\tau})} \\ - \frac{1}{2c^*}\ln\left(\frac{2\eta - (b^* + \eta)(1 - e^{-\eta\tau})}{2\eta}\right). \end{aligned} \tag{12.29}$$

We finally have a complete characterization of the indirect utility function, via (12.21, 12.22, 12.27–12.29). Maybe more interestingly, (12.23) shows the investor's optimal investment policy in the risky asset. The first part depends on risk aversion and the subsistence level, W_*. To be able to compare directly with the Merton formula (12.12) which assumes CRRA utility, let us focus on the case with $W_* = 0$, which together with the fact that $\hat{\mu}_t = r + X_t\sigma$ leads to

$$\alpha = \frac{1}{\gamma}\left(\frac{\hat{\mu}_t - r}{\sigma^2} + \frac{\sigma_X \rho_{SX}}{\sigma}(B(\tau) + C(\tau)X)\right). \tag{12.30}$$

So, when $\rho_{SX} = 0$, the formula is instantaneously the same as that in Merton (1969), i.e., the investor behaves myopically, choosing the same formula as in Merton, based on the instantaneous value of expected returns $\hat{\mu}_t$.

When $\rho_{SX} \neq 0$, the investor's behavior is richer. For the specific value $X = X^* = -\frac{B(\tau)}{C(\tau)}$, the myopic portfolio is chosen. One can verify that C, C', B, and B' are all positive if $\gamma < 1$ and negative if $\gamma > 1$, which in turn means that $X^* < 0$ regardless of γ. So the nonmyopic investor behaves just like a myopic investor, when $X = X^* < 0$, i.e., at a point where the risky asset has a negative risk premium.

We assume $\rho_{SX} < 0$. In this case a run-up of stock prices is associated with future lower expected stock returns, whereas a run-down is associated with future higher expected returns, compared with the uncorrelated case. The future therefore, in some sense, provides a partial hedge against current events through time diversification.

For an agent with $\gamma > 1$, when $X > X_*$ more is invested in the risky asset than when $\rho_{SX} = 0$, and an increase in X is associated with a further increase in the amount invested in the risky asset (since $C(\tau) < 0$ when $\gamma > 1$). The risk-averse investor appreciates the hedge the future offers against current bad events, and is therefore willing to increase immediate investments. Note that the effect is more pronounced, the longer the horizon of the investor (since $C' < 0$). For an agent with low risk aversion, the effect goes in the opposite direction. Such an agent values the hedging the future offers less that the agent with high risk aversion, and is actually more interested in the convexity offered from "return momentum," where high returns are followed by more high returns in the near future. It is therefore when $\rho_{SX} > 0$ (so that there is "momentum") that the investor with low risk aversion invests more, compared with the myopic investor when X is high. Note that as $\tau \to 0$, the dynamic effects disappear (since $B(\tau) \to 0, C(\tau) \to 0$), because the model is becoming closer and closer to the static model. This fully dynamic model offers a lot of intuition that cannot be captured in the two-period setting in section 4.7.

Another interesting effect that may arise when $\rho_{SX} > 0$ is the existence of nirvana solutions in finite time. We have seen nirvana solutions before in the infinite horizon economy, but here they may actually arise in finite time under the right conditions. A hint of why this may happen is given by the functional form of $C(\tau)$ in (12.27). Note that if

$$2\eta = (b^* + \eta)(1 - e^{-\eta\tau}), \tag{12.31}$$

then this function formally evaluates to infinity, suggesting that at that horizon, the investor's utility function tends to (plus or minus) infinity, and that the portfolio choice defined in (12.23) becomes extremely aggressive.

What is needed for (12.31) to be satisfied? Recall that we are analyzing the normal case with real distinct roots, so $\eta = \sqrt{(b^*) - 4a^*c^*} > 0$. The right-hand side of (12.31) is zero when $\tau = 0$, and it is positive for $\tau > 0$ if and only if $b^* + \eta > 0$, which is the case if and only if $b^* > 0$ (since $b^2 - \eta^2 > 0$). In that case, we get that (12.31) is satisfied when

$$\tau^* = \frac{1}{\eta} \ln\left(\frac{b^* + \eta}{b^* - \eta}\right).$$

The condition $b^* > 0$ is satisfied if

$$a^* \rho_{SX} \sigma_X > \lambda.$$

For $\gamma < 1$ and $\rho_{SX} > 0$, this occurs when the mean reversion parameter λ is sufficiently low. In this case, shocks to X tend to be very persistent, and together with the positive feedback between dS and dX, at a sufficient long horizon, the upside of investing is so high from the perspective of the investor with a low risk-aversion coefficient, γ, that the indirect utility function becomes unbounded, and infinitely aggressive investment behavior is optimal. Of course, we have seen such infinitely aggressive behavior before: a risk-neutral investor will be infinitely aggressive whenever there is an investment opportunity with positive risk premium, regardless of investment horizon.

The conditions for nirvana solutions are a bit more subtle when $\gamma > 1$ and $\rho_{SX} < 0$, but they do exist. In this case, $A(\tau) \to -\infty$ as $\tau \to \tau^*$, which makes the indirect utility function tend to 0 (recall that when $\gamma > 1$, utility is negative so the nirvana solution occurs when $J = 0$).

12.1.2 Solution with Intermediate Consumption

As mentioned, the stochastic environment in Kim and Omberg (1996) does not in general admit a closed-form solution when utility is of the form

$$U = E_0\left[\int_0^T e^{-\rho t} u(c_t)\, dt\right], \tag{12.32}$$

so that there is intermediate consumption. Wachter (2002) shows that in the special case when $\rho_{SX} = -1$, so that $dV^2 = -dV^1 \stackrel{\text{def}}{=} dV$, a closed-form solution does exist with CRRA utility. In this case, the investor's indirect utility function J is defined as

$$J(W, X, t) = \max_{\{\alpha_s\}_s, \{c_s\}_s} E_t\left[\int_0^T e^{-\rho s} \frac{c_s^{1-\gamma}}{1-\gamma}\, ds\right],$$

subject to (12.1), repeated below for convenience:

$$dW_t = (W_t(r + \alpha_t(\hat{\mu} - r)) - c_t)\, dt + W_t \alpha_t \sigma\, dV_t, \tag{12.33}$$

and the terminal condition $W_T = 0$ (there is no bequest motive).[6] This leads to the Bellman equation

$$0 = \max_{\alpha_t, c_t}\Big(\frac{c_t^{1-\gamma}}{1-\gamma} + J_t + J_W(W(r+\alpha_t\sigma X) - c_t) + J_X\lambda(\bar{X} - X)$$
$$+ \frac{1}{2}(J_{WW}W^2\alpha_t^2\sigma^2 + 2J_{WX}W\alpha_t\sigma\sigma_X\rho_{SX} + J_{XX}\sigma_X^2)\Big).$$

The FOC in α_t leads to the same expression as in the previous setting (12.18),

$$\alpha = -\frac{1}{W}\Big(\frac{J_W}{J_{WW}}\frac{X}{\sigma} + \frac{J_{WX}}{J_{WW}}\frac{\sigma_X\rho_{SX}}{\sigma}\Big) = -\frac{1}{WJ_{WW}\sigma}(J_W X - J_{WX}\sigma_X), \tag{12.34}$$

and the FOC in c_t yields, as in Merton (1969), $c^{-\gamma} = J_W$, altogether leading to the PDE

$$0 = J_t + \frac{\gamma}{1-\gamma}J_W^{\frac{\gamma-1}{\gamma}} + J_W Wr$$
$$+ J_X\lambda(\bar{X} - X) + \frac{1}{2}J_{XX}\sigma_X^2 - \frac{1}{2}J_{WW}W^2\sigma^2\alpha^2. \tag{12.35}$$

It is unclear how to proceed from here on since we have a nonlinear PDE with two space dimensions, and the trick used in Merton (1969) is not directly applicable. We therefore take another approach. A key difference between this special setting with $\rho_{SX} = -1$ and the more general one is that there is effectively only one source of risk here, so the market is complete. There is thus a unique SDF process, M_t, that prices the asset as well as any contingent claim on V_t risk, including any contingent claim on the realization of X_t.

Moreover, since the market is complete, the investor can generate any (adapted) consumption policy $\{c_s\}_s$ that satisfies the constraint that the price of consumption equals total wealth,

$$W_0 = E_0\Big[\int_0^T \frac{M_t}{M_0}c_t\,dt\Big]. \tag{12.36}$$

This is the complete market SDF version of the budget constraint. So the agent maximizes (12.32) subject to (12.36), which is an equivalent formulation to the optimization with respect to (12.33) that works because the market is complete (otherwise we could not be sure that the optimal policy derived for this problem would actually be feasible).

This optimization is similar to what we did in the Lucas model, and leads to the FOC (5.33). In continuous time, we get

$$\frac{M_t}{M_0} = e^{-\rho t}\frac{u'(c_t)}{u'(c_0)},$$

or equivalently, since $M_0 = 1$,

$$u'(c_t) = e^{\rho t}M_t u'(c_0). \tag{12.37}$$

This condition must hold, since otherwise the investor would have an incentive to either increase consumption today, financed by decreasing consumption at time t in some state (if the left-hand side is greater than the right-hand side), or the other way round. This redistribution of consumption can be done in a budget neutral way (keeping (12.36) satisfied) so this consumption

[6] Note that for notational consistency, we use ρ to represent the personal discount factor, which should not be confused with ρ_{SX} which represents the correlation between stock returns and X_t.

redistribution would be feasible. If we know M_t, the only thing we need to do is therefore to find c_0 such that (12.36) is satisfied when c_t is defined via (12.37).

Just like the Lucas economy introduced a powerful method for equilibrium asset pricing, the approach described above introduces a powerful way to solve portfolio choice problems in complete markets. The technical conditions needed to justify the approach were analyzed in Cox and Huang (1989) and Karatzas, Lehoczky, and Shreve (1987). The following theorem summarizes this novel approach.

Theorem 12.1. *In a complete market with SDF $\{M_t\}_t$, the investor's optimal consumption policy, $\{c_t\}$, can be determined by finding c_0, such that $\{c_t\}_t$, defined by solving* (12.37), *satisfies* (12.36).

Again, the interpretation is that we are basically rewriting the problem as a complete-market state-price problem, like we did in the Lucas economy (and before that in the static Arrow–Debreu model).

Let us now apply this approach to our portfolio choice problem. We first need to find the SDF. The relevant state variable here is X_t, which determines the stock's drift term. Indeed, from example 9.12 (the time-dependent version; one can show that Novikov's condition is satisfied), we know that

$$M_t = e^{-rt}\xi_t, \quad \text{where } \xi_t = e^{-\int_0^t X_s\, dV_s - \frac{1}{2}\int_0^t X_s^2\, ds},$$

is the likelihood ratio function, and from before we also know that $d\xi_t = -X_t\xi_t\, dV_t$.

The FOC, together with $u'(c_t) = c_t^{-\gamma}$ for the CRRA utility function, give us

$$M_0 c_t^{-\gamma} = e^{\rho t} M_t c_0^{-\gamma},$$

so that

$$c_t = e^{\frac{r-\rho}{\gamma}t + \frac{1}{\gamma}\int_0^t X_s\, dW_s + \frac{1}{2\gamma}\int_0^t X_s^2\, ds} c_0,$$

where c_0 is chosen such that

$$W_0 = E_0\left[\int_0^T \frac{M_t}{M_0} c_t\, dt\right] = E_0\left[\int_0^T e^{-\frac{\rho}{\gamma}t}\left(\frac{M_t}{M_0}\right)^{1-\frac{1}{\gamma}} dt\right] c_0.$$

We derived this formula from the agent's decision problem at $t = 0$, but it must also hold at any later point in time since the decision problem is the same at any point, although with different investment horizons. So we have

$$\frac{W_t}{c_t} = E_t\left[\int_t^T e^{-\frac{\rho}{\gamma}(s-t)}\left(\frac{M_s}{M_t}\right)^{1-\frac{1}{\gamma}} ds\right], \quad 0 \le t < T.$$

As a step toward calculating the right-hand side, let us define $q_t = \xi_t^{1-\frac{1}{\gamma}}$, and

$$F(t, q, X) \stackrel{\text{def}}{=} E_t[q_T | q_t = q, X_t = X].$$

Obviously, $F(T, q, X) = q$ for all X. Itô calculus gives us

$$\frac{dq_t}{q_t} = -\left(1 - \frac{1}{\gamma}\right)X_t\, dV_t - \frac{1}{2\gamma}\left(1 - \frac{1}{\gamma}\right)X_t^2\, dt,$$

$$(dq_t)^2 = \left(1 - \frac{1}{\gamma}\right)^2 X_t^2 q_t^2\, dt,$$

$$(dq)(dX) = \left(1 - \frac{1}{\gamma}\right) q_t X_t \sigma_X\, dt,$$

and Feynman–Kac's theorem therefore leads to

$$0 = F_t + F_X\lambda(\bar{X} - X) - \frac{1}{2\gamma}\Big(1 - \frac{1}{\gamma}\Big)X^2 q F_q$$
$$+ \frac{1}{2}\Big(F_{XX}\sigma_X^2 + 2F_{Xq}\Big(1 - \frac{1}{\gamma}\Big)qX\sigma_X + q^2 F_{qq}\Big(1 - \frac{1}{\gamma}\Big)^2 X^2\Big).$$

Now, since $E_t[q_T | q_t, X_t = X] = q_t E_t[\frac{q_T}{q_t} | q_t, X_t]$, and the distribution of

$$\frac{q_T}{q_t} = e^{-(1-\frac{1}{\gamma})(\int_t^T X_s\, dV_s - \frac{1}{2}\int_t^T X_s^2\, ds)}$$

does not depend on q_t, it follows that $F(t, q, X) = q\widehat{F}(T - t, X)$, i.e., that the function F is separable and linear in q. Note that we switched to the reflected coordinates $\tau = T - t$ here, in line with what we did in the previous analysis when we solved the terminal wealth problem. The PDE for $\widehat{F}(\tau, X)$ is then

$$\widehat{F}_\tau = \lambda(\bar{X} - X)\widehat{F}_X - \frac{1}{2\gamma}\Big(1 - \frac{1}{\gamma}\Big)X^2\widehat{F} + \frac{1}{2}\Big(\widehat{F}_{XX}\sigma_X^2 + 2\widehat{F}_X\Big(1 - \frac{1}{\gamma}\Big)X\sigma_X\Big),$$

with initial condition $\widehat{F}(0, X) = 1$. We now use the ansatz $\widehat{F}(\tau, X) = e^{\frac{1}{\gamma}Z(\tau, X)}$ which, using the fact that $\rho_{SX} = -1$, leads to

$$\Big(\frac{1}{\gamma}Z_\tau\Big) = \lambda(\bar{X} - X)\Big(\frac{1}{\gamma}Z_X\Big) - \frac{1}{2\gamma}\Big(1 - \frac{1}{\gamma}\Big)X^2$$
$$+ \frac{1}{2}\Big(\Big(\frac{1}{\gamma}Z_{XX}\Big) + \Big(\frac{1}{\gamma}Z_X\Big)^2\Big)\sigma_X^2 + \Big(1 - \frac{1}{\gamma}\Big)X\sigma_X\Big(\frac{1}{\gamma}Z_X\Big).$$

By multiplying this expression by γ, we arrive at

$$Z_\tau = \lambda(\bar{X} - X)Z_X - \frac{1}{2}\Big(1 - \frac{1}{\gamma}\Big)X^2 + \frac{1}{2}\Big(Z_{XX} + \frac{1}{\gamma}Z_X^2\Big)\sigma_X^2 + \Big(1 - \frac{1}{\gamma}\Big)X\sigma_X Z_X.$$

This equation is actually in the same form as (12.25) when $\rho_{SX} = -1$, since in this case

$$\begin{aligned} Z_\tau &= \lambda(\bar{X} - X)Z_X + \frac{1}{2}\sigma_X^2(Z_{XX} + Z_X^2) + \frac{1}{2}\frac{1-\gamma}{\gamma}(X - \sigma_X Z_X)^2 \\ &= \lambda(\bar{X} - X)Z_X + \frac{1}{2}\sigma_X^2(Z_{XX} + Z_X^2) + \frac{1}{2}\frac{1-\gamma}{\gamma}(X^2 - 2\sigma_X X Z_X + \sigma_X^2 Z_X^2) \\ &= \lambda(\bar{X} - X)Z_X - \frac{1}{2}\Big(1 - \frac{1}{\gamma}\Big)X^2 + \frac{1}{2}\Big(Z_{XX} + \frac{1}{\gamma}Z_X^2\Big)\sigma_X^2 + \Big(1 - \frac{1}{\gamma}\Big)X\sigma_X Z_X. \end{aligned}$$

Also, the terminal condition is the same, $Z(0, X) = 0$. We therefore know that the solution is in the form $Z(\tau, X) = A(\tau) + B(\tau)X + C(\tau)\frac{X^2}{2}$, where C, B, and A, are defined by (12.27, 12.28, 12.29).

We can finally use this solution to calculate

$$\begin{aligned}
\frac{W_t}{c_t} &= E_t\left[\int_t^T e^{-\frac{\rho}{\gamma}(s-t)}\left(\frac{M_s}{M_t}\right)^{1-\frac{1}{\gamma}} ds\right],\\
&= \int_t^T e^{-\frac{\rho}{\gamma}(s-t)} e^{-r(1-\frac{1}{\gamma})(s-t)} \frac{E_t[\xi_s^{1-\frac{1}{\gamma}}]}{\xi_t^{1-\gamma}} ds\\
&= \int_t^T e^{-\frac{\rho}{\gamma}(s-t)} e^{-r(1-\frac{1}{\gamma})(s-t)} \frac{\xi_t^{1-\frac{1}{\gamma}}\widehat{F}(s-t,X_t)}{\xi_t^{1-\gamma}} ds\\
&= \int_t^T e^{-\frac{\rho}{\gamma}(s-t)} e^{-r(1-\frac{1}{\gamma})(s-t)}\widehat{F}(s-t,X_t)\, ds\\
&= \int_0^{T-t} e^{-\frac{\rho}{\gamma}\tau} e^{-r(1-\frac{1}{\gamma})\tau}\widehat{F}(\tau,X_t)\, d\tau,
\end{aligned}$$

where

$$\widehat{F}(\tau,X) = e^{\frac{1}{\gamma}(A(\tau)+B(\tau)X+C(\tau)\frac{X^2}{2})}.$$

Equivalently, defining $\hat{A}(\tau) = A(\tau) + r(1-\gamma) - \rho$, and $H(\tau,X) = e^{\frac{1}{\gamma}(\hat{A}(\tau)+B(\tau)X+C(\tau)\frac{X^2}{2})}$, we can write

$$\frac{W_t}{c_t} = \int_0^{T-t} H(\tau,X_t)\, d\tau.$$

So, in this special setting studied by Wachter (2002), with a complete market, we also get a closed-form solution for the problem with intermediate consumption. The analysis also shows how powerful the approach of rewriting the portfolio choice problem in terms of Arrow–Debreu securities can be in the complete market setting.

12.2 Intertemporal Capital Asset Pricing Model, ICAPM

A continuous-time extension of the CAPM was introduced in Merton (1971, 1973). Consider an investor who lives between 0 and T, with expected utility of consumption

$$U = E_0\left[\int_0^T e^{-\rho t}u(c_t)\, dt\right].$$

Here, u is an increasing, smooth, and concave utility function. There is one risk-free bond, and the discount rate is constant, r. So the dynamics for the bond price, B, is

$$\frac{dB}{B} = r\, dt.$$

There are also N risky stocks, with dynamics

$$\frac{dS_i}{S_i} = \hat{\mu}_i\, dt + \sigma_i\, d\omega_i,$$

where ω_i are Wiener processes, $i = 1, \ldots, N$. The instantaneous covariances between stock returns are $\mathrm{Cov}(\frac{dS_i}{S_i}, \frac{dS_j}{S_j}) = \sigma_{ij}\, dt = \sigma_i\sigma_j\rho_{ij}\, dt$, where $\rho_{ij}\, dt = \mathrm{Cov}(d\omega_i, d\omega_j)$. We define the covariance matrix $\Sigma = [\sigma_{ij}]_{ij}$. As described below, variances and covariances may be stochastic and time varying, as long as they are adapted diffusion processes.

The investor's wealth at time t is W_t. The agent invests the fractions $\alpha_t = (\alpha_{1t}, \alpha_{2t}, \ldots, \alpha_{Nt})'$ in the risky assets and the rest in the risk-free asset, and consumes c_t. The budget constraint is then

$$dW_t = \left(W_t \left(r + \sum_{i=1}^{N} \alpha_{it}(\hat{\mu} - r) \right) - c_t \right) dt + W_t \sum_{i=1}^{N} \alpha_{it} \sigma_i \, d\omega_{it},$$

and the expected change in wealth is

$$E[dW_t] = \left(W_t \left(r + \sum_{i=1}^{N} \alpha_{it}(\hat{\mu} - r) \right) - c_t \right) dt.$$

We allow drift and volatility to be stochastic and time dependent in that they also follow diffusion processes:

$$d\hat{\mu}_i = a_i \, dt + b_i \, dx_i,$$

$$d\sigma_i = e_i \, dt + h_i \, dy_i.$$

Here, $x_1, \ldots, x_n$, $y_1, \ldots, y_n$ are Wiener processes, which may be correlated with each other and with ω_i, so these equations are written in correlated form. Consider the three N-vectors $\mathbf{S}_t = (S_{1t}, S_{2t}, \ldots, S_{Nt})'$, $\mu_t = (\hat{\mu}_{1t}, \ldots, \hat{\mu}_{Nt})'$, $\sigma_t = (\sigma_{1t}, \ldots, \sigma_{Nt})'$. The vector $\mathbf{Y}_t = (S_{1t}, \ldots, S_{Nt}, \hat{\mu}_{1t}, \ldots, \hat{\mu}_{Nt}, \sigma_{1t}, \ldots, \sigma_{Nt})' = (\mathbf{S}_t, \mu_t, \sigma_t)'$ has $M = 3N$ elements, and follows the vector diffusion process

$$d\mathbf{Y}_t = \mathbf{f}_t \, dt + \operatorname{diag}(\mathbf{g}_t) \, d\mathbf{q}_t.$$

The adapted vector of drift coefficients,

$$\mathbf{f}_t = (f_1, \ldots, f_M)' = (\hat{\mu}_{1t} S_{1t}, \ldots, \hat{\mu}_{Nt} S_{Nt}, a_{1t}, \ldots, a_{Nt}, e_{1t}, \ldots, e_{Nt})',$$

may, for example, be of the form $\mathbf{f}_t = \mathbf{f}(t, \mathbf{Y}_t)$, but could also be path dependent. This is also the case for the M-vector of volatility coefficients,

$$\mathbf{g}_t = (g_1, \ldots, g_M)' = (\sigma_{1t} S_{1t}, \ldots, \sigma_{Nt} S_{Nt}, b_{1t}, \ldots, b_{Nt}, h_{1t}, \ldots, h_{Nt})'.$$

The variance covariance matrix $\Xi \, dt = d\mathbf{q}_t \, d\mathbf{q}_t'$ has elements $[\Xi_{ij}] = \eta_{ij}$, where $\eta_{i,j,t} \, dt = \langle d\mathbf{q}_{it}, d\mathbf{q}_{jt} \rangle$. A special case arises if the covariance matrix is in the Markovian form $\Xi_t = \mathbf{Q}(t, \mathbf{Y}_t)$, as is the vector of drift coefficients, in which case $\mathbf{Y}$ satisfies the SDE

$$d\mathbf{Y} = \mathbf{f}(t, \mathbf{Y}) \, dt + \mathbf{Q}(t, \mathbf{Y}) \, d\mathbf{Y}. \tag{12.38}$$

Note that with this notation, it follows that $\rho_{ij} = \eta_{ij}$, $i, j = 1, \ldots, N$.

We postulate the existence of a smooth indirect utility function of the form $J(t, W, \mathbf{Y})$, with the associated investment and consumption policies α_t and c_t. A similar argument to that in Merton (1969), but using the multivariate version of Itô's lemma, then leads to the Bellman equation,

$$\begin{aligned} 0 = \max_{\alpha_{1t}, \ldots, \alpha_{Nt}, c_t} \; & u(c_t) - \rho J + J_t + J_W \left(W \left(r + \sum_{i=1}^{N} \alpha_{it}(\hat{\mu}_i - r) \right) - c_t \right) \\ & + \sum_{j=1}^{M} J_j f_j + W^2 J_{WW} \frac{1}{2} \sum_{i=1}^{N} \sum_{j=1}^{N} \alpha_{it} \alpha_{jt} \sigma_{ij} + W \sum_{i=1}^{N} \sum_{j=1}^{M} J_{jW} \alpha_{it} \sigma_i h_j \eta_{ij} \\ & + \frac{1}{2} \sum_{i=1}^{M} \sum_{j=1}^{M} J_{ij} h_i h_j \eta_{ij}. \end{aligned}$$

Here we have written J_{ij} for the cross derivatives of $\mathbf{Y}$ terms, instead of $J_{Y_iY_j}$.

We next define $s_i^j = \sigma_i h_j \eta_{ij}$, $\mathbf{s}^j = [s_i^j]_{i=1,\ldots,N}$, $j = 1, \ldots, M$, and $\mu_e = \hat{\mu} - r\mathbf{1}$. We have

$$\alpha_t' \hat{\mu}_e = \sum_{i=1}^{N} \alpha_{it}(\hat{\mu}_i - r),$$

$$\alpha_t' \Sigma \alpha_t = \sum_{i=1}^{N} \sum_{j=1}^{N} \alpha_{it}\alpha_{jt}\sigma_{ij},$$

$$\sum_{j=1}^{M} J_{jW} \alpha_t' \mathbf{s}^j = \sum_{i=1}^{N} \sum_{j=1}^{M} J_{jW} \alpha_{it} h_j \sigma_i \eta_{ij}.$$

Note, again, that Σ may be time dependent, but that we suppress this dependence for notational convenience. This rewriting allows us to rewrite Bellman equation as

$$0 = \max_{\alpha_{1t},\ldots,\alpha_{Nt},c_t} u(c_t) - \rho J + J_t + J_W(Wr - c_t) + \frac{1}{2}\sum_{i=1}^{M}\sum_{j=1}^{M} J_{ij} h_i h_j \eta_{ij}$$

$$+ WJ_W(\alpha_t' \mu_e) + W^2 J_{WW} \frac{1}{2}(\alpha_t' \Sigma \alpha_t) + W \sum_{j=1}^{M} J_{jW}(\alpha_t' \mathbf{s}^j).$$

We take the first-order condition with respect to α, which gives us the vector equation

$$\alpha_t = -\frac{1}{WJ_{WW}}\left(J_W \Sigma^{-1}\mu_e + \sum_{j=1}^{M} J_{jW}\Sigma^{-1}\mathbf{s}^j\right).$$

We thus have an $(M+1)$-fund separation theorem! Indeed, the first fund is the (instantaneous) mean–variance-efficient portfolio $\Sigma^{-1}\mu_e$ that we saw in the static CAPM. The other M funds relate to $\mathbf{s}^j$ factors, $j = 1, \ldots, M$. These represent *hedging portfolios*, which the agent uses to hedge the risk of future changes in expected returns because of the q_i shocks. Specifically, the $\Sigma^{-1}\mu_e$ portfolio is what a myopic investor focuses on, maximizing the instantaneous Sharpe ratio. This is the myopic part of the portfolio. We have encountered hedging portfolios before, in sections 4.4.2 and 4.7. The $\Sigma^{-1}\mathbf{s}^j$ portfolios here allow the investor to hedge q_j shocks that affect future expected returns. Indeed, if the q_j shocks are correlated with the returns on individual stocks ($\eta_{im} \neq 0$), then a change in q_j which decreases future expected returns can be partially offset by investing in stocks that tend to have high immediate returns when such shocks arrive.

In the general case, the number of hedging portfolios is large, larger than the number of stocks, since $M = 3N$. However, if the number of risks that impact drift and volatility is much smaller than M, then so is the number of hedging portfolios. Specifically, consider the special case when $\hat{\mu}$ and σ can be written as

$$\hat{\mu}_t = \hat{\mu}(t, \mathbf{X}_t), \quad \sigma_t = \sigma(t, \mathbf{X}_t),$$

where $\mathbf{X}_t \in \mathbb{R}^K$ follows the diffusion process

$$d\mathbf{X}_t = \hat{\mathbf{f}}(t, \mathbf{X}_t)\, dt + \mathrm{diag}(\hat{\mathbf{g}}(\mathbf{X}_t))\, d\hat{\mathbf{q}}_t.$$

Here, $K \ll M$ represents a much lower-dimensional space of factors that affect the drift and volatility coefficients of stock returns. The correlation coefficients are $\hat{\eta}_{ij} = \mathrm{Cov}(d\hat{\mathbf{q}}_i, d\hat{\mathbf{q}}_j)$, $i, j = 1, \ldots, K$, and $\hat{v}_{ij} = \text{Cov}(d\hat{\mathbf{q}}_i, d\omega_j)$, $i = 1, \ldots, K$, $j = 1, \ldots, N$. Postulating $J = J(t, W_t, \mathbf{X}_t)$ then leads to the Bellman equation

$$0 = \max_{\alpha_{1t}, \ldots, \alpha_{Nt}, c_t} u(c_t) - \rho J + J_t + J_W(Wr - c_t) + \frac{1}{2} \sum_{i=1}^{K} \sum_{j=1}^{K} J_{ij} h_i h_j \eta_{ij}$$

$$+ WJ_W(\alpha_t' \mu_e) + W^2 J_{WW} \frac{1}{2} (\alpha_t' \Sigma \alpha_t) + W \sum_{j=1}^{K} J_{jW}(\alpha_t' \mathbf{s}^j),$$

where $s_i^j = \sigma_i h_j \hat{\eta}_{ij}$, $\mathbf{s}^j = [s_i^j]_{i=1,\ldots,N}$, $j = 1, \ldots, K$, and the first-order conditions lead to

$$\alpha_t = -\frac{1}{WJ_{WW}} \left(J_W \Sigma^{-1} \mu_e + \sum_{j=1}^{K} J_{jW} \Sigma^{-1} \mathbf{s}^j \right).$$

In this case, we get a $(K+1)$-fund separation.

In the special case when $K = 0$, so that $\hat{\mu}_t$ and σ_t are not stochastic (they can still be time varying), we get one-fund separation into the instantaneous mean–variance-efficient portfolio. When, in addition, $\hat{\mu}$ and Σ are constant over time, the mean–variance-efficient portfolio is also constant, and we get the time-invariant portfolio

$$\alpha_t = -\frac{J_W}{WJ_{WW}} \Sigma^{-1} \mu_e$$

and

$$\mathbf{w}_t = \mathbf{w} = \frac{\alpha_t}{\mathbf{1}' \alpha_t} = \frac{1}{\mathbf{1} \Sigma^{-1} \mu_e} \Sigma^{-1} \mu_e.$$

So the same mean–variance-efficient risky portfolio as in the static model is held at each point in time by all investors. Note that we made no assumptions about the utility function, expect for it being increasing, smooth, and concave. So all agents hold the same risky portfolio in this setting, and therefore the CAPM holds regardless of utility functions. This dynamic diffusion setting thus corresponds to having multivariate normally distributed risks in the static setting—an environment in which all agents behave as mean–variance optimizing agents with respect to the portfolio composition, regardless of their utility function in the class $\mathcal{U}_2$; see chapter 3.

LOGARITHMIC UTILITY In the special case when the agent has logarithmic utility,

$$U = E\left[\int_0^T e^{-\rho t} \ln(C_t)\, dt \right],$$

the case with a general stochastic investment opportunity set is significantly simplified. In this case, one can show that the indirect utility function will be of the form

$$J = J(t, W_t, \mathbf{Y}) = A(t) \ln(W_t) + F(t, \mathbf{Y}),$$

where

$$A(t) = \frac{1 - e^{\rho(T-t)}}{\rho},$$

$$C_t = \frac{W_t}{A(t)},$$

$$J_{jW} = 0, \quad \forall j.$$

Here, $\mathbf{Y}$ summarizes the state of the economy, representing the fact that the investment opportunity set is not constant. But the investor's consumption still does not depend on the investment opportunity set, since C_t only depends on $A(t)$ and W_t. Note that when $T=\infty$, we get $A(t)=\frac{1}{\rho}$ at all times.

It also follows that the investor is myopic and chooses the portfolio

$$\mathbf{w}_t=\frac{\alpha_t}{\mathbf{1}'\alpha_t}=\frac{1}{\mathbf{1}\Sigma^{-1}\mu^e}\Sigma_t^{-1}\mu_t^e, \tag{12.39}$$

an expression that only depends on the instantaneous covariance matrix and vector of expected excess returns. So the case with logarithmic utility provides an extremely convenient benchmark, where the agent's behavior at any point is completely characterized by instantaneous dynamics.

12.3 Continuous-Time Lucas Model

The standard dynamic exchange economy model used in finance, the one-tree Lucas model, builds on the ideas in Lucas (1978) discussed in chapter 5, although there are some differences. The model is developed in continuous time, has only one tree, includes growth (so there is no stationary solution), and unbounded utility functions, from below and/or from above. The easiest equilibrium argument in this case is to simply calculate the price function of the tree,[7]

$$P(Y)=E\left[\int_0^T e^{-\rho t}u'(Y_t)Y_t\,dt\right],$$

and verify that the price function leads to a well-defined value function for the representative agent.

The setting is as follows: There is one firm, $N=1$, time is continuous and infinite horizon, $t\geq 0$ (so $T=\infty$), and aggregate dividends evolve according to GBM dynamics, as

$$\frac{dY_t}{Y_t}=\hat{\mu}\,dt+\sigma\,dW_t, \tag{12.40}$$

where $\hat{\mu}=\mu+\frac{\sigma^2}{2}$, and $\sigma>0$. There is a representative investor with CRRA expected utility, so that

$$U=E\left[\int_0^\infty e^{-\rho t}\frac{C_t^{1-\gamma}}{1-\gamma}\,dt\right],\quad \gamma>0. \tag{12.41}$$

As in the original model, equilibrium is defined by the agent's consumption demand being equal to supply,

$$C_t=Y_t,\quad \forall\, t,$$

at all points in time.

The continuous-time version of the SDF pricing relation for the price of an asset that generates the consumption flow X_t is then

$$p_t=E_t\left[\int_t^\infty \frac{M_s}{M_t}X_s\,ds\right],$$

where the SDF is defined by

$$M_t=e^{-\rho t}C_t^{-\gamma}.$$

[7] In the discrete model we relied on a fixed-point argument when determining equilibrium prices.

Since this pricing relation holds at any point in time, it also follows that

$$p_t = E_t\left[\int_t^T \frac{M_s}{M_t} X_s\, ds + \frac{M_T}{M_t} p_T\right], \tag{12.42}$$

for arbitrary $T > t$. Note that the SDF here, M_t, corresponds to $M_{0,t}$ in the discrete model.

Using a log-transformation, see example 9.5, we can write

$$Y_t = e^{\mu t + \sigma W_t} Y_0,$$

which leads to the following formula for the price of the firm:

$$\begin{aligned}
p_t &= E_t\left[\int_t^\infty \frac{M_s}{M_t} Y_s\, ds\right] \\
&= E_t\left[\int_t^\infty e^{-\rho(s-t)} \frac{Y_s^{1-\gamma}}{Y_t^{-\gamma}}\, ds\right] \\
&= Y_t E_t\left[\int_t^\infty e^{-\rho(s-t)+(1-\gamma)(\mu(s-t)+\sigma(W_s - W_t))}\, ds\right] \\
&= \frac{Y_t}{\rho + (\gamma-1)\mu - (\gamma-1)^2\frac{\sigma^2}{2}}.
\end{aligned}$$

The market's dividend yield, as well as the consumption ratio in the economy (since dividends equal consumption in the model), is

$$\frac{Y_t}{p_t} = \rho + (\gamma - 1)\mu - (\gamma - 1)^2 \frac{\sigma^2}{2}. \tag{12.43}$$

For the total expected return on the market, note first that since p_t is proportional to Y_t,

$$E\left[\frac{dp_t}{p_t}\right] = E\left[\frac{dY_t}{Y_t}\right] = \left(\mu + \frac{\sigma^2}{2}\right) dt.$$

We then get the total expected return formula

$$\begin{aligned}
r_m\, dt &= E\left[\frac{dp_t + Y_t\, dt}{p_t}\right] \\
&= \left(\mu + \frac{\sigma^2}{2}\right) dt + \left(\rho + (\gamma-1)\mu - (\gamma-1)^2\frac{\sigma^2}{2}\right) dt \\
&= \left(\rho + \gamma\hat{\mu} - \gamma(\gamma-1)\frac{\sigma^2}{2}\right) dt,
\end{aligned}$$

so

$$r_m = \rho + \gamma\hat{\mu} - \gamma(\gamma - 1)\frac{\sigma^2}{2}. \tag{12.44}$$

These formulas are the same as those we derived in the static Arrow–Debreu model in chapter 5; see equations (5.25–5.28).

We next look at risk-free bond yields. Consider a bond that pays out one unit of the good at time T. Given the price $p(T)$ of such a bond, the risk-free rate (technically, the time-t zero coupon yield) is such that

$$p(T) = e^{-y_T T},$$

leading to

$$p(T) = e^{-y_T T} = E[e^{-\rho T}(e^{v_T})^{-\gamma}]$$
$$= e^{-(\rho+\gamma\mu-\frac{\sigma^2}{2}\gamma^2)T}$$
$$= e^{-(\rho+\gamma\hat{\mu}-\frac{\sigma^2}{2}\gamma(\gamma+1))T}.$$

We arrive at

$$y_T = r^f = \rho + \gamma\hat{\mu} - \frac{\sigma^2}{2}\gamma(\gamma+1), \tag{12.45}$$

regardless of maturity, T. So again, the risk-free rate is the same as in the AD model, and the risk premium is therefore

$$r^e = r_m - r^f = \gamma\sigma^2.$$

So the equity premium puzzle is also present in the dynamic model, just like in the static AD model. Indeed, this equity premium is based on the instantaneous properties of the SDF, which are the same in the static and dynamic models, and will therefore in general be present in dynamic models.

Now consider the instantaneous expected return on an arbitrary risky asset with price P_t. For simplicity, we assume that the asset does not pay dividends. The instantaneous expected return is then

$$\hat{\mu}_p\,dt = E\Big[\frac{dP_t}{P_t}\Big].$$

We assume that P_t evolves according to a diffusion process, i.e.,

$$\frac{dP_t}{P_t} = \hat{\mu}_p\,dt + \sigma_p\,dZ,$$

for some Wiener process, Z.

The pricing relation (12.42) implies

$$P_t = E\Big[\frac{M_{t+dt}}{M_t}P_{t+dt}\Big],$$

and thus

$$1 = E\Big[\frac{M_{t+dt}P_{t+dt}}{P_t M_t}\Big]$$
$$= E\Big[\frac{M_t p_t + d(M_t P_t)}{P_t M_t}\Big]$$
$$= E\Big[\frac{M_t P_t + M_t dP_t + dM_t P_t + dM_t dP_t}{P_t M_t}\Big]$$
$$= 1 + E\Big[\frac{dP_t}{P_t}\Big] + E\Big[\frac{dM_t}{M_t}\Big] + \Big(\frac{dM_t}{M_t}\Big)\Big(\frac{dP_t}{P_t}\Big).$$

Here, $(\frac{dM_t}{M_t})(\frac{dP_t}{P_t}) = \gamma\sigma\sigma_p\rho_{WZ}\,dt$ is the instantaneous covariance between $\frac{dM_t}{M_t}$ and $\frac{dP_t}{P_t}$, and ρ_{WZ} is the (instantaneous) correlation coefficient between innovations in W_t and Z_t, in line with the product rule for Itô processes. So

$$\hat{\mu}_p\,dt = -E\Big[\frac{dM_t}{M_t}\Big] - \gamma\sigma\sigma_p\rho_{WZ}\,dt.$$

Since $M_t = e^{-\rho t} C_t^{-\gamma}$, it follows that

$$\frac{dM_t}{M_t} = -\Big(\rho + \gamma\hat{\mu} - \frac{\sigma^2}{2}\gamma(\gamma+1)\Big)\,dt - \gamma\sigma\,dW_t$$
$$= -r^f\,dt - \gamma\sigma\,dW_t. \tag{12.46}$$

The expected change of the SDF is in general related to the short interest rate through the formula

$$E\Big[\frac{dM_t}{M_t}\Big] = -r_t\,dt,$$

where $r_t = \lim =_{T\searrow t} r_T^f$ is the short-rate process, see (10.5), which in the continuous-time Lucas model equals r^f. This holds because for the SDF to correctly price a short-lived risk-free bond, it must be that

$$1 = E\Big[\frac{M_t + dM_t}{M_t}(1 + r_t\,dt)\Big]$$
$$= 1 + r_t\,dt + E\Big[\frac{dM_t}{M_t}\Big].$$

For this formula we used (12.42) in differential form. Using this relation between the expected change of the SDF and the risk-free rate, we arrive at

$$\hat{\mu}_p - r_t = -\gamma\sigma\sigma_p\rho_{WZ}. \tag{12.47}$$

This is the formula for the risk premium of an arbitrary asset in the continuous-time Lucas model. Similar to the CAPM, the expression says that the risk premium is determined by the (instantaneous) covariance between the asset's returns and a factor. However, whereas the factor in the CAPM is defined by the return on the market portfolio, in this Lucas model (and more generally within consumption-based asset pricing) it is determined by aggregate consumption.

Assets that tend to have high returns when aggregate consumption *increases*, i.e., when the representative investor's marginal utility *decreases*, will not be demanded as highly, and will have lower prices and *higher* expected returns than assets that tend to have high returns when aggregate consumption *decreases*. Such assets will have a *negative* covariance with the SDF, and the right-hand side of (12.47) is then *positive*, in line with a positive risk premium for such assets. Assets that have high returns when consumption decreases will have a positive covariance with the SDF, and therefore have a negative risk premium. The latter assets offer insurance against negative consumption shocks. This is the same intuition as we saw in section 5.4.

Equation (12.47) also provides us with the continuous-time version of the *Hansen and Jagannathan (1991)* bound. Note that the volatility of the SDF is $\sigma_M = \gamma\sigma$, so, taking absolute values on both sides of that equation, noting that $\rho_{WZ} \leq 1$, and dividing by σ_p, leads to

$$\frac{|\hat{\mu}_p - r_s|}{\sigma_p} \leq \sigma_M. \tag{12.48}$$

So for the market to admit high Sharpe ratios in this model, the volatility of the SDF needs to be high,just like we saw earlier.

12.4 Economies with Production

12.4.1 Extending the One-Tree Model to Include Production

So far, we have been very simplistic in our treatment of the operational side of firms in the economy. The goods these firms produce and the dividends they pay have been treated as exogenous, e.g., in the continuous-time one-tree model; see (12.40). In reality, most firms constantly make investment decisions, investing short-term cash flows to generate long-term growth. We extend the one-tree models to include such decisions, with the aim of being as close as possible to the one-tree model to allow for a comparison.

Assume that there is one infinitely lived firm in the economy, which needs capital to produce consumption goods and to grow in the future. As before, there is also an infinitely lived representative investor, with CRRA utility function $u = \frac{c^{1-\gamma}}{1-\gamma}$, and expected utility

$$U = E_0\left[\int_0^\infty e^{-\rho t}\frac{c_t^{1-\gamma}}{1-\gamma}\,dt\right]. \tag{12.49}$$

The consumption good is generated by the representative firm, which pays out the (real) dividend stream Y_t. In equilibrium, consumption must equal dividends at each point, $c_t \equiv Y_t$ for all t. In contrast to the one-tree model, the firm actively decides how much of the surplus to use to produce the consumption good, which is then paid out as a dividend, and how much to reinvest into future growth. Specifically, the firm owns *real capital*, the amount of which at time t is denoted K_t. Real capital here represents "physical things"—for example factories, land, and machines—as opposed to financial capital which we have mainly considered up until this point.

Real capital grows at a stochastic rate

$$dK_t = gK_t\,dt + \sigma K_t\,dW_t.$$

The parameters g and σ are constant and, especially, they do not depend on K, consistent with a *linear production technology*. The parameter g includes potential depreciation of capital—its value could potentially be negative. The real capital also generates a dividend flow of the consumption good, so that $Y_t = \kappa K_t$. The amount of capital can never be negative: $K_t \geq 0$ for all t.

So far, everything is completely in line with the one-tree model. Indeed, we can interpret the one-tree model as a version of this model where the real capital part was hidden. The growth of dividends would just be g, i.e., g replaces $\hat{\mu}$ in the one-tree model (since $Y = \kappa K$, so capital and dividends only differ by a constant factor). The novel assumption, which makes this a production economy, is that dividends can also be instantaneously reinvested, leading to additional capital growth, at the cost of instantaneously decreasing dividends. Specifically, I represents the amount of dividends that are reinvested. We allow for a general "exchange rate" between the consumption good and the investment, so that one unit of the consumption good generates v units of capital. This is again a linear relation, i.e., there are no decreasing returns to scale. We allow for disinvestments (negative investments), so that it is possible that $I < 0$. We can think of the firm's reinvestment, I, as representing *retained earnings*, which the company uses to buy more real capital.

The relations between capital, dividends, and investments then become

$$Y_t = \kappa K_t - I_t, \tag{12.50}$$

$$dK_t = gK_t\,dt + \sigma K_t\,dW_t + vI_t\,dt. \tag{12.51}$$

These two relations define the economy's real budget constraint, in terms of how current dividends and consumption may be traded off for growth in capital, which in turn generates future dividends and consumption. As in the one-tree model, only the consumption good can be consumed by the investor, so in equilibrium we must have

$$c_t = Y_t, \tag{12.52}$$

for all t. Note that if the investment is $I_t = \kappa K_t$, i.e., if all dividends are reinvested and $Y_t = 0$, we get

$$\frac{dK_t}{K_t} = (g + \nu\kappa)\, dt + \sigma\, dW_t.$$

We therefore define

$$G \stackrel{\text{def}}{=} g + \nu\kappa$$

as the real growth rate under complete reinvestment.

If we also define the instantaneous consumption (dividend) rate, $y_t = \frac{Y_t}{K_t}$, and the investment rate, $i_t = \frac{I_t}{K_t}$ (observe that these variables are defined in terms of a fraction of the capital, K_t), we get from (12.50),

$$y_t + i_t = \kappa$$

and

$$\frac{dK_t}{K_t} = (G - \nu y_t)\, dt + \sigma\, dW_t$$
$$= (g + \nu i_t)\, dt + \sigma\, dW_t.$$

This economy is friction-free in that the transformation from capital to consumption is done instantaneously and without costs. The firm is competitive, owns the capital, and chooses the investment strategy that maximizes shareholder value.[8] That is, given the stochastic discount factor $\{M_t\}_t$, the firm makes the investment decision that maximizes its market value,

$$V_t = \frac{1}{M_t} E_t\left[\int_t^{\infty} M_s Y_s\, ds\right]. \tag{12.53}$$

A production economy version of the first welfare theorem, theorem 5.6, can now be applied, and it follows that the Walrasian complete market equilibrium outcome in this economy will implement the solution to the social planner's problem. That is, we may derive the equilibrium capital growth equation in this economy by solving the social planner's problem,

$$\max_{\{c_s\}} E_t\left[\int_0^{\infty} e^{-\rho s} u(c_s)\, ds\right], \tag{12.54}$$

subject to (12.50–12.52), and such that $K_t \geq 0$ for all t.

Now, it may seem almost like magic that the firm's narrow objective function, to maximize its market value, leads to an investment strategy that coincides with what is welfare optimal in the economy. Indeed, given what we know about the functional form of the equilibrium SDF from the exchange economy analysis, $M_s = e^{-\rho s} u'(c_s)$, so the optimization in (12.54) is with respect to $e^{-\rho s} u(Y_s)$ (because the social planner must choose $c_s \leq Y_s$ at each point in time, and will of course

[8] Several variations of these assumptions are possible here, all leading to similar real outcomes. For example, one may alternatively assume that agents have direct access to the production technology and make their own investment decisions.

never choose c_s below Y_s which would mean the disposal of utility-creating consumption goods), whereas the optimization in (12.53) is with respect to $e^{-\rho s}u'(Y_s)Y_s$, so the functional forms of these two optimization problems seem different. Why would we expect them to give the same solution?

The following result provides an explanation of why the solutions are the same:[9]

Proposition 12.1. *Consider the optimization problem*

$$\mathcal{Y} = \arg\max_{\{Y_t\}_t \in \mathcal{A}} \int_0^T e^{-\rho t} u(Y_t)\, dt,$$

and assume $\mathcal{Y}$ is nonempty. Here, $u\colon [0,T] \to \mathbb{R}$ is a continuously differentiable function and $\mathcal{A}$ denotes a convex set of bounded functions $Y\colon [0,T] \to \mathbb{R}$. For $Y^* \in \mathcal{Y}$, define

$$\mathcal{Y}' = \arg\max_{\{Y_t\}_t \in \mathcal{A}} \int_0^T e^{-\rho t} u'(Y_t^*) Y_t\, dt.$$

Then $Y^* \in \mathcal{Y}'$.

The proposition thus shows that the socially optimal choice is also an optimal choice for the firm, which takes the SDF as given, providing the link between the two solutions we are looking for.

Proof. Denote the functional $\mathcal{F}(Y) = \int_0^T e^{-\rho t} u(Y_t)\, dt$, and also $Y^\epsilon = Y^* + \epsilon(Y^{**} - Y^*)$, where $Y^{**} \in \mathcal{Y}'$. Note that $Y^\epsilon \in \mathcal{A}$, since $\mathcal{A}$ is convex. Also, define $U = \mathcal{F}(Y^*)$, which is finite since $\mathcal{Y}$ is nonempty, and which also is a finite upper bound on $\mathcal{F}(Y)$ for all $Y \in \mathcal{A}$.

We study $\mathcal{F}(Y^\epsilon)$ for small $\epsilon > 0$. Taylor's theorem allows us to write

$$\left| u(Y^\epsilon(t)) - \left(u(Y^*(t)) + \epsilon u'(Y^*(t))(Y^{**}(t) - Y^*(t)) \right) \right| \le C\epsilon^2,$$

for small $\epsilon > 0$, where the constant C does not depend on $t \in [0,T]$. This is where a technical condition on the joint behavior of u and $\mathcal{A}$ is needed to ensure that such an expansion is possible. It holds, for example, if $\mathcal{A}$ is bounded, or if u is bounded. We therefore get

$$\begin{aligned} \mathcal{F}(Y^\epsilon) &= \int_0^T e^{-\rho t} u(Y^*)\, dt + \epsilon \int_0^T e^{-\rho t} u'(Y^*)(Y^{**} - Y^*)\, dt + O(\epsilon^2) \\ &> U, \end{aligned}$$

for small enough ϵ—which would mean that $Y^* \notin \mathcal{Y}$—unless

$$\int_0^T e^{-\rho t} u'(Y^*) Y^{**}\, dt = \int_0^T e^{-\rho t} u'(Y^*) Y^*\, dt,$$

i.e., unless $Y^* \in \mathcal{Y}'$. Since, $Y^* \in \mathcal{Y}$, it therefore follows that $Y^* \in \mathcal{Y}'$. □

The above result provides an economic rationale for the net present value (NPV) rule, used in corporate finance. The rule states that (under ideal conditions) firms should maximize the NPV of their investments, which will then lead to maximal shareholder value (because a firm's shareholder value reflects its fundamentals). Equivalently, a firm should make the choice that maximizes (12.53). Under the aforementioned conditions, this will then lead to a Pareto-efficient outcome,

[9] We state the result in finite horizon with no uncertainty. Under some technical conditions, which are satisfied here, it can be extended to our stochastic infinite horizon production economy.

i.e., the decentralized economy, in which firms maximize NPV, implements the social planner's problem also in the production economy.

Note, however, that the result does not imply that Y^* is the *only* solution to the firm's problem. It may be that there are many solutions in $\mathcal{Y}'$, because fixing the pricing kernel $(u'(Y^*))$ in the optimization problem makes the problem "less concave" than the social planner's problem. Indeed, uniqueness must come from properties of $\mathcal{A}$, which we make few assumptions about. If $\mathcal{A}$ contains linear production technologies, for example, as in our model, there will typically be a whole range of reshuffling of investments and consumption across time that from a firm's perspective are all zero NPV, but which would be socially costly if made in aggregate. This is similar to when an investor buys a bond at its market value, which changes the timing of cash flows the investor receives over time, and thereby increases the investor's utility, while still being a zero NPV transaction. The idea is then that the representative firm is guided to choose the "right" $Y^* \in \mathcal{Y}'$, consistent with NPV maximization, to meet agent demand for the consumption good in the product market.

Due to this equivalence result, we may henceforth focus on the social planner's problem. Because the CRRA utility function is homogeneous and the production technology is linear in K and does not depend on time, it can be shown that the optimal consumption rate is constant in this case, so $y_t \equiv y$; see, for example, Betermeier, Calvet, Jo, and Walden (2023). Therefore, capital dynamics in equilibrium follows a geometric Brownian motion,

$$K_t = K_0 e^{(G - vy - \frac{\sigma^2}{2})t + \sigma W_t},$$

and since $c_t = Y_t = yK_t$, the planner's maximization problem becomes

$$\begin{aligned} U &= \max_y E_0\left[\int_0^\infty e^{-\rho t} \frac{(K_0 y e^{(G - vy - \frac{\sigma^2}{2})t + \sigma W_t})^{1-\gamma}}{1-\gamma} dt\right] \\ &= \max_y \frac{(K_0 y)^{1-\gamma}}{1-\gamma} \int_0^\infty e^{-\rho t} e^{(1-\gamma)(G - vy - \frac{\sigma^2}{2})t + (1-\gamma)^2 \frac{\sigma^2}{2} t} dt \\ &= \max_y \frac{K_0^{1-\gamma}}{1-\gamma} \times \frac{y^{1-\gamma}}{\rho - ((1-\gamma)(G - vy) + \gamma(\gamma - 1)\frac{\sigma^2}{2})}. \end{aligned}$$

Here we need to impose the condition

$$\rho - \left((1-\gamma)G + \gamma(\gamma - 1)\frac{\sigma^2}{2}\right) > 0, \tag{12.55}$$

for there to be a well-defined solution to the problem.[10]

From the FOC in y, one derives the optimal consumption share,

$$vy = \frac{\rho}{\gamma} + G\left(1 - \frac{1}{\gamma}\right) + (1-\gamma)\frac{\sigma^2}{2} > 0,$$

and expected growth rate of capital,

$$\hat{\mu} \stackrel{\text{def}}{=} G - vy = \frac{G - \rho + \gamma(\gamma - 1)\frac{\sigma^2}{2}}{\gamma} = \frac{g + v\kappa - \rho + \gamma(\gamma - 1)\frac{\sigma^2}{2}}{\gamma}.$$

[10] If the condition is violated when $\gamma < 1$, there will exist nirvana solutions with positively infinite expected utility, and if the condition is violated when $\gamma > 1$, expected utility will be negatively infinite regardless of the choice of y.

So

$$\frac{dc}{c} = \frac{dY}{Y} = \frac{dK}{K} = \hat{\mu}\,dt + \sigma\,dW_t,$$

i.e., on the consumption side, we end up with dynamics identical to those in the one-tree economy (12.40).

All the SDF pricing relations will be the same as in the one-tree economy, including the expressions for the risk-premium and risk-free rates. So it may seem like we did not gain much from introducing production into the economy. On the contrary, we have now linked asset prices and returns to real variables in the economy, and specifically to real productivity. For example, from (12.44) we get

$$r_m = G,$$

that is, the equilibrium expected return on the market is the same as the expected real growth rate of capital in the economy in the hypothetical scenario that all real capital returns were reinvested, and nothing consumed.

The consumption ratio (12.43) takes the form

$$\begin{aligned}
\frac{Y_t}{p_t} &= \rho + (\gamma - 1)\Big(\hat{\mu} - \frac{\sigma^2}{2}\Big) - (\gamma - 1)^2\frac{\sigma^2}{2}\\
&= \rho + (\gamma - 1)\Big(\Big(\frac{G - \rho + \gamma(\gamma - 1)\frac{\sigma^2}{2}}{\gamma}\Big) - \frac{\sigma^2}{2}\Big) - (\gamma - 1)^2\frac{\sigma^2}{2}.\\
&= \nu y\\
&= \nu\frac{Y_t}{K_t}.
\end{aligned}$$

So

$$p(K_t) = \frac{1}{\nu}K_t,$$

i.e., when the firm is viewed through the prism of the capital it owns, every unit of capital is worth $\frac{1}{\nu}$ (and, specifically, 1 when $\nu = 1$). This is intuitive, since the consumption good can be invested/transformed into capital at the transformation rate $\Delta Y \mapsto \Delta K = \nu\Delta Y$. At any price of a unit of capital other than $\frac{1}{\nu}$, it would be optimal for the firm to either increase or decrease the amount invested (given that the equilibrium investment is strictly positive, which is ensured by (12.55)).

Finally, if we think of K as the real assets of the company, $p(K)$ is their market value, and $\frac{1}{\nu}$ is the per-unit replacement cost of these assets. If we define *Tobin's* q as their ratio, we get

$$q = \frac{\text{market value of assets}}{\text{replacement cost of assets}} = \frac{1/\nu}{1/\nu} = 1.$$

So, in this friction-free model, Tobin's q is equal to 1.

So-called q-theory is important within investments, for example, in understanding real investment flows. Our model above is a bit too simplistic to allow for variation in q. First, it does not allow for intangible capital (for example, patents and human capital) in addition to physical capital. Second, its production technology is linear.

In a model with decreasing returns to scale, one would need to separate average q, i.e., the ratio of the market value of the firm's total capital to total replacement value of capital, from marginal q, i.e., the ratio of the market value of a marginal increase in firm capital to the marginal replacement cost. We would expect the latter to be equal to 1, at least if there are no frictions, whereas the former may deviate from 1 in that setting; see Hayashi (1982). One such friction may be convex readjustment costs, which make v increase in $|I|$.

12.4.2 Cox–Ingersoll–Ross (CIR) Economy

The Cox–Ingersoll–Ross (CIR) model (see Cox, Ingersoll, and Ross 1985) and associated interest rate dynamics, which we discussed in the context of term structure models in section 10.3, is actually the equilibrium short-rate process in a production economy. We sketch the key ingredients of the equilibrium model.

There are N linear production technologies, which may be thought of as representing those of N "firms." These technologies are specified by their stochastic return on capital:

$$\frac{dK_n}{K_n} = \hat{\mu}_n(Y_t)\,dt + \sigma_n(Y_t)\,dV_n.$$

Here, K_n represents the real capital invested in the nth technology. The state variable, $Y_t \in \mathbb{R}$, follows a diffusion process:

$$dY_t = a(t, Y_t)\,dt + b(t, Y_t)\,dq.$$

So we see that this stochastic environment is much richer than in our model in the previous section, in that it may vary over time and states and it is multidimensional.

All agents have access to these technologies, and can choose their own capital mix. Also, capital can instantaneously be reallocated between the technologies. Capital can also be used for consumption. Equivalently, capital K can be transformed into a consumption good, and vice versa, in a one-to-one fashion, so that the effect of instantaneously consuming $C\,dt$ is to decrease K by the same amount, $dK = -C\,dt$.

The economy is set up in such a way that the dynamic maximization problem for an agent who has access to capital is very similar to the portfolio choice problem with N assets we studied before in the ICAPM model, with a constant investment opportunity set. Indeed, given that the agent with total capital/wealth K_t chooses the investment portfolio of how much to allocate to the different technologies, and also how much to instantaneously consume ($C_t\,dt$), where such consumption depletes capital, the structure of the problem is the same as before, although the investments here represent real investments, not investments in financial capital.

As known from the Lucas model, the price of financial assets in a complete market will be determined by aggregate consumption. This is the case in the CIR economy too. Indeed, all the pricing arguments in the exchange economy will hold in the complete market production economy, since the first-order conditions on the consumption side must also hold in the friction-free production economy. Also, actual real growth will be determined as an equilibrium outcome, and not be exogenously specified as it is in the Lucas economy. We discussed both these points in the previous section.

There is a complete market of contingent claims, justifying the existence of a representative agent with utility

$$U = E\left[\int_0^T e^{-\rho t} u(C_t)\,dt\right].$$

Moreover, because the market is complete, equilibrium can be derived as the solution to the social planner's problem. From here on, we therefore work with aggregate variables. The financial claims, including risk-free assets, are in zero net supply. They will still be priced correctly, since the SDF pricing relationship holds for all traded assets in the economy, regardless of their supply.

In an interior equilibrium, the aggregate wealth at time t is

$$W_t = \sum_{n=1}^{N} K_{n,t}.$$

This follows from the fact that all real capital can be transferred back and forth with the consumption good, $dK = -C\,dt$, so in equilibrium the price of a unit of capital and a unit of the consumption good—which is the numeraire we used earlier in this chapter—is the same.

To take advantage of the similarities with previous portfolio choice problems, we define the investment share in technology n: $\alpha_{n,t} = \frac{K_{n,t}}{W_t}$, and the vector of portfolio weights $\alpha_t = (\alpha_{1,t}, \ldots, \alpha_{N,t})'$. The aggregate budget constraint for the planner is then

$$dW = W\Big(\sum_{n=1}^{N} \alpha_n(\hat{\mu}_n\,dt + \sigma_n\,dV_t)\Big) - C_t\,dt,$$

and the optimization problem is $\max_{C_t,\alpha_{1,t},\ldots,\alpha_{N,t}} U$, such that $\sum_n \alpha_{n,t} = 1$.

We assume that the representative investor has log-utility. From section 12.2, it follows that the indirect utility function is of the form

$$J(W,t) = A(t)\ln(W_t) + F(t, Y_t),$$

where

$$A(t) = \frac{1 - e^{-\rho(T-t)}}{\rho},$$

$$C_t = \frac{W_t}{A(t)},$$

where the function F does not depend on wealth, but only on time and the state variable, Y, and where α_t only depends on the instantaneous investment opportunity set at t.

Since the cross derivative $J_{WY} = 0$ with this specification, the Bellman equation for J is then

$$0 = \max_{C_t,\alpha_t}\Big(\ln(C_t) - \rho J + J_t + J_W W\alpha_t'\hat{\mu}_t + \frac{1}{2}J_{WW}W^2\alpha_t'\Sigma_t\alpha_t + J_Y a + \frac{b^2}{2}J_{YY}\Big),$$

and, as before, the instantaneous FOCs with respect to C_t yield

$$J_W = \frac{A(t)}{W}.$$

The portfolio weights are chosen to solve

$$\max_{\alpha}\Big(A(t)\alpha_t'\hat{\mu}_t - \frac{1}{2}A(t)\alpha_t'\Sigma_t\alpha_t\Big), \quad \text{s.t. } \alpha'\mathbf{1} = 1,$$

leading to

$$\alpha_t = \Sigma_t^{-1}\hat{\mu}_t - \frac{\mathbf{1}'\Sigma^{-1}\hat{\mu}_t - 1}{\mathbf{1}'\Sigma_t^{-1}\mathbf{1}}\Sigma_t^{-1}\mathbf{1}.$$

Given that we now know how capital is allocated between the firms in the economy, we get the following evolution dynamics for capital:

$$\frac{dK}{K} = \sum_{n=1}^{N} \alpha_{n,t}(\hat{\mu}_n(Y_t)\,dt + \sigma_n(Y_t)\,dV_n) - c_t\,dt \stackrel{\text{def}}{=} z(Y_t)\,dt + s(Y_t)\,dV - c_t\,dt,$$

where $c_t = \frac{C_t}{K_t}$ is the consumption share at time t.

In equilibrium, net demand for the (short-lived) risk-free asset is zero, so the short rate, r_t, must adjust so that the representative investor does not change the α_t weights, even if short-lived bonds are available, i.e.,

$$\alpha_t = \Sigma_t^{-1}(\hat{\mu}_t - r_t\mathbf{1}).$$

This leads to

$$r_t = \frac{\mathbf{1}'\Sigma_t^{-1}\hat{\mu}_t - 1}{\mathbf{1}'\Sigma_t^{-1}\mathbf{1}}.$$

Now assume $\hat{\mu}_t = \hat{\mu} Y_t$ and $\Sigma_t = \Sigma Y_t$, so that

$$r_t = \frac{\mathbf{1}'\Sigma^{-1}\hat{\mu} - 1}{\mathbf{1}'\Sigma^{-1}\mathbf{1}} Y_t = \tau Y_t.$$

We assume that the parameters are such that $\tau > 0$. Note that with this choice of production technologies,

$$\alpha_t = \Sigma^{-1}\hat{\mu} - \tau\Sigma^{-1}\mathbf{1},$$

independently of Y_t. So the investor chooses the same portfolio weights at each point in time. Finally, assume

$$dY = (-\kappa Y + \zeta)\, dt + \nu\sqrt{Y}\, dq, \quad \text{where } \kappa, \zeta, \nu > 0.$$

This is a square-root process which we saw in the term structure section 10.3, and its behavior is well known. For example, if $Y_0 > 0$, then Y_t always stays weakly positive, $Y_t \geq 0$. For some parameter choices, Y_t also stays strictly positive. Indeed, the so-called *Feller condition*,

$$2\zeta > \nu^2,$$

ensures that the positive drift component is high enough that random shocks cannot drive Y_t to zero; see Feller (1951). It follows that

$$\begin{aligned} dr &= \tau\, dY \\ &= \tau(-\kappa Y + \zeta)\, dt + \tau\nu\sqrt{Y}\, dq \\ &= \kappa(\theta - r)\, dt + \sigma\sqrt{r}\, dq. \end{aligned} \tag{12.56}$$

This interest rate process, which is indeed the CIR process we saw in section 10.3, is thus a stochastic short-rate process that arises as an equilibrium outcome (although in section 10.3 the process was defined in the risk-neutral measure). The process is mean reverting and oscillates around θ. It is "wilder" than the Ornstein–Uhlenbeck process, which is of the form $dr = \kappa(\theta - r)\, dt + \sigma\, dq$, for large r, and the CIR process therefore has heavier unconditional right tails than the Ornstein–Uhlenbeck process.

In the left tail, the volatility decreases as r approaches zero, and the positive drift term for such small r's takes over, thereby keeping it nonnegative. Compared with another process, the GBM with $dr = \kappa\theta r\, dt + \sigma r\, dt$, the CIR process has higher drift and volatility close to zero, and will therefore tend to "bounce back" from very small r's faster than the GBM (because of the higher drift), in a wilder manner (because of the higher volatility).

If we assume $T = \infty$, i.e., that the economy is an infinite horizon economy, we get $A(t) \equiv 1$, $C_t = \rho K_t$. Also, the SDF is

$$M_t = e^{-\rho t}\frac{1}{C_t},$$

as usual with log-utility. The capital dynamics is $\frac{dK}{K} = (\alpha'\hat{\mu} Y - \rho)\, dt + \sqrt{\alpha'\Sigma\alpha}\sqrt{Y}\, dV$.

The key to understanding why the interest rate varies in this economy, but not in the Lucas one-tree economy, is that the varying productivity of capital forces the interest rate to adjust, so that the representative investor's net demand for bonds is always zero. When productivity is high (Y_t is high), the interest rate needs to adjust upward to keep the investor from borrowing in the bond market and investing in a leveraged equity portfolio. Similarly, when productivity is low, the interest rate must be low to avoid positive demand for bonds.

Note that the whole argument leading up to (12.56) could have been done with one firm ($N = 1$) and a scalar portfolio weight $\alpha = 1$. This would have been simpler if the only goal was to derive the interest rate process. Having a workhorse production economy with N production technologies is useful in other applications, however, which is why we followed the original argument in Cox, Ingersoll, and Ross (1985), with $N \geq 1$ production technologies, quite closely.

Finally, note that the pricing side of this economy comes from the same SDF relation we derived in the Lucas economy. We could have postulated the process for C_t and derived the same interest rate process. As mentioned before, this equivalence arises in production economies without frictions, since the FOCs on the consumption side are the same in this production economy as in the exchange economy.

CHAPTER 13 More Derivative Pricing

13.1 Constant Elasticity of Variance (CEV) Model

Although very tractable, the assumption of geometric Brownian motion (GBM) dynamics for stock prices, which we relied heavily on in Part II, is usually too bare bones to provide a rich enough description of real-world dynamics. A stylized fact about stock returns is that they are typically more volatile when the stock has recently lost a lot of value, i.e., when the stock price is low. This can, for example, be explained by leverage. If the company has debt, then as it approaches the point where its total asset value falls below the face value of its debt, stock returns will become increasingly volatile.

The *constant elasticity of variance* (CEV) model, originally studied by Cox (1975), provides a convenient way of modeling such volatility dependence on stock prices. Specifically, assume that

$$dS_t = rS_t\,dt + \sigma S_t^{1-\alpha}\,dW_t^Q, \tag{13.1}$$

where $0 \leq \alpha < 1$. Note that when $\alpha = 0$ we have the standard GBM, when $\alpha = 1$ (and $r < 0$) we have the Ornstein–Uhlenbeck process (although outside the range we study), and when $\alpha = \frac{1}{2}$ we have the CIR process. When $\alpha > 0$,

$$\left(\frac{dS}{S}\right)^2 = \sigma^2 S^{-2\alpha}\,dt,$$

which is decreasing in S, in line with the stylized fact often observed in practice, of decreasing return volatility with price.

How do we derive an option pricing formula under CEV dynamics? The model (13.1) falls within the Black–Scholes framework with state-dependent coefficients, so we should be able to use risk-neutral pricing. But, of course, when $\alpha > 0$, the distribution of S_t will be different from the classic Black–Scholes setting.

Consider a process $\{X_t\}_t$ that has the same volatility dynamics as S_t but zero drift,

$$dX_t = \sigma X_t^{1-\alpha}\,dZ_t^Q, \tag{13.2}$$

for some Wiener process, Z_t^Q. Define the time transformation function,

$$\tau(t) = \frac{1 - e^{-2r\alpha t}}{2r\alpha},$$

which has $\tau'(t) = e^{-2r\alpha t}$. Finally, define

$$S_t = e^{rt} X_{\tau(t)}. \tag{13.3}$$

From the Itô product rule and the time transformation relation provided in the hint for exercise 3 at the end of chapter 10, we get

$$\begin{aligned} dS_t &= d(e^{rt} X_{\tau(t)}) \\ &= d(e^{rt}) X_{\tau(t)} + e^{rt} d(X_{\tau(t)}) \\ &= re^{rt} X_{\tau(t)}\, dt + e^{rt} \sqrt{e^{-2r\alpha t}} \sigma X_{\tau(t)}^{1-\alpha}\, dW_t^Q \\ &= rS_t\, dt + \sigma e^{(1-\alpha)rt} X_{\tau(t)}^{1-\alpha}\, dW_t^Q \\ &= rS_t\, dt + \sigma S_t^{1-\alpha}\, dW_t^Q, \end{aligned}$$

which is of the form (13.1). So a characterization of the distributional properties of the process (13.2) can be used to characterize S_t via the relation (13.3).

Now, the behavior of the process (13.2) close to zero depends on α. The larger is α, the more slowly the volatility of X_t decreases as the process approaches 0, and the more "force" there is therefore for randomness to move X_t all the way to 0. Indeed, when $\alpha = 0$, we know from our analysis of GBMs that $X_t > 0$ (a.s.) for all t when $X_0 > 0$. However, when $\alpha = 1$ (the Ornstein–Uhlenbeck case), we know that there is a strictly positive probability that $X_t < 0$ for any $t > 0$, and therefore that X_t has "hit" the origin by time t, regardless of how large X_0 is. This is also the case for any $\alpha > 0$.

We specify that if the process hits 0 at some time, τ, this corresponds to a default of the firm from which it never recovers, so then $X_s = 0, s > \tau$ (and therefore $S_q = 0$ for $q > t$), i.e., the process is "killed" when the boundary at 0 is hit.

The process (13.2) is closely related to the so-called *Bessel process*, with dynamics

$$dY = \left(\frac{1 - \frac{1}{\alpha}}{2Y}\right) dt + dW_t;$$

see Linetsky and Mendoza (2010) and also Hull (2018). Indeed, the $\{X_t\}_t$ process can be defined as a power of such a Bessel process:

$$X_t = CY_t^{\frac{1}{\alpha}},$$

for some constant $C > 0$. This leads us to the following probability density function, ϕ^X, for $X_t = x$ (where $x > 0$):

$$\phi^X(x|X_0, t) = \frac{X_0^{\frac{1}{2}} x^{2\alpha - \frac{2}{3}}}{a^2 \alpha t} I_{-a}\left(\frac{X_0^\alpha x^\alpha}{a^2 \alpha^2 t}\right) e^{-\frac{X_0^{2\alpha} + x^{2\alpha}}{2a^2\alpha^2 t}}, \quad a = \frac{1}{2}\left(1 - \frac{1}{\alpha}\right).$$

Here, I_{-a} is the *modified Bessel function* of the first kind, of order $-a$. Transforming this expression back to the S_t process, we get the (risk-neutral) density, ϕ^S, for $S_t = s$,

$$\phi^S(s|S_0, t) = e^{-rt} \phi^X(e^{-rt} s|s, \tau(t)).$$

Moreover, the (risk-neutral) probability that the S_t process has hit 0 by t, i.e., that the asset has defaulted by then, is

$$1 - \Gamma\left(\frac{1}{2\alpha}, \frac{rS_0^{2\alpha}}{a^2 \alpha (e^{-2\alpha t} - 1)}\right),$$

where $\Gamma(c, x)$ is the *incomplete Gamma function*.

Putting it all together, we have a full specification of the risk-neutral probability distribution of the CEV process (13.1) when $\alpha \in (0, 1)$, which allows us to price any simple contingent claim with the usual risk-neutral pricing formula

$$P_t = e^{-r(T-t)} E_t^{\mathbb{Q}}[\Phi(S_T)].$$

This formulation can be used to price plain vanilla options, as well as more complex contingent claims within the CEV setting.

13.2 Jumps

As we have seen, geometric Brownian motions and more generally diffusion processes, as modeled by the dynamics $dS_t = \mu_t\, dt + \sigma_t\, dV_t$, can capture many important features of asset prices. The diffusion model allows for random shocks at various frequencies (the $\sigma_t\, dV_t$ term), time-varying expected returns (the $\mu_t\, dt$ term), and with multiple assets it allows for covariation of returns (as described by $dV_i\, dV_j$ terms for assets i and j). However, several stylized facts about asset prices are challenging to capture well by diffusion processes, like the shape of so-called implied volatility curves, very large price movements over very short time periods, and higher moments in general, which tend to suggest heavier tails over short time periods than what a model with diffusion processes can generate.

In figure 13.1, the value of the S&P 500 index between roughly 1985 and 1989 is shown (upper panel). We see that the index had a dramatic drop toward the end of 1987. Indeed, on "Black Monday," October 19, 1987, the market dropped by over 20% in one day. In the lower panel of the figure, daily index returns are shown, and we can appreciate what an outlier event this index drop was. The daily volatility was about 1% before the crash, so the Black Monday crash corresponded to a 20+ standard deviation event. Clearly, for the diffusion process to explain such a shock, volatility would have to "explode" very quickly.[1] Rather, it looks like the market "jumped" on that day.

Tests for the presence of jumps for general so-called *Lévy processes* were developed in Ait-Sahalia (2004). These tests use fairly high frequency data, and therefore need to take potential market microstructure issues into account. Ait-Sahalia and Jacod (2009) test for jumps in the Dow Jones Industrial Average (DJIA) during the calendar year 2005, using five-second intervals. They find strong evidence in favor of the presence of jumps.

How should we model jumps? After the Wiener process, the Poisson (point) process is the second most important process within continuous-time asset pricing. Recall that a Poisson-distributed random variable, $X \sim \text{Po}(\mu)$, is a discrete random variable, $X \in \{0, 1, 2, \ldots\}$, such that

$$\mathbb{P}(X = k) = \frac{e^{-\mu}\mu^k}{k!}.$$

Such a distribution is closed under additions, in that if $X_1 \sim \text{Po}(\mu_1)$ and $X_2 \sim \text{Po}(\mu_2)$ are independent, then $X_1 + X_2 \sim \text{Po}(\mu_1 + \mu_2)$. This is similar to how the class of normal distributions is closed under additions. Note that for small μ, the probability that $X > 1$ is very small (of order μ^2), and to a first-order approximation, $\mathbb{P}(X = 1) \approx \mu$ and $\mathbb{P}(X = 0) \approx 1 - \mu$.

[1] A 20 standard deviation event (at the daily frequency) for a normally distributed random variable would on average occur once in about 10^{86} years.

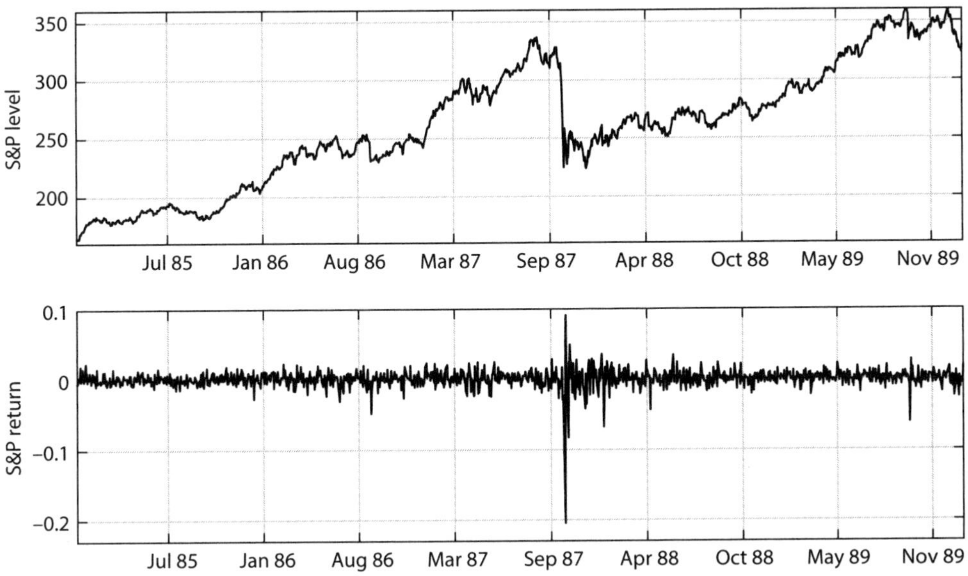

Figure 13.1: October 1987 crash. Source: Center for Research in Security Prices, CRSP.

A *Poisson process* with intensity λ is a counting process: $J(t) \in \{0, 1, 2, \ldots\}$ (we also write J_t), such that

1. $J(0) = 0$,
2. $J(t)$ has independent increments,
3. for all $t > 0$ and $\tau > 0$, $J(t+\tau) - J(t) \sim \text{Po}(\lambda t)$.

Note that this definition has similarities with that of a Wiener process. Indeed, both the Wiener process (and associated Brownian motion) and the Poisson process share several properties, e.g., the linear scaling of expectation and variance over time. Of course, there is also the fundamental difference that the Wiener process moves around all the time in a continuous fashion, whereas the Poisson process stays constant most of the time, occasionally makes a jump, and is always nondecreasing.

We write $dJ_t = J(t+dt) - J(t)$, and it follows that $dJ = 1$ with probability $\lambda\, dt$, and $dJ = 0$ with probability $1 - \lambda\, dt$ over infinitesimal time periods. By convention, the process is *right continuous* (with left limits), i.e., a jump at t occurs at t^-. In figure 13.2, we see an example of a Poisson process with intensity 1.

In the first paper to introduce jumps in an option pricing framework, Merton (1976) assumes the underlying stock follows a *jump-diffusion process*, thus combining diffusion dynamics with jumps. The risk-neutral process is assumed to be

$$dS = (r - \lambda\xi)S\, dt + \sigma S\, dW^Q + S\, dZ^Q. \tag{13.4}$$

Here, Z^Q is a so-called compound Poisson process, with intensity λ, which is independent of the Wiener process, dW^Q. The Z^Q process is made up of two parts: the first part is a Poisson process J_t with intensity λ, which determines whether a jump occurs, so that $dZ_t = 0$ when $dJ_t = 0$.

The second part determines the size of the jump, if it occurs. Given a jump between t and $t + dt$ ($dJ = 1$), $dZ = Y - 1$, where the nonnegative random variable Y has p.d.f. $p(y)$, and

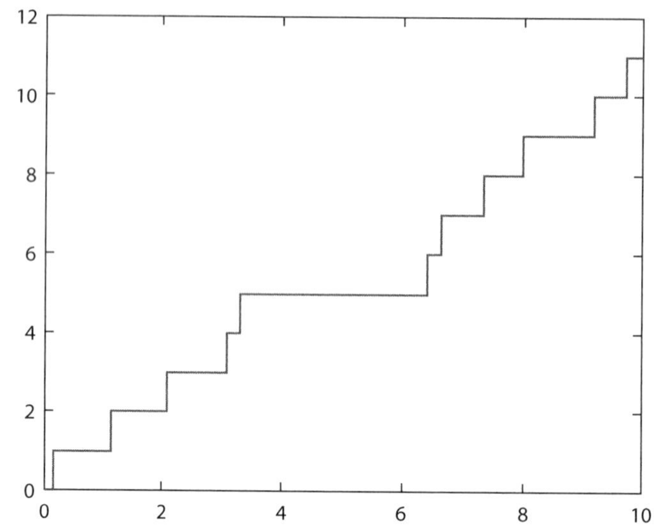

Figure 13.2: Sample path of a Poisson process.

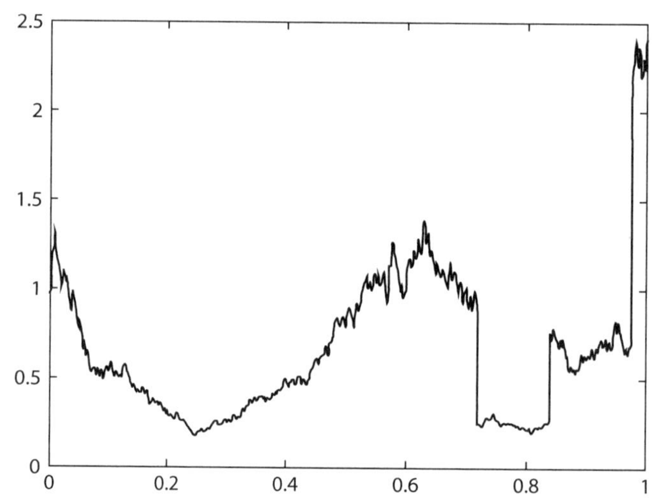

Figure 13.3: Jump diffusion process, with three jumps between $t=0$ and $t=1$.

$\xi+1 \stackrel{\text{def}}{=} E[Y]=\int_0^\infty yp(y)\,dy$. Also, $Y_1, Y_2, \ldots$, associated with the different jumps have i.i.d. distributions across these jumps. An example is when Y is log-normally distributed, $Y \sim \mathrm{Ln}(\gamma, \delta^2)$, i.e., Y has p.d.f.

$$p(y)=\frac{1}{y\sqrt{2\pi\delta^2}}e^{-\frac{(\ln(y)-\gamma)^2}{2\delta^2}}, \quad \text{so that } \xi=e^{\gamma+\frac{\delta^2}{2}}-1.$$

An example of a jump-diffusion process is shown in figure 13.3.

Going back to (13.4), we see that the right-hand side has two modifications compared with the standard risk-neutral diffusion process. The term $S\,dZ^Q$ is zero at all times, except when there is a jump. Since $dZ^Q \geq -1$ (because $Y \geq 0$), S cannot jump more than -100% on the downside. Specifically, if $dZ_t^Q=-1$, then at that very moment, the change in S is $dS_t=-S$, since the dt and

dW^Q terms will not have time to move the stock price during the infinitesimal period between t^- and t. This means that

$$S_t = S_{t^-} - S_{t^-} = 0,$$

at t, and also at any time after t. If $dZ_t^Q > -1$, on the other hand, then $S_t > 0$, and S "lives on" after t, with possible jumps at later points in time.

Also, note the adjustment to the drift term in (13.4). The drift coefficient is no longer r, but $r - \lambda\xi$. This is so that the risk-neutral instantaneous drift is still $rS\,dt$:

$$\begin{aligned} E^{\mathbb{Q}}[dS] &= (r - \lambda\xi)S\,dt + SE^{\mathbb{Q}}[dZ^Q] \\ &= (r - \lambda\xi)S\,dt + S\lambda\,dt\,E^{\mathbb{Q}}[Y - 1|dJ = 1] \\ &= (r - \lambda\xi)S\,dt + S\lambda\xi\,dt \\ &= rS\,dt. \end{aligned}$$

A natural way to approximate the dynamics over short time horizons is

$$S_{t+\Delta t} = S_t + (r - \lambda\xi)S_t\Delta + \sigma\sqrt{\Delta t}\eta_t + S_t(Y_t + 1)B_t, \tag{13.5}$$

where $\eta_t \sim N(0, 1)$ has a standard normal distribution, $B_t \sim \text{Ber}(\lambda\Delta t)$ is Bernoulli distributed, and Y_t has the aforementioned distribution when $B_t = 1$, all random variables being independent.

We have described the dynamics of S directly in the risk-neutral measure. In contrast to the case of diffusion process dynamics, the stock and the bond are in general no longer sufficient to make the market complete. Intuitively, there are now two sources of risk at each point in time (dW risk and dJ risk), but only one risky asset, suggesting that this is not sufficient for the market to be complete. If $Y \equiv y$ for some constant y, our intuition suggests that additionally adding an option to the trading portfolio would be sufficient to complete the market. However, if the distribution of Y is nondegenerate, for example having support on a whole interval, then there will be many possible outcomes over the next dt period, and many additional assets seem to be needed. The replicating portfolio argument therefore becomes quite involved.

It is therefore natural to make additional assumptions about the pricing of dZ risk, beyond what can be derived from no-arbitrage arguments alone. Merton (1976) assumes that the jump-risk component does not have a risk premium, so that the risk-neutral and objective measures are the same for such risk, i.e., $dZ^Q = dZ$. This means that $E^{\mathbb{Q}}[dJ] = E^{\mathbb{P}}[dJ]$, so λ is the same under the risk-neutral and objective probability measures, and also $E^{\mathbb{Q}}[Y] = E^{\mathbb{P}}[Y] = \xi$.

What is the rationale for the assumption that $dZ = dZ^Q$ in this case, when we have spent so much effort on distinguishing risk-neutral from objective probability measures? One such rationale may be that jumps at the individual firm level represent idiosyncratic risk—huge events for a firm, but marginal from the aggregate economy's perspective. For example, the CEO of the company may step down after a scandal, or a class action lawsuit against the firm may be announced. Such idiosyncratic risk can be diversified away, and is therefore not priced.

The risk-neutral pricing formula is then well defined, with the diffusion process part being priced according to our no-arbitrage methodology in the diffusion model, and the jump process part being priced such that risk-neutral and objective probabilities are the same.

The risk-neutral pricing formula for a simple contingent claim is formally the same as before:

$$C = e^{-rT}E^{\mathbb{Q}}[\Phi(S_T)],$$

in differential form,

$$E^{\mathbb{Q}}[dC] = rC\,dt.$$

However, calculating the price will naturally be more challenging than before. Consider, for example, using the law of motion to find a solution. Under diffusion dynamics, this led to the Black–Scholes PDE. It is clear from (13.5) that the law of motion here is much less local, because of the jumps. Indeed, if Y has a continuous probability density function, then the price of the underlying may instantaneously move to an infinite number of new levels. As a consequence, the Kolmogorov equations become more involved.

We can understand heuristically what the law of motion will look like. Given the price function $C(S,t)$, where we may focus on a European call option, we have that over a very short time period, dt, the price of the underlying does not jump with probability $1-\lambda\,dt$, in which case C follows diffusion dynamics:

$$dC = C_t\,dt + C_S S((r-\lambda\xi)\,dt + \sigma\,dW^{\mathbb{Q}}) + \frac{\sigma^2}{2} C_{SS} S^2\,dt \Big| dJ = 0.$$

With probability $\lambda\,dt$ the price does jump, $dJ = 1$, and in this case the expected change of C is

$$E^{\mathbb{Q}}[dC|dJ=1] = \int_0^\infty (C(t^-, Sy) - C(t^-, S))p(y)\,dy = \int_0^\infty C(t^-, Sy)p(y)\,dy - C(t^-, S).$$

We do not need to include the changes because of diffusion drift and volatility here, since the jump will be of order 1, whereas the diffusion part is negligible over the dt period.

When we add these two contributions together, we get in total,[2]

$$\begin{aligned} E^{\mathbb{Q}}[dC] &= E^{\mathbb{Q}}[dC|dJ=0] \times \mathbb{P}(dJ=0) + E^{\mathbb{Q}}[dC|dJ=1] \times \mathbb{P}(dJ=1) \\ &= \left(C_t\,dt + C_S S(r-\lambda\xi)\,dt + \frac{\sigma^2}{2} C_{SS} S^2\,dt\right)(1-\lambda\,dt) \\ &\quad + \lambda\,dt\left(\int_0^\infty C(t, Sy)p(y)\,dy - C\right). \end{aligned}$$

Disregarding higher-order terms, and relying on the EMM relation $E^{\mathbb{Q}}[dC] = rC\,dt$, then gives us

$$\begin{aligned} E^{\mathbb{Q}}[dC] &= \left(C_t + C_S S(r-\lambda\xi) + \frac{\sigma^2}{2} C_{SS} S^2 + \lambda \int_0^\infty C(t, Sy)p(y)\,dy - \lambda C\right) dt \\ &= rC\,dt. \end{aligned}$$

We arrive at the following so-called *partial integro-differential equation, PIDE,* for the option price,

$$C_t + C_S S(r-\lambda\xi) + \frac{\sigma^2}{2} C_{SS} S^2 - (r+\lambda)C + \lambda \int_0^\infty C(t, Sy)p(y)\,dy = 0. \tag{13.6}$$

Because of the rightmost integration term, we expect this law of motion to be a lot more challenging to solve than the Black–Scholes PDE, in general.

Under clever additional assumptions about jump distributions, the analysis simplifies considerably. Assume, as in Merton (1976), that the jump size is log-normally distributed, $Y \sim \mathrm{Ln}(\gamma, \delta^2)$. Let us first assume that we know that there will be exactly one jump immediately, at $t = 0^+$, after which the underlying diffusion dynamics is a standard (GBM) diffusion process. In this case, $S_{0^+} = YS_0$:

$$C = e^{-rT} E_0\left[E^{\mathbb{Q}}_{0^+}[\Phi[S_T]]\right] = E_0[\mathcal{BS}(YS_0, K, r, \sigma, T)], \tag{13.7}$$

where, as before, $\mathcal{BS}$ denotes the Black–Scholes plain vanilla call option formula.

[2]Since $\lambda\,dt$ multiplies the $E^{\mathbb{Q}}[dC|dJ=1]$ term, any terms including dt or $dW^{\mathbb{Q}}$ will be higher-order terms.

Now, in practice, we do not know how many jumps there will be, nor when they will occur. Indeed, the total number of jumps between 0 and T, is $J_T \sim \text{Po}(\lambda T)$. If there are k jumps, then we know that the total jump size is distributed as

$$\widehat{Y}(k) = \prod_{i=1}^{k} Y_i \sim \text{Ln}(k\gamma, k\delta^2).$$

This follows because the total jump size is the product of k i.i.d. jumps, and the product of log-normal distributed risks is log-normally distributed. It is easy to see that the risk-neutral distribution of S_T does not depend on when the k jumps occur, and therefore neither does the risk-neutral expectation. We may actually assume that they all occur almost instantaneously, clustered at $t = 0^+$, in which case (13.7) implies that

$$C(S, 0|J_T = k) = E[\mathcal{BS}(S\widehat{Y}(k)e^{-\lambda\xi T}, K, r, \sigma, T)].$$

Recalling that $\mathbb{P}(J_T = k) = \frac{e^{-\lambda T}(\lambda T)^k}{k!}$, we arrive at the unconditional option pricing formula,

$$C = \sum_{k=0}^{\infty} \frac{e^{-\lambda T}(\lambda T)^k}{k!} E[\mathcal{BS}(S\widehat{Y}(k)e^{-\lambda\xi T}, K, r, \sigma, T)]. \tag{13.8}$$

This formula may look complicated, but it is actually straightforward to handle numerically, as long as λT is sufficiently low so that the probability is very high that the number of jumps is moderate (say, no more than 100 jumps).

Another way to think about (13.8) is to define $\widehat{S}_t$, the price of the stock at t if the jumps are not considered,

$$\frac{d\widehat{S}}{\widehat{S}} = (r - \lambda\xi)\, dt + \sigma\, dW^Q,$$

and then define the actual price through the adjustment

$$S_T = Y_1 \times Y_2 \times \cdots \times Y_{J_T} \times \widehat{S}_T = \widehat{Y}(J_T)\widehat{S}_T.$$

The total price is then the sum of the conditional expectation given the number of jumps, k, multiplied by the probability for k jumps, $k \geq 0$, which leads to (13.8).

An example is shown in figure 13.4, where we study the *implied volatility* curve. Consider a call option with strike price K and price C. The implied volatility, $\sigma(K)$, solves the equation $C(K) = \mathcal{BS}(S, K, r, \sigma(K), T)$, i.e., it is the volatility that is consistent with the Black–Scholes option pricing formula. Note that S and T are known, and r can be calculated using the price of a T-bond, $p(T) = e^{-rT}$, so $\sigma(K)$ is the only unobservable in this equation. The implied volatility curve is the function $\{\sigma(K)\}$, as a function of K, which can then be constructed by observing many options with different strike prices.

If the Black–Scholes model holds, the implied volatility curve is a flat line, $\sigma(K) \equiv \sigma$. In practice, the curve is often convex, sometimes looking like a "smile"—decreasing for low K's, reaching a minimum somewhere near the at-the-money option, for which $K = S$, end then increasing—and sometimes like a "smirk"—decreasing, but flattening out for high K's.

We see in the figure that the model can generate a volatility smirk. This is because the possibility of jumps may instantaneously move the price of the underlying stock to very low values, increasing the risk-neutral probability of ending up at such values compared with what the instantaneous volatility, σ, suggests.

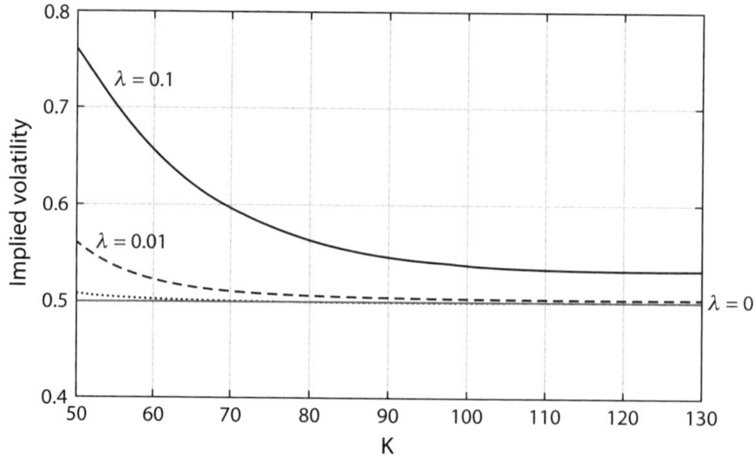

Figure 13.4: Implied volatility curve. Parameters: $S=100$, $T=0.3$, $r=0.03$, $\sigma=0.5$, $\gamma=2$, and $\delta=1$.

As mentioned earlier, the presence of implied volatility smirks is a common feature in real markets. Formula (13.8) holds whether or not Y is log-normally distributed, although the log-normal distribution makes it especially straightforward to calculate, because this class of distributions is closed under multiplication. In general, as long as the distribution of $\widehat{Y}(k)=\prod_{i=1}^{k} Y_i$ can be efficiently calculated, the formula can be used.

A special case arises when a jump makes the underlying asset worthless, i.e., $\mathbb{P}(Y=0)=1$ when $dJ=1$. Similar arguments to before lead to

$$\begin{aligned}
C &= e^{-rT}E_0[\mathcal{BS}(Se^{\lambda T}, K, r, \sigma, T) \times \chi_{J_T=0}] \\
&= e^{-rT}\mathcal{BS}(Se^{\lambda T}, K, r, \sigma, T) \times e^{-\lambda T} \\
&= e^{-(r+\lambda)T}\mathcal{BS}(Se^{\lambda T}, K, r, \sigma, T) \\
&= \mathcal{BS}(S, K, r+\lambda, \sigma, T).
\end{aligned}$$

This expression is in the same closed-form as the Black–Scholes formula, but with a higher discount rate ($r+\lambda$ replaces r). An advantage with this special case is then that there exists a closed-form solution! A disadvantage is that the qualitative behavior of the option's price as a function of the strike price is the same in this special case as for Black–Scholes' classical formula without jumps, implying a constant implied volatility curve. So we will not be able to explain volatility smiles or smirks under this specific specification.

13.3 Further Classification of Processes and Distributions

Jump-diffusion processes fall within the more general class of processes with the Markov property and stochastically continuous sample paths, as shown in figure 13.5. We have discussed the Markov property before, namely that the future dynamics of the process only depends on the current state—the historical path is irrelevant. A process with a stochastically continuous sample path may have jumps, but the probability for a jump at any given time is 0, i.e.,

$$\lim_{\Delta t \searrow 0} \mathbb{P}(|X_{t+\Delta t} - X_t| > \epsilon) = 0, \tag{13.9}$$

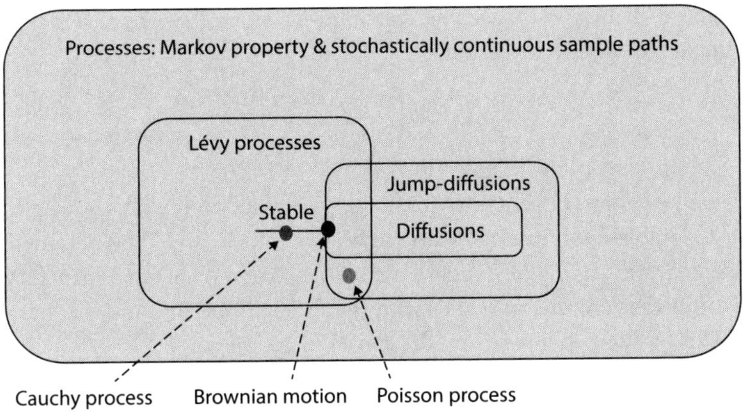

Figure 13.5: Classification of stochastic processes.

for all $\epsilon > 0$. Clearly, Poisson processes and jump-diffusion processes have stochastically continuous sample paths, since the probability for one or more jumps of the Poisson process between t and $t + \Delta t$ is $1 - e^{-\lambda \Delta t} \approx \lambda \Delta t$, which tends to 0 when Δt tends to 0, and since diffusion processes have continuous sample paths.

Lévy processes define a subclass of the processes satisfying the Markov property with stochastically continuous sample paths. For the process X_t to qualify as a Lévy process, it must satisfy the following conditions:

1. *Start at origin*: $X_0 = 0$.
2. *Independent increments*: For all $r < s \leq t < u$, $X_u - X_t$ is independent of $X_s - X_r$.
3. *Stationary increments*: For any $s < t$, $X_t - X_s$ has the same distribution as X_{t-s}.
4. *Stochastically continuous sample paths*: Defined by (13.9).

We see that conditions 1 and 2 are the same as for a Wiener process, whereas conditions 3 and 4 are weaker. With respect to condition 3, for the Wiener process the stationary increments need to be standard Gaussian, $X_{t-s} \sim N(0, t - s)$, whereas here the distribution is not specified. Finally, the almost surely continuous sample path requirement for the Wiener process is here replaced by the weaker condition of stochastically continuous sample paths in condition 4.

The Wiener process, and more generally, any Brownian motion that starts at 0, is a Lévy process, as is the Poisson process, but note that Lévy processes do not allow for time-varying distributions. So diffusions with variable coefficients do not fall within the class of Lévy processes. The so-called Lévy–Itô decomposition shows that any Lévy process can be thought of as the sum of a Brownian motion and a jump process that is the sum of independent Poisson processes with at most a countable number of jumps on any interval.

Within the class of Lévy processes, the *α-stable processes* are especially important. Here, $\alpha \in (0, 2]$ is a parameter that characterizes such a process. These processes are generated by random variables with *stable distributions*. A continuous random variable is said to have a stable distribution if its distribution is closed under summation. Specifically, consider two random variables, $\widetilde{Y}_1 = \mu_1 + \sigma_1 \widetilde{X}_1$, $\widetilde{Y}_2 = \mu_2 + \sigma_2 \widetilde{X}_2$, where $\widetilde{X}_1$ and $\widetilde{X}_2$ are i.i.d. random variables, with probability density function ϕ. If the probability density function of $\widetilde{Y} = \widetilde{Y}_1 + \widetilde{Y}_2$ is of the form $\phi(y)^Y = \phi(\frac{y-\mu}{\sigma})$ for some parameters μ and σ (that may depend on μ_1, μ_2, σ_1, and σ_2), then $\widetilde{X}_1$ belongs to the class of stable distributions.

Clearly, normal distributions are stable distributions since $\widetilde{Y}_1 + \widetilde{Y}_2 \sim N(\mu_1 + \mu_2, \sigma_1^2 + \sigma_2^2)$, i.e., the sum's probability density function is

$$\phi^Y(x) = \phi\left(\frac{x - \mu_1 - \mu_2}{\sqrt{\sigma_1^2 + \sigma_2^2}}\right),$$

when $\widetilde{X}_1$ and $\widetilde{X}_2$ are standard normal distributions, with associated p.d.f.'s ϕ. The class of normal distributions are α-stable distributions, with parameter value $\alpha = 2$. The parameter α here corresponds to the quadratic scaling of standard deviations, $(\sigma_1, \sigma_2) \mapsto (\sigma_1^2 + \sigma_2^2)^{1/2}$. One can show that normal distributions are the only ones with the index $\alpha = 2$, and indeed the only ones with finite variance. This basically follows from the central limit theorem.

For each $\alpha \in (0, 2)$, there is also a class of stable distributions, defined by their probability density function ϕ_α. Except for $\alpha = \frac{1}{2}$, $\alpha = 1$, and $\alpha = 2$ (the normal case), there is no closed-form expression for ϕ_α. But the Fourier transform of the function has a closed-form expression. Recall that the Fourier transform of a function $\phi: \mathbb{R} \to \mathbb{R}$ is defined as

$$\hat{\phi}(\omega) = \int_{-\infty}^{\infty} \phi(x) e^{i\omega x}\, dx,$$

and that this transform defines a bijection on the Hilbert space L^2, with inverse

$$\phi(x) = \frac{1}{2\pi} \int_{-\infty}^{\infty} \hat{\phi}(\omega) e^{-i\omega x}\, dx.$$

We discuss the Fourier transform further in section 13.4.

The Fourier transform of the probability density function for the α-stable distribution is then defined as

$$\hat{\phi}_\alpha(\omega; \beta) = e^{-|\omega|^\alpha (1 - i\beta\, \mathrm{sign}(\omega) \tan(\pi \frac{\alpha}{2}))}, \quad \beta \in \mathbb{R},\ \alpha \neq 1.$$

Here, β is a so-called generalized skewness parameter that influences the shape of the distribution. When $\beta = 0$, the distribution is symmetric around 0.

The α-stable distributions with $\alpha < 2$ are extremely heavy tailed, to the point that they have infinite variances. Indeed, the tail behavior of an α-stable distribution is that of a Pareto distribution with tail index α:

$$\phi_\alpha(x; 0) \sim \frac{1}{|x|^{1+\alpha}}, \quad |x| \gg 1.$$

The scaling of the sum of two random variables for general α is such that $\sigma_1 \widetilde{X}_1 + \sigma_2 \widetilde{X}_2$ has the distribution

$$\phi^Y(x) = \phi_\alpha\left(\frac{x}{(|\sigma_1|^\alpha + |\sigma_2|^\alpha)^{1/\alpha}}\right).$$

Note here that σ can no longer be interpreted as a standard deviation parameter when $\alpha < 2$, since the variance is infinite in this case. Rather, it is a spread parameter. Just like with standard deviation, a higher σ means that the distribution is more spread out (riskier).

We can now use α-stable distributions to define α-stable processes, just like we use normal distributions to define Brownian motions. Because of the closedness of the class of α-stable distributions under summation, it follows that an α-stable distribution can be written as an arbitrarily large sum of i.i.d. α-stable distributions:

$$\widetilde{Y} = \widetilde{X}_1 + \widetilde{X}_2 + \widetilde{X}_3 + \cdots + \widetilde{X}_N.$$

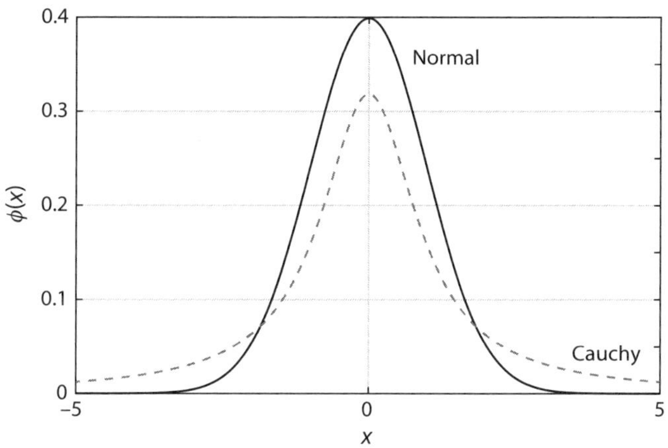

Figure 13.6: Cauchy distribution (dash-dotted line) and normal distribution (solid line).

In other words these distributions are *infinitely divisible*. It means that it is straightforward to interpret any distribution $X_t - X_s$ as a sum of small increments $(X_{s+\Delta t} - X_s) + (X_{s+2\Delta t} - X_{s+\Delta t}) + \cdots + (X_t - X_{t-\Delta t})$.

The scaling of the σ-parameter will be different when $\alpha < 2$, and σ no longer corresponds to standard deviation. Let us, for example, consider the case $\alpha = 1$. One can show that the symmetric α-stable distribution with $\alpha = 1$ is the so-called Cauchy distribution, with probability density function

$$\phi_1(x; 0) = \frac{1}{\pi(1 + x^2)}.$$

The slow algebraic decay of this density function means that there will be much higher risk of tail events compared with normal distributions. The probability density functions of the Cauchy and normal distributions are shown in figure 13.6. As seen in the figure, the decay in the tails is much slower for the Cauchy distribution.

Also, in this case the scaling for $Y = X_1 + X_2$ leads to the probability density function

$$\phi^Y(x; 0) = \phi_1\left(\frac{x}{2}; 0\right).$$

So, instead of the spread parameter increasing sublinearly to $\sqrt{2}$ when we add two i.i.d. random variables as it does for normal distributions, it actually increases linearly. This means that the associated Cauchy process will increase in riskiness faster over time than the Wiener process.[3]

The heavy-tailed behavior of increments over short time associated with the Cauchy process is impossible to obtain without jumps. Indeed, the Cauchy process frequently jumps. In figure 13.7, the sample paths of a Brownian motion and a Cauchy process are compared. We see

[3]The different scaling also has implications for portfolio diversification. Recall Samuelson's (1967) result that diversification always pays. Strictly speaking, this was only under the assumption of finite variance. With Cauchy-distributed risks, the diversified portfolio $\frac{1}{2}\widetilde{X}_1 + \frac{1}{2}\widetilde{X}_2$ has the *same* distribution as the undiversified portfolio $\widetilde{X}_1$. When $\alpha < 1$, diversification actually *increases risk*. This was noted in Mandelbrot (1963) and Fama (1965); see also Ibragimov and Walden (2007) and Ibragimov, Ibragimov, and Walden (2015). So putting all one's eggs in one basket is basically optimal when $\alpha < 1$ for anyone who is risk averse. Intuitively, since the risks are so heavy tailed, one wants to be exposed to as few of them as possible.

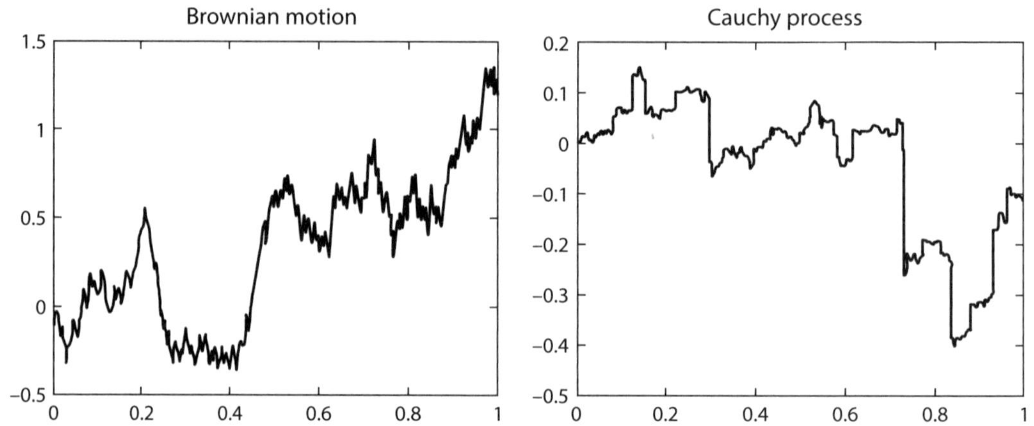

Figure 13.7: Brownian motion and a Cauchy process.

that the behavior of the Cauchy process is quite different in that the process is heavily influenced by jumps, whereas the Brownian motion shows the "continuous-but-wiggly" behavior we have become used to.

As discussed in Ibragimov, Ibragimov, and Walden (2015), many financial time series do indeed show much heavier-tailed behavior than what is suggested by normal and log-normal distributions, at various frequencies, suggesting that the α-stable processes may provide a fruitful alternative to the diffusion or jump-diffusion process setting.

13.4 Stochastic Volatility

As we discussed in section 13.1, return volatilities of stocks vary over time. The CEV model imposes a direct relation between the level of the stock price, S_t, and the magnitude of the volatility. Although such a relation can be motivated, for example, by leverage, in practice volatility also varies for other reasons, not directly related to S_t. Volatility itself is stochastic.

Heston (1993) introduces a model that incorporates such stochastic volatility into asset pricing. Specifically, the dynamics for the stock is

$$dS_t = \hat{\mu} S_t\, dt + \sqrt{v_t} S_t\, dV_1.$$

There is also a bond with constant risk-free returns:

$$dB = rB\, dt.$$

In the classical Black–Scholes model, we would have the instantaneous variance $v_t \equiv \sigma^2$, but here we let the variance be stochastic. Specifically, we assume the following Ornstein–Uhlenbeck process for (signed) volatility, $x_t \stackrel{\text{def}}{=} \sqrt{v_t}$:

$$dx_t = -\beta x_t\, dt + \delta\, dV_2.$$

Just like in the jump-diffusion model, dynamic trading in the stock and bond will not make the market complete in this model, since there are two sources of risk, dV_1 and dV_2. In contrast to that model, we want to allow the second risk factor to be associated with a risk premium. Indeed, we would expect an important driver of shocks to individual stock volatility to be market-wide volatility changes. So the volatility risk would not be idiosyncratic. We also allow the two risks to be correlated,

$$\mathrm{Cov}(dV_1, dV_2) = \rho\, dt, \quad \rho \in (-1, 1).$$

Itô's lemma gives us the following dynamics for v_t:

$$\begin{aligned} dv = d(x^2) &= 2x\, dx + \frac{1}{2} 2(dx)^2 \\ &= 2x(-\beta x\, dt + \delta\, dV_2) + \delta^2\, dt \\ &= (\delta^2 - 2\beta v)\, dt + 2\delta \sqrt{v}\, dV_2 \\ &= \kappa(\theta - v)\, dt + \sigma \sqrt{v}\, dV_2, \end{aligned}$$

where $\kappa = 2\beta$, $\theta = \frac{\delta^2}{2\beta}$, and $\sigma = 2\delta$. So variance follows a square-root (CIR) process. Recall that the Feller condition,

$$2\kappa\theta > \sigma^2,$$

is needed if we want to ensure that v_t stays strictly positive for this process. Here,

$$2\kappa\theta = 2(2\beta)\frac{\delta^2}{2\beta} = 2\delta^2 = \frac{\sigma^2}{2} < \sigma^2,$$

so the Feller condition is violated. This is unsurprising, since the signed volatility process, x_t, is an Ornstein–Uhlenbeck process. Ornstein–Uhlenbeck processes pass zero occasionally, at which point instantaneous variance, v_t, being the square of the volatility, is then also zero.

We use the same trick as when deriving the Black–Scholes PDE and the PDE in the one-factor term structure models. Specifically, we find a portfolio that is locally risk-free, and then use no-arbitrage arguments to derive the PDE for the asset's price. Here we have two sources of risk, so we will need three assets. Specifically, consider two simple contingent claims on the stock price, with maturities T_1 and T_2, and assume that their prices are $C^1(t, S, v)$ and $C^2(t, S, v)$, respectively, where C^1 and C^2 are smooth functions. Itô's lemma gives, for $i = 1, 2$,

$$\begin{aligned} dC^i &= C^i_t\, dt + C^i_S\, dS + C^i_v\, dv + \frac{1}{2}(C^i_{SS}(dS)^2 + 2C^i_{Sv}(dS)(dv) + C^i_{vv}(dv^2)) \\ &= \left(C^i_t + C^i_S \hat{\mu} S + C^i_v \kappa(\theta - v) + \frac{v}{2}(C^i_{SS} S^2 + 2C^i_{Sv}\rho\sigma S + \sigma^2 C^2_{vv})\right) dt \\ &\quad + C^i_S S\sqrt{V}\, dV_1 + C^i_v \sigma \sqrt{v}\, dV_2. \end{aligned}$$

Now consider the portfolio $\mathbf{h} = (C^1_S C^2_v - C^2_S C^1_v, -C^2_v, +C^1_v)'$, where $\mathbf{h} = (\#S, \#C^1, \#C^2)'$, i.e., it is the vector with three elements: the number of shares of the stock, of the first contingent claim, and of the second contingent claim. The value of this portfolio is

$$V = (C^1_S C^2_v - C^2_S C^1_v)S - C^2_v C^1 + C^1_v C^2,$$

and Itô's lemma gives us

$$\begin{aligned} dV &= (C^1_S C^2_v - C^2_S C^1_v) S(\hat{\mu}\, dt + \sqrt{v}\, dV_1) \\ &\quad - C^2_v \Big(\Big(C^1_t + C^1_S \hat{\mu} S + C^1_v \kappa(\theta - v) + \frac{v}{2}(C^1_{SS} S^2 + 2C^1_{Sv}\rho\sigma S + \sigma^2 C^1_{vv})\Big)\, dt \\ &\quad + C^1_S S\sqrt{V}\, dV_1 + C^1_v \sigma \sqrt{v}\, dV_2\Big) \end{aligned}$$

$$+ C_v^1\Big(\Big(C_t^2 + C_S^2\hat{\mu}S + C_v^i\kappa(\theta - v) + \frac{v}{2}(C_{SS}^2 S^2 + 2C_{Sv}^2\rho\sigma S + \sigma^2 C_{vv}^2)\Big)\,dt$$

$$+ C_S^i S\sqrt{V}\,dV_1 + C_v^i\sigma\sqrt{v}\,dV_2\Big)$$

$$= C_v^1\Big(C_t^2 + C_v^2\kappa(\theta - v) + \frac{v}{2}(C_{SS}^2 S^2 + 2C_{Sv}^2\rho\sigma S + \sigma^2 C_{vv}^2)\Big)\,dt$$

$$- C_v^2\Big(C_t^1 + C_v^1\kappa(\theta - v) + \frac{v}{2}(C_{SS}^1 S^2 + 2C_{Sv}^1\rho\sigma S + \sigma^2 C_{vv}^1)\Big)\,dt$$

$$= r((C_S^1 C_v^2 - C_S^2 C_v^1)S - C_v^2 C^1 + C_v^1 C^2)\,dt.$$

Here, in the last step, we used the no-arbitrage argument that since the portfolio is locally risk-free, its instantaneous return must be $rV\,dt$.

We rearrange terms and divide by $C_v^1 C_v^2$ to get

$$\frac{1}{C_v^1}\Big(C_t^1 + C_v^1\kappa(\theta - v)C_S^1 S + \frac{v}{2}(C_{SS}^1 S^2 + 2C_{Sv}^1\rho\sigma S + \sigma^2 C_{vv}^1) - rC^1\Big)$$

$$= \frac{1}{C_v^2}\Big(C_t^2 + C_v^2\kappa(\theta - v)C_S^2 S + \frac{v}{2}(C_{SS}^2 S^2 + 2C_{Sv}^2\rho\sigma S + \sigma^2 C_{vv}^2) - rC^2\Big)$$

$$\stackrel{\text{def}}{=} \lambda(t, S, v)\sigma.$$

Since the equality must hold for arbitrary contingent claims, the function $\lambda(t, S, v)$ must be the same for any such contingent claim. This leads to the following PDE, which must be satisfied for all contingent claims:

$$C_t + C_v(\kappa(\theta - v) - \lambda(t, S, v)\sigma) + rSC_S + \frac{v}{2}(C_{SS}S^2 + 2C_{Sv}\rho\sigma S + \sigma^2 C_{vv}) - rC = 0. \tag{13.10}$$

Via the multidimensional Feynman–Kac theorem, we also have the risk-neutral dynamics

$$dS_t = rS_t\,dt + \sqrt{v_t}S_t\,dV_1^Q, \tag{13.11}$$

$$dv_t = (\kappa\theta - (\kappa + \lambda\sigma)v_t)\,dt + \sigma\sqrt{v_t}\,dV_2^Q$$

$$= \hat{\kappa}(\hat{\theta} - v_t)\,dt + \sigma\sqrt{v_t}\,dV_2^Q, \quad \text{where } \hat{\kappa} = \kappa + \lambda\sigma, \hat{\theta} = \frac{\kappa\theta}{\kappa + \lambda\sigma}. \tag{13.12}$$

In general, we need to resort to two-dimensional PDE solvers to calculate the solution to (13.10). However, in the special case when $\lambda(t, S, v) = \lambda v$, where $\lambda \in \mathbb{R}$ is a constant, we can push the analysis further. Note that the objective and risk-neutral measures have the same functional form in this case: GBM for S_t, and CIR for v_t, but with different parameters.

The PDE is now

$$C_t + C_v\hat{\kappa}(\hat{\theta} - v) + C_S S + \frac{v}{2}(C_{SS}S^2 + 2C_{Sv}\rho\sigma S + \sigma^2 C_{vv}) - rC = 0. \tag{13.13}$$

Consider the plain vanilla call option, with terminal payoff $\Phi(S, T) = \max(S - K, 0)$, as usual. To guarantee uniqueness, we need additional boundary conditions here. As discussed in Heston (1993), we impose the following conditions:

$$C(t, 0, v) = 0,$$

$$C_S(t, \infty, v) = 1,$$

$$C(t, S, \infty) = S,$$

$$C_t(t, S, 0) + rSC_s(t, S, 0) + \kappa\theta C_v(t, S, 0) - rC(t, S, 0) = 0.$$

The last two conditions are new compared with classical Black–Scholes. The third condition can be understood by realizing that when v is very large, it will most likely stay very large until T. So (13.11) implies that C is bounded below by the Black–Scholes formula with a very high σ^2. It is easy to verify that the Black–Scholes call option price tends to S as $\sigma^2 \to \infty$, so this must also be the call option price in this model, for very large v (the price can obviously not be higher than S). The last term is what (13.10) reduces to when $v \to 0$.

Inspired by the approach we took when proving the pricing formula in the classical model, see theorem 9.12, we conjecture that the solution is of the form

$$C(t, S, v) = SF - Ke^{-r(T-t)}G, \tag{13.14}$$

with the associated terminal conditions $F(T, S, v) = G(T, S, v) = \chi_{S \geq K}$. Following the same approach as in that proof, we use the chain rule to expand the partial derivatives of C, plug them into the PDE (13.10), and collect terms, to get the two PDEs

$$F_t + (r + v^2)SF_S + (\kappa\theta - (\kappa + \lambda\sigma - \rho\sigma)v)F_v + \frac{v}{2}(S^2F_{SS} + 2\rho\sigma SF_{Sv} + \sigma^2F_{vv}) = 0,$$

$$G_t + rSG_s + (\kappa\theta - (\kappa + \lambda\sigma)v)G_v + \frac{v}{2}(S^2G_{SS} + 2\rho\sigma SG_{Sv} + \sigma^2G_{vv}) = 0.$$

These PDEs still look quite complicated. In particular, they contain S and S^2 for the derivatives with respect to the spot price, because of the geometric nature of the S process, but not for v which is in CIR form. We transform to log-coordinates in S, defining $f(t, x, v) = F(t, S, v)$ and $g(t, x, v) = G(t, S, v)$, where $x = \ln(S)$, as we have done before for the Black–Scholes PDE, which leads to the following PDEs for f and g:

$$f_t + \left(r + \frac{v}{2}\right)f_x + (\kappa\theta - (\kappa + \lambda\sigma - \rho\sigma)v)f_v + \frac{v}{2}(f_{xx} + 2\rho\sigma f_{xv} + \sigma^2 f_{vv}) = 0,$$

$$g_t + \left(r - \frac{v}{2}\right)g_x + (\kappa\theta - (\kappa + \lambda\sigma)v)g_v + \frac{v}{2}(g_{xx} + 2\rho\sigma g_{xv} + \sigma^2 g_{vv}) = 0,$$

with terminal conditions $f(t, x, v) = g(t, x, v) = \phi(x) = \chi_{x \geq \ln(K)}$. Note that the PDEs for f and g have identical structures. The only differences are in parameter values.

This is beginning to look pretty good! We still have two two-dimensional PDEs but, importantly, the terminal conditions are actually one-dimensional in that they only depend on x, not on v. Moreover, in the x-direction, the PDE has constant coefficients (for fixed v). This is a setting well suited for so-called Fourier methods, i.e., methods that use the *Fourier transform.*

13.4.1 Fourier Transform and Fourier Methods

The Fourier transform of a function $f \in L^1(\mathbb{R})$ is defined as

$$\hat{f}(w) = \int_{-\infty}^{\infty} f(x)e^{ix\omega}\, dx. \tag{13.15}$$

We write $\hat{f} = \mathcal{F}(f)$.[4] One can show that the inverse transform is given by

$$f(x) = \mathcal{F}^{-1}(\hat{f})(x) = \frac{1}{2\pi} \int_{-\infty}^{\infty} \hat{f}(\omega) e^{-ix\omega}\, d\omega. \tag{13.16}$$

The definition can also be defined over $L^2(\mathbb{R})$ (using a continuity argument, as shown in standard textbooks on Fourier transforms), over which it is a bijection, $\mathcal{F}\colon L^2 \leftrightarrow L^2$. A constructive way of thinking about the inversion formula is that the function $f(x)$ can be viewed as being made up by basis functions, similar to an orthogonal eigenvector decomposition. Specifically, think of the function $q_\omega(x) = e^{-i\omega x}$ as a basis function and consider the finite linear combination

$$\sum_{n=1}^{N} k_n q_n(x).$$

The representation (13.16) is basically a version of such a linear combination where the basis functions are defined for all values of $n \in \mathbb{R}$ (rather than just over a finite number of values), now represented by the variable ω, as are the coefficients, k_i, which are now represented by the function $\hat{f}(\omega)$. A thorough introduction to Fourier transforms and Fourier series is given in Katznelson (1976).

Note that $\hat{f}$ is in general a complex-valued function, and that if f is real valued, then $\hat{f}(-\omega) = \overline{\hat{f}(\omega)}$, since $e^{i\omega x} = \cos(\omega x) + i\sin(\omega x)$, so $e^{-i\omega x} = \cos(\omega x) - i\sin(\omega x) = \overline{e^{i\omega x}}$. This also means that the Fourier inversion formula for the Fourier transform of real-valued functions can be written

$$\begin{aligned} f(x) &= \frac{1}{2\pi} \int_{-\infty}^{\infty} \hat{f}(\omega) e^{-ix\omega}\, d\omega \\ &= \frac{1}{2\pi} \int_{0}^{\infty} \hat{f}(\omega) e^{-ix\omega} + \overline{\hat{f}(\omega)} e^{ix\omega}\, d\omega \\ &= \frac{1}{\pi} \int_{0}^{\infty} \Re\mathfrak{e}(\hat{f}(\omega) e^{-ix\omega})\, d\omega. \end{aligned} \tag{13.17}$$

Here, $\Re\mathfrak{e}(z)$ represents the real part of the complex number z, $\Re\mathfrak{e}(a + ib) = a$, where $a, b \in \mathbb{R}$.

One can also show that the q_ω's essentially make up an orthonormal basis of $L^2(\mathbb{R})$. Specifically, the following isometry result holds:

$$\|f\|^2 = \frac{1}{2\pi} \|\hat{f}\|^2,$$

where the L^2 norms $\|g\|^2 = \int |g|^2\, dx$, $\|\hat{f}\|^2 = \int |\hat{f}|^2\, d\omega$ are used. This is the famous Plancherel theorem (a generalization of Parseval's theorem, which provides the same result when $f \in L^1 \cap L^2$). We denote the x-domain the physical domain, and the ω-domain the Fourier domain, or the frequency domain. As a consequence, we can "build" L^2 functions from the q_ω functions with appropriate coefficients, so that $\hat{f} \in L^2$. The Fourier transform is a linear operator, which makes it very helpful for some linear—and especially constant-coefficient—PDEs. Efficient computational methods for calculating option prices using Fourier methods are described in Carr and Madan (1999).

[4] There are several equivalent, alternative definitions, e.g., $\int_{-\infty}^{\infty} f(x) e^{-ix\omega}\, dx$, i.e., replacing $e^{ix\omega}$ with $e^{-ix\omega}$. Here we choose the definition in (13.15), since it coincides with the definition of the characteristic function in probability theory.

13.4.2 Solving the Stochastic Volatility Problem

Inspired by the Fourier methodology and following Heston (1993), for the generic form of the PDE

$$h_t + (r + uv)h_x + (a - bv)h_v + \frac{v}{2}(h_{xx} + 2\rho\sigma h_{xv} + \sigma^2 h_{vv}) = 0, \tag{13.18}$$

let us conjecture a solution of the form

$$h^\omega(t, x, v; T, \omega) = e^{C(T-t;\omega)+D(T-t;\omega)v} e^{i\omega x},$$

and see what the functions C and D need to look like for h^ω to solve the PDE. This is a similar exercise to what we did when identifying the ODEs in the affine term structure models. The $e^{i\omega x}$ term here defines the basis function part, whereas the $e^{C(T-t;\omega)+D(T-t;\omega)v}$ term is the associated coefficient, which we allow to change with time and v. We will need many such basis functions to match the terminal conditions, because no individual h^ω alone matches the conditions in general.

Taking partial derivatives, and separating coefficients that depend on v from those that do not, just like we did in the affine term structure model (proposition 10.1), we get the following ODEs that need to be satisfied:

$$D' + (i\rho\sigma\omega - b)D + \frac{1}{2}D^2 + iu\omega - \frac{\sigma^2}{2}\omega^2 = 0,$$

$$C' + aD + ir\omega = 0.$$

The solution should not depend on v when $T - t = 0$, so $C(0) = 0$, and we can also normalize so that $D(0) = 0$. One verifies that the solution to this system of ODEs is

$$C(\tau;\omega) = ir\omega\tau + \frac{a}{\sigma^2}\Big((b - i\rho\sigma\omega + d)\tau - 2\ln\Big(\frac{1 - ge^{d\tau}}{1 - g}\Big)\Big), \tag{13.19}$$

$$D(\tau;\omega) = \frac{b - i\rho\sigma\omega + d}{\sigma^2}\Big(\frac{1 - e^{d}\tau}{1 - ge^{d}\tau}\Big), \tag{13.20}$$

where

$$g = \frac{b - i\rho\sigma\omega + d}{b - i\rho\sigma\omega - d}$$

and

$$d = \sqrt{(i\rho\sigma\omega - b)^2 - \sigma^2(2iu\omega - \omega^2)}.$$

This looks quite complicated, but the functions are straightforward to evaluate numerically, just like for the affine term structure models. Note that the expression for d is the square root of a complex number, which has two possible values (for real numbers the square root is always defined as the positive root). One needs to ensure that one chooses the right root; see Albrecher et al. (2007). Also, note that as $\omega \to 0$, $d \to b$, so that $g \to \infty$, and also $C \to 0$ and $D \to 0$ for all τ. We define

$$q^\omega = e^{C(T-t;\omega)+D(T-t;\omega)v}, \tag{13.21}$$

so that $h^\omega = q^\omega e^{ix\omega}$. It follows that $h^0 = 1$ for all t and v.

We now have a set of solutions to the PDE (13.18), but none of them satisfy the terminal condition $h(T, x, v) = \chi_{x \geq y}$, for $y = \ln(K)$. This is where we impose the "building block argument":

We find a linear combination of solutions, using the building blocks $\ell(\omega)h^{\omega}$, to define the total function $H=\int \ell(\omega)h^{\omega}\,d\omega$ that does satisfy the terminal condition. Then H is the solution we are looking for, since it also satisfies the PDE (because all building blocks do, and linear combinations of solutions are also solutions by the superposition principle).

How should we choose $\ell(\omega)$? Well, recall that $h^{\omega}=q^{\omega}e^{i\omega x}$, where $q^{\omega}(T,v)=1$ for all ω and v. So the terminal condition becomes

$$\int_{-\infty}^{\infty} \ell(\omega)e^{i\omega x}\,d\omega=\chi_{x\geq y},$$

which via the Fourier inversion formula implies that

$$\ell(\omega)=\mathcal{F}^{-1}(\chi_{x\geq y})(\omega)=\frac{1}{2\pi}\int_{-\infty}^{\infty}\chi_{x\geq y}e^{-i\omega x}\,dx$$

(note that the roles of x and ω have been switched in this argument compared with how the Fourier transform was defined in the previous section). It is a standard result, which we can look up in a table of Fourier transforms (see Gradshteyn and Ryzhik 2000, page 1110), that the solution is

$$\ell(\omega)=\frac{1}{2}e^{-i\omega y}\Big(\delta_0(\omega)+\frac{1}{i\pi\omega}\Big),$$

where δ_0 is the Dirac distribution centered at 0. There are some subtleties with this expression in general, but they cause no troubles in this setting.[5]

The solution is now defined as

$$\begin{aligned}
H(t,x,v)&=\int_{-\infty}^{\infty}\frac{1}{2}e^{-i\omega y}\Big(\delta_0(y)+\frac{1}{i\pi\omega}\Big)q^{\omega}(T-t,v)e^{i\omega x}\,d\omega\\
&=\frac{1}{2}+\frac{1}{2\pi}\int_{-\infty}^{\infty}e^{i\omega(x-y)}\frac{q^{\omega}(T-t,v)}{i\omega}\,d\omega\\
&=\frac{1}{2}+\frac{1}{\pi}\int_{0}^{\infty}\mathfrak{Re}\Big(e^{i\omega(x-y)}\frac{q^{\omega}(T-t,v)}{i\omega}\Big)\,d\omega. \qquad (13.22)
\end{aligned}$$

Expression (13.22) needs to be evaluated numerically. It describes a one-dimensional integral that can be efficiently calculated using standard numerical quadrature formulas. We need to calculate two such integrals numerically, once for f with parameters

$$u=\frac{1}{2}, \qquad (13.23)$$

$$b=\kappa+\lambda\sigma-\rho\sigma, \qquad (13.24)$$

and once for g with parameters

$$u=-\frac{1}{2}, \qquad (13.25)$$

$$b=\kappa+\lambda\sigma. \qquad (13.26)$$

In both cases, $a=\kappa\theta$.

[5]The Dirac distribution, which we have seen before, is not technically a function, but is still straightforward to apply in our context. The second term is technically defined as a so-called principal value and can, given the setting here, also be directly applied.

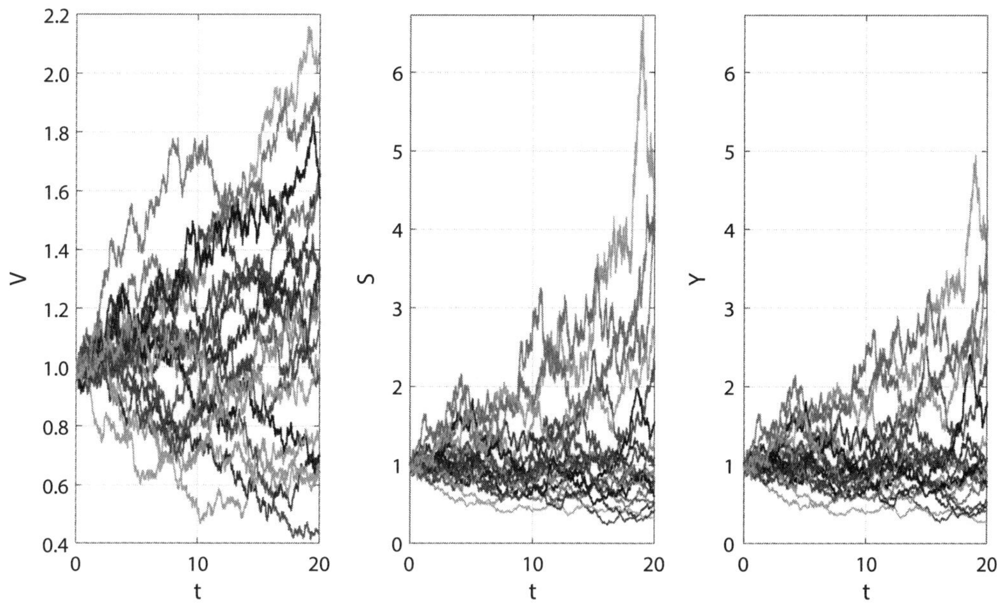

Figure 13.8: Stochastic volatility model, 20 sample paths. Leftmost panel shows realized volatility, v_t. Middle panel shows realized stock price, S_t. Rightmost panel shows realized stock price under GBM dynamics.

To summarize, the option price is given by (13.14). Here, $F(t,S,v) = f(t,\ln(S),v)$, where $f(t,x,v)$ is calculated by the integral (13.22), where q^{ω} is defined by (13.19, 13.20, 13.21), and with parameters given by (13.23, 13.24). Similarly, $G(t,S,v) = g(t,\ln(S),v)$, where g is defined the same way, from (13.19, 13.20, 13.21), but with parameters given by (13.25, 13.26).

An example of dynamics in the stochastic volatility model is shown in figure 13.8, with parameters $\kappa = 0.1, \theta = 1, \hat{\mu} = 0.15, \rho = 0.5$. The leftmost panel in the figure shows 20 simulations of v_t over a 20-year period, whereas the middle panel show the realization of S_t for the simulations. The rightmost panel shows the realization of a hypothetical stock with GBM dynamics Y_t, where $Y_0 = S_0$, and

$$\frac{dY_t}{Y_t} = \hat{\mu}\, dt + \sigma_Y\, dV_t, \quad \sigma_Y = \sqrt{\theta}.$$

Thus, the hypothetical stock has constant variance equal to the long-term mean variance of stochastic variance: $\sigma_Y^2 = E[v_\infty]$. We see that the extreme paths of S_t, because they are associated with higher volatility, are even more extreme in the stochastic volatility model than in the classical Black–Scholes model with GBM dynamics. So, just like in the jump-diffusion model, the tails are heavier in this model than in the classical Black–Scholes model, which will affect option prices. In addition, the risk premium $\lambda\sigma$ will affect derivative prices, allowing for further differences compared with the Black–Scholes model, an effect that was not present in the jump-diffusion model, which assumed idiosyncratic (nonpriced) jump risk.

13.5 Variance Gamma Model

The *variance gamma model* was introduced in Madan, Carr, and Chang (1998) as an extension of the classical Black–Scholes model that allows for better control of the (risk-neutral) skewness and kurtosis of the underlying return distribution. Recall that changes in log-prices in the classical

Black–Scholes model are normally distributed. The first and second moments completely characterize a normally distributed random variable, so there is no additional role for higher moments in that model. Indeed, if $\tilde{x} \sim N(\mu, \sigma^2)$, then skewness μ_3, and kurtosis μ_4, are

$$\mu_3 = E\left[\left(\frac{\tilde{x}-\mu}{\sigma}\right)^3\right] = 0,$$

$$\mu_4 = E\left[\left(\frac{\tilde{x}-\mu}{\sigma}\right)^4\right] = 3,$$

so there is no flexibility in their values. This is another consequence of the implied volatility curve being flat in the Black–Scholes model.

The variance gamma model provides a clever way of generalizing the Black–Scholes model. In the variance gamma model, time increases randomly, which leads to different price functions from the classical Black–Scholes setting. We have already seen time transformations in chapter 10, and in this chapter when analyzing the CEV model, but those transformations were deterministic. Here, time changes are random. This also implies that the market is generically incomplete. The pricing formulas will therefore not be based on no-arbitrage arguments, but rather on a specification of the risk-neutral measure, quite similarly to the approach we took in the term structure analysis.

We begin with some preliminaries on gamma distributions and gamma processes. A *gamma-distributed* random variable, $\tilde{x} \sim \Gamma(\alpha, \lambda)$, has probability density function defined by

$$\phi(x) = \frac{\lambda^\alpha}{\Gamma(\gamma)} e^{-\lambda x} x^{\alpha-1}, \quad x > 0,$$

where $\Gamma(\gamma)$ is the gamma function defined by $\Gamma(\gamma) = \int_0^\infty t^{\alpha-1} e^{-t}\, dt, \alpha > 0$. It follows that $E[\tilde{x}] = \frac{\alpha}{\lambda}$, and $\mathrm{Var}(\tilde{x}) = \frac{\alpha}{\lambda^2}$.

The *gamma process* $\{X_t\}_t \in \mathcal{G}(\alpha, \lambda)$ is a Lévy process, such that $X_t - X_s \sim \Gamma(\alpha t, \lambda)$ distributed, $t > s$. It follows that $E_s[X_t - X_s] = \frac{\alpha(t-s)}{\lambda}$, $\mathrm{Var}(X_t - X_s) = \frac{\alpha(t-s)}{\lambda^2}$, $t > s$. Note that the realized path of a gamma process is monotone; it never decreases. One can show that the gamma process always moves by jumps. Indeed, it has an infinite number of (mostly very small) jumps over any finite time period. From this perspective, it behaves quite differently from a Brownian motion. It is more like a Poisson process, but with many more jumps that are mostly very small. Also note that the lower λ is, the higher is the expectation and variance of the gamma process, at any given time.

One way of characterizing the gamma process, which provides some further intuition, is that it can be viewed as a "sum" of Poisson processes of different sizes, where the arrival rate of jumps of size Y occurs with intensity $\frac{\alpha}{Y} e^{-\lambda Y}$. Clearly, the intensity of small jumps is much higher than the intensity of large jumps, but of course they are smaller so each of them does not contribute as much to X_t.

Defining $Q(Y)$ as the expected fraction of the total change in X_t made up by jumps of size Y or smaller, we get

$$Q(Y) = \frac{\int_0^Y \frac{\alpha t}{x} e^{-\lambda x}\, dx}{\int_0^\infty \frac{\alpha t}{x} e^{-\lambda x}\, dx} = 1 - e^{-\lambda Y}. \tag{13.27}$$

The function $Q(Y)$ is convex, so the total expected contribution to X_t, over any interval of jump sizes, is higher the smaller the jump size.

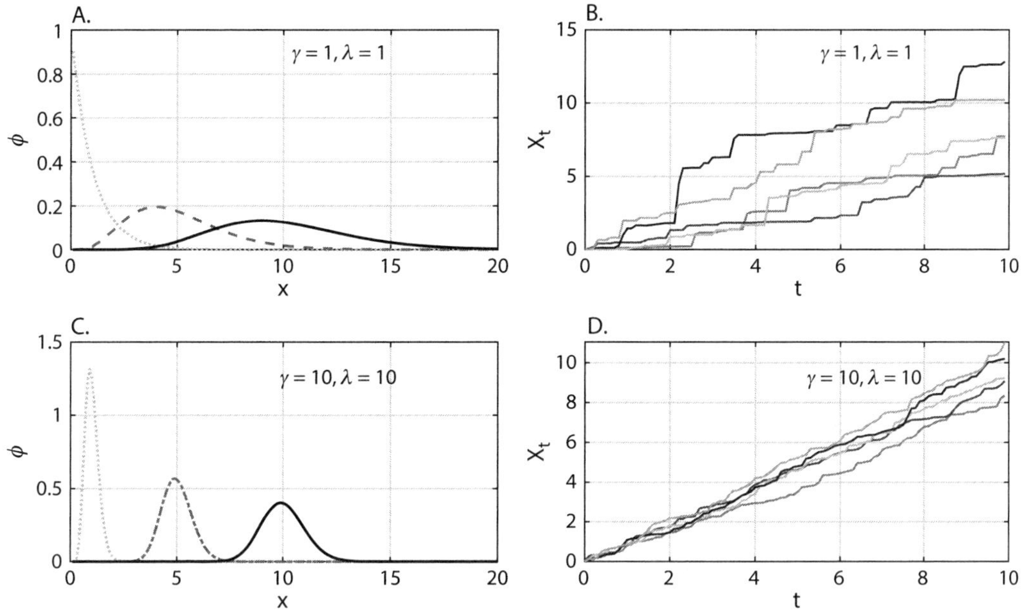

Figure 13.9: Examples of gamma processes. Top panels: High volatility process ($\gamma = \lambda = 1$). Bottom panels: Low volatility process ($\gamma = \lambda = 10$). Left panels: Probability density functions at $t = 1$ (dotted), $t = 5$ (dashed), and $t = 10$ (solid). Right panels: Five realized sample paths, $0 \le t \le 10$.

In figure 13.9, we see the probability distributions and realized sample paths of high-volatility (upper panels) and low-volatility (lower panels) gamma processes. The sample paths of the low-volatility processes seem to be fairly close to straight lines, although they technically jump an infinite number of times on any interval. The sample paths of the high volatility processes (upper panels) have more pronounced jumps.

The *variance gamma process* (VG process), $\{Z_t\}_t \in \mathcal{VG}(\sigma, \nu, \theta)$, is defined as follows:

$$Z_t = \theta g_t + \sigma W_{g_t},$$

where

$$g_t \in \mathcal{G}\left(\frac{1}{\nu}, \frac{1}{\nu}\right),$$

and W_t is a standard Wiener process that is independent of $\{g_t\}_t$.

So the variance gamma process behaves like a Brownian motion that is evaluated at stochastic times, g_t. Note that $E[g_t] = t$, and $\mathrm{Var}(g_t) = \nu$ with this definition. So for ν close to zero, the dynamics of Z_t will in many ways be similar to that of a Brownian motion.[6] When ν is large, however, the variance gamma function will look much "wilder" than the Brownian motion, with large jumps that lead to heavier tails (and thereby higher kurtosis) than the Brownian motion, and potentially also nonzero skewness.

An example of a VG process is given in figure 13.10. We see that Z_t, shown in the lower-left panel C, is more "jumpy" than the Brownian motion, shown in the lower-right panel D.

[6]Not in every way though, since even for small but positive ν, the gamma process has an infinite number of jumps on any interval, which carries over to the gamma variance process. So, under sufficient magnification, the variance gamma process will look very "jumpy," whereas the sample path of the Brownian motion is continuous but wiggly.

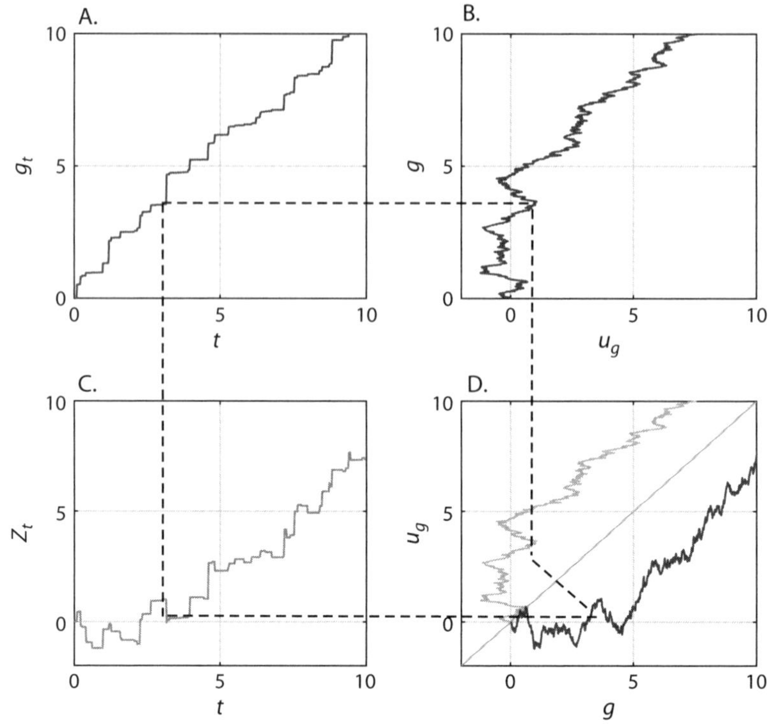

Figure 13.10: Examples of sample paths of gamma variance processes, $Z_t \in \mathcal{VG}(\sigma = 1, \nu = 0.5, \theta = 0.7)$. Panel A shows the realization of the time transformation, g_t. Panel C shows the realization of the VG process, Z_t. Panels B and D show the realization of the Brownian motion $u_g = \theta g + \sigma W_g$ on different axes, as a function of g. The graph of Z_t can be interpreted through the lens of the dashed "loop." Moving from C to A, we identify the value of g_t associated with Z_t. Moving from A to B, we identify the value of u associated with g_t. Moving from B to D, the axes are flipped, which corresponds to reflecting the graph in the 45-degree line representing the unit mapping $u \equiv g$. Finally, the horizontal line between C and D represents the identity $Z_t = u_{g_t}$.

The following property of the VG process is useful for our subsequent analysis:

Proposition 13.1. *For the process $Z_t \in \mathcal{VG}(\sigma, \nu, \theta)$, we have*

$$E_0[E^{Z_t}] = e^{-\omega t},$$

where

$$\omega \stackrel{def}{=} \frac{1}{\nu} \ln\left(1 - \theta\nu - \frac{\sigma^2}{2}\nu\right).$$

Proof. See Madan, Carr, and Chang (1998). □

Note that a Taylor expansion of $\ln(1+x)$ around $x = 0$ yields $\ln(1+x) = x + O(x^2)$, which immediately implies

$$\lim_{\nu \to 0} \omega(\nu) = -\left(\theta + \frac{\sigma^2}{2}\right).$$

The risk-neutral dynamics of the stock's price is now assumed to be of the form

$$S_t = S_0 e^{rt + Z_t + \omega t},$$

where $Z_t \in \mathcal{VG}(\sigma, \nu, \theta)$. Here, r is the short risk-free rate which, as in the classical Black–Scholes model, is assumed to be constant. The dynamics are defined in the risk-neutral measure, in the usual sense that the price of a contingent claim with payoff function $\Phi(S_T)$ is

$$P_0 = e^{-rt} E_0^{\mathbb{Q}}[\Phi(S_T)],$$

where $Z_t \in \mathcal{VG}(\sigma, \nu, \theta)$ under the $\mathbb{Q}$-expectation operator.

We verify that the T-bond and stock are correctly priced under this assumption:

$$P^B = e^{-rT} E_0^{\mathbb{Q}}[e^{rT}] = 1,$$
$$P^S = e^{-rt} E_0^{\mathbb{Q}}[S_0 e^{rt+Z_t+\omega t}] = S_0 e^{-rt+rt-\omega t+\omega t} = S_0.$$

Note that when $\nu \to 0$, $Z_t \to \theta t + \sigma W_t$ (since $g_t \to t$), and therefore in the limit, the stock price dynamics becomes

$$S_t = S_0 e^{(r-\frac{\sigma^2}{2})t+\sigma W_t}.$$

This is the same as in the classical Black–Scholes setting where the risk-neutral drift of the log-stock price is $r - \frac{\sigma^2}{2}$. The following moment conditions for Z_t are shown in Madan, Carr, and Chang (1998):

$$E[Z_t] = \theta t,$$
$$\mathrm{Var}(Z_t) = (\theta^2 \nu + \sigma^2)t,$$
$$E[(Z_t - E[Z_t])^3] = (2\theta^3 \nu^2 + 3\sigma^2 \theta \nu)t,$$
$$E[(Z_t - E[Z_t])^4] = (3\sigma^4 \nu + 12\sigma^2\theta^2\nu^2 + 6\theta^4\nu^3)t + (3\sigma^4 + 6\sigma^2\theta^2\nu + 3\theta^4\nu^2)t^2.$$

Therefore, θ and ν can be used to affect the skewness and kurtosis of the risk-neutral distribution in the VG model. The authors also derive a closed-form solution for the plain vanilla call option, using the risk-neutral pricing formula

$$C = e^{-rt} E^{\mathbb{Q}}[\max(S_T - K, 0)].$$

13.6 Volatility Index, VIX

We have discussed the importance of volatility. Risk-averse investors dislike volatility, and especially market volatility, since it is in aggregate not hedgeable (someone needs to take it on). Individuals who are more risk averse than average may want to buy insurance against future market volatility, however. Similarly, individuals who are less risk averse may be willing to provide insurance against future market volatility.

In a complete market, the primitive assets can be used to generate claims on future realized volatility, but this may require designing complex dynamics trading strategies. To mitigate such needs, the *volatility index*, the VIX, was introduced. It provides a cleverly constructed index that should be closely related to investors' expectations of market volatility in the near future (over the next 30 days). In figure 13.11, the realization of VIX between 2006 and 2024 is shown. We see that the VIX spiked around 2009, during the financial crises, and in 2020, during the outbreak of COVID-19. These were both periods of extreme uncertainty.

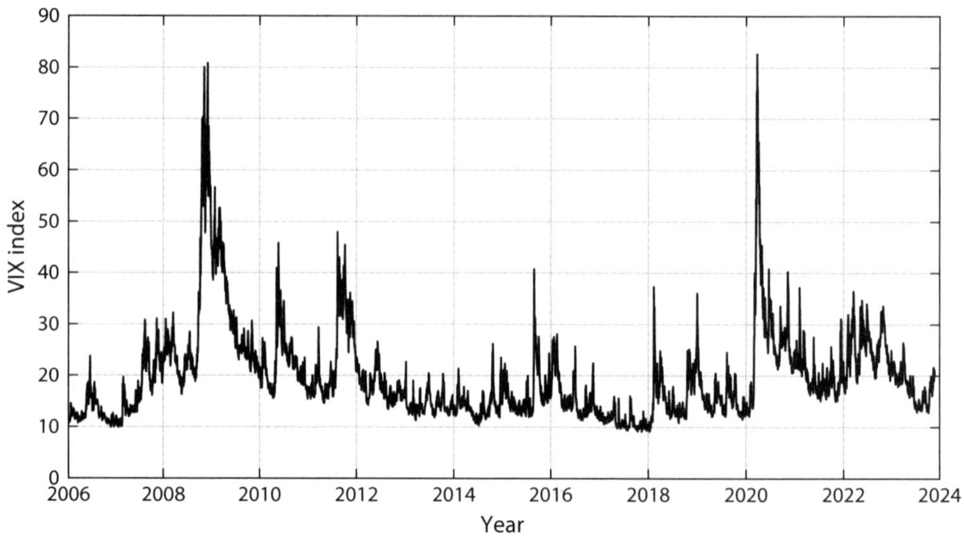

Figure 13.11: Realization of VIX between 2006 and 2024. Source: Federal Reserve Bank of St. Louis.

The definition of VIX relies on call and put option prices on the future value of the S&P 500 index, with maturity 30 days ahead. The VIX is defined as

$$\text{VIX} = 100 \times s, \tag{13.28}$$

where

$$s^2 = \frac{1}{T}\sum_i \frac{K_{i+1} - K_i}{K_i^2} e^{rT} Y(K_i) - \frac{1}{T}\left(\frac{H_0}{K_0} - 1\right)^2. \tag{13.29}$$

Here, the K_i's represent strike prices of traded options (puts and calls) on the S&P 500 index, H_0 is the (current) futures price on the S&P 500, which is observable, and K_0 is chosen as the strike price closest to H_0. The function Y represents the call option price when $K_i > K_0$, and the put option price when $K_i < K_0$, as explained below.

At first sight, it is not easy to see how this definition has any relation to expected market volatility between times 0 and T. To see that there is indeed such a relation, let us begin with the futures pricing formula:

$$H_0 = H_{0,T} = E_0^{\mathbb{Q}}[H_{T,T}] = E_0^{\mathbb{Q}}[S_T],$$

i.e., the (current) futures price, H_0, is the risk-neutral expectation of the price of the underlying (the S&P index in this case) at T. In the diffusion setting, the martingale representation theorem then implies that

$$dH_t = \sigma_t H_t \, dW_t^{\mathbb{Q}},$$

for some volatility process, σ_t. Our definition of the market's expected variance between 0 and T is then

$$s^2 \stackrel{\text{def}}{=} \frac{1}{T} E_0^{\mathbb{Q}}\left[\int_0^T \sigma_t^2 \, dt\right]. \tag{13.30}$$

The variable s^2 thus defines the $\mathbb{Q}$-expectation of the per-period variance of the returns on the futures index.

Note that σ_t is not the same volatility as that of the underlying asset. Indeed, even if discount rates are constant, $r_t \equiv r$, the two volatilities will differ. In that case we have

$$\frac{dS_t}{S_t} = r\,dt + \hat{\sigma}_t\,dW_t^Q,$$

where S_t is the price of the underlying asset (the index in this case), which leads to

$$S_t = e^{-r(T-t)} E_t^{\mathbb{Q}}[S_T] = e^{-r(T-t)} H_t.$$

So in this case we get

$$dS_t = rS_t\,dt + \hat{\sigma}_t S_t\,dW_t^Q = d(e^{-r(T-t)} H_t) = rS_t\,dt + dH_t,$$

which together with $dH_t = \sigma_t H_t\,dW_t^Q$ leads to

$$\sigma_t = \hat{\sigma}_t e^{r(T-t)}.$$

Thus, σ_t will be higher than $\hat{\sigma}_t$, and put more weight on volatility near the terminal date, T.

When the short risk-free rate, r_t, is stochastic, the covariance between interest rate changes and dW^Q creates another wedge between the volatility of the underlying asset and that of the futures contract. Finally, note that the definition of s^2 relies on the risk-neutral probability measure when calculating the expectation, which we know in general deviates from the physical measure.

We show how (13.29) and (13.30) are related. To this end, let us begin with defining $Z_t = Z(H_t) = \ln(H_t)$, $t \le T$. Itô's lemma gives us

$$dZ_t = \frac{dH_t}{H_t} - \left(\frac{dH_t}{H_t}\right)^2 = \frac{dH_t}{H_t} - \sigma_t^2\,dt,$$

and thus

$$Z_T - Z_0 = \ln\left(\frac{H_T}{H_0}\right) = \int_0^T dZ_t = \int_0^T \frac{dH_t}{H_t} - \int_0^T \sigma_t^2\,dt.$$

Taking the expectation on both sides and using the $\mathbb{Q}$-martingale property of $\frac{dH_t}{H_t}$, $E_0^{\mathbb{Q}}[\frac{dH_t}{H_t}] = 0$, then yields

$$E_0^{\mathbb{Q}}[\ln(H_T)] - \ln(H_0) = -Ts^2. \tag{13.31}$$

Our next goal is to express the term on the left-hand side of (13.31), $E_0^{\mathbb{Q}}[\ln(H_T)]$, in terms of current option prices. Intuitively, this should be possible since option prices contain information about $\mathbb{Q}$ probabilities via the fundamental theorem of asset pricing. For this derivation, we start with the following lemma from (classical) calculus:

Lemma 13.1. *Consider a twice continuously differentiable function, $f\colon \mathbb{R}_{++} \to \mathbb{R}$. For arbitrary $x, y \in \mathbb{R}_{++}$,*

$$f(y) = f(x) + f'(x)(y-x) + \int_0^x f''(v)(v-y)_+\,dv + \int_x^\infty f''(v)(y-v)_+\,dv.$$

Proof. Consider the case when $y > x$. In this case, $v - y < 0$ for all $v \le x$, so the third term on the right-hand side is irrelevant (i.e., it is 0) because of the $(\cdot)_+$ operator. Moreover, for similar reasons, the rightmost term is only relevant for $v \le y$. The expression therefore reduces to

$$f(y) = f(x) + f'(x)(y-x) + \int_x^y f''(v)(y-v)\,dv$$

in this case. The integration by parts rule for the rightmost term in this expression then yields

$$\int_x^y f''(v)(y-v)\,dv = [f'(v)(y-v)]_x^y - \int_x^y f'(v)(-1)\,dv = -f'(x)(y-x) + f(y) - f(x),$$

leading to the desired result when $y > x$. A similar argument leads to the result when $y < x$. □

We apply the lemma to the logarithmic function, $f(x) = \ln(x)$, to get

$$\ln(H_T) = \ln(H_0) + \frac{H_T - H_0}{H_0} - \int_0^{H_0} \frac{(K - H_T)_+}{K^2}\,dK - \int_{H_0}^{\infty} \frac{(H_T - K)_+}{K^2}\,dK.$$

Note that this is a relation that follows from the lemma, and has nothing to do with the dynamics of H_t. Rather, it is a relation that holds for the logarithmic function, for arbitrary integration intervals.

Plugging this formula into the expectation on the left-hand side of (13.31), we get

$$\begin{aligned} &E_0^{\mathbb{Q}}[\ln(H_T)] - \ln(H_0) \\ &\quad = E_0^{\mathbb{Q}}\left[\ln(H_0) + \frac{H_T - H_0}{H_0} - \int_0^{H_0} \frac{(K - H_T)_+}{K^2}\,dK - \int_{H_0}^{\infty} \frac{(H_T - K)_+}{K^2}\,dK\right] - \ln(H_0) \\ &\quad = -E_0^{\mathbb{Q}}\left[\int_0^{H_0} \frac{(K - H_T)_+}{K^2}\,dK\right] - E_0^{\mathbb{Q}}\left[\int_{H_0}^{\infty} \frac{(H_T - K)_+}{K^2}\,dK\right]. \end{aligned}$$

Here we used the fact that $E_0^{\mathbb{Q}}[H_T] = H_0$.

Finally, note that

$$P(K) = e^{-rT} E_0^{\mathbb{Q}}[(K - H_T)_+], \quad C(K) = e^{-rT} E_0^{\mathbb{Q}}[(H_T - K)_+],$$

where P and C represent put and call option prices on the underlying asset. Here, r is inferred from the price of a bond with maturity T, $B = e^{-rT}$. Putting it all together gives us

$$s^2 = -\frac{1}{T}(E_0^{\mathbb{Q}}[\ln(H_T)] - \ln(H_0)) = \frac{1}{T} e^{rT} \left(\int_0^{H_0} \frac{P(K)}{K^2}\,dK + \int_{H_0}^{\infty} \frac{C(K)}{K^2}\,dK \right). \tag{13.32}$$

Equation (13.29) is the discrete approximation of the integral in (13.32), using numerical quadrature formulas to approximate the integrals, and recalling that the function Y represents put option prices for $K_i < K_0$, and call option prices for $K_i > K_0$. The rightmost term in (13.29) is a correction term, needed because the available option strike K_0 is used instead of the actual futures price H_0 (when the two are the same, the term evaluates to 0).

CHAPTER 14 Recovery Theorem

A key theme throughout this text is that one needs to distinguish between objective and risk-neutral probability distributions. State prices alone are not sufficient for inferring the probabilities for states to occur. Indeed, the state-price equation,

$$\psi_n = \frac{1}{R} E^{\mathbb{Q}}[\chi_{\omega_n}] = M_n p_n, \tag{14.1}$$

shows that the state price is a product of the SDF, M_n, and the objective probability, p_n (technically, p_n is the market's beliefs about the probability for state n to occur). The SDF, in turn, is in equilibrium related to investor risk aversion, as discussed earlier. Recovering M_n and p_n from their product, ψ_n, therefore seems impossible.

On a related note, in the continuous-time Black–Scholes model, the call option formula does not require knowledge of the expected return on the stock, $\hat{\mu}$. This is great, since that parameter is difficult to estimate, but it also means that call option prices, as well as the associated risk-neutral probabilities, are uninformative about $\hat{\mu}$. Since $\hat{\mu}$ depends on the objective return distribution, it seems impossible to recover the objective probability distribution from the risk-neutral distribution.

This limitation has been an accepted fact within asset pricing, so it was quite surprising when Ross (2015) turned it upside down by introducing a framework in which knowledge about state prices allowed for the *recovery* of the SDF, M, and market beliefs about objective probabilities, p. Being able to do such recovery would of course be very helpful for both policymakers and investors.

Markets are in general viewed as being good at incorporating information. So the market beliefs would be valuable to know for a policymaker, e.g., in understanding the risk for a forthcoming recession, oil price shock, etc., as would understanding the degree of risk aversion of the market. For an investor, knowing the market's views about the probability for different events to occur would obviously be very helpful when choosing the investment portfolio.

In the one-period binomial tree model, knowledge about the risk-neutral probabilities will not allow recovery. Let us check why. Consider the example shown in figure 14.1, where the returns on investing in two assets are shown in a future up-state (above) and down-state (below). This is a complete market, with two assets and two states, so we can calculate the risk-free rate, state prices,

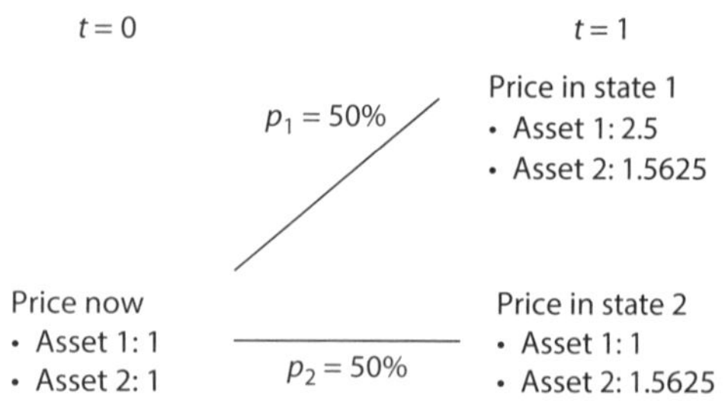

Figure 14.1: Parameters in a binomial tree model.

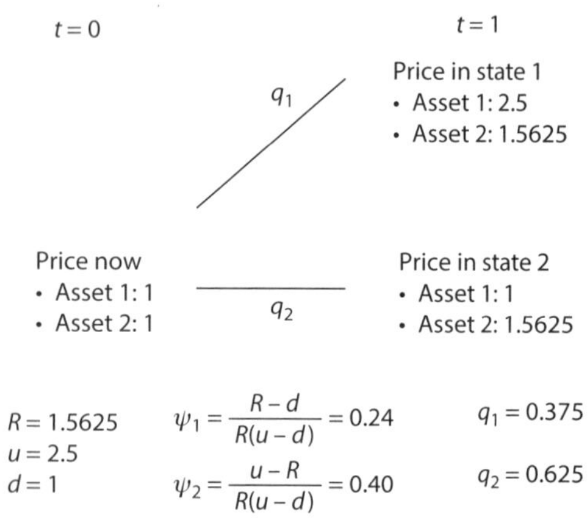

Figure 14.2: Binomial tree model: state prices when starting in the down-state, so that $m_2 = m_0$.

and risk-neutral probabilities. The results are shown in figure 14.2. The values of p_1 and p_2 are not used in the calculations, so we would be very surprised if we could recover them from state prices alone.

Let us put the problem into an equilibrium framework and see if that helps. Consider the representative agent Arrow–Debreu model from section 5.4, in which the representative agent's utility function is u, aggregate consumption at time 0 is C_0, and at $t = 1$ is C_1, C_2 in states 1 and 2, respectively. The agent's utility is then $U = u(C_0) + \delta E^{\mathbb{P}}[u(C_1)]$, which via the Euler equations leads to equilibrium state prices

$$\psi_1 = \delta \frac{u'(C_1)}{u'(C_0)} p_1,$$

$$\psi_2 = \delta \frac{u'(C_2)}{u'(C_0)} p_2,$$

or, equivalently,

$$\psi_1 = \delta \frac{m_1}{m_0} p_1, \tag{14.2}$$

$$\psi_2 = \delta \frac{m_2}{m_0} p_2, \tag{14.3}$$

where $m_i = u'(C_i)$.

If we know the utility function and aggregate consumption in the different states, then we know the SDF, as well as ψ_1, ψ_2, so we can recover p_1 and p_2 via this equilibrium argument. But we do not want to assume knowledge of the SDF.

Remember that expected utility preferences are invariant to linear scaling, so without loss of generality we may assume that $m_0 = 1$. Equivalently, we only need to know the ratios $\frac{m_1}{m_0}$ and $\frac{m_2}{m_0}$, in addition to δ, for a full characterization of the SDF. So we would like to infer $\frac{m_1}{m_0}, \frac{m_2}{m_0}, p_1, p_2$, as well as δ from market prices alone. But this is obviously impossible, since we have five unknowns, and together with the total probability constraint

$$p_1 + p_2 = 1,$$

only three equations. So the equilibrium argument does not help us much so far.

If we assume that the aggregate consumption in the down-state is the same as at $t = 0$, then it must be that $m_2 = m_0$, so that $\frac{m_2}{m_0} = 1$. This reduces the number of unknowns from five to four, but we still only have three equations, and in general cannot expect to find a unique solution. Indeed, the equilibrium relations (14.2, 14.3), without further knowledge about δ and u, are really no more helpful than the likelihood ratio relations

$$\psi_1 = \frac{1}{R} L_1 p_1, \tag{14.4}$$

$$\psi_2 = \frac{1}{R} L_2 p_2, \tag{14.5}$$

which we know hold based on pure no-arbitrage arguments; see equation (7.10) in an earlier chapter. It is clear that further assumptions are needed for recovery to be feasible.

14.1 The Ross Recovery Model

Ross (2015) assumes a representative investor with increasing utility function, u, and personal discount rate, δ. This leads to the equilibrium SDF

$$M = \delta \frac{u'(C_1)}{u'(C_0)};$$

see section 5.4.3.

The stochastic environment is governed by an N-state Markov process with time-invariant transition matrix Φ, $N < \infty$. Specifically, the process $s_t \in \{1, 2, \ldots, N\}$ describes the evolution of states, and $\mathbb{P}(s_{t+1} = j | s_t = i) = \Phi_{ij}$. For simplicity, we assume that $\Phi_{ij} > 0$ for all i and j, i.e., that it is possible to move from any state to any state with strictly positive probability, in the next period. The results hold more generally if the stochastic matrix is *irreducible*, meaning that it is possible to get from any state to any other state with strictly positive probability, even if it takes more than one time period, i.e., for all i, j, there is a $t > 0$, such that $(\Phi^t)_{ij} > 0$.

The consumption of the representative agent at any time depends on the state, s_t, $C_t = C(s_t)$. We define the marginal utilities $m_j = u'(C(j))$, and the vector $\mathbf{m} = (m_1, \ldots, m_N)'$. The one-period equilibrium state prices ψ_{ij}, defined as the price of obtaining a dollar in state j in the next period, given that the current state is i, are then

$$\psi_{ij} = M_{ij} \Phi_{ij}, \tag{14.6}$$

where

$$M_{ij} = \delta \frac{m_j}{m_i}. \tag{14.7}$$

Ross (2015) denotes an SDF that satisfies (14.7), a *transition-independent* pricing kernel. Let us define the $N \times N$ matrix $\Psi = [\psi_{ij}]_{ij}$ that contains all the different state prices across all current (i) and next-period (j) states.

If the market is complete, then for each current state i, the state-price vectors,

$$\psi_{i1}, \psi_{i2}, \ldots, \psi_{iN},$$

are observable, and if the economy is observed for sufficiently long, all the state prices will then eventually be observed (the transition matrix is irreducible), so we may assume knowledge of Ψ. This is where we depart from the binomial tree example, where we only observed one set of state prices. We will subsequently provide an alternative method through which the whole Ψ-matrix is recovered at one point in time.

Let us summarize the information we are allowed to use to try to recover actual probabilities, Φ, the personal discount rate, δ, and marginal utilities, $\mathbf{m}$:

1. The state-price matrix, Ψ, is known.
2. Equilibrium prices are such that (14.6, 14.7) hold for some stochastic matrix Φ representing the representative agent's belief, personal discount factor $\delta > 0$, and vector of marginal utilities $\mathbf{m} \gg \mathbf{0}$.

Importantly, we are *not* allowed to make assumptions about Φ, δ, and $\mathbf{m}$ further than those above. The problem of recovering Φ, δ, and $\mathbf{m}$ from Ψ is the *Ross recovery problem*.

Consider an example with two states, and see how far we get. Assume the following state-price matrix:

$$\Psi = \begin{bmatrix} \psi_{11} & \psi_{12} \\ \psi_{21} & \psi_{22} \end{bmatrix}.$$

We actually have quite a bit of information:

$$\Psi_{ij} = \delta \frac{m_j}{m_i} \Phi_{ij}, \quad i, j = 1, 2,$$

$$\Phi_{11} + \Phi_{12} = 1,$$

$$\Phi_{21} + \Phi_{22} = 1.$$

This provides us with 6 equations for 7 unknowns (four probabilities, two ms, and δ). However, recall that the utility specification is invariant to positive scaling $u \mapsto cu$, $c > 0$, so the vectors $\mathbf{m}$ and $c \times \mathbf{m}$ actually represent the same utility function. We are therefore allowed to normalize, for example, imposing the condition $m_1 = 1$, which provides another equation. From a pure equation-counting perspective, we therefore have the same number of equations as unknowns.

Note, though, that the equation for Ψ is nonlinear, so it is unclear how far the equation-counting intuition will take us. We can actually rewrite the system of equations in a much more convenient form. Define the matrix

$$\Lambda_{\mathbf{m}} = \text{diag}(\mathbf{m}).$$

One can then verify that the four probability equations can be conveniently written as the matrix equation

$$\Psi = \delta \Lambda_{\mathbf{m}}^{-1} \Phi \Lambda_{\mathbf{m}},$$

and equivalently,

$$\Phi = \delta^{-1} \Lambda_{\mathbf{m}} \Psi \Lambda_{\mathbf{m}}^{-1}. \tag{14.8}$$

We can also use the fact that the total probability equations can be written

$$\Phi \mathbf{1} = \mathbf{1}.$$

In other words, $\mathbf{1}$ is an eigenvector of Φ. But via (14.8), it then follows that

$$\mathbf{1} = \Phi \mathbf{1} = \delta^{-1} \Lambda_{\mathbf{m}} \Psi \Lambda_{\mathbf{m}}^{-1} \mathbf{1},$$

and therefore that

$$\delta^{-1}(\Lambda_{\mathbf{m}}^{-1} \mathbf{1}) = \Psi(\Lambda_{\mathbf{m}}^{-1} \mathbf{1}). \tag{14.9}$$

Defining the vector $\mathbf{z} = \Lambda_{\mathbf{m}}^{-1} \mathbf{1}$, with elements $\mathbf{z}_i = \frac{1}{m_i}$, (14.9) can now be written as an eigenvector problem:

$$\delta \mathbf{z} = \Psi \mathbf{z}. \tag{14.10}$$

So $\mathbf{z}$ is an eigenvector of the state-price matrix Ψ, and δ a corresponding eigenvalue! Of course, if we know $\mathbf{z}$ and δ, we can calculate $\mathbf{m}$ and Φ (from 14.8). Now, this argument has already taken us very far. We know from the fundamental theorem of algebra that there are at most N solutions to the general eigenvector problem (remember that there can be a multiplicity of some eigenvalues in general, which may lead to fewer than N eigenvectors).

Let us check what it does for us in the two-state example we looked at earlier in this section. In the Ross model, we also observe the state prices when starting in the up-state. Let us assume that the returns when starting in the up-state are as in figure 14.3, leading to the state prices shown in the figure, $\psi_1 = 0.32$, $\psi_2 = 0.80$.

Solving the eigenvector problem for

$$\Psi = \begin{bmatrix} 0.32 & 0.80 \\ 0.24 & 0.40 \end{bmatrix},$$

we get the solutions

$$\delta^1 = 0.8, \qquad \mathbf{z}^1 = \begin{bmatrix} 1.666 \\ 1 \end{bmatrix},$$

$$\delta^2 = -0.08, \quad \mathbf{z}^2 = \begin{bmatrix} -2 \\ 1 \end{bmatrix}.$$

Here, the eigenvectors are unique up to a scaling factor. So there are $N = 2$ candidate solutions, but here we can use the knowledge that $\mathbf{z} \gg \mathbf{0}$ (since $\mathbf{m} \gg \mathbf{0}$) to rule out the second solution and conclude that the first eigenvector must be the right one. We therefore end up with the *unique* solution

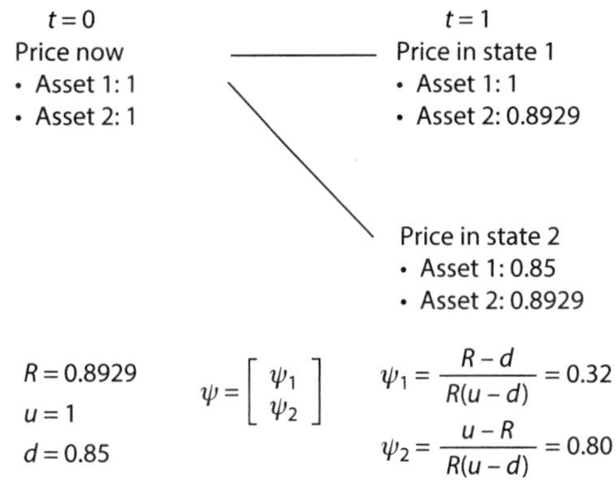

Figure 14.3: Ross model with two states: state prices when starting in the up-state, so that $m_0 = m_1$.

$$\delta = 0.8, \quad m_1 = \frac{1}{\mathbf{z}_1^1} = \frac{1}{1.666} = 0.6, \quad m_2 = \frac{1}{\mathbf{z}_2^1} = \frac{1}{1} = 1,$$

$$\Phi = \frac{1}{\delta}\Lambda_{\mathbf{m}}\Psi\Lambda_{\mathbf{m}}^{-1} = \frac{1}{0.8}\begin{bmatrix} 0.6 & 0 \\ 0 & 1 \end{bmatrix}\begin{bmatrix} 0.32 & 0.8 \\ 0.24 & 0.4 \end{bmatrix}\begin{bmatrix} 0.6 & 0 \\ 0 & 1 \end{bmatrix}^{-1} = \begin{bmatrix} 0.4 & 0,6 \\ 0.5 & 0.5 \end{bmatrix}.$$

We have recovered Φ, δ, and $\mathbf{m}$!

It turns out that this methodology always works, because out of all the N eigenvectors in the general case, there will be exactly one, $\mathbf{z}$, that has only strictly positive elements.[1] Specifically, we can apply a version of the so-called Perron–Frobenius theorem:

Theorem 14.1 (Perron–Frobenius theorem)**.** *Consider a square matrix Ψ with strictly positive elements. Then, the matrix has a unique eigenvector with strictly positive elements and associated positive eigenvalue δ^1.*

- *All other eigenvalues, $\delta^2, \ldots, \delta^N$, have $|\delta^i| \leq \delta^1$ (eigenvalue is maximal).*
- *All other eigenvectors have at least one nonpositive element.*

This then immediately implies the *Ross recovery theorem*:

Theorem 14.2 (Ross recovery theorem)**.** *Consider an N-state economy with a transition-independent pricing kernel, governed by a Markov process, with $\Psi_{ij} > 0$, representing the price of an asset that in the current state i pays \$1 in state j in the next period. Then the pricing kernel, $\delta\frac{m_j}{m_i}$, and transition probabilities, Φ_{ij}, are recovered by the strictly positive solution to the eigenvector problem $\delta\mathbf{z} = \Psi\mathbf{z}$,*

$$m_j = \frac{1}{\mathbf{z}_j},$$

$$\Phi = \delta^{-1}\Lambda_{\mathbf{m}}\Psi\Lambda_{\mathbf{m}}^{-1},$$

where $\Lambda_{\mathbf{m}} = \text{diag}(m_1, m_2, \ldots, m_N)$ and $\Phi = [\Phi_{ij}]_{ij}$.

The assumption that all N^2 state prices, Ψ_{ij}, are observable may seem the weakest in the argument so far. Indeed, at any given point in time the market will be in one state, so how can one know the other state prices? As discussed in Ross (2015), in the multiperiod market the whole matrix Ψ can actually be inferred from multiperiod state prices, as observed at one point in time.

[1] Or, technically with all elements being nonzero and having the same sign, since, of course, $-\mathbf{z}$ is also an eigenvector with the same eigenvalue.

Specifically, consider an AD security, ψ_{ij}^2, that pays a dollar in state j at $t=2$, given that the state at $t=0$ is i. We then have

$$\psi_{ij}^2 = \delta^2 \frac{m_j}{m_i} \mathbb{P}(s_2 = j | s_0 = i) = \delta^2 \frac{m_j}{m_i} \Phi_{ij}^2,$$

where $\Phi^2 = \Phi \times \Phi$, i.e., the two-period transition matrix, which is obtained by multiplying Φ by itself. This leads to the matrix of time-2 AD security prices

$$\delta^2 \Lambda_{\mathbf{m}}^{-1} \Phi^2 \Lambda_{\mathbf{m}} = (\delta \Lambda_{\mathbf{m}}^{-1} \Lambda_{\mathbf{m}})(\delta \Lambda_{\mathbf{m}}^{-1} \Lambda_{\mathbf{m}}) = \Psi^2.$$

More generally, the t-period-ahead AD security prices are given by Ψ^t, $t = 1, 2, 3, \ldots$.

Now assume, without loss of generality, that $s_0 = 1$, and that AD security prices ψ_{1j}^t are observed for $j = 1, \ldots, N$, $t = 1, \ldots, N$. So N^2 prices are observed, but instead of Ψ, these are

$$\psi^1 = [\Psi]_{1,:}, \quad \psi^2 = [\Psi^2]_{1,:}, \quad \ldots \quad , \psi^N = [\Psi^N]_{1,:}.$$

We can use this information to find Ψ. Indeed, we have N^2 equations for N^2 unknowns, and we can actually set this up as a system of N^2 linear equations.

We focus on the case with three states; the extension to general N is immediate. In this case, the state prices

$$\begin{aligned}
\psi_1^1 &= \Psi_{11}, \quad \psi_2^1 = \Psi_{12}, \quad \psi_3^1 = \Psi_{13}, \\
\psi_1^2 &= \Psi_{11}^2, \quad \psi_2^2 = \Psi_{12}^2, \quad \psi_3^2 = \Psi_{13}^2, \\
\psi_1^3 &= \Psi_{11}^3, \quad \psi_2^3 = \Psi_{12}^3, \quad \psi_3^3 = \Psi_{13}^3,
\end{aligned}$$

are observed. Now, one can then verify that the recursive relation $\Psi^{t+1} = \Psi^t \Psi$ leads to the following system of equations:

$$\begin{bmatrix} \psi_1^1 \\ \psi_2^1 \\ \psi_3^1 \\ \psi_1^2 \\ \psi_2^2 \\ \psi_3^2 \\ \psi_1^3 \\ \psi_2^3 \\ \psi_3^3 \end{bmatrix} = \begin{bmatrix} 1 & 0 & 0 & 0 & 0 & 0 & 0 & 0 & 0 \\ 0 & 1 & 0 & 0 & 0 & 0 & 0 & 0 & 0 \\ 0 & 0 & 1 & 0 & 0 & 0 & 0 & 0 & 0 \\ \psi_1^1 & 0 & 0 & \psi_2^1 & 0 & 0 & \psi_3^1 & 0 & 0 \\ 0 & \psi_1^1 & 0 & 0 & \psi_2^1 & 0 & 0 & \psi_3^1 & 0 \\ 0 & 0 & \psi_1^1 & 0 & 0 & \psi_2^1 & 0 & 0 & \psi_3^1 \\ \psi_1^2 & 0 & 0 & \psi_2^2 & 0 & 0 & \psi_3^2 & 0 & 0 \\ 0 & \psi_1^2 & 0 & 0 & \psi_2^2 & 0 & 0 & \psi_3^2 & 0 \\ 0 & 0 & \psi_1^2 & 0 & 0 & \psi_2^2 & 0 & 0 & \psi_3^2 \end{bmatrix} \times \begin{bmatrix} \Psi_{11} \\ \Psi_{12} \\ \Psi_{12} \\ \Psi_{21} \\ \Psi_{22} \\ \Psi_{23} \\ \Psi_{31} \\ \Psi_{32} \\ \Psi_{33} \end{bmatrix}.$$

This is a standard matrix equation of the form $\mathbf{y} = \mathbf{A}\mathbf{x}$, which can be solved by calculating $\mathbf{x} = \mathbf{A}^{-1}\mathbf{y}$. So all information needed for recovery is indeed available at $t = 0$.

Ross (2015) uses S&P 500 index options with different strike prices and maturities to find the state prices ψ_j^t for different j and t. The assumption is thus that the state space is given by the level of the index. The discrete version of the method of Breeden and Litzenberger (1978) is used to approximate state prices, since option prices are only available at discrete strike prices.

Jackwerth and Menner (2020) investigate the methodology proposed in Ross (2015) for estimating the state-price matrix, Ψ. They find that the matrix inversion problem is ill posed, leading to dramatic amplification of errors. As a possible consequence, the calculated state prices may be very noisy, for example negative, if no further constraints are imposed. Possible additional constraints may be nonnegativity, unimodality, and solving an overdetermined system of equations (choosing $t > N$) using minimum least squares.

Even with such additional constraints, Jackwerth and Menner (2020) find that the recovered probability distribution does not predict future returns well in the data. It is an open question whether this is because the recovery model does not provide a good representation of the real world, or whether the estimated state prices are too noisy.

14.2 Recovery for Diffusion Processes

A crucial difference with Ross's approach compared with the binomial tree model is that we here have an N-state Markov chain, where all state prices are known for each of the N initial states. So there are N^2 state prices, allowing enough equations to uniquely determine δ, $\mathbf{m}$, and Φ. Compare this with the recombining binomial tree model (with constant parameters u, d, and r), where the one-period model has one initial state, two possible outcomes at $t = 1$, three possible outcomes at $t = 2$, etc. Every time we add a time period, we increase the number of possible outcomes, and thereby the number of state prices to calculate.

As the number of periods increases, the maximum and minimum values of the log-price of the underlying tend to $\pm\infty$, i.e., the price is unbounded in the limit in the binomial model. We know that recovery is possible in neither the binomial tree model, nor the Black–Scholes model. The increasing number of states in the discrete setting, and the unboundedness of the process in the continuous setting, are potentially important for the difference between these models and Ross's approach.

To introduce a continuous-time version of the recovery model, assume that the state evolves as a time-homogeneous diffusion process:

$$dX_t = \mu(X_t)\,dt + \sigma(X_t)\,dW_t, \quad t \geq 0.$$

Here, the coefficients μ and σ may depend on the state, but not on time. This restriction is the continuous-time equivalent of the time invariance of the transition matrix assumed in the discrete setting. We define the transition density function of X_t, $f^t(x, y)$, such that

$$\mathbb{P}(X_t \in [y, y + dy] | X_0 = x) = f^t(x, y)\,dy.$$

The Fokker–Planck equation then leads to the following dynamics for f:

$$\frac{\partial f^t}{\partial t} = \mathcal{L}^* f^t,$$

$$f^0(x, y) = \delta_x(y),$$

where

$$\mathcal{L}^* f = -\frac{d}{dy}(\mu(y) f(y)) + \frac{d^2}{dy^2}\Big(\frac{\sigma^2(y)}{2} f(y)\Big).$$

The transition density function is the continuous-time equivalent of the transition matrix Φ in the discrete model.

The equivalent property of the time-invariant Markov chain, that

$$\mathbb{P}(s_{k+t} = j | s_k = i) = [\Phi^t]_{ij},$$

in the continuous-time model is captured by the *semigroup property*,

$$f^{t+s}(x, y) = \int f^t(x, z) f^s(z, y)\,dz.$$

This property is very intuitive, stating that the total probability of moving from x to y between 0 and $t+s$ is equal to the sum (i.e., integral) of the probabilities of all the paths that go from x to z from 0 to t and then from z to s from t to $t+s$, over all z.

The state price of an AD security paying $\delta_y(X_t)$ at t, given that $X_0 = x$, is defined as $p^t(x,y)$. In line with the discrete model, we assume that the function $p^t(x,y)$ is known for all x, y, and $t \le t_0$, where $t_0 > 0$. The continuous-time SDF is now assumed to be of the form

$$M_t = e^{-\rho t}\frac{m(X_t)}{m(X_0)},$$

where $m(x) = u'(x)$ is the representative agent's marginal utility function. This specification is in line with the functional forms of the SDF in our earlier equilibrium. This is then the continuous-time version of a transition-independent pricing kernel.

The equilibrium state price is

$$p^t(x,y) = e^{-\rho t}\frac{m(y)}{m(x)}f^t(x,y). \tag{14.11}$$

The recovery problem under a diffusion process is to recover ρ, the functions $m(x)$, and $f^t(x,y)$ from knowledge of $p^t(x,y)$. Equivalent to recovering f^t is, of course, recovering the drift function μ in the objective probability measure and the volatility function σ (since f^t can then be calculated by solving Fokker–Planck's equation).

Given what we know about quadratic variation and volatility, we expect the function σ to be observable from state prices. Indeed, assume the risk-neutral process for X_t,

$$dX_t = \kappa(X_t)\,dt + \sigma(X_t)\,dW_t^Q. \tag{14.12}$$

Then the volatility function $\sigma(X_t)$ should be the same in both measures. Note that X_t is not a traded asset here, so we do in general expect the function κ to be different from the short risk-free rate. Also, note that the time invariance of the process in the physical measure will carry over to time invariance in the risk-neutral measure, because of the transition-independent form of the SDF.

It will be useful to define the functions

$$q(x) = \frac{m'(x)}{m(x)} \quad \text{and} \quad D(x) = \frac{\sigma(x)^2}{2}.$$

Note that q corresponds to (minus) the absolute risk-aversion coefficient, and is therefore invariant to affine transformations $u \mapsto au+b$. Also, note that $q'(x) = \frac{m''(x)}{m(x)} - q(x)^2$.

It is straightforward to recover the short risk-free rate from state prices. Recall that the yield $y_{\Delta t}$ is such that the price of a Δt-bond, $P^{\Delta t}$, equals

$$P^{\Delta t} = e^{-y_{\Delta t}\Delta t}.$$

Of course,

$$P^{\Delta t} = \int p^{\Delta t}(X_t, y)\,dy,$$

and $e^{-y_{\Delta t}\Delta t} \approx 1 - y_{\Delta t}\Delta t$. Finally, the short rate is the same as the limit of the yield at the short-end of the yield curve,

$$r = \lim_{\Delta t \searrow 0} y_{\Delta t},$$

altogether leading to the following functional expression for the short rate:

$$r(x) = \lim_{\Delta t \searrow 0} \frac{1 - \int p^{\Delta t}(x, y)\, dy}{\Delta t},$$

which can be used to recover the short-rate function from AD prices.

The SDF pricing relation implies

$$\begin{aligned}
P^{\Delta t} &= e^{-\rho \Delta t} + E\Big[\frac{M_{t+\Delta t}}{M_t}\Big] \\
&= (1 - \rho \Delta t) E\Big[\frac{m(x) + m'(x)\, dX + D(x) m''(x)\, dt}{m(x)}\Big] + o(\Delta t) \\
&= (1 - \rho \Delta t)\big(1 + q(x)\mu(x)\, dt + D(x)(q'(x) + q(x)^2)\, dt\big) + o(\Delta t) \\
&= 1 - \big(\rho - q(x)\mu(x) - D(x)(q'(x) + q(x)^2)\big)\Delta t + o(\Delta t).
\end{aligned}$$

Since we also have that $P^{\Delta t} = 1 - r\Delta t + o(\Delta t)$, we get

$$r(x) = \rho - q(x)\mu(x) - D(x)(q'(x) + q(x)^2). \tag{14.13}$$

To recover $\sigma(x)$, consider the approximate pricing for the AD security $p^{\Delta t}(x, x + \Delta t)$. We have

$$\begin{aligned}
p^{\Delta t}(x, x + \Delta t) &= e^{-\rho \Delta t} \frac{m(x + \Delta t)}{m(x)} E[\delta_{x+\Delta t}(X_{\Delta t} | X_0 = x)] \\
&\approx (1 - \rho \Delta t)(1 + q(x)\Delta t) E[\delta_{x+\Delta t}(X_{\Delta t} | X_0 = x)] \\
&\approx (1 - \rho \Delta t)(1 + q(x)\Delta t) \frac{1}{\sqrt{2\pi \sigma(x)^2 \Delta t}} e^{-\frac{(\mu(x)\Delta t)^2}{2\sigma(x)^2 \Delta t}} \\
&\approx (1 - \rho \Delta t)(1 + q(x)\Delta t) \frac{1}{\sqrt{2\pi \sigma(x)^2 \Delta t}} \Big(1 - \frac{\mu(x)^2}{2\sigma(x)^2} \Delta t\Big) \\
&= \frac{1}{\sqrt{2\pi \sigma(x)^2 \Delta t}} (1 + O(\Delta t)) \\
&= \frac{1}{\sqrt{4\pi D(x) \Delta t}} (1 + O(\Delta t)).
\end{aligned}$$

This leads to the formula

$$D(x) = \lim_{t \searrow 0} \frac{1}{4\pi t} \times \Big(\frac{1}{p^t(x, x + t)}\Big)^2,$$

so the functions $D(x)$ and $\sigma(x)$ can be recovered from AD prices.

Finally, consider the price of an asset that pays off X_{dt}, given that $X_0 = x$,

$$\begin{aligned}
P_X^{dt} &= E\Big[e^{-\rho\, dt} \frac{M(X_{dt})}{M(X_0)} X_{dt}\Big] \\
&= (1 - \rho\, dt) E\Big[\frac{m(x) + m'(x)\, dX + m''(x) D(x)\, dt}{m(x)} (x + dX)\Big] \\
&= (1 - \rho\, dt) E\Big[(1 + q(x)\, dX + D(x)(q'(x) + q(x)^2)\, dt)(x + dX)\Big] \\
&= (1 - \rho\, dt)\big(x(1 + q(x)\mu(x) + D(x)(q'(x) + q(x)^2)\, dt) + \mu(x)\, dt + 2q(x)D(x)\, dt\big)
\end{aligned}$$

$$
\begin{aligned}
&= x - x(\rho - q(x)\mu(x) - D(x)(q'(x) + q(x)^2))\,dt + (\mu(x) + 2q(x)D(x))\,dt \\
&= x(1 - r(x)\,dt) + \underbrace{(\mu(x) + 2q(x)D(x))}_{\kappa(x)}\,dt.
\end{aligned}
$$

Now, since the risk-neutral pricing formula for P_X^{dt} is

$$
\begin{aligned}
P_X^{dt} &= \int p^{dt}(x,y)y\,dy \\
&= e^{-r(x)\,dt}E^{\mathbb{Q}}[X_{t+dt}] \\
&= (1 - r(x)\,dt)(x + \kappa(x)\,dt) \\
&= x(1 - r(x)\,dt) + \kappa(x)\,dt,
\end{aligned}
$$

it follows that

$$\kappa(x) \stackrel{\text{def}}{=} \mu(x) + 2q(x)D(x)$$

is actually the risk-neutral drift of X_t. Thus, we can recover the risk-neutral drift from AD prices:

$$\kappa(x) = r(x)x + \lim_{\Delta t \searrow 0} \frac{\int p^{\Delta t}(x,y)y\,dy - x}{\Delta t}. \tag{14.14}$$

The recovery problem in the (time-homogeneous) diffusion process setting can then be formulated as follows:

Definition 14.1 (Recovery problem in the diffusion process setting)**.** Recover the personal discount rate ρ, the $m(x)$ function, and the $\mu(x)$ function from knowledge of the functions $r(x)$, $D(x)$, and $\kappa(x)$.

How do we proceed? Let us begin with the risk-free rate equation (14.13), which needs to hold for all x. It actually represents a nonlinear first-order ODE, a Riccati equation, for q. Such equations can be transformed into second-order linear ODEs; see proposition 9.4. In this case, we define $z(x) = \frac{1}{m(x)}$ (similar to the **z**-vector in the discrete case), which is well defined and strictly positive, since $m(x)$ is strictly positive. Differentiating z, we get

$$
\begin{aligned}
z' &= -\frac{m'}{m^2} = \frac{-q}{m}, \\
z'' &= -\frac{m''}{m^2} + 2\frac{(m')^2}{m^3} = -\left(\frac{m''}{m^2} + 2q\frac{m'}{m^2}\right) = -\left(\frac{m''}{m^2} + 2qz'\right).
\end{aligned}
$$

We rewrite (14.13) as

$$\frac{r-\rho}{m} = -\mu\frac{m'}{m^2} - \frac{m''}{m^2}D(x).$$

Rewriting this expression in z, z', and z'' yields

$$
\begin{aligned}
r - \rho z &= \mu z' + D(x)(z'' + 2qz') \\
&= \kappa z' + D(x)z'',
\end{aligned}
$$

and by moving around some terms we get a second-order linear ODE for z:

$$z'' + \frac{\kappa}{D}z' + \frac{\rho - r}{D}z = 0.$$

Note that everything is observable in this ODE, except for ρ. So we know that $z(x)$ must be the solution to the following *fundamental ODE* for the recovery problem:

$$z'' + \frac{\kappa}{D}z' + \frac{\lambda - r}{D}z = 0, \quad \lambda \in \mathbb{R}. \tag{14.15}$$

Defining the $\mathcal{W}$ operator on an arbitrary twice continuously differentiable function, $u(x)$, as

$$\mathcal{W}[u|\lambda] \overset{\text{def}}{=} \frac{d^2u}{dx^2} + \frac{\kappa}{D}\frac{du}{dx} + \frac{\lambda - r}{D}u,$$

the fundamental ODE can then be conveniently written as

$$\mathcal{W}[u|\rho] = 0.$$

The argument has already taken us pretty far. Instead of an arbitrary strictly positive smooth function $m(x)$, we now know that the marginal utility function must be given by $m(x) = \frac{1}{z(x)}$, where $z(x)$ is a strictly positive solution to (14.15) for some $\lambda \in \mathbb{R}$, the value of λ corresponding to the unobservable personal discount factor, ρ.

From the theory of linear ordinary differential equations, we know that there are typically two linearly independent solutions to (14.15), let us call them $z_1^\lambda(x)$ and $z_2^\lambda(x)$, such that any linear combination $az_1^\lambda + bz_2^\lambda$ is also a solution, suggesting two potential degrees of freedom for every λ; see Simmons (1988). However, since z and αz effectively represent the same utility function, because of the invariance of expected utility preferences under linear scaling of the utility function, there is really only one degree of freedom, i.e., for a given λ, the set of potential solutions is spanned by the functions $\beta z_1^\lambda + (1-\beta)z_2^\lambda$, $\beta \in \mathbb{R}$. So there are no more than two degrees of freedom in total among the class of candidate z functions, one for λ and one for β.

We still have not used the positivity condition on m. Recall that this was what implied uniqueness of the solution in the discrete problem, via the Perron–Frobenius theorem. In this setting, we can replace the Perron–Frobenius theorem with Sturm–Liouville theory for second-order linear ODEs; see Simon (2005). Walden (2017) explores the conditions under which the positivity condition is sufficient to ensure a unique solution to the recovery problem. The following result is key:

Proposition 14.1. *Consider the set* $\mathcal{S}^\lambda = \{u : \mathcal{W}[u|\lambda] = 0\}$. *Define the* scale function $Q(x) = e^{-\int_0^x \frac{\mu(s)}{D(s)}\,ds}$. *Then necessary and sufficient conditions for the two conditions*

1. $\mathcal{S}^\rho$ *contains exactly one strictly positive function,*
2. $\mathcal{S}^\lambda$ *contains no strictly positive functions when* $\lambda > \rho$,

to hold jointly are that

$$\int_{-\infty}^{0} Q(x)\,dx = \infty \quad \textit{and} \quad \int_0^\infty Q(x)\,dx = \infty. \tag{14.16}$$

Proof. See Walden (2017). □

An immediate consequence of this proposition is that when (14.16) holds, m can be recovered by finding the maximal λ for which $\mathcal{S}^\lambda$ contains a positive solution. Then $\rho = \lambda^*$, and the unique positive solution $z^* \in \mathcal{S}^{\lambda^*}$ is the reciprocal of the marginal utility function $m = \frac{1}{z^*}$. Transition densities can then be calculated by using (14.11), leading to

$$f^t(x, y) = e^{\rho t}\frac{m(x)}{m(y)}p^t(x, y).$$

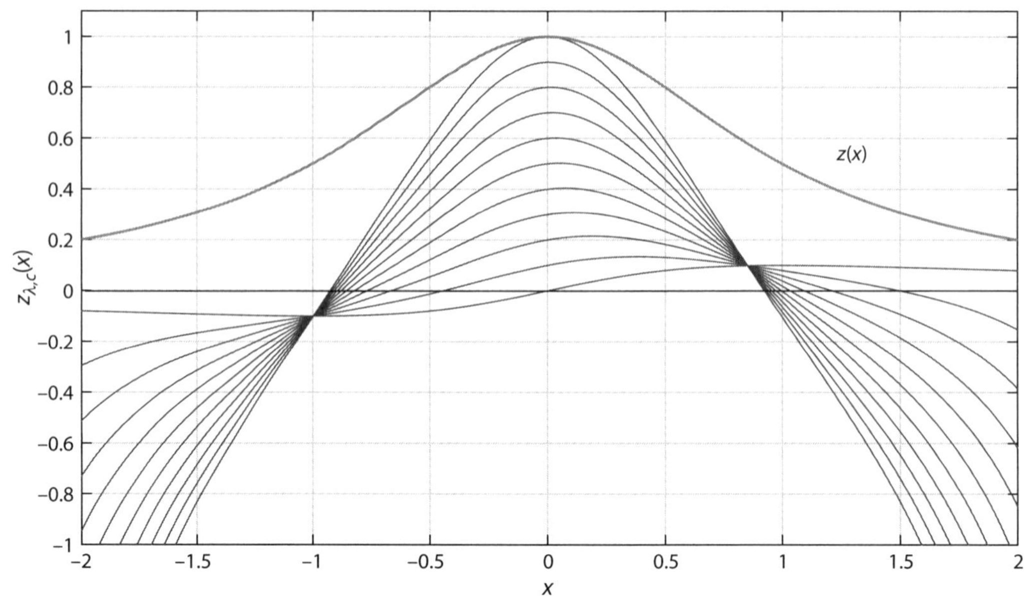

Figure 14.4: Candidate functions, z, solving $\mathcal{W}[z|\lambda]$. Thick line: Correct solution $z = \frac{1}{m}$, where $m(x) = 1 + x^2$ (the only positive solution when $\lambda = \rho = 0.01$). Thin lines: Candidate solutions when $\lambda = 0.02 > \rho$. All candidate solutions eventually become negative when $\lambda > \rho$, and therefore cannot represent $\frac{1}{m}$. Process: $dX_t = -0.01X_t\, dt + 0.1\, dW_t$. Example from Walden (2017).

In the finite-state model studied before, irreducibility is necessary to guarantee recovery. Here, the condition is given by (14.16). This condition has a fruitful stochastic interpretation. Define a process X_t to be *recurrent* if

$$\mathbb{P}(X_t = y \text{ for some } t > s | X_s = x) = 1, \quad \forall s \geq 0, \forall x, \forall y.$$

As discussed in Pinsky (1995), (14.16) is a necessary and sufficient condition for the process X_t to be recurrent (see also Karlin and Taylor 1981). So the proposition could equivalently have been stated in terms of recovery being possible if and only if the underlying process is recurrent in the objective measure. A process that is not recurrent is said to be *transient.*

Examples of recurrent processes we have encountered so far include the Ornstein–Uhlenbeck process and the Wiener process. The Brownian motion with a nonzero drift, on the other hand, is not recurrent. If the drift is positive, for example, it is quite likely that the process starting at $x = 0$ will never reach a state $y \ll 0$. Over time the process will likely move higher and higher, so there will be a last point in time that it reaches any finite x. The Brownian motion with nonzero drift is therefore transient.

In figure 14.4, we show an example with an Ornstein–Uhlenbeck process that governs the dynamics of X_t. Since the Ornstein–Uhlenbeck process is recurrent, it should allow for recovery. Indeed, it is straightforward to verify that the process satisfies condition (14.16). In this example, we assume a nonstandard utility function, with $m(x) = 1 + x^2$. Recall that the marginal utility function, m, being strictly positive and smooth are our only constraints on the utility function. The thick line in the figure, and the associated parameter ρ, is the unique maximal solution to the fundamental ODE, which indeed identifies the reciprocal of the marginal utility function, $z(x) = \frac{1}{1+x^2}$. Thus, recovery worked in this case!

The necessary condition (14.16) also sheds light on the apparent paradox that no information about the stock's expected return $\hat{\mu}$ is needed to calculate option prices in the Black–Scholes model. Indeed, since different expected returns are consistent with the same option prices (and thereby state prices), it must be impossible to recover the drift term in the physical measure from state prices in the Black–Scholes model.

Now define the state in the Black–Scholes model by the log-stock price, $X_t = \ln(S_t)$, so that

$$dX_t = \left(\hat{\mu} - \frac{\sigma^2}{2}\right) dt + \sigma \, dW_t. \tag{14.17}$$

The condition for a Brownian motion to be recurrent is that its drift term is 0, so the only process that satisfies the recurrence condition is the Brownian motion for which $\hat{\mu} = \frac{\sigma^2}{2}$. This is the drift term that will be "recovered" regardless of whether condition (14.16) is actually satisfied. In general, when the underlying processes contain long-term growth, the recovery methodology will therefore have limitations.

For processes that have long-term growth, one may consider a "fix," namely redefining the state variable to filter out the growth part. For example, we could define $\widehat{X}_t = e^{-(\hat{\mu}-\frac{\sigma^2}{2})t}X_t$ in the previous example. However, this requires us to know what the growth is, something we have tried to avoid when taking the recovery approach. Moreover, redefining the state variable may generate challenges with respect to the assumption of a transition-independent pricing kernel (14.11). If the pricing kernel is transition independent under the original specification, it will not be transition independent when time-varying growth is added. If a constant growth rate is added, then the wrong discount rate ρ will be recovered.

Indeed, with CRRA utility, separating ρ from $\hat{\mu}$ under GBM dynamics of aggregate consumption, $X_t = X_0 + \mu t + \sigma W_t$, $C_t = e^{X_t}$, will be impossible. This is easily seen: note that this is the dynamics of a standard Lucas one-tree economy, so the risk-free rate will be given by (12.45). Moreover, since $u'(X_t) = e^{-\gamma X_t}$, it follows that $q(x) = -\gamma$, and therefore

$$\kappa = \mu + 2(-\gamma)\frac{\sigma^2}{2} = \mu - \gamma\sigma^2,$$

which is the standard formula for the risk-neutral drift in the Lucas one-tree economy with CRRA preferences. Of course, σ is observable in the continuous-time setting, from the quadratic variation, whereas ρ, μ, and γ are not. From the formulas for the risk-free rate and risk-neutral drift, we have

$$r = \rho + \gamma\mu - \gamma^2\frac{\sigma^2}{2},$$
$$\kappa = \mu - \gamma\sigma^2,$$

so given observations of r, σ^2, and κ, any triplet (γ, μ, ρ) with

$$\mu = \kappa + \gamma\sigma^2, \quad \rho = r - \gamma\kappa - \gamma^2\frac{\sigma^2}{2}$$

is consistent with observed state prices, whereas the recovery method will single out the special case with

$$\mu = 0, \quad \gamma = -\frac{\kappa}{\sigma^2}, \quad \rho = r + \frac{\kappa^2}{2\sigma^2}.$$

The situation is thus a lot more complicated for the recovery methodology with a diffusion process when (14.16) fails. An additional challenge is that (14.16) is defined with respect to the drift term in the objective measure, which we assume no knowledge about. There is therefore no simple way of taking a stand on whether (14.16) is satisfied from observed state prices alone.

An alternative approach, which we now consider, is to restrict the class of marginal utility functions. Indeed, so far the only restriction we impose is that they need to be smooth and strictly positive. If we consider a smaller class of candidate utility functions, it should be easier to find cases where the set of such candidate functions that satisfy the pricing relations contains a unique element. One such class mentioned in Ross (2015), and further explored in Walden (2017), is that of utility functions with bounded marginal utility strictly above zero and below infinity, i.e., with associated functions $m(x)$ such that

$$0 < \underline{c} \leq m(x) \leq \bar{c} < \infty, \quad x \in \mathbb{R}.$$

We denote the class of such utility functions by $\mathcal{B}$.

It can then be shown that the following proposition holds:

Proposition 14.2. *Unique recovery in $\mathcal{B}$ is possible if and only if at least one of the conditions in* (14.16) *is satisfied.*

Proof. See Walden (2017). □

So, instead of both of the scale coefficient conditions in (14.16) being satisfied, as is required for unique recovery within the larger class of utility functions, here only one of the conditions needs to be satisfied. This actually makes a major difference, since relaxing one of the conditions on the scale function allows for long-term growth in the process (either toward infinity or toward minus infinity, but not both). The classical Black–Scholes economy will therefore be solvable within the class $\mathcal{B}$ of utility functions.

An example is given in figure 14.5, where we have the classical GBM Black–Scholes dynamics, in log-coordinates $dX_t = \mu\, dt + \sigma\, dW_t$, and with bounded marginal utility function,

$$m(x) = \frac{1}{1 + \frac{\tan^{-1}(x)}{\pi}}.$$

We choose positive growth $\mu = 0.01$, so this example does not admit recovery within the full class of utility functions, since the integral $\int_0^\infty Q(x)\, dx < \infty$, while $\int_{-\infty}^0 Q(x)\, dx = \infty$. It does admit recovery within $\mathcal{B}$ though, according to proposition 14.2, since one of the conditions in (14.16) is satisfied.

In figure 14.5, the left-hand panel shows candidate functions z, being solutions to $\mathcal{W}[z|\lambda] = 0$, when $\lambda = \rho = 0.01$. Of course, $z \in \mathcal{B} \Leftrightarrow m \in \mathcal{B}$, so only bounded z functions qualify, and as shown in the left-hand panel there is only one such solution, represented by the thick line. This is indeed the reciprocal of the marginal utility function, $z = \frac{1}{m}$. In the right-hand panel, candidate solutions for $\lambda > \rho$ are shown, all of which are either disqualified because they are unbounded or at some point turn negative (or both). We have recovered m!

14.3 Error Bounds under Bounded Observations

The diffusion process recovery model provides insight beyond the discrete model. However, it takes us one step further away from the real world, in assuming an infinite number of state prices. In practice, only a finite number of state prices are observed, as in Ross (2015), where the states represent the levels of a market index, and there is a finite number of option strike prices from which state prices may be inferred.

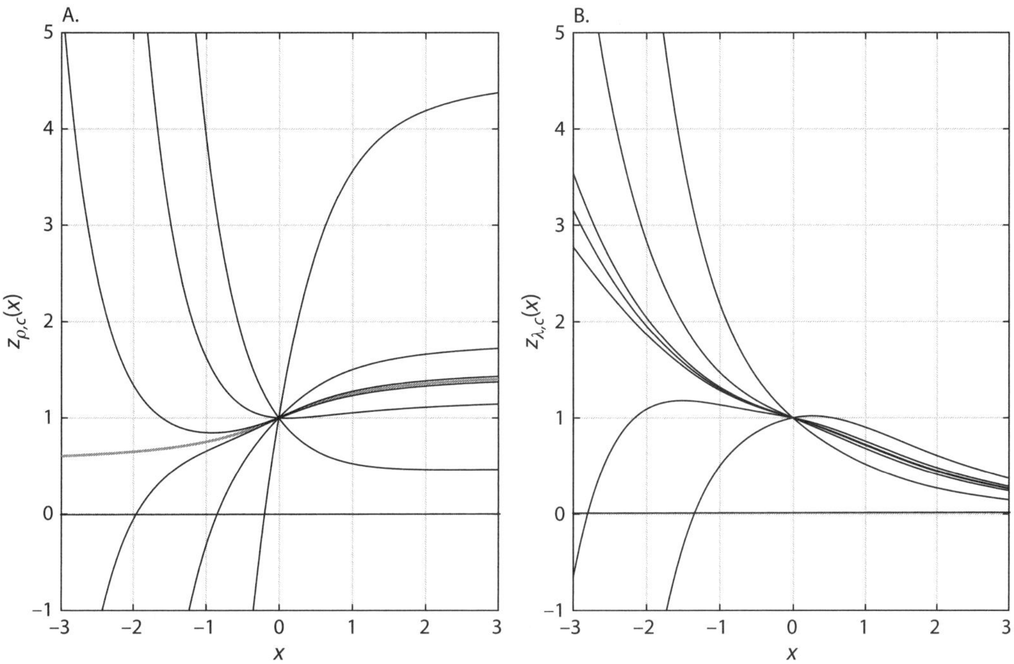

Figure 14.5: Candidate functions, z, solving $\mathcal{W}[z|\lambda]$. Left panel: Candidate solutions when $\lambda = \rho$. The thick line represents the unique bounded nonnegative solution. Right panel: Candidate solutions when $\lambda > \rho$. All solutions are either unbounded or turn negative (or both). Process: $dX_t = 0.01\,dt + 0.1\,dW_t$, $\rho = 0.01$. Example from Walden (2017).

The mapping between discrete observations of option prices and continuous pricing kernels has been extensively investigated; see, e.g., Ait-Sahalia and Lo (1998). However, the additional challenge that arises in the recovery setting, of having only *bounded* observations, is novel and important, given what we know about how important the behavior of the process for asymptotically large values is for whether recovery is even feasible. How do we think about recovery when we only observe state prices on a bounded domain, say on the interval $A = [-N, N]$ for some finite number N?

The case we have studied so far is the limit case when $N \to \infty$. It follows immediately that in the limit, the set of candidate recovery solutions reduces to one, as long as (14.16) is satisfied. However, when $N < \infty$, this set will contain multiple candidate solutions, because there are many possible state prices outside A. How much can these candidate solutions vary within A? This question is studied in von Sydow and Walden (2020), where it is shown that the convergence rate toward the correct solution as $N \to \infty$ depends on how quickly the integrals in (14.16) tend to infinity as the integration bounds grow.

To solve the fundamental ODE at x, $\kappa(x)$ is needed. An *approximate recovery problem* can be solved by assuming that $z > 0$ in the interior of A, and then studying the set of positive candidate solutions that satisfy the ODE in A, with some arbitrary boundary conditions at $\pm N$. It is especially convenient to choose $z(-N) = z(N) = 0$, as discussed in von Sydow and Walden (2020), leading to the approximate recovered solution $\bar{z}$. The authors show that given that recovery is feasible on the whole of $\mathbb{R}$, approximate recovery will be feasible for $\lambda = \rho$ in that the set of candidate functions will be nonempty when $\lambda = \rho$. For some $\bar{\lambda} > \rho$ the set will contain a unique solution, and for even larger λ's no positive solution exists within A. The solution to the approximate recovery solution on $[-N, N]$ is then the pair $(\bar{\lambda}^N, \hat{z}^N)$ that solves the problem for the maximum possible $\bar{\lambda}^N$. The following result can then be shown:

Proposition 14.3. *Define the functions*

$$Q(x) = e^{-\int_0^x \frac{\mu(s)}{D(s)}\, ds},$$

$$R(x) = \int_0^x Q(s)\, ds,$$

$$T(x) = \min\{-R(-x), R(x)\},$$

$$Z(x, N) = \min\left\{\frac{R(N)}{R(x)}, \frac{R(-N)}{R(-x)}\right\}.$$

The approximation errors between the approximate recovered and true solutions, $(\bar{\lambda}^N, z^N)$ and (ρ, z), satisfy the following bounds:

$$0 \le \bar{\lambda}^N - \rho \le C_1 \frac{1}{T(N) - \epsilon}, \tag{14.18}$$

$$\left|\frac{z^N(x) - z(x)}{z(x)}\right| \le C_2 \frac{1}{Z(x, N) - 1}. \tag{14.19}$$

Here, the positive constant C_1 depends on μ and σ, and on $\epsilon > 0$, and the positive constant C_2 depends on μ, σ, and x, but neither constant depends on N.

Proof. See von Sydow and Walden (2020). □

This result confirms the numerical investigation in Walden (2017) that found faster convergence to the true solution, the faster the mean reversion of the stochastic process for X; see figure 14.6.

Another approach is taken in Carr and Yu (2012). They assume a bounded process for the state price, and impose boundary conditions at the upper and lower bounds that allow for unique recovery. A challenge with their approach is that it is unclear how those boundary conditions would be identified through economic arguments, at least without making additional assumptions about the utility specification. The analysis here makes no such assumptions, the downside being that only an approximate solution can be identified with this approach.

14.4 Misspecified Recovery

The recovery methodology developed by Ross builds on an earlier literature that uses Perron–Frobenius theory to study pricing kernels; see, Alvarez and Jerman (2005), Hansen and Scheinkman (2009), and Hansen (2012). The transition-independent pricing kernels assumed by Ross make up a subset of the larger class of pricing kernels studied in this literature. The literature has mainly focused on the long-term properties of the economy and pricing kernel, for example in terms of risk premia. This is somewhat different from our focus on recovery.

Borovička, Hansen, and Scheinkman (2016) point out that the recovery theorem will not be able to uniquely recover the pricing kernel within the larger class of such kernels defined in this earlier literature. In Ross's discrete N-state economy, consider the class of pricing kernels,

$$\mathcal{K} = \left\{\mathbf{M} : \mathbf{M}_{ij} = \delta \frac{m_j}{m_i} \mathbf{H}_{ij}\right\},$$

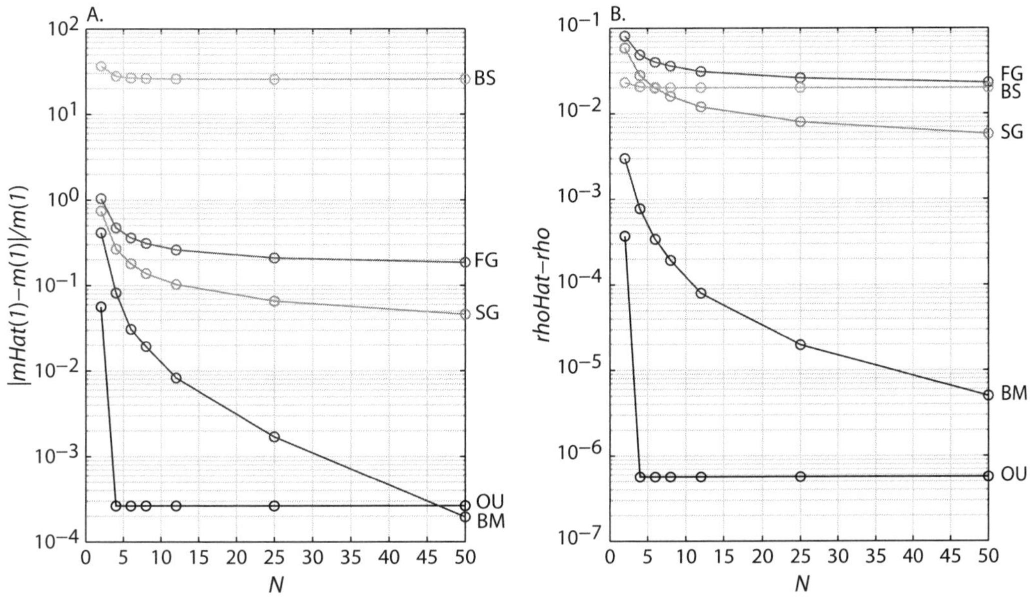

Figure 14.6: Approximate recovery for different diffusion processes: (1) Ornstein–Uhlenbeck process (OU). (2) Brownian motion without drift (BM). (3) Slow growth process (SG). (4) Faster growth process (FG). (5) Brownian motion with positive drift, which does not converge (BS). The left-hand panel shows the error (in logarithmic scale) of the estimated $m(1)$ as N grows; the right-hand panel shows the error (in logarithmic scale) of the estimated ρ as N grows. Example from Walden (2017).

where $\mathbf{H} \in \mathbb{R}_+^{N \times N}$ satisfies

$$\sum_j \mathbf{H}_{ij}\Phi_{ij} = 1, \quad \forall\, i, \tag{14.20}$$

and with the associated SDF process

$$\frac{M(t+1)}{M(t)} = \mathbf{M}_{s_t, s_{t+1}}.$$

Equivalently, we can define the process $h_0 = 1$ and $h_{t+1} = \mathbf{H}_{s_t, s_{t+1}}$. The condition (14.20) then states that h_t is a martingale:

$$E[h_{t+1}|h_t] = \sum_j \mathbf{H}_{s_t,j}\Phi_{s_t,j}h_t = h_t,$$

i.e., the condition can be viewed as a *martingale condition.* With this definition, and also writing m_t for the marginal utility at t, instead of m_{s_t} (so that m is viewed as a process rather than a vector), the SDF can be written as

$$\frac{M_{t+1}}{M_t} = \delta \frac{m_{t+1}h_{t+1}}{m_t h_t}. \tag{14.21}$$

Note that whether a given $\mathbf{H}$ satisfies the martingale condition depends on Φ, and therefore cannot be verified without further knowledge about the economic environment.

A special case is when

$$\mathbf{H} = \mathbf{1}\mathbf{1}', \tag{14.22}$$

i.e., $\mathbf{H}$ is a matrix of 1s, in which case $h_t \equiv 1$ and the martingale condition is trivially satisfied. We may consider the subclass $\mathcal{K}^0 \subset \mathcal{K}$ of pricing kernels that satisfies this condition (14.22). This subset is the set that Ross (2015) studies and shows unique recovery within. Unique recovery within $\mathcal{K}$, however, is more challenging, since the set of candidate SDFs is larger

Borovička, Hansen, and Scheinkman (2016) point out that unique recovery is no longer possible within the larger class $\mathcal{K}$. Specifically, the pricing relation within this larger class of SDFs is

$$\Psi_{ij} = \delta \frac{m_j}{m_i} \mathbf{H}_{ij} \Phi_{ij}. \tag{14.23}$$

Now, defining the matrix $\mathbf{R}$, with

$$[\mathbf{R}]_{ij} = \mathbf{H}_{ij} \Phi_{ij},$$

the martingale condition on $\mathbf{H}$ implies that $\mathbf{1}$ is an eigenvector of $\mathbf{R}$, with eigenvalue 1. So a similar argument to that leading to (14.9) in the Ross model then implies that

$$\mathbf{z} = \Lambda_{\mathbf{m}}^{-1} \mathbf{1}$$

is the only strictly positive eigenvector of Ψ, and is associated with the eigenvalue δ.

However, neither the SDF, M_t, nor the transition density, Φ, is correctly identified here. Rather, $\mathbf{R}$ is identified, since

$$\mathbf{R} = \delta^{-1} \Lambda_{\mathbf{m}} \Psi \Lambda_{\mathbf{m}}^{-1}.$$

So, instead of $\mathbf{H}$ being part of the pricing kernel, as defined by (14.21), it is incorporated into the inferred transition density, so that $\mathbf{R}$ is identified rather than Φ. In other words, given Ψ, there are an infinite number of solutions, $(\mathbf{M}, \Phi)$, each with $\mathbf{H}$ satisfying (14.20), and such that (14.23) holds. The approach in Ross (2015) selects the solution that satisfies (14.22). Borovička, Hansen, and Scheinkman (2016) note that when a consumption-based pricing kernel is used, the martingale component of the form (14.22) is rejected in the data. So Ross recovery, which focuses on the class of SDFs $\mathcal{K}_0 \subset \mathcal{K}$, does not account for the martingale component that is present in the data. The authors call this *misspecified recovery.*

CHAPTER 15 Information and Disagreement

One of the main stylized facts in financial markets is that trading volumes are huge. Indeed, the annual turnover of the average publicly traded stock is above 100%, meaning that in some sense firm ownership shifts hands once per year. Trading volumes in derivatives markets, e.g., future and forward markets on interest rates, indexes, and currencies, are much higher. What drives these large trading volumes? We have discussed hedging demands, but much also seems to be due to speculation, different views, and heterogeneous information among market participants. Indeed, many people associate financial markets with "stock tips," and making fortunes via clever "bets."

Our main focus has been on the representative agent setting so far, which does not allow us to say much about such trading, since there is only one agent who therefore does not have anyone to trade against. A different framework is needed to model trading between investors with different information and how their information is incorporated into asset prices. Fortunately, there is a huge field within financial economics that focuses on these questions—*market microstructure*. We only have space to scratch the surface of this important field here, by covering a few seminal contributions.

To better understand some modeling choices made in this literature, it is helpful to discuss some results that were derived around the time these models were developed—results that show that it is actually not that easy to get rational agents to trade with each other for informational purposes. The reason is that because the investors are rational, they will try to infer other investors' information from the trades those investors are willing to take on. Without some friction, they tend to be very good at making such inferences, and all agents are able to infer the information of all other agents. This is good in the sense that it makes prices *informationally efficient*, but it kills any trading incentives—once investors have the same information, they all behave the same and we are back in the representative agent setting.

To provide a very simple example that captures some of the intuition, imagine that you are a speculator in a market for rare collectibles, for example, stamps. You are risk neutral and purely in the business to make profits, i.e., you associate no personal (private) value with owning the stamp. You only care about expected price appreciation. After some detailed research, you conclude that you can expect to sell the stamp for \$1000 five years from now (which is your investment horizon).

You know a seller who is just like you: risk neutral, and purely in the business to make money, who is willing to sell the stamp to you for \$200. Sounds like a great deal? The crux is that you know that the seller is a world expert on stamps, and clearly has much more information about future prices than you have.

So, in this situation, it seems rational for you to infer that the seller, based on his/her superior information, believes that the price will be much lower than you think, and based on this you will update your own beliefs. How much should you update? Well, if the seller's information nests yours (i.e., the seller knows everything you know, and more), and both of you measure the value of the transaction in terms of expected profits, you may reasonably conclude that whatever price you are offered leads to an expected loss (or at least not a profit), and as a result you decide not to trade with the expert.

15.1 Agreeing to Disagree

We first discuss a related result, namely the difficulty of getting rational agents to agree to disagree. Aumann (1976) showed that agents who initially have the same (prior) beliefs, and who then get private informative signals, will never be able to disagree about the probability for an event, as long as each agent's posterior beliefs are *common knowledge*. Common knowledge here means that not only do the agents know each other's posterior beliefs, each agent knows that the other agent knows these posterior beliefs, and also that the other agent knows that the agent knows that the other agent knows, etc.

In the previous stamp example, we could imagine that the two collectors view the prices the counterparty is willing to trade for as a signal about their beliefs of the expected value of the stamp, suggesting that they must ultimately agree on the stamp's expected value. So, although Aumann's result does not assume a market, it is clear that it is also important for the type of environments we have in mind.

Following Aumann (1976), we show the result formally, beginning with an example. Recall how in section 8.4 we introduced sigma-algebras and equivalently (in the finite-state case) partitions to represent the information available to traders. Now, assume that there are two agents, 1 and 2, who have different information. Specifically, assume that the state space is $\Omega = \{\omega_1, \omega_2, \omega_3, \omega_4, \omega_5, \omega_6, \omega_7, \omega_8\}$.

Before receiving any information, the two agents agree on the probability for different states to occur, i.e., define $p^k_m = \mathbb{P}^k(\{\omega_m\})$, where $k \in \{1, 2\}$ represents the agent, and $m \in \{1, 2, 3, 4, 5, 6, 7, 8\}$ the state. The common prior assumption is then $p^1_m = p^2_m$, $m = 1, \ldots, 8$.

Agents now receive private information, represented by the two partitions

$$\mathcal{P}^k = \{B^k_1, B^k_2, B^k_3, B^k_4\}, \quad k = 1, 2,$$

where

$$B^1_1 = \{\omega_1, \omega_2, \omega_3\}, \quad B^1_2 = \{\omega_4, \omega_5, \omega_6\}, \quad B^1_3 = \{\omega_7\}, \quad B^1_4 = \{\omega_8\},$$
$$B^2_1 = \{\omega_1, \omega_4, \omega_5\}, \quad B^2_2 = \{\omega_2, \omega_3\}, \quad B^2_3 = \{\omega_6, \omega_7\}, \quad B^2_4 = \{\omega_8\}.$$

The interpretation here is that given that ω_m is the true state, each agent knows that the state is one in B^k_ℓ, for the information (partition) set B^k_ℓ that ω_m belongs to. So, if the true state happens to be ω_2, then agent 1 knows that one of the states ω_1, ω_2, ω_3 (since $\omega_2 \in B^1_1$) is the true state, whereas agent 2 knows that either ω_2 or ω_3 is the true state (since $\omega_2 \in B^2_2$). These two partitions

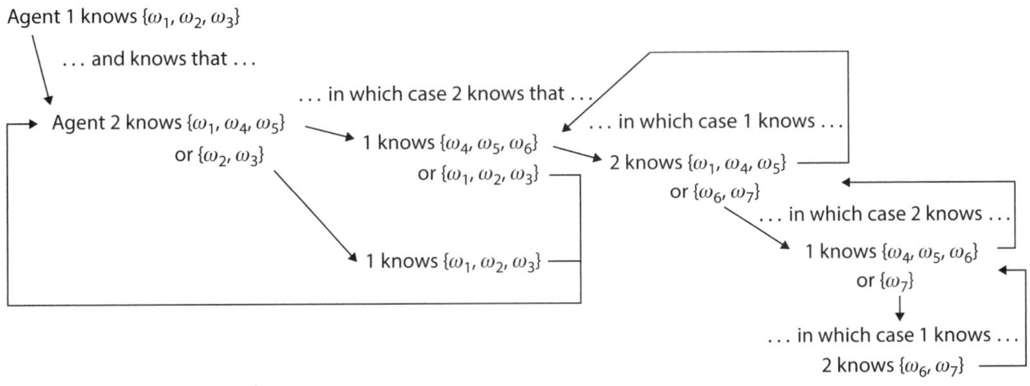

Figure 15.1: Common-knowledge example.

define the *information structure.* Both agents know the other agent's partition, and can thus draw some inferences about the other agent's information set from their own information set. But both can only perfectly infer the other agent's information set when the true state is ω_8, in which case $\omega_8 \in B_4^1 = B_4^2$.

Now, assume that ω_1 is the true state. We want to understand which events are common knowledge in this case among the two agents, in the sense informally defined above. We proceed according to the sequence in figure 15.1, starting in the upper-left corner. Agent 1 knows that any state in the event $B_1^1 = \{\omega_1, \omega_2, \omega_3\}$ is possible (first-order beliefs), and therefore that agent 2 must either know that event B_1^2 or B_2^2 contains the true state (second-order beliefs). If agent 2 happens to know that B_1^2 is correct, then (s)he knows that agent 1 knows that either B_1^2 or B_1^1 contains the true state. But, if agent 2 thinks that agent 1 may know that the state is in B_2^2, then agent 2 believes that agent 1 may believe that agent 2 may know $B_3^2 = \{\omega_6, \omega_7\}$.

The argument can be continued to higher and higher orders of beliefs, but as shows from the figure, there is no way for either agent to believe the other agent may believe that state ω_8 is "in play," at any order of beliefs. In other words, the smallest event that is common knowledge at ω_1 is $E = \{\omega_1, \omega_1, \omega_2, \omega_3, \omega_4, \omega_5, \omega_6, \omega_7\}$. Moreover, one sees from the figure that the same argument can be applied to any state in E, leading to the same minimal common-knowledge set. For example, assume that agent 1 knows the event is B_3^1, i.e., that the state is ω_7, as in the lower-right part of the figure. Then (s)he knows that agent 2 knows the state lies in $B_3^2 = \{\omega_6, \omega_7\}$, so the mutual knowledge set, $B_3^1 \cup B_3^2 = \{\omega_6, \omega_7\}$, is much smaller than E. Agent 2, however, thinks that agent 1 may believe $B_2^1 = \{\omega_4, \omega_5, \omega_6\}$ is correct, and from there on it unravels so that eventually the common-knowledge set is again E.

In the case of the only remaining state, ω_8, the same argument immediately implies that the set $E' = \{\omega_8\}$ is the minimal one that is common knowledge, i.e., at ω_8, the actual state is common knowledge, $E' = \{\omega_8\}$. So the (minimal) common sets form a coarser partition of the state space, such that $\Omega = E \cup E'$. Upon some further thought, one sees that this partition is the so-called meet of the two individual partitions, defined as follows:

Definition 15.1. The *meet*, $\mathcal{P}$, of a number of partitions, $\mathcal{P}^1, \dots, \mathcal{P}^K$, of a state space, Ω, is defined as the finest partition that is coarser than each of the partitions, i.e., the finest partition such that for each $B_\ell^k \in \mathcal{P}^k$ and $B_{\ell'} \in \mathcal{P}$, either $B_\ell^k \cap B_{\ell'} = B_\ell^k$, or $B_\ell^k \cap B_{\ell'} = \emptyset$.

We write $\mathcal{P} = \mathcal{P}^1 \wedge \mathcal{P}^2 \wedge \cdots \wedge \mathcal{P}^K$. It is easy to verify that our (minimum) common-knowledge set partition of $\Omega = E \cup E'$ is obtained by the meet $\mathcal{P} = \mathcal{P}^1 \wedge \mathcal{P}^2$.

The common-knowledge posterior assumption made in Aumann (1976) is now that both (all if there are more than two) agents' posterior beliefs about (the probability for) an event, $A \subset 2^{\Omega}$, are common knowledge, leading to the following result:

Theorem 15.1 (Aumann 1976). *If agents have common prior beliefs, and the posterior beliefs about an event are common knowledge, then all agents have the same posterior beliefs about the event.*

The result is known as the impossibility of agreeing to disagree (within the information structure environment of Aumann (1976)).

Proof. The proof is actually really straightforward (the main challenge was to define an appropriate environment in which this important question could be asked and analyzed). Assume the actual state is ω_m, and $\omega_m \in B$, where B belongs to the meet $\mathcal{P}$. For an arbitrary agent, k, we have $B = \bigcup_{j \in J} B_j^k$ for some sets $B_j^k \in \mathcal{P}^k$, $J = \{j_1, j_2, \ldots, j_v\}$. Now, since the agent's posterior beliefs about an event A are common knowledge, they must be the same for each B_j^k, i.e., using Bayes' rule, the conditional probability

$$q^k = \frac{\mathbb{P}(A \cap B_j^k)}{\mathbb{P}(B_j^k)}$$

is the same for all $j \in J$. It follows that

$$\mathbb{P}(A \cap B_j^k) = q^k \mathbb{P}(B_j^k),$$

for all j. By the law of total probability,

$$\mathbb{P}(A \cap B) = \sum_{j \in J} \mathbb{P}(A \cap B_j^k) = \sum_{j \in J} q^k \mathbb{P}(B_j^k) = q^k \mathbb{P}(B).$$

So

$$q^k = \frac{\mathbb{P}(A \cap B)}{\mathbb{P}(B)}.$$

But this conditional probability is then the same regardless of agent, k, since agents have the same priors and therefore agree on $\mathbb{P}(A \cap B)$ and $\mathbb{P}(B)$. Thus, agents have the same posterior beliefs about the event A. □

Now, it may not be immediately clear how this relates to the earlier example with the stamp collectors. The key here is that the common knowledge of posterior beliefs about an event typically comes about via some type of information exchange. In the stamp example, the exchange would occur when agents negotiate the stamp price. We provide an example with a coin toss, a simplified version of an environment mentioned in Aumann (1976). Consider a coin that may be unfair, i.e., the probabilities for heads and tails may be different. Two agents have been told that there is $\frac{1}{3}$ chance each that the coin favors heads (an H-coin, HC), that it favors tails (a T-coin, TC), or that it is fair, with the same probability for heads and tails (an F-coin, FC). The actual coin-type is an element in the set {HC, FC, TC}. A coin that favors an outcome has a probability of $\frac{3}{4}$ to land on that outcome. All this information is common knowledge, and determines the agents' common priors.

Each agent potentially receives some private information. Specifically, with probability $z = \frac{54}{79}$ each agent (independently) gets to observe two coin tosses, which may then show two heads, one heads and one tails, or two tails. With probability $\frac{25}{79}$, an agent does not receive any private information. Finally, the coin is tossed once under the observation of both agents, with the possible outcomes H (heads) or T (tails).

Denote the four possible observations of an agent by the set $A = \{\emptyset, HH, HT, TT\}$, where HT represents one heads and one tails, regardless of the order of observations. The state space is now $\Omega = \{\text{HC}, \text{FC}, \text{TC}\} \times A \times A \times \{H, T\}$, representing the actual coin type, agent 1's and 2's private observations, respectively, and the outcome of the final coin toss.

We are interested in agents' beliefs about the probability for heads in the final coin toss, represented by the event $B = \{\text{HC}, \text{FC}, \text{TC}\} \times A \times A \times \{H\}$. This event thus represents all combinations of coin types, and observations of the two agents, for which the final observed coin toss lands on heads. The agents' common prior beliefs about the probability for this event are

$$\begin{aligned}\mathbb{P}(B) &= \mathbb{P}(\text{HC}) \times \mathbb{P}(H|\text{HC}) + \mathbb{P}(\text{FC}) \times \mathbb{P}(H|\text{FC}) + \mathbb{P}(\text{TC}) \times \mathbb{P}(H|\text{TC}) \\ &= \frac{1}{3} \times \frac{3}{4} + \frac{1}{3} \times \frac{1}{2} + \frac{1}{3} \times \frac{1}{4} = \frac{1}{2}.\end{aligned}$$

Obviously, once agents make their private observations, they will update their beliefs about the coin types, $\mathbb{P}(\text{HC})$, $\mathbb{P}(\text{FC})$, and $\mathbb{P}(\text{TC})$. For example, an agent who observes $HH \in A$ uses Bayes' rule to compare the conditional probabilities $\mathbb{P}(HH|\text{HC}) = \frac{9}{16}$, $\mathbb{P}(HH|\text{FC}) = \frac{4}{16}$, and $\mathbb{P}(HH|\text{TC}) = \frac{1}{16}$, and update to the posterior beliefs $\mathbb{P}(\text{HC}|HH) = \frac{9}{14}$, $\mathbb{P}(\text{FC}|HH) = \frac{4}{14}$, and $\mathbb{P}(\text{TC}|HH) = \frac{1}{14}$, leading to

$$\mathbb{P}(B|HH) = \frac{9}{14} \times \frac{3}{4} + \frac{4}{14} \times \frac{1}{2} + \frac{1}{14} \times \frac{1}{4} = \frac{9}{14}.$$

Without any information sharing, the two agents will end up with different posterior beliefs if they receive different private information. However, this situation violates the common knowledge about posteriors assumption.

To generate common knowledge, we assume that agents alternate in announcing their current beliefs, $p^k = \mathbb{P}^k(B)$, $k \in \{1, 2\}$, given the information they have at that point. They do this an infinite number of times or, equivalently, until neither agent updates their beliefs further when hearing the other agent's beliefs. The situation is shown in figure 15.2, where a tree of beliefs of the form (p^1, p^2) is shown, starting with the agent's common priors on the left and then traversing to the right as the agents alternately announce their beliefs. In the first step, agent 1 makes the observation, and announces his/her updated belief, which is $\frac{9}{14}$ after observing two heads, $\frac{5}{14}$ after observing two tails, and remains at $\frac{1}{2}$ after either observing HT or not observing any coin tosses.

If agent 1 announces $\frac{9}{14}$, agent 2 can then infer that agent 1 got to observe coin tosses and observed HH. Agent 2 now also gets to potentially observe coin tosses. Assume that agent 2 also observed HH. Agent 2 then knows that in total the outcome of the four coin tosses was $HHHH$ and, using Bayes' rule, updates to the belief

$$\mathbb{P}(B|HHHH) = \frac{81}{98} \times \frac{3}{4} + \frac{16}{98} \times \frac{1}{2} + \frac{1}{98} \times \frac{1}{4} = \frac{69}{98}.$$

Upon announcing these beliefs, agent 1 understands that there were in total four observations with realization $HHHH$, and updates to the same posterior as agent 1. At that point the two agents' beliefs are the same, and further announcements have no effect, so they may as well stop announcing their beliefs. This sequence of events then leads to node (a) in the figure. Here, the node value of $(\frac{69}{98}, \frac{69}{98})$ in node (a) represents agent 1's and 2's ultimate beliefs, respectively.

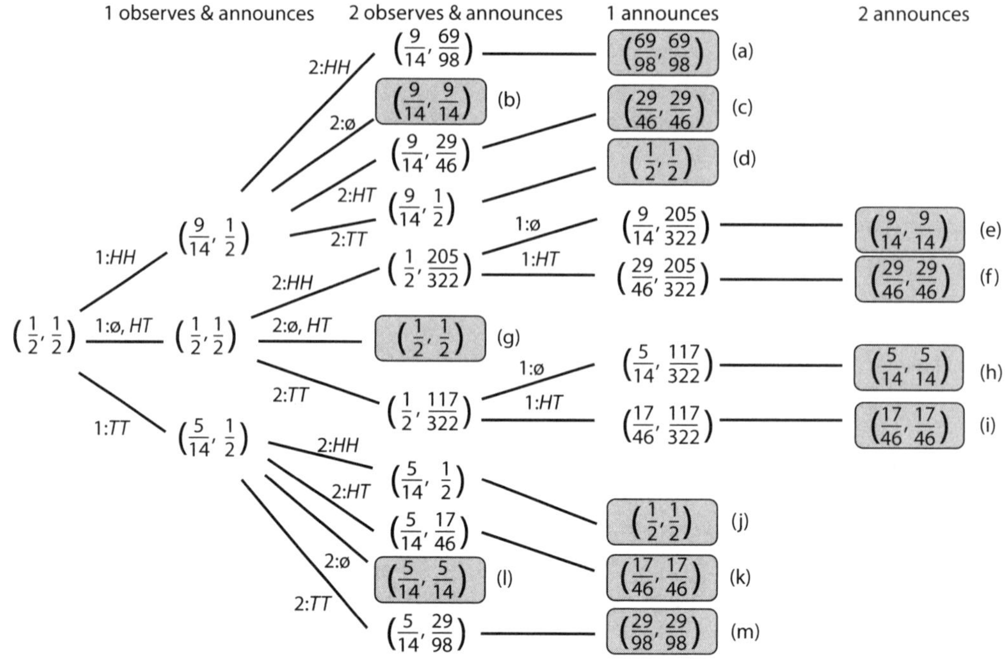

Figure 15.2: Coin toss example.

In this case, the two agents completely infer each others' information from the announcements, but this is not the case in general. Consider, for example, the middle branch, where agent 1 observes either *HT*, or does not get to make any observations. In either case (s)he sticks with the same posterior $p^1 = \frac{1}{2}$.

Assume also that agent 2 is in the same situation, and either observes nothing or *HT*. Agent 2 then argues that regardless of whether agent 1's state is Ø or *HT*, there is no basis for revising the belief away from $\frac{1}{2}$, either based on agent 1's announcement or on agent 2's own potential observation. Agent 2 also announces a belief of $\frac{1}{2}$, and agent 1 then makes the same argument as agent 2. Again, no further belief announcements will affect the agents' beliefs. We end up in node (g). Also, again, the two agents end up with the same posteriors.

However, they do not share the same information set in this case, since it is still private information to each agent whether they observed coin tosses or not. Indeed, they may well disagree about the conditional probability that the coin is of a specific type, e.g., $\mathbb{P}(\text{FC})$, where an agent who makes an *HT* observation will view this probability as being higher than $\frac{1}{3}$, based on Bayesian updating.

Going through all the different variations in the figure (13 altogether, (a)–(m)), we see that under each scenario, the two agents end up having the same beliefs, once the common-knowledge node is reached, i.e., they never agree to disagree, in line with Aumann's result.

Before we move on, let us also check scenario (e), which is the one that takes the longest before the agents converge on the same posterior beliefs. Under this scenario, agent 1 did not get to make any observations, and agent 2 observes *HH*. Agent 2 initially does not know whether agent 1's state is Ø or *HT*. Using Bayes' rule, agent 2 calculates the relative likelihood of these two different states, as follows: First, the agent calculates the conditional probability of observing *HT*, given that the agent gets to observe coin tosses, as

$$q=\frac{1}{3}\times\frac{4}{9}+\frac{1}{3}\times\frac{1}{2}+\frac{1}{3}\times\frac{4}{9}=\frac{25}{54}.$$

Then (s)he calculates

$$\mathbb{P}(1 \text{ observed } HT|p^1=\tfrac{1}{2})=\frac{(1-z)q}{(1-z)q+z}+\frac{\frac{54}{79}\times\frac{25}{54}}{\frac{54}{79}\times\frac{25}{54}+\frac{25}{79}}=\frac{1}{2}.$$

So the two likelihoods, that agent 1 observed Ø or HT, are the same. Agent 2's updated belief is therefore the average of the beliefs under observations HH and $HHHT$, i.e.,

$$p^2=\frac{1}{2}\times\frac{9}{14}+\frac{1}{2}\times\frac{29}{46}=\frac{205}{322}.$$

Upon agent 2's announcement, agent 1 immediately understands that agent 2 must have observed HH, updates to either $p^1=\frac{9}{14}$ (if agent 1 observed Ø) or $\frac{29}{46}$ (if (s)he observed HT), and announces. This allows agent 2 to infer which of agent 1's two states was the correct one, and convergence is obtained to node (e) in this case, since agent 1 observed Ø.

The argument so far provides some intuition for why heterogeneous information may not immediately lead to heterogeneous behavior of investors and high trading volume. Let us see what happens in a simple market with heterogeneous information. We take the model in section 5.1 as a starting point. Recall that there are K CARA investors and the risky asset pays the liquidating dividend $\widetilde{D}\sim N(\bar{X},\sigma^2)$. Here, we have changed notation for expected payoff from a to $\bar{X}$ and for variance from b^2 to σ^2, to be consistent with notation in the literature.

We study a slightly generalized version of that model, in which investors are allowed to have different risk aversion, so that γ_k denotes the risk-aversion coefficient of investor k. We also restrict ourselves to the case when the risk-free rate is $R^f=1$. A similar market-clearing argument to before then implies that

$$P_0=\bar{X}-\frac{S}{K}\bar{\gamma}\sigma^2, \tag{15.1}$$

where

$$\bar{\gamma}=\left(\frac{1}{K}\sum_{k=1}^{K}\frac{1}{\gamma_k}\right)^{-1}$$

is the harmonic average of the agents' risk-aversion coefficients.

Now assume that there is some more information available about $\widetilde{D}$. Specifically, there are K noisy signals about $\widetilde{D}$:

$$y_k=\widetilde{D}+\tilde{\epsilon}_k. \tag{15.2}$$

Here, $\epsilon_k\sim N(0,s^2)$ are i.i.d. and independent of $\widetilde{D}$. Clearly, such a signal is useful for drawing inferences about $\widetilde{D}$, especially if the noise term $\tilde{\epsilon}_k$ has low variance, s^2. In the extreme case where $s=0$, the signal perfectly reveals $\widetilde{D}$.

As a benchmark, assume that all investors observe all the signals, $\tilde{y}_1,\ldots,\tilde{y}_K$. What will they learn about $\widetilde{D}$? This is a problem of Bayesian updating, which the *projection theorem* solves for us:

Theorem 15.2 (Projection theorem). *Consider the multivariate normal distribution*

$$\begin{pmatrix}\tilde{\mathbf{x}}\\ \tilde{\mathbf{y}}\end{pmatrix}\sim N\left(\begin{pmatrix}\mu_x\\ \mu_y\end{pmatrix},\begin{pmatrix}\Sigma_{xx} & \Sigma_{xy}\\ \Sigma_{yx} & \Sigma_{yy}\end{pmatrix}\right),$$

where $\tilde{\mathbf{x}} \in \mathbb{R}^K$, $\tilde{\mathbf{y}} \in \mathbb{R}^L$. *Then the conditional distribution of* $\tilde{\mathbf{x}}$ *given* $\tilde{\mathbf{y}}$ *is*

$$\tilde{\mathbf{x}}|\tilde{\mathbf{y}} \sim N(\mu_x + \Sigma_{xy}\Sigma_{yy}^{-1}(\tilde{\mathbf{y}} - \mu_y), \Sigma_{xx} - \Sigma_{xy}\Sigma_{yy}^{-1}\Sigma_{yx}).$$

Note that the conditional variance does not depend on the realization of $\tilde{\mathbf{y}}$, which is very helpful for the analysis and results.

In our case, $\tilde{\mathbf{x}} = \widetilde{D}$, and $\tilde{\mathbf{y}} = (\tilde{y}_1, \ldots, \tilde{y}_K)'$, and therefore $\mu_x = \bar{X}$, $\mu_y = \bar{X}\mathbf{1}$, $\Sigma_{xx} = \sigma^2$, $\Sigma_{yx} = \Sigma'_{xy} = \sigma^2\mathbf{1}$, and $\Sigma_{yy} = s^2\mathbf{I} + \sigma^2\mathbf{1}\mathbf{1}'$. Note that $\Sigma_{yy}^{-1} = \frac{1}{s^2}\mathbf{I} - \frac{\sigma^2}{s^2(s^2+\sigma^2 K)}\mathbf{1}\mathbf{1}'$. This leads to

$$\widetilde{D}|\tilde{\mathbf{y}} \sim N\left(\bar{X} + \frac{\sigma^2}{\sigma^2 + \frac{s^2}{K}}(\bar{y} - \bar{X}), \sigma^2 - \frac{\sigma^4}{\sigma^2 + \frac{s^2}{K}}\right), \tag{15.3}$$

where $\bar{y} = \frac{1}{K}\sum_k \tilde{y}_k$ is the average of the signals.

Thus, the investors use the information provided by the signals to update to the new expectation of payout $\bar{X} + \frac{\sigma^2}{\sigma^2+s^2/K}(\bar{y} - \bar{X})$ and the new variance $\sigma^2 - \frac{\sigma^4}{\sigma^2+s^2/K}$. Since the posterior is also normally distributed, the price conditional on the updated beliefs is

$$P_0 = \bar{X} + \frac{\sigma^2}{\sigma^2 + \frac{s^2}{K}}(\bar{y} - \bar{X}) - \frac{S}{K}\bar{\gamma}\left(\sigma^2 - \frac{\sigma^4}{\sigma^2 + \frac{s^2}{K}}\right). \tag{15.4}$$

It is unsurprising that only the average of the signals, $\bar{y}$, is used in the updating, since the signals are all equally informative. Indeed, one verifies easily that in this setting, the same equilibrium arises if agents, instead of the K signals, simply observe $\bar{y} \sim N(\widetilde{D}, \frac{s^2}{K})$. In other words, $\bar{y}$ is a sufficient statistic for the information provided by the $\tilde{y}_k$ signals.

Note also that an individual agent's demand, measured in number of shares, is $\frac{S}{K}\frac{\bar{\gamma}}{\gamma_k}$, which is easy to see from the market-clearing condition. This is the agent's equilibrium demand regardless of whether the signals are observed by agents or not. Under another interpretation, consider a setting where agents initially do not observe any signals. The asset is then traded at price (15.1). Agents then simultaneously observe the K signals, and the price jumps to (15.4), based on their more precise information. However, *no trade occurs*.

Similar to the stamp example, if the agents are equally well informed and the initial allocation is Pareto efficient, there is no reason for them to trade when new information arrives. A *no trade theorem* based on such an argument in a more general setting was derived in Milgrom and Stokey (1982). In such a setting, large trading volume will therefore not be explained by the arrival of new information alone.

Now, let's move to the situation where the agents' get different pieces of information. Specifically, assume that agent k observes only the signal $\tilde{y}_k$. At first sight, this seems promising if the goal is to generate trade. In this situation, it seems like agents arrive at different posterior distributions of $\widetilde{D}$ when using the projection theorem to update. They should therefore submit different demand schedules, potentially generating trade and speculation.

This environment is basically the one introduced in Grossman (1976) who shows that, quite surprisingly, the equilibrium under this alternative setting is identical to the one we just studied, where all agents observe all signals. A key clue to this result is that agents get additional information from the market-clearing price, just like in the case with the two stamp collectors. Indeed, agent k, who submits a so-called *limit order* that allows the number of shares demanded to depend on P_0, can condition the trade on the information set $\{\tilde{y}_k, P_0\}$, not just the signal information, $\{\tilde{y}_k\}$.

What will the market-clearing price be in this case? A priori, this is unclear. It may well be that the price function is such that an agent's posterior belief is not normally distributed, in which case the CARA agent's demand function may look quite different from $\frac{\mu-r}{\gamma_k\sigma^2}$, i.e., different from the ratio of (conditional) expected excess returns to variance, scaled with the reciprocal of the risk-aversion coefficient.

Fortunately, it turns out that because of the specific setting, the equilibrium price function is linear in all the signals, which allows us to stay in the multivariate normal setting. The way to verify this is to conjecture a linear price function, and verify that it works. We proceed as follows: We assume that the equilibrium price function is of the form

$$P_0 = \pi_0 + \sum_{k=1}^{K} \pi_k \tilde{y}_k. \tag{15.5}$$

Agents know this, and therefore use P_0 to gain information about $\widetilde{D}$. Specifically, an agent uses the projection theorem to calculate $\widetilde{D}|\{\tilde{y}_k, P_0\}$. We define $\pi = \sum_{k=1}^{K} \pi_k$ and the vector $(\widetilde{D}, \tilde{y}_k, P_0)$, to get

$$\mu = \begin{bmatrix} \bar{X} \\ \bar{X} \\ \pi_0 + a\pi \end{bmatrix}, \quad \Sigma = \begin{bmatrix} \sigma^2 & \sigma^2 & \pi\sigma^2 \\ \sigma^2 & \sigma^2 + s^2 & \pi\sigma^2 + \pi_k s^2 \\ \pi\sigma^2 & \pi\sigma^2 + \pi_k s^2 & \pi^2\sigma^2 + s^2 \sum_{k=1}^{K} \pi_k^2. \end{bmatrix}.$$

Using the projection theorem, each agent then calculates the conditional expectation and variance of $\widetilde{D}$, which will be of the form

$$\bar{D}_k = E[\widetilde{D}|\tilde{y}_k, P_0] = \alpha_{0k} + \alpha_{1k}\tilde{y}_k + \alpha_{2k}P_0,$$
$$\beta_k = \mathrm{Var}(\widetilde{D}|\tilde{y}_k, P_0).$$

The actual expressions for the coefficients α_{0k}, α_{1k}, α_{2k}, and β_k may in general be messy. Also, even though the signal distributions, $\tilde{y}_k$, are identical, the coefficients will in general vary across agents, depending on π_k.

Based on agents' posterior beliefs about $\bar{D}_k$ and β_k, they choose their demands, z_k, $k = 1, \dots, K$, to maximize

$$E[u(W_{0,k} + z_k(\widetilde{D} - P_0))].$$

Here, z_k represents the number of shares they demand,[1] and since $\widetilde{D}$ is conditionally normally distributed, this leads to demand

$$z_k = \frac{1}{P_0} \times \frac{\frac{\bar{D}_k}{P_0} - R^f}{\gamma_k \frac{\beta_k}{P_0^2}} = \frac{\alpha_{0k} + \alpha_{1k}\tilde{y}_k + (\alpha_{2k} - R^f)P_0}{\gamma_k\beta_k}.$$

Recall that, per assumption, $R^f = 1$. The market-clearing condition therefore becomes

$$S = \sum_{k=1}^{K} z_k = \sum_{k=1}^{K} \frac{1}{\gamma_k\beta_k}(\alpha_{0k} + \alpha_{1k}\tilde{y}_k + (\alpha_{2k} - 1)P_0).$$

We define $\eta = \sum_{k=1}^{K} \frac{\alpha_{2k}-1}{\gamma_k\beta_k}$ and reorganize the terms to get

$$\eta P_0 = \left(\sum_{k=1}^{K} \frac{\alpha_{0k}}{\gamma_k\beta_k} - S\right) + \sum_{k=1}^{K} \frac{\alpha_{1k}}{\gamma_k\beta_k}\tilde{y}_k. \tag{15.6}$$

[1] We follow the notation in the literature, which uses α_{1k} and α_{2k} to represent the demand schedule coefficients, and therefore use z_k here for the demand, instead of the α-notation used in previous chapters.

Comparing (15.5) and (15.6), it is clear that the necessary and sufficient conditions for the $\{\pi_k\}_k$ coefficients to define an equilibrium are

$$\eta\pi_k = \frac{\alpha_{1k}}{\gamma_k\beta_k}, \quad k=1,\ldots,K, \tag{15.7}$$

$$\eta\pi_0 = \left(\sum_{k=1}^{K}\frac{\alpha_{0k}}{\gamma_k\beta_k} - S\right). \tag{15.8}$$

An equilibrium is then defined as a set of coefficients, $\{\pi_k\}_k$, $k=0,\ldots,K$, and associated pricing function defined by (15.5), such that when agents use the projection theorem to derive the coefficients $\{\alpha_{0k}\}_k$, $\{\alpha_{1k}\}_k$, and $\{\alpha_{2k}\}_k$, these coefficients satisfy the system of equations defined by (15.7, 15.8). In words, agents form posterior beliefs and demands based on the pricing function, and their aggregate demand is such that market clearance occurs at the postulated price, for all realizations of the signals, $\{\tilde{y}_k\}_k$.

We now have the following result:

Theorem 15.3 (Grossman 1976). *There exists an equilibrium with coefficients*

$$\pi_k = \frac{\sigma^2}{K\sigma^2+s^2}, \quad k=1,\ldots,K,$$

$$\pi_0 = \frac{s^2}{K\sigma^2+s^2}\bar{X} - \frac{S}{K}\bar{\gamma}\beta,$$

where $\beta = \sigma^2(1-\frac{K\sigma^2}{K\sigma^2+s^2})$.

Proof. We need to verify that under the postulated coefficients defined in the theorem, agent aggregate demand is such that the market clears at the postulated price. Note that $\pi_k = \Pi$ is the same for all k in this case, and therefore $\pi = K\Pi$. So each agent's unconditional expected return vector and covariance matrix are of the form

$$\mu = \begin{bmatrix} \bar{X} \\ \bar{X} \\ \pi_0 + \bar{X}K\Pi \end{bmatrix} = \begin{bmatrix} \bar{X} \\ \bar{X} \\ \pi_0 + \bar{X}\frac{K\sigma^2}{K\sigma^2+s^2} \end{bmatrix}$$

and

$$\Sigma = \begin{bmatrix} \sigma^2 & \sigma^2 & K\Pi\sigma^2 \\ \sigma^2 & \sigma^2+s^2 & K\Pi\sigma^2+\Pi s^2 \\ K\Pi\sigma^2 & K\Pi\sigma^2+\Pi s^2 & K^2\Pi^2\sigma^2+s^2K\Pi^2. \end{bmatrix} = \begin{bmatrix} \sigma^2 & \sigma^2 & \frac{K\sigma^4}{K\sigma^2+s^2} \\ \sigma^2 & \sigma^2+s^2 & \sigma^2 \\ \frac{K\sigma^4}{K\sigma^2+s^2} & \sigma^2 & \frac{K\sigma^4}{K\sigma^2+s^2}. \end{bmatrix}.$$

Some algebra gives us

$$\Sigma_{yy}^{-1} = \frac{1}{\sigma^4 s^2(K-1)}\begin{bmatrix} K\sigma^4 & -\sigma^2(K\sigma^2+s^2) \\ -\sigma^2(K\sigma^2+s^2) & (\sigma^2+s^2)(K\sigma^2+s^2) \end{bmatrix},$$

and since $\Sigma_{xy} = (\sigma^2, \frac{K\sigma^4}{K\sigma^2+s^2})$, and therefore $\Sigma_{xy}\Sigma_{yy}^{-1} = (0,1)$, using the projection theorem we arrive at

$$E[\widetilde{D}|\tilde{y}_k, P_0] = \bar{X} - \pi_0 + P_0 - \bar{X}\frac{K\sigma^2}{K\sigma^2+s^2} = \bar{X}\frac{s^2}{K\sigma^2+s^2} - \pi_0 + P_0.$$

It follows that

$$\alpha_{0k} = \bar{X}\frac{s^2}{K\sigma^2+s^2} - \pi_0, \quad \alpha_{1k} = 0, \quad \text{and} \quad \alpha_{2k} = 1,$$

for $k=1,2,\ldots,K$. Moreover, $\Sigma_{xy}\Sigma_{yy}^{-1}\Sigma_{yx}=\frac{K\sigma^4}{K\sigma^2+s^2}$, so $\beta_k=\beta$, where

$$\beta=\Sigma_{xx}-\Sigma_{xy}\Sigma_{yy}^{-1}\Sigma_{yx}=\sigma^2\Big(1-\frac{K\sigma^2}{K\sigma^2+s^2}\Big),\quad k=1,2,\ldots,K.$$

Now, since $\alpha_{2k}=1$, it follows that $\eta=0$, and since $\alpha_{1k}=0$, (15.7) is satisfied for all k, so the coefficients π_k, $k=1,\ldots,K$, are consistent with equilibrium. It remains to determine π_0, such that (15.8) is satisfied, i.e., such that

$$0=\sum_{k=1}^{K}\frac{\alpha_{0k}}{\gamma_k\beta_k}-S.$$

When the expressions for α_{0k} are plugged in, we get

$$S=\frac{1}{\beta}\Big(\frac{s^2}{K\sigma^2+s^2}-\pi_0\Big)\sum_{k=1}^{K}\frac{1}{\gamma_k},$$

and equivalently,

$$\pi_0=\frac{s^2}{K\sigma^2+s^2}-\frac{S}{K}\bar{\gamma}\beta,$$

which is the expression for π_0 in the theorem. We are done. □

Corollary 15.1. *Equilibrium is fully revealing, in the sense that the equilibrium price is the same as when all agents receive all signals.*

This result immediately follows from verifying that the equilibrium pricing functions in the two economies, (15.4) and (15.5), are identical. A key observation for understanding the result is that when all the π_k coefficients are the same, then observing P_0 is actually equivalent to observing $\bar{y}$, which in turn is a sufficient statistic for the posterior return distribution, as we discussed before. Thus, the equilibrium price provides all agents with all relevant information available, even if they each just observe one of the $\tilde{y}_k$ signals.

The result is closely related to the idea introduced in Hayek (1945) that markets serve a valuable role in aggregating information. Here, the price P_0 aggregates *all* the information that decentralized investors are sitting on. The result may therefore be viewed as very reassuring: not only do friction-free markets lead to Pareto-efficient allocations given that all investors are equally well informed, they also seem to resolve informational asymmetries, so that there is also information efficiency.

The markets are so efficient that investors do not even care about their private signals, which is why the α_k coefficients are all equal to zero. Now, upon some reflection, this is actually very strange. If no agent uses his/her own information when submitting the demand function, how are these signals then incorporated into the prices?

Another challenge with the result is that if this is how the market works in practice, individual agents will have no incentives to acquire costly information. Indeed, we may think of the private signals as being the outcome of an information-gathering process, where individual agents spend resources (for example, time, purchasing a proprietary dataset, or interviewing experts) to obtain the information. The reason they do this is because they wish to obtain an informational advantage over the rest of the market, and thereby increase their expected profits (and expected utility).

However, if all private information is reflected in prices, why would anyone spend any resources on information gathering? There is a huge free-rider problem, as discussed in Grossman and Stiglitz (1980). In the absence of any possibility to make profits from gathering private information, we may then actually expect the market to be really uninformative in the current model, leading to the opposite outcome to that described in Hayek (1945). For these reasons, we may therefore search for a model that is not quite as dramatic with respect to the informational efficiency of the equilibrium outcome.

15.2 Noisy Rational Expectations Equilibrium (NREE) Models

A way to get away from the "dramatic" informational efficiency of the model in the previous section is to introduce some additional noise that "hides" some private information in equilibrium. A very useful approach is to assume that the risky asset's supply is stochastic, and not known by the market participants. As a consequence, when an agent sees a high price, (s)he does not know how much is because of a high realization of other agents' signals and how much is due to low asset supply. This idea was formalized in Hellwig (1980), in a setting that builds upon that in Grossman (1976).

We make the same assumptions as before about the K CARA agents, with risk-aversion coefficients γ_k, who consume at $t=1$. We also assume that there is a risk-free asset in elastic supply, offering returns normalized to $R^f=1$. Similarly, the risky asset has the payoff $\widetilde{D}\sim N(\bar{X},\sigma^2)$ at $t=1$, and is traded at time 0 at price P_0. Each agent receives a noisy private signal about the asset's value:

$$\tilde{y}_k=\widetilde{D}+\tilde{\epsilon}_k, \quad k=1,\ldots,K,$$

$\epsilon_k\sim N(0,s_k^2)$, and the signals $\{\epsilon_i\}_k$, and $\widetilde{D}$ are jointly independent. So far, everything looks like before, except that we have allowed a more general signal structure than in the previous model, in that the signal precision may vary, hence the subscript in s_k^2.

Our main deviation from the previous model is in assuming that the asset is in stochastic supply. There are $\widetilde{Z}\sim N(\bar{Z},\Delta^2)$ shares available for trade, where $\widetilde{Z}$ is independent of $\widetilde{D}$ and $\{\epsilon_k\}_k$. Agents do not observe $\widetilde{Z}$ and are not allowed to condition on the variable when submitting their demand schedules. When $\Delta=0$, we have the previous model, with $S=\bar{Z}$. Here we assume $\Delta^2>0$. We will not dwell upon what the source of the stochastic supply is; several motivations have been discussed in the literature, e.g., that supply is net of so-called *noise traders* who trade for exogenous reasons (for example, for liquidity needs), or more generally that it is a reduced-form assumption that represents random risk-bearing capacity of the market.

As before, we assume that agents are price takers who submit demand functions $z_i(\tilde{y}_i,P_0)$, but here we postulate that the price function is linear, not only in signal realizations, but also in realized supply, so that

$$P_0=\pi_0+\sum_{k=1}^{K}\pi_k\tilde{y}_k-q\widetilde{Z}, \quad \pi=\sum_{k=1}^{K}\pi_k.$$

As before, the vector $(\widetilde{D},\tilde{y}_k,P_0)$ is then jointly normally distributed, with mean $(\bar{X},\bar{X},\pi_0+\pi\bar{X}-q\bar{Z})$ and associated covariance matrix

$$\Sigma=\begin{bmatrix}\sigma^2 & \sigma^2 & \pi\sigma^2\\ \sigma^2 & \sigma^2+s_k^2 & \pi\sigma^2+\pi_k s_k^2\\ \pi\sigma^2 & \pi\sigma^2+\pi_k s_k^2 & \pi^2\sigma^2+\sum_k\pi_k^2 s_k^2+q^2\Delta^2\end{bmatrix}.$$

The covariance matrix has an identical structure to the previous model, except for the minor difference that signal variance s_k^2 may vary across agents, and the major difference that additional variance from the stochastic supply increases the price variance, $\mathrm{Var}(P_0) = (\Sigma)_{3,3}$, by $q^2\Delta^2$ compared with the model with known supply.

As before, we use the projection theorem to infer that $\widetilde{X}|\{\tilde{y}_k, P_0\}$ is normally distributed and such that

$$E[\widetilde{X}|\tilde{y}_k, P_0] = \alpha_{0k} + \alpha_{1k}\tilde{y}_k + \alpha_{2k}P_0,$$

$$\mathrm{Var}(\widetilde{X}|\tilde{y}_k, P_0) = \beta_k,$$

and as before, this leads to agent demand

$$z_k = \frac{\alpha_{0k} + \alpha_{1k}\tilde{y}_k + (\alpha_{2k} - 1)P_0}{\gamma_k\beta_k}$$

(here, β_k varies across agents because of the different signal precisions). Market clearing then implies

$$P_0(\widetilde{Z}, \{\tilde{y}_k\}_k) = \left[\sum_k \frac{1-\alpha_{2k}}{\gamma_i\beta_i}\right]^{-1}\left[\sum_k \frac{\alpha_{0k} + \alpha_{1k}\tilde{y}_k}{\gamma_k\beta_k} - \widetilde{Z}\right].$$

The consistency conditions that need to be satisfied for the coefficients $\{\pi_k\}_k$ and q to define an equilibrium are

$$q = \left[\sum_k \frac{1-\alpha_{2k}}{\gamma_k\beta_k}\right]^{-1},$$

$$\pi_k = q\frac{\alpha_{1k}}{\gamma_k\beta_k},$$

$$\pi_0 = q\sum_k \frac{\alpha_{0k}}{\gamma_k\beta_k}.$$

In contrast to the previous model, closed-form expressions for the values of the coefficients are in general unobtainable. However, the existence of an equilibrium is in general guaranteed, as shown by the following:

Theorem 15.4 (Hellwig 1980). *There exist coefficients π_0, $\{\pi_k\}_k$, $k = 1, \ldots, K$, and q, and an associated equilibrium pricing function*

$$P_0 = \pi_0 + \sum_{k=1}^{K} \pi_k\tilde{y}_k - q\widetilde{Z}.$$

Proof. The proof can be found in Hellwig (1980). It is based on Brouwer's fixed-point theorem, just like our proof of equilibrium existence in the Arrow–Debreu economy. □

When the number of agents, K, tends to infinity, one can obtain a closed-form solution in the limit, under appropriate assumptions. Specifically, we define the *large economy* as the limit when $K \to \infty$, in a sequence of economies where we keep per-agent supply fixed, i.e., so that supply in the economy with K agents is $\widetilde{Z}(K) = K\widetilde{Z} \sim N(KZ^*, K^2\Delta^{*2})$. We assume that

$$A^* = \lim_{K\to\infty} \frac{1}{K}\sum_{k=1}^{K}\frac{1}{\gamma_k},$$

$$B^* = \lim_{K\to\infty} \frac{1}{K}\sum_{k=1}^{K} \frac{1}{\gamma_k s_k^2}$$

are well-defined limits. We then have the following result:

Theorem 15.5. *When $K \to \infty$, the price function converges to*

$$P_0^* = \pi_0^* + \pi^* \widetilde{D} - q^* \widetilde{Z}, \tag{15.9}$$

where

$$\pi_0^* = \frac{\bar{X}\Delta^{*2}A^* + \sigma^2 Z^* A^* B^*}{A^*\Delta^{*2} + \sigma^2 B^* \Delta^{*2} + \sigma^2 A^* B^{*2}},$$

$$q^* = \frac{\sigma^2\Delta^{*2} + \sigma^2 A^* B^*}{A^*\Delta^{*2} + \sigma^2 B^* \Delta^{*2} + \sigma^2 A^* B^{*2}},$$

$$\pi^* = B^* q^*.$$

Individual agent demand converges to

$$z_k = \frac{1}{\gamma_k \sigma^2(\Delta^{*2} + A^*B^*)}(Z^*B^*\sigma^2 + \Delta^{*2}(\bar{X} - P_0)) + \frac{\tilde{y}_k - P_0}{\gamma_k s_k^2}. \tag{15.10}$$

Proof. The proof can be found in Hellwig (1980). □

To explore the differences between equilibrium in this model and the one without noise traders, let us first focus on the special case when $s_k = s$ is the same for all agents, as is $\gamma_k = \gamma$. In this case $A^* = \frac{1}{\gamma}$ and $B^* = \frac{1}{\gamma s^2}$. For a constructive comparison, we should keep the per-agent supply of the asset constant when we increase the number of agents in Grossman's model, i.e., in the market with K agents we set the supply to SK. It then follows from theorem 15.3 that $\lim_{K\to\infty} \pi_k(K) = 0$, $\lim_{K\to\infty} \pi_0(K) = 0$, and $\lim_{K\to\infty} \sum_{k=1}^{K} \pi_k = 1$.

Moreover, from the LLN, we have $\lim_{K\to\infty} \bar{y}(K) \equiv \widetilde{D}$ (almost surely). Consequently, in that limit of the model without noise traders, we get the pricing

$$P_0 = \bar{y} \equiv \widetilde{D}.$$

So there is no residual uncertainty about the asset's value in the large economy version of Grossman's model.

In Hellwig's model, the large economy limit behaves quite differently. Indeed, assume that $\bar{X} \geq 0$. Then all of the coefficients

$$\pi_0^* = \frac{\bar{X}\Delta^{*2}\frac{1}{\gamma} + \sigma^2 Z^* \frac{1}{\gamma^2 s^2}}{\frac{1}{\gamma}\Delta^{*2} + \frac{1}{\gamma s^2}\sigma^2\Delta^{*2} + \sigma^2\frac{1}{\gamma^3 s^4}},$$

$$q^* = \gamma s^2\left(1 - \frac{s^2}{s^2 + \sigma^2 + \frac{\sigma^2}{\Delta^{*2}\gamma^2 s^2}}\right),$$

$$\pi^* = 1 - \frac{s^2}{s^2 + \sigma^2 + \frac{\sigma^2}{\Delta^{*2}\gamma^2 s^2}},$$

are strictly positive, and also $\pi^* < 1$. So the price defined in (15.9) does not incorporate all the information jointly contained by the signals, and it is also affected by the realization of the supply shock. The equilibrium is not fully revealing. For small γ, however, the equilibrium is close to revealing, since it is easy to show that $\pi_0^* \to 0$, $q^* \to 0$, and $\pi^* \to 1$, when $\gamma \to 0$.

Another contrast with Grossman's model is that investor demand, as defined in (15.10), depends on the private signal, avoiding the "strangeness" of the fully revealing equilibrium in the former model. Indeed, the rightmost term in (15.10) is the demand associated with a CARA agent who believes that $\widetilde{D} \sim N(\tilde{y}_k, s^2)$, and the smaller s^2 is, the more aggressive this part is with respect to differences between the market price and the signal. An agent with a precise signal (low s^2) will, all else being equal, be more aggressive and—as one can show—have higher expected utility. Thus, in the Hellwig model, agents have incentives to find out information about the asset's value. We conclude that NREE models provide important insights beyond what is obtained in equilibrium models that fully reveal information.

15.3 Strategic Investors

One assumption we have made throughout our equilibrium analysis is that agents are price takers. This is often a (sufficiently) realistic assumption, and it simplifies our lives a lot. There are important situations, however, when the assumption is too simplistic. Consider, for example, a fairly small firm with a limited number of investors. One investor—an *insider*—finds out important private information about the future prospects of the firm. There are also noise traders in the market. How will the market behave? The term insider should not be confused with "insider trading," which is illegal. The term within the context of this model simply means that the insider has superior information.

We first use Hellwig's model to solve the problem, assuming that all agents have the same risk-aversion coefficient and that the other agents receive extremely noisy signals, i.e., with very high s_k^2. In the large economy, this leads to $B^* \approx 0$,

$$\pi_0^* \approx \bar{X},$$
$$q^* \approx \gamma\sigma^2,$$
$$\pi^* \approx 0,$$

and the corresponding approximate pricing function,

$$P_0 \approx \bar{X} - \gamma\sigma^2\widetilde{Z}.$$

This is the same as in the model with no private signals (15.1), taking into account that $\widetilde{Z}$ is the per-agent supply of the asset. The informed agent, who has a small s_k^2, then submits demand according to (15.10), which because $B^* \approx 0$ is

$$z_k \approx \frac{1}{\gamma}\left(\frac{\bar{X} - P_0}{\sigma^2} + \frac{\tilde{y}_k - P_0}{s_k^2}\right). \tag{15.11}$$

This makes sense. The second part of the demand function allows the agent to earn higher expected profits than the other agents.

Now, what if the informed agents actually make up a nonnegligible fraction of the total investor population? Maybe 0.1% of the population have extremely precise information, so that s_k^2 is very close to zero for these agents. A similar analysis shows that in this case, we get $\pi_0 \approx 0$, $q^* \approx 0$, and $\pi^* \approx 1$. So, just like in the situation when the risk-aversion coefficient was low, we are basically back to the fully revealing equilibrium with $P_0 \approx \widetilde{D}$. As a consequence, the well-informed agents make almost no profits: they compete away almost all their informational advantage.

The previous argument assumed that the informed agents were price takers. What if they realized that their trades had an impact on prices, and could also coordinate so they did not compete against each other? Would they not submit less aggressive demand schedules, so that equilibrium prices were less revealing and profits therefore higher? This would be similar to the behavior we find in a market with a monopolist. The questions are really interesting, and very relevant when the mass of informed investors is large enough so that they affect prices, and small enough so that they can cooperate.

Unfortunately, the NREE model we have studied so far is not easily adapted to such a setting, where an informed agent strategically takes price impact into account. Kyle (1985) solves the problem in a different type of model, which we now discuss. We focus on the static version of the model with two dates, $t=0,1$. We will then briefly discuss the continuous-time version, which is often used.

There is a risky asset, with time-1 value

$$\tilde{v} \sim N(\bar{X}, \sigma^2).$$

There is also a noise trader, in total demanding $\tilde{u}$ shares of the assets, where

$$\tilde{u} \sim N(0, \sigma_u^2),$$

and where $\tilde{u}$ and $\tilde{v}$ are independent. As before, this noise trader trades for exogenous reasons, and is not modeled in detail.

In addition, there is a risk-neutral insider, who knows the realization of $\tilde{v}$. In contrast to the previous models, the insider here submits a *market order*, i.e., (s)he commits to buying or selling a fixed number of shares, x, regardless of the market-clearing price. The insider thus has perfect information about $\tilde{v}$, but it is assumed that (s)he does not know the realization of $\tilde{u}$.

Finally, there is competitive risk-neutral *market maker*, who does not know $\tilde{v}$ but who observes the total order of the insider and noise trader, $z=\tilde{u}+x$. The market maker takes the opposite position to the total insider and noise-trader demand, in total holding the position $-z$. Being competitive, which in practice means representing a large number of identical market makers, (s)he sets the market price equal to the expected value of $\tilde{v}$, given the information contained in z.

Both the insider and the market maker know the structure of the economy. In contrast to the previous model, where all agents were price takers, here the insider understands that his/her market order x affects the price: the higher x is, the higher the price. This provides an incentive for the insider to trade less. Altogether, the insider comes up with the demand function $x(\tilde{v})$. As we will see, it will follow naturally that this demand function is strictly increasing, i.e., the higher $\tilde{v}$ is, the more shares the insider demands.

The market maker's inference problem is to understand how much of total demand is due to x. If the market maker knew x, and the insider's demand function is invertible (for example, because it is strictly increasing), the actual value, $\tilde{v}$, could be inferred. But since the market maker observes $z=x(\tilde{v})+\tilde{u}$ rather than $x(\tilde{v})$, (s)he faces an inference problem, finding $E[\tilde{v}|z]$. The solution to this inference problem leads to the competitive maker's price function, $p(z)=E[\tilde{v}|z]$.

An equilibrium is now defined as a demand function and a price function that are jointly consistent, in the following sense:

Definition 15.2. An equilibrium is given by a demand function, $x\colon \mathbb{R}\to\mathbb{R}$, and a price function $p\colon \mathbb{R}\to\mathbb{R}$, so that jointly,

- given the market maker's price function, the demand function maximizes expected profits for all realizations of $\tilde{v}$:

$$x(\tilde{v}) = \arg\max_x E[(\tilde{v} - p(x + \tilde{u}))x|\tilde{v}],$$

- given the insider's demand function, price equals the expected value of the asset, conditioned on total demand:

$$p(z) = E[\tilde{v}|\tilde{u} + x(\tilde{v}) = z].$$

We can now show the following result:

Theorem 15.6 (Kyle 1985, static model). *Define* $\beta = \frac{\sigma_u}{\sigma}$, *and* $\lambda = \frac{1}{2\beta}$. *Then there exists an equilibrium in which both x and p are linear functions:*

$$x(\tilde{v}) = \beta(\tilde{v} - \bar{X}), \quad p(z) = \bar{X} + \lambda z.$$

This equilibrium is unique among the set of equilibrium pairs (x, p), *for which at least one of the two functions is linear.*

Proof. We conjecture price and demand functions, of the linear form $x(v) = \beta v + x_0$ and $p(z) = p_0 + \lambda z$, $\beta > 0$, $\lambda > 0$, and show that these functions are consistent, in that if the insider has a linear strategy, the market maker's pricing function will be linear, and vice versa. We then find the coefficients that make the two functions jointly consistent.

We first start with the insider, who, given the market maker's pricing function and knowledge of $\tilde{v}$, maximizes

$$\begin{aligned}\Pi &= \max_x E[(\tilde{v} - p(x + \tilde{u}))x|\tilde{v}]\\ &= \max_x E[(\tilde{v} - p_0 - \lambda(x + \tilde{u}))x|\tilde{v}]\\ &= \max_x (\tilde{v} - p_0)x - \lambda x^2.\end{aligned}$$

The solution is

$$x = \frac{\tilde{v} - p_0}{2\lambda}.$$

So, indeed, x is linear in $\tilde{v}$ if the market maker's price function is linear, and

$$\beta = \frac{1}{2\lambda}.$$

We next solve the market maker's problem, to set the price such that

$$p = E[\tilde{v}|\underbrace{\tilde{u} + \beta(\tilde{v} - p_0)}_{z}],$$

where we plugged in the insider's demand function that we just derived. The joint distribution of $\tilde{v}$ and $\tilde{u} + \beta(\tilde{v} - p_0)$ is

$$\begin{pmatrix}\tilde{v}\\ \tilde{u} + \beta(\tilde{v} - p_0)\end{pmatrix} \sim N\left(\begin{pmatrix}\bar{X}\\ \beta(\bar{X} - p_0)\end{pmatrix}, \begin{pmatrix}\sigma^2 & \beta\sigma^2\\ \beta\sigma^2 & \sigma_u^2 + \beta^2\sigma^2\end{pmatrix}\right).$$

Using the projection theorem, we get

$$E[\tilde{v}|z] = \bar{X} + \frac{\beta\sigma^2}{\sigma_u^2 + \beta^2\sigma^2}(z - \beta(\bar{X} - p_0)),$$

which gives us

$$\lambda = \frac{\beta\sigma^2}{\sigma_u^2 + \beta^2\sigma^2},$$

$$p_0 = \bar{X} - \frac{\beta\sigma^2}{\sigma_u^2 + \beta^2\sigma^2}\beta(\bar{X} - p_0).$$

The second of these equations implies that

$$p_0 = \bar{X},$$

and in the first equation, we use the previously derived relation, $\lambda = \frac{1}{2\beta}$, to write

$$\frac{1}{2\beta} = \frac{\beta\sigma^2}{\sigma_u^2 + \beta^2\sigma^2},$$

which leads to

$$\beta^2 = \frac{\sigma_u^2}{\sigma^2},$$

and therefore (since $\beta > 0$) to

$$\beta = \frac{\sigma_u}{\sigma}.$$

These unique linear demand and pricing functions therefore jointly define an equilibrium. Moreover, if one assumes one of the two functions to be linear, one infers that the other function is linear; uniqueness within the class defined in the theorem follows. □

The parameter λ, which is often denoted *Kyle's lambda*, has the natural interpretation of *liquidity*. It determines how much changes in demand impact prices. In equilibrium,

$$\text{Var}(\tilde{v}|p) = \frac{1}{2}\sigma^2.$$

So, on average, half of the insider's information is incorporated into the price. The market is therefore not informationally efficient. The reason is that the insider cannot reveal all information since it would take away any profit opportunity.

The insider's expected profits are

$$E[\tilde{\pi}] = \frac{1}{2}\sigma\sigma_u.$$

Thus, higher uncertainty, both about the value of the asset and about noise-trader demand, helps generate higher expected profits for the insider. Indeed, we would expect precise knowledge about $\tilde{v}$ to be more valuable if the market (represented by the market maker) has less information (σ is higher). With respect to uncertainty in noise-trader demand, two observations help provide intuition for the result: First, the insider "hides" his/her trades behind the noise traders, since the market maker observes $x + \tilde{u}$. A higher σ_u allows the insider to "hide" better.

Second, the market maker does not have any expected losses—the insider's expected profits are "paid" by the expected losses by the noise traders. If the noise traders were not present, the market would break down, since the market maker would not be willing to trade with the insider at any price. This is similar to the earlier example with the stamp collectors, where the market maker is at a fundamental disadvantage compared with the insider. Finally, note that the price is a sufficient statistic for $x + \tilde{u}$ in equilibrium. So, when the insider sees the market-clearing price, (s)he knows what the noise-trader demand was.

Kyle (1985) also develops a multiperiod model and, as the limit when the number of periods tends to infinity, a continuous-time model. We sketch the equilibrium in the continuous-time model, in which trading occurs continuously over time, $t \in [0, 1]$. In this case, the cumulative noise-trader demand between 0 and t is u_t, and over the infinitesimally short time period between t and $t + dt$, their increment in demand is

$$du_t = \sigma_u \, dW_t.$$

The market price at t is p_t, and the insider's profit generated from t to 1 is defined as π_t. Thus, π_0 represents the actual profit generated between 0 and 1, which no one knows at time 0 (including the insider), so it is random. In addition to the asset's value, $\tilde{v}$, the profit will depend on the realized noise-trader demand, $\{u_t\}_t, 0 \leq t \leq 1$. At $t = 1$, the asset's value, $\tilde{v}$, will be revealed, so $p_1 = \tilde{v}$. Moreover, at $t = 0$, no information has been incorporated into the price, so $p_0 = \bar{X}$.

The cumulative insider demand until t is x_t. This demand is conjectured to be a linear function of the difference between the instantaneous price, p_t, and the asset's value, $\tilde{v}$, with instantaneous slope coefficient, β_t, that is a deterministic function of t. Note that this specification is consistent with the linear specification we arrived at in the static model. So

$$dx_t = \beta_t(\tilde{v} - p_t) \, dt.$$

The cumulative total order flow between 0 and t, z_t, then satisfies

$$dz_t = dx_t + du_t.$$

Similarly, the market maker's pricing function is conjectured to be such that

$$dp_t = \lambda_t(dx_t + du_t),$$

i.e., the liquidity function λ_t, which is also assumed to be deterministic in the dynamic setting, determines the instantaneous price impact of instantaneous order flow.

The contribution to the insider's expected profit from trades in the remaining period from t to 1, π_t, then satisfies

$$d\pi_t = (\tilde{v} - p_t) \, dx_t,$$

i.e., the contribution to the total profit generated at t is $(\tilde{v} - p_t) \, dx_t$ (the change in market value generated by the position taken on at t is $(p_1 - p_t) \, dx_t$, and recall that $p_1 \equiv \tilde{v}$). The total value is then

$$\pi_t = \int_t^1 d\pi_t,$$

so the insider's problem at t is to maximize

$$E[\pi_t | \{p_s\}_{s \in \{0,t\}}, \tilde{v}] = E\left[\int_t^1 d\pi_s\right].$$

Moreover, the market maker sets the price at t so that the expected profit of time-t trades, given all public information at time t, is zero, i.e., such that

$$p_t = E[\tilde{v} | \{dz_s\}_{s \in \{0,t\}}].$$

An equilibrium is then given by functions $\lambda \colon [0, 1] \to \mathbb{R}$ and $\beta \colon [0, 1] \to \mathbb{R}$, such that the insider's and market maker's behavior are jointly consistent with these functions. The following result can be shown:

Theorem 15.7 (Kyle 1985, continuous-time model). *Equilibrium is given by the price and demand functions defined by*

$$\lambda_t = \frac{\sigma}{\sigma_u},$$

$$\beta_t = \frac{1}{\lambda(1-t)}.$$

The theorem provides a nice characterization of equilibrium, with several consequences. First, the asset's liquidity is the same over time (λ is a constant), i.e., the price impact of an additional unit of demand is the same, regardless of t. Second, the insider becomes increasingly aggressive in trading against deviations of prices from $\tilde{v}$ as time progresses (the $\frac{1}{1-t}$ part of the demand function, as characterized by β_t). One may think that this leads to dramatic trading volumes as $t \to 1$, but this intuition is actually false. Indeed, over time, price is becoming more and more informative, in such a way that p_t tends to $\tilde{v}$ as t tends to 1, offsetting the increased aggressiveness.

It is straightforward to verify that in equilibrium $\{dp_s\}_s$ and $\{dx_s + du_s\}_s$ contain the same information, in that one may infer one from the other. So, at t, the insider who has observed the price dynamics knows the realized noise-trader demand up until t. A measure of the market's *price informativeness* at time t is then given by the residual variance in the value of the asset, given what is publicly known. One can show that

$$\operatorname{Var}(\tilde{v}|\{dx_s + du_s\}_{s\in[0,t]}) = (1-t)\sigma^2.$$

Thus, the residual uncertainty in the asset's value decreases linearly in time, offsetting the increased aggressiveness of the insider's demand function. Note that the measure is lower the more informative prices are—it is zero when there is no residual uncertainty about the value of the asset.

The time-0 unconditional expected profits of the insider are

$$E[\pi_0] = \sigma\sigma_u,$$

thus having the same form as in the static model, but being twice as high. Intuitively, the continuous inflow of noise-trader demand allows the insider to hide more efficiently behind that demand.

So, to summarize some fundamental insights provided by the continuous-time model,

(i) the insider trades such that informativeness increases gradually over time, at a constant speed;
(ii) the price converges to the fundamental value as $t \to 1$, in such a way that price "looks" like a martingale from the uninformed market maker's perspective, whereas the time-1 price is known by someone with the insider's information;
(iii) the insider becomes increasingly aggressive in trading against mispricing over time;
(iv) liquidity—as measured by Kyle's lambda—is constant over time;
(v) welfare analysis is out of reach in this model, without further assumptions. From the risk-neutral insider's perspective, higher expected profits are of course always better, and the risk-neutral market maker always breaks even in expectation. But for a complete welfare analysis, the noise traders—who are losing money—also need to be explicitly modeled.

Acknowledgments

I have been very fortunate to have the support of great advisors and mentors throughout my academic career. Bertil Gustafsson, my thesis advisor in applied mathematics at the Department of Scientific Computing, Uppsala University, shared his deep knowledge of numerical analysis and many other insights, but also encouraged me to think independently and learn from my own mistakes. Leif Abrahamsson, who held a joint position at the Swedish Defense Research Agency (FOA) and Uppsala University during my years as a doctoral student, was also very helpful and supportive during this period. Björn Engquist and Gregory Beylkin hosted visits, to UCLA in 1994 and to the University of Boulder Colorado in 1995, respectively.

Raphy Coifman, invited me to do a postdoc at the Department of Mathematics, Yale University, between 1997 and 1999, and was, in addition to being a great mentor and collaborator, always very supportive—even lending me his car before I could purchase one myself. Peter Jones at the Yale math department also took me under his wing, sharing his tremendously deep knowledge of analysis, and also helping my wife Petronella and me get over the homesickness we might occasionally feel. Working with my office mate, Moshe Israeli, on computer tomography algorithms was a great pleasure during this period. I also had many great discussions with Petter Kolm and Michel Nahon, who were then doctoral students at the Yale math department.

During my years at McKinsey & Company, between 1999 and 2002, Attila Aranyos, Johan Fahlén, Steffen Karlsson, Henrik Mella, Jacob Michlewicz, and Anna Wallin were good colleagues and friends.

When I returned to Yale in 2002, for my graduate studies in financial economics, my thesis advisor Jon Ingersoll, my committee members Will Goetzmann and Zhiwu Chen, and also Matt Spiegel, managed to perfectly fine-tune the trade-off between providing guidance and still letting me (over-)confidently push my own thinking and ideas. Rick Antle, Nick Barberis, Arturo Bris, Ed Kaplan, Avri Ravid, and Ivo Welch were also very inspiring teachers during this period.

During my years as assistant, associate, and full professor at Berkeley Haas, Christine Parlour has been a valuable mentor and collaborator, as well as a role model. Jonathan Berk has been a source of inspiration and a highly valued coauthor, as have my senior colleagues Richard Stanton and Nancy Wallace. David Sraer has been a great colleague and finance group cochair. Eben Lazarus has provided helpful feedback on this manuscript, while using it in the MFE 230A investments course.

I have benefited tremendously from interactions with my many collaborators over the years, beginning within applied mathematics—in chronological order—Mats Holmström, Raphy Coifman, Amir Averbuch, Dave Donoho, and Moshe Israeli; and then subsequently within finance, Will Goetzmann, Peter Jones, Mauro Maggioni, Rustam Ibragimov, Dwight Jaffee, Christine Parlour, Han Ozsoylev, Eric Talley, Yurii Fedyk, Christian Heyerdahl-Larsen, Richard Stanton, Sebastien Betermeier, Thomas Jansson, Marcus Opp, Nancy Wallace, Uday Rajan, David Hirshleifer, Bing Han, Raman Uppal, Harjoat Bhamra, Lina von Sydow, Philipp Illeditsch, Karen Pence, You Suk Kim, Laurent Calvet, Evan Jo, Artem Prokhorov, and Eben Lazarus.

I have had many constructive interactions with the faculty at a number of great finance departments, during my extended visits at Oxford University, INSEAD, NYU, Koç University, and—most extensively—at the Swedish House of Finance, Stockholm School of Economics. Especially, thanks to Per Strömberg, Magnus Dahlquist, Anders Andersson, Irina Zviadadze, Tobias Sichert, Peter Englund, Xavier Gabaix, Eduardo Davila, Cecilia Parlatore, Steijn van Nieuwerburgh, Laura Veldkamp, Bernard Dumas, and Adrian Buss.

During what ended up being my one-year visit at the University of Lausanne, UNIL, I had the pleasure to have as colleagues and hang out with Theo Dimopoulos, Amit Goyal, Boris Nikolov, Michael Rockinger, and Norman Schürhoff. Also, many thanks to Paul Ehling, Willie Fuchs, Nicolae Gârleanu, Brett Green, Terry Hendershott, Hayne Leland, Dmitry Livdan, Steve Ross, and Jacob Sagi, all of whom I have had many stimulating research discussions with. Tomas Björk, Dwight Jaffee, and Mark Rubinstein were good friends as well as outstanding finance scholars, who all significantly impacted my academic path, and who sadly passed away too early.

I have enjoyed teaching the material in this manuscript to many MFE and PhD cohorts at UC Berkeley, Haas. Especial thanks to Minghao Yang, Bernardo Maciel, Chad Wildman, Labeed Almani, Gurmeet Bedi, Travis Cable, Anjali Jha, Jiaxun Paw, Anudeep Nallamothu, Daniel Trivino, Jackson Walker, Morteza Aghajanzadeh, Jake Moore, Patrik Räty, Jack Ryan, Matteo Santamaria, Abdul Salako, and Hanna Yu for providing helpful feedback on the manuscript. Thanks to Christian Heyerdahl-Larsen for reading the whole manuscript and providing encouraging feedback. Also, thanks to Linda Kreitzman, who in her role as executive director of the MFE program provided lots of help and support over the years.

Finally, I would not be where I am today without the support from my parents, Lars Johan and Jennifer; my sister, Susanne; and most of all my wife and life companion, Petronella, and my children, Tintin, Felix, and Theodore.

APPENDIX A Sets and Functions

A.1 Sets

According to a standard definition, a *set* is "a collection of distinct objects, considered as an object in its own right." The objects are also called elements. Each element appears only once (otherwise the collection is a multiset). Elements are not ordered, which distinguishes a set from a vector.

As an example, the set $A = \{8, 4, 9\}$ consists of the three elements 4, 8, and 9, and the set $B = \{1, 3, 4, 7, 9\}$ contains five elements. A special set is the empty set, $\emptyset = \{\}$, which contains no elements. Sets can be very general, since they can contain anything: numbers, animals, other sets, etc. The number of elements in a set can be infinite, e.g., the set of natural numbers, $\mathbb{N} = \{1, 2, 3, \ldots\}$. Many standard operations on sets may be defined, e.g., the union and the intersection of two sets, see Rudin (1976).

We use the following notation:

- Member of a set: $4 \in A$.
- Not a member of a set: $3 \notin A$.
- Union of sets: $A \cup B = \{1, 3, 4, 7, 8, 9\}$.
- Intersection of sets: $A \cap B = \{4, 9\}$.
- Set difference: $B \backslash A = \{1, 3, 7\}$.
- Subset: The set A is a subset of B, $A \subset B$, if $x \in A \Rightarrow x \in B$.
- Equality: $A = B$ if $A \subset B$ and $B \subset A$, i.e., if A is a subset of B and B is a subset of A.
- Number of elements (*cardinality*) of a set: $|A| = 3$.
- Product set: $A \times B = \{(a, b) : a \in A,\ b \in B\}$.

To put more structure on a set, we can introduce an *order* of its elements, which captures the intuition of inequality of numbers. We write $x = y$ if x and y are the same element, and define an order as follows:

Definition A.1. An *order* (also called a strict total order) on the set A is a relation, $<$, between pairs of elements in A, such that for all $x, y \in A$ the order is

- trichotomous: exactly one of $x < y$, $y < x$, and $y = x$ holds,
- transitive: $x < y$ and $y < z \;\Rightarrow\; x < z$.

We also define

- $x \leq y$ if $x < y$ or $x = y$,
- $x > y$ if $\neg(x \leq y)$, i.e., if $\neg(x < y)$ and $\neg(x = y)$ (i.e., it is not the case that $x < y$, and not the case that $x = y$).

Consider the sets $A \subset S$, where S is an ordered set. We say that

- A is *bounded above* by $s \in S$, if $a \leq s$ for all $a \in A$,
- s is the least upper bound, *supremum*, of A if all other bounds, s', have $s < s'$. We write

$$s = \sup A.$$

Similarly, we define the concept of A being bounded *below*, and its greatest lower bound, *infimum*,

$$s = \inf A.$$

We say that S has the *least-upper-bound property* if every nonempty $E \subset S$ that is bounded from above has a supremum in S.

An important type of set is the *power set* of another set: $2^A = \{B : B \subset A\}$. For example, $2^{\{1,2\}} = \{\emptyset, \{1\}, \{2\}, \{1,2\}\}$. We can also think of the power set of A as the set of all functions that map A to $\{0,1\}$, $2^A = \{f : A \to \{0,1\}\}$. The equivalence between these two definitions is then such that for a set $B \in 2^A$, the corresponding function f_B maps elements in B to 1, and elements not in B to 0.

We have the following properties of power sets:

- $|2^A| = 2^{|A|}$.
- $A \in 2^A$.
- $A \not\subset 2^A$.
- 2^A does not naturally have a total order, even if A has a total order.

Some other important sets are the following *number systems*:

- Natural numbers: $\mathbb{N} = \{1, 2, 3, \ldots\}$.
- Integers: $\mathbb{Z} = \{\ldots, -3, -2, -1, 0, 1, 2, 3, \ldots\}$.
- Rational numbers: $\mathbb{Q} = \{\frac{q}{p} : q \in \mathbb{Z},\ p \in \mathbb{N},\ q \text{ and } p \text{ no common factors}\}$.
- Real numbers: $\mathbb{R}$.
- Extended natural numbers: $\bar{\mathbb{N}} = \mathbb{N} \cup \{\infty\}$.
- Extended set of integers and the extended real line $\bar{\mathbb{Z}} = \mathbb{Z} \cup \{-\infty, \infty\}$, $\bar{\mathbb{R}} = \mathbb{R} \cup \{-\infty, \infty\}$.
- Real plane: $\mathbb{R}^2 = \mathbb{R} \times \mathbb{R} = \{(x_1, x_2) : x_1, x_2 \in \mathbb{R}\}$.
- Complex number system: $\mathbb{C} = \{x + iy : x \in \mathbb{R},\ y \in \mathbb{R}\}$.

Defining the "size" of an infinite set, corresponding to the "number of elements" for a finite set, $|A|$, is trickier than for such finite sets. For finite sets, we have

1. A and B are the same size if and only if $|A| = |B|$,
2. if B is a strict subset of A, $|B| < |A|$, i.e., B is smaller than A,
3. $|A| < |2^A|$.

Consider the two sets $A = \mathbb{N}$ and $B = \mathbb{N} \backslash \{1\}$.

- One the one hand, B is a strict subset of A, so B is "smaller" than A.
- On the other hand, we may relabel all elements in B, so that $2 \mapsto 1$, $3 \mapsto 2$, etc. Then the two sets are the same. So one may argue that the two sets have the same size.

It is clear that not all properties of finite sets can carry over to infinite sets. It turns out that it is more constructive to define the two sets A and B to have the same "size" (cardinality). Indeed, being able to "relabel" the elements of two sets in an invertible manner is taken as the definition for two sets to have the same size. This definition also works for finite sets: two finite sets have the same number of elements if and only if one can relabel their elements in an invertible manner.

So two sets—finite or infinite—are said to have the same *cardinality* if and only if a bijection $f: A \leftrightarrow B$ exists between the two (see the definition of bijection in the next section). This definition generates a sequence of infinite cardinalities. We have $|\mathbb{N}| = \aleph_0$, which is *countably infinite* in that the set's elements can be enumerated in a sequence. It is a famous result that a set, finite or infinite, always has fewer elements than its power set, $|A| < |2^A|$. We therefore have the following cardinality ordering:

- $0 < 1 < 2 < 3 \cdots < \aleph_0 < 2^{\aleph_0} < 2^{2^{\aleph_0}} \cdots$.
- Implication: $\aleph_0 = |\mathbb{N}| = |\mathbb{Z}| = |\mathbb{Q}| < |\mathbb{R}| = 2^{\aleph_0}$. So there are *many* more real numbers than rational numbers!

The *continuum hypothesis* states that there is no cardinality of infinity between $\aleph_0$ and $2^{\aleph_0}$. The continuum hypothesis can be shown to be equivalent to the so-called *axiom of choice* within the standard axiomatic approach to set theory, the so-called Zermelo–Fraenkel set theory. When the axiom of choice is included in the Zermelo–Fraenkel set theory, ZFC set theory is obtained (the "C" standing for "choice"), which is nowadays the standard axiomatic approach to set theory. The continuum hypothesis then holds per assumption.

A.2 Functions

- A *relation* (correspondence), R, is a subset of a product set, $R \subset A \times B$:
  - $R = \{(x, y) \in \mathbb{R}_+ \times \mathbb{R} : x \leq y\}$.
  - $R = \{(x, y) \in \mathbb{R}_+ \times \mathbb{R} : x = y^2\}$.
- A *function*, $f: A \rightarrow B$, is a relation on $A \times B$, such that each element in A is related to exactly one element in B:
  - $f: x \mapsto \sqrt{x}$: relation $R_f = \{(x, y) \in \mathbb{R}_+ \times \mathbb{R}_+ : y = \sqrt{x}\}$.
  - A is the *domain*.
  - B is the *range*.
  - Write $b = f(a)$, if $(a, b) \in R_f$.
  - *Image*, $f(A_0)$, $A_0 \subset A$, is $\{f(a) : a \in A_0\}$.
  - *Inverse image*, $f^{-1}(B_0)$, $B_0 \subset B$, is $\{a : f(a) \in B_0\}$.
- A function is
  - *onto* (surjective, a surjection) if $f(A) = B$,
  - *one-to-one* (injective, an injection) if $a_1 \neq a_2 \;\Rightarrow\; f(a_1) \neq f(a_2)$,
  - a *bijection* (one-to-one correspondence) if it is onto and one-to-one, $f: A \leftrightarrow B$:
    - A bijection is invertible: there exists a function $f^{-1}: B \rightarrow A$ such that $f(f^{-1}(b)) = b$ for all $b \in \mathbb{B}$, and $f^{-1}(f(a)) = a$ for all $a \in \mathbb{A}$.

APPENDIX B Topology and Linear Algebra

B.1 Metric Spaces

Metric spaces generalize the concept of distance and related concepts such as convergence of sequences, and sums, etc.

Definition. A set X is a *metric space* if it is associated with a distance function (metric) $d\colon X \times X \to \mathbb{R}_+$, such that we have

- $d(p,q) = 0 \;\Leftrightarrow\; p = q$,
- symmetry: $d(p,q) = d(q,p)$,
- triangle inequality: $d(p,q) \leq d(p,r) + d(r,q)$ for any $r \in X$.

Examples.

- $\mathbb{R}$ with metric $d(x,y) = |x - y|$.
- $\mathbb{R}^2$ with metric $d((x_1,y_1),(x_2,y_2)) = \sqrt{(x_1 - x_2)^2 + (y_1 - y_2)^2}$.
- $\mathbb{Q}$ with metric $d(x,y) = 0$ if $x = y$, and 1 otherwise.

Consider a metric space, X, a point $x \in X$, and a set $E \subset X$. The following concepts are defined for X:

- *Open neighborhood* of x: $N_r(x) = \{y : d(x,y) < r\}$, $r > 0$.
- x is a *limit point* of E if for all $r > 0$, there exists $y \neq x$ such that $y \in N_r(x) \cap E$.
- x is a *boundary point* of E if for all $r > 0$, there exist $y, y' \in N_r(x)$, $y \in E$, and $y' \notin E$.
- E is *open* if it contains no boundary points.
- E is *closed* if it contains all boundary points.
- The interior of E, $\text{int}(E)$, is obtained by removing all the boundary points from E. It is also defined as the union of all open subsets of E.
- The closure of E, $\bar{E}$, is obtained by including all E's boundary points. It is also defined as the intersection of all closed supersets of E.
- E is *dense* in X if for all $\epsilon > 0$, for all $x \in X$, there exists $e \in E$ such that $d(x,e) < \epsilon$.
- A *Cauchy sequence* in X is a sequence, $x_1, x_2, \ldots$, such that, for all $\epsilon > 0$, there exists N such that $M \geq N \;\Rightarrow\; d(x_N, x_M) < \epsilon$.
- A metric space is *complete* if all Cauchy sequences converge within X.
- The *complement* of E is $E^c = X \backslash E$.
- A set is *bounded* if there exist $M < \infty$ and $p \in E$, such that $d(p,x) \leq M$ for all $x \in X$.

Consider a metric space, X:

- A *sequence* is a function, $f\colon \mathbb{N} \to X$, represented by $x_1, x_2, x_3, \ldots$.
- A sequence *converges* to a point $x \in X$ if

$$\forall \epsilon > 0, \exists N : n \geq N \;\Rightarrow\; d(x_n, x) < \epsilon.$$

We write $\lim_{n\to\infty} x_n = x$, or $\lim x_n = x$.

- Equivalently, the sequence converges to x if for every open neighborhood of x, $N_r(x)$, all but a finite number of x_n's belong to $N_r(x)$.

Important properties of sets in metric spaces:

- $\emptyset$ and X are open and closed.
- $N_r(x)$ is open for all $r > 0$, for all $x \in X$.
- E open $\Leftrightarrow$ E^c closed.
- $E_1, E_2, \ldots,$ open $\Rightarrow \bigcup_n E_n$ open (arbitrary unions).
- $E_1, E_2, \ldots, E_N$ open $\Rightarrow \bigcap_{n=1}^N E_n$ open (finite intersections).
- $E_1, E_2, \ldots,$ closed $\Rightarrow \bigcap_n E_n$ closed (arbitrary intersections).
- $E_1, E_2, \ldots, E_N$ closed $\Rightarrow \bigcup_{n=1}^N E_n$ closed (finite unions).

Examples in $\mathbb{R}$ with standard distance function $d(x, y) = |x - y|$:

- Finite sets are closed.
- (a, b) is open.
- $[a, b]$ is closed.

B.2 Vector Spaces

Vector spaces (linear spaces) generalize the concept of vectors from geometry. Before defining a vector space, we define a field, which captures the generic properties of addition and multiplication of real and complex numbers:

Definition B.1. A *field* is a set, F, with operations $+ : F \times F \to F$ and $\times : F \times F \to F$, that satisfy the following properties:

- Commutative addition and multiplication: $x + y = y + x$, $x \times y = y \times x$.
- Associative addition and multiplication: $(x + y) + z = x + (y + z)$, $(x \times y) \times z = x \times (y \times z)$.
- There is an element $0 \in F$, such that for all $x \in F$, $0 + x = x$. There is an element $1 \in F$, such that for all $x \in F$, $1 \times x = x$. For all $x \in F$, there is an element $-x \in F$, such that $x + (-x) = 0$.
- For all $x \in F$, such that $x \neq 0$, there is an element $1/x \in F$, such that $x \times (1/x) = 1$.
- Distributive law: For all $x, y, z \in F$, $x \times (y + z) = x \times y + x \times z$.

Definition B.2. A set V is a *vector space*, associated with the operations $\times : F \times V \to V$ and $+ : V \times V \to V$, where F is a field, if it satisfies the following conditions:

- Associative addition: $u + (v + w) = (u + v) + w$.
- Commutative addition: $u + v = v + u$.
- Identity addition: there exists an element 0 such that $0 + u = u$, for all u.
- Inverse addition: for all u, there exists an element $-u$ such that $u + (-u) = 0$.
- Associative multiplication: $a(bv) = (ab)v$.
- Identity multiplication: $1v = v$.
- Distributive rule 1: $a(u + v) = (au) + (av)$.
- Distributive rule 2: $(a + b)u = (au) + (bu)$.

An example of a vector space is $\mathbb{R}^k$, $k \in \mathbb{N}$.

Note that a vector space in itself has no topological properties associated with it. A vector space with an associated topology (a generalization of a metric) is called a *topological vector space*. We mainly deal with metric vector spaces, i.e., vector spaces for which the topology is a metric. In fact, we mainly deal with the even more special case under which the metric is a so-called *norm*. In this case the vector space is called a normed space.

Definition B.3. A vector space V is a *normed space* if it is associated with a *norm function*, $\|\cdot\|: V \to \mathbb{R}_+$, such that

- $u \neq 0 \;\Rightarrow\; \|u\| > 0$,
- $\|au\| = |a|\,\|u\|$,
- $\|u + v\| \leq \|u\| + \|v\|$.

The norm turns V into a special kind of metric space, since the distance function $d(u, v) = \|u - v\|$ satisfies the axioms of a metric. A complete normed space is called a *Banach space*.

An example of a Banach space is $\mathbb{R}^2$ with the norm $\|u\| = |u_1| + |u_2|$.

A specific type of normed space is an *inner product space*. Such spaces have a more well-defined geometric interpretation, since not only can one tell whether vectors in such spaces are close or far away, but the *angles* between vectors (e.g., whether they are perpendicular, i.e., *orthogonal*) are also well defined.

Definition B.4. A vector space V is an *inner product space* if it is associated with a *inner product*, $\langle \cdot, \cdot \rangle: V \times V \to \mathbb{R}$, with the following properties:

- Commutative: $\langle u, v \rangle = \langle v, u \rangle$.
- Linearity 1: $\langle au, v \rangle = a\langle u, v \rangle$.
- Linearity 2: $\langle u + v, w \rangle = \langle u, w \rangle + \langle v, w \rangle$.
- Positiveness: $\langle u, u \rangle \geq 0$ with equality only if $u = 0$.

We have the following relations between normed and inner product spaces:

- The inner product makes V into a special kind of normed space, since the function $\|u\| = \sqrt{\langle u, u \rangle}$ satisfies the norm axioms.
- A complete inner product space is called a *Hilbert space*.

An example of a Hilbert space is $\mathbb{R}^2$ with the inner product $= \langle u, v \rangle = u_1 v_1 + u_2 v_2$.

More examples.

- $\mathbb{R}^k$, $\mathbb{C}^k$ (Hilbert spaces)
  - $\langle x, y \rangle = \sum_{n=1}^{k} x_k \overline{y_k}$.
- ℓ^1: $\{x \in \mathbb{R}^\infty : \sum_k |x_k| < \infty\}$ (Banach space)
  - $\|x\| = \sum_k |x_k|$.
- ℓ^∞: $\{x \in \mathbb{R}^\infty : \sup_k |x_k| < \infty\}$ (Banach space)
  - $\|x\| = \sup_k |x_k|$.
- ℓ^2: $\{x \in \mathbb{R}^\infty : \sum_k |x_k|^2 < \infty\}$ (Hilbert space)
  - $\langle x, y \rangle = \sum_k x_k y_k$.

- C: $\{f: [0, 1] \to \mathbb{R} : f \text{ is continuous}\}$ (Banach space)
  - $d(f,g) = \sup_{x \in [0,1]} |f(x) - g(x)|$.
- $L^2 = L^2(\mathbb{R})$: $\{f: \mathbb{R} \to \mathbb{R} : \int_{-\infty}^{\infty} |f(x)|^2\, dx < \infty\}$ (Hilbert space)
  - $\langle f, g\rangle = \int f(x)g(x)\, dx$.
- $L^1 = L^1(\mathbb{R})$: $\{f: \mathbb{R} \to \mathbb{R} : \int_{-\infty}^{\infty} |f(x)|\, dx < \infty\}$ (Banach space)
  - $\|f\|_1 = \int_{-\infty}^{\infty} |f(x)|\, dx$.

In infinite dimensions, Hilbert spaces are about as close as we get to the finite-dimensional space $\mathbb{R}^k$. In inner product spaces, we have the *Cauchy–Schwarz* inequality, which states that $|\langle \mathbf{x}, \mathbf{y}\rangle| \leq \|\mathbf{x}\|\, \|\mathbf{y}\|$. Also, the concept of an *angle* between two elements of a Hilbert space is well defined, in contrast to a normed space, via the relation $\cos(\phi) = \frac{\langle \mathbf{x}, \mathbf{y}\rangle}{\|\mathbf{x}\|\, \|\mathbf{y}\|}$. Specifically, when $\langle \mathbf{x}, \mathbf{y}\rangle = 0$, the two elements are *orthogonal*.

An important theorem in economics and finance, which we use to prove the fundamental theorem of asset pricing, is the *separating hyperplane theorem*:

Theorem B.1 (Separating hyperplane theorem)**.** *Suppose A and B are convex subsets of $\mathbb{R}^n$ with no interior point in common. Then there exists a vector, $\mathbf{x} \in \mathbb{R}^n$, and a constant, c, such that $\mathbf{x}^T\mathbf{a} \leq c$ for all $\mathbf{a} \in A$ and $\mathbf{x}^T\mathbf{b} \geq c$ for all $\mathbf{b} \in B$. If A is closed and B is compact (i.e., closed and bounded) and A and B are disjoint, the inequality can be made strict.*

Another very useful theorem is the Heine–Borel theorem for finite-dimensional inner product spaces (which are isomorphic to $\mathbb{R}^k$ for some k):

Theorem B.2 (Heine–Borel theorem)**.** *The following two statements about the set $E \subset \mathbb{R}^k$ are equivalent:*

(a) *E is closed and bounded.*
(b) *Every infinite subset of E has a limit point in E.*

An implication of the theorem is that any sequence in E has a subsequence that converges to a point in E.

The following is a counterexample to the Heine–Borel theorem in an infinite-dimensional space: Consider the ℓ^2 space,

- ℓ^2: $\{x \in \mathbb{R}^{\infty} : \sum_k |x_k|^2 < \infty\}$,
- $\|x\|^2 = \sum_k |x_k|^2$.

Consider the set $E = \{x \in \ell^2 : \|x\| \leq 1\}$. This is a closed set. In fact, one can show that any "ball" in a metric space, of the form $\bar{N}_r(x) = \{y : d(x,y) \leq r\}$, where $r > 0$, is closed, just like $N_r(x)$ is always open. The following properties of E are easy to show:

(a) E is bounded.
(b) The elements $\delta_1, \delta_2, \delta_3, \ldots$, where δ_i has its ith element equal to 1 and all other elements equal to 0, so that, e.g., $\delta_2 = (0, 1, 0, \ldots)$, all belong to E, and this sequence does *not* have a convergent subsequence.

In light of (a) and (b), the Heine–Borel theorem does *not* generalize to ℓ^2.

B.3 Vectors and Matrices

A matrix $\mathbf{A}$ is an element of $\mathbb{R}^{M\times N}$, represented by a "box" of numbers

$$\mathbf{A} = [\mathbf{A}_{ij}]_{i,j} = \begin{bmatrix} a_{11} & \cdots & a_{1N} \\ \vdots & & \vdots \\ a_{M1} & \cdots & a_{MN} \end{bmatrix},$$

where $a_{ij} \in \mathbb{R}$. We use the notation $\mathbf{A}_{ij} = (\mathbf{A})_{ij} = a_{ij}$. The following operations are defined:

- Addition: $\mathbf{C} = \mathbf{A} + \mathbf{B} \in \mathbb{R}^{M\times N}$, $\mathbf{C}_{ij} = \mathbf{A}_{ij} + \mathbf{B}_{ij}$.
- Scalar multiplication: $\mathbf{C} = \alpha\mathbf{A}$, $\mathbf{C}_{ij} = \alpha\mathbf{A}_{ij}$.
- Matrix multiplication: $\mathbf{C} = \mathbf{AB}$, $\mathbf{A} \in \mathbb{R}^{M\times P}$, $\mathbf{B} \in \mathbb{R}^{P\times N}$, $\mathbf{C} \in \mathbf{R}^{M\times N}$,

$$\mathbf{C}_{ij} = \sum_{k=1}^{P} \mathbf{A}_{ik}\mathbf{B}_{kj}.$$

We define the following special matrices:

- Diagonal matrix: $\mathbf{A} \in \mathbb{R}^{M\times M}$ is diagonal if $\mathbf{A}_{ij} = 0$ for $i \neq j$.
- Identity matrix: $\mathbf{I} = \mathbf{I}_M \in \mathbb{R}^{M\times M}$ is a diagonal matrix, with $\mathbf{I}_{ii} = 1$, for $i = 1, \ldots, M$.
- Property of the identity matrix: $\mathbf{I}_M\mathbf{A} = \mathbf{A}$ for all $\mathbf{A} \in \mathbb{R}^{M\times N}$.

Matrices satisfy the following properties:

- Addition is commutative and associative:
  - $\mathbf{A} + \mathbf{B} = \mathbf{B} + \mathbf{A}$.
  - $\mathbf{A} + (\mathbf{B} + \mathbf{C}) = (\mathbf{A} + \mathbf{B}) + \mathbf{C}$.
- Multiplication is associative:
  - $\alpha(\beta\mathbf{A}) = (\alpha\beta)\mathbf{A}$.
  - $\mathbf{A}(\mathbf{BC}) = (\mathbf{AB})\mathbf{C}$.
- Multiplication is in general *not* commutative:
  - $\mathbf{AB} \neq \mathbf{BA}$.
- Matrix $\mathbf{C} \in \mathbb{R}^{N\times M}$ is transpose to $\mathbf{A} \in \mathbb{R}^{M\times N}$, $\mathbf{C} = \mathbf{A}^T = \mathbf{A}'$, if $\mathbf{C}_{ij} = \mathbf{A}_{ji}$ for all i and j.
- $\mathbf{A}$ is *symmetric* if $\mathbf{A} = \mathbf{A}^T$.
- Rule: $(\mathbf{AB})^T = \mathbf{B}^T\mathbf{A}^T$.

A (column) vector is a special case of a matrix $\mathbf{v} \in \mathbb{R}^{N\times 1}$, $\mathbf{v} = \begin{bmatrix} a_1 \\ \vdots \\ a_N \end{bmatrix}$. We use the notation $\mathbf{v}_i = (\mathbf{v})_i = a_i$. The transpose of a column vector is a row vector. The inner product of two vectors is

$$\langle \mathbf{x}, \mathbf{y} \rangle = \mathbf{x}^T\mathbf{y}.$$

Some special vectors are $\mathbf{1} = \mathbf{1}_N = (1, 1, \ldots, 1)' \in \mathbb{R}^N$, and δ_i: $(\delta_i)_j = 0$, $i \neq j$; $(\delta_i)_i = 1$.

A matrix can be partitioned into column and row vectors:

- Column partition of $\mathbf{A} \in \mathbb{R}^{M \times N}$,

$$\mathbf{A} = \begin{bmatrix} \mathbf{v}^1 & \mathbf{v}^2 & \cdots & \mathbf{v}^N \end{bmatrix} \quad \text{or} \quad \mathbf{A} = \begin{bmatrix} \vdots & \vdots & & \vdots \\ \mathbf{v}^1 & \mathbf{v}^2 & \cdots & \mathbf{v}^N \\ \vdots & \vdots & & \vdots \end{bmatrix}.$$

- Row partition of $\mathbf{A}$:

$$\mathbf{A} = \begin{bmatrix} (\mathbf{w}^1)'; & (\mathbf{w}^2)'; & \cdots; & (\mathbf{w}^M)' \end{bmatrix} \quad \text{or} \quad \mathbf{A} = \begin{bmatrix} \cdots & (\mathbf{w}^1)' & \cdots \\ \cdots & (\mathbf{w}^2)' & \cdots \\ \vdots & \vdots & \vdots \\ \cdots & (\mathbf{w}^M)' & \cdots \end{bmatrix}.$$

If $\mathbf{A} \in \mathbb{R}^{N \times N}$ is a square matrix, then $\mathbf{B} \in \mathbb{R}^{N \times N}$ is the *inverse* to $\mathbf{A}$ if $\mathbf{BA} = \mathbf{I}_N$. We write $\mathbf{B} = \mathbf{A}^{-1}$ (note that the inverse does not always exist, just like the inverse $y \in \mathbb{R}$ to the equation $xy = 1$ does not exist when $x = 0$). If $\mathbf{BA} = \mathbf{I}_N$, then, equivalently, $\mathbf{AB} = \mathbf{I}_N$.

Example. $\mathbf{A} = \begin{bmatrix} 1 & 2 \\ 2 & 0 \end{bmatrix} \Rightarrow \mathbf{A}^{-1} = \begin{bmatrix} 0 & \frac{1}{2} \\ \frac{1}{2} & -\frac{1}{4} \end{bmatrix}$.

For the vector $\mathbf{v} = (a_1, a_2, \ldots, a_N)' \in \mathbb{R}^N$, we define

$$\operatorname{diag}(\mathbf{v}) = \Lambda_{\mathbf{v}} = \begin{bmatrix} a_1 & 0 & 0 & \cdots & 0 \\ 0 & a_2 & 0 & \cdots & 0 \\ 0 & 0 & a_3 & \cdots & 0 \\ & & & \ddots & 0 \\ 0 & 0 & 0 & \cdots & a_N \end{bmatrix} \in \mathbb{R}^{N \times N}.$$

We have the multiplication rule,

$$\Lambda_{\mathbf{v}} \mathbf{1} = \mathbf{v},$$

and the inverse rule when $a_n \neq 0$ for all n,

$$\Lambda_{\mathbf{v}}^{-1} = \Lambda_{\mathbf{1}./\mathbf{v}},$$

where $\mathbf{1}./\mathbf{v} = (1/v_1, 1/v_2, \ldots, 1/v_N)'$.

The determinant of the square matrix $\mathbf{A}$, $\det(\mathbf{A})$, is defined recursively:

- $\mathbf{A} = a \in \mathbb{R}^{1 \times 1} \Rightarrow \det(\mathbf{A}) = a$.
- $\mathbf{A} \in \mathbb{R}^{(N+1) \times (N+1)} \Rightarrow \det(\mathbf{A}) = \sum_{j=1}^{N+1} (-1)^{i+j} \mathbf{A}_{ij} \det(\mathbf{A}^{ij})$, for any $i = 1, \ldots, N+1$.
  - $\mathbf{A}^{ij}$ is the matrix obtained by deleting the ith row and jth column of $\mathbf{A}$.
- $\det(\mathbf{A}) \neq 0 \Leftrightarrow \mathbf{A}$ is invertible.

Assume $\mathbf{A}, \mathbf{B} \in \mathbb{R}^{N \times N}$. We then have the following rules:

- $(\mathbf{AB})^{-1} = \mathbf{B}^{-1}\mathbf{A}^{-1}$ (if both are invertible).
- $(\mathbf{A}^T)^{-1} = (\mathbf{A}^{-1})^T$.
- $\det(\mathbf{AB}) = \det(\mathbf{A}) \det(\mathbf{B})$.
- $\det(\mathbf{A}^T) = \det(\mathbf{A})$.
- $\det(\alpha \mathbf{A}) = \alpha^N \det(\mathbf{A})$.

B.4 Linear Algebra

A useful application of matrices is in defining linear functions on vector spaces. Specifically, the matrix $\mathbf{A} \in \mathbb{R}^{M\times N}$ can be viewed as a linear function (operator) that maps vectors in $\mathbb{R}^N$ to vectors in $\mathbb{R}^M$:

$$\mathbf{A}: \mathbb{R}^N \to \mathbb{R}^M,$$
$$\mathbf{x} \mapsto \mathbf{Ax}.$$

The operator satisfies the linearity properties

- $\mathbf{A}(\mathbf{x}+\mathbf{y}) = \mathbf{Ax}+\mathbf{Ay}$,
- $\mathbf{A}(\alpha\mathbf{x}) = \alpha\mathbf{Ax}$.

We write $\mathbf{A} \in \mathcal{L}(\mathbb{R}^N, \mathbb{R}^M)$. Here, $\mathcal{L}(\mathbb{R}^N, \mathbb{R}^M)$ is the set of all linear operators from $\mathbb{R}^N$ to $\mathbb{R}^M$.

The *column space* (*span, range, image*) of a matrix $\mathbf{A} \in \mathbb{R}^{N\times M}$ is the subspace in $\mathbb{R}^N$, $\{\mathbf{Ax}: \mathbf{x} \in \mathbb{R}^M\}$. The *row space* is the subspace in $\mathbb{R}^M$, $\{\mathbf{A}^T\mathbf{x}: \mathbf{x} \in \mathbb{R}^N\}$. The *rank* of $\mathbf{A}$, $\text{rank}(\mathbf{A})$, is the dimension of the column space. We have $\text{rank}(\mathbf{A}) = \text{rank}(\mathbf{A}^T)$. The null space (*kernel*) of $\mathbf{A}$, is the space of M-vectors that map to the zero vector, $\{\mathbf{x}: \mathbf{Ax} = \mathbf{0}\}$. The dimension of the null space is denoted by $\text{null}(\mathbf{A})$. The rank theorem from linear algebra states that $\text{rank}(\mathbf{A}) + \text{null}(\mathbf{A}) = M$.

The left null space is the subspace of $\mathbb{R}^N$, $\{\mathbf{x}: \mathbf{A}^T\mathbf{x} = \mathbf{0}\}$. Clearly, the left null space is the orthogonal complement of the column space of $\mathbf{A}$ and the null space is the orthogonal complement of the row space of $\mathbf{A}$. A cone is a set in $\mathbb{R}^n$ that is closed under multiplication by positive scalars.

Definition B.5. A matrix $\mathbf{P} \in \mathbb{R}^{N\times N}$ is a *projection operator* if

- $\mathbf{P}$ is symmetric, $\mathbf{P}^T = \mathbf{P}$,
- $\mathbf{P}$ is *idempotent*, $\mathbf{P}^2 = \mathbf{P}$.

Recall that the vectors $\mathbf{x}$ and $\mathbf{y}$ are defined to be orthogonal if $\langle \mathbf{x}, \mathbf{y}\rangle = 0$. It is straightforward to show that if $\mathbf{P}$ is a projection operator, then $\mathbf{Px} \perp (\mathbf{I}-\mathbf{P})\mathbf{x}$.

An important property of a projection operator is that $\mathbf{Pv}$ minimizes the distance between $\mathbf{v}$ and the subspace spanned by $\mathbf{P}$. An example of a one-dimensional projection operator is $\mathbf{P} = \frac{1}{\|\mathbf{x}\|^2}\mathbf{xx}^T$, for a vector $\mathbf{x} \neq \mathbf{0}$.

It is often important to measure distances between matrices, just as between vectors. We can do this by introducing a matrix norm. Consider the matrix $\mathbf{A} \in \mathbb{R}^{M\times N}$. The following matrix norms are useful:

- Frobenius norm: $\|\mathbf{A}\|_F = \sqrt{\sum_{m=1}^{M}\sum_{n=1}^{N} |\mathbf{A}_{mn}|^2}$.
  - Generalization of the $\|\cdot\|_2$ norm for a vector.
- p norms: $\|\mathbf{A}\|_p = \sup_{\mathbf{x}\neq\mathbf{0}} \frac{\|\mathbf{Ax}\|_p}{\|\mathbf{x}\|_p}$.
  - Here, the vector p norm, $1 \le p \le \infty$, induces a matrix p norm.
  - The following algebraic inequality holds: $\|\mathbf{AB}\|_p \le \|\mathbf{A}\|_p\|\mathbf{B}\|_p$ as long as the dimensionalities match.
  - $\|\mathbf{A}\|_2^2 \le \|\mathbf{A}\|_1\|\mathbf{A}\|_\infty$.

The vector space of matrices $\{\mathbf{A} \in \mathbb{R}^{M\times N}\}$, with the vector space operations defined by $\mathbf{A} \mapsto \alpha\mathbf{A}$, and $\mathbf{A}, \mathbf{B} \mapsto \mathbf{A}+\mathbf{B}$, is a Banach space under all the above norms. Moreover, all these norms are equivalent in that there are uniform bounds on any of the norms in terms of any other of the norms. We have

- $\|\mathbf{A}\|_2 \leq \|\mathbf{A}\|_F \leq \sqrt{\min(M,N)}\|\mathbf{A}\|_2$,
- $\frac{1}{\sqrt{N}}\|\mathbf{A}\|_\infty \leq \|\mathbf{A}\|_2 \leq \sqrt{M}\|\mathbf{A}\|_\infty$,
- $\frac{1}{\sqrt{M}}\|\mathbf{A}\|_1 \leq \|\mathbf{A}\|_2 \leq \sqrt{N}\|\mathbf{A}\|_1$,
- $\|\mathbf{A}\|_1 = \max_{1\leq n\leq N}\sum_{m=1}^{M}|\mathbf{A}_{mn}|$,
- $\|\mathbf{A}\|_\infty = \max_{1\leq m\leq M}\sum_{n=1}^{N}|\mathbf{A}_{mn}|$.

So far, we have interpreted a matrix $\mathbf{A}\in\mathbb{R}^{M\times N}$ as a linear operator in $\mathcal{L}(\mathbb{R}^N,\mathbb{R}^M)$.

- For a square matrix, $\mathbf{A}\in\mathbb{R}^{N\times N}$, we can also interpret it as the *quadratic form* $\mathbf{A}\colon \mathbb{R}^N\to\mathbb{R}$, defined by $\mathbf{x}\mapsto\mathbf{x}^T\mathbf{A}\mathbf{x}$.
- For any nonsymmetric matrix $\mathbf{A}$, define $\mathbf{B}\overset{\text{def}}{=}\frac{1}{2}(\mathbf{A}+\mathbf{A}^T)$.
- Then $\mathbf{B}$ is symmetric and $\mathbf{x}^T\mathbf{A}\mathbf{x}=\mathbf{x}^T\mathbf{B}\mathbf{x}$.

Consider a square matrix $\mathbf{A}\in\mathbb{R}^{N\times N}$. The (complex) number λ is said to be an *eigenvalue* of $\mathbf{A}$ if the matrix $\mathbf{A}-\lambda\mathbf{I}_N$ is singular, i.e., if $\det(\mathbf{A}-\lambda\mathbf{I}_N)=0$.

- From the rank theorem, there exists an *eigenvector* $\mathbf{x}$ associated with λ, i.e., a vector such that $\mathbf{A}\mathbf{x}=\lambda\mathbf{x}$.
- The set of eigenvalues $\Lambda=\{\lambda:\det(\mathbf{A}-\lambda\mathbf{I}_N)=0\}$ is called the *spectrum* of $\mathbf{A}$.
- From the fundamental theorem of algebra, there are N eigenvalues (when accounting for algebraic multiplicity).
- A matrix $\mathbf{Q}\in\mathbb{R}^{N\times N}$ is orthogonal if $\mathbf{Q}^T\mathbf{Q}=\mathbf{I}$.
- The columns of an orthogonal matrix form an orthonormal basis of $\mathbb{R}^N$.

Theorem B.3 (Spectral theorem). *If* $\mathbf{A}$ *is a symmetric matrix, then*

- $\mathbf{A}$ *can be diagonalized by an orthogonal matrix, i.e.,*

$$\mathbf{A}=\mathbf{Q}\Lambda\mathbf{Q}^T,$$

- *all of* $\mathbf{A}$*'s eigenvalues are real.*

An interpretation of the spectral theorem is that in the orthonormal basis $\mathbf{Q}$, $\mathbf{A}$ is a diagonal operator.

A symmetric matrix $\mathbf{A}$ is said to be

- positive definite if $\mathbf{x}^T\mathbf{A}\mathbf{x}>0$ for all $\mathbf{x}\neq\mathbf{0}$,
- positive semidefinite if $\mathbf{x}^T\mathbf{A}\mathbf{x}\geq 0$ for all $\mathbf{x}$,
- negative definite if $\mathbf{x}^T\mathbf{A}\mathbf{x}<0$ for all $\mathbf{x}\neq\mathbf{0}$,
- negative semidefinite if $\mathbf{x}^T\mathbf{A}\mathbf{x}\leq 0$ for all $\mathbf{x}$.

The signature of $\mathbf{A}$ is the triplet

$$(\text{\# of negative eigenvalues, \# of 0 eigenvalues, \# of positive eigenvalues}).$$

We have the following relationships between the definiteness of $\mathbf{A}$ and its signature:

- Positive definite $\Leftrightarrow$ signature $(0,0,N)$.
- Positive semidefinite $\Leftrightarrow$ signature $(0,r,N-r)$.

- Negative definite $\Leftrightarrow$ signature $(N, 0, 0)$.
- Negative semidefinite $\Leftrightarrow$ signature $(N-r, r, 0)$.

Theorem B.4 (Sylvester's law of inertia). *If* $\mathbf{A}$ *is symmetric and* $\mathbf{X}$ *is invertible, then the signature of* $\mathbf{X}^T\mathbf{A}\mathbf{X}$ *is the same as the signature of* $\mathbf{A}$.

- *Note that if* $\mathbf{A}$ *is symmetric, then so is* $\mathbf{X}^T\mathbf{A}\mathbf{X}$*, since*

$$(\mathbf{X}^T\mathbf{A}\mathbf{X})^T = \mathbf{X}^T\mathbf{A}^T\mathbf{X} = \mathbf{X}^T\mathbf{A}\mathbf{X}.$$

Theorem B.5 (Singular value decomposition). *Any real matrix,* $\mathbf{A} \in \mathbb{R}^{M\times N}$*, can be factorized as* $\mathbf{A} = \mathbf{U}\Sigma\mathbf{V}^T$*, where* $\mathbf{U} \in \mathbb{R}^{M\times M}$ *and* $\mathbf{V} \in \mathbb{R}^{N\times N}$ *are real orthogonal matrices, and* $\Sigma \in \mathbb{R}_+^{M\times N}$ *is a real diagonal matrix, i.e., such that* $[\Sigma]_{mn} \neq 0$ *when* $m \neq n$.

The elements $\sigma_i = [\Sigma]_{ii}$, $i \leq k$, where $k = \min(M, N)$, are called the singular values of $\mathbf{A}$, and are ordered so that $\sigma_1 \geq \sigma_2 \geq \cdots \geq \sigma_k$. If $\sigma_r > 0$, and $\sigma_{r+1} = 0$, then $\mathbf{A}$ is of rank r, $\text{rank}(\mathbf{A}) = r$.

Theorem B.6 (Eckhart–Young theorem). *Consider the minimization problem*

$$\min_{\substack{\mathbf{B}\in\mathbb{R}^{M\times N}\\ \text{rank}(\mathbf{B})=t}} \|\mathbf{A}-\mathbf{B}\|_F,$$

i.e., of finding a rank-t approximation of the matrix $\mathbf{A} \in \mathbb{R}^{M\times N}$ *that is as close to the matrix* $\mathbf{A}$ *as possible in the Frobenius norm,* $t \leq \min(M, N)$*. The solution to this problem is*

$$\mathbf{B} = \mathbf{U}\widehat{\Sigma}\mathbf{V}^T,$$

where $\mathbf{U}$ *and* $\mathbf{V}$ *are defined by the singular value decomposition of* $\mathbf{A}$*, and* $\widehat{\Sigma}$ *is derived from* Σ *in this decomposition by replacing the diagonal elements* $[\Sigma]_{qq}$ *with zeros for* $q = t+1, \ldots, r$.

There are many other useful matrix factorizations. Here are a few examples:

- A square matrix $\mathbf{A} = \mathbf{L}\mathbf{U}$, where $\mathbf{L}$ is the unit lower diagonal and $\mathbf{U}$ is an upper diagonal matrix:
  - This factorization is useful for solving the linear equation $\mathbf{A}\mathbf{x} = \mathbf{b}$.
  - The factorization does not always exist.
  - If $\mathbf{A}$ is symmetric, a factorization $\mathbf{L}\mathbf{D}\mathbf{L}^T$ always exists.
- A general square matrix $\mathbf{A}$ can be factorized as $\mathbf{A} = \mathbf{Q}\mathbf{R}$, where $\mathbf{Q}$ is an orthogonal matrix and $\mathbf{R}$ is upper triangular:
  - The factorization always exists.
  - Gram–Schmidt orthogonalization leads to one such factorization.
- A *symmetric positive definite matrix* $\mathbf{A}$ can be factorized as $\mathbf{A} = \mathbf{G}\mathbf{G}^T$, where $\mathbf{G}$ is a (unique) lower triangular matrix with positive diagonal elements:
  - This is the so-called Cholesky factorization.

B.5 Stochastic Matrices

Stochastic matrices are useful in representing finite state Markov processes. A matrix $\Phi \in \mathbb{R}^{N\times N}$ is a *stochastic* matrix if it (i) has nonnegative elements: $\Phi_{ij} \geq 0$ for all i, j, and (ii) elements sum to 1 over rows: $\sum_j \Phi_{ij} = 1$ for each row, i. The elements of Φ are interpreted as representing transition probabilities of an N-state Markov process, i.e.,

$$\mathbb{P}(s_{t+1} = n | s_t = m) = \Phi_{mn}, \quad s \in \{1, 2, \ldots, N\}.$$

The matrix $\Phi^2 = \Phi\Phi$ then represents the transition probabilities between t and $t+2$. For example, consider the 3-state Markov process,

$$\Phi = \begin{bmatrix} 0.8 & 0.2 & 0 \\ 0 & 0 & 1 \\ 0.05 & 0.95 & 0 \end{bmatrix}. \tag{B.1}$$

Then

$$\Phi^2 = \begin{bmatrix} 0.64 & 0.16 & 0.2 \\ 0.05 & 0.95 & 0 \\ 0.04 & 0.01 & 0.95 \end{bmatrix}$$

represents the transition probability over two periods. Consider, e.g., the element $[\Phi^2]_{1,2} = 0.16$, which states that if the process is in state 1 at t, there is a 16% chance that it will be in state 2 at $t+2$. This is indeed correct, since there is only one way the process can transition from states 1 to 2 in two periods: In the first period it must remain in state 1, which it does with an 80% chance. Then, in the second period, it must move to state 2, which it does with a 20% probability. So the total probability is $16\% = 80\% \times 20\%$. In general, we have

$$[\Phi^{T-t}]_{ij} = \mathbb{P}(s_T = j | s_t = i).$$

We use the Kolmogorov backward equation in the continuous-time part of the text. The discrete version, for Markov processes, states that for an arbitrary function $F: \{1, \ldots, N\} \to \mathbb{R}$, defining $F(j) = \mathbf{f}_j$, $\mathbf{f} \in \mathbb{R}^N$, it is the case that

$$E[F(s_T)|s_t = j] = [\Phi^{T-t}\mathbf{f}]_j, \quad T > t.$$

For the matrix defined in (B.1), we calculate

$$\Phi^{1000} = \begin{bmatrix} 0.111 & 0.444 & 0.444 \\ 0.111 & 0.444 & 0.444 \\ 0.111 & 0.444 & 0.444 \end{bmatrix}.$$

We note that all elements in each column are the same, the interpretation being that whichever state the process starts in at $t = 0$, the probability of being in another state much later is the same. In other words, the long-term (limiting) distribution is $\mathbf{p} = (0.111, 0.444, 0.444)'$ regardless of initial state. This convergence to the same long-term distribution regardless of initial state is not satisfied for any stochastic matrix.

A counterexample is given by the 2×2 matrix that represents moving back and forth between the two states:

$$\Phi = \begin{bmatrix} 0 & 1 \\ 1 & 0 \end{bmatrix}, \quad \Phi^2 = \begin{bmatrix} 1 & 0 \\ 0 & 1 \end{bmatrix}, \quad \Phi^3 = \begin{bmatrix} 0 & 1 \\ 1 & 0 \end{bmatrix}, \quad \ldots.$$

We call a vector $\mathbf{p} \in \mathbb{R}^N$ a *probability vector* if

- $\mathbf{p}_i \geq 0$,
- $\sum_i \mathbf{p}_i = 1$.

A probability vector is a *stationary distribution* for a stochastic matrix Φ if $\mathbf{p} = \Phi'\mathbf{p}$, i.e., if $\mathbf{p}$ is an eigenvector of Φ' with eigenvalue 1:

- Here, Φ' is the transpose of Φ, which satisfies $\langle \mathbf{a}, \Phi\mathbf{b} \rangle = \langle \Phi'\mathbf{a}, \mathbf{b} \rangle$ for all $\mathbf{a}$ and $\mathbf{b}$.
- Equivalently, we say that $\mathbf{p}$ is a *left eigenvector* of Φ with eigenvalue 1.

If the probability vector at t is $\mathbf{p}^t$, then at T it is $(\Phi')^{T-t}\mathbf{p}^t$. This is the Kolmogorov forward equation for a time-invariant N-state Markov process.

One can show that any stochastic matrix has a stationary distribution. However, there may be more than one. The *Perron–Frobenius theorem* provides the conditions needed for a unique stationary distribution to exist.

Definition B.6. A stochastic matrix is said to be *irreducible* if for each i, j, there exists $k > 0$ such that $(\Phi^k)_{ij} > 0$.

Definition B.7. The *period* of state i is k_i, the greatest common divisor of the set $\{n : (\Phi^n)_{ii} > 0\}$.

Definition B.8. If $k_i = 1$ for $i = 1, \ldots, N$, then Φ is said to be *aperiodic*. Otherwise it is said to be *periodic*.

The intuition here is that a periodic state can only be revisited at regular intervals, even after a long while.

Theorem B.7 (Perron–Frobenius theorem). *Consider an irreducible stochastic matrix Φ. Then Φ has a unique stationary distribution with strictly positive elements:*

- *All other left eigenvalues of Φ, $\lambda_2, \ldots, \lambda_N$, have $|\lambda_i| < 1$.*
- *All other left eigenvectors of Φ have at least one nonpositive element.*

If, in addition to irreducibility, the matrix is aperiodic, then regardless of initial state, the long-term distribution exists and is the same as the unique stationary distribution. Note that if Φ is strictly positive, $\Phi_{ij} > 0$ for all i, j, then it is both irreducible and aperiodic. If Φ is merely nonnegative, a stationary distribution exists, but

- there may exist multiple stationary distributions,
- the long-term distribution may not exist for some (or all) initial states.

APPENDIX C Real Analysis

C.1 Limits of Sequences and Series

Definition C.1. The *limit inferior* of a sequence, $\{x_n\}$, $n = 1, 2, \ldots$, is defined as

$$\liminf x_n = \lim_{n\to\infty} \inf\{x_m\}_{m\geq n}$$

and the *limit superior* as

$$\limsup x_n = \lim_{n\to\infty} \sup\{x_m\}_{m\geq n}.$$

It follows that

- lim inf and lim sup are always defined on the extended real line, $\bar{\mathbb{R}} = [-\infty, \infty]$,
- $\lim x$ exists in $\bar{\mathbb{R}}$ if and only if $\liminf x_n = \limsup x_n$, in which case

$$\lim x_n = \liminf x_n = \limsup x_n.$$

Important Limits

- If $p > 0$ then $\lim_{n\to\infty} \frac{1}{n^p} = 0$.
- If $p > 0$ then $\lim_{n\to\infty} \sqrt[n]{p} = 1$.
- $\lim_{n\to\infty} \sqrt[n]{n} = 1$.
- If $p > 0$ then $\lim_{n\to\infty} \frac{n^\alpha}{(1+p)^n} = 0$.
- If $|x| < 1$ then $\lim_{n\to\infty} x^n = 0$.

Calculus of Limits

If $s_n \to s \in \mathbb{R}$ and $t_n \to t \in \mathbb{R}$, then

- $\lim_{n\to\infty}(s_n + t_n) = s + t$,
- $\lim_{n\to\infty}(s_n t_n) = st$,
- $\lim_{n\to\infty} \frac{1}{s_n} = \frac{1}{s}$, if $s_n \neq 0$ and $s \neq 0$,
  - so $\lim_{n\to\infty} \frac{t_n}{s_n} = \frac{t}{s}$.

Series

- Consider the sequence $x_1, x_2, \ldots$.
- Denote by s_n the sum

$$s_n = \sum_{k=1}^{n} x_k.$$

- Consider the sequence $s_1, s_2, \ldots$.

- If $s_n \to s$, i.e., if
$$\lim_{n\to\infty} \sum_{k=1}^{n} x_k \to s,$$
we say that the *series*, s_n, converges to s and we write
$$\sum_{n=1}^{\infty} x_n = s.$$

A necessary condition for convergence of a series is that
$$x_n \to 0.$$
However, this is not a sufficient condition! A counterexample is given by $x_n = \frac{1}{n}$, for which the associated series can be shown to be bounded below by the logarithmic function.

Important Limits of Series, and Testing for Convergence

- For all $x \neq 1$, $\sum_{n=0}^{N} x^n = \frac{1-x^{N+1}}{1-x}$.
- If $|x| < 1$, then $\sum_{n=0}^{\infty} x^n = \frac{1}{1-x}$.
- $\sum_n \frac{1}{n^p}$ converges if $p > 1$ and diverges if $p \le 1$.
- $\sum_{n=2}^{\infty} \frac{1}{n(\log n)^p}$ converges if $p > 1$ and diverges if $p \le 1$.
- Here, $\log(n) = \ln(n) = \log_e(n)$ (natural logarithm).

Consider the series $s_n = \sum_{k=1}^{n} x_k$:

- *Root test*: Define $\alpha = \lim\sup \sqrt[n]{|x_n|}$:
  - If $\alpha < 1$, the series converges.
  - If $\alpha > 1$, the series diverges.
  - If $\alpha = 1$, the test is inconclusive.
- *Ratio test*: If $\lim\sup |\frac{x_{n+1}}{x_n}| < 1$, the series converges.

Of these two tests, the ratio test is typically easier to perform, but the root test is more general in that it can be used to show convergence in more cases.

An extremely important class of series is the class of so-called *power series*. Such series provide the basis for analytic functions in the mathematical field of complex analysis.

Given a sequence, $c_0, c_1, c_2, \ldots$, and a complex (or real) number z, formally define the function
$$F(z) = \sum_{n=0}^{\infty} c_n z^n,$$
for z such that the series converges.

- As in the root test, define $\alpha = \lim\sup^n \sqrt{|c_n|}$, and $R = \frac{1}{\alpha}$.
- It follows that for any z, such that $|z| < R$, $F(z)$ is defined.
- Within the radius of convergence, F is a *very* well-behaved (analytic) function.
  - For example, termwise differentiation always works: $F'(z) = \sum_{n=1}^{\infty} n c_n z^{n-1}$.

C.2 Continuity

Consider a function $f: X \to Y$, where X and Y are metric spaces:

- f is *continuous* at $x_1 \in X$ if for all $\epsilon > 0$, there exists $\delta > 0$, such that $d(f(x_1), f(x_2)) < \epsilon$ if $d(x_1, x_2) < \delta$.

- If f is continuous for all x, then f is said to be continuous on X.
- Important intuition: If f is a continuous function, and x_1 is close to x_2, then $f(x_1)$ is close to $f(x_2)$.

Theorem C.1 (Continuous function theorem). *Assume $f: X \to Y$ is continuous at $x \in X$, and consider the sequence $\{x_n\}_n$, such that $x_n \to x$. Then the sequence $f(x_1), f(x_2), f(x_3), \ldots$, converges to $f(x)$,*

$$f(x_n) \to f(x).$$

The extension of the continuous function theorem to random variables is the *continuous mapping theorem.*

A function $f: X \to Y$ is said to be *uniformly* continuous on X if for all ϵ, there exists $\delta > 0$, such that $d(x_1, x_2) < \delta \Rightarrow d(f(x_1), f(x_2)) < \epsilon$.

- Compare with continuity on X: for all $x \in X$, for all $\epsilon > 0$, there exists $\delta > 0$ such that $d(x, x_2) < \delta \Rightarrow d(f(x), f(x_2)) < \epsilon$.
- Thus, δ is *not* allowed to depend on x for uniform continuity!

Theorem C.2 (Rudin 1976, theorem 7.12). *If $\{f_n\}$ is a sequence of continuous functions on some set $E \subset \mathbb{R}$, $f_n: E \to \mathbb{R}$, and $f_n \to f$ uniformly on E, then f is continuous on E.*

Proof. See Rudin for a full proof. The result follows by checking that

$$\begin{aligned}|f(y) - f(x)| &= |f(y) - f_n(y) + f_n(y) - f_n(x) + f_n(x) - f(x)| \\ &\leq |f(y) - f_n(y)| + |f_n(y) - f_n(x)| + |f_n(x) - f(x)|.\end{aligned}$$

The first and third terms are small when n is large, say $\leq \frac{\epsilon}{3}$, regardless of x and y. For a given n, by choosing x and y close, the middle term is also smaller than $\frac{\epsilon}{3}$, so the total is small, $|f(y) - f(x)| \leq \epsilon$, and f is therefore continuous. □

Remark C.1. A counterexample, where a sequence of functions converges but the convergence is not uniform, is $E = [0, 1]$, $f_n(x) = x^n$. The functions are continuous for all n and the sequence converges (pointwise) to a function, f, but that function is discontinuous at 1: $f(x) = 0$ for $0 \leq x < 1$, and $f(1) = 1$.

C.3 Derivatives and Taylor Expansions

Consider the function $f: [a, b] \to \mathbb{R}$:

- f is said to be differentiable at x, $a \leq x \leq b$, if

  $$y = \lim_{h \to 0} \frac{f(x+h) - f(x)}{h}$$

  exists and is finite.
- We write $y = f'(x)$, and say that y is the derivative of f at x.
- We also write $y = \frac{df}{dx}(x)$.

The following properties of derivatives are good to know:

- $(f+g)'(x) = f'(x) + g'(x)$.
- Product rule: $(fg)'(x) = f'(x)g(x) + f(x)g'(x)$.

- Chain rule: $g(f(x))' = g'(f(x))f'(x)$:
  - $(\frac{1}{g})'(x) = -\frac{g'(x)}{g^2(x)}$ if $g(x) \neq 0$.
  - $f(ax)' = af'(ax)$.
- $(x^n)' = nx^{n-1}$, $n \neq 0$.
- $\sin(x)' = \cos(x)$.
- $\cos(x)' = -\sin(x)$.
- $(e^x)' = e^x$.
- $\log(x)' = \frac{1}{x}$, $x > 0$.

Theorem C.3 (Mean value theorem). *If f is continuous on $[a,b]$, and differentiable in (a,b), then there is a point $x \in (a,b)$, such that*

$$\frac{f(b)-f(a)}{b-a} = f'(x).$$

Theorem C.4 (L'Hospital's rule). *Assume that f and g are differentiable in (a,b), and $g'(x^*) \neq 0$ for some $x \in (a,b)$. Suppose*

$$\frac{f'(x)}{g'(x)} \to A, \quad x \to x^*,$$

and $f(x) \to 0$, $g(x) \to 0$ when $x \to x^*$. Then

$$\frac{f(x)}{g(x)} \to A, \quad x \to x^*.$$

We define higher-order derivatives iteratively:

- Second-order derivative: $f'' = (f')' = f^{(2)} = \frac{d^2 f}{dx^2}$.
- nth-order derivative $f^{(n)} = (f^{(n-1)})'$.

For smooth functions (i.e., those that have many derivatives), Taylor's theorem provides an extremely powerful method of providing a very close local approximation by a polynomial:

Theorem C.5 (Taylor's theorem). *Consider a function $f : [a,b] \to \mathbb{R}$, such that $f^{(n-1)}$ is continuous on $[a,b]$ and $f^{(n)}(x)$ exists for all $x \in (a,b)$. Let α, β be distinct points in (a,b) and define*

$$P^{(n-1)}(\beta) = \sum_{k=0}^{n-1} \frac{f^{(k)}(\alpha)}{k!}(\beta-\alpha)^k.$$

Then there exists a point y between α and β, such that

$$f(\beta) = P^{n-1}(\beta) + \frac{f^{(n)}(y)}{n!}(\beta-\alpha)^n.$$

For x close to α, the error of approximating f with $P^{(n-1)}$, $|f(x) - P^{(n-1)}(x)|$, is bounded by $C(x-\alpha)^n$, for some finite constant, $C > 0$.

C.4 Multivariate Calculus

- Consider the mapping $f : X \to \mathbb{R}^M$, where $X \subset \mathbb{R}^N$ is an open set.
- If there exists $\mathbf{A} \in \mathcal{L}(\mathbb{R}^N, \mathbb{R}^M)$ such that

$$\lim_{\mathbf{h}\to\mathbf{0}} \frac{\|f(\mathbf{x}+\mathbf{h}) - f(\mathbf{x}) - \mathbf{A}\mathbf{h}\|}{\|\mathbf{h}\|} = 0,$$

then f is *differentiable* at $\mathbf{x}$ and $f' = \mathbf{A}$ is the *total derivative* of f at $\mathbf{x}$.

- For a function $f\colon \mathbb{R}^N \to \mathbb{R}^M$, define the *partial derivative*

$$a_{nm} = \frac{\partial f(\mathbf{x})_m}{\partial x_n} = D_n(f)_m.$$

Theorem C.6. *If the function f is differentiable at a point $\mathbf{x}$, then the function's total derivative at that point is given by $\mathbf{A} \in \mathbb{R}^{M\times N}$, where*

$$\mathbf{A} = \begin{bmatrix} a_{11} & \cdots & a_{1N} \\ \vdots & & \vdots \\ a_{M1} & \cdots & a_{MN} \end{bmatrix}.$$

A caveat here is that the partial derivatives may exist even when the total derivative does not. For the special case when $M = 1$, where $f\colon \mathbb{R}^N \to \mathbb{R}^1$ is differentiable,

- the gradient operator is $\mathbf{A} = \nabla f = \begin{bmatrix} \frac{\partial f}{\partial x_1} & \cdots & \frac{\partial f}{\partial x_N} \end{bmatrix}$,
- $\lim_{t\to 0} \frac{f(\mathbf{x}+t\mathbf{u})-f(\mathbf{x})}{t} = (\nabla f)(\mathbf{x})\mathbf{u}$,
- $f(\mathbf{x}+t\mathbf{u}) \approx f(\mathbf{x}) + t\nabla f(\mathbf{x})\mathbf{u}$.

Definition C.2. The function f is continuously differentiable on E, written $f \in C^1(E)$, if f' is a continuous mapping of E into $\mathcal{L}(\mathbb{R}^N, \mathbb{R}^M)$, i.e., if for all $\epsilon > 0$, there exists $\delta > 0$ such that

$$\|f'(\mathbf{y}) - f'(\mathbf{x})\| < \epsilon \quad \text{whenever } \|\mathbf{x}-\mathbf{y}\| < \delta.$$

One can show that $f \in C^1$ if and only if all its partial derivatives exist and are continuous. Continuous differentiability is stronger than just differentiability.

Theorem C.7 (Inverse function theorem). *Suppose $E \subset \mathbb{R}^N$ and $f\colon E \to \mathbb{R}^N$ is a C^1 mapping such that $f'(\mathbf{a})$ is invertible and $f(\mathbf{a}) = \mathbf{b}$. Then there exists a C^1 mapping $g\colon U \to V$, where U and V are open neighborhoods with $\mathbf{a} \in V$, $\mathbf{b} \in U$, such that*

$$g(f(\mathbf{x})) = \mathbf{x} \quad \forall \mathbf{x} \in V.$$

Definition C.3. The function $f\colon \mathbb{R}^N \to \mathbb{R}^M$ is C^2 if all partial derivatives exist and are C^1.

- In this case $D_{nk}(f_m) = D_{kn}(f_m)$.
- The function f is C^3 if all partial derivatives exist and are C^2 and so on....
- The mth-order partial derivative $D_{\mathbf{k}}$, where $\mathbf{k} \in \{1,\dots,N\}^m$, is given by

$$D_{k_1,\dots,k_m} = \frac{\partial^m f}{\partial x_{k_1}\partial x_{k_2}\cdots\partial x_{k_m}}.$$

We define the set $K_{NM} = \{\mathbf{k} \in \{0,1,2,\dots,M\}^N : 0 \le \sum_i k_i \le M\}$:

- $p\colon \mathbb{R}^N \to \mathbb{R}$ is an Mth-order *multivariate polynomial* on $\mathbb{R}^N$ if

$$p(\mathbf{x}) = \sum_{\mathbf{k}\in K_{NM}} c(\mathbf{k}) \prod_{n=1}^{N} x_n^{k_n}.$$

- Example: $p(x_1,x_2,x_3) = 5 + 3x_1 + 2x_1x_3 + x_2^4$ is a 4th-order ($M = 4$) multivariate polynomial on $\mathbb{R}^3$ ($N = 3$), $p\colon \mathbb{R}^3 \to \mathbb{R}$.
- The class of multivariate polynomials of order no more than M on $\mathbb{R}^N$ is denoted by $\mathcal{P}_N^M$.

Theorem C.8 (Multivariate Taylor expansion). *Consider a C^{M+1} function $f\colon \mathbb{R}^N \to \mathbb{R}$, and define the polynomial $p \in \mathcal{P}_N^M$ by*

$$p(\mathbf{y}) = \sum_{\mathbf{k}\in K_{NM}} \frac{1}{\mathbf{k}!}(D_{\mathbf{k}}f)(\mathbf{x}) \prod_{n=1}^{N} (y_n - x_n)^{k_n}.$$

Then $|f(\mathbf{y}) - p(\mathbf{y})| \le C\|\mathbf{y} - \mathbf{x}\|^{M+1}$ in a neighborhood of $\mathbf{x}$.

We define the *Hessian* as the matrix $\mathbf{H} \in \mathbb{R}^{N\times N}$ that contains all the second-order partial derivatives, D_{nk}:

$$\mathbf{H} = \begin{bmatrix} \frac{\partial^2 F}{\partial x_1^2} & \frac{\partial^2 F}{\partial x_1 \partial x_2} & \cdots & \frac{\partial^2 F}{\partial x_1 \partial x_N} \\ \frac{\partial^2 F}{\partial x_2 \partial x_1} & \frac{\partial^2 F}{\partial x_2^2} & \cdots & \frac{\partial^2 F}{\partial x_2 \partial x_N} \\ \vdots & \vdots & \cdots & \vdots \\ \frac{\partial^2 F}{\partial x_N \partial x_1} & \frac{\partial^2 F}{\partial x_N \partial x_2} & \cdots & \frac{\partial^2 F}{\partial x_N^2} \end{bmatrix}.$$

We also write $\mathbf{H}(\mathbf{x})$ if we want to emphasize the dependence of the Hessian on $\mathbf{x}$.

The second-order multivariate Taylor expansion can then conveniently be written as

$$p(\mathbf{y}) = f(\mathbf{x}) + (\nabla f)(\mathbf{x})(\mathbf{y} - \mathbf{x}) + \frac{1}{2}(\mathbf{y} - \mathbf{x})'\mathbf{H}(\mathbf{y} - \mathbf{x}).$$

The multidimensional chain rule takes the following form. Consider the functions $f\colon \mathbb{R}^N \to \mathbb{R}^M$ and $g\colon \mathbb{R}^M \to \mathbb{R}^K$, where both functions are differentiable. Define $h(\mathbf{x}) = g(f(\mathbf{x})) = g \circ f(\mathbf{x})$. Then

$$\underbrace{h'(\mathbf{x}_0)}_{\mathbf{C}\in\mathbb{R}^{K\times N}} = \underbrace{g'(f(\mathbf{x}_0))}_{\mathbf{A}\in\mathbb{R}^{K\times M}} \times \underbrace{f'(\mathbf{x}_0)}_{\mathbf{B}\in\mathbb{R}^{M\times N}} \quad \in \mathbb{R}^{K\times N},$$

that is,

$$\mathbf{C} = \mathbf{AB}.$$

C.5 Optimization

Definition C.4. A set $E \subset \mathbb{R}^N$ is said to be *convex* if for all $\lambda \in (0, 1)$, for all $x \in E$, for all $y \in E$, $\lambda x + (1 - \lambda)y \in E$.

Definition C.5. A function $f\colon E \to \mathbb{R}$, where $E \subset \mathbb{R}^N$ is convex, is said to be

- *concave* if for all $\lambda \in (0, 1)$, $x, y \in E$,

$$f(\lambda x + (1 - \lambda)y) \ge \lambda f(x) + (1 - \lambda)f(y),$$

- *convex* if for all $\lambda \in (0, 1)$, $x, y \in E$,

$$f(\lambda x + (1 - \lambda)y) \le \lambda f(x) + (1 - \lambda)f(y),$$

- *strictly concave* if for all $\lambda \in (0, 1)$, $x, y \in E$,

$$f(\lambda x + (1 - \lambda)y) > \lambda f(x) + (1 - \lambda)f(y),$$

- *strictly convex* if for all $\lambda \in (0, 1)$, $x, y \in E$,

$$f(\lambda x + (1 - \lambda)y) < \lambda f(x) + (1 - \lambda)f(y).$$

Theorem C.9. *Consider a C^1 function $f\colon [a,b] \to \mathbb{R}$, which satisfies $f'(x^*) = 0$ for some $x^* \in [a,b]$. If*

- *f is concave, then x^* is a maximum,*
- *f is strictly concave, then x^* is the unique maximum,*
- *f is convex, then x^* is a minimum,*
- *f is strictly convex, then x^* is the unique minimum.*

The multivariate version of this theorem is as follows:

Theorem C.10. *Consider a C^2 function $f\colon E \to \mathbb{R}$ for a convex set $E \subset \mathbb{R}^N$, where f satisfies $\nabla f(\mathbf{x}^*) = \mathbf{0}$ for some $\mathbf{x}^* \in E$. If*

- *f is concave, then $\mathbf{x}^*$ is a maximum,*
- *f is convex, then $\mathbf{x}^*$ is a minimum,*
- *f is strictly concave, then $\mathbf{x}^*$ is a unique maximum,*
- *f is strictly convex, then $\mathbf{x}^*$ is a unique minimum.*

If the function is smooth, in that $f\colon E \to \mathbb{R}$ is C^2 (twice continuously differentiable), then

- if f concave, its Hessian, **H**, is negative semidefinite.
- if f is strictly concave, its Hessian, **H**, is negative definite.
- if f is convex, its Hessian, **H**, is positive semidefinite.
- if f strictly convex, its Hessian, **H**, is positive definite.

We next focus on constrained optimization, i.e., optimization under which some constraints need to be satisfied. There are many variations. Here we focus on what may be the simplest one, where the constraint is an equality. Consider the problem of finding $\max f(\mathbf{x})$, subject to the requirement that $g(\mathbf{x}) = 0$ for some smooth function $g\colon \mathbb{R}^N \to \mathbb{R}$:

Theorem C.11. *Consider the problem*

$$\max f(\mathbf{x}),$$
$$\text{s.t. } g(\mathbf{x}) = 0,$$

for C^1 functions $f, g\colon E \to \mathbb{R}$ and a convex set $E \subset \mathbb{R}^N$.

A necessary condition for $\mathbf{x}^* \in \text{int}(E)$ to be an optimum is that for some $\lambda \in \mathbb{R}$ we have

- *$\nabla f(\mathbf{x}^*) = \lambda \nabla g(\mathbf{x}^*)$, and*
- *$g(\mathbf{x}^*) = 0$.*

An equivalent formulation to the theorem is to solve the *Lagrangian optimization problem*

$$\max_{\mathbf{x},\lambda} f(\mathbf{x}) - \lambda g(\mathbf{x}),$$

leading to the equivalent first-order conditions

- $\frac{\partial}{\partial \mathbf{x}}\colon \nabla f - \lambda \nabla g = \mathbf{0}$,
- $\frac{\partial}{\partial \lambda}\colon g(\mathbf{x}) = 0$.

APPENDIX D Lebesgue–Stieltjes Integral

One may ask whether the issue with defining certain stochastic integrals is that we have used the Riemann approach to integration, instead of the Lebesgue approach. This is *not* the case. Lebesgue integrals are good at taking care of irregularities of functions that occur on sets of small length (measure). The Stieltjes integral approach, however, breaks down everywhere for the type of functions we are studying, and the Lebesgue approach will therefore be of little help.

To focus on the core difference between the Riemann and Lebesgue integrals, we follow the Daniell approach, as discussed in Riesz and Nagy (1990). An advantage for us of this approach is that it avoids the whole measure-theoretic machinery needed in the standard approach, and therefore makes the core difference from the Riemann (Stieltjes) integral quite transparent.

Consider a set $E \subset \mathbb{R}$. A finite covering of E is a set $C = \bigcup_{i \in X}[a_i, b_i]$, such that $E \subset C$, where $|X| < \infty$. Similarly, a countable covering is defined when X is countable. If, for every $\epsilon > 0$, E can be covered by a countable covering such that $\sum_i (b_i - a_i) < \epsilon$, E is said to be a *null set*, or of *measure zero*. A property that holds for all x, except on a null set, is said to hold *almost everywhere* (a.e.), or *for almost all* x.

A function, $\phi\colon [a, b] \to \mathbb{R}$, is a step function if there is an interval partition, $\mathcal{P}$, such that $\phi(x)$ is constant for all $x_i \le x < x_{i+1}$, for all i. The set of all such step functions is S. For such a step function, it is trivial to define the integral $\int_a^b \phi\, dx = \sum_i \phi(x_i)(x_{i+1} - x_i)$.

For an arbitrary nonnegative function, $f\colon [a, b] \to \mathbb{R}$, if there is an increasing sequence of step functions, ϕ^n, with partitions $\mathcal{P}^n = \{x_1^n, \ldots, x_{N_n}^n\}$, $n = 1, \ldots,$ such that

- $\phi^n(x) \nearrow f(x)$ almost everywhere,
- $\lim_{n\to\infty} \int \phi^n\, dx = M < \infty$,

then we say that f is *Lebesgue measurable* and *Lebesgue integrable* (since $M < \infty$) and that its *Lebesgue integral* is $\int_a^b f\, dx = M$.

We extend the integral to arbitrary signed functions, f, by defining $f = f^+ - (-f^-)$, where $f^+(x) = \max(f(x), 0)$ and $f^-(x) = \min(f(x), 0)$, $\int f\, dx = M^+ + M^-$, where $M^+ = \int f^+\, dx$, $M^- = -\int -(f^-)\, dx$, and we require that M^+ and M^- are finite. For a signed integrable function, we write $f \in L^1([a, b])$.

Remark D.1. The key difference between the Lebesgue and Riemann integrals is that the convergence needs only to hold almost everywhere for the Lebesgue integral. Therefore, the function may behave quite wildly in many places, as long as these are of measure zero. For the Riemann integral, on the other hand, since we take the supremum and infimum on each interval, in the limit, they can only fail to match on a zero measure set. Another way of stating this is that for the Riemann sums to converge, $\lim_{n\to\infty} \sum_{i=1}^n \sup_{x \in [x_i, x_{i+1})} |f(x) - \phi^n(x_i)|(x_{i+1} - x_i)$ must converge to zero, whereas for the Lebesgue integral to be defined, $\lim_{n\to\infty} |f(x) - \phi^n(x)|$ must converge to zero for almost all x. The first convergence implies the second, since for arbitrary $\epsilon > 0$, the total length of the intervals where sup $|f - \phi^n|$ is larger than ϵ must eventually become small, otherwise convergence cannot occur.

Remark D.2. A classic example of a function that is Lebesgue integrable but not Riemann integrable on [0, 1] is the function that is zero everywhere but on the rational field, where it is 1, i.e.,

$$f(x) = 1, \quad x \in \mathbb{Q},$$
$$f(x) = 0, \quad x \in \mathbb{R} \backslash \mathbb{Q}.$$

The Lebesgue integral $\int_0^1 f\, dx$ is 0, since the sequence $\phi^n \equiv 0$, $n = 1, 2, \ldots$, converges to f almost everywhere. The Riemann integral is undefined since the lower sum is 0, whereas the upper sum is 1, regardless of the partition, so there is no convergence between the two sums as the partitions are refined.

Remark D.3. It is possible to show that the Riemann integral is defined if and only if f is continuous almost everywhere.

Remark D.4. To show that the Lebesgue integral is well defined, we would need to show that the sum over any sequence of interval partitions converges to the same M. This is done in Riesz and Nagy (1990).

Remark D.5. For a nonnegative function, f, it is easy to show that $\int f\, dx = \sup_{\phi \in S, \phi \leq f \text{ a.e.}} \int \phi\, dx$. This argument can be extended to signed functions, using the sign decomposition above. Once the integral is defined, the supremum of the ϕ's can be taken over function spaces other than the step functions, e.g., all continuous functions, $\phi \in C([a, b])$, and since the Riemann integral is defined for such functions, and Lebesgue and Riemann coincide when both integrals are defined, the Riemann integral can also be used in the definition, over these function spaces.

Remark D.6. For those who have taken a course in measure theory, this definition of the Lebesgue above integral is equivalent to the standard measure-theoretic definition, and is therefore defined over Borel-measurable functions, $f^{-1}(I) \in \mathcal{B}(\mathbb{R})$, as well as for Lebesgue-measurable functions, $f^{-1}(I) \in \mathcal{M}_{\lambda_*}(\mathbb{R})$. Here, $\mathcal{M}_{\lambda_*}(\mathbb{R})$ denotes the completion of the Borel sigma-algebra with respect to Lebesgue measure, $\mathcal{B}(\mathbb{R}) \subset \mathcal{M}_{\lambda_*}(\mathbb{R})$.

The methodology is easy to extend to the *Lebesgue–Stieltjes* integral, for an arbitrary Borel-measurable, integrable, function, f, and a function of bounded variation, α. Once again, without loss of generality we can assume that f is nonnegative. The idea is to use a similar definition to remark D.5, but instead of the Riemann integral use the Riemann–Stieltjes integral, i.e., $\underline{\int} f\, d\alpha = \sup_{\phi \in C,\, \phi \leq f \text{ a.e.}} \int \phi\, d\alpha$, using the standard Riemann–Stieltjes definition for the integral on the right-hand side. Similarly, $\overline{\int} f\, d\alpha = \inf_{\phi \in C,\, \phi \geq f \text{ a.e.}} \int \phi\, d\alpha$. If $\overline{\int} f\, d\alpha = \underline{\int} f\, d\alpha$, then it is said to be the *Lebesgue–Stieltjes* integral. It can be shown that the integral is always defined for Borel-measurable functions (if $\pm\infty$ is included in the range of the integral).

Remark D.7. It is clear that for a continuous function, f, the Lebesgue–Stieltjes definition adds nothing compared with the Riemann–Stieltjes definition, since f can be chosen in the upper and lower integrals and it then just collapses to the standard Riemann–Stieltjes integral. Thus, if the Riemann–Stieltjes integral is not defined for a continuous function, f, because of the behavior of α, it will not be defined for the Lebesgue–Stieltjes integral either. So "'moving to Lebesgue" will not help with the issues we faced when trying to define the Riemann–Stieltjes integral for Itô processes.

An important theorem within the theory of Lebesgue integration is the *dominated convergence theorem*, which allows one to switch the order of taking limits and integration:

Theorem D.1 (Dominated convergence theorem). *Consider a sequence of Lebesgue measurable functions, f_n, $n = 1, 2, \ldots$, that converges pointwise to the function f (i.e., $\lim_{n\to\infty} f_n(x) = f(x)$ for all x), such that there is a Lebesgue-integrable function g that dominates the sequence in the sense that $f_n(x) \leq g(x)$ for all x. Then f is Lebesgue integrable, and*

$$\lim_n \int f_n(x)\,dx = \int \lim_n f_n(x)\,dx = \int f(x)\,dx.$$

APPENDIX E MATLAB Code

Construction of a Wiener Process

```
%function BrownianMotion(J,Choice)
%
%Creates a standard Wiener process at dyadic discretizations k2^{-J}, using
%three approaches:
% Choice=1 => noninterpolating
% Choice=2 => interpolating ("filling in holes"), vector version
% Choice=3 => interpolating, Haar matrix version
function [t,W,dW,Z]=BrownianMotion(J,Choice)
N=2^J;
t=(0:N)/N;
Z=[];
if (Choice==1) %Noninterpolating
   dW=sqrt(1/N)*randn(1,N);
   W=[0,cumsum(dW)];
end;
if (Choice==2) %Interpolating
  W=[0,randn(1,1)];
  n=1;dT=1;
  for j=1:J
    Wnew=zeros(1,2*n+1);
    for k=1:n
      Wnew(2*k+1)=W(k+1);
    end;
    xi=randn(1,n)*sqrt(dT)/2;
    for k=1:n
      Wnew(2*k)=(Wnew(2*k-1)+Wnew(2*k+1))/2+xi(k);
    end;
    n=2*n;dT=dT/2;
    W=Wnew;
  end;
  dW=W(2:n+1)-W(1:n);
end;
if (Choice==3)
  %Haar basis: Important points:
  %(i) 2^{j/2}Z is an orthogonal matrix, so when xi
```

```
  %is independent normal, so is Zxi leading to independent increments
  %(ii) for N-step matrix, $Z(N)_{k,j}=Z(N+1)_{2k,j}$, so value does
  %not change at dyadic points as number of elements is increased
  A=zeros(N,N,J);
  for j=1:J
    Del=2^(j-1);
    for k=2*Del+1:N
      A(k,k,j)=1; %Part not resolved yet
    end;
    for k=0:Del-1
      A(2*k+1,k+1,j)=1/2;
      A(2*k+1,k+1+Del,j)=-1/(2*sqrt(Del));
      A(2*k+2,k+1,j)=1/2;
      A(2*k+2,k+1+Del,j)=1/(2*sqrt(Del));
    end;
  end;
  Z=eye(N);
  for j=1:J
    Z=A(:,:,j)*Z;
  end;
  U=triu(ones(N,N));
  Zcum=U*Z;
  xi=randn(N,1);
  dW=Z*xi;
  W=[0,cumsum(dW)'];
end;
```

Bibliography

Abel, A., 1990, Asset prices under habit formation and catching up with the Joneses, *American Economic Review, Papers and Proceedings* 80, 38–42.

Admati, A. R., 1985, A noisy rational expectations equilibrium for multi-asset securities markets, *Econometrica* 53, 629–658.

Aït-Sahalia, Y., 2004, Disentangling diffusion from jumps, *Journal of Financial Economics* 74, 487–528.

Aït-Sahalia, Y., and J. Jacod, 2009, Testing for jumps in a discretely observed process, *Annals of Statistics* 37, 184–222.

Aït-Sahalia, Y., and A. W. Lo, 1998, Nonparametric estimation of state-price densities implicit in financial asset prices, *Journal of Finance* 53, 499–547.

Albrecher, H., P. Mayer, W. Shoutens, and J. Tistaert, 2007, The little Heston trap, *Wilmott Magazine* 1, 83–92.

Allais, M., 1953, Le comportement de l'homme rationell devant le risque: Critique des postulats et axioms de l'ecole Américaine, *Econometrica* 21, 503–546.

Alvarez, F., and J. Jerman, 2005, Using asset prices to measure the persistence of the marginal utility of wealth, *Econometrica* 73, 1977–2016.

Anderson, R. M., and R. C. Raimondo, 2008, Equilibrium in continuous-time financial markets: Endogenously dynamically complete markets, *Econometrica* 76, 841–907.

Ang, A., R. J. Hodrick, Y. Xing, and X. Zhang, 2006, The cross-section of volatility and expected returns, *Journal of Finance* 61, 259–299.

Arrow, K. J., 1951, An extension of the basic theorems of classic welfare economics, in *Proceedings of the Second Berkeley Symposium of Mathematical Statistics and Probability* (University of California Press).

Arrow, K. J., 1971, *Essays in the theory of risk bearing* (Markham).

Aumann, R. J., 1976, Agreeing to disagree, *Annals of Statistics* 4, 1236–1239.

Back, K., and S. R. Pliska, 1991, On the fundamental theorem of asset pricing with an infinite state space, *Journal of Mathematical Economics* 20, 1–18.

Bansal, R., and A. Yaron, 2005, Risks for the long run: A potential resolution of asset pricing puzzles, *Journal of Finance* 59, 1481–1509.

Banz, R. W., 1981, The relationship between return and market value of common stocks, *Journal of Financial Economics* 9, 3–18.

Barro, R. J., 2006, Rare disasters and asset markets in the twentieth century, *Quarterly Journal of Economics* 121, 211–221.

Basak, S., 2005, Asset pricing with heterogeneous beliefs, *Journal of Banking & Finance* 29, 2849–2881.

Bellman, R. E., 1957, *Dynamic programming* (Princeton University Press).

Berk, J. B., 1995, A critique of size-related anomalies, *Review of Financial Studies* 8, 275–286.

Berk, J. B., and J. H. van Binsbergen, 2025, The impact of impact investing, *Journal of Financial Economics*, forthcoming.

Betermeier, S., L. Calvet, E. Jo, and J. Walden, 2023, Two trees and a gardener, Working Paper, UC Berkeley.

Bizid, A., and E. Jouini, 1995, Equilibrium pricing in incomplete markets, *Journal of Financial and Quantitative Analysis* 40, 833–848.

Björk, T., 2009, *Arbitrage theory in continuous time* (Oxford University Press).

Black, F., and R. Litterman, 1991, Asset allocation: Combining investor views with market equilibrium, *Journal of Fixed Income* 1, 7–18.

Black, F., and R. Litterman, 1992, Global portfolio optimization, *Financial Analyst Journal* 48, 28–43.

Black, F., and M. Scholes, 1973, The pricing of options and corporate liabilities, *Journal of Political Economy* 81, 637–654.

Blackwell, D., 1965, Discounted dynamic programming, *Annals of Mathematical Statistics* 36, 226–235.

Borodin, A. N., and P. Salminen, 2000, *Handbook of Brownian motion—Facts and formulae* (Birkhäuser).

Borovička, J., L. P. Hansen, and J. A. Scheinkman, 2016, Misspecified recovery, *Journal of Finance* 71, 2493–2544.

Breeden, D. T., 1979, An intertemporal asset pricing model with stochastic consumption and investment opportunities, *Journal of Financial Economics* 7, 265–296.

Breeden, D. T., and R. H. Litzenberger, 1978, Prices of state-contingent claims implicit in option prices, *Journal of Business* 51, 621–651.

Brunnermeier, M. K., A. Simsek, and W. Xiong, 2014, A welfare criterion for models with distorted beliefs, *Quarterly Journal of Economics* 129, 1753–97.

Campbell, J. Y., 2003, Consumption-based asset pricing, in R. M. Stultz, G. Constantinides, and M. Harris, eds., *Handbook of the economics of finance*, volume 1B. (North Holland).

Campbell, J. Y., and J. H. Cochrane, 1999, By force of habit: A consumption-based explanation of aggregate stock market behavior, *Journal of Political Economy* 107, 205–251.

Campbell, J. Y., and L. M. Viceira, 1999, Consumption and portfolio decisions when expected returns are time varying, *Quarterly Journal of Economics* 114, 433–495.

Carhart, M. M., 1997, On persistence in mutual fund performance, *Journal of Finance* 52, 57–82.

Carr, P., and R. A. Jarrow, 1990, The stop-loss start-gain paradox and option valuation: A new decomposition into intrinsic and time value, *Review of Financial Studies* 3, 469–492.

Carr, P., and D. B. Madan, 1999, Option valuation using the fast Fourier transform, *Journal of Computational Finance* 2, 61–73.

Carr, P., and J. Yu, 2012, Risk, return, and Ross recovery, *Journal of Derivatives* 20, 38–59.

Cass, D., and J. Stiglitz, 1970, The structure of investor preferences and asset returns, and separability in portfolio allocation: A contribution to the pure theory of mutual funds, *Journal of Economic Theory* 2, 122–160.

Cocco, J. F., F. J. Gomes, and P. J. Maenhout, 2005, Consumption and portfolio choice over the life cycle, *Review of Financial Studies* 18, 491–533.

Cochrane, J. H., 1996, A cross-sectional test of an investment-based asset pricing model, *Journal of Political Economy* 104, 572–621.

Cochrane, J. H., F. A. Longstaff, and P. Santa-Clara, 2008, Two trees, *Review of Financial Studies* 21, 347–385.

Constantinides, G. M., and D. Duffie, 1996, Asset pricing with heterogeneous consumers, *Journal of Political Economy* 104, 219–240.

Copeland, T., T. Koller, and J. Murrin, 1994, *Valuation: Measuring and managing the value of companies* (Wiley).

Cover, T. M., 1991, Universal portfolios, *Mathematical Finance* 1, 1–29.

Cox, J. C., 1975, Notes on option pricing I: Constant elasticity of variance diffusion, Working Paper, Stanford University.

Cox, J. C., and C.-H. Huang, 1989, Optimal consumption and portfolio policies when asset prices follow a diffusion process, *Journal of Economic Theory* 49, 33–83.

Cox, J. C., J. E. Ingersoll, and S. A. Ross, 1981, A reexamination of traditional hypotheses about the term structure of interest rates, *Journal of Finance* 73, 321–346.

Cox, J. C., J. E. Ingersoll, and S. A. Ross, 1985, An intertemporal general equilibrium model of asset prices, *Econometrica* 53, 363–384.

Cox, J. C., J. E. Ingersoll, and S. A. Ross, 1985, A theory of the term structure of interest rates, *Econometrica* 53, 385–407.

Cox, J. C., and S. A. Ross, 1976, The valuation of options for alternative stochastic processes, *Journal of Financial Economics* 3, 145–166.

Cox, J. C., S. A. Ross, and M. Rubinstein, 1979, Option pricing: A simplified approach, *Journal of Financial Economics* 7(3), 229–263.

Cvitanic, J., H. Pham, and N. Touzi, 1999, Super-replication in stochastic volatility models under portfolio constraints, *Journal of Applied Probability* 36, 523–545.

Danthine, J. P., and J. B. Donaldson, 2002, Labor relations and asset returns, *Review of Economic Studies* 69, 41–64.

Danthine, J. P., and J. B. Donaldson, 2015, *Intermediate financial theory* (Academic Press).

Debreu, G., 1951, The coefficient of resource utilization, *Econometrica* 19, 273–292.

Debreu, G., 1959, *Theory of value* (Yale University Press).

Delbaen, F., and W. Schachermayer, 1994, A general version of the fundamental theorem of asset pricing, *Mathematische Annalen* 300, 463–520.

Delbaen, F., and W. Schachermayer, 1998, The fundamental theorem of asset pricing for unbounded stochastic processes, *Mathematische Annalen* 312, 215–250.

DeMiguel, V., L. Garlappi, and R. Uppal, 2009, Optimal versus naive diversification: How inefficient is the $1/N$ portfolio strategy, *Review of Financial Studies* 22, 1915–1953.

Duffie, D., and L. G. Epstein, 1992, Stochastic differential utility, *Econometrica* 60, 353–394.

El Karoui, N., and M. C. Quenez, 1995, Dynamic programming and pricing of contingent claims in an incomplete market, *SIAM Journal of Control and Optimization* 33, 29–66.

Ellsberg, D., 1961, Risk, ambiguity, and the savage axioms, *Quarterly Journal of Economics* 75, 643–669.

Epstein, L. G., and S. E. Zin, 1989, Substitution, risk aversion, and the temporal behavior of consumption and asset returns: A theoretical framework, *Econometrica* 57, 937–969.

Fabozzi, F. J., S. M. Focardi, and P. N. Kolm, 2006, *Financial modeling of the equity market* (Wiley).

Fama, E. F., 1965, The behavior of stock-market prices, *Journal of Business* 38, 34–105.

Fama, E. F., and K. R. French, 1993, Common risk factors in the returns on stocks and bonds, *Journal of Financial Economics* 33, 3–56.

Fama, E. F., and K. R. French, 2015, A five-factor asset pricing model, *Journal of Financial Economics* 116, 1–22.

Feller, W., 1951, Two singular diffusion problems, *Annals of Mathematics* 54, 173–182.

Friedman, M., 1953, *Essays in positive economics* (University of Chicago Press).

Friedman, M., 1957, *A theory of the consumption function* (Princeton University Press).

Gilboa, I., and D. Schmeidler, 1989, Maxmin expected utility with non-unique prior, *Journal of Mathematical Economics* 18, 141–153.

Gradshteyn, I. S., and I. M. Ryzhik, 2000, *Table of integrals, series, and products*, sixth edition (Academic Press).

Graham, B., and D. Dodd, 1934, *Security analysis* (McGraw Hill).

Grossman, S., 1976, On the efficiency of competitive stock markets where traders have diverse information, *Journal of Finance* 31, 573–585.

Grossman, S. J., and J. E. Stiglitz, 1980, On the impossibility of informationally efficient markets, *American Economic Review* 70, 393–408.

Hakansson, N., 1970, Optimal investment and consumption strategies under risk for a class of utility functions, *Econometrica* 38, 587–607.

Hansen, L. P., 2012, Dynamic valuation decomposition within stochastic economies, *Econometrica* 80, 911–967.

Hansen, L. P., and R. Jagannathan, 1991, Implications of security market data for models of dynamic economies, *Journal of Political Economy* 99, 225–262.

Hansen, L. P., and J. A. Scheinkman, 2009, Long-term risk: An operator approach, *Econometrica* 77, 177–234.

Harrison, J. M., and D. M. Kreps, 1979, Martingales and arbitrage in multiperiod securities markets, *Journal of Economic Theory* 20, 381–408.

Harrison, J. M., and S. R. Pliska, 1981, Martingales and stochastic integrals in the theory of continuous trading, *Stochastic Processes and Their Applications* 11, 215–260.

Hart, O. D., 1975, On the optimality of equilibrium when the market structure is incomplete, *Journal of Economic Theory* 11, 418–443.

Hayashi, F., 1982, Tobin's marginal q and average q: A neoclassical interpretation, *Econometrica* 50, 213–224.

Hayek, F. A., 1945, The use of knowledge in society, *American Economic Review* 35, 519–530.

He, G., and R. Litterman, 2002, The intuition behind Black–Litterman model portfolios, available at SSRN, https://ssrn.com/abstract=334304.

Hellwig, M. F., 1980, On the aggregation of information in competitive markets, *Journal of Economic Theory* 22, 477–98.

Heston, S. L., 1993, A closed-form solution for options with stochastic volatility with application to bond and currency options, *Review of Financial Studies* 6, 327–343.

Hou, K., C. Xue, and L. Zhang, 2015, Digesting anomalies: An investment approach, *Review of Financial Studies* 28, 650–705.

Hull, J., 2018, *Options, futures, and other derivatives*, tenth edition (Pearson).

Hörmander, L., 2003, *The analysis of linear partial differential operators I* (Springer).

Ibragimov, M., R. Ibragimov, and J. Walden, 2015, *Heavy-tailed distributions and robustness in economics and finance* (Springer).

Ibragimov, R., and J. Walden, 2007, The limits of diversification when losses may be large, *Journal of Banking and Finance* 31, 2551–2569.

Ingersoll, J. E., 1987, *Theory of financial decision making* (Rowman & Littefield).

Jackwerth, J. C., and M. Menner, 2020, Does the Ross recovery theorem work empirically?, *Journal of Financial Economics* 137, 723–739.

Jagannathan, R., and Z. Wang, 1996, The conditional CAPM and the cross-section of expected returns, *Journal of Finance* 51, 3–53.

Jegadeesh, N., and S. Titman, 1993, Returns to buying winners and selling losers: Implications for stock market efficiency, *Journal of Finance* 48, 65–91.

Jensen, C. S., D. Lando, and L. H. Pedersen, 2019, Generalized recovery, *Journal of Financial Economics* 133, 154–174.

Kahneman, D., and A. Tversky, 1979, Prospect theory: An analysis of decision under risk, *Econometrica* 47, 263–292.

Kamrad, B., and P. Ritchken, 1991, Multinomial approximation models for options with k state variables, *Management Science* 37, 1640–1652.

Karatzas, I., J. P. Lehoczky, and S. E. Shreve, 1987, Optimal portfolio and consumption decisions for a "small investor" on a finite horizon, *SIAM Journal on Control and Optimization* 25, 1557–1586.

Karlin, S., and H. M. Taylor, 1981, *A second course in stochastic processes* (Academic Press).

Katznelson, Y., 1976, *An introduction to harmonic analysis*, second edition (Dover).

Kelly, J. L.,1956, A new interpretation of information rate, *Bell System Technical Journal* 35, 917–926.

Kim, T. S., and E. Omberg, 1996, Dynamic nonmyopic portfolio behavior, *Review of Financial Studies* 9, 141–161.

Kreps, D. M., and E. L. Porteus, 1978, Temporal resolution of uncertainty and dynamic choice theory, *Econometrica* 46, 185–200.

Kyle, A. S., 1985, Continuous auctions and insider trading, *Econometrica* 53, 1315–36.

Laibson, D., 1997, Golden eggs and hyperbolic discounting, *Quarterly Journal of Economics* 112, 443–477.

Lamont, O. A., and R. H. Thaler, 2003, Can the market add and subtract? Mispricing in tech stock carve-outs, *Journal of Political Economy* 111, 227–268.

Leland, H. E., 1968, Savings and uncertainty: The precautionary demand for saving, *Quarterly Journal of Economics* 82, 465–473.

Linetsky, V., and R. Mendoza, 2010, The constant elasticity of variance model, in *Encyclopedia of quantitative finance* (Wiley).

Lintner, J., 1965, The valuation of risk assets and the selection of risky investments in stock portfolios and capital budgets, *Review of Economics and Statistics* 47, 13–37.

Lucas, R. E., 1978, Asset prices in an exchange economy, *Econometrica* 46, 1429–1445.

Madan, D. B., P. P. Carr, and E. C. Chang, 1998, The variance gamma process and option pricing, *European Finance Review* 2, 79–105.

Malamud, S., 2008, Universal bounds for asset prices in heterogeneous economies, *Finance and Stochastics* 12, 411–422.

Mandelbrot, B., 1963, The variation of certain speculative prices, *Journal of Business* 36, 394–419.

Markowitz, H., 1952, Portfolio selection, *Journal of Finance* 7, 77–91.

Mehra, R., and E. C. Prescott, 1985, The equity premium: A puzzle, *Journal of Monetary Economics* 15, 145–161.

Merton, R. C., 1969, Lifetime portfolio selection under uncertainty: The continuous-time case, *Review of Economics and Statistics* 51, 247–257.

Merton, R. C., 1971, Optimum consumption and portfolio rules in a continuous-time model, *Journal of Economic Theory* 3, 373–413.

Merton, R. C., 1973, An intertemporal capital asset pricing model, *Econometrica* 41, 867–887.

Merton, R. C., 1976, Option pricing when underlying stock returns are discontinuous, *Journal of Financial Economics* 3, 125–144.

Milgrom, P., and N. Stokey, 1982, Information, trade, and common knowledge, *Journal of Economic Thoery* 26, 17–27.

Nash, J., 1951, Non-cooperative games, *Annals of Mathematics* 54, 286–295.

Oksendahl, B., 1998, *Stochastic differential equations* (Springer).

Parlour, C. A., R. Stanton, and J. Walden, 2011, Revisiting asset pricing puzzles in an exchange economy, *Review of Financial Studies* 24, 629–674.

Pastor, L., and R. F. Stambaugh, 2012, Are stocks really less volatile in the long run?, *Journal of Finance* 67, 431–478.

Petajisto, A., 2009, Why do demand curves for stocks slope down?, *Journal of Financial and Quantitative Analysis* 44, 1013–1044.

Pinsky, R. G., 1995, *Positive harmonic functions and diffusion* (Cambridge University Press).

Pratt, J. W., 1964, Risk aversion in the small and in the large, *Econometrica* 32, 122–136.

Qin, L., and V. Linetsky, 2016, Positive eigenfunctions of Markovian pricing operators: Hansen–Scheinkman factorization, Ross recovery, and long-term pricing, *Operations Research* 64, 99–117.

Riesz, R., and B. Nagy, 1990, *Functional analysis*, reprint edition (Dover).

Ross, S. A., 1976, The arbitrage theory of capital asset pricing, *Journal of Economic Theory* 13, 341–360.

Ross, S. A., 1978, A simple approach to the valuation of risky streams, *Journal of Business* 51, 453–475.

Ross, S., 2015, The recovery theorem, *Journal of Finance* 70, 615–648.

Rothschild, M., and J. E. Stiglitz, 1970, Increasing risk: I. A definition, *Journal of Economic Theory* 2, 225–243.

Rothschild, M., and J. E. Stiglitz, 1971, Increasing risk II: Its economic consequences, *Journal of Economic Theory* 3, 66–84.

Roy, A. D., 1952, Safety first and the holding of assets, *Econometrica* 20, 431–449.

Rubinstein, M., 1974, An aggregation theorem for securities markets, *Journal of Financial Economics* 1, 225–244.

Rudin, W., 1976, *Principles of mathematical analysis*, third edition (McGraw Hill).

Rudin, W., 1991, *Functional analysis*, second edition (McGraw Hill).

Samuelson, P. A., 1967, General proof that diversification pays, *Journal of Financial and Quantitative Analysis* 2, 1–13.

Sandroni, A., 2000, Do markets favor agents able to make accurate predictions, *Econometrica* 68, 1303–1341.

Savage, L., 1954, *The foundations of statistics* (Wiley).

Schachermayer, W., 1994, Martingale measures for discrete-time processes with infinite horizon, *Mathematical Finance* 4, 25–55.

Sharpe, W. F., 1964, Capital asset prices: A theory of market equilibrium under conditions of risk, *Journal of Finance* 19, 425–442.

Shiller, R. J., 1981, Do stock prices move too much to be justified by subsequent changes in dividends, *American Economic Review* 71, 421–436.

Simmons, G., 1988, *Differential equations* (McGraw Hill).

Simon, B., 2005, Sturm oscillation and comparison theorems, in W. O. Amrein, A. M. Hinz, and D. B. Pearson, eds., *Sturm–Liouville theory: Past and present* (Birkhäuser, Basel, Switzerland).

Stoll, H. R., 1969, The relationship between put and call option prices, *Journal of Finance* 24, 801–824.

Treynor, J. L., 1961, Market value, time, and risk, available at SSRN: https://papers.ssrn.com/sol3/papers.cfm?abstract_id=2600356, revised version 4.29.2015.

von Neumann, J., and O. Morgenstern, 1944, *Theory of games and economic behavior* (Princeton University Press).

von Sydow, L., and J. Walden, 2020, Numerical Ross recovery for diffusion processes using a PDE approach, *Applied Numerical Finance* 27, 46–66.

Wachter, J. A., 2002, Portfolio and consumption decisions under mean-reverting returns: An exact solution for complete markets, *Journal of Financial and Quantitative Analysis* 37, 63–91.

Walden, J., 2017, Recovery with unbounded diffusion processes, *Review of Finance* 21, 1403–1444.

Wang, J., 1996, The term structure of interest rates in a pure exchange economy with heterogeneous investors, *Journal of Financial Economics* 41, 75–110.

Weil, P., 1989, The equity premium puzzle and the risk-free rate puzzle, *Journal of Monetary Economics* 24, 401–421.

Yosida, K., 1995, *Functional analysis*, sixth edition (Springer).

Young, L. C., 1936, An inequality of the Hölder type, connected with Stieltjes integration, *Acta Mathematica* 67, 251–282.

Index